Net Zero and Natural Resources Law

Academic Advisory Group (AAG) of the Section on Energy, Environment, Resources and Infrastructure Law (SEERIL) of the International Bar Association (IBA)

General Editors

TITLES IN THE SERIES

Human Rights in Natural Resource Development: Public Participation in the Sustainable Development of Mining and Energy Resources **(2002)**

Energy Security: Managing Risk in a Dynamic Legal and Regulatory Environment **(2004)**

Regulating Energy and Natural Resources **(2006)**

Beyond the Carbon Economy: Energy Law in Transition **(2008)**

Property Law in Energy and Natural Resources **(2010)**

Energy Networks and the Law: Innovative Solutions in Changing Markets **(2012)**

The Law of Energy Underground: Understanding New Developments in Subsurface Production, Transmission, and Storage **(2014)**

Sharing the Costs and Benefits of Energy and Resource Activity **(2016)**

Innovation in Energy Law and Technology **(2018)**

Energy Justice and Energy Law: Distributive, Procedural, Restorative and Social Justice in Energy Law **(2020)**

Resilience in Energy, Infrastructure, and Natural Resources Law **(2022)**

Net Zero and Natural Resources Law

Sovereignty, Security, and Solidarity in the Clean Energy Transition

Edited by

DAMILOLA S. OLAWUYI

Professor and UNESCO Chair on Environmental Law and Sustainable Development, Hamad Bin Khalifa University, Qatar

JOSÉ JUAN GONZÁLEZ

Full Professor and Researcher of Energy and Environmental Law, Metropolitan Autonomous University, Mexico

HANRI MOSTERT

DST/NRF SARChI Research Chair: Mineral Law in Africa, and Professor of Law; Professional Integral Coach, University of Cape Town, South Africa

MILTON FERNANDO MONTOYA

Director, Mining and Energy Law Institute, Externado de Colombia University, Colombia

CATHERINE BANET

Professor of Law, Department of Energy and Resources Law, University of Oslo, Norway

OXFORD
UNIVERSITY PRESS

OXFORD
UNIVERSITY PRESS

Great Clarendon Street, Oxford, OX2 6DP,
United Kingdom

Oxford University Press is a department of the University of Oxford.
It furthers the University's objective of excellence in research, scholarship,
and education by publishing worldwide. Oxford is a registered trade mark of
Oxford University Press in the UK and in certain other countries

Published in the United States of America by Oxford University Press
198 Madison Avenue, New York, NY 10016, United States of America

British Library Cataloguing in Publication Data

Data available

Library of Congress Control Number: 2024936304

ISBN 9780198925002

DOI: 10.1093/9780198925033.001.0001

Preface

In Memoriam Donald N. Zillman

This is the twelfth book within a fruitful and long-standing collaboration among the International Bar Association's Section on Energy, Environment, Natural Resources, and Infrastructure Law (IBA SEERIL), the Oxford University Press (OUP), and the Academic Advisory Group (AAG) of the IBA SEERIL. The International Bar Association is the world's largest association of lawyers and bar associations. As an active section of the IBA, the IBA-SEERIL spearheads public interest initiatives to keep members informed on significant developments relating to the Section's six committees: Environment, Health and Safety Law; International Construction Projects; Mining Law; Oil and Gas Law; Power Law; and Water Law fields. The AAG is a network of academics that carry out research and teaching in the areas pertinent to SEERIL.

This latest book is designed to inform a worldwide audience of practitioners, policy-makers, scholars, researchers, and students on the fundamental implications of ongoing net zero emission reduction pledges and targets for natural resources law. As countries seek to recover from the impacts of the COVID-19 pandemic and enhance resilience to future disruptive events, the urgent need to accelerate efforts to address the climate change emergency has become ever more pressing. With several state and non-state actors announcing plans to bring down global emissions of greenhouse gases (GHGs) that contribute to climate change to net zero by the year 2060 or earlier, the AAG-SEERIL wanted to be at the forefront of proposing legal solutions to enhance the legitimacy, transparency, and coherent implementation of such net zero targets. Our aim is to shed new light on the often-neglected question of the place and role of innovative natural resources law and policy in addressing fundamental sovereignty, security, and solidarity questions posed by the net zero transition across the world.

In 2023, the AAG members met at Hamad Bin Khalifa University (HBKU), Doha, Qatar, for an intensive three-day workshop to present draft chapters and refine the book's focus. In addition to serving as an important opportunity to frame the book project, the mid-term meeting also marked the 40th anniversary of the establishment of the AAG-SEERIL. The meeting therefore also provided a momentous occasion to reflect upon and renew the focus of the AAG. For over forty years, the IBA, SEERIL, and the AAG have been involved in a productive circle of ideas, practices, joint publications, and public events. With a marked expansion in the range of nations represented by the AAG, as evident from the fact that the current book has representatives from different continents among its authors, the Doha meeting offered a timely platform to celebrate such an important milestone. Special thanks are due to Florencia Heredia, the Chairperson of SEERIL, and her predecessors in office for their exceptional support to the AAG over the last several years. We also extend our most sincere appreciation to our marvellous hosts, Dean Susan L Karamanian, Professor Damilola Olawuyi, SAN, Sandhya Monis, and Nisha Duggal at the HBKU College of Law for their efficient help and dedication in making that mid-term workshop very successful and memorable.

We would also like to thank the editorial staff of Oxford University Press (OUP), especially Fay Gibbons, for the thoughtful, constructive, and professional review process which guided this book through to its timely completion. Elena Athwal (Harvard Law School) deserves special appreciation for providing remarkable and thoughtful research assistance. She assisted greatly in collating chapters at submission, review, and editing stages. We also acknowledge the dedication and collegiality of all the contributing authors, whose substantial research and commitment to leading-edge scholarship in this field has been pivotal to the production of this book.

In July 2023, just a few weeks before the submission of the final manuscripts to OUP, a monumentally sad circumstance shook the AAG. Donald Zillman, a longstanding member of the AAG and former president of the University of Maine at Presque Isle, passed away at the age of seventy-nine. A globally regarded expert and thought leader on energy law, military law, tort law, and legal writing for over fifty years, Don was the Edward Godfrey Professor of Law at the University of Maine School of Law. He was our great friend, our beloved colleague, and a pillar of the AAG, to which he made an enormous contribution. In addition to his calm, cheerful, and warm personality, Don provided kind and remarkable leadership to several of the previous publications of the AAG. As lead or co-editor of our previous books, Don's vast and deep knowledge, as well as his generous and assuring mentorship and support to AAG members, was so pivotal.[1] We have lost a kind, thoughtful, and friendly unifying force of the AAG and a great scholar. We will miss him so very much.

We dedicate this book to him with all of our admiration and affection.

The Editors
30 August 2023

[1] Don's most recent contributions as lead or co-editor on previous AAG books include: *Innovation in Energy Law and Technology* (OUP 2018); *Energy Justice and Energy Law* (OUP 2020).

Contents

List of Abbreviations

AC	Alternating Current
ACER	Agency for the Cooperation of Energy Regulators
AEEP	Africa-EU Energy Partnership
AfCFTA	African Continental Free Trade Area
ASSELLAU	Association of Environmental Law Lecturers in African Universities
ASSELLMU	Association of Environmental Law Lecturers in Middle East and North African Universities
BCA	Border Carbon Adjustment
BITs	Bilateral Investment Treaties
BRP	Balancing Responsible Party
BSP	Balancing Service Provider
CAC	Command-and-control
CBAM	Carbon Border Adjustment Mechanism
CBD	Convention on Biological Diversity
CBDR-RC	Common but Differentiated Responsibilities and Respective Capabilities
CBI	Climate Bonds Initiative
CCUS	Carbon Capture Utilization and Storage
CDM	Clean Development Mechanism
CDS	Closed Distribution System
CEC	Citizen Energy Community
CEQ	Council of Environmental Quality
CFC	Chlorofluorocarbon
CFE	Carbon Pollution-Free Electricity
CH_4	Methane
CITES	Convention on International Trade in Endangered Species of Wild Fauna and Flora
CJEU	Court of Justice of the European Union
COP	Conference of the Parties
CORESO	Coordination of Electrical System Operators
COVID-19	Coronavirus Disease 2019
DC	Direct Current
DFI	Development Finance Institutions
DRC	Democratic Republic of Congo
DSM	Dispute Settlement Mechanism
DSO	Distribution System Operator
EC	Extractive Company
ECJ	European Court of Justice
ECL	European Climate Law
ECT	Energy Charter Treaty
EEZ	Exclusive Economic Zone
EIA	Environmental Impact Assessment
EITI	Extractive Industries Transparency Initiative
ENTSO-E	European Network of TSOs for Electricity

EPA	Environmental Protection Agency
ESD	Education for Sustainable Development
ESG	Environmental, Social, Governance
ET	Emission Trading
ETMs	Energy Transition Minerals
ETS	Emissions Trading Systems
EU	European Union
EV	Electric Vehicle
FDE	Energy Development Fund
FDI	Foreign direct investment
FIT	Feed-in Tariffs
FPIC	Free, Prior, and Informed Consent
GCC	Gulf Cooperation Council
GDP	Gross Domestic Product
GECF	Gas Exporting Countries Forum
GEI	Global Entrepreneurship Index
GHG	Greenhouse Gases
H_2O	Water Vapour
HDI	Human Development Index
HFC	Hydrofluorocarbons
HLEG	High-Level Expert Group on the Net-Zero Emissions Commitments of Non-State Entities
HRDD	Human Rights Due Diligence
HRIA	Human Rights Impact Assessment
IATA	International Air Transport Association
IBA	Impact Benefit Agreement
ICCPR	International Covenant on Civil and Political Rights
ICESCR	International Covenant on Economic, Social and Cultural Rights
ICJ	International Court of Justice
IEA	International Energy Agency
IET	Impossible Energy Trinity
ILO	International Labour Organisation
IMF	International Monetary Fund
INDC	Intended Nationally Determined Contributions
IOCs	International Oil Companies
IPCC	Intergovernmental Panel on Climate Change
IRA	Inflation Reduction Act
IRENA	International Renewable Energy Agency
IsDB	Islamic Development Bank
JCPOA	Joint Comprehensive Plan of Action
JDA	Joint Development Agreement
JI	Joint Implementation
JOA	Joint Operating Agreement
LAS	League of Arab States
LC	Local Content
LCRs	Local Content Requirements
LEED	Leadership in Energy and Environmental Design
MASEN	Moroccan Agency for Solar Energy
MBA	Market-Based Approaches

MDB	Multilateral Development Bank
MEAs	Multilateral Environmental Agreements
MENA	Middle East and North Africa
MEPS	Minimum Energy Performance Standards
MERS	Middle East Respiratory Syndrome
MFN	Most Favored Nation
mHRDD	mandatory Human Rights Due Diligence
N_2O	Nitrous Oxide
NAFTA	North American Free Trade Agreement
NCF	National Climate Funds
NDCs	Nationally Determined Contributions
NDP	National Development Plan
NEVs	New Energy Vehicles
NGO	Non-Governmental Organization
NGPB	National Green Participative Banks
NOCs	National Oil Companies
NOx	Nitrogen Oxide
NRA	National Regulatory Authority
NRGI	Natural Resource Governance Institute
O_3	Tropospheric Ozone
OECD	Organisation for Economic Co-operation and Development
OFTO	Offshore Transmission Owners
OHCHR	Office of the United Nations High Commissioner for Human Rights
OIC	Organization of Islamic Cooperation
OPEC	Organization of Petroleum Exporting Countries
OPT	Occupied Palestine Territories
PCI	Project of common interest
PFC	Perfluorocarbons
PGMs	platinum group metals
PIA	Petroleum Industry Act
PPP	Public Private Partnership
PSC	Production Sharing Contract
PSNR	Permanent Sovereignty of Natural Resources
RCC	Regional Coordination Centre
RCPs	Responsible Contracting Principles
REC	Renewable Energy Community
RECREEE	Regional Centre for Renewable Energy and Energy Efficiency
REDD+	Reducing Emissions from Deforestation and Forest Degradation
REE	rare earth elements
RES	Renewable Energy Source
RSC	Regional Security Coordinator
RSCI	Regional Security Coordination Initiative
SDG	Sustainable Development Goal
SE4All	Sustainable Energy for All
SER	Sufficiency, Efficiency, and Renewables
SF_6	Sulphur Hexafluoride
SIDS	Small Island Developing States
SLCP	Short-lived Climate Pollutants
SMEEs	Small- and Medium-Scale Entrepreneurial Eco-Ventures

SMR	steam-methane reforming
SO_2	Sulphur Dioxide
SSA	Sub-Saharan Africa
SWF	Sovereign Wealth Funds
TEN-E	Trans-European networks for energy
TSC	TSO Security Cooperation
TSO	Transmission System Operator
UN	United Nations
UNCCD	United Nations Convention to Combat Desertification
UNCED	United Nations Conference on Environment and Development
UNCLOS	UN Convention on the Law of the Sea
UNDP	United Nations Development Programme
UNEP	United Nations Environment Programme
UNESCO	United Nations Educational, Scientific and Cultural Organization
UNFCCC	United Nations Framework Convention on Climate Change
UNGPs	United Nations Guiding Principles on Business and Human Rights
UNOCHA	United Nations Office for the Coordination of Humanitarian Affairs
UNOPS	United Nations Office for Project Services
UNSC	United Nations Security Council
UNWG-BHR	United Nations Working Group on Business and Human Rights
USMCA	Canada-United States-Mexico Agreement
USMCA	United States–Mexico–Canada Agreement
VCLT	Vienna Convention on the Law of Treaties
VOCs	Volatile Organic Emissions
WFP	World Food Programme
WTO	World Trade Organization
ZCL	Zoonotic Cutaneous Leishmaniasis

List of Contributors

Nadia B. Ahmad is Associate Professor of Law, Barry University, Orlando, United States, Yale School of the Environment, United States. https://orcid.org/0000-0003-2446-2886

Adenike Adebukola Akinsemolu, PhD is Vanguard Fellow, Institute of Advanced Studies, University of Birmingham, Birmingham, United Kingdom, Afe Babalola University, Ado-Ekiti, Nigeria. https://orcid.org/0000-0001-6360-9356

Elodie Annamayer is Research Assistant, UMR 6031 TREE (CNRS, UPPA), Université de Pau et des Pays de l'Adour, France

Mehrnoosh Aryanpour, Doctor of law (SJD) candidate is Doctor of Law (S.J.D) candidate at the University of Pennsylvania Carey Law School, Founder and CEO of Green Swan, University of Pennsylvania Carey Law School, Philadelphia, United States

Elena I. Athwal is LLM Candidate, International Environmental & Energy Law, Harvard Law School, Cambridge, Massachusetts, United States

Catherine Banet is Professor of Law, Department of Energy and Resources Law, University of Oslo, Norway

Barry Barton, BA, LLM is Professor, Te Piringa Faculty of Law, University of Waikato, Hamilton, New Zealand. https://orcid.org/0000-0002-2394-4384

Anatole Boute, PhD is Professor, Faculty of Law, The Chinese University of Hong Kong, Hong Kong, Hong Kong SAR China

Louis de Fontenelle, PhD is Associate Professor in Public Law, University of Pau and Pays de l'Adour, CNRS,TREE, Pau, France

Íñigo del Guayo, PhD is Professor of Administrative Law, Law Department, University of Almería, Almería, Spain. https://orcid.org/0000-0002-4918-2533

Tengi George-Ikoli, LLB, LLM is Senior Officer, Nigeria Program, Natural Resource Governance Institute, New York, United States of America

Lee Godden, PhD is Dean Faculty of Law, Victoria University of Wellington, Wellington, New Zealand

José Juan González is Full Professor and Researcher of Energy and Environmental Law, Metropolitan Autonomous University, Mexico. https://orcid.org/0000-0002-8029-9457

Ana Paola Gutiérrez Rico, PhD, LLM is Research Director of the Mining and Energy Law Department, Externado University, Bogotá, Colombia

Qaraman M. Hasan, PhD is a Postdoctoral fellow, School of Advanced International Studies (SAIS), Johns Hopkins University, 555 Pennsylvania Avenue NW, Washington, DC

Alastair R. Lucas, Professor Emeritus, and Senior Research Fellow, Canadian Institute of Resources Law, Faculty of Law, University of Calgary, Canada

Anthony Moffa, JD is Associate Dean and Professor of Law, University of Maine School of Law, Portland, United States

Milton Fernando Montoya is Director, Mining and Energy Law Institute, Externado de Colombia University, Colombia

Lindsay Taylah Moses, LLB, LLM is Doctoral Researcher, DST/NRF South African Research Chair Initiative: Mineral Law in Africa, Private Law Department, University of Cape Town, South Africa. https://orcid.org/0000-0003-0570-0826

Hanri Mostert is DST/NRF SARChI Research Chair: Mineral Law in Africa, and Professor of Law; Professional Integral Coach, University of Cape Town, South Africa. https://orcid.org/0000-0001-8224-0056

Walters Nsoh, PhD, LLM (Dist), BSc is Associate Professor in Law, Birmingham Law School, University of Birmingham, Birmingham, United Kingdom, Durban University of Technology, Durban, South Africa. https://orcid.org/0000-0001-5892-7050

Damilola S. Olawuyi is Professor and UNESCO Chair on Environmental Law and Sustainable Development, Hamad Bin Khalifa University, Qatar. https://orcid.org/0000-0003-0700-981X

Akinbobola Olukayode Olugbemi, LLB, BL (Nigeria), LLM (Aberdeen), LLM (Calgary) is Research Fellow, Canadian Institute of Resources Law, University of Calgary, Calgary, Canada

Ana María Pacheco Ruiz is Research assistant, master's degree student, Metropolitan Autonomous University, Mexico City, Mexico

LeRoy Paddock, Juris Doctorate is Distinguished Professorial lecturer in Environmental Law, The George Washington University Law School, Washington, D.C., USA

José Antonio Redondo Torres, LLB is Spanish Governmental Scholarship recipient to assist Professor Del Guayo in his teaching and research activities, Administrative Law Department., University of Almeria, Spain

Martha M. Roggenkamp, PhD is Prof. Emeritus in energy law, University of Groningen, Groningen, Netherlands, Université de Pau et des Pays de l'Ardour, Pau, France

Aaron Sayne is Lead, Domestic Energy Transitions, Natural Resource Governance Institute (NRGI), United States

Sara Soini, LLM in Energy and Environmental Law is Project Development Manager, Nordic Ren-Gas Oy, Finland

Kim Talus is a Professor of European Energy Law at UEF Law School and a Director of its Center for Climate Change, Energy and Environmental Law (CCEEL) (Finland) as well as a Professor of Energy Law at University of Helsinki (Finland). He is also a Partner in a Swiss energy law consultancy Energy and Regulation Partners.

Hugo Meyer van den Berg, BAHons LLB LLM PhD is Adjunct Associate Professor, NRF/DST SARChI Research Chair: Mineral Law in Africa, University of Cape Town, South Africa, Ellis Shilengudwa Inc, Windhoek, Namibia

Hao Zhang is Associate Professor of Law, Faculty of Law, The Chinese University of Hong Kong, Hong Kong, Hong Kong. https://orcid.org/0000-0003-2429-5336

Donald Zillman (deceased) was Emeritus Godfrey Professor of Law at the University of Maine Law School, Portland, Maine, United States

1

Introduction

The New Age of Natural Resources Law and Policy: From Resource Conservation to Net Zero

Damilola S. Olawuyi, José Juan González, Hanri Mostert, Milton Fernando Montoya, and Catherine Banet

I. Introduction

This book examines the fundamental transformations to natural resources law as a result of ongoing widespread adoption of net zero programmes. It offers a structured and systematic analysis of the natural resource sovereignty, security, and solidarity trilemma and risks that the ongoing net zero transition pose to legal and regulatory systems. It explores the coherence gaps that remain in regulatory efforts to address those risks; and nexus governance approaches for addressing such gaps in the design, approval, financing, and implementation of natural resource investments in a net zero era.

For several centuries, the production of natural resources—that is, items or materials, such as air, land, forests, water, flora, fauna, and minerals, that occur naturally in the environment and are useful in economic, industrial, or day-to-day human activities—has remained the bedrock of modern societies and the global economy.[1] While natural resources are often classified based on a wide range of characteristics such as their exhaustibility, economic value, pattern of distribution, and pricing, this book discusses two categories of natural resources, namely: renewable and non-renewable natural resources.[2] Renewable natural resources (such as sun, air, water, wind, and heat) are resources that generally self-replenish naturally, and are therefore infinite in their availability and supply, while non-renewable natural resources are generally not replenished by natural means, so their availability and supply is for a finite amount of time.[3] Examples of non-renewable natural resources include extractive resources, such as petroleum (oil and natural gas) and solid minerals.[4] Consequently, given

[1] The natural resource industry consists of people, companies, financial institutions, trade organizations, and national authorities involved in the production, distribution, and sale of natural resources. The natural resource industry consists of three key sectors: production (upstream), networks (midstream), and retail (downstream). There are various sub-industries encompassed in each key sector, including the petroleum (oil and gas) industry; mineral and mining industry; electrical power industry; renewable energy industry; forest industry; hunting, fishing, and water industry; drilling, equipment, and service industry; and the refining and marketing industry amongst others. See World Trade Organization (WTO), 'Natural resources: definitions, trade patterns and globalization' (World Trade Report, 2010) <https://www.wto.org/english/res_e/booksp_e/anrep_e/wtr10-2b_e.pdf> accessed 14 August 2023; also Damilola Olawuyi, *Extractives Industry Law in Africa* (Springer 2018) 1–5.

[2] See the African Convention on the Conservation of Nature and Natural Resources, art 5, which defines natural resources as 'renewable resources, tangible and nontangible, including soil, water, flora and fauna and non-renewable resources'.

[3] Christine A Klein and others, *Natural Resources Law: A Place-Based Book of Problems and Cases* (4th edn, Aspen Publishing 2018) 1–15.

[4] ibid.

Damilola S. Olawuyi, José Juan González, Hanri Mostert, Milton Fernando Montoya, and Catherine Banet, *Introduction* In: *Net Zero and Natural Resources Law*. Edited by: Damilola S. Olawuyi, José Juan González, Hanri Mostert, Milton Fernando Montoya, and Catherine Banet, Oxford University Press. © International Bar Association 2024. DOI: 10.1093/9780198925033.003.0001

the importance of natural resources to modern economies and societies, ensuring their conservation and protection from threats resulting from their unsustainable management and illicit use has been a fundamental aspect of legal and regulatory systems worldwide.[5]

The discipline of natural resources law has therefore grown as the network of laws, institutions, and fiscal policies and frameworks established to regulate the safe, orderly, and sustainable development of renewable and non-renewable natural resources.[6] This includes strategies, rules, and procedures relating to: the exploration, exploitation, or commercialization of natural resources, especially extractive resources such as oil, gas, or minerals; the acquisition or holding of a permit, licence, lease, or any other authorization to carry out resource development and commercialization; and the institutions established at national, regional, and supranational levels to oversee safe, orderly, and sustainable resource development.[7]

However, with the rapid development of environmental law, the last decade has seen an ongoing transformation in the fundamental law and policy frameworks that have for several decades governed the development, commercialization, use, and management of natural resources.[8] With increased manifestation of extreme weather events such as Cyclone Pam in Vanuatu, devastating floods in Tuvalu, droughts in South Sudan, water scarcity in northern Mexico, and fatal heat waves across the United States, amongst others, there is now increased consensus by the scientific community that climate change is real and that the continuous anthropogenic (human-induced) emission of greenhouse gases (GHG) is a principal cause.[9] To avert the climate crisis, several studies, including reports of the Intergovernmental Panel on Climate Change, point to an urgent need to reduce human dependence on the combustion of fossil fuels, such as coal, oil, and gas that emit GHGs.[10] In response, more than 2,000 jurisdictions and governments worldwide have now declared a climate emergency, resulting in increased legislation and regulatory action to bring down emissions of GHGs that contribute to climate change to net zero by the year 2060 or earlier.[11]

[5] See Nico Schrijver, 'Advancements in the Principles of International Law on Sustainable Development' in Marie Claire Cordonier Segger and Christopher G Weeramantry (eds), *Sustainable Development Principles in the Decisions of International Courts and Tribunals, 1992–2012* (Routledge 2017) 99–102.

[6] Generally, there are four key sources of natural resources law: international law, domestic legislation, judicial decisions, and scholarly publications. See Chapter 2 of this book. See also Robert L Fischman, 'What Is Natural Resources Law?' (2007) <https://www.repository.law.indiana.edu/facpub/197> accessed 27 August 2023.

[7] Olawuyi, *Extractives* (n 1).

[8] See Donald Zillman and others, 'Introduction: How Technological and Legal Innovation Are Transforming Energy Law' in Donald Zillman and others (eds), *Innovation in Energy Law and Technology: Dynamic Solutions for Energy Transitions* (OUP 2018) 1–16.

[9] ibid 10–15; also Damilola Olawuyi (ed), *Climate Change Law and Policy in the Middle East and North Africa Region* (Routledge 2021) 3–10.

[10] Preyadarshi R Shukla and others (eds), 'Climate Change 2022: Mitigation of Climate Change: Working Group III Contribution to the Sixth Assessment Report of the Intergovernmental Panel on Climate Change' <https://www.ipcc.ch/report/ar6/wg3/downloads/report/IPCC_AR6_WGIII_FullReport.pdf> accessed 1 May 2023.

[11] 'More than 70 countries, including the biggest polluters—China, the United States, and the European Union—have set a net-zero target, covering about 76% of global emissions', see United Nations, 'For a livable climate: net zero commitments must be backed by credible action' <https://www.un.org/en/climatechange/net-zero-coalition> accessed 1 May 2023. In Africa, Gambia, Ghana, Nigeria, and South Africa are among the first few countries to have adopted net zero targets. Oil- and gas-rich MENA countries such as Bahrain, Iraq, Kuwait, Oman, Saudi Arabia, and the United Arab Emirates—have also committed to achieve net zero by 2060 or earlier. See Energy and Climate Intelligence Unit, 'Net Zero Tracker' <https://eciu.net/netzerotracker> accessed 1 May 2023. See also Climate Emergency Declaration, 'Climate emergency declarations in 2,309 jurisdictions and local governments cover 1 billion citizens' <https://climateemergencydeclaration.org/climate-emergency-declarations-cover-15-million-citizens/> accessed 1 May 2023.

Net zero in this context therefore refers to two things. First, reducing anthropogenic GHG emissions in energy and industrial systems to as close to zero as possible, and second, removing any residual atmospheric GHG emissions through natural or artificial measures.[12] By implementing both GHG emission reduction and removal programmes, net zero initiatives aim to cut GHGs in the atmosphere to zero.[13] Despite debates on the adequacy and practicability of net zero targets to effectively halt the climate emergency, the ambitions and pledges to transition towards net zero are already resulting in increased divestments from non-renewable natural resource projects such as oil and gas.[14] At the same time, net zero targets are resulting in increased investment in renewable and decarbonization projects, especially solar, wind, hydro, and storage technologies and infrastructure. Several countries are also emphasizing more stringent economic diversification, resource efficiency, and climate-smart infrastructure standards, such as net zero buildings, as well as more stringent environment impact assessment programmes to screen out high GHG-emitting projects, all with the aim of accelerating net zero and clean energy transition.[15] Net zero goals have also increasingly been integrated into financing and sustainability reporting requirements by commercial banks and development finance institutions, trade and investment agreements, as well as procurement practices, with the aim of screening out projects that do not advance net zero.[16] Over the last decade, net zero has therefore become the new central and organizing paradigm of natural resources law and policy.[17]

The widespread adoption of efforts towards net zero, and the associated changes in the demand and supply patterns of natural resources, is altering the development and practice of natural resources law and policy. First, while nations have permanent sovereignty over their natural resources, the growing social, economic, and environmental risks of extreme dependence on hydrocarbons have become more apparent in the net zero era. For example, the European Union (EU), one of the world's largest energy importers, announced plans to achieve a 55 per cent reduction of GHG emissions, at least a 32 per cent increase in renewable energy, and net zero emission status by the year 2050, all of which raise key questions for EU's energy suppliers and connected stakeholders.[18] While the need for a low-carbon economy is incontrovertible, a sudden global divestment from fossil fuel as an energy source

[12] See Intergovernmental Panel on Climate Change (IPCC), 'Glossary of Climate Change terms' <https://www.ipcc.ch/site/assets/uploads/2018/11/sr15_glossary.pdf> accessed 1 May 2023, stating that 'Net zero emissions are achieved when anthropogenic emissions of greenhouse gases to the atmosphere are balanced by anthropogenic removals over a specified period.' See also the Paris Agreement, art 4(1) calling for efforts to 'achieve a balance between anthropogenic emissions by sources and removals by sinks of greenhouse gases in the second half of this century'.

[13] While net zero targets and ambitions are increasingly announced, a recent UN report emphasizes that net zero targets may alone not be sufficient to halt the climate emergency. It calls on countries and businesses to adopt more ambitious zero carbon plans, including ending carbon offsets and new coal, oil and gas investments. See United Nations Working Group on Business and Human Rights (UN WGBHR), 'Extractive Sector, Just Transition and Human Rights' (2023) UN General Assembly Report A/78/155.

[14] Share Action, 'HSBC Announces it will No Longer Finance New Oil and Gas Fields—Share Action Response' <https://www.shareaction.org/news/hsbc-announces-it-will-no-longer-finance-new-oil-and-gas-fields-shareaction-response?token=IcQ5WS9tht8-TEEQvxuwEDe-2weKKnYd&s=09> accessed 1 May 2023.

[15] Damilola Olawuyi, *Environmental Law in Arab States* (OUP 2022) 133–59.

[16] Share Action (n 14); see also Kelly Levin and others, 'Designing and Communicating Net Zero Targets' (World Res Inst Working Paper, July 2020).

[17] Shelley Welton, 'Neutralizing the Atmosphere' (2022) 132 Yale Law Journal 171.

[18] European Commission, *2030 Climate and Energy Framework* <https://www.climate.ec.europa.eu/eu-action/climate-strategies-targets/2030-climate-energy-framework_en#tab-> accessed 27 August 2023; European Commission, 'EU 2050 Long-term Strategy' <https://www.ec.europa.eu/clima/policies/strategies/2050_en> accessed 1 May 2023.

may have catastrophic development impacts in some parts of the world. Commentators have already expressed the fear that developing countries in Africa, Asia, and Latin America may become the 'involuntary sacrificial lamb for net zero'.[19] The reference is, specifically, to the expected escalation of energy poverty levels in these regions that the drive to net zero might exacerbate as more countries continue to divest investments from oil, gas, and coal industries that have powered the economies of these regions.[20] The clean energy transition and the resulting socio-economic challenges in resource-dependent countries raise fundamental questions on the need to reimagine the application of established principles of natural resources law, such as permanent sovereignty and jurisdiction over natural resources, intergenerational equity principle, energy solidarity, energy security, and energy justice, amongst others.

Second, debates on environment, social, governance, and justice risks in the supply of transition minerals raise salient questions as to whether extant natural resource law and policy frameworks can coherently balance net zero ambitions with broader goals of energy justice and security. For example, a recent report of the Australian Clean Energy Council documents the growing evidence that clean energy projects are linked to human rights violations, modern slavery, and forced labour.[21] Recent reports also show how children as young as seven years old work in dangerous artisanal cobalt mines in the Democratic Republic of Congo (DRC).[22] DRC accounts for more than half (60%) of the global supply of cobalt, an essential transition mineral needed to manufacture batteries for electric vehicles, solar, wind, and other renewable energy infrastructure.[23] As clean energy policies and projects ramp up in scale and ambition, global demand for cobalt, and other transition minerals, are projected to significantly increase, which may further exacerbate human rights violations in mine fields across the world, especially in Global South countries such as the DRC, where the legal and institutional framework on human rights is currently weak.[24] Net zero and the clean energy transition also raise fundamental questions of policy and practice for the management of renewable natural resources that will play essential

[19] UN WGBHR Report (n 13), also G Moore, 'Africa must not be the West's sacrificial lamb for net zero at Cop26' <https://www.african.business/2021/10/energy-resources/africa-must-not-be-the-wests-sacrificial-lamb-for-net-zero-at-cop26/> accessed 1 May 2023.

[20] S Zubairu, 'COP26: Africa charts a complex road to net zero' <https://www.african.business/2021/10/energy-resources/africas-complex-road-to-net-zero/> accessed 1 May 2023.

[21] Clean Energy Council, 'Addressing Modern Slavery in the Clean Energy Sector' <https://www.cleanenergycouncil.org.au/resources/resources-hub/addressing-modern-slavery-in-the-clean-energy-sector> accessed 1 May 2023.

[22] See Chapter 11 of this book. Also, Amnesty International, 'Democratic Republic of Congo: "This is what we die for": Human rights abuses in the Democratic Republic of the Congo power the global trade in cobalt' (2016) <https://www.amnesty.org/en/documents/afr62/3183/2016/en/> accessed 1 May 2023. See also UN Security Council Resolution on the Democratic Republic of Congo, Resolution 1952 (2010) <https://www.documents-dds-ny.un.org/doc/UNDOC/GEN/N10/655/23/PDF/N1065523.pdf?OpenElement> accessed 1 May 2023, which calls on all companies purchasing, processing, and consuming minerals in the DRC to apply and implement rights-based due diligence standards.

[23] Amnesty International, 'Amnesty challenges industry leaders to clean up their batteries' <https://www.amnesty.org/en/latest/press-release/2019/03/amnesty-challenges-industry-leaders-to-clean-up-their-batteries/> accessed 1 May 2023.

[24] Robin Goad, 'New cobalt supply central to growing electric vehicle market' Canadian Mining Journal (January 2019) <https://www.s1.q4cdn.com/337451660/files/doc_downloads/in-the-media/190101-Canadian-Mining-Journal-Cobalt-Commentary.pdf> accessed 27 August 2023, stating that regardless of its history of poor human rights record, corruption, instability, and environmental concerns, DRC will continue to be the world's largest producer of cobalt.

roles in the transition towards a net zero energy future. For example, while green hydrogen, solar, wind, and hydro projects have been discussed for their low carbon potential, the social, environmental, and human rights impacts associated with their development must be carefully weighed.

Apart from the foregoing concerns that feed into the discourse of energy justice, the net zero agenda also raises questions on energy security. For example, a reimagination of natural resource law and policy is required to ensure the reliability, security, and stability of the supply of critical and strategic mineral resources, such as cobalt, copper, manganese and lithium, in light of projected exponential growth in demand in the net zero era. At the same time, the world is facing one of the most serious threats to the international peace since the Second World War, following the invasion of Ukraine by the Russian Federation. The war in Ukraine is revealing a complex security of supply threat for energy, critical raw materials as well as other natural resources (including food supply), and the need to speed up the energy transition. While the REPowerEU package of the European Commission aims to do just that, questions remain as to the implications of the ambitious EU programmes for energy security worldwide.[25]

The undertone of conflict between the net zero agenda and the coherent implementation of natural resources law raises fundamental and pressing questions of policy and practice. It will be difficult to achieve a just, inclusive, and orderly global energy transition without a more precise understanding of the nature, scope, and guiding principles of natural resources law that is required to coherently balance the net zero agenda with broader sustainability aims.[26] This book provides a multijurisdictional and systematic exposition of how legal and regulatory systems are responding, and can better respond, to the wide range of sovereignty, security, and solidarity questions raised by net zero pledges. With case studies from Africa, Asia, Europe, North America, South America, and Australasia, it provides comparative analyses of the key implementation challenges and risks that arise, and legal and contract negotiation techniques for managing those challenges.

This chapter provides foundational information on both the contours and significance of the net zero discourse, and the fundamental questions on resource sovereignty, security, and solidarity that ongoing net zero programs and initiatives raise. After this general introduction, Section II provides conceptual clarification on resource sovereignty, security, and solidarity dimensions of net zero. Section III outlines the overall aim, methodology, and structure of the book, providing information on the work that the twenty-two chapters of the book have done to clarify the nature, scope, and guiding principles of natural resources law and policy in a net zero era. Section IV is the concluding section.

[25] European Commission, 'REPowerEU: affordable, secure and sustainable energy for Europe' <https://www.commission.europa.eu/strategy-and-policy/priorities-2019-2024/european-green-deal/repoweu-affordable-secure-and-sustainable-energy-europe_en> accessed 1 May 2023.

[26] Recognizing the lack of clear, transparent, and comprehensive regulatory standards on net zero, the UN Secretary-General in 2022 established the High-Level Expert Group on the Net-Zero Emissions Commitments of Non-State Entities (HLEG) to 'develop stronger and clearer standards for net-zero emissions pledges' and to speed up implementation. United Nations Climate Action, 'Credibility and Accountability of Net-Zero Emissions Commitments of Non-State Entities' (2022) <https://www.un.org/en/climatechange/high-level-expert-group> accessed 27 August 2023.

II. The Net Zero Trilemma: Defining Sovereignty, Security, and Solidarity Risks of the Clean Energy Transition

The global ambition to advance net zero has wide-ranging implications for the commercialization, management, and use of natural resources. Given the range of intersecting issues worldwide, this book focuses on three grand themes of natural resources law that are most impacted by net zero efforts, namely permanent sovereignty over natural resources, security, and solidarity.[27]

The interplay of the key trade-offs and decisions facing resource-dependent countries in the global energy transition has been described as an attempt to achieve an 'impossible energy trinity' of energy security, sustainable energy, and energy sovereignty.[28] The net zero trilemma—that is, the challenge of balancing resource sovereignty, security of supply, and solidarity in the clean energy transition—is the task of the century for natural resources law and practice.

A. Sovereignty

First are sovereignty questions which relate to how net zero targets and pledges may impact the abilities of resource-dependent countries to freely use and dispose of their natural resources in light of increased global defunding of non-renewable assets. Generally, the starting point of natural resources law and policy is that every country has the authority to make decisions with respect to the use, control, and disposal of natural resources within its territory.[29] This is the idea of permanent sovereignty of natural resources (PSNR) which has for several decades remained the bedrock of international law and diplomacy. For example, article 2.1 of the United Nations Charter specifically recognizes 'the principle of the sovereign equality of all its Members', while the UN General Assembly has adopted several instruments that recognize 'the right of peoples freely to use and exploit their natural wealth and resources is inherent in their sovereignty and is in accordance with the Purposes and Principles of the Charter of the United Nations'.[30] In addition to non-binding resolutions, several core and legally binding treaties recognize the permanent sovereignty of states over their natural resources. For example, article 1 (2) of the International Covenant on Economic, Social and Cultural Rights (ICESCR) expressly recognizes the right of countries to 'freely dispose of their natural wealth and resources' and that 'in no case may a people be deprived of its own means of subsistence'. Article 1 (2) of the International Covenant on Civil and Political Rights (ICCPR) contains the same express recognition. PSNR has,

[27] See eg *The UNESCO Declaration of Ethical Principles in relation to Climate Change* (13 November 2017) which, though not legally binding, outlines 'globally-agreed ethical principles that should guide decision-making and policy-making at all levels' on climate change.

[28] Philipp Thaler and Benjamin Hofmann, 'The Impossible Energy Trinity: Energy Security, Sustainability, and Sovereignty in Cross-Border Electricity Systems' (2022) 94 Political Geography 102579.

[29] Jérémie Gilbert, 'The Right to Freely Dispose of Natural Resources: Utopia or Forgotten Right?' (2013) 31(2) Netherlands Quarterly of Human Rights 314; Lillian Miranda, 'The Role of International Law in Intrastate Natural Resource Allocation: Sovereignty, Human Rights, and Peoples-Based Development' (2012) 45 Vanderbilt Journal of Transnational Law 785.

[30] UN Resolution 523 (VI) of 12 January 1952; Resolution 626 (VII) of 21 December 1952. See also resolutions 37/135, 36/173, 35/110, 34/136, and 32/161 and, with variations, resolutions 31/186, 3336 (XXIX), 3175 (XXVIII), and 3005 (XXVII).

therefore, come to signify the inalienable right of countries to freely determine legislation, policies, and fiscal frameworks for the management and use of their natural resources in accordance with their own objectives and priorities of sustainable development, without any external interference.[31] Sovereignty debates focus on avoiding or reducing foreign control over crucial domestic decisions on energy security and the management of natural resources.[32]

A rapidly evolving net zero drive, which is already resulting in the defunding and write down of fossil fuel resources and the associated risks of fossil fuel assets becoming stranded assets, therefore trigger questions on how to reconcile and balance net zero ambitions with the quest for resource sovereignty, economic subsistence, and social development by resource-dependent states. A key question is how to ensure the fair and equitable allocation of the financial, governance, and contractual risks of the net zero agenda to ensure it does not worsen social, economic, and environmental vulnerabilities in resource-dependent countries, especially in the Global South. This question is often framed in recent scholarship as cosmopolitan justice, which is the need to address the cross-border impacts of climate change and energy transition programmes and policies so as to avoid unintended adverse human rights impacts in already vulnerable countries.[33] For instance, host governments who heavily rely on revenues from fossil fuels are prone to financial and subsistence risks resulting from an inability to commercialize their natural resources. Also, net zero is already resulting in governance risks in many parts of the world, especially so in rentier economies in the Middle East, where governance is closely tied to the ability of states to provide subsidies and benefits to the people.[34] Efforts to eliminate fossil fuel subsidies and liquidity stress resulting from net zero induced budgets and spending cuts are already triggering a wave of public protests, discontent, and political instability in this and other world regions.[35] In response, some countries are asserting resource sovereignty rights by approving new coal, oil and gas, and carbon intensive projects, despite announcing net zero plans.[36] The deepening difficulties and failure to align net zero targets with natural resource politics, policies, and legislation remains a major threat to the clean energy transition.

Furthermore, the net zero transition raises the need for countries to renegotiate natural resource concessions, contracts, bilateral investment treaties, and procurement practices that may constrain their own abilities to advance net zero or result in complex disputes. Studies already show how stabilization provisions in extractive contracts, which freeze the abilities of states to update existing laws or contracts, may constrain the regulatory space

[31] United Nations Draft Declaration on the Right to International Solidarity <https://www.ohchr.org/sites/default/files/DraftDeclarationRightInternationalSolidarity.pdf> accessed 1 May 2023.

[32] Marti Rosas-Casals and others, 'Sovereignty, Robustness and Short-term Energy Security Levels: The Catalonia Case Study' (12 May 2014) 2(16) Frontiers in Energy Research 1–10.

[33] Inigo Del Guayo and others (eds), *Energy Law and Energy Justice* (OUP 2020) 1–25; Raya Salter, Carmen G Gonzalez, and Elizabeth Kronk Warner, *Energy Justice: US and International Perspectives* (Edward Elgar 2018) 73–104.

[34] Damilola Olawuyi, 'Advancing Innovations in Renewable Energy Technologies as Alternatives to Fossil Fuel Use in the Middle East: Trends, Limitations, and Ways Forward' in Donald Zillman and others (eds), *Innovation in Energy Law and Technology: Dynamic Solutions for Energy Transitions* (OUP 2018) 354–70.

[35] ibid; see also 'Report: Political instability biggest threat to net-zero transition' (15 November 2022) <https://www.thenational.scot/news/23124775.report-political-instability-biggest-threat-net-zero-transition/> accessed 14 August 2023.

[36] See Chapter 7 of this book. See also 'UK Energy Minister maintains country can still meet net-zero targets despite oil and gas licences' (2 August 2023) <https://www.offshore-technology.com/news/uk-energy-minister-net-zero-new-oil-gas/> accessed 14 August 2023.

for governments to advance net zero.[37] Such contractual risks resulting from net zero are already triggering new waves of disputes. As countries enact net zero legislation that constrain investment in non-renewable resource projects, investors may rely on stabilization and dispute resolution clauses to seek protection against any unilateral modifications to the terms of the agreed natural resource contracts by host states which prevents them from investing in such projects.[38] For instance, in the case of *Westmoreland Mining Holdings v Canada*, the claimant, a mineral licence holder, challenged the decision of the government of Alberta, Canada, to phase out coal-generated electricity by 2030. Westmoreland claimed that the Province of Alberta's Climate Leadership Plan (CLP), which aims to eliminate all electricity produced from coal by 2030, has abridged the lifespan of Westmoreland's mines in Alberta and treated Westmoreland unfairly in the process. Although the claim was dismissed for lack of jurisdiction, it shows the potential for new net zero regulations and environmental, social, and governance (ESG) requirements in the energy and mining sector to trigger disputes.[39] Another example is the case of *RWE AG and RWE Eemshaven Holding II BV v Kingdom of the Netherlands*.[40] The Netherlands Authority had proposed to abolish all coal-fired power plants by 2030. RWE filed an arbitration claim for €1.4 billion as compensation for 'expropriation of their investments' resulting from such new regulations that prohibit them from maximizing the coal mining investments under the issued licences.[41] The issue for determination therefore was whether or not the Netherlands' plan to phase out coal by 2030 violates the Energy Charter Treaty. While final determination of the substantive matters is still pending, this case shows the new forms of energy disputes that may begin to occur over the next few years as net zero obligations become fully implemented worldwide. This ongoing trend highlights the need for states and investors alike to reimagine natural resource contracts in the net zero era to address legal risks that may result from net zero efforts in a transparent manner.[42]

Furthermore, the global rush for energy transition minerals (ETMs) needed to drive the energy transition, and the rise of resource nationalism in many resource-rich countries reveal how resource politics are shaping the energy transition, and the need for a reimagination of natural resource contracts to better manage such political risks.[43] The exercise of resource sovereignty in the distribution of ETMs and other transition-related risks are bound to increase as countries worldwide adopt climate-change-focused laws and regulations. Existing and new contractual arrangements in the natural resource industry will therefore need to respond to the financial, governance, and contractual risks of net zero transition across the entire natural resource value chain. On the part of investors, there is a need to carefully negotiate and review new contracts to avoid costs associated with complying with net zero obligations as well as to address new and emerging transition risks.

[37] See Chapter 4 of this book.

[38] For more on stabilization clauses, see P Cameron, *International Energy Investment Law: The Pursuit of Stability* (2nd edn, OUP 2022) 1–25; also V Nalule, 'What is the Problem with Stabilization Clauses in Petroleum Agreements?' (2022) 13(1) Journal of Sustainable Development Law and Policy 85.

[39] ICSID Case No UNCT/20/3.

[40] ICSID Case No Arb/21/4.

[41] ibid.

[42] See, on the role of contract transparency in addressing contractual risks from net zero, Siân Bradley, *Transparency in Transition: Climate Change, Energy Transition and the EITI* (Chatham House, April 2020).

[43] See Chapter 4 of this book. See also Damien Nyer and Silvia Marchili, 'A new wave of resource nationalism in the mining & metals industry' (15 September 2021) <https://www.whitecase.com/insight-our-thinking/new-wave-resource-nationalism-mining-metals-industry> accessed 14 August 2023.

B. Security

Given the significance of the natural resource industry to the global economy, the search for security—that is, availability, affordability, accessibility, and reliability of supply of natural resources, and reducing the vulnerability of vital resource infrastructure systems to natural and ecological disasters—have been some of the most important objectives of natural resource law and policy.[44] Natural resource law aims to address challenges that impact the security of supply of water, energy, food, and other natural resources. Natural resource law provides a legal framework for ensuring security of supply. This includes regulating demand side management; balancing supply and sustainable consumption; ensuring resilience of supply networks and infrastructure to disaster risks; mitigating ESG impacts in the resource value chain; addressing climate change impacts on security; addressing business and human rights impacts including price distortion and modern slavery in production processes; and addressing resource curse concerns in a coherent and integrated manner amongst other things.[45]

Net zero specifically has three key implications for energy security, which are the focus of this book. First, is the direct concern that net zero initiatives may constrain efforts to address the energy poverty crisis—defined as the inability of households to access electricity and modern energy services at an affordable cost—facing many parts of the world, especially in the Global South.[46] In many countries of the Global North, where electrification rates are close to 100 per cent, energy transition is often framed in terms of a 'shift from high-carbon energy sources such as oil, gas and coal to low-carbon and zero-carbon energy sources such as renewables'.[47] Whereas in countries of the Global South, where there is still a heavy dependence and reliance on biomass and non-commercial fuels, such as charcoal, coal dust, wood, animal dung, and crop residues, for cooking, lighting, heating, and commercial activities, the current goal of energy transition is to achieve a shift from toxic and environmentally unsafe biomass fuels to modern commercial energy, such as natural gas-powered electricity and cooking stoves.[48] For example, despite the abundant natural gas wealth of the Middle East and North African region with 45 per cent of the world's proven natural gas reserves, the region is home to a significant portion of the world's energy-poorest people.[49] About 30 per cent of the people living in the MENA region still lack access to electricity, while an additional 30 per cent suffer from prolonged power outages and undersupply.[50]

[44] Raphael Heffron and others, 'A Treatise for Energy Law' (2018) 11 Journal of World Energy Law and Business 34–48.

[45] Catherine Banet and others (eds), *Resilience in Energy, Infrastructure, and Natural Resources Law: Examining Legal Pathways for Sustainability in Times of Disruption* (OUP 2022) 1–15.

[46] Damilola Olawuyi, 'Energy Poverty in the Middle East and North African (MENA) Region: Divergent Tales and Future Prospects' in Inigo Del Guayo and others (eds), *Energy Law and Energy Justice* (OUP 2020) 254–72.

[47] Anna Zinecker and others, *Real People, Real Change—Strategies for Just Energy Transitions* (The International Institute for Sustainable Development 2018) 1.

[48] International Renewable Energy Agency (IRENA) and African Development Bank (AfDB), *Renewable Energy Market Analysis: Africa and Its Regions* (IRENA and AfDB 2022) 31–40.

[49] Daniel Camos and others, *Shedding Light on Electricity Utilities in the Middle East and North Africa: Insights from a Performance Diagnostic* (World Bank Group 2017) 2–5, describing the paradox of energy poverty in the MENA region.

[50] In North Africa, about one in ten people do not have access to electricity. See Todd Lindeman, '1.3 Billion are Living in the Dark' (*Washington Post*, 6 November 2015); International Energy Agency (IEA), 'Access to Electricity' (2022) <https://www.iea.org/reports/sdg7-data-and-projections/access-to-electricity> accessed 10 August 2023.

Similarly, Sub-Saharan Africa has an average electrification rate of 24 per cent, meaning that about 76 per cent of the people living in the region still lack access to electricity, while an additional 30 per cent suffer from prolonged power outages and undersupply.[51] In resource-rich, but energy-poor countries, expanding access to modern forms of energy, such as electricity and modern fuels, remains a key focus and priority of the energy transition. With recent natural gas discoveries in countries such as South Africa, Mozambique, Senegal, Tanzania, and Nigeria, Global South countries are seeking new ways to leverage abundant natural gas resources to accelerate infrastructure development, reduce current energy poverty levels, and widen access to modern energy services in a manner that does not worsen the climate change emergency.[52]

However, with reduced financing for non-renewable natural resource projects, including natural gas infrastructure, efforts to accelerate energy access projects to combat energy poverty face an uncertain future and will require net zero-aligned financing and technology solutions.[53] Furthermore, worsening energy poverty and increasing energy cost which is exacerbated considerably by the Russia–Ukraine conflict, is already triggering sustainability reversals in a number of countries where there is now increased reliance on coal and biomass to meet urgent energy needs.[54] Such a disjunctive approach to the pursuit of net zero raises a fundamental question on how to design and implement innovative natural resource laws and policies that balance and advance energy security without delaying net zero transition goals.

Second, as demand for critical and strategic minerals needed to advance net zero transition increase, there is an urgent need for law and policy frameworks to ensure the security of their supply in order to avoid delays and missed targets for net zero. For example, as discussed in this book, the global effort to drive the energy transition has placed an increasing demand on lithium, which is crucial to manufacturing lithium-ion batteries used in energy storage and electric vehicles (EV).[55] Such a rush for transition minerals may result in heightened ESG concerns and human rights violations in the sourcing and supply of transition minerals, especially in developing countries in Africa, Asia, and South America.[56] There is therefore a need for innovative natural resource law and policy to advance the security and reliability of the supply of critical transition minerals in a manner that does not exacerbate energy poverty, gender, and energy injustice, or worsen ESG risks.

Third, the injection of new and cleaner sources of energy such as renewables and green hydrogen, into the energy networks and grids could result in damage to existing electricity infrastructure. A comprehensive legal framework is required to clarify licensing and

[51] Lindeman (n 50); also IRENA and AfDB (n 48) 31–40.

[52] IRENA and AfDB (n 48); see also Oleg E Aksyutin and others, 'The Role of Natural Gas in Achieving Sustainable Development Goals' (2020) 10(4) International Journal of Energy Economics and Policy 463; Damilola Olawuyi, 'The Role of Natural Gas in a Just and Equitable Energy Transition' in Damilola Olawuyi and Eduardo Pereira, *The Palgrave Handbook of Natural Gas and Global Energy Transitions* (Palgrave Macmillan 2022) 73–95.

[53] See Chapter 14 of this book on the role of green hydrogen technologies in advancing energy security. See also Damilola Olawuyi, 'Can MENA Extractive Industries Support the Global Energy Transition? Current Opportunities and Future Directions' (2020) Extractive Industry and Society Journal 100685.

[54] Yuru Guan and others, 'Burden of the Global Energy Price Crisis on Households' (2023) 8 Nature Energy 304.

[55] See Chapter 6 of this book. See also International Energy Agency (IEA), 'The Role of Critical Minerals in Clean Energy Transitions' (May 2021) <https://www.iea.org/reports/the-role-of-critical-minerals-in-clean-energy-transitions/executive-summary> accessed 10 August 2023.

[56] See Chapter 11 of this book.

permitting processes for hydrogen production, storage, commercialization, and export; while health, safety, and design standards for hydrogen infrastructure will need to be elaborated to ensure reliability and prevent environment, social, and governance risks. Furthermore, given that the focus of network laws has been on energy generation from centralized power plants, there is now an urgent need to refocus energy network regulations to advance net zero goals. Natural resources law must be reimagined to ensure that energy supply from a significant share of decentralized renewable sources does not outstrip demand by consumers, a situation that could result in system overloading or grid collapse. Furthermore, the increased adoption of energy efficiency and ESG requirements, such as net zero building standards, could result in increased compliance costs for investors, all of which may result in complex disputes.

Existing and new legal and regulatory standards in the natural resource industry will therefore need to respond to the foregoing legal challenges resulting from net zero initiatives.

C. Solidarity

Several of the sustainability challenges facing our world cannot be addressed in isolation. Natural resources law therefore emphasizes the continued importance of, and need for, solidarity and cooperation between key stakeholders, individuals, organizations, and countries in order to advance resource security.[57] For example, the obligation of states to cooperate in order to resolve problems that concern the international community has been a cornerstone and *raison d'être* of international law on energy, environment, and natural resources for many years.[58] Solidarity encompasses the 'union of interests, purposes and actions and the recognition of different needs and rights to achieve common goals'.[59] To advance solidarity in the management of natural resources, a number of international organizations such as the Organization of Petroleum Exporting Countries (OPEC), Gas Exporting Countries Forum (GECF), International Renewable Energy Agency (IRENA), and the Energy Charter Treaty, amongst others, have emerged to promote cooperative action to address common threats to energy security.[60] However, the ongoing energy transition has created an uncertain and complex outlook on the continued relevance and future roles of OPEC and GECF in advancing global solidarity in a net zero era.[61]

[57] See the *Germany v Poland* case (15 July 2021), in which the Court of Justice of the European Union (CJEU) affirmed that the principle of solidarity is a cornerstone of EU energy law. See Max Munchmeyer, 'The Principle of Energy Solidarity: *Germany v. Poland*' (2022) 59(3) Common Market Law Review 915; also Damilola Olawuyi, 'International Cooperation in Oil and Gas: The Role of OPEC and the GECF' in MM Roggenkamp, KJ de Graaf, and RC Fleming (eds), *Encyclopedia—Energy Law and the Environment* (Edward Elgar 2021).

[58] See Principle 24 of the Stockholm Declaration, United Nations (1971); also, Principles 7 and 14 of the Rio Declaration, United Nations (1992).

[59] See United Nations Special Mechanism on International Solidarity <https://www.ohchr.org/en/special-procedures/ie-international-solidarity> accessed 27 August 2023; the UNESCO Declaration of Ethical Principles in Relation to Climate Change, art 6 (13 November 2017), which, though not legally binding, emphasizes the need for solidarity between states and other pertinent actors to address climate change. See also Kaisa Huhta and Leonie Reins, 'Solidarity in European Union Law and Its Application in the Energy Sector' (2023) International and Comparative Law Quarterly 1–2.

[60] Olawuyi, 'International Cooperation (n 57); Munchmeyer (n 57).

[61] Thijs Van de Graaf, 'Is OPEC Dead? Oil Exporters, The Paris Agreement and the Transition to a Post-Carbon World' (2017) 23 Energy Research & Social Science 182.

The international dimensions of net zero transition, and the geopolitical dimensions of implementing net zero programmes, call for a reimagination of natural resources law and policy to further revitalize global solidarity and cooperative approaches.[62] First is the concern that increased net zero legislation in some countries may result in relocation of pollution-intensive industries to countries with lax environmental enforcement—the so-called 'pollution haven hypothesis' or carbon dumping—which may decelerate global progress in achieving net zero. On the other hand, is the concern that increased measures, unilateral policies, and rules aimed at advancing net zero might act as barriers to trade and investment. For example, governments might introduce carbon tax, Carbon Border Adjustment Mechanism (CBAM), energy efficiency standards, or eco-labelling requirements, which might have indirect impacts on international trade and the growth of domestic economies. Such measures risk also coming in conflict with the World Trade Organization (WTO) regime, which largely emphasizes the need to prohibit all trade restrictions other than tariffs.[63] Yet, due to the different levels of technology, capacity, and resource availability in different countries and regions, and the geopolitics of the net zero agenda, efforts to cooperatively address the impact of net zero in trade, investment, and environmental sustainability have not been easily forthcoming. These scenarios raise the need to reimagine natural resources law and policy through net zero-aligned trade and investment agreements, and market-based mechanisms, such as CBAM and regional Emissions Trading Systems (ETS) to advance collective solidarity and multilateral action on net zero. Furthermore, international energy organizations such as OPEC and the GECF must strategically evolve to play lead roles in promoting coherence and solidarity in the ongoing clean energy transition process.[64]

Solidarity is also required at the domestic level to promote a holistic approach in designing and implementing net zero programmes. As chapters of this book demonstrate, regulatory fragmentation and incoherence, meaning the existence of diverse and unaligned standards, metrics, requirements, and supervisory structures and institutions on net zero, remains a key threat to coherent implementation and progress.[65] Furthermore, power politics, isolationism, and lack of cross-sectoral synergy in aligning net zero goals with the management of water, energy, food, and other natural resources could slow down the clean energy transition process.[66] This book discusses the nexus governance approach to resource management as a framework for promoting the systemic and cross-sectoral solidarity required to advance net zero goals across the entire natural resource value chain a coordinated, coherent, and holistic manner.[67]

[62] See the Paris Agreement, art 6, which recognizes cooperative approaches and coordination in advancing climate goals.

[63] Daniel Bethlehem and others (eds), *Oxford Handbook of International Trade Law* (2nd edn, OUP 2022) 674–92.

[64] Van de Graaf (n 61); also Chapter 22 of this book.

[65] See also UN Climate Action (n 26).

[66] See Chapters 20 and 21 of this book. See also Damilola Olawuyi, 'Sustainable Development and the Water-Energy-Food Nexus: Legal Challenges and Emerging Solutions' (2020) 103(1) Journal of Environmental Science & Policy.

[67] See Chapter 22 of this book.

III. Aim, Methodology, and Structure of the Book

A. Aim

While earlier works have offered country-focused analyses and surveys of the implications of net zero transitions for the natural resources sector, the multidimensional, multijurisdictional, and intersectional nature of fundamental changes to natural resources law and policy as a result of net zero initiatives has yet to receive detailed, book-length exposition. This book fills this gap.

First, it examines the implications of net zero targets for established principles of natural resources law such as permanent sovereignty and jurisdiction over natural resources, do-no-harm, energy security, and energy justice, amongst others. Second, it evaluates how natural resources law and policy can coherently respond to, and manage, the wide range of interconnected energy security, energy justice, gender justice, network regulation, and other broad sustainability challenges posed by net zero. Third, it provides practical recommendations on how natural resources stakeholders can better align globally, regionally, and nationally in solidarity, to develop risk-informed, holistic, and cross-sectoral policies needed to advance just, orderly, and inclusive transition to net zero in the natural resource sector.

The twenty-two chapters unpack the sovereignty, security, and solidarity dimensions of the net zero transition; the legal and institutional barriers that hinder the coherent management of such risks; and legal pathways, including contract negotiation techniques, for promoting nexus governance in managing net zero transition risks across the entire natural resource value chain.

B. Methodology

While this book offers an in-depth examination of the sources and principles of natural resources law in a net zero era, it is clearly acknowledged that the substantive chapters cannot unpack and analyse every applicable piece of legislation and instrument in all natural resource-rich countries. Given the sheer number of legislation, regulations, policies, and contracts around the world, this book focuses on select case study countries with historically active levels of natural resources investment activity, especially in the extractive sector, and with publicly accessible legal instruments and information on their net zero ambitions and strategies.

In Africa, comparative examples are drawn from Nigeria, Malawi, South Africa, Kenya, and Zambia,[68] while China's role as the world largest supplier of lithium, a critical transition mineral, makes it an ideal case study in Asia.[69] Case studies from Chile, Colombia, and Mexico in Latin America,[70] as well as discussion of resource efficiency and ESG governance in the Middle East and North Africa region offer additional perspectives from resource-rich

[68] See Chapters 9 and 10.
[69] Chapter 6.
[70] Chapters 5, 8, and 18.

developing countries.[71] On the other hand, substantive chapters on the United States, United Kingdom, Canada, and Australia, Global North countries with ambitious clean energy transition programmes, as well as the EU,[72] offer balanced and representative perspectives from different legal traditions (common law, civil law, and mixed jurisdictions) on how natural resource stakeholders are responding to the wide range of sustainability questions posed by net zero. All the chapters adopt a comparative and lessons learned approach aimed at unpacking regulatory responses to the net zero trilemma. In parallel with these national and regional case studies, the book includes thematic chapters that distill the nature, scope, and guiding principles of natural resources law in a net zero era and future directions for the practice and development of the discipline.[73]

C. Structure

This book is organized into three parts, consisting of twenty-two chapters. Part I of the book examines how net zero targets and pledges are impacting the exercise of natural resource sovereignty, especially decision making on resource development, contracting, mining of ETMs, and strategies for risk allocation. After this introduction, Chapter 2 discusses the core principles of natural resources law, such as permanent sovereignty and jurisdiction over natural resources, do-no-harm, energy solidarity, energy security, and just transition, amongst others, and how the ongoing net zero transition is already altering their scope and application. Building on Chapter 2, Chapter 3 assesses the legal dimensions of sovereignty risks and trends that are associated with the clean energy transition and their implications for energy security and solidarity. It discusses the need for net zero-aligned natural resources law to address stranded assets, divestments, resource nationalism, procurement, and supply chain risks that are fast emerging. In response to these risks and trends, how should resource-rich countries update existing resource contracts to safeguard the use of their resources while advancing their net zero goals? Chapter 4 examines how clauses and provisions, such as stabilization and dispute resolution clauses in long-term resource contracts, may constrain or even freeze the sovereign rights and abilities of states to advance net zero. It also examines emerging changes to contractual and fiscal frameworks in response to sovereignty questions on the management of natural resources in a net zero era. Chapter 5 provides an overview of the different mineral strategies and legislation that are being developed by countries to maintain national sovereignty over their critical transition mineral resources in the face of increased demand fuelled by net zero ambitions.

Disputes and debates on PSNR and net zero strategies are bound to increase as countries adopt transition-focused laws and regulations aimed at addressing the net zero trilemma, including the supply of ETMs. Building on the first part, Part II of the book evaluates how natural resources law can foster regulatory coherence in responding to, and managing, the wide range of energy security, energy justice, gender justice, network regulation, and other

[71] See Chapters 11 and 13.

[72] Chapters 15, 16, and 17 on the EU; Chapter 10 on the United Kingdom; Chapters 12 and 20 on the United States; Chapter 21 on Australia.

[73] See Chapters 2–5, 11, 19, and 22 of this book.

broad sustainability challenges posed by net zero. Drawing lessons from China, Chapter 6 examines strategies and frameworks to promote regulatory coherence in the security and reliability of supply of ETMs such as lithium. Chapter 7 examines the implications of net zero for intergenerational equity in the development of natural resources. It examines how the regulatory disconnect between the ambitious net zero goals and the continued licensing of fossil fuel projects in Canada may worsen intergenerational injustice. Chapter 8 focuses on the question of how to coherently balance net zero, energy diversification and energy security goals in resource-dependent countries. Drawing lessons from Colombia, it considers the consequences of transition policies for the national energy matrix and the transformations to natural resource law needed to achieve carbon neutrality while ensuring energy security.

The need for regulatory coherence in balancing net zero goals with wider justice and human rights concerns in the net zero transition process are explored in the next set of chapters. Chapter 9 examines the role of law in advancing the exploration and development of energy transition minerals in a manner that does not exacerbate human rights violations, social exclusions, and inequity. Chapter 10 examines gender-based vulnerabilities and risks in the net zero transition and how natural resources law and policy can better balance and address those concerns. Chapter 11 examines ESG risks in natural resource investments including human rights challenges associated with net zero projects. It unpacks the drivers and dimensions of ESG risks in a net zero era, the nexus governance approaches, as well as corporate governance strategies, required to address such risks in an integrated manner.

Legislative reforms and enhanced due diligence processes are required to coherently address the sustainability, security, and justice risks of the net zero transition process. Chapter 12 analyses the need for standardized and more rigorous environmental impact assessment (EIA) processes and legal environmental baseline limits as key requirements for addressing the disconnect between net zero goals and the continued approval of fossil fuel projects in the United States. Still exploring the need for regulatory coherence between net zero goals and the design and approval of infrastructure projects, Chapter 13 highlights the prevailing disconnect between net zero goals and the continued reliance on carbon intensive fuels and technologies in buildings. It examines the role of environmentally sustainable technologies in lowering GHG emissions from buildings, and the need for net zero-aligned laws to promote climate-smart buildings and infrastructure across the entire natural resource sector value chain.

Green hydrogen technologies are increasingly discussed as important for net zero and the clean energy transition. The legal challenges associated with the introduction of green hydrogen as alternative to fossil fuel is examined in Chapter 14. It discusses the need for coherent and integrated policy measures for hydrogen production, infrastructure, and applications to effectively address legal, institutional, and technology challenges of green hydrogen production. Chapter 15 explores the legal challenges posed by a rapid increase of renewable energy sources to the existing transmission and distribution energy systems. It discusses natural resources law and policy transformations that are emerging in the EU to address security and reliability risks posed to electricity systems by the net zero transition.

The sovereignty and security questions raised by the net zero transition cannot be addressed in isolation. Part III of the book offers reflections on the importance of regulatory coherence and systemic solidarity at international, regional, and local levels in mitigating transition risks in the natural resources sector. Chapter 16 argues that a pragmatic mix of market-based measures such as emissions trading, can ensure greater coherence and progress towards net zero goals. It reviews various existing ETS in different parts of the world; the gaps to the coherent implementation to advance net zero objectives; and the reforms that are being carried out in the EU to advance the efficiency of ETS. Still on the subject of market-based mechanisms, Chapter 17 discusses the potential of CBAM as an instrument choice for promoting international solidarity for net zero. It evaluates the key opportunities and challenges associated with the EU CBAM, and the legal innovations required to enhance their coherent design and implementation of CBAMs. Advancing net zero will also require addressing the disconnect between net zero targets and regional and bilateral trade and investment treaties and agreements. Chapter 18 unpacks the role of regional free trade agreements, with clear and comprehensive natural resource and environmental provisions, as an instrument choice for advancing multilateral solidarity for net zero. Chapter 19 examines the role of international investment treaty and market reforms as tools through which investors in the natural resource sector can collaboratively reduce and manage financial, legal, and investment risks associated with net zero-driven fossil phase out decisions. It proposes reform measures that are required to bring investment treaties in line with the decarbonization urgency, and in particular to integrate net zero transition considerations in damage quantification.

Chapter 20 discusses multisectoral solidarity and nexus approaches to resource governance that will be required at national levels to advance coherence in the design and implementation of net zero programmes. Drawing lessons from the United States, it discusses how power politics, increasing partisan divisions, and the rise of nationalism and America first policies are weakening the required solidarity for advancing net zero and the clean energy transition. The regulatory incoherence resulting from power politics in Australia, including the dismantling of decarbonization regulations in 2014, are examined in Chapter 21. The chapter discusses the potential for climate litigation to propel faster and systemic change across various sectors, particularly in relation to Australia's continuing high levels of fossil fuel exports.

Chapter 22 (Conclusion) provides a synthesis of the drivers of fragmentation and regulatory incoherence in addressing the interconnected sovereignty, security, and solidarity challenges of net zero and the clean energy transition. It examines the role of a nexus governance approach to resource management in addressing such drivers; the legal, institutional, and technology barriers to achieving nexus and systemic governance in the natural resource sector; and the guiding principles for addressing such barriers.

Together, these twenty-two chapters interrogate the adequacy and coherence of extant natural resource law in frontier jurisdictions to deal with sovereignty, security, and solidarity dimensions of the ongoing global transition to net zero, and they do so in an in-depth, systematic, and practical manner. They propose forward-looking analyses of how the net zero agenda can be balanced with wider sustainability objectives in a coherent, just, and inclusive manner that sustains progress towards the safe, orderly, and sustainable use of natural resources for the development of our societies.

IV. Conclusion

Natural resource industries worldwide are undergoing rapid transformations driven mainly by ongoing transition to net zero in response to the problem of climate change and the need to diversify to low carbon energy sources.

The structural implications of this transition for resource sovereignty, energy security, and solidarity in resource-rich countries can be mitigated through innovative legal, contractual, and investment approaches that balance net zero ambitions with wider sustainability efforts. Furthermore, net zero targets and programmes will need to be clearly and systemically integrated into the mandates, processes, and work of all actors and stakeholders in the natural resource industry in order to avoid incoherent and duplicative implementation. A comprehensive analysis and study of structural and non-structural challenges that arise in the design, application, and implementation of net zero initiatives in the context of the energy transition can help us plot a comprehensive path for achieving policy coherence and reform.

The systematic and multijurisdictional assessment offered by this book can simplify the task of negotiating comprehensive, coherent, and enforceable natural resource contracts that minimize sovereignty, security, and solidarity risks in natural resource industries.

PART I
SOVEREIGNTY: INTRODUCTORY CONTEXT AND PRINCIPLES

2

Sources and Principles of Natural Resources Law and Policy in a Net Zero Era

Mehrnoosh Aryanpour

I. Introduction

This chapter examines the key sources of law, as well as principles, governing the ownership, commercial development, production, and supply of natural resources and how the ongoing net zero transition is fundamentally altering their scope and application.

In 2017, 195 countries adopted a set of ethical principles relating to climate change and the clean energy transition.[1] Though not legally binding, this resolution is part of ongoing efforts aimed at clarifying and addressing the wide range of sovereignty, security, and solidarity challenges associated with the ongoing clean energy transition.[2] Since the 2017 declaration, further questions have arisen as to why even though more than two-thirds of the global economy have released net zero targets, only less than 5 per cent of such targets are robust enough to halt the climate emergency or advance sustainability.[3] The lack of clarity and coherence in quantifying, verifying, and reporting on net zero targets and programmes raise the need for regulators, financing institutions, business enterprises, and other stakeholders to connect net zero targets with existing laws, licensing requirements, bidding guidelines, and policies in the natural resource sector in order to achieve coherent outcomes. For example, releasing net zero targets, while at the same time asserting permanent sovereignty over carbon-intensive natural resources, such as coal or oil and gas, and investing in new projects may not only escalate the climate emergency but could also delay the attainment of net zero targets.[4]

On the other hand, the diverse transition-related targets and obligations as well as the increased emphasis on environment, social, and governance (ESG) and human rights standards in natural resource development are rapidly widening the scope and application of existing principles of natural resources law, especially those relating to

[1] The declaration recognizes six important ethical principles relating to climate change: prevention of harm; precautionary approach; equity and justice; sustainable development; solidarity; and scientific knowledge and integrity in decision-making. See *The UNESCO Declaration of Ethical Principles in relation to Climate Change* <https://en.unesco.org/themes/ethics-science-and-technology/ethical-principles> accessed 10 August 2023.

[2] See Chapter 1 of this book. See also Frédéric G Sourgens and Leonardo Sempertegui, *Principles of International Energy Transition Law* (OUP 2023) chs 7–12.

[3] SEI, 'It's time to regulate standards and criteria for net-zero pledges' (10 October 2022) <https://www.sei.org/perspectives/regulating-net-zero-pledges/> accessed 26 August 2023.

[4] See Chapter 7 of this book. See also Offshore Technology, 'UK Energy Minister maintains country can still meet net-zero targets despite oil and gas licences' (2 August 2023) <https://www.offshore-technology.com/news/uk-energy-minister-net-zero-new-oil-gas/> accessed 10 August 2023.

Mehrnoosh Aryanpour, *Sources and Principles of Natural Resources Law and Policy in a Net Zero Era* In: *Net Zero and Natural Resources Law.* Edited by: Damilola S. Olawuyi, José Juan González, Hanri Mostert, Milton Fernando Montoya, and Catherine Banet, Oxford University Press.
 DOI: 10.1093/9780198925033.003.0002

do-no-harm, intergenerational equity, and energy justice, amongst others. For example, the scope and volume of climate change litigation brought against natural resource operators and licensees shows the increased colouration of natural resources law by international environmental and climate change law. Several of such claims relate to failure to mitigate greenhouse gas (GHG) emissions that cause climate change, non-compliance with net zero targets, lack of climate-smart infrastructure and technologies, legal liability for greenwashing and deceptive marketing, and inadequate compensation for climate loss and damage, amongst others.[5] These claims show that in a net zero era, just 'doing no harm' may not be enough. Investors and governments are expected to embed just transition, as well as responsible and rights-based practices into licensing requirements and contracting practices.[6] As net zero becomes the forefront and priority of natural resources law in the coming decades, effective risk management requires a renewed understanding of the key sources of natural resources law, and how the established guiding principles of natural resources law are changing due to net zero ambitions and targets.

Following this introduction, Section II provides an overview of the primary sources of law on natural resources development and commercialization. It examines the increasing role of international law, especially multilateral environmental agreements (MEAs), in the development and application of natural resources law at domestic and regional levels. Section III analyses how increased focus on net zero is resulting in a reimagination of well-established principles of natural resources law in light of the global energy transition. Key principles examined include permanent sovereignty and jurisdiction over natural resources, the do-no-harm principle, sustainable resource development and intergenerational equity, environmental justice (PANEL) principles, and the principle of cooperation (solidarity). Section IV explores barriers that limit the coherent integration of net zero principles in natural resources law. Section V proposes a dynamic legal innovation that would be required to better mainstream emerging norms on net zero in the (re)design of natural resources law, especially to address the fulfilment of net zero ambitions within the context of the decentralized commercialization of natural resources. The chapter concludes in Section VI.

II. Sources of Natural Resources Law

Natural resources law is generally derived from four key sources: (1) international law; (2) regional and domestic legislation; (3) judicial decisions; and (4) scholarly publications. This section provides an overview of these sources and examines the varying degrees in which the net zero transition has informed transformations in their interpretation and application in the natural resources industry.

[5] See Chapters 1 and 4 of this book. See also United Nations Environment Programme, 'Global Climate Litigation Report: 2023 Status Review' (27 July 2023), showing that more than 2,000 climate and net zero-related cases have been filed in sixty-five jurisdictions and international or regional courts and tribunals as of December 2022.

[6] See Chapter 4 of this book.

A. International Law

Although states have sovereignty and control over natural resources, international law has always played a key role in cooperative trade and the distribution of natural resources beyond borders. As Bilder rightly notes, 'international law provides a process, a set of techniques and a body of experience which can help nations to forge better solutions to resource problems'.[7] The sources of international law that shape the management and distribution of natural resources are derived from primary sources identified in article 38(1) of the Statute of the International Court of Justice, namely, international treaties or MEAs, customs, general principles of law, and judicial decisions and teachings of highly qualified publicists.[8]

1. Multilateral Environmental Agreements

With the rapid development of international environmental and climate change law over the last decades, natural resources law is now highly influenced by a wider range of MEAs that provide legal principles relating to the management of renewable and non-renewable natural resources.[9] MEAs address a broad range of environmental issues, but here we will focus only on those targeting climate change and clean energy transition.[10] MEAs and their commitments are upheld on the principle of *pacta sunt servanda* ('let agreements be kept') enshrined in article 26 of the 1968 Vienna Convention on the Law of Treaties (VCLT).[11] Thus, when a sovereign state joins an MEA, it commits to uphold the treaty's principles, including in the development and management of its natural resources.

As indicated in Table 2.1, a wide range of MEAs codify legal principles relating to pollution control, drastic reduction of GHGs that cause climate change, conservation of natural resources, protection of the ozone layer, and the integrated and sustainable management of water, energy, land, and agricultural resources for future generations, amongst others. For example, the 1987 Montreal Protocol on Substances that Deplete the Ozone Layer (Montreal Protocol) exemplifies a successful MEA that garnered broad support and accomplished its goals, namely, to mitigate the production and import of ozone-depleting substances and to reduce their concentration in the atmosphere in order to protect and restore the ozone layer as a natural resource. In addition to its importance in mitigating climate change, the Montreal Protocol is widely regarded as one of the most successful MEAs due to the relative success in achieving broad support, promoting the use of flexible mechanisms, and establishing a system of compliance and dispute resolution.[12]

Learning from that success, in 1994 the United Nations (UN) established the United Nations Framework Convention on Climate Change (UNFCCC), which was tasked with

[7] Richard B Bilder, 'International Law and Natural Resources Policies' (1980) 20(3) Natural Resources Journal 45.

[8] Statute of the International Court of Justice (signed 26 June 1945, entered into force 24 October 1945) 33 UNTS 993.

[9] Secretariat of the Pacific Regional Environment Programme (SPREP), 'What Are Global and Regional Multilateral Environmental Agreements (MEAs)?' (SPREP 2020) 5.

[10] ibid.

[11] Vienna Convention on the Law of Treaties (opened for signature 23 May 1969, entered into force 27 January 1980) 1155 UNTS 331.

[12] Guus JM Velders and others, 'The Importance of the Montreal Protocol in Protecting Climate' (2007) 104(2) Proceedings of the National Academy of Sciences of the United States of America 4814; Sean Cumberledge, 'Multilateral Environmental Agreements: From Montreal to Kyoto-A Theoretical Approach to an Improved Climate Change Regime' (2009) 37 Denver Journal of International Law & Policy 303, 313.

the goal of 'stabili[zing] greenhouse gas (GHG) concentrations in the atmosphere at a level that would prevent dangerous anthropogenic interference with the climate system'.[13] Today, the UNFCCC, with nearly 200 signatory nations, and the subsequent climate protocols that operationalize its provisions, namely, the 2005 Kyoto Protocol and the 2015 Paris Agreement, provide the institutional framework for combatting climate change.[14] The Paris Agreement formally recognized the necessity of limiting the global temperature increase to 1.5 degrees Celsius by capping cumulative totals of carbon dioxide (CO_2) to 40 gigatonnes by 2050.[15] The net zero drive is directly linked to article 4(1) of the Paris Agreement, which calls for efforts to 'achieve a balance between anthropogenic emissions by sources and removals by sinks of greenhouse gases in the second half of this century'.[16] As discussed in Chapter 1 of this book, signatories to the Paris Agreement have increasingly announced plans to achieve net zero emissions through both reductions in the carbon intensity of their activities as well as investment in negative-emission projects (ie those which are in the aggregate carbon reducing), as well as the acquisition of the requisite emissions offsets for any residual exigent CO_2.

Similarly, in line with the principle of Common but Differentiated Responsibilities and Respective Capabilities (CBDR-RC),[17] the UNFCCC encourages developed countries to take the lead in advancing climate mitigation and adaption efforts, including through the provision of finance, technologies, and capacity development for developing countries. The Paris Agreement also emphasizes the need to ensure that net zero efforts proceed 'on the basis of equity, and in the context of sustainable development and efforts to eradicate poverty'.[18]

2. International Trade Agreements and the World Trade Organization

In addition to MEAs, international trade agreements include a wide range of provisions relating to natural resource management, environmental protection, and climate change mitigation.[19] The WTO was built upon the achievements of the General Agreement on Tariffs and Trade (GATT) to establish a more comprehensive and formalized international organization dedicated to promoting global trade and resolving trade disputes.[20] Since the WTO's establishment, the organization has seen a growing focus on environmental issues. While the intersection of WTO and natural resources law is often discussed mainly in relation to the trade of natural resources or trade policies impacting their extraction and export, the WTO also recognizes the clear link between trade and climate issues.[21] However, the need to balance the conflict between environmental and climate change efforts and the

[13] United Nations Framework Convention on Climate Change, art 3, para 1, opened for signature 4 June 1992, S Treaty Doc No 102-38, 1771 UNTS 107; ibid art 4, para 1.

[14] Clare Breidenich and others, 'The Kyoto Protocol to the United Nations Framework Convention on Climate Change' (1998) 92(2) American Journal of International Law.

[15] Conference of the Parties, Adoption of the Paris Agreement, 12 December 2015, Paris Agreement to the United Nations Framework Convention on Climate Change, 12 December 2015, TIAS No 16-1104.

[16] See Chapter 1 of this book.

[17] UNFCCC (n 13).

[18] Paris Agreement (n 15); also Breidenich and others (n 14).

[19] See Damilola Olawuyi, 'Environment' in Isabelle Van Damme and others (eds), *Oxford Handbook of International Trade Law* (2nd edn, OUP 2022).

[20] Daniel Bodansky and Jessica C Lawrence, 'Trade and Environment' in Daniel Bethlehem and others (eds), *The Oxford Handbook of International Trade Law* (1st edn, OUP 2009) 505, 513–15.

[21] ibid.

Table 2.1 Core multilateral agreements applicable to net zero and natural resources law

International treaty	Key provisions
United Nations Framework Convention on Climate Change 1992	The ultimate aim of the Convention, as set out in art 2, is to reduce the emission of greenhouse gases (GHGs) that cause climate change.
Kyoto Protocol, 2005	Establishes legally binding targets for industrialized nations to limit the emission of GHGs. It also allows for flexibility by providing for the use of emissions trading and other market-based mechanisms.
Paris Agreement, 2015	The Paris Agreement sets the target of holding the increase in the global average temperature to well below 2°C above pre-industrial levels and to limit the temperature increase to 1.5°C above pre-industrial levels. Net zero is underpinned by art 4(1) which calls for efforts to 'achieve a balance between anthropogenic emissions by sources and removals by sinks of greenhouse gases in the second half of this century'.
Convention on Biological Diversity (CBD) 1992	The CBD is the principal MEA that seeks to protect and conserve biodiversity. It calls on countries to implement environmental impact assessment and other measures to prevent adverse impacts of economic activities, including energy development, on flora, fauna, and other aspects of the ecosystem.
UN Convention on the Law of the Sea (UNCLOS) 1982	UNCLOS aims to address the pollution of the marine environment from resource development, shipping (especially the transportation of oil and gas), and other economic activities. It emphasizes the sustainable management and conservation of living marine resources within national and international waters.
The International Convention for the Prevention of Pollution from Ships, 1973 as modified by the Protocol of 1978 (MARPOL 73/78)	MARPOL aims to prevent pollution of the marine environment by ships from operational or accidental causes.
International Convention on Civil Liability for Oil Pollution Damages	An auxiliary regulatory framework which stipulates that adequate compensation is available to persons who suffer oil pollution damage resulting from maritime casualties involving oil-carrying ships.
International Convention on establishing an international fund for Compensation of Oil Pollution Damages	It necessitates that there be adequate financial resources to provide the compensation demanded in cases where oil or hydrocarbons have demonstrably been leaked into nature.
Vienna Convention on the Protection of the Ozone Layer, the Montreal Protocol, and amendments thereof	A multiparty framework that encourages countries to stop the use of ozone-depleting substances. The Convention was supplemented by the Montreal Protocol, which requires countries to take concerted actions to protect the ozone layer. Both of the foregoing acknowledge that GHG emissions from hydrocarbons also contribute to ozone depletion.
Basel Convention on Hazardous Materials and Trans-border Movement thereof	It prescribes actions to limit the transboundary movement of hazardous chemicals and materials, some of which are by-products of energy activities.

(*continued*)

Table 2.1 Continued

International treaty	Key provisions
The Rotterdam Convention on the Prior Informed Consent Procedure for Certain Hazardous Chemicals and Pesticides in International Trade (PIC Convention)	This framework acknowledges the health risks of chemicals, including an exhaustive set of hydrocarbons and petroleum-based by-products. It establishes a prior informed consent procedure with which countries must comply when moving hazardous chemicals to other jurisdictions.
Stockholm Convention on Persistent Organic Pollutants (POPs) 2001	It aims to protect human health and the environment from chemicals and toxic organic pollutants, several of which are by-products of energy production processes, such as incineration of waste.
United Nations Convention to Combat Desertification	Considering the importance of lands and forests as natural resources, this Convention aims to combat desertification and mitigate the effects of droughts on forests and sustainable land use.
Non-binding international declarations and guidelines	**Key provisions**
United Nations Sustainable Development Goals (SDGs)	A collection of seventeen interlinked objectives designed to address a wide range of sustainability concerns facing the world. It includes natural resource sector-related targets such as energy for all, climate change mitigation, health and wellbeing, clean air and water, biodiversity, and the protection of the marine environment.
United Nations Guiding Principles on Business and Human Rights	The United Nations Guiding Principles on Business and Human Rights are a set of thirty-one principles that provide a framework for states and businesses to prevent and address human rights abuses linked to business activity, including natural resource development.
UN Resolution (A/76/L.75) on the human right to a clean, healthy, and sustainable environment	This UN Resolution expressly recognizes the human right to a clean, healthy, and sustainable environment and the duty of stakeholders in all economic sectors, including the natural resource sector, to protect, promote, and fulfil it.

Source: Compiled by author

WTO regime, which largely prohibits all trade restrictions other than tariffs, has been one of the most charged debates in international law.[22]

The Most Favored Nation (MFN) principle broadly requires member nations to 'immediately and unconditionally' grant any 'advantage, favor, privilege or immunity' granted to one WTO member to 'like products' from all other WTO member states[23] and to treat foreign goods and 'like products' equal to their local counterparts.[24] For example, in the case

[22] See Chapter 17 of this book. See also Joost Pauwelyn and David Kleimann, 'Trade Related Aspects of a Carbon Border Adjustment Mechanism. A Legal Assessment' (European Parliament Directorate-General for External Policies, Policy Department 2020); Felicity Deane, 'The WTO, the National Security Exception and Climate Change' (2012) 6(2) Carbon & Climate Law Review 157.

[23] See General Agreement on Tariffs and Trade (GATT) (30 October 1947) 61/Stat A-11/55 UNTS 194, art 1; General Agreement on Trade in Services (GATS) (15 April 1994) Marrakesh Agreement Establishing the World Trade Organization, Annex 1B, 1869 UNTS 183/33 ILM 1167 (1994) art 2; see also Kati Kulovesi, 'International Trade: Natural Resources and the World Trade Organization' in Elisa Morgera and Kati Kulovesi (eds), *Research Handbook on International Law and Natural Resources* (Edward Elgar Publishing Limited 2016) 52.

[24] Kulovesi (n 23) 52.

of *U.S.—Gasoline*,[25] it was determined that the US measure to apply differing baseline rules to imported and domestic gasoline violated GATT's MFN provision.[26]

However, while the WTO requires members to align domestic legislation and regulations with WTO obligations, the general exceptions article of GATT[27] recognizes that important public policy objectives, including, ostensibly, climate change, may justify a member state's derogation from international trade rules as well as principles such as MFN and proportionate national treatment. As such, article XX(b) allows member states to invoke policies contrary to international trade rules that are nonetheless 'necessary to protect human, animal or plant life and health'. Similarly, article XX(g) is invoked to justify derogations and deviations from international trade rules pertaining to the 'conservation of exhaustible natural resources if such measures are effective in conjunction with restrictions on domestic production or consumption', provided that the requisite criteria are met.[28]

Notably, in some cases involving natural resources, exceptions based on public policy listed in article XX GATT have been accepted as valid justifications for measures that would otherwise violate international trade laws, which bolsters the national remit to protect natural resources and the environment notwithstanding certain limiting case law.[29] However, the use of preferential local content policies in the natural resource sector, especially in renewable energy projects, has been challenged as a violation of WTO principles in several cases.[30] Debates over how net zero legislation and targets may be in conflict with WTO principles have already been raised in different countries.[31]

There is a need for greater coherence in trade and natural resource instruments in a manner that advances the clean energy transition and avoids complex disputes. Net zero and climate-aligned trade agreements that integrate just transition and sustainable resource management provisions are required.[32] At the regional level, the North American Free Trade Agreement (NAFTA) has included a separate parallel agreement on the environment, which, with the introduction of the Canada–United States–Mexico Agreement (CUSMA) that replaced NAFTA in 2020, incorporated environmental provisions directly within the new agreement.[33] CUSMA builds upon the principles of NAFTA with a chapter on environmental commitments and with a provision that environmental matters will be subject to the same adjudication process as disputes under the general trade agreement.[34] CUSMA, however, 'falls short on the crucial issue of climate change'[35] by including

[25] Appellate Body Report, *United States—Standards for Reformulated and Conventional Gasoline*, 7, WTO Doc WT/DS/AB/R (adopted 29 April 1996).

[26] Kulovesi (n 23) 53.

[27] Art 20 GATT.

[28] Kulovesi (n 23) 54.

[29] ibid.

[30] See Appellate Body Reports, *Canada: Certain Measures Affecting the Renewable Energy Generation Section, Canada: Measures Relating to the Feed-in Tariff Program*, 5.85, WTO Doc WT/DS412/AB/R, WT/DS426/AB/R (adopted 24 May 2013) (finding that Canada's LCR programmes—'Minimum Required Domestic Content Levels'—violate art III:4 GATT 1994 standards).

[31] See Chapter 4 of this book. See also David Kleimann and others, 'How Europe should answer the US Inflation Reduction Act' (2023) 4 Bruegel <https://www.bruegel.org/sites/default/files/2023-02/PB%2004%202023_0_1.pdf> accessed 26 August 2023.

[32] See Chapter 18 of this book.

[33] ibid.

[34] Silvia Maciunas, 'Environmental Provisions in CUSMA: A New Approach' Centre for International Governance Innovation, 16 July 2020. Policy Brief No 161.

[35] ibid 1.

provisions for protecting the planet but failing to mention climate change and neglecting collaboration on GHG emissions.[36]

The gaps in regional and international trade agreements show the herculean tasks that remain in integrating climate change and net zero targets in natural resource-related trade agreements.

3. International Investment Laws

International investment laws, often established through multilateral or bilateral investment treaties (BITs), aim to streamline the cross-border flow of foreign capital and investment into key economic sectors, including the natural resource sector.[37] Traditionally, investment laws focus on protecting foreign investors in host nations through various means, such as safeguarding investments from appropriation, providing incentives such as tax relief, and providing effective dispute resolution mechanisms.[38] However, in the net zero era, the rise of responsible investment and ESG principles that aim to uphold sound human rights and good governance policies in investments is rapidly changing the application of international investment law in the natural resource sector.[39] Not only are states and civil society actors checking whether an investment is net zero or zero carbon, they also want to measure whether the investment will promote just transition and sound ESG outcomes, while safeguarding the human rights of vulnerable groups such as women, youth, indigenous peoples, and local communities.[40]

A number of international investment agreements have emerged that expressly introduce responsible investment principles, including environmental protection, land rights, and climate change mitigation.[41] However, such increased focus on just transition principles has also resulted in a wide range of investment disputes with some investors challenging the decision of countries to introduce stringent net zero legislation and policies.[42] For instance, the Energy Charter Treaty (ECT), which established a 'legal framework to promote long-term co-operation in the energy field'[43] and has served as the largest energy-related MEA frequently invoked in investor–state dispute settlements,[44] has historically curtailed the ability of states to implement meaningful climate policies and instead protected the interests of investors, particularly in the hydrocarbon sector.[45]

[36] ibid 5.

[37] Rudolf Dolzer and Christoph Schreuer, *Principles of International Investment Law* (2nd edn, OUP 2012) 11.

[38] ibid.

[39] See Chapter 11 of this book. See also Nelson Goh, 'ESG and Investment Arbitration: A Future with Cleaner Foreign Investment?' (2022) 15 The Journal of World Energy Law & Business 485.

[40] Goh (n 39). See also Lorenzo Cotula, 'Rethinking Investment Treaties to Advance Human Rights' (2016) IIED Briefing.

[41] See Hafiz Mirza, William Speller, and Grahame Dixie, 'The Practice of Responsible Investment Principles in Larger- Scale Agricultural Investments: Implications for Corporate Performance and Impact on Local Communities' (World Bank Report Number 86175- GLB, World Bank and UNCTAD 2014).

[42] See Chapter 4 of this book.

[43] Energy Charter Treaty, art 2 (opened for signature 17 December 1994, entered into force 16 April 1998) 2080 UNTS 95.

[44] As of 1 May 2023, 158 arbitration claims are known to have been brought under the ECT. International Energy Charter, 'Statistics' (Energy Charter Treaty, 1 May 2023) <https://www.energychartertreaty.org/cases/statistics/> accessed 28 July 2023.

[45] Martin Dietrich Brauch, 'Should the European Union Fix, Leave or Kill the Energy Charter Treaty?' (Columbia Centre on Sustainable Investment Staff Publication 2021) <https://scholarship.law.columbia.edu/sustainable_investment_staffpubs/190> accessed 28 July 2023; see also Kyla Tienhaara and Lorenzo Cotula, 'Raising the Cost of Climate Action? Investor-State Dispute Settlement and Compensation for Stranded Fossil Fuel Assets' (International Institute for Environment and Development 2020) 32.

There is a need for greater coherence in the negotiation of investment treaties in a manner that does not constrain net zero programmes. As discussed further in Chapter 19 of this book, international investment law will also play a key role in mitigating revenue loss and damages associated with net zero.

Net zero and climate-aligned investment agreements that integrate just transition and sustainable resource management provisions can enable countries and investors to clarify net zero ambitions and obligations and to cooperatively implement them. Announcing net zero targets without updating long-term natural resource investment agreements exacerbates regulatory incoherence which may reduce the competitiveness of a country to attract foreign direct investment needed to advance the clean energy transition.

B. Regional and Domestic Legislation

Regional and national regulatory regimes also play important roles in the creation of rules and norms impacting natural resource development. The EU's climate governance regime ranges from the 2003 emissions trading scheme directive that established carbon pricing for large industrial power plants to domestic aviation and instruments, such as the largest ever stimulus package adopted, providing a €750 billion commitment to creating a 'greener Europe' under the NextGeneration initiative.[46] The European Green Deal passed in 2020 intends to reshape the European Union (EU) into a resource-efficient and competitive economy, achieving net zero GHG emissions by 2050 with significant investment allocation from the NextGenerationEU Recovery Plan and the EU's seven-year budget to support its implementation.[47] Outside Europe, in the Middle East region, each member of the Gulf Cooperation Council has formed a National Committee on Climate Change, with reasonably harmonized financial and governance commitments to achieve net zero.[48] Similarly, in Africa, state commitments to propose and implement rigorous carbon reduction measures have coalesced in the form of the Africa Nationally Determined Contribution (NDC) Hub,[49] which as of October 2021, has been endorsed by thirty-eight of fifty-four constituent members.

Such rapid development of regional and community laws on net zero is resulting in increased regulatory action at the domestic level. As discussed in Chapter 1 of this book, more than 2,000 jurisdictions and governments worldwide have now declared a climate emergency, resulting in increased legislation and regulatory action to achieve net zero by the year 2060 or earlier.[50] A good example is the Inflation Reduction Act (IRA), passed in 2022 with over US$400 billion in spending over the next decade including for climate

[46] Marco Giuli and Sebastian Oberthür, 'Third Time Lucky? Reconciling EU Climate and External Energy Policy During Energy Security Crises' (2023) 45 Journal of European Integration 395.

[47] European Commission, 'Recovery Plan for Europe' <https://commission.europa.eu/strategy-and-policy/recovery-plan-europe_en> accessed 29 May 2023.

[48] The World Bank, 'Gulf Economic Update: Achieving Climate Change Pledges' (World Bank Publications 2022).

[49] African Development Bank, 'Africa's NDC Journey and the Imperative for Climate Finance Innovation' (India Environment Portal, 11 August 2021).

[50] See Climate Emergency Declaration 'Climate emergency declarations in 2,309 jurisdictions and local governments cover 1 billion citizens' (21 August 2023) <https://climateemergencydeclaration.org/climate-emergency-declarations-cover-15-million-citizens/> accessed 26 August 2023.

change mitigation and clean energy projects.[51] Countries such as the United Kingdom, Norway, Nigeria, and Kenya, amongst others, have also enacted specific climate legislation that provides a clear legal framework for GHG emission reduction and the transition to cleaner energy sources.[52] In Nigeria, for example, the climate legislation requires every private business with more than fifty employees to appoint a Climate Change Officer and to submit periodic Action Plans on climate change efforts. It also prescribes fines for non-compliance.[53] The legislation shows the need for investors to carefully examine the increasing forms of ESG obligations that are arising in climate change and net zero-related legislation in order to avoid non-compliance risks.

However, despite the increase in climate legislation, the continued approval of carbon-intensive natural gas projects, especially coal, oil, and gas, show the challenges that remain in aligning net zero targets with climate change and natural resource legislation and policies.[54] Regulatory incoherence and the misalignment of natural resources law with net zero targets would not only delay the path to the clean energy transition but could also result in complex disputes and risks for investors.

C. Judicial Decisions and Scholarly Publications

In addition to the primary sources of international law discussed above, natural resources also remain influenced by the judicial decisions of domestic courts, as well as the scholarly works of qualified experts and institutions, such as the World Bank, the UN Intergovernmental Panel on Climate Change (IPCC), International Energy Agency (IEA), International Bar Association, and the International Law Association, amongst others.[55]

In common law jurisdictions, such as the United States, United Kingdom, and most of the commonwealth where the *stare decisis* principles apply, the judgment of courts may be invoked as a binding source of law.[56] However, in civil law countries, such as the Middle East and North Africa region, as well as in several European states, case law does not constitute a binding source of law but may be regarded as persuasive authority for the formation of norms.[57]

The role of courts in the formation of just transition and net zero principles has been accentuated over the last decade. As of December 2022, more than 2,000 climate and net zero-related cases have been filed in sixty-five jurisdictions and international or regional courts and tribunals.[58] Governments and investors have been challenged for

[51] House of Representatives, Congress. HR 812 (IH), 'Inflation Reduction Act of 2023' 2022 (IRA) 136 Stat 1818.

[52] United Kingdom: Climate Change Act 2008; Norway: Climate Change Act 2017; Nigeria: Climate Change Act 2021; Kenya: Climate Change Act 2016. See London School of Economics and the Grantham Research Institute on Climate Change and the Environment, 'The Climate Change Law of the World' <https://www.climate-laws.org> accessed 26 August 2023.

[53] Government of Nigeria, Climate Change Act 2021, art 24 (18 November 2021) <https://www.ilo.org/dyn/natlex/natlex4.detail?p_isn=112597&p_lang=en> accessed 26 August 2023.

[54] See Chapter 7 of this book. See also Offshore Technology (n 4).

[55] For a discussion of the importance of scholarly publications as a source of law, see *Paquete Habana case* 175 US 677 (1900).

[56] Joseph Dainow, 'The Civil Law and the Common Law: Some Points of Comparison' (1966–67) 15 American Journal of Comparative Law 419.

[57] ibid; also Damilola S Olawuyi, *Environmental Law in Arab States* (OUP 2022) 52–55.

[58] See United Nations Environment Programme (UNEP), 'Global Climate Litigation Report: 2023 Status Review' (27 July 2023) <https://www.unep.org/resources/report/global-climate-litigation-report-2023-status-review> accessed 26 August 2023.

inadequate net zero programmes or approving new investments that are inconsistent with their obligations under the Paris Agreement.[59] Furthermore, some natural resource operators have been challenged for greenwashing and misleading consumers on the scope and impact of their net zero programmes and products.[60] These cases highlight the importance of regulatory alignment and coherence in protecting natural resources, achieving net zero goals, and implementing responsible investment practices, especially by addressing ESG risks. Failure to align natural resource legislation and policies with net zero targets will not only increase the scope and scale of such disputes but could significantly delay the implementation of clean energy transition projects.[61] An in-depth understanding of the rapidly changing scope of natural resources laws and principles will help investors design more up-to-date and net zero-aligned risk management strategies.

The next section analyses how net zero and clean energy transition is expanding the scope and application of well-established principles of natural resources law.

III. Net Zero and the General Principles of Natural Resources Law

Natural resources law has its roots in principles and concepts that aim to advance the safe, orderly, sustainable, and efficient development and management of natural resources for the benefit of current and future generations.[62] Despite some debates on the legal status of some of these principles, they are widely recognized and have become the bedrock of natural resources law and policy in several jurisdictions.[63]

A. Permanent Sovereignty over Natural Resources (PSNR)

As discussed in Chapter 1 of this book, while the PSNR principle aims to prevent foreign influence over domestic policies on the use of natural resources, the increased internationalization of climate change governance impacts the very foundation of PSNR.[64]

Tensions arise regarding a state's ability to shift away from traditional dominance over natural resources while maintaining its sovereignty. Furthermore, as the rush for energy transition minerals (ETMs) escalates, countries with abundant ETMs are increasingly

[59] See *Earthlife Africa v Minister of Environmental Affairs* (65662/16) [2017] ZAGPPHC 58; BVwG Wien 2.2.2017 W109 2000179-1/291E; *Milieudefensie et al. v Royal Dutch Shell plc.*, The Hague District Court, C/09/571932/HA ZA 19-379, 25 April 2022 (Netherlands).

[60] See 'Environmental NGO wins greenwashing lawsuit against TotalEnergies' (5 April 2023) <https://www.cleanenergywire.org/news/environmental-ngo-wins-greenwashing-lawsuit-against-totalenergies> accessed 26 August 2023; also *Advertising Standards Authority UK v Shell UK Ltd* <https://www.asa.org.uk/rulings/shell-uk-ltd-g22-1170842-shell-uk-ltd.html> accessed 26 August 2023.

[61] Anna-Julia Saiger, 'Domestic Courts and the Paris Agreement's Climate Goals: The Need for a Comparative Approach' (2020) 9 Transnational Environmental Law 37.

[62] Christine A Klein and others, *Natural Resources Law: A Place-Based Book of Problems and Cases* (4th edn, Aspen Publishing 2018) 1–15; Robert L Fischman, 'What Is Natural Resources Law?' (2007) 78 University of Colorado Law Review 717 <https://www.repository.law.indiana.edu/facpub/197> accessed 26 August 2023.

[63] Klein and others (n 62) 1–15.

[64] See Raphael J Heffron and others, 'A Treatise for Energy Law' (2018) 11 The Journal of World Energy Law & Business 34; also Benjamin Sovacool and others, 'Energy Decisions Reframed as Justice and Ethical Concerns' (2016) 1 Nature Energy 16024.

updating their mining laws to assert great control over ETMs.[65] The shift in the application of PSNR and the increasing resource politics associated with the clean energy transition raise cosmopolitan justice questions which require collaborative dialogue and solidarity by the international community.[66]

Chapter 3 discusses the wide range of financial, economic, and socio-political decisions that face carbon-intensive economies and societies, as they try to decarbonize, address energy poverty, and create clean energy jobs in a just and inclusive manner that leaves no one behind. Asserting resource sovereignty by approving carbon-intensive projects, or through resource nationalism, will not only worsen the climate crisis but could significantly delay the clean energy transition.

There is therefore a need for net zero and climate-aligned legislation, fiscal regimes and policies that enhance coherence between national visions and ambitions on net zero, and the laws, practices, and guidelines on natural resource development.

B. Do-No-Harm Principle

As a foundational principle of international environmental law, the do-no-harm principle imposes upon states the positive obligation to prevent, mitigate, and control environmental harm arising from activities within their territorial borders.[67] The do-no-harm principle requires robust and extensive environmental impact assessments and human rights due diligence aimed at preventing transboundary environmental harm.

Initially invoked by a tribunal in the context of a US–Canada transboundary border dispute, the 1941 *Trail Smelter* dispute found Canada responsible for environmental damages inflicted upon US farmers from fumes emitted from a copper smelter company on Canadian land.[68] The tribunal noted that, as a principle of international law, 'no State has the right to use or permit the use of its territory in such a manner as to cause injury by fumes in or to the territory of another'.[69] This principle was later reasserted in the *Corfu Channel* dispute, which held that it is 'every State's obligation not to allow knowingly its territory to be used for acts contrary to the rights of other States',[70] and by the International Court of Justice (ICJ) in *Pulp Mills*, which held that states must use all means at their disposal to prevent activities within their borders from inflicting environmental harm.[71]

Principle 21 of the Stockholm Declaration notes that states have the 'responsibility to ensure that activities within their jurisdiction or control do not cause damage to the environment of other States or of areas beyond the limits of national jurisdiction',[72] as is echoed by Principle 2

[65] See Chapters 1 and 4 of this book. See also Damien Nyer and Silvia Marchili, 'A new wave of resource nationalism in the mining & metals industry' (White & Case, 15 September 2021).

[66] Sovacool and others (n 64).

[67] See *Legality of the Threat or Use of Nuclear Weapons* (Advisory Opinion) [1996] ICJ Rep (I) 242, para 29, which identified this principle as customary international law.

[68] Trail Smelter Case (*United States of America v Canada*) (1938 & 1941) 3 Rep Intl Arbitral Awards 1905, 1965.

[69] ibid.

[70] Corfu Channel Case (*United Kingdom v Albania*) (Merits) [1949] ICJ Rep 4, 22.

[71] Pulp Mills on the River Uruguay (*Argentina v Uruguay*) (Judgment) [2010] ICJ Rep 14.

[72] 'Report of the United Nations Conference on the Human Environment' UN Conference on the Human Environment (Stockholm 5–16 June 1972) UN Doc A/CONF.48/14/Rev.1.

of the Rio Declaration.[73] Though not legally binding, the UNESCO Declaration also emphasizes that states should 'anticipate, avoid or minimize harm, wherever it might emerge, from climate change, as well as from climate mitigation and adaptation policies and actions'.[74]

The implication is that in a net zero era, 'harm' may no longer be thought of in the context of large projects alone, but now includes policies or projects by a state that may exacerbate climate change, such as approval of carbon-intensive projects.[75] Similarly, in addition to taking steps to reduce GHG emissions, development institutions and investors are elaborating policies that focus on the principle of 'do good beyond do no harm', which aim to promote respect for human rights and social inclusion.[76] In defining the 'do good beyond do no harm' principle, the Inter-American Development Bank requires its borrowers to not only demonstrate 'ways in which harms will be avoided, but also consider and report on ways in which project design will enhance both the social and the environmental good'.[77] The increasing recognition of obligations relating to just transition, ESG, responsible contracting, and green procurements shows that in a net zero era, do-no-harm includes the need to conduct human rights due diligence (HRDD) aimed at addressing social impacts of clean energy transition programmes.[78]

To avoid legal, contractual, and reputational risks relating to environment and social harm, investors will not only need to conduct extensive environmental impact assessments (EIAs) and HRDDs to mitigate GHG emissions and all forms of pollution, but they must also play active roles in advancing clean energy innovation, green procurements, research, awareness, and empowerment programmes that enhance social and environmental good.

C. Sustainable Resource Development and Intergenerational Equity

Ever since the Brundtland Commission report defined sustainable development as 'development that meets the needs of the present without compromising the ability of future generations to meet their own needs', the principle has remained a core foundation of natural resources law.[79] Sustainable resource development includes *intragenerational equity*, which means the fair, equitable, and efficient use of resources to meet the needs of the current generation. It also includes *intergenerational equity* which emphasizes the importance of fairness and justice in the utilization and preservation of the environment and its natural resources for future generations.[80] While intergenerational equity debates over the years

[73] 'Report of the United Nations Conference on Environment and Development' UN Conference on Environment and Development (Rio de Janeiro 3–14 June 1992) (12 August 1992) UN Doc A/CONF.151/26/Rev.1.

[74] Art 2 UNESCO Declaration (n 1).

[75] Benoît Mayer, 'The Relevance of the No-Harm Principle to Climate Change Law and Politics' (2016) 19 Asia Pacific Journal of Environmental Law 79.

[76] See Inter-American Development, Environmental and Social Policy Framework (September 2020) 7–8; see also Responsible Business Alliance, 'Decarbonization' <https://www.responsiblebusiness.org/initiatives/rei/decarbonization/> accessed 26 August 2023.

[77] Inter-American Development (n 76) 6.

[78] See United Nations Working Group on Business and Human Rights (UN WGBHR), 'Extractive Sector, Just Transition and Human Rights' (2023) UN General Assembly Report A/78/155.

[79] World Commission on Environment and Development, *Our Common Future* (OUP 1987).

[80] Simon Caney, 'Climate Change, Intergenerational Equity and the Social Discount Rate' (2014) 13(4) Politics, Philosophy and Economics 320; see also Theo Henckens, 'Mineral Resources Ethics' in Theo Henckens, *Governance of the World's Mineral Resources* (Elsevier 2021) 71–98.

tend to focus on resource conservation and management, its application in a net zero era includes taking concrete steps to halt the climate emergency, and doing so in a manner that ensures the sustainable use of geologically scarce energy transition mineral resources.[81]

As discussed in Chapter 7 of this book, the intergenerational equity principle requires sovereign states to balance decisions on energy security and hydrocarbon development, with net zero targets in a manner that safeguards the environment for future generations. The increasing misalignment between net zero targets and approval of carbon-intensive projects raises significant intergenerational equity questions. Net zero and climate aligned policy-making should prioritize choices and actions that reduce the future cost of delayed transition, in terms of the adverse social, environmental, and economic impacts of climate change, for the future generation. Achieving intergenerational equity will also require addressing barriers to active youth participation in decision-making on energy transition to ensure that future generations play the lead role in decision-making processes on net zero.[82]

D. Just Transition (Energy and Environmental Justice)

The clean energy transition is projected to result in significant social, economic, and environmental burdens for communities, especially at-risk groups such as women, youth, indigenous peoples, and workers in emissions-intensive sectors.[83] Furthermore, the implementation of clean energy transition projects have increasingly been linked with racial capitalism, compulsory acquisition of lands as project sites, forced displacements, social exclusions, concentration of projects in poor and vulnerable communities, governmental repression, and other complex human rights violations in many countries.[84]

Debates on just transition therefore aim to ensure the fair, inclusive, and equitable implementation of clean energy transition programmes in a manner that upholds the human rights of impacted peoples and communities and ensures that no one is left behind.[85] Just transition draws on longstanding principles relating to climate justice, energy justice, and environmental justice, all of which require that natural resource laws, regulations, and policies be designed and implemented in a right-based manner, with meaningful participation of all people regardless of income, race, colour, creed, or national origin.[86] The Paris Agreement expressly recognizes the 'imperatives of a just transition of the workforce', and

[81] Henckens (n 80); also Bill Anderson-Samways and John Hobby, 'On Borrowed Time: Future Generations and the Net Zero Transition' Briefing Paper (June 2022) Social Market Foundation/Intergenerational Foundation <https://www.smf.co.uk/wp-content/uploads/2022/06/On-Borrowed-Time-June-2022.pdf> accessed 26 August 2023.

[82] See Simon Caney, 'Global Climate Governance, Short-Termism, and the Vulnerability of Future Generations' (2022) 36(2) Ethics & International Affairs 137, 147–48.

[83] Catherine Saget and others, 'Jobs in a Net-Zero Emissions Future in Latin America and the Caribbean' (Inter-American Development Bank and International Labour Organization, Washington DC 2020).

[84] See Carmen G Gonzalez, 'Racial Capitalism, Climate Justice, and Climate Displacement' (2021) 11(1) Oñati Socio-Legal Series 108; also Damilola Olawuyi, 'Energy (and Human Rights) for All: Addressing Human Rights Risks in Energy Access Projects' in Raya Salter, Carmen G Gonzalez, and Elizabeth Kronk Warner (eds), *Energy Justice: US and International Perspectives* (Edward Elgar 2018) 73.

[85] See UN WGBHR (n 78); also Raphael J Heffron, 'The Role of Justice in Developing Critical Minerals' (2020) 7 The Extractive Industries and Society 855.

[86] Heffron and others (n 64) 40–43, see also Inigo Del Guayo and others (eds), *Energy Law and Energy Justice* (OUP 2020) 1–15; Ryan Holifield and others, *Handbook of Environmental Justice* (Routledge 2017) 567–78.

the need for all Parties to 'respect, promote and consider their respective obligations on human rights' when taking action to address climate change.[87]

A wide range of other international instruments emphasize the need to integrate five core human rights principles (the PANEL Principles) in the design and implementation of clean energy transition programmes in order to advance just transition.[88] In the context of net zero, *Public participation* recognizes that clean energy transition policies must be developed and implemented with the participation of the 'public' (ie all those who have been or are susceptible to be impacted by clean energy transition programmes), in accordance with the free, prior, informed consent (FPIC) principle. *Accountability* requires a positive obligation on behalf of states and participants to demonstrate that climate change mitigation efforts and goals are faithfully monitored and executed in accordance with the prescribed rules and standards. *Non-discrimination and equality* means that climate efforts and policies should include clear vulnerability assessments and guidelines to identify adverse human rights effects on marginalized groups, while continuously establishing internal guidelines to monitor and reduce social exclusions in implementation. *Empowerment and access to information* recognizes the importance of equipping the public with knowledge and accessible information and resources to engage meaningfully in decision-making on net zero and energy transition. Finally, *Legality and access to justice* requires addressing all barriers to meaningful and effective legal remedies for victims of pollution and other human rights violations in natural resource development activities, including clean energy transition.[89]

As discussed in Chapter 4 of this book, just transition clauses are now increasingly inserted in natural resource contracts, legislation, and policies to underpin the obligations of investors and state-owned enterprises to coherently address gender justice, environmental justice, ESG, and other justice risks associated with natural resource investments.[90] To reduce the burdens of the transition, especially on workers in emissions-intensive sectors, a just transition also requires concrete programmes that create new economic opportunities through green jobs, green transportation, and eco-entrepreneurship to promote cleaner technologies, such as green hydrogen, electric vehicles, biofuels and carbon capture utilization and storage (CCUS).

E. Solidarity

As discussed in Chapter 1, solidarity, that is, broad-based cooperation and collaboration, through knowledge exchange, technology transfer, and capacity development,

[87] See Preamble to the Paris Agreement, also arts 2.2 and 4.1.

[88] See the International Labour Organisation (ILO), 'Outcome of the General Discussion Committee on a Just Transition: Proposed resolution and Conclusions submitted to the Conference for adoption', 111th Session, 2023 (15 June 2023) <https://www.ilo.org/wcmsp5/groups/public/---ed_norm/---relconf/documents/meetingdocument/wcms_885375.pdf> accessed 26 August 2023; see also ILO, 'Guidelines for a Just Transition' (2015) <https://www.ilo.org/wcmsp5/groups/public/---ed_emp/---emp_ent/documents/publication/wcms_432859.pdf> accessed 26 August 2023.

[89] See ILO, 'Outcome of the General Discussion Committee on a Just Transition' (n 88); ILO, 'Guidelines for a Just Transition' (n 88); also Sourgens and Sempertegui (n 2); Holifield and others (n 86); Damilola S Olawuyi, 'Local Content and the Sustainable Development Nexus' in Damilola S Olawuyi (ed), *Local Content and Sustainable Development in Global Energy Markets* (CUP 2021) 8; Damilola S Olawuyi, 'Corporate Accountability for the Natural Environment and Climate Change' in Ilias Bantekas and Michael Ashley Stein (eds), *The Cambridge Companion to Business and Human Rights Law* (CUP 2021) 237.

[90] See also the Chancery Lane Project, 'Just Transition in Climate Clauses' (last updated 3 November 2022) <https://chancerylaneproject.org/wp-content/uploads/2022/11/Just-Transition-in-Climate-Clauses-V1.pdf> accessed 10 June 2023.

is required to advance the clean energy transition.[91] A number of international instruments, including Sustainable Development Goal 17, underscore the need for enhanced partnerships—globally, regionally, nationally, and locally—as a required step for advancing development goals, including the clean energy transition, across all sectors.[92]

However, the rise of nationalism, regional political uprisings, and the increased weakening of multilateralism shake the very foundation of international climate solidarity.[93] A good example is the ongoing Russia–Ukraine crisis which has not only impacted energy security in many parts of the world, but has also fundamentally weakened collaborative efforts to advance clean energy transition.[94] There is also consensus in scholarly literature that economic sanctions applied against some countries may stunt global energy transition and net zero efforts in the targeted jurisdiction.[95] While sanctions are not directly designed to halt environmental protection efforts, in practice that is often the inevitable result.[96] Furthermore, at the domestic level, deepening power politics, political fragmentations, and sectoral approaches have complicated the process of advancing collaborative solutions and decisions needed to advance net zero.[97]

The increasing fragmentation and weakening of solidarity at international, regional, and domestic levels calls for a new form of resource politics that prioritizes the urgency of climate change and fosters the required collaboration to address it. Net zero and climate-aligned diplomacy that enhances collaboration on knowledge exchange, technology transfer, and capacity development, especially from the Global North to the Global South, are urgently required to bridge the current technology and financing gaps that limit progress on net zero.[98]

IV. Moving from Principles to Practice: Lessons Learned

As discussed in the previous sections, while net zero targets and clean energy transition policies are increasingly prevalent across the world, progress in advancing net zero remains

[91] See also art 6 UNESCO Declaration (n 1); also Eva Kassoti and Narin Idriz (eds), *The Principle of Solidarity: International and EU Law Perspectives* (Asser Press 2023) 76.

[92] Marianne Beisheim and Nils Simon, 'Multistakeholder Partnerships for Implementing the 2030 Agenda: Improving Accountability and Transparency', Analytical paper for the 2016 ECOSOC Partnership Forum (11 March 2016).

[93] Shekhar Aiyar and others, *Geo-economic Fragmentation and the Future of Multilateralism* (International Monetary Fund 2023) 1–10.

[94] ING, 'How the Ukraine war has affected Asia's race to net zero' (1 August 2022) <https://think.ing.com/bundles/how-the-ukraine-war-has-affected-asias-race-to-net-zero/> accessed 10 June 2023.

[95] See Mohsen Abdollahi, 'Economic Sanctions and the Effectiveness of the Global Climate Change Regime: Lessons from Iran' in Damilola S Olawuyi (ed), *Climate Change Law and Policy in the Middle East and North African Region* (Routledge 2021) 119–36; Kaveh Madani, 'How International Economic Sanctions Harm the Environment' (2020) 8(12) Earth's Future <https://agupubs.onlinelibrary.wiley.com/doi/full/10.1029/2020EF001829> accessed 30 July 2023.

[96] Madani (n 95); also Ali Saberpour, Masoud Akhavan Fard, and Gholamhossein Masoud, 'Impact of Sanctions from the Perspective of International Environmental Commitments with Emphasis on Iran' (2021) 15 Legal Innovation 417.

[97] See Chapter 20 of this book.

[98] UNCTAD, 'Investing in the Sustainable Development Goals: An Action Plan' (United Nations 2014).

slow in many countries.[99] This section offers some recommendations on how to move net zero norms and principles from theory to practice.

First, there is a need for more ambitious and stringent application of net zero and just transition principles. Policy stringency 'is defined as the degree to which climate actions and policies [effectively] incentivise or enable GHG emissions mitigation at home or abroad'.[100] Stringency entails raising current ambition levels in natural resource legislation to accelerate clean energy transition. The effectiveness of net zero regulations also heavily depends on their enforcement, including the implementation of prescribed penalties and maximizing their application. Regulators will need to address all gaps to the monitoring of net zero programmes and the enforcement of the wide range of legislation and principles relating to just energy transition and responsible investment.

Second, efforts to articulate functional roadmaps to net zero suffer from deficiencies in compliance mechanisms. The Paris Agreement, for instance, encompasses a broad range of commitments, including mitigation, adaptation, funding, and technology access. Yet, notably, many of these are self-determined, such as the Nationally Determined Contributions (NDCs), which parties submit every five years.[101] The 'coupling of weak substantive commitments with an incomplete compliance response' has proven underwhelming, failing to incentivize 'ambitious NDC targets... and present indications suggest that this is unlikely to change'.[102] And although article 15 of the Paris Agreement establishes a mechanism aimed at promoting compliance via 'non-adversarial and non-punitive' methods, that aspect remains controversial.[103] By contrast, more effective compliance systems include those of the Montreal Protocol[104] and the Convention on International Trade in Endangered Species of Wild Fauna and Flora (CITES) which use facilitative approaches to non-compliance, supplemented by more coercive measures, such as the suspension of trade privileges, which have proven to be potent deterrents.[105]

Third, both stringency and compliance are as much about data as they are about regulations. Data, in turn, forms the basis of transparency and accountability. Without adequate information to ascertain just how well states are keeping up with their commitments, it is difficult to monitor progress, allocate rewards, and assign penalties. Laws should thus, at a minimum, mandate a reporting mechanism to ensure transparency and accountability for monitoring environmental impacts and GHG emissions. It is especially important that this be imposed on those jurisdictions' state-controlled National Oil Companies' (NOCs) own natural resources. Such transparency could, theoretically, accrue to the benefit of the NOCs in the sense that improved performance on the environmental front may well lead to

[99] Yasemin Kaya, 'Reconsidering the Effectiveness of International Environmental Regimes in the Anthropocene' (2022) 24 Insight Turkey 113.

[100] Daniel Nachtigall and others, 'The Climate Actions and Policies Measurement Framework: A Structured and Harmonised Climate Policy Database to Monitor Countries' Mitigation Action' (2022) Organisation for Economic Co-operation and Development Working Paper No 203, 26 <https://doi.org/10.1787/2caa60ce-en> accessed 30 July 2023.

[101] Meinhard Doelle, 'Compliance in Transition: Facilitative Compliance Finding Its Place in the Paris Climate Regime' (2018) 12 Carbon & Climate Law Review 229.

[102] Anna Huggins, 'The Paris Agreement's Article 15 Mechanism: An Incomplete Compliance Strategy' in Benoit Mayer and Alexander Zahar (eds), *Debating Climate Law* (CUP 2021) 105.

[103] Paris Agreement (n 15) art 15.

[104] Montreal Protocol on Substances that Deplete the Ozone Layer (adopted 16 September 1987, entered into force 1 January 1989) 1552 UNTS 3.

[105] Huggins (n 102) 104.

monetizable economic benefit, such as lower borrowing costs, improved equity valuations (if applicable), or even the realization of gains of demonstrable emissions reductions that could result in the accretion of carbon credits or other forms of offsets.

Fourth, there are fundamental misalignments between existing laws (and their interpretation) and ostensibly agreed upon net zero goals, which represents a significant deficiency. As illustrative examples, we refer to the judgments of the US Supreme Court in *West Virginia v Environmental Protection Agency*[106] and *Sackett v Environmental Protection Agency*,[107] which collectively weaken and place into question the regulatory power of the Environmental Protection Agency (EPA) with respect to natural resource management and the ability of the United States to meaningfully commit to its climate targets and ambitions.

In *West Virginia* and through the introduction of the 'major questions doctrine', the Court opens the doors to a re-examination of the EPA's ability to unilaterally propose regulations within its regulatory framework—in this case, its ability to devise emission caps based upon the generation-shifting approach implemented under the EPA's Clean Power Plan. Requiring the EPA to cite to 'clear congressional authority' for proposed actions, the Court finds the proposals to fall outside the scope and reach of the agency, debunking previous assumptions of regulatory autonomy and a level of free will and agency on behalf of the EPA. These cases show the need for greater regulatory coherence in legislative efforts aimed at advancing net zero and clean energy transition.

V. Conclusion

This chapter has examined the regulatory frameworks and principles that shape our approach to natural resources in the context of net zero and clean energy transition. The slow pace of progress in advancing net zero is clearly not due to lack of laws, principles, or policies. Rather, a deep disconnect between adopted net zero targets and their integration into natural resources frameworks, contracts, and legislation remains prevalent in many countries. There is an urgent need for dynamic legal innovation to advance net zero and climate aligned legislation, policies, and practices in the natural resource sector.

At a national level, natural resources laws and policies should align with the Paris Agreement, and regulators and judges should interpret and enforce them with attention to environmental protection principles, especially the intergenerational equity principle. By prioritizing climate considerations in natural resources laws and policy, stakeholders in the natural resource sector would be able to make natural resource and energy decisions that do not worsen the climate crisis.

As the next chapter demonstrates, the task of balancing resource sovereignty with energy security and justice concerns will not be easy, especially in resource-dependent developing countries. This raises the need for all stakeholders at international, regional, and domestic levels to jettison competitive and restrictive resource politics and advance the multistakeholder solidarity needed to accelerate net zero and the clean energy transition.

106 *West Virginia v Environmental Protection Agency* 577 US 1126 (2016).
107 *Sackett v Environmental Protection Agency* 143 S Ct 1322 (2023).

3

Net Zero Transition and Resource Sovereignty

Emerging Trends and Changing Landscape

Tengi George-Ikoli, Aaron Sayne, and Damilola S. Olawuyi

I. Introduction

This chapter examines the potential impacts of net zero transitions for the development, management, and control of natural resources. This includes a discussion of the resource sovereignty risks such as stranded assets, divestments, bankruptcies, resource nationalism, procurement, and supply chain challenges, that are emerging as a result of net zero and the clean energy transition, and legal pathways for managing such risks.

The starting point of natural resources law and policy is the idea of permanent sovereignty over natural resources (PSNR), which recognizes the right of every nation to make decisions about the use, control, and disposal of resources within its territory.[1] With the phase-out of colonization and efforts by resource-rich countries to build fiscal regimes that maximized returns, the idea of PSNR became widely recognized,[2] and enshrined in international, regional, and domestic instruments.[3] Virtually all national constitutions recognize outright ownership of natural resources by the state and the authority of the government to utilize such resources as a means of subsistence and economic, social, and cultural development.[4] Recognition of PSNR, in turn, places a fundamental responsibility on governments to adopt good governance policies that protect the interests of the people in natural resources.[5] It also creates an obligation to design policies that promote equitable resource rent distribution based on notions of common ownership and environmental justice and to allocate resource wealth properly.[6]

Despite the widespread recognition of PSNR, however, natural resource sovereignty has been a battle for many countries seeking to retain control over decision-making and to avoid international agreements, concessionary systems, or policies that curtail resource sovereignty.[7] As countries seek to maximize the use of natural resources to advance sustainable

[1] See Chapter 1 of this book.

[2] Emeka Duruigbo, 'Permanent Sovereignty Over Natural Resources and People's Ownership of Natural Resources in International Law' (2006) 38 George Washington International Law Review 33.

[3] See United Nations General Assembly (UN GA) Resolution 1803 (XVII) of 1962 GA Res 523 (VI), at 20, UN Doc A/2052 (12 January 1952). Similarly, the International Covenant on Civil and Political Rights (ICCPR), art 1 expressly recognizes the right of countries to 'freely dispose of their natural wealth and resources', and that 'in no case may a people be deprived of its own means of subsistence'.

[4] Yinka Omorogbe and Peter Oniemola, 'Property Rights in Oil and Gas under Dominial Regimes' in A McHarg and others (eds), *Property and the Law in Energy and Natural Resources* (OUP 2010) 115–39.

[5] Lillian A. Miranda, 'The Role of International Law in Intrastate Natural Resource Allocation: Sovereignty, Human Rights, and Peoples-Based Development' (2012) 45 Vanderbilt Journal of Transnational Law 785.

[6] Damilola Olawuyi and Temitope Onifade, 'Promoting Functional Distributive Justice in the Nigerian Sovereign Wealth Fund System: Lessons from Alaska and Norway' in Chile Eboe-Osuji (ed) *Nigerian Yearbook of International Law* (Springer 2018) 317–54.

[7] Jérémie Gilbert, 'The Right to Freely Dispose of Natural Resources: Utopia or Forgotten Right?' (2013) 31(2) Netherlands Quarterly of Human Rights 314.

Tengi George-Ikoli, Aaron Sayne, and Damilola S. Olawuyi, *Net Zero Transition and Resource Sovereignty* In: *Net Zero and Natural Resources Law.* Edited by: Damilola S. Olawuyi, José Juan González, Hanri Mostert, Milton Fernando Montoya, and Catherine Banet, Oxford University Press.
 DOI: 10.1093/9780198925033.003.0003

development and reduce poverty, they also face pressures to balance their national interests with the urgent need to halt the climate emergency,[8] as well as the associated changing economic landscape and other emerging geopolitical trends in other parts of the world.

As the world transitions towards cleaner sources of energy, natural resource sovereignty has become a crucial issue for many fossil fuel-producing countries. In resource-dependent countries in Africa, the Middle East, and Latin America, significant portions of gross domestic product (GDP), revenues, and foreign exchange earnings remain tied to oil and gas extraction.[9] Given these shifts, calls for a just, inclusive, and equitable global energy transition that protects the sovereignty of peoples over natural resources and leaves no one behind will become an even more critical issue for resource-rich countries.[10] The global net zero drive is already resulting in the reduced demand for fossil fuels, leading to defunding and write-down of extractive resources and associated losses of government revenue and jobs.[11] At the same time, research has also suggested links between the financial stress caused by declining extractives revenues and rising energy poverty levels in some parts of Africa, Asia, and Latin America.[12] As discussed in Chapter 1 of this book, the trade-offs and decisions facing resource-dependent countries in the global energy transition have been described as an attempt to achieve an 'impossible energy trinity' (IET) of energy security, sustainable energy, and energy sovereignty.[13] The sovereignty challenges of net zero may also contribute to economic governance risks in many parts of the world, especially in rentier economies in Africa and the Middle East, where states provide subsidies and benefits to people.[14] These stresses are already triggering a wave of public protests, discontent, and political instability in these and other parts of the world.[15]

How can resource-dependent countries balance the demands of global energy markets and international climate concerns with their national interests and ensure that resource benefits accrue to the public? What are the innovative natural resources law frameworks and governance models through which countries can address resource sovereignty risks in a net zero era? These are the questions that this chapter aims to answer.

[8] More than seventy countries have set a net zero target. See Chapter 1 of this book.

[9] Alexander Ezenagu, 'Boom or Bust, Extractives Are No Longer Saviours: The Need for Robust Tax Regimes in Gulf Countries' (2021) 8(2) The Extractive Industries and Society 100848. See also International Monetary Fund (IMF), *Trade and Foreign Investment—Keys to Diversification and Growth in the GCC* (IMF 2018) 3–6.

[10] See United Nations Working Group on Business and Human Rights, *Extractive Sector, Just Transition and Human Rights* (2023) UN General Assembly Report, <https://www.ohchr.org/en/documents/thematic-reports/a78155-extractive-sector-just-transition-and-human-rights> accessed 12 May 2024.

[11] ILO, 'Jobs in a Net-Zero emissions future in Latin America and the Caribbean', <https://www.ilo.org/wcmsp5/groups/public/---americas/---ro-lima/documents/publication/wcms_752069.pdf> accessed 12 August 2023.

[12] G Moore, 'Africa must not be the West's sacrificial lamb for Net Zero at Cop26' <https://www.african.business/2021/10/energy-resources/africa-must-not-be-the-wests-sacrificial-lamb-for-Net-Zero-at-cop26/> accessed 12 August 2023; S Zubairu, 'COP26: Africa charts a complex road to Net Zero' <https://www.african.business/2021/10/energy-resources/africas-complex-road-to-Net-Zero/> accessed 12 August 2023.

[13] See also Philipp Thaler and Benjamin Hofmann, 'The Impossible Energy Trinity: Energy Security, Sustainability, and Sovereignty in Cross-Border Electricity Systems' (2022) 94 Political Geography 102579.

[14] Jose Alberto Fuinhas and Antonio Cardoso Marques, 'Rentierism, Energy and Economic Growth: The Case of Algeria and Egypt (1965–2010)' (2013) 62 Energy Policy 1165–71; also Damilola Olawuyi, 'Advancing Innovations in Renewable Energy Technologies as Alternatives to Fossil Fuel Use in the Middle East: Trends, Limitations, and Ways Forward' in Donald Zillman and others (eds), *Innovation in Energy Law and Technology: Dynamic Solutions for Energy Transitions* (OUP 2018) 354–70.

[15] Jane McLeod, 'Report: Political instability biggest threat to Net-Zero transition' (15 November 2022) <https://www.thenational.scot/news/23124775.report-political-instability-biggest-threat-Net-Zero-transition/> accessed 12 August 2023.

This chapter discusses the legal dimensions of sovereignty risks and trends in the net zero transition process. After this general introduction, Section II clarifies the nature and scope of sovereignty risks of net zero and the clean energy transition. It unpacks the social, economic, and environmental implications of the net zero transition for natural resource decisions in resource-dependent countries. Section III examines legal and policy barriers to effective responses to such sovereignty risks. Section IV proposes some natural resources law options for addressing the barriers and maximizing the use of natural resources to advance the energy trinity of energy security, sustainable energy, and energy sovereignty. Section V is the concluding section.

II. Resource Sovereignty Risks of Net Zero

'Resource sovereignty risk' in this chapter refers to the risk of a government becoming unable to make autonomous decisions on the sustainable management of its country's natural resources, and the associated social, economic, and environmental implications. As noted above, the changing landscape of global energy markets in the context of net zero is deepening sovereignty risks for extraction-dependent countries.

A. Main Drivers of Resource Sovereignty Risks in Fossil Fuel-Dependent Countries

There are four key drivers of sovereignty risk associated with the net zero transition. The first is reduced demand for non-renewable natural resources like oil and gas.[16] Extraction is demand-driven, with countries making supply decisions based on local and international interest projections. However, the uncertainty associated with the global net zero drive means that such decisions now depend more than ever on factors outside the producer countries' control. Such uncertainty and the associated price volatility can have severe economic consequences for extraction-dependent economies.[17] For instance, after the 2014 decline in world oil prices, GDP growth declined sharply in many resource-rich countries, with governments forced to implement austerity measures to address the resulting fiscal deficit.[18] Similarly, during the COVID-19 pandemic, when demand slumped from slowed global activity, several oil- and gas-producing countries had to increase their borrowing to deliver support to their populations, especially those living in extreme poverty.[19] The worldwide shift towards net zero is already causing rapid decline in fossil fuel investments.[20]

[16] Ezenagu (n 9).

[17] Damilola Olawuyi, 'Advancing Resilience to Price Volatility in Oil and Gas Markets: Current Challenges and Ways Forward in the MENA Region' in Catherine Banet and others (eds), *Resilience in Energy, Infrastructure, and Natural Resources Law: Examining Legal Pathways for Sustainability in Times of Disruption* (OUP 2022) 135–49.

[18] See Hanen Keskes, 'How Cheap Oil and The Pandemic Threaten Economies and the Energy Transition in the Middle East and North Africa' (Natural Resource Governance Institute 2020).

[19] R Arezki and H Nguyen, 'Coping with a Dual Shock: COVID-19 and Oil Prices' <https://www.worldb ank.org/en/reg ion/mena/brief/coping-with-a-dual-shock-coronavirus-covid-19-and-oil-prices> accessed 12 August 2023. See also UN Department of Economic and Social Affairs (UN DESA), 'Covid 19 and Sovereign Debt, Policy Brief No 72' (May 2020).

[20] Auke Plantinga and Bert Scholtens, 'The Financial Impact of Fossil Fuel Divestment' (2021) 21(1) Climate Policy 107.

There is already evidence of increasing reversal or postponement of energy infrastructure projects in many resource-dependent countries in the Middle East and North African (MENA) region, for example.[21]

A second driver of resource sovereignty risk is the increased global harmonization of natural resources regulation and policy to focus on net zero. The growth in worldwide pledges and commitments to net zero, and the associated changes to the demand and supply of fossil fuels, mean that domestic natural resource decisions are increasingly subjected to, and bound by, decisions taken abroad.[22] The rise of new importation requirements, environmental labelling, health and safety, and environmental, social, and governance (ESG) requirements that countries and foreign investors are now placing on imports means that resource-rich countries must reimagine and re-evaluate their natural resource laws and standards to ensure their products are not left behind.[23] The increased globalization of natural resource governance may also spur competition between countries, potentially leading to geopolitical tensions and conflicts. In Nigeria, for example, tensions exist between local communities and foreign oil companies over access to oil resources and benefits, which may be exacerbated as demand for oil declines.[24] As international oil companies continue to diversify their interests, the legacies of resulting underdevelopment and environmental degradation in resource-rich regions may further exacerbate already high tensions. International solidarity is therefore important for countries to collaboratively address competitive geopolitics associated with net zero in a fair, inclusive, and ethical manner.[25]

A third driver of net zero-related sovereignty risk is the potential of existing long-term extractive contracts to keep countries from making decisions that support their own net zero transitions. For example, stabilization provisions in extractive contracts, which freeze the abilities of states to update existing laws or contracts, may constrain regulatory space for governments to advance net zero or address its social and economic impacts.[26] The number of cases in which government decisions on net zero are challenged by investors relying on stabilization and dispute resolution clauses is already rising.[27] This type of sovereignty risk calls for innovative responses by countries to renegotiate concessions, contracts, and bilateral investment treaties (BITs) that may constrain their abilities to make independent and sustainable resource management decisions.

A fourth driver of sovereignty risk is the lack of economic diversification in extraction-dependent countries. With the rise of climate change mitigation measures—primarily those targeted at reducing global dependence on fossil fuels—the side effects of excessive dependence on oil and gas revenue will be felt hardest by countries that have failed to use resource wealth to develop other key sectors over time. For example, the transition

[21] See Keskes (n 18); also IMF, *Policy Responses to Covid-19* <https://www.imf.org/en/topics/imf-and-covid19/policy-responses-to-covid-19> accessed 12 August 2023.

[22] Thaler and Hofmann (n 13).

[23] See Chapter 11 of this book for a more in-depth discussion of the issues.

[24] Anthony I Osawe and Goddy Uwa Osimen, 'Natural Resource Governance and Conflicts in Nigeria' (2023) 4(1) British Journal of Multidisciplinary and Advanced Studies: Arts, Humanities and Social Sciences 17.

[25] See art 6 UNESCO, 'Declaration of Ethical Principles in relation to Climate Change' <https://www.unesco.org/en/legal-affairs/declaration-ethical-principles-relation-climate-change?hub=66535> accessed 12 August 2023.

[26] Natural Resource Governance Institute (NRGI), 'Tying Their Hands? How Petroleum Contract Terms May Limit Governments' Climate Policy Flexibility' <https://www.resourcegovernance.org/analysis-tools/publications/tying-their-hands-how-petroleum-contract-terms-may-limit-gov-climate-policy-flexibility> accessed 12 August 2023.

[27] See Chapter 1 of this book for a discussion of such cases.

to a net zero economy will require adopting new technologies and implementing new regulations and policies, which may be challenging for countries with limited infrastructure, human capacity, or technological capabilities.[28] This is especially true for hydrocarbon-dependent countries that envision rapid transitions to solar energy, electric vehicles, and hydrogen for energy sources without adequate technology or infrastructure to achieve such goals. The increased reliance on technology transfer for net zero-aligned technologies may require support from technology-rich countries, which may result in technology dependence and a loss of control over the transition process or the ability to make technology-related choices that are free from foreign influence or interference. For example, while many African and Middle East countries are placing increased emphasis on energy citizenship—that is, the engagement of citizens in the development of clean and decentralized energy solutions—the lack of homegrown technologies has made designing and implementing such initiatives complex and difficult.[29] To advance net zero and to address sovereignty risks, there is an urgent need for countries to put in place regulatory measures to incentivize and facilitate small- and medium-scale entrepreneurial eco-ventures (SMEs) to unlock locally made technologies, tools, and products needed to advance net zero, energy security, and export diversification. By promoting eco-entrepreneurship and energy citizenship, resource-dependent countries can take better control of their energy futures by advancing homegrown energy solutions and technologies needed to expand energy access and resilience to several of the complex social, economic, and environmental vulnerabilities resulting from net zero and the clean energy transition.[30]

B. Emerging Trends Related to Sovereignty Risks

As energy transition gathers steam and countries navigate the impacts on their national sovereignty, some sovereignty risks have begun to emerge. These risks encompass a range of interconnected factors that are shaping the global landscape of economic and political sovereignty. Among these trends are stranded assets, fossil fuel divestments, resource nationalism, procurement challenges, and supply-side complexities.

1. Stranded Assets

Stranded assets refer to fossil fuel assets that may become uneconomical or unusable in a low-carbon economy, resulting in a significant loss of value and revenue for countries that depend on them. Adopting new, clean energy technologies and regulations can raise the risks of asset stranding. In countries and regions that adopt long-term decarbonization strategies for power and transport—for example through switching from gas-powered power plants to solar or petrol-fueled cars to electric vehicles—the

[28] Damilola Olawuyi, 'Advancing Innovations in Renewable Energy Technologies as Alternatives to Fossil Fuel Use in the Middle East: Trends, Limitations, and Ways Forward' in Donald Zillman and others (eds), *Innovation in Energy Law and Technology: Dynamic Solutions for Energy Transitions* (OUP 2018) 354–70.

[29] Damilola Olawuyi, 'From Energy Consumers to Energy Citizens: Legal Dimensions of Energy Citizenship' in K Hunter and others (eds), *Sustainable Energy Democracy and the Law* (Brill 2021) 101–23.

[30] International Energy Agency (IEA), 'Net Zero by 2050: A Roadmap for the Global Energy Sector' (2021) <https://www.iea.blob.core.windows.net/assets/deebef5d-0c34-4539-9d0c-10b13d840027/NetZeroby2050-ARoadmapfortheGlobalEnergySector_CORR.pdf> accessed 12 August 2023.

infrastructure supporting the old energy systems would eventually become obsolete.[31] Expensive requirements to retrofit infrastructure with new technologies such as carbon capture and storage may also lead to the early retirement of fossil fuel assets, resulting in significant financial losses for countries that have invested heavily in them.[32] In some cases, significant revenue losses from stranded assets could lead to social unrest and political instability.[33] Additionally, these countries may be forced to rely more heavily on external sources of finance and investment, potentially leading to a loss of control over the development and management of their natural resources in instances where those assets are leveraged.

Addressing these risks will require a comprehensive approach considering the transition's economic, social, and environmental implications. Countries may need to diversify their economies, invest in new technologies, and explore alternative sources of revenue to mitigate the impact of stranded assets.[34] Effective regulation and international cooperation will ensure a just and equitable energy transition towards net zero.

2. Fossil Fuel Divestments

The net zero drive is resulting in increased divestment from fossil fuel assets by countries and international oil companies (IOCs). Royal Dutch Shell, in 2020, announced a new strategy to become a net zero emissions company by 2050, including investments in renewable energy and a reduction in oil and gas production.[35] In recent years, Shell has divested some of its Nigerian assets as part of a broader global divestment programme likely to be accelerated with its strategic inclusion of renewables. In 2015, for example, Shell sold its stake in the OML 29 oil block to a Nigerian consortium for US$2.5 billion.[36] In 2019, Exxon Mobil announced a similar agreement to sell its 60 per cent stake in Mobil Oil Nigeria to NIPCO plc.[37]

These growing divestments by IOCs put pressure on national oil companies (NOCs) to take over operations.[38] Many NOCs are relatively inexperienced, however, with less access to international capital markets and technological resources. They may also not be subject to private firms' governance standards. Principles and standards such as the Equator Principles, the International Finance Corporation (IFC) Performance Standards, and the

[31] David Manley, 'Oil Companies Face Stranded Assets, But Producer Countries Have It Worse' (27 January 2017) <https://www.resourcegovernance.org/articles/oil-companies-face-stranded-assets-producer-countries-have-it-worse> accessed 12 August 2023.

[32] Bartosz Dziejarski and others, 'Current Status of Carbon Capture, Utilization, and Storage Technologies in the Global Economy: A Survey of Technical Assessment' (2023) 342 Fuel 127776.

[33] G Semieniuk and others, 'Stranded Fossil-Fuel Assets Translate to Major Losses for Investors in Advanced Economies' (2022) 12 Nature Climate Change 532.

[34] Zainab Usman, *Economic Diversification in Nigeria: The Politics of Building a Post-Oil Economy* (Bloomsbury Publishing 2022) 1–15.

[35] Ron Bousso and Shadia Nasralla, 'Shell Sets Net-Zero Emissions Target for 2050, with Customer Help (Reuters 16 April 2020) <https://www.reuters.com/article/us-shell-emissions-idUSKCN21Y0MW#> accessed 12 August 2023.

[36] William Clowes and Laura Hurst, 'Shell Resumes Talks in Nigeria Oil Fields Sale to Local Firm' (Bloomberg, 31 July 2023). Shell, ND Western Resume Talks Over Nigeria Oil Fields Sale - Bloomberg.

[37] NIPCO PLC, 'NIPCO Acquires 60% Equity in Mobil Oil' <https://www.nipcoplc.com/nipco-acquires-60-equity-in-mobil-oil-2/> accessed 12 August 2023.

[38] Stakeholder Democracy Network, 'Report: Divesting from the Delta: Implications for the Niger Delta as international oil companies exit onshore production' (October 2021) <https://www.stakeholderdemocracy.org/wp-content/uploads/2021/11/Full-report-Delta-Divestments.pdf> accessed 12 August.

United Nations Guiding Principles on Business and Human Rights provide tools to assess and manage the environmental, social, and human rights risks associated with lending and investment activities. Thus, with growing divestments, the standards and sustainability fossil fuel businesses could be threatened.

Divestment by IOCs also raises concerns over legacy environmental degradation caused by these companies over their six decades-long exploitation. For example, IOCs operating in Nigeria's oil-producing communities have been accused of causing significant damage to the local environment through oil spills, gas flaring, and other activities.[39] They have been slow to address the issues, however, leading to calls from oil communities for increased accountability by the international community to address environmental degradation that may be left behind by oil and gas companies in a rushed and incoherent net zero divestment process.[40]

The failure of IOCs to address legacy environmental pollution has been addressed in Nigeria's petroleum sector reform law the Petroleum Industry Act (PIA) 2021.[41] The PIA incorporates several mechanisms to address these concerns by establishing a Decommissioning and Abandonment Fund, and also requiring operators to make financial provisions for the costs of decommissioning and abandonment at the end of the life of an oil and gas field.[42] One important significant limitation is that the Act's provisions address new and future environmental issues, not past pollution.[43] And ultimately, while the PIA does offer a framework for addressing legacy issues associated with net zero which could provide useful lessons for regulators in other jurisdictions, its overall effectiveness will depend on implementation and enforcement to hold defaulting IOCs responsible.[44]

3. Resource Nationalism

Resource nationalism emphasizes that a country and its citizens should be the main decision-makers and beneficiaries of their natural resource wealth, for instance, through dominant government or local private sector ownership.[45] As a response to concerns about resource sovereignty, resource nationalism can be a double-edged sword. On the one hand, it can help countries assert greater control over their natural resources to accelerate economic development, energy security, and sustainable resource management.[46] On the other hand, exercise of resource sovereignty through increased licensing of new fossil fuel investments could significantly delay the path to net zero and the clean energy transition.[47]

Furthermore, as demand for energy transition minerals (ETMs) grow in the clean energy sector, especially to meet increasing demands for electric vehicles, solar homes, wind

[39] Damilola Olawuyi, 'Corporate Accountability for the Natural Environment and Climate Change' in Ilias Bantekas and MA Stein (eds), *Cambridge Companion to Business and Human Rights* (CUP 2021).

[40] Stakeholder Democracy Network (n 38).

[41] Government of Nigeria, 'The Petroleum Industry Act 2021' <http://www.petroleumindustrybill.com/wp-content/uploads/2021/09/Official-Gazette-of-the-Petroleum-Industry-Act-2021.pdf> accessed 18 August.

[42] Stakeholder Democracy Network, 'Opportunities to Improve the Host Community Development Trusts under Nigeria's Petroleum Industry Act' (2023) <https://www.stakeholderdemocracy.org/wp-content/uploads/2023/05/PIA-and-HCDT-Report.pdf> accessed 18 August 2023.

[43] Government of Nigeria (n 41).

[44] Stakeholder Democracy Network (n 38).

[45] S Pryke, 'Explaining Resource Nationalism' (2017) 8 Global Policy 474.

[46] ibid.

[47] Freddie Hospedales, 'Energy Nationalism—A Stumbling Block to Net Zero Ambitions?' (26 July 2022) <https://www.environment-analyst.com/global/108300/expert-opinion-energy-nationalism-a-stumbling-block-to-net-zero-ambitions> accessed 18 August 2023.

farms, and other renewable sector needs, the quest and tendency for resource nationalism also grows.[48] For example, countries such as Nigeria, Zimbabwe, and the DRC, amongst others, that are home to significant quantities of ETMs, have announced plans to review the terms and conditions for the development and supply of such minerals in order to prioritize domestic value creation.[49] The geopolitical dimensions of the supply of ETMs is also brought to the fore by recent concerns over the potential disruptions of uranium supply to the European Union (EU) by the military government of Niger Republic.[50] In the case of Nigeria, the focus is on the need to avoid the consequences of revenue and job flight and to fully harness its clean energy minerals for the benefit of local communities.[51] In this regard, Nigeria asserts control through majority stake ownership, and by putting in place new regulatory frameworks to ensure greater transparency and coherence in the natural resource industry.[52] Nigeria also applies a stringent local content law which mandates that Nigerian companies carry out a certain percentage of work in the industry and a percentage of the equipment used in the industry be locally sourced.[53] As global drive for net zero increases in scale and ambition, the exercise of resource sovereignty, through resource nationalism with respect to the flow of ETMs, is bound to increase with many of such decisions becoming influenced more by geopolitical considerations rather than legal principles. Resource nationalism, especially by unilaterally cancelling or amending resource contracts and licences, could lead to conflicts with foreign investors and potentially discourage investment, resulting in reduced access to financing and expertise needed to accelerate net zero.[54]

As governments consider their renewables governance approaches, therefore, a less political approach is essential to attract the technologies and foreign direct investment needed for advancing the clean energy transition and sustainable development of ETMs. Natural resource investors will also need to negotiate contracts that avoid resource nationalism risks carefully, especially risks relating to the unliteral termination of mining contracts.[55] For example, as part of a due diligence search, it is important to investigate and determine the ownership structure in specific countries; the nature of legislative power conferred on the national oil company; and the nature of investment protection and tenure security

[48] CMS Law, 'Resource Nationalism in Battery Metals: Risks and Mitigation' <https://www.cms-lawnow.com/en/media/law-now/files/resource-nationalism-in-battery-metals-risks-and-mitigation> accessed 18 August 2023.

[49] See Chapter 4 of this book.

[50] Giorgio Leali, 'Niger coup sparks concerns about French, EU uranium dependency' (*Politico*, 31 July 2023) <https://www.politico.eu/article/niger-coup-spark-concerns-france-uranium-dependency/> accessed 18 August 2023.

[51] Government of Nigeria, Nigeria Energy Transition Plan <https://www.energytransition.gov.ng/#Key> accessed 18 August 2023.

[52] See Government of Nigeria (n 41). See also Timothy Choji, 'Nigeria to Introduce New Mining Law' (*Voice of Nigeria*, 5 April 2023) <https://von.gov.ng/nigeria-to-introduce-new-mining-law/> accessed 12 May 2024. Nigeria to introduce new Mining Law – Voice of Nigeria (von.gov.ng)

[53] Nigerian Content Monitoring Development Board Act 2010; Damilola Olawuyi and Ayobami Olaniyan, 'Local Content and the Sustainable Development of Oil and Gas Resources in Nigeria' in Damilola Olawuyi (ed), *Local Content and Sustainable Development in Global Energy Markets* (CUP 2022) 167–87.

[54] Nafisa Sherida, Rawshan Begum, and Shahidur Rahman, 'The Effects of National Oil Companies' Power on International Relations and Investment in the Oil Industry' (2018) 13(10) International Journal of Business and Management 74.

[55] Damilola Olawuyi, 'Legal Strategies and Tools for Mitigating Legal Risks Associated with Oil and Gas Investments in Africa' (2015) 39(3) OPEC Energy Review 247.

guaranteed to potential investors. During contract negotiations, it is also pertinent to ensure that stabilization, adaptation, and foreign arbitration clauses are established as part of any agreements with the host state.[56]

4. Procurement

Procurement is a critical component of net zero and the clean energy transition. As countries and companies move towards decarbonization, they need to procure materials, equipment, and services that support their goals. Such procurement processes raise several questions that could undermine net zero efforts without adequate legal and governance frameworks to balance sovereignty risks in this regard.

One challenge is the availability of ETMs, low-carbon raw materials, and clean energy technologies. As demand for these grows, there is a risk that the reliability of supply chains may not be sustained, leading to higher costs and potential supply chain disruptions.[57] Additionally, the high cost of low-carbon technologies may present a barrier to adoption, particularly for fossil fuel low-income countries with limited financial and technological resources. In this context, even when some carbon intensive countries agree on the need for net zero transition, the restrictive application of local content policies, as well as inadequate availability of goods, services, and clean energy technologies may impact or delay their energy transition decisions and efforts. Natural resources law must integrate resilience principles to minimize disruptions to the supply of goods and services needed to drive the transition.[58]

Another potential challenge of net zero-aligned procurement is balancing environmental sustainability with social and economic considerations. Some low-carbon technologies may require rare earth metals that are associated with human rights abuses and environmental damage in their extraction and production. The tendency of resource-dependent countries to lower environment and human rights standards to attract foreign investments, especially in the extractive sector, may become more apparent as demands increase for transition minerals.[59] Procurement policies and practices should carefully integrate ESG safeguards to ensure that net zero transitions are not achieved at the expense of human rights and environmental sustainability.[60]

Several countries and organizations have developed procurement policies and practices to support net zero and the clean energy transition. The EU has established a sustainable procurement criteria called the EU Green Public Procurement' (GPP) criteria, that prioritizes the use of low-carbon materials and technologies.[61] Similarly, the United States Federal Acquisition Regulation and the Green Procurement Compilation provide guidance and tools for US federal agencies to implement green and environmentally preferable

[56] ibid. See also Chapter 4 of this book.

[57] See Chapter 10 of this book. See also Mokbul Ahmad and Jahan Chowdhury, 'Supply Chain Disruption: Risks and Opportunities for a Net Zero Transition' (CUP 14 October 2021) <http://www.cambridgeblog.org/2021/10/supply-chain-disruption-risks-and-opportunities-for-a-net-zero-transition/> accessed 18 August 2023.

[58] Catherine Banet and others (eds), *Resilience in Energy, Infrastructure, and Natural Resources Law: Examining Legal Pathways for Sustainability in Times of Disruption* (OUP 2022) 1–15.

[59] See UN WGBHR (n 10).

[60] ibid; see also Chapter 14 of this book.

[61] European Union, 'EU Green Public Procurement Criteria' <http://www.ec.europa.eu/environment/gpp/pdf/brochure.pdf> accessed 18 August 2023.

purchasing practices.[62] Nigeria has also developed guidelines for sustainable procurement that prioritizes use of environmentally friendly products and services.[63] Accelerating the implementation of such guidelines while also addressing regulatory barriers, such as restrictive local content laws and policies, which may delay green procurement will be essential. Natural resources law should to promote greater coherence between net zero targets and the domestic availability of low-carbon goods, services, and innovation that is required to drive such transition.

5. Supply-Side Challenges

The shift to net zero energy systems will require significant diversification and decentralization of energy systems to ensure progress in energy transition while addressing supply-side challenges to energy security.[64] This includes diversifying the source and type of energy to reduce dependence on hydrocarbons, promoting investment in renewable energy sources, and deploying low-carbon technologies such as green hydrogen and carbon capture technologies.[65]

The Russia–Ukraine crisis has already shown the challenges associated with extreme dependence on one type or source of energy, as European countries attempt to navigate the impact of the war on their ability to meet domestic energy needs.[66] While a sudden shift from fossil fuels can reduce dependence on Russia and other hydrocarbon majors, a rapid demand for ETMs and renewable energy technologies could also result in the growth of new 'renewable energy super powers' which may also impact the cost and speed of the transition.[67] Addressing the geopolitical dimension of the energy transition, including ETM dependency risks, will therefore require a nexus governance approach to balance sustainability, resource sovereignty, and energy security concerns.[68] Similarly, infrastructure constraints, such as inadequate pipeline networks or storage capacity, can limit the ability of countries to access and transport clean energy resources, which may exacerbate dependence on other countries to meet energy needs.[69] The Nigerian context illustrates this well, with its perennial problems of oil pipeline vandalism, sabotage, and ageing, poorly maintained infrastructure.[70]

Overall, managing sovereignty risks of supply-side challenges requires a multifaceted approach that addresses the underlying issues related to energy production and ETM supply, while accelerating energy diversification. So far, countries have implemented various strategies and policies to promote the reliable supply of critical minerals, as well as advance

[62] US General Service Administration, Green Procurement <https://www.sftool.gov/greenprocurement> accessed 18 August 2023. See also US Government, Executive Order 14057 on Catalyzing American Clean Energy Industries and Jobs Through Federal Sustainability <https://www.whitehouse.gov/briefing-room/presidential-actions/2021/12/08/executive-order-on-catalyzing-clean-energy-industries-and-jobs-through-federal-sustainability/> accessed 18 August 2023.

[63] Nigeria's Sustainable Procurement, Environmental and Social Standards Project <https://www.documents1.worldbank.org/curated/en/257211582340515134/pdf/Nigeria-Sustainable-Procurement-Environmental-and-Social-Standards-Enhancement-Project.pdf> accessed 12 August 2023.

[64] IEA (n 30).

[65] See Chapter 14 of this book.

[66] Caroline Kuzemko and others, 'Russia's War on Ukraine, European Energy Policy Responses and Implications for Sustainable Transformations' (2022) 93 Energy Research & Social Science 102842.

[67] International Renewable Energy Agency (IRENA), *The Geopolitics of the Energy Transition: Critical Minerals* (IRENA 2023) 1–10.

[68] Ibid; see also Chapter 22 of this book.

[69] Thaler and Hofmann (n 13); also Michael Rodi, *Energy Infrastructure and Policy Options for Sustainable Future* (Lexxion 2012) 1–15.

[70] Afe Babalola and Damilola Olawuyi, 'Overcoming Regulatory Failure in the Design and Implementation of Gas Flaring Policies: The Potential and Promise of an Energy Justice Approach' (2022) 14(11) Sustainability 6800.

energy diversification, energy efficiency, and energy security.[71] For example, Nigeria's National Renewable Energy and Energy Efficiency Policy aims to increase the share of renewable energy in the country's energy mix, improve mineral sector diversification, and advance energy efficiency.[72] On a larger scale, the EU's Energy Security Strategy seeks to reduce dependence on imported fossil fuels and promote energy efficiency and renewable energy.[73]

Implementing legal and governance reforms to address these drivers and trends related to sovereignty risk has become, and will remain, a fundamental objective of natural resources law in a net zero era. The next section assesses the main legal and institutional barriers to this task.

III. Legal and Policy Barriers to Effective Responses to Sovereignty Risks

Addressing the wide-ranging challenges to resource sovereignty resulting from net zero will require a coherent and integrated approach that balances implementing net zero programmes with broader sustainability targets and objectives. The pursuit of sustainability remains a common theme that cuts across net zero, energy security, sustainable resource development, and resource sovereignty objectives. Despite these intersections, the lack of coordination in the design and implementation of net zero programmes could exacerbate sovereignty risks. Some of the main challenges are discussed below.

A. Regulatory Incoherence

The legal frameworks for furthering net zero objectives, whether found in policy documents or climate-related legislation, will need to be better aligned with existing natural resource policies and laws.[74] For instance, in many countries the different sectors and stages of generating and distributing renewable energy, water, agriculture, forestry, and transport are not often linked to net zero pledges and plans.[75] This can leave net zero ambitions either vaguely or insufficiently reflected in the negotiation of concessions, contracts, and bilateral agreements relating to the natural resource sector, resulting in sovereignty risks.[76] In Nigeria, for example, the lack of coordination of the relevant legislation, policies, institutions, and sectors has created a deep sense of fragmentation in the country's energy transition drive and regulations.[77]

Governments and other stakeholders have options to address these barriers to ensure effective responses to sovereignty risks and promote sustainable development. First, they should

[71] See Chapter 5 of this book on critical mineral strategies. See also Chapters 7, 8, and 13.

[72] National Renewable Energy and Energy Efficiency Policy (NREEEP) 2013 <https://www.fao.org/faolex/results/details/en/c/LEX-FAOC211220/> accessed 12 August 2023.

[73] EU, 'Energy Strategy' <https://www.energy.ec.europa.eu/topics/energy-strategy_en> accessed 12 August 2023.

[74] Joeri Rogelj, 'Net-zero emissions targets are vague: three ways to fix' (*Nature*, 16 March 2021) <https://www.nature.com/articles/d41586-021-00662-3> accessed 12 August 2023.

[75] ibid.

[76] NRGI (n 26); see also UN WGBHR (n 10).

[77] Babalola and Olawuyi (n 70).

carefully negotiate any bilateral agreements that could limit their ability to enact policies that prioritize their citizens' interests, particularly in the case of foreign investment in fossil fuel resources. For example, the Energy Charter Treaty (ECT) is a multilateral agreement between the EU and other countries that potentially serves as a risk to African countries in the implementation of their energy transition. The ECT is an agreement that aims to promote international cooperation in the energy sector. However, critics have argued that the treaty prioritizes investors' interests over states' sovereignty. The treaty includes provisions that require signatory states to protect foreign investors and their investments, including the right to seek compensation for any perceived losses. African countries, including Nigeria, have been particularly affected by the ECT's provisions. Some African countries have sought to review or withdraw from the treaty, arguing that it limits their ability to enact policies. The EU itself was in the process of reviewing the ECT to determine whether to continue its implementation.

Renegotiation of extractive contracts and concessions could, in some instances, also be used to better reflect net zero objectives. Obsolete contracts that do not reflect net zero dynamics constitute a major risk and negatively impact the country and communities they were intended to advance. Old policies may fail to comply with new laws and regulations, or they may not embrace new dynamics and address emerging concerns and needs. This is why evaluating sovereignty risks in existing contracts is important and exploring renegotiation tools that may be embedded in such contracts.[78]

B. Regulatory and Administrative Barriers to Eco-Entrepreneurship

One reason for the slow pace of economic diversification in hydrocarbon-dependent countries is the absence of comprehensive legal frameworks for stimulating entrepreneurship and investment across other sectors, especially clean technology.[79] In the 2022 Global Entrepreneurship Index (GEI), virtually all African and Middle East countries scored low on having adequate legal frameworks that foster entrepreneurship.[80] This partly reflects a lack of clear rules for licensing and registration of energy ventures. The proliferation of regulatory licences and approvals by various ministries and the associated administrative barriers make the process of developing and commercializing net zero-aligned technologies difficult and leaves countries reliant on technology imports. Reforms to allow for broad-based public participation in energy innovation and streamlining the process of venture registration will be vital to promoting the development of energy SMEs.

C. Institutional Fragmentation

Fragmented institutions can also hinder the integration of net zero objectives with broader sustainability aims of a country. This is a result of various governmental departments

[78] See Chapter 4 of this book.

[79] Damilola Olawuyi, 'Advancing Resilience to Price Volatility in Oil and Gas Markets: Current Challenges and Ways Forward in the MENA Region' in Catherine Banet and others (eds), *Resilience in Energy, Infrastructure, and Natural Resources Law: Examining Legal Pathways for Sustainability in Times of Disruption* (OUP 2022) 135–49.

[80] Global Entrepreneurship and Development Institute (GEDI), 'Global Entrepreneurship Index' (2022) <http://www.thegedi.org/global-entrepreneurship-and-development-index/?> accessed 18 August 2023.

explicitly and implicitly influencing regulations. For example, integrating net zero plans into resource investment will require the coordination of climate, energy, environment, trade, and foreign affairs ministries and institutions.[81] Furthermore, leveraging climate-smart infrastructure in the natural resource sector will require concerted planning by infrastructure, technology, planning and development agencies.[82] However, the reality in many countries is that developing energy transition and environmental legislation continue to occur independently and incoherently with various sectors operating in institutional silos.[83] This leads to fragmentation in planning and the absence of integrative planning when drafting and implementing renewable energy legislation that mirrors environmental law principles. There is a need to address such fragmentation by creating national working groups that bring together stakeholders in different sectors to jointly elaborate and implement net zero programmes in natural resource activities and projects.

D. Inadequate Consultation with Affected Communities and Other Stakeholders

The need for robust consultation as a country prepares for its energy transition cannot be overemphasized. There is a need to develop an open and transparent public outreach strategy, with appropriate and well-publicized procedures for effective and timely inputs from relevant national and foreign parties and other stakeholders such as businesses, trade unions, and wider interest groups who are crucial to decision-making with respect to net zero. Consultation improves the quality of rules and programmes, improves compliance, and reduces enforcement costs for both governments and those subject to the rules. While it is not always possible to define public interest as the sum of interests of individual stakeholders, adopting a public-oriented perspective on net zero regulatory policy should be a goal to assess the design, review, and implementation of clean energy policies and regulation. Open government can also promote public scrutiny, safeguard against corruption, promote trust in government, and further non-discrimination by supporting equal access and treatment for everyone under the law.[84]

E. Limited Potential for Joint Resource Development and Cross-Border Energy Cooperation

Achieving global and national level net zero ambitions will require international solidarity and cooperation focused on addressing barriers to clean technology access, cross-border energy, and natural resource trade and climate-smart investment. For example, the Paris Agreement encourages countries to uphold and promote regional cooperation to mobilize

[81] Geraldine Ang and Hannah Copeland, *Integrating Climate Change-related Factors in Institutional Investment* (OECD 2018) 1–15.

[82] ibid.

[83] UN GA Report (n 10); see also Damilola Olawuyi and Zibima Tubondenyefa, 'Review of the Environmental Guidelines and Standards for the Petroleum Industry in Nigeria (EGASPIN)' Technical Report, Institute for Oil, Gas, Energy, Environment and Sustainable Development (OGEES Institute 2019) 1–25.

[84] Michael Canares and Denis G Calleja, 'The Role of Open Government Data in Combating Corruption' (2018) 53 Transylvanian Review of Administrative Sciences Journal 5.

more robust and more ambitious action on climate change mitigation and adaptation by all parties.[85] However, geopolitical contentions and tensions associated with net zero and political factors such as the Russian invasion of Ukraine, means that the multilateral solidarity and cooperation required to address net zero is not always forthcoming.[86] Balancing resource sovereignty with wide sustainability goals will require a new form of multilateralism that reduces conflict-based energy geopolitics between countries. International cooperation and solidarity are required to address the sovereignty risks of net zero in a manner that does not worsen social and economic vulnerabilities in developing countries especially.

It is also crucial for countries to develop bilateral trade and investment agreements that promote efficient and mutually beneficial joint resource development. For example, in the net zero era, one of the key tools that can unlock the efficient, orderly, and sustainable use of transboundary natural resources, including water, wind, and green hydrogen, is the promotion of joint development agreements (JDAs).[87] JDAs can provide a framework for two or more countries to jointly develop their natural resources in a manner that promotes resource efficiency and conservation while addressing energy security needs. However, lack of solidarity and cooperation in implementing such agreements remains an issue, especially in the absence of clear implementation structures, regional knowledge-sharing platforms, or best practices.[88] There is thus a strong need for countries to put in place adequate supervisory mechanisms and institutions to oversee the collaborative management of natural resources, especially those straddling different countries.

IV. Responding to Sovereignty Risks in Natural Resource Investments

A nexus governance approach is required to reduce regulatory incoherence and effectively respond to the wide range of resource sovereignty risks that net zero poses to resource-dependent countries.[89] As the mining sector gains momentum due to rising demand for ETMs needed to unlock the clean energy transition, it is important for mineral-rich countries to avoid the same mistakes that resulted in resource curse, environmental pollution, and incoherent planning in many countries in the boom years of global focus on hydrocarbons. In a net zero era, therefore, there is a need for an imaginative natural resources law framework that coherently maximizes the use of natural resources to advance the energy trinity of energy security, sustainable energy, and energy sovereignty.

First is the need for countries to harmonize national net zero policy with natural resource legislation and guidelines. Clear and consistent laws provide the foundation for

[85] Conference of the Parties to the United Nations Framework Convention on Climate Change, Paris Agreement, Twenty-first session Paris, 30 November–11 December 2015 <https://www.unfccc.int/resource/docs/2015/cop21/eng/l09.pdf> accessed 21 June 2023.

[86] Manfred Hafner and Simone Tagliapietra, 'The Geopolitics of the Global Energy Transition' (2020) 73 'Implications of the Global Energy Transition in Russia' 93.

[87] JDAs for renewable energy projects have been announced. See eg 'Masdar signs joint development agreements with Azerbaijan's state oil company to develop wind, solar projects' (*Arabian Business*, 18 January 2023) < https://www.prnewswire.com/in/news-releases/masdar-partners-with-azerbaijans-socar-to-develop-renewable-energy-projects-with-4-gw-capacity-301723457.html> accessed 12 May 2024. Masdar Partners with Azerbaijan's SOCAR to Develop Renewable Energy Projects with 4 GW Capacity (prnewswire.com).

[88] Eduardo G Pereira, *Joint Operating Agreements: Mitigating Operational and Contractual Risks in Exclusive Operations* (Globe Law and Business 2013).

[89] See Chapter 22 of this book for in-depth discussion of nexus governance in natural resource management.

regulators to integrate decarbonization considerations into investment decision-making and long-term planning, promoting regulatory certainty, and supporting the transition to a sustainable low-carbon future.[90] Regulatory certainty supports countries' navigation of the complex interplay between sustainable development, climate objectives, and responsible utilization of natural resources, increasing investor confidence. This will provide investors with a clear understanding of the critical information and data necessary for investment decision-making, such as efficiency standards, project approval process, eligible renewable technologies, and registration and certification requirements for projects verification, validation, reporting, and monitoring.[91]

Second is the need to put in place clear and specific laws on net zero and climate action in key sectors, including the natural resource sector. While several countries have adopted net zero pledges, the lack of a clear regulatory framework for measuring progress has resulted in the proliferation of different ESG reporting and investing standards.[92] Specific laws and regulations designed to encourage the adoption of low-carbon technologies, promote energy efficiency, and incentivize the development of renewable energy sources locally are critical elements needed to foster a sustainable transition. For instance, Nigeria recently enacted a Climate Change Act to lower GHGs and a National Energy Transition Plan 2023, which outlines Nigeria's commitment to achieving carbon neutrality by 2060.[93] However, its new oil and gas law, the PIA 2021 simultaneously promotes new and continued investments in fossil fuels in contradiction to the climate change frameworks. Such regulatory incoherence reflects ongoing challenges at national levels in balancing resource sovereignty with net zero ambitions. Failure to address such incoherence could result in heightened non-compliance risks for investors, and regulatory fines which may, at the same time, reduce the investment competitiveness and attractiveness of a country for mining and other resource investments. Enacting coherent net zero legislation may provide a sound basis for harmonizing such incoherence by stipulating the standards and requirements that all natural resource sector actors must meet.

Third is the need to reform concessions and contracts to align with net zero. Many countries are currently designing or refining their net zero pathways. A critical element should focus on negotiations for new contracts or the renegotiating of existing contracts. On the part of investors, there is a need to carefully negotiate resource contracts that minimize the risk of resource nationalism, stranded assets, or unrealistic ESG or clean technology requirements.[94] Negotiating net zero-aligned contracts for renewable projects, mining, or other resource contracts provide a great opportunity to include flexible review clauses and adaptation provisions to navigate infrastructure or project lock-in as demand for fossil fuel projects diminishes.[95] Host countries must also avoid stabilization clauses or bilateral agreements that penalize and impede long-term energy transition strategies. For example, the ECT penalizes countries that vary fossil fuel contracts in line with their energy transition or

[90] Ruven Fleming, Kaisa Huhta, and Leonie Reins, *Sustainable Energy Democracy and the Law* (Brill 2021) 116–17.

[91] Damilola Olawuyi, *Energy Poverty in the Middle East and North African (MENA) Region: Divergent Tales and Future Prospects* (OUP 2022).

[92] See Chapter 14 of this book.

[93] Climate Change Act 2021, Laws of the Federal Republic of Nigeria.

[94] See Chapter 4 of this book.

[95] ibid. See also NRGI (n 26).

low-carbon policies.[96] It is important for countries to scrutinize bilateral agreements of this nature before entering into them. Stabilization clauses that tie countries to fossil fuel agreements should be reviewed and jettisoned for more flexible arrangements.

Fourth, resource-dependent countries will need to accentuate fiscal incentives and legislation to promote economic diversification. In a net zero era, diversifying from extreme hydrocarbon dependence is no longer a choice, but rather, a necessity for all countries. Countries should design and implement tax incentives, tax waivers, breaks, grants, and other financial mechanisms to stimulate and accelerate entrepreneurship in non-fossil fuel sectors, especially renewable sectors.[97] Fiscal incentives that encourage tax breaks for industries focused on research and development, locally grown energy solutions, sustainable technologies, innovations, and ventures foster a sustainable, just energy transition. Countries must ensure that fiscal incentives are well-targeted, monitored, and evaluated to avoid misuse or unintended consequences. They should engage in regular policy reviews to adapt to changing economic dynamics and emerging opportunities. Complementary pro-diversification laws that facilitate access to capital, streamline business registration processes, access to profits, protect intellectual property rights, and promote fair competition are critical components to fostering sustainable economic development. While adopting fiscal incentives, counties should introduce fiscal disincentives such as carbon tax and others to dissuade investments in new fossil fuel-related projects to limit the potential for stranded assets and infrastructure lock-ins.[98]

Fifth is the need for regional solidarity, cooperation, and knowledge-sharing. Several of the resource sovereignty risks and challenges cannot be addressed in isolation. Countries will need to come together to facilitate knowledge-sharing, joint resource development, and to accelerate innovation, uptake, and scale of renewable energy technologies. Such cooperation should proceed at continental and international levels. Regional cooperation can support wider regional economic growth where countries leverage regional treaties and laws to exploit their economic comparative advantages. The African Continental Free Trade Act is an example of a regional instrument that provides opportunities to exploit regional cooperative benefits. Technology transfer and knowledge-sharing partnerships with international entities should be leveraged to enhance local capabilities and promote innovation, and research and development are important. These policies create an ecosystem that strengthens the country's capacity to diversify their economies, support economic growth, and mitigate against the risks associated with natural resource sovereignty. There is also a need to look beyond the continent as international energy law emphasizes the continued importance of, and need for, political cooperation to advance regional, as well as global, energy security.[99] International energy institutions such as the International Energy Agency, Organization of Petroleum Exporting Countries (OPEC), and the Gas Exporting Countries Forum (GECF), amongst others, have key roles to play in promoting knowledge sharing on how resource-dependent countries can

[96] Energy Charter Treaty (ECT) <https://www.energycharter.org/process/energy-charter-treaty-1994/energy-charter-treaty/> accessed 18 August 2023.

[97] Ezenagu (n 9).

[98] David Manley and Patrick Heller, 'Risky Bet: National Oil Companies in the Energy Transition' (Natural Resource Governance Institute, 9 February 2021).

[99] For see Chapter 2 of this book for a discussion of the principle of solidarity and cooperation.

cooperatively navigate the wide range of resource sovereignty risks facing the natural resource sector.[100]

V. Conclusion

As countries and businesses divest from non-renewable resources like oil and gas, decision-making by resource-rich countries on the development and use of their natural resources to advance energy security, address energy poverty, and accelerate the attainment of the UN's Sustainable Development Goals has become the most complex task of the century.

Transition-related challenges concerning stranded assets, financial and revenue constraints, resource nationalism, especially transition minerals, inadequate access to clean energy technologies, and supply chain challenges are already transforming the scope and application of natural resources law in many resource-dependent countries. Yet, regulatory incoherence, institutional fragmentation, insufficient national coordination and weak sustainability, and resource sovereignty continue to complicate the ability of countries to effectively manage resource sovereignty risks and to balance the aims of energy justice and security with net zero.

Natural resource laws and policies are required to effectively address these and other emerging resource sovereignty risks. Failing to manage these risks undermines the ability of countries to protect their national interests, build resilient economies, ensure sustainable governance, and effectively manage the challenges arising from the energy transition. First, there is a need for countries to ensure clarity and consistency of legal frameworks to accommodate the global energy transition, its complexities, and changing dynamics to provide clarity and certainty for investors, companies, and other stakeholders. Secondly, policy-makers need to prioritize the development of robust regulatory frameworks that encourage investment in low-carbon initiatives while safeguarding national interests. Thirdly, enhanced regional cooperation fosters cooperation in sharing best practices, harmonizing regulations, and establishing multilateral agreements to facilitate a smooth and coordinated energy transition. Fourthly, strengthening enforcement mechanisms and fostering transparency in reporting and monitoring progress on disclosure can help mitigate sovereignty risks. Governments should ensure that investment decision-making and long-term planning are aligned. Finally, engaging affected communities and marginalized groups and fostering inclusive decision-making are important to ensuring any net zero action or policy has buy-in from citizens and local communities, thus enhancing the prospects for coherent, successful, and sustainable implementation.

[100] See Chapter 22 of this book.

4

Natural Resource Contracts and Net Zero

Kim Talus, Qaraman M. Hasan, and Damilola S. Olawuyi

I. Introduction

The chapter argues that regulatory regimes on natural resources in general, and natural resources contracts in particular, require a radical shift to be consistent with net zero objectives. It examines provisions and clauses in long-term resource contracts that may constrain or even freeze the sovereign rights and abilities of states to advance net zero; the legal and institutional barriers facing resource-rich countries in adapting existing contract forms to accommodate new realities in a net zero era; and how such barriers can be addressed going forward.

With the exception of Canada and the United States where some form of private ownership of natural resources is recognized, in virtually all countries, sovereign rights over natural resources are vested exclusively in the state.[1] Natural resource contracts are therefore the dominant fiscal tools through which countries allocate or transfer their sovereign rights over natural resources.[2] Natural resource contracts contain the terms and conditions under which parties (typically state and international investor) agree to develop, produce, commercialize, and transport natural resources.[3] The primary aim when resource-rich countries contract with foreign investors is to turn natural resources into financial assets.[4] For example, the focus of the contracts was economic development during the seventies of the last century. By the 1980s and 1990s, these contracts became more investment-friendly, and stabilization clauses were major characteristics of these contracts.[5] Then, host countries attempted to insert provisions in favour of them, such as a local content requirement, in the last two decades. However, with the rapid development of international climate change and environmental laws, the aims, terms, and conditions of these contracts are rapidly changing. The transition to a carbon neutral energy system is currently taking place globally and an increasing number of countries have introduced net zero targets.[6] In this transition, fossil

[1] Yinka Omorogbe and Peter Oniemola, 'Property Rights in Oil and Gas under Dominial Regimes' in A McHarg and others (eds), *Property and the Law in Energy and Natural Resources* (OUP 2010) 115–39.

[2] Environmental Law Alliance Worldwide, 'Natural Resource Contracts: A Practical Guide' (2013) <https://www.elaw.org/sites/default/files/images_content/general_page_images/publications/Natural_Resource_Contracts_Guide.pdf> accessed 27 August 2023.

[3] ibid. See also David Kienzler and others, 'Natural Resource Contracts as a Tool for Managing the Mining Sector' (2015) <https://scholarship.law.columbia.edu/sustainable_investment_staffpubs/21> accessed 12 May 2024.

[4] Kienzler and others (n 3).

[5] ibid.

[6] To date, eighty-five Parties to the Paris Agreement have communicated a net zero target through their nationally determined contributions (NDCs), long-term low greenhouse gas (GHG) emissions development strategy, domestic law, policy, or high-level political pledge such as head of state commitment. They represent eighty-nine countries and 75.3% of global GHG emissions. See Chapter 1 of this book. See also Climate Watch, 'Net Zero Tracker' <https://www.climatewatchdata.org/netzero-tracker> accessed 2 June 2023.

Kim Talus, Qaraman M. Hasan, and Damilola S. Olawuyi, *Natural Resource Contracts and Net Zero* In: *Net Zero and Natural Resources Law*. Edited by: Damilola S. Olawuyi, José Juan González, Hanri Mostert, Milton Fernando Montoya, and Catherine Banet, Oxford University Press.
 DOI: 10.1093/9780198925033.003.0004

fuels are being replaced by clean and renewable energy sources and the sun is slowly setting on industries that produce the most polluting types of primary energy sources. Rethinking the contracting system to align with these emerging market realities have become crucial, particularly, long-term natural resource contracts negotiated prior to the adoption of the Paris Agreement in 2015, which may constrain the abilities of countries and investors to implement more pro-environment requirements with ambitious zero carbon targets in the natural resource industry.[7]

Furthermore, with increasing demand for transition minerals, especially cobalt, lithium, copper, nickel, rare earth elements (REEs), and vanadium, amongst others, as well as the growing importance of natural gas as a transition fuel, there is a clear need for states and investors to address new and emerging environment, social, and governance (ESG) risks associated with the rush for transition fuels and minerals.[8] The urgent need to address ESG and human rights challenges, increase transparency, eliminate corruption along the natural resource supply value chain, and avoid complex contractual disputes requires countries and investors to adapt existing contracts in order to accommodate new realities in a net zero era.[9]

Moving towards net zero and climate-aligned natural resource contracts requires a strong regulatory framework and institutional capacity that enables regulators and investors to better negotiate and implement climate-conscious provisions that advance net zero and mitigate ESG risks.[10] In this regard, some countries are attempting to have more control over their resources and use their sovereign rights by putting clauses related to contract renegotiations, local content requirements, and increasing royalties in the contract.[11] These are major developments in public sector contracts, but private sector contracts are not less important. Most energy transition studies focus on public sector regulation driving the transition towards net zero. There is no shortage of studies on the legal and regulatory framework driving the sustainable energy transition or its impact on energy markets and energy investments.[12] Traditional legal and policy research focuses on the detail of the regulatory instruments involved and the market impact of emission reduction policies and related regulations.

However, there are no significant studies focusing on the impact of natural resource contracts on the sustainable energy transition or the need to adapt these contracts amid the

[7] Natural Resource Governance Institute (NRGI), 'Tying Their Hands? How Petroleum Contract Terms May Limit Governments' Climate Policy Flexibility' <https://www.resourcegovernance.org/analysis-tools/publications/tying-their-hands-how-petroleum-contract-terms-may-limit-gov-climate-policy-flexibility> accessed 27 August 2023.

[8] See Chapter 10 and 12 of this book for a discussion of justice, security, and ESG risks associated with the rush for energy transition minerals.

[9] Qaraman M Hassan, Ibrahim M Khudir, and Damilola S Olawuyi, 'Regulating Corporate Social Responsibility in Energy and Extractive Industries: The Case of International Oil Companies in a Developing Country' (2023) 83 Resources Policy 103607.

[10] See the Chancery Lane Project which provides a Net Zero Toolkit as 'a set of practical tools to help professionals implement climate-conscious clauses in their organisation' <https://www.chancerylaneproject.org/toolkit/> accessed 27 August 2023.

[11] See Chapter 3 of this book. See also Abel Kinyondo and Christopher Huggins, 'Resource Nationalism in Tanzania: Implications for Artisanal and Small-Scale Mining' (2019) 6 The Extractive Industries and Society 181.

[12] Among many others, Geert Van Calster, Geert Vandenberghe, and Leonie Reins (eds), *Research Handbook on Climate Change Mitigation Law* (Edward Elgar 2015); Tade Oyewunmi and others (eds), *Decarbonisation and the Energy Industry: Law, Policy and Regulation in Low-Carbon Energy Markets* (Hart Publishing 2020); Ruven Fleming, 'Clean or Renewable—Hydrogen and Power-to-Gas in EU Energy Law' (2021) 39(1) Journal of Energy & Natural Resources Law 43.

accelerating transition to net zero. The only study touching this area appears to be from Boute, which focuses on coal bans and force majeure clauses in coal supply agreements.[13] More generally, the dominant approach to energy law studies especially in the European Union (EU) has been that of public law, with only few notable exceptions focusing on private law aspects of natural gas contracts and EU energy market liberalization such as Almeida.[14] Considering the crucial roles of natural resource contracts as the dominant fiscal tool through which countries allocate or transfer their sovereign rights over natural resources, it is essential to understand the impact of natural resource contracts on net zero and clean energy transition. This chapter contributes to filling a gap in this regard.

This chapter mainly concentrates on the government's natural resource contracts and licences, but it also discusses the private law elements of energy transition and the relationship between the commercial efforts to reach net zero and the existing and future private energy commodity supply and purchase contracts. After this introduction, Section II discusses the nature and scope of existing natural resource contracts, with focus on gaps that may accentuate risks for both the contractual parties as well as for the sovereignty of governments driving the transition. Section III discusses the challenges facing countries and investors in efforts to move towards net zero and climate-aligned natural resource contracts. The critical issue of resource-rich countries, which is the lack of institutional capacity, will be discussed in this section. Section IV mainly provides possible solutions and opportunities to deal with these challenges. Section V is the concluding section.

II. Existing Natural Resource Contracts and the Search for Alignment

A. Background and Context

Although there are several fiscal arrangements that have been developed across the world to govern the development and commercialization of natural resources, the two main arrangements relied on by state-owned enterprises and governments to convey titles and interests in petroleum, mineral, and other natural resources are: concessions and contracts.[15] A concession, also known as a lease, permit, or licence, is generally a right granted by the state to an investor to explore, develop, or produce natural resources from a defined area of land over a stipulated time period.[16] Concession agreements were major contracting types in the early twentieth century when most of the natural resource-rich countries were under the significant influence of colonial powers.[17] The quest by resource-rich jurisdictions to assert

[13] Anatole Boute, 'Environmental Force Majeure: Relief from Fossil Energy Contracts in the Decarbonisation Era' (2021) 33(2) Journal of Environmental Law 339.

[14] Lucila Almeida, 'Integration through Self-standing European Private Law: Insights from the Internal Point of View to Harmonization in Energy Market' (European University Institute 2017). Hans Micklitz has also touched upon private energy contracts, see eg Marta Gamito and Hans Micklitz, *The Role of the EU in Transnational Legal Ordering: Standards, Contracts and Codes* (Edward Elgar 2020).

[15] Damilola Olawuyi, *Extractives Industry Law in Africa* (Springer 2018) 191–95.

[16] ibid 205–08. See also NRGI, 'Fiscal regime design: what revenues the Government will be entitled to collect' (2015) <https://www.resourcegovernance.org/sites/default/files/nrgi_Fiscal-Regime-Design.pdf> accessed 12 June 2018.

[17] James Otto and John Cordes, *The Regulation of Mineral Enterprises: A Global Perspective on Economics, Law and Policy*, vol 34 (Rocky Mountain Mineral Law Foundation 2002).

greater control over their resources and to foster more mutually beneficial and long-term partnerships with foreign companies led progressively to the emergence of a contractual model.[18] Natural resource contracts provide a framework for the development and commercialization of natural resources. These contractual agreements range from production sharing contracts (PSCs), joint venture contracts (JVCs), joint operating agreements, and service agreements, to participation agreements such as farmout contracts, pooling and unitization contracts, sale and purchase agreements, transportation contracts, as well as community or impact benefit agreements.[19]

As natural resource law covers various resources such as fossil fuels, including oil and natural gas, water, mineral deposits, and timber, the laws and types of contracts are continuously changing.[20] As well as the variety of natural resources, selecting particular types of contracts 'depends on the stage of the mining process, the legal regime of the host country, the governments and companies involved and their needs, and even the political and economic dynamics of the era in which they were concluded'.[21] No matter the regulatory regime or types of contracts, from the perspective of an investor, negotiating the right fiscal arrangement that maximizes the profitability and sustainability of the investment, while minimizing regulatory risks is typically the priority. For the host state, maximizing revenue from its natural resources, avoiding adverse social, human rights, and environmental side effects, while at the same time providing sufficient incentives to foreign investors to participate is the ultimate aim.[22] However, the rise of net zero targets and ambitions across the world are increasingly complicating the process of balancing and aligning these aims and objectives of resource-rich states and investors.

B. How Net Zero Is Impacting the Scope and Application of Natural Resource Contracts

First, resource extraction projects are primarily governed by long-term contracts which may range for twenty to thirty years or even more, which may create lock-in effects that constrain net zero efforts.[23] For example, sale and purchase agreements commonly used in the natural gas sector often contain highly restrictive clauses that are designed to ensure stability of supply and demand, which makes them suitable for acquiring the project financing necessary for large capital-intensive energy projects.[24] Their intention is to lock parties into a specific transaction under defined conditions for long periods of time, typically ten to

[18] M Likosky, 'Contracting and Regulatory Issues in the Oil and Gas and Metallic Minerals Industries' (2009) 18 (1) Transnational Corporations 1; also Kienzler and others (n 3) 9.

[19] Olawuyi, *Extractives Industry Law in Africa* (n 15) 191–95. See also Alastair R Lucas and David K Laidlaw, 'Oil and Gas Sector Local Content Decision Processes: Canadian Indigenous Participation' in D Olawuyi (ed), *Local Content and Sustainable Development in Global Energy Markets* (CUP 2021) 343–60.

[20] Richard J Lazarus, 'Changing Conceptions of Property and Sovereignty in Natural Resources: Questioning the Public Trust Doctrine' (1985) 71 Iowa Law Review 631.

[21] Kienzler and others (n 3) 17.

[22] NRGI, 'Fiscal Regime' (n 16).

[23] Environmental Law Alliance Worldwide (n 2).

[24] Kim Talus, Scott Looper, and Luke Burns, 'Long-Term Take-or-Pay Agreements in Natural Gas: Past, Present and Future' (2020) OGEL 3; more generally on energy investment protection, see Peter Cameron, *International Energy Investment Law: The Pursuit of Stability* (2nd edn, OUP 2022) 1–25.

twenty-five years.[25] These agreements often have the effect of locking in the supply of natural gas (pipeline gas or LNG) for significant periods of time, unless both parties agree otherwise or one party is willing to pay for cancellation of the contract. Since the adoption of the Paris Agreement in 2015, investors and countries face increasing challenges in efforts to integrate net zero objectives into natural resource contracts signed prior to 2015.[26] The lock-in effect concerns the buyer in circumstances where it endeavours to move to more sustainable energy supplies (eg green or clean hydrogen) and the seller/producer, which may not be able to cancel its natural gas purchase or supply obligations when it wants to move to other types of energy activity or where the government bans natural gas production or exports. It also concerns gas transporters that may want to move to transport green hydrogen, which can be done without major changes to the pipeline infrastructure and is something that the public sector is promoting and supporting (eg the EU Hydrogen Strategy[27]). The lock-in effect becomes even more complicated when a government-mandated change is imposed upon a party which would potentially lead to the invocation of the legal doctrines of frustration, force majeure, fait du prince, or government compulsion, amongst others.[28] This question connects with the detail of the contracts involved and how legal risk is allocated, as well as whether a government would unilaterally impose restrictions on the continued operation of a contract, in light of what such a step might do to that government's international (investment treaty) obligations or the obligations of private parties subject to its sovereign jurisdiction.[29] The problem caused by the sanctity of existing long-term agreements (and other similar contract law doctrines) to net zero efforts is therefore very real and tangible.

Second, and closely related, is the impact of dispute resolution provisions on net zero. As discussed in Chapter 1 of this book, the ongoing global net zero transition is resulting in a wide range of disputes.[30] In addition to contentions over how the introduction of such new ESG regulations and standards by States may constitute breach of contract, other claims include the potential breach of stabilization provisions by government measures to reduce or phase out extractive operations, and how the introduction

[25] As just one example, in October 2021, the Hungarian government signed a fifteen-year contract with Russian Gazprom for deliveries of significant natural gas volumes to the country. See Reuters, 'Hungary agrees on option for more Russian gas shipments, oil transit fees' (11 April 2023) <https://www.reuters.com/business/energy/hungary-agrees-option-more-russian-gas-shipments-oil-transit-fees-2023-04-11/> accessed 21 August 2023.

[26] NRGI, 'Fiscal Regime' (n 16).

[27] Communication from the Commission to the European Parliament, the Council, the European Economic and Social Committee and the Committee of the Regions, A hydrogen strategy for a climate-neutral Europe (COM/2020/301 final).

[28] See Chapter 1 of this book on the rise of disputes in which investors rely on stabilization and dispute resolution clauses to seek protection against any unilateral modifications to the terms of the agreed natural resource contracts by host states which prevents them from investing in such projects.

[29] Kyra Tienhaara, 'Regulatory Chill in a Warming World: The Threat to Climate Policy Posed by Investor-State Dispute Settlement' (2017) 7 Transnational Environmental Law 229. Examples of investment disputes that focus on existing hydrocarbon investments and government climate change related regulation include *Rockhopper Exploration Plc, Rockhopper Italia S.p.A. and Rockhopper Mediterranean Ltd v Italian Republic*, ICSID Case No ARB/17/14, *RWE AG and RWE Eemshaven Holding II BV v Kingdom of the Netherlands*, ICSID Case No ARB/21/4, and *Uniper SE, Uniper Benelux Holding B.V. and Uniper Benelux N.V. v Kingdom of the Netherlands*, ICSID Case No ARB/21/22. The case involving Italy was decided in favour of the claimant, the Uniper case against Netherlands was discontinued as a part of the German government's rescue package for Uniper, and the case involving RWE is facing headwinds with the judgment from the Higher Regional Court of Cologne on 1 September 2022 declaring the case inadmissible due to its intra-EU nature.

[30] See also Jack Ballantyne, 'Climate change: a "strong recipe" for disputes' (28 September 2021) <https://www.globalarbitrationreview.com/article/climate-change-strong-recipe-disputes> accessed 27 August 2023.

of incentive regimes for renewables energy may be a violation of international trade law requirements on non-discrimination.[31] As new forms of disputes relating energy transition and net zero emerge, it is essential to ensure that dispute resolution provisions in natural resource contracts provide a framework for fair, timely, and effective resolution of such disputes in a manner that does not result in costly delays to time-sensitive transition projects.[32] Arbitration is growing in prominence as an essential mechanism for ensuring that disputes relating to transition projects are not unduly delayed.[33] However, in many resource-rich countries, lack of clear and enforceable arbitration provisions in natural resource contracts, as well as arbitration laws that limit the scope of arbitrable disputes continues to hinder the timely and effective resolution of transition-related disputes in the energy and mining sectors.[34] There is a need for lawyers and advisors to ensure the insertion of clear and enforceable arbitration clauses for the resolution of disputes resulting from natural resource investments, including disputes relating to net zero and climate response programmes.[35]

Third, as governments are creating policies and laws that aim at a transition, global demand for transition minerals are projected to increase fivefold by the year 2050.[36] As discussed in Chapter 3 of this book, such significant rise in demand for transition minerals are already resulting in increased risk of resource nationalism in the mineral sector.[37] Countries such as Argentina, Bolivia, Chile, Madagascar, Nigeria, Zimbabwe, Niger Republic, and the Democratic Republic of Congo (DRC), amongst others, that are home to significant quantities of transition minerals, have increasingly announced plans to review the terms and conditions of mining contracts in order to address informal mining and increase local content and domestic value creation.[38] Some have already banned the export of critical minerals, while others have unilaterally announced the suspension of mining contracts.[39] With rising resource nationalism risks in the net zero era, investors will need to carefully integrate contractual mechanisms to mitigate such risks.[40] On the part of states, there is a need to carefully assess the disadvantages of resource nationalism and the unilateral assertion of resource sovereignty, in terms of competitiveness and investment climate, and how

[31] See Sven Volkmer, Michel Selim Djandji and Taylor Gillespie, 'Energy Transition and Investor-State Disputes' (8 April 2022) <https://www.whitecase.com/insight-alert/energy-transition-and-investor-state-disputes> accessed 08 July 2023. See also Qaraman Mohammed Hasan and Hemin Mohammed Ismael, 'International Trade Rules and Natural Gas Export: Trends and Challenges in National Markets' (2022) The Palgrave Handbook of Natural Gas and Global Energy Transitions 483.

[32] Catherine Dixon, 'Achieving a Net Zero World: What is the Role of ADR?' (2021) 4 The Resolver 7.

[33] Queen Mary University and Pinsent Mason, 'The Future of International Energy Arbitration Survey Report' (2022) <https://www.arbitration.qmul.ac.uk/media/arbitration/docs/Future-of-International-Energy-Arbitration-Survey-Report.pdf> accessed 27 August 2023.

[34] Victoria Nalule and Damilola Olawuyi, *The Palgrave Handbook of Arbitration in the African Energy and Mining Sectors* (Palgrave Macmillan 2023) 1–10.

[35] ibid.

[36] World Bank, *Minerals for Climate Action: The Mineral Intensity of the Clean Energy Transition* <https://www.pubdocs.worldbank.org/en/961711588875536384/pdf/Minerals-for-Climate-Action-The-Mineral-Intensity-of-the-Clean-Energy-Transition.pdf> accessed 27 August 2023.

[37] See also Carole Nakhle, 'The energy transition and the risk of resource nationalism' (12 May 2023) <https://www.gisreportsonline.com/r/resource-nationalism/> accessed 27 August 2023.

[38] Damien Nyer and Silvia Marchili, 'A new wave of resource nationalism in the mining & metals industry' (15 September 2021) <https://www.whitecase.com/insight-our-thinking/new-wave-resource-nationalism-mining-metals-industry> accessed 27 August 2023.

[39] ibid.

[40] CMS Law, 'Resource Nationalism in Battery Metals: Risks and Mitigation' <https://www.cms-lawnow.com/en/media/law-now/files/resource-nationalism-in-battery-metals-risks-and-mitigation> accessed 27 August 2023.

unpredictability may weaken foreign direct investment and the flow of resources needed to advance sustainability programmes and infrastructure.

Fourth, is the rise of local content requirements (LCRs) in the natural resource sector as countries seek to advance net zero objectives and transition to our low-carbon economy. LCRs are 'regulatory measures, contractual provisions and policies that require energy market participants and operators to give priority to nationals, domestic companies and locally produced materials, in the procurement of goods and services used for energy operations'.[41] The Inflation Reduction Act (IRA) 2022 in the United States is an obvious example that requires significant local content and support for domestic products inside the United States to promote renewable energy and reduce climate emissions.[42] Scholars argue that several provisions of the IRA violate World Trade Organization (WTO) laws and regulations.[43] Disputes over the compatibility of LCR clauses with WTO requirements have also been raised in Canada and other jurisdictions.[44] In the context of developing countries, a key concern is how LCRs may constrain net zero and sustainability objectives. For example, complying with LCRs and product requirements could mean project delays or higher costs on the part of the operator, especially when suitable and reasonably priced clean technologies are not immediately available locally.[45] With the rapid rise of LCRs in natural resource contracts in many parts of the world and the associated increase in compliance costs,[46] investors will need to carefully integrate contractual mechanisms to mitigate such LCR risks. On the part of states, there is a need to carefully assess the implications of LCRs, in terms of competitiveness and investment climate, and how mandatory LCRs may weaken foreign direct investment and the flow of resources needed to advance sustainability programmes and infrastructure.

Fifth, the global drive towards net zero has seen rapid regulatory developments relating to the integration of responsible contracting principles (RCPs) such as just transition and equity, transparency, resource efficiency, as well as standards relating to ESG in natural resource contracts.[47] Just transition clauses aim to maximize the benefits of clean energy transition to local and indigenous communities by ensuring inclusive, responsible, and right-based net zero programmes and investments across the natural resource development value chain.[48] The key requirement is to integrate provisions on just transition and

[41] Damilola Olawuyi, *Local Content and Sustainable Development in Global Energy Markets* (CUP 2022) 3–15.

[42] United States Congress, 'Inflation Reduction Act of 2022'.

[43] David Kleimann and others, 'How Europe should answer the US Inflation Reduction Act' (JSTOR 2023) <https://www.bruegel.org/sites/default/files/2023-02/PB%2004%202023_0_1.pdf> accessed 27 August 2023.

[44] See Appellate Body Reports, Canada: Certain Measures Affecting the Renewable Energy Generation Section, Canada: Measures Relating to the Feed-in Tariff Program, 5.85, WTO Doc WT/DS412/AB/ R, WT/DS426/AB/ R (adopted 24 May 2013) (finding that Canada's LCR programmes—'Minimum Required Domestic Content Levels'—violate art III:4 GATT 1994 standards).

[45] J-C Kuntze and T Moerenhout, 'Local Content Requirements and the Renewable Energy Industry: A Good Match?' (2013) International Centre for Trade and Sustainable Development 6.

[46] S Stone, J Messent, and D Flaig, 'Emerging Policy Issues: Localisation Barriers to Trade' (2015) 180 OECD Trade Policy Papers 10.

[47] See the Chancery Lane Project, 'Just Transition in Climate Clauses' <https://www.chancerylaneproject.org/wp-content/uploads/2022/11/Just-Transition-in-Climate-Clauses-V1.pdf> accessed 27 August 2023; see also UN Principle of Responsible Investment (UNPRI), 'Climate change and the just transition: A guide for investor action' <https://www.unpri.org/download?ac=9452>, noting that RCPs 'provide investors with a practical tool for protecting their investments in renewable infrastructure and green real estate. These cover issues such as fair wages and benefits, diversity, union participation, training and skills, as well as regulatory compliance.'

[48] See the Chancery Lane Project (n 47); Qaraman Hasan, Raphael J. Heffron, Soran Mohtadi, Brian D. Blankenship, Indra Overland, and Johannes Urpelainen, 'Stepping into the just transition journey: The energy transition in petrostates' (2024) 113 Energy Research & Social Science 103553.

mandatory human rights and environmental due diligence (mHREDD) in natural resource contracts, in order to promptly anticipate and address risks.[49] As discussed in Chapter 2 of this book, by integrating just transition principles into resource contracts, investors and host states can ensure that natural resource development projects, especially the sourcing of transition minerals, proceed with full respect for international human rights law.[50] Failing to properly understand and integrate just transition and mHREDD provisions in natural resource contracts may significantly expose investors to community protests, regulatory fines, project suspension, and reputational damage all of which could significantly increase project costs and reduce the viability of resource investments, including clean energy programmes.[51] There is therefore a strong business case, in terms of risk anticipation and management, for investors to clarify during contract negotiation stage, the regulatory requirements and expectations of the host state with respect to mHREDD. While clear and harmonized standards in this regard are emerging in the EU and North America, lack of clarity with respect to mHREDD requirements remains a significant risk point while investing in Africa, Asia, Middle East, and Latin American markets.[52]

The acceleration of the transition and the legal liabilities and uncertainties that the foregoing gaps can create make it necessary to adapt existing natural resource agreements to new realities, especially those relating to net zero, which may not have been contemplated by the contracting parties. At a general level, there is clearly a need for net zero and climate-aligned contracts that anticipate and address new and emerging transition-related risks. Increasing transparency, greater public participation, and prioritizing environmental goals would be major changes in natural resources law, and mining law in particular. While the natural gas industry has already seen such flexibility being introduced into these contracts,[53] there is a need to understand the contextual reality and the details of the necessary conceptual changes across the entire natural resources sector. Similarly, there is a clear need to rethink certain contract law doctrines, such as force majeure, impossibility to take, frustration, and so on.[54] Legal and institutional barriers facing resource-rich countries and investors in negotiating and adopting net zero and climate-aligned contracts are examined in the next section.

III. Net Zero and Climate-Aligned Contracts: Limitations and Challenges

Natural resource law in general, and natural resource contracts in particular, require a radical shift to be aligned with net zero objectives. There is an urgent need to adapt existing

[49] See United Nations Working Group on Business and Human Rights (UN WGBHR), 'Extractive Sector, Just Transition and Human Rights' (2023) UN General Assembly Report.

[50] ibid; see also ILO Guidelines for a just transition towards environmentally sustainable economies and societies for all, calling on countries to 'integrate provisions for a just transition into national plans and policies . . . and national environmental and climate change action plans' (2016).

[51] Damilola Olawuyi, 'Climate Justice and Corporate Responsibility: Taking Human Rights Seriously in Climate Actions and Projects' (2016) 34(1) Journal of Energy & Natural Resources Law 27.

[52] United Nations Development Programme (UNDP), A Baseline Assessment on Business and Human Rights in Africa: From the First Decade to the Next (10 October 2022) 45–50.

[53] Kim Talus, 'Asian Liquified Natural Gas Markets: The Tomorrow Will Look Very Different from Yesterday' in T Hunter and M Taylor (eds), *Handbook of Oil and Gas Law* (Elgar Research 2022).

[54] Anatole Boute, 'Environmental Force Majeure: Relief from Fossil Energy Contracts in the Decarbonisation Era' (2021) 33(2) Journal of Environmental Law 339.

contract forms of natural resource contracts for future use in a net zero era, and move towards more net zero and climate-aligned natural resource contracts that accommodate new realities. Net zero and climate-aligned natural resource contracts mainstream climate-conscious provisions that advance just energy transition targets and mitigate ESG risks.[55] The task of evolving net zero and climate-aligned natural resource contracts is not easy for resource-rich countries, particularly those lacking robust legal frameworks and solid institutional capacity. Legal and institutional barriers facing resource-rich countries in adapting existing contract forms to accommodate new realities in a net zero era include the following.

A. Legal and Institutional Barriers in Adapting Existing Contracts

1. Stabilization Provisions as Constraints to Change

A stabilization clause preserves the sanctity of a contract against the sovereign right to change the law.[56] Governments as sovereign actors can, either directly or through state-owned enterprises, agree on contract stabilization that protects the investor and stabilizes the original bargain to the time the agreement was signed. As a consequence, such clauses are valid and binding upon the state, and neither national nor international law can have the effect of undermining a contractual stabilization clause.[57] In the event of a specific stabilization provision, a change in laws that would have a negative impact on the investor may not be possible to the extent that (1) these changes would apply to the investment; or (2) it changes the original economic equilibrium established in the contract.[58]

While stabilization provisions enable foreign investors to mitigate risks associated with a sudden or unilateral change of law by the host state, such provisions may, however, constrain the ability of host states to introduce energy transition laws, especially new provisions relating to resource efficiency, transparency, just transition, and mHREDD as required in a net zero era.[59] Despite the challenges and constraints of stabilization clauses, they remain prevalent even in natural resource contracts adopted in the aftermath of the Paris Agreement.[60] One could argue, however, that the likelihood of states agreeing to stabilize climate change-related regulation is fairly low. However, lack of specificity on the scope of obligations covered by broadly framed stabilization provisions may constrain efforts to

[55] See the Chancery Lane Project (n 47); see also UNPRI (n 47).

[56] P Cameron, *International Energy Investment Law: The Pursuit of Stability* (OUP 2010) 69.

[57] Rudolf Dolzer, *Petroleum Contracts and International Law* (OUP 2018) 207.

[58] eg the Host Government Agreement, art 7(x) between the project parties and the government of Turkey of 17 October 2000, provides that 'the State Authorities shall take all actions available to them to restore the Economic Equilibrium established under the Project Agreements if and to the extent the Economic Equilibrium is disrupted or negatively affected, directly or indirectly, as a result of any change (whether the change is specific to the Project or of general application) in Azerbaijan Law . . .'.

[59] Victoria R Nalule, 'What Is the Problem with Stabilization Clauses in Petroleum Agreements?' (2022) 13(1) Journal of Sustainable Development Law and Policy 85.

[60] eg recent contracts in Egypt and Ivory Coast still include stabilization provisions. See the 2021 Egyptian Model Contract Concession, art XIX which provides for stabilization. See <https://www.resourcecontracts.org/contract/ocds-591adf-3622348341/view#/> accessed 27 August 2023; see also the Chevron Egypt Holdings B PTE Ltd, Tharwa Petroleum Company S A E, North El Dabaa Offshore Area, Concession 2021, art XIX <https://www.resourcecontracts.org/contract/ocds-591adf-5541913618/view#/> accessed 27 August 2023; the BP Exploration, Kosmos Energy Cote d'Ivoire, Petroci Holding, Block CI-603, PSA, 2017, art 36 <https://www.resourcecontracts.org/contract/ocds-591adf-9188516395/view#/> accessed 27 August 2023.

advance net zero. This is especially so with the traditional freezing or intangibility clauses which have, because of their restricting impact on sovereignty, been largely replaced more generally by economic stabilization clauses that provide for reestablishment of the original economic equilibrium in case of new regulations.[61] Under the intangibility or immutability clause, 'the state agrees not to amend or terminate the contract without the mutual consent of the contracting parties'.[62] While intangibility provisions may protect investors from resource nationalism risks, it may also constrain the ability of a host state to modify the terms and conditions of mining agreements to get more domestic value especially in light of the new high market valuations of ETMs.

Even without a specific stabilization clause, the international investor may enjoy a degree of protection against new government regulation. This protection may come from international investment treaties that the government may have concluded. Governments can also limit their sovereignty through conclusion of international agreements with more general scope. By concluding international investment treaties which shield investors from new regulations, a state may limit the scope of its action with respect to net zero and clean energy transition in the future.[63] State action introducing more stringent and limiting regulations aimed at addressing human rights and ESG risks, reducing harmful emissions, and moving towards net zero can be limited under the obligations of an investment treaty.[64]

In light of the foregoing constraints on stabilization provisions, there is a need for countries to review and examine existing long-term contracts to determine to what extent they may undermine or constrain net zero targets and objectives. It is imperative to explore provisions in contracts that may enable a mutually beneficial break free from such provisions, while adopting great care when negotiating future contracts to ensure that they are aligned the net zero objectives of both parties. [65]

2. Unclear or Misaligned Net Zero Provisions

Net zero and climate-aligned natural resource contracts should clearly reference the obligation of investors to conduct mHREDD prior to the commencement of resource development or renewable energy projects. Such contracts should also stipulate the need for responsible practices and conduct that address ESG risks in accordance with the United Nations (UN) Guiding Principles on Business and Human Rights.[66]

However, while countries are adopting net zero targets and ambitions, several of the natural resource contracts adopted after 2015 are yet to reference just transition, mHREDD, transparency, resource efficiency, as well as standards relating to ESG.[67] Failure to integrate net zero provisions in natural resource contracts can create obstacles to coherent

[61] Paul Griffin, *Liquefied Natural Gas* (3rd edn, Globe Law and Business 2017) 100.

[62] Damilola Olawuyi, 'Legal Strategies and Tools for Mitigating Legal Risks Associated with Oil and Gas Investments in Africa' (2015) 39(3) OPEC Energy Review 247.

[63] Nalule (n 59), also Katja Gehne and Romulo Brillo, 'Stabilization Clauses in International Investment Law: Beyond Balancing and Fair and Equitable Treatment' (2014) Working Paper No 2013/46.

[64] Lorenzo Cotula, *Regulatory Takings, Stabilization Clauses and Sustainable Development, OECD VII Global Forum on International Investment* <http://www.oecd.org/dataoecd/45/8/40311122.pdf> accessed 27 August 2023.

[65] Kim Talus, 'Revocation and Cancellation of Concessions, Operating Licenses and Other Beneficial Administrative Acts' in Stephan Schill (ed), *International Investment Law and Comparative Public Law* (OUP 2010) 466.

[66] See Chapter 12 of this book on ESG. See also UN WGBHR (n 49); UNPRI (n 47).

[67] eg recent contracts in Egypt and Ivory Coast do not include these net zero-related provisions. See n 60.

implementation and could result in significant ESG risks for investors. For example, lack of clearly defined requirements on the verification and reporting of net zero-related efforts is resulting in increased litigation relating to greenwashing in the energy sector.[68] To mitigate net zero-related risks, a new generation of natural resource contracts must clearly define what is meant by net zero, zero carbon, climate neutral, or just transition.[69] Such contracts should also clearly specify GHG reduction and the net zero obligations of both parties. They should also allocate responsibilities and risks, timelines, and indicators for measuring success with respect to implementing and reporting net zero efforts. Such contracts should include comprehensive and enforceable arbitration provisions that will enhance the timely resolution of disputes that may arise.

Net zero and climate-aligned natural resource contracts could also provide opportunities to address misalignments that may result from restrictive LCRs. While LCRs will continue to play key roles in efforts by developing countries to advance domestic value creation in mineral development and the implementation of renewable energy projects, it is essential to ensure flexibility in their use. This could include providing adequate flexibility for the investor to source goods and services abroad when suitable and reasonably priced alternatives are not immediately available locally. For example, this flexible model is found in the Qatari production-sharing contract (PSC), which provides that the contractor shall, *when possible*, give first consideration or preference to locally manufactured or locally available goods.[70] Negotiating flexible LCRs will enable an IOC to consider other goods and services needed for renewable energy projects in cases where such goods, services or technologies are not available locally.[71]

Furthermore, given the long-term nature of natural resource contracts, there is a need for clarity on how unforeseen ESG and transition risks will be allocated and dealt with throughout the contract. As Sauvant and Wells have rightly argued, resource contracts need mechanisms to allow for the prospect of future events such as unanticipated price changes and windfalls. Such uncertain events will include those relating to the future value and pricing of ETMs.[72] For example, price review mechanisms can allow parties to adjust the contract when, due to sharp changes in prices, the price formula in the contract no longer reflects the prevailing fair market value.[73] Another related risk mitigation clause is the force majeure clause. A force majeure clause is an important contractual provision that 'entitles a party to suspend or terminate the contract on the occurrence of an event which is beyond the control of the parties and which prevents, impedes, or delays the performance of

[68] See 'Environmental NGO wins greenwashing lawsuit against TotalEnergies' <https://www.cleanenergywire.org/news/environmental-ngo-wins-greenwashing-lawsuit-against-totalenergies> accessed 27 August 2023.

[69] See the Net Zero drafting checklist offered by the Chancery Lane Project <https://www.chancerylaneproject.org/wp-content/uploads/2022/11/TCLP-Net-zero-drafting-checklist-V3.pdf> accessed 27 August 2023.

[70] State of Qatar: Model Development and Production Sharing Agreement (2002), art 23.

[71] Olawuyi, *Local Content* (n 41) 242–45.

[72] Karl P Sauvant and Louis T Wells, 'Obsolescence of the Obsolescing Bargain: Why Governments Must Get Investor-State Contracts Right' (Columbia FDI Perspectives, Perspectives on Topical Foreign Direct Investment Issues No 298, 22 February 2021); see also K Berger 'Renegotiation and Adaptation of International Investment Contracts: The Role of Contracts Drafters and Arbitration' (2003) 36 VJTL 1347, 1352.

[73] An example of this clause is as quoted in Lord Justice Leggatt, 'Negotiation in Good Faith: Adapting to Changing Circumstances in Contracts and English Contract Law', Jill Poole Memorial Lecture (Aston University, 19 October 2018), if Seller or Buyer desires a review of the prices set out in this Agreement due to a change in relevant circumstances resulting in such prices being significantly disadvantageous to either Seller or Buyer compared with the prices for other LNG sold into Japan on similar terms to this Agreement, then . . . Buyer and Seller shall meet and discuss in good faith to review such prices.

the contract'.[74] Such events may include climate-induced extreme weather events such as flood, storms, or droughts which should be clearly included in natural resource contracts as events that may entitle a party to suspend or terminate the contract.[75] A third and equally important contractual mitigation clause for long-term contracts is the hardship clause. The hardship clause allows parties to a contract to renegotiate all or certain aspects of the agreement in the event of unforeseen changes or regulatory restrictions which render the continued performance of the contract more burdensome than could have been reasonably foreseen and fundamentally alters the economic equilibrium of the contract.[76] Unlike a force majeure clause, which allows a party suspend or terminate the contract, the hardship clause allows the disadvantaged party to request a renegotiation of the contract.

Generally, in order to provide contractual relief, there is a need to carefully align contractual provisions with the new market realities of net zero in order to mitigate emerging transition risks. A careful contract negotiation is necessary to arrive at a protective provision that will allow both parties to conceptualize unforeseen and unavoidable events relating to net zero that would make the performance of the contract fundamentally burdensome.

3. Capacity Constraints

Negotiating net zero and climate-aligned natural resource contracts will require a clear understanding of legal principles relating to net zero and climate change.[77] One of the key factors that heighten contractual and implementation risks relating to net zero is weak domestic capacity, especially in developing countries.[78] While many developing countries have increasingly outsourced contract negotiation work to law firms to match the expertise of international investors, there is a need to expand the domestic capacity of natural resource sector officials through training and capacity development on net zero. Though not legally binding, article 6 of the UNESCO Declaration on Ethical Principles Relating to Climate Change calls on developed and other states to strengthen international solidarity and timely cooperative action on capacity development on climate change and responses to it.[79] Addressing capacity constraints relating to the negotiation and implementation of net zero and climate-aligned natural resource contracts will therefore require knowledge exchange and targeted training aimed at improving the capacity of key stakeholders across the natural resource value chain. For example, in addition to improving the capacity of energy negotiators on climate change and net zero, arbitral tribunals and judges before whom net

[74] Anatole Boute, 'Environmental Force Majeure: Relief from Fossil Energy Contracts in the Decarbonisation Era' (2021) 33(2) Journal of Environmental Law 339; see also H Konarski, 'Force Majeure and Hardship Clauses in International Contractual Practice' (2003) 4 International Business Law Journal 405, 405–504.

[75] Boute (n 74). See also NRGI, 'Tying Their Hands' (n 7).

[76] Talal Abdulla Al-Emadi, 'The Hardship and Force Majeure Clauses in International Petroleum Joint Venture Agreements' (Oxford Student Legal Research Paper Series Paper no 02/2011 (July 2011).

[77] The UK Law Society, *The Impact of Climate Change on Solicitors* (19 April 2023) <https://www.lawsociety.org.uk/topics/climate-change/impact-of-climate-change-on-solicitors#h3-heading2> accessed 27 August 2023.

[78] See High-Level Expert Group on the Net Zero Emissions Commitments of Non-State Entities (HLEG) <https://www.un.org/sites/un2.un.org/files/high-levelexpertgroupupdate7.pdf> accessed 27 August 2023; see also Qaraman M Hasan and Karwan A Perot, 'Production Sharing Contracts and Rentierism: Reforming Transparency Gaps in Kurdistan's Oil and Gas Contracts' (2021) 8 The Extractive Industries and Society 100899; Qaraman Mohammed Hasan, 'The Power of Constitution for Enacting Energy Law and Managing Natural Resources: The Case of the Kurdistan Regional Government's Oil Contracts' (2019) 128 Energy Policy 744.

[79] UNESCO, 'The UNESCO Declaration of Ethical Principles in relation to Climate Change' (13 November 2017) <https://www.unesco.org/en/legal-affairs/declaration-ethical-principles-relation-climate-change?hub=66535> accessed 27 August 2023.

zero-related disputes come must be equipped with latest information and knowledge on net zero concepts and transition-related contractual techniques.

Barriers to international solidarity and cooperation with respect to capacity development on net zero will have to be carefully addressed. As discussed in Chapter 2 of this book, conflicting geopolitics, international sanctions, and increased weakening of international cooperation on climate change weaken the abilities of North–South cooperation on capacity development relating to negotiating and implementing net zero and climate-aligned natural resource contracts.

IV. Towards Net Zero and Climate-Aligned Natural Resource Contracts: Need for Dynamic Legal Innovation

Improving regulatory regimes on natural resources in general, and natural resource contracts in particular, requires a legal, fiscal, and institutional reform agenda aimed at mainstreaming net zero and climate change into the design and implementation of natural resource investments. This would be done by infusing natural resource investments and programmes with legal principles and norms relating to net zero.

A starting point is the need for regulators and industry associations to collaboratively design model contracts and toolkits that define and conceptualize essential provisions to be included in net zero and climate-aligned natural resource contracts. There is an ongoing cooperation between the International Bar Association (IBA), Section for Energy, Environment, Natural Resources and Infrastructure Law Section (SEERIL), and the Association of International Energy Negotiators (AIEN) focusing on developing an energy transition model clause for future agreements within the energy industry. The objective of this cooperation is to 'create standard contractual provisions the oil and gas industry can rely on to implement their emissions reductions and decarbonization goals and that will help enable an energy transition that is timely, just, sustainable, and efficient'.[80] The work will focus on three different model clauses all addressing different aspects of the energy transition. First, operational Emissions Model Clauses to enable oil and gas companies to reduce the emissions of their oil and gas operations, including through the supply chains of those operations. Second, Hydrogen/Low Carbon Energy Sources Model Clauses to enable oil and gas companies to tap new sources of low carbon or zero (or near-zero) carbon sources of energy. Third, carbon capture, usage and storage and Carbon Market Model Clauses to enable oil and gas companies to reduce a project's 'carbon footprint' through the addition of carbon capture and storage capabilities and purchase of credits that remove carbon from the environment. These clauses aim to offer multiple energy transition-related purposes that could be adapted to a wide range of natural resource agreements. Similar initiatives such as the Chancery Lane Project (TCLP) aimed at providing model clauses on net zero are key to improving current understanding on mitigating transition-related risks in the natural resource sector.[81] Natural resource lawyers should not only integrate net zero

[80] Andrea Forabosco and others, 'The Future is Form: AIEN and IBA Launch Joint Collaboration on New Model Clauses for a Successful Energy Transition' <https://www.ibanet.org/document?id=Megastand-brochure-IBA-Oil-and-gas> accessed 12 May 2023.

[81] See the net zero drafting checklist offered by the Chancery Lane Project <https://www.chancerylaneproject.org/wp-content/uploads/2022/11/TCLP-Net-zero-drafting-checklist-V3.pdf> accessed 27 August 2023.

provisions in contracts, they must also provide early counsel to clients on the importance of mHRDD and ESG investing in order to properly anticipate and address the wide range of just transition risks associated with natural resource investments in a net zero era.

In addition to specific contractual provisions in new contracts, there is a need for countries to review existing long-term contracts to ensure alignment and to introduce climate-conscious provisions. Contractual provisions that act as barriers to just transition or constrain the abilities of the state to introduce GHG emission reduction obligations should be reformed to ensure that natural resource investments align with sovereign decisions relating to net zero. The ability of a state to make decisions relating to natural resource use is the hallmark of resource sovereignty, which must be persevered in contractual arrangements and investment treaties. Furthermore, improving coordination among the various ministries responsible for contract negotiation, fiscal coordination, and natural resource development, such as national oil companies, national investment authorities, and environment ministries is also essential. Such inter-ministerial coordination will significantly streamline contract negotiation processes to ensure that new contracts reflect national strategies and ambition on net zero. As discussed in Chapter 3 of this book, the increasing tendency of conflict and overlap between net zero targets announced, and new resource contracts for oil and gas and coal projects signed by countries creates market uncertainties which may impact the realization of net zero ambitions. There is a need to mainstream net zero and climate thinking into all aspects of the natural resource value chain, especially contract negotiation, policy development, and investment decision-making.

Third is the need for all stakeholders across the natural resource sector to place greater emphasis on capacity development and knowledge-sharing on net zero. Investors and countries will need to develop and implement targeted capacity development programmes in areas relating to contract negotiation and development to progressively improve the in-house expertise of boards, managers, and officers that are involved in contract negotiation, procurement, and management. Special attention should also be paid to providing training for members of the judiciary, bar associations, and industry associations on the essential guiding principles of quantifying, reporting, and monitoring net zero programmes to avoid greenwashing and to ensure compliance with industry standards and regulations. International development agencies, academia, and bar associations have key roles to play in spearheading tailored courses that enhance capacity for the negotiation and implementation of net zero and climate-aligned natural resource contracts.

V. Conclusion

Governments as sovereign actors have the right and the obligation to ensure the transition to net zero. Contractual and treaty level obstacles to this transition are real and tangible. There is an increasing awareness of this, illustrated in the increased call for countries to update natural resource contracts to address clauses that constrain the exercise of sovereign decision-making authority with respect to net zero, just transition, and mandatory human rights due diligence in natural resource development.

The task of renegotiating and implementing net zero and climate-aligned natural resource contracts is often complicated by lack of coherent legal frameworks and limited institutional capacity. Failure to align net zero targets with contractual clauses such as stabilization, dispute resolution, LCRs and force majeure provisions, amongst others, can create obstacles to coherent implementation and could result in significant ESG risks for investors. Such incoherence could also weaken the competitiveness and investment climate of a country. Addressing these gaps will require increased international solidarity through the development of model contractual clauses, capacity development, and knowledge-sharing on negotiating and integrating net zero obligations in resource contracts. There is also a need to ensure inter-ministerial coordination and cooperation in order to effectively mainstream net zero and climate thinking into all aspects of the natural resource value chain, especially contract negotiation, investment decision-making, and the development and implementation of critical mineral strategies.

The next chapter provides an overview of the different mineral strategies and legislation being developed by countries to maintain national sovereignty over their critical transition mineral resources in the face of increased demand fuelled by net zero ambitions.

5

Critical Minerals Strategies, Net Zero, and Natural Resources Law

Barry Barton

I. Introduction

Northeast of Winnipeg in Canada, the Tanco mine produced tantalum, lithium, and cesium for fifty years before closing in 2009 because the market for these niche products was slow.[1] But in 2022 it reopened under the ownership of a Chinese firm called Sinomine, with refurbished facilities to produce lithium spodumene concentrates, all of which are being shipped to a sister company in China, although the company aims to supply the burgeoning North American market as well. On a broader level, the change that this mine's story demonstrates is seen in the reports from mining industry sources that auto industry executives are turning up in large numbers at their events, anxious to talk about supplies of materials for electric vehicles.[2] Equally, the International Energy Agency (IEA), a leading energy policy institution, has quickly focused on minerals as a key part of the net zero energy transition.[3] At their meeting in Hiroshima in May 2023, the Group of Seven (G7) leaders—consisting of Canada, France, Germany, Italy, Japan, the United Kingdom, and the United States—who do not usually address anything as specific as minerals policy, spent time discussing the diversification of critical minerals supplies.[4] Something unusual is going on; the attention being given to the minerals needs of the net zero transition is unprecedented.

This chapter enquires into the critical minerals strategies that a number of countries are producing as part of this change, and the effects that they may have on natural resources law, and mining law specifically. The influence of these strategies is a significant aspect of the relationship between natural resources law and the net zero energy future, representing an exercise of national sovereignty in an internationally competitive situation. Yet, in the existing literature, there is almost no examination of critical minerals strategies and policies and their legal effects, something that may come as no surprise since the strategies are such a recent development, appearing only in 2022 and 2023.[5] Certainly the new need for critical minerals for the net zero transition has been closely examined,[6] and so too have

[1] Naimul Karim, 'Historic Tanco mine in Manitoba producing lithium again—this time under China's Sinomine' (*The Northern Miner*, 16–29 May 2022).

[2] 'Carmaker investment gives McEwen Copper more time to go public' (*Mining Weekly*, 1 March 2023).

[3] International Energy Agency (IEA), *Securing Clean Energy Technology Supply Chains* (2022).

[4] Group of Seven, 'G7 Hiroshima Leaders' Communiqué' (20 May 2023) <http://www.g7hiroshima.go.jp> accessed 18 August 2023.

[5] Only Sam Kalen, 'Mining Our Future Critical Minerals: Does Darkness Await Us?' (2021) 51 Environmental Law Reporter 11006 appears to have addressed them, and only in the United States.

[6] Morgan D Bazilian, 'The Mineral Foundation of the Energy Transition' (2018) 5 The Extractive Industries and Society 93.

Barry Barton, *Critical Minerals Strategies, Net Zero, and Natural Resources Law* In: *Net Zero and Natural Resources Law*.
Edited by: Damilola S. Olawuyi, José Juan González, Hanri Mostert, Milton Fernando Montoya, and Catherine Banet,
Oxford University Press. DOI: 10.1093/9780198925033.003.0005

the risks that new levels of activity present to environmental, cultural, and indigenous values.[7]

Work is, therefore, needed to analyse the new policies and strategies specifically, for the influence that they can foreseeably exert over natural resources law.

The chapter begins by outlining the context in which these strategies have appeared, firstly the new materials needs of the net zero transition, then market and commercial responses, and the responses in international relations. It goes on to consider the strategies that Canada, Australia, the United States, and the European Union (EU) have put forward, and the lithium strategy of Chile. The next section explores the effects that these strategies are likely to have in natural resources law, having regard to the structure of mining law, and considering the foreseeable consequences for communities and the environment. Recycling and the circular economy are part of the picture that some of the strategies provide for, but so too is the risk that the drive for increased minerals supply will clash with the imperative of staying within planetary boundaries. The chapter concludes by identifying the lessons to be learned from the increasing occurrence of critical mineral strategies, the likely positive effects they will have on the exercise of resource sovereignty, and the possible negative effects that policy-makers and law reformers should avoid.

II. Context: Net Zero and the New Demand for Minerals

A. The Materials Needed to Electrify and to Harvest Energy

The clean energy technologies required for decarbonization need a mix of minerals, materials, and metals that is different from what the old technologies needed. Coal and natural gas-fired power stations need a lot of steel and a certain amount of copper.[8] In contrast, wind turbines need much more copper per megawatt of capacity, especially in cabling, and more zinc. Offshore wind turbines, which are generally larger and employ direct drive permanent magnet synchronous generators without gearboxes, need a variety of rare earth elements (REEs) for the magnets, and more copper again, seven or eight times as much as a coal or gas power station.[9] Solar photovoltaic (PV) installations vary in their technology and may require crystalline silicon, cadmium telluride, copper indium gallium diselenide, or amorphous silicon, and they also need copper, steel, and aluminium for inverters, mounts, and the like. As for energy use, a car using petrol or diesel is made mainly of steel (with manganese for alloys) and aluminium, and copper for its electrical parts; in contrast, an electric vehicle (EV) uses twice as much copper, and it usually needs REEs for its motor;

[7] Raphael J Heffron, 'The Role of Justice in Developing Critical Minerals' (2020) 7 The Extractive Industries and Society 855; Teresa Kramarz and others, 'Governing the Dark Side of Renewable Energy: A Typology of Global Displacements' (2021) 74 Energy Research & Social Science 101902; Laura Berglan and others, 'The Clean Energy Dilemma: How the Push for Clean Energy Could Threaten Indigenous Communities and an Exploration of Potential Alternatives' (2022) 33 Colorado Environmental Law Journal 285; Roger E Meiners and Andrew P Morriss, 'Addressing Green Energy's "Resource Curse"' (2022) 33 Duke Environmental Law & Policy Forum 35; Kate R Finn and Christina AW Stanton, 'The (Un)just Use of Transition Minerals: How Efforts to Achieve a Low-Carbon Economy Continue to Violate Indigenous Rights' (2022) 33 Colorado Environmental Law Journal 341.

[8] International Energy Agency (IEA), *The Role of Critical Minerals in Clean Energy Transitions* (2021). https://www.iea.org/reports/the-role-of-critical-minerals-in-clean-energy-transitions

[9] IEA, *Role* (n 8) 66, also 56 and 88. However, the growing size and efficiency of turbines has reduced the materials intensity of wind power in kg of material per MW of output: p 64.

all EVs need lithium, nickel, and graphite, and (depending on their battery technology) varying amounts of manganese and cobalt. Different batteries are required for grid-scale storage, to complement intermittent generation and manage peak demand, and manufacturers are experimenting with technologies not constrained by weight. Electrolyzers for hydrogen come in different types; some require nickel and zirconium, others need lanthanum and yttrium as well, and others again use platinum, palladium, and iridium. (In niches like this there is a greater possibility of technical change and disruption, so demand is less predictable.[10]) Fuel cells need platinum. Electrification of any kind invariably calls for more copper and aluminium.

The net zero transition therefore leads to a greatly increased demand for minerals, for different minerals than hitherto, and for a much wider range of minerals, some common but some quite exotic and in limited production at present. The supply of copper, lithium, nickel, cobalt, and REEs will be of particular importance.[11] Demand for lithium under the IEA's Sustainable Development Scenario could grow forty times by 2040.[12]

There is a reason for all this, which is obvious if one reflects on the basic human activity of harvesting energy and gathering it together in the form of fuels. Coal, oil, and natural gas are astonishingly energy dense, whether one measures the density in joules per kilogramme or joules per cubic metre.[13] Those fuels and their sources also have high power density, in watts per square metre of the earth's surface required, so, to transition to renewable energy, society will have to rely on concentrating energy flows several orders of magnitude more diffuse than fossil fuel equivalents. It takes more effort to harvest usable energy from the sun or the wind, where it is more diffuse, and the tools we need to do the work are more complicated. The tools and technologies we need to move into a net zero world often have a higher mineral intensity.[14] It is therefore plain to see that the minerals concerns of the transition to net zero are no accident; indeed, they are central and inevitable. Moreover, they are layered on top of the additional demand caused by the growth of human population and advancement of economic development.

Price changes are inevitable too. The prices of lithium and cobalt more than doubled in 2021, and those for copper, nickel, and aluminium all rose by about 25 to 40 per cent. Lithium went up again in the first three months of 2022, so that it rose 738 per cent over fifteen months. Mineral prices are volatile at the best of times, but these major increases are so large that they threaten the long-term trend towards cheaper renewables and electrification.[15]

The IEA has seen the need to engage with the policy implications of these changes, realizing that clean energy chains largely depend on minerals, not fossil fuels.[16] The net zero transition redefines global energy security; as the transition progresses, security will be less about oil politics and more about the supply chains for finding and extracting critical

[10] Kirsten Hund and others, *Minerals for Climate Action: the Mineral Intensity of the Clean Energy Transition* (World Bank Group 2020).

[11] IEA, *Securing* (n 3) 11.

[12] IEA, *Role* (n 8) 8.

[13] Vaclav Smil, *Power Density: A Key to Understanding Energy Sources and Uses* (MIT Press 2015) 12, strictly J/kg is called specific energy; more generally, see p 202.

[14] IEA, *Securing* (n 3) Fig 5, p 12.

[15] Tae-Yoon Kim, 'Critical minerals threaten a decades-long trend of cost declines for clean energy technologies' (IEA, 18 May 2022) <http://www.iea.org> accessed 26 May 2023.

[16] IEA, *Securing* (n 3) 4. The IEA hosted a Critical Minerals and Clean Energy Summit in Paris in September 2023.

minerals, processing them, and readying them for the manufacturers of clean energy systems. Wind, sun, water, and geothermal heat are domestic energy resources, which implies a level of energy security and resilience,[17] but the supply chains for the technology to harness them are less secure. Production and processing operations for many minerals are highly concentrated, making supplies vulnerable to political instability, geopolitical risks, export controls, and natural disasters. South Africa accounts for around 70 per cent of world platinum production, and the Democratic Republic of Congo about the same proportion of cobalt.[18] China dominates the production of EV batteries and PV wafer to a degree that it is a key reason for much of the international action we consider shortly.

B. Company Responses and Implications for Transactions

In the face of these changes, we are seeing major shifts in company behaviour. General Motors, for example, has invested US$650 million in a company building a lithium mine in Nevada, with exclusive access to its Phase 1 production and a right of first offer on Phase 2.[19] Stellantis is investing US$207 million in an Argentinian copper project, and a part of the deal is a copper cathodes and concentrates purchase rights agreement.[20] Ford Motor Co has entered into non-binding memoranda of understanding for lithium and nickel with nine mining companies, followed up in some cases with binding offtakes.[21] Indeed, there are reports of many such deals now. What is so striking about them is that usually companies stick to the niches where they can do well, where they have technical, marketing, and commercial expertise that gives them a competitive advantage; broad conglomerates are out of fashion. So when these car makers move into the business of financing and supporting mine development, they are entering a field well outside their usual skillset, several steps away from their factories up the supply chain. Evidently, their need to secure raw materials is urgent. For the miners, these equity investments and purchase agreements furnish capital and give convincing proof of financial viability at a crucial stage in the mine development process, allowing them to secure other finance from investors and lenders.

Fresh legal issues may arise from these new commercial arrangements. Shareholder relationships between the very different participants require careful negotiation, and the arrangements must comply with competition law. Offtake agreements are usually for concentrates or material in the form of personal property and are usually for reasonably short terms, such as five years. However, the product does not begin to flow until the mine comes into operation, so the agreement must include conditions to deal with different

[17] Discussed in Barry Barton, 'Building Resilience from the Ground Up: Local Supply and Demand Management with Renewables, Prosumers, Energy Efficiency, Critical Minerals, and the Circular Economy' in Catherine Banet and others (eds), *Resilience in Energy, Infrastructure, and Natural Resources Law: Examining Legal Pathways for Sustainability in Times of Disruption* (OUP 2022) 327.

[18] IEA, *Securing* (n 3) 24.

[19] 'Lithium Americas provides General Motors transaction details and update on construction plan for Thacker Pass' (31 January 2023) <https://www.lithiumamericas.com/news/lithium-americas-provides-general-motors-transaction-details-and-update-on-construction-plan-for-thacker-pass> accessed 17 February 2023.

[20] 'McEwen Copper Closes ARS $30 Billion Investment by Stellantis' (press release from McEwen Mining Inc, 27 Feb 2023) <http://www.mcewenmining.com> accessed 2 March 2023. The deal includes a commitment by the miner to achieve net zero carbon emissions from the project (Los Azules) by 2038.

[21] Blair McBride, 'Ford goes directly to miners for lithium, nickel to support EV ambitions' (*The Northern Miner*, 8–21 August 2022).

contingencies including force majeure events, failure of the project, and transfer of ownership of the project. They may include elements such as a take-or-pay structure to reassure the bankers. No doubt they must also address the intermediate steps that the car maker must arrange to have the mine concentrates processed and fabricated into components that they can use in their factories.

C. International Responses: Market Dominance and De-risking

Along with the general surge in demand for certain minerals, stands the role of China, which holds a significant lead in the processing of a number of critical minerals, especially lithium and rare earth elements. Seventy-five per cent of the world's battery production capacity is in China, and so is 97 per cent of global capacity for wafer manufacturing for PV cells.[22] In such sectors China is not merely the leader, it is utterly dominant. In the mining stages of the supply chain it is much less dominant, except in graphite. Its position is not accidental, but the result of national effort over a long period. Zhang's chapter in this volume explains the laws and policies that China has used to plan systematically to secure its lithium supply chain and increase its dominance in EV materials and manufacturing.[23] With few lithium mineral resources of its own it has acted vigorously to acquire mine assets in Argentina, Chile, Australia, Mexico, and other countries; Chinese companies have been willing to pay a premium to safeguard their security of supply for the future. This buying spree has left other countries anxious about their own lithium supplies. But China's strategizing is not confined to lithium; it has made similar efforts in relation to REEs and a number of other materials.[24] Its dominance, in a world order that has become more competitive, causes other countries to worry about their dependence, apprehensive not only of confrontation but also of disruption such as that caused by strict COVID-19 lockdowns.

As a result, international responses in the developed world are driven not only by the general demand for critical minerals, but also more specifically by the desire to reduce dependence on China, and, less pressingly, other countries that are the lead suppliers of particular minerals. The atmosphere is affected by the fact that some of the largest manufacturing countries—the EU, Japan, South Korea, and (in respect of many materials) China—do not host much mining activity. Manufacturing countries are experiencing fear of missing out; they see themselves as engaged in a 'global race' for critical raw materials.[25]

The international response in the developed world is seen in the work of specialist institutions but also at the highest political levels. The IEA work noted above has led to recommendations for diversification, technological innovation, recycling, resilience, market transparency, higher environmental, social and corporate governance (ESG) standards, and international collaboration.[26] The World Bank has offered similar advice.[27] The theme of the 2022 meeting of the Intergovernmental Forum on Mining, Minerals, Metals and Sustainable Development

[22] IEA, *Securing* (n 3) 10, 22; IEA, *World Energy Outlook 2022* 174.
[23] See Chapter 6 of this book.
[24] See Barton, 'Resilience' (n 17).
[25] European Commission Statement, 'Critical Raw Materials Act: securing the new gas & oil at the heart of our economy' Blog of Commissioner Thierry Breton, 14 September 2022.
[26] IEA, *Role* (n 8) 18.
[27] Hund and others (n 10) 16.

was Critical Minerals and the Energy Transition.[28] A Sustainable Critical Minerals Alliance has been formed to pursue environmentally-sound and responsible mining.[29] The G7 leaders, also noted above, addressed critical minerals in May 2023, supporting the Minerals Security Partnership and the IEA's Voluntary Critical Mineral Security Program.[30] The meeting emphasized de-risking in its relations with China (not de-coupling), preventing economic coercion, and diversifying supplies of critical minerals. Alongside the market and commercial responses, these international efforts to coordinate action on critical minerals run in parallel with action at the national level, to which this discussion can now turn.

III. Critical Minerals Strategies: National Exercises of Sovereignty over Natural Resources

Against that background, this section considers the legal and policy actions being taken at the national and subnational levels, mainly in the developed world, exercising national sovereignty over non-renewable resources. Governments are now paying more attention to the supply of minerals and other raw materials than they have for many years. As at the international level, countries are concerned to improve their energy security, and to secure a place for their industries as the net zero transition takes place, particularly as to participation in high technology industries, employment opportunities, and regional development. Concerns about human rights and international development also put a sharper focus on the sources of raw materials. The IEA can now list dozens of policy measures in different countries to address critical minerals issues.[31] Some of the measures being taken are narrow in their scope, for example taking a direct equity stake in a mining company to head off foreign direct investment by non-market state-oriented entities,[32] or entering into a memorandum of understanding with motor vehicle manufacturers with respect to their materials needs.[33] Other measures reach further, for example Mexico's decision in 2022 to declare lithium a strategic mineral and nationalizing it.[34]

However, the intention here is to examine the critical minerals strategies that several developed countries have proposed or put in place in 2022 or 2023, usually building on previous work that they have had in train. These strategies are becoming common in developed countries; even countries with little mining activity are considering them.[35] The

[28] *IGF Bulletin* (International Institute for Sustainable Development, 13 November 2022) <http://www.enb.iisd.org/igf-agm-2022-mining-minerals-metals> accessed 2 March 2023.

[29] 'Sustainable Critical Minerals Alliance announced at COP15' (*Mining Magazine*, 13 December 2022) https://miningmagazine.com.au/sustainable-critical-minerals-alliance-announced-at-cop15/, accessed 2 May 2024. Australia, Canada, France, Germany, Japan, the United Kingdom, and the United States are members.

[30] G7 Communiqué (n 4). On the Minerals Security Partnership, see Vlado Vivoda, 'Friend-shoring and Critical Minerals: Exploring the Role of the Minerals Security Partnership' (2023) 100 Energy Research & Social Science 103085.

[31] IEA, 'Policies Database' <https://www.iea.org/policies?topic=Critical%20Minerals> accessed 26 May 2023.

[32] Cecilia Jamasmie, 'U.S. Grabs Stake in Battery Minerals Miner to Fight Chinese Control' (*The Northern Miner*, 12–25 October 2020) (TechMet nickel-cobalt development in Brazil).

[33] Henry Lazenby, 'Canada inks MOUs with German automakers to help meet clean transport demand' (*The Northern Miner*, 5–18 September 2022).

[34] Cecilia Jamasmie, 'Mexico passes bill nationalizing lithium industry' (*The Northern Miner*, 2–15 May 2022).

[35] eg United Kingdom: *Resilience for the Future: the United Kingdom's Critical Minerals Strategy* (2022); New Zealand: NZ Petroleum and Minerals, 'Crown Minerals Amendment Bill introduced' (6 December 2022) <https://www.nzpam.govt.nz/about/news/crown-minerals-amendment-bill-introduced/> accessed 9 February 2023.

strategies list the minerals or raw materials that have been determined to be critical or strategic. (Materials like lithium, cobalt, and REEs appear on most lists, but other materials such as copper and aluminium appear on some countries' lists but not others.) The particular interest of this chapter is not so much the lists themselves as the possible legal significance of the strategies, and its concern is with the application of the strategies to mineral exploration and development, rather than processing and manufacturing.

It should be recognized that the perspective of countries in the developing world or the Global South is very different. Only some of them have a manufacturing base that is hungry for critical mineral raw materials, and many of them have mineral resources that they look to for the improvement of their citizens' wellbeing. There are important stories to be told about the effects of the net zero transition on people and communities already experiencing hardship from mining, such as in the artisanal mining of cobalt.[36] Which minerals are understood to be critical is a contestable concept; although it can be analysed through technical indicators,[37] the perspective of the Global South, especially of the citizens of producer countries, is different from that of the consumers of the Global North.[38]

A. Canada

The *Canadian Critical Minerals Strategy* of 2022[39] operates primarily through the coordinated spending of public funds. Funds (CAN$3.5 billion) are being found for public geoscience, research and development (R&D) in government labs, support for private-sector R&D on critical minerals in the upstream and midstream, and roading and power supply for remote areas (CAN$1.5 billion); and the Strategic Innovation Fund will have an additional CAN$1.5 billion to invest in critical minerals projects. Apart from the power of the purse, the *Strategy* seeks to expedite regulatory processes for environmental and other impacts, while recognizing that responsible regulation is vital; it walks a fine line. The Critical Minerals Centre of Excellence (within the federal agency Natural Resources Canada) will help project developers navigate regulatory processes. However no law reform is proposed for these purposes. The *Strategy* seeks to grow the workforce, and to advance reconciliation with indigenous peoples, ensuring that they are active partners in development. Internationally, it proposes to pursue collective action to maintain supply chain security and ESG standards, and to work with 'like-minded partners' to protect national security in the supply of critical minerals.[40]

[36] Benjamin K Sovacool, 'The Precarious Political Economy of Cobalt: Balancing Prosperity, Poverty, and Brutality in Artisanal and Industrial Mining in the Democratic Republic of the Congo' (2019) 6 The Extractive Industries and Society 915; and Benjamin K Sovacool and others, 'The Decarbonisation Divide: Contextualizing Landscapes of Low-Carbon Exploitation and Toxicity in Africa' (2020) 60 Global Environmental Change 102028.

[37] TE Graedel and others, 'Methodology of Metal Criticality Determination' (2012) 46 Environmental Science & Technology 1063, dx.doi.org/10.1021/es203534z; Christoph Helbig and others, 'Selecting and Prioritizing Material Resources by Criticality Assessments' (2021) 4 One Earth 339, doi.org/10.1016/j.oneear.2021.02.006.

[38] Susan Nakanwagi, 'Just Criticality: A Justice Framework for Critical Minerals Value Chains' (PhD thesis, University of Dundee, 2022).

[39] Natural Resources Canada (2022) <https://www.canada.ca/content/dam/nrcan-rncan/site/critical-minerals/Critical-minerals-strategyDec09.pdf> accessed 12 August 2023.

[40] The Strategy refers to the problem of relying on non-market economies (at 35).

Foreign direct investment rules relating to critical minerals, as defined on the government's list, were tightened up in late 2022. The 'net benefit' economic regime is now applied on the basis that investments in the critical mineral sector by foreign state-owned and state-linked enterprises pose an inherent economic risk, and under a new national security regime the participation of a state-owned enterprise or a foreign-influenced private investor in an investment in a critical minerals business in Canada will support a finding that the investment could be injurious to national security.[41] In November 2022, the government applied this new policy to order divestiture of three critical minerals investments made by Chinese investors, even though they were minority stakes, and even though in one case the company's operations were entirely outside Canada.[42]

There is a new tax credit; the Critical Mineral Exploration Tax Credit encourages investment in critical minerals exploration.[43] If an expenditure is made under a plan of exploration certified by a qualified engineer or geoscientist as primarily targeting critical minerals (which are listed in the Income Tax Act) then a 30 per cent tax credit is available to the company's shareholders, making the investment a very attractive one. It will have its difficulties, however. For example, many base metal mineral deposits host multiple metals, and even after several years' exploration effort it may not be clear what will be the primary target and what will be the by-products; is it a copper mine with some gold values, or is it the other way around, and if so do the credits have to be repaid? A similar tax credit for equipment for critical minerals extraction and processing and battery and EV manufacturing was included in the March 2023 Budget.[44]

Because mineral rights on public lands are mostly administered by the provinces, provincial action is important. The Ontario *Critical Minerals Strategy*[45] pursues policies similar to the federal one. It includes a tax credit which does not, however, target critical minerals. It speaks of improving the regulatory framework but makes no new proposals, and its desire to improve Aboriginal participation is based on existing programmes, although it says that success will be measured by an increase in the number of agreements that share provincial mining revenue with First Nations. The Québec strategy has a particular emphasis on geoscience, recycling in a circular economy perspective, and foreign investment.[46] Alberta has developed a strategy and amended its natural resources laws to facilitate the extraction of minerals like lithium from the brines found in petroleum

[41] Government of Canada, 'Guidelines on the National Security Review of Investments', 24 March 2021, and 'Policy Regarding Foreign Investments from State-Owned Enterprises in Critical Minerals under the Investment Canada Act' (28 October 2022) <http://www.ised-isde.canada.ca> accessed 2 March 2023. Under the Investment Canada Act RSC 1985 c 28 (1st Supp) national security reviews are provided for under ss 25.1–25.6, and guidelines under s 38.

[42] McCarthy Tétrault, 'Government of Canada Orders Divestitures in the Critical Minerals Sector' (7 November 2022) <http://www.mccarthy.ca> accessed 2 March 2023.

[43] Income Tax Act, RSC 1985 c 1 (5th Supp), s 127(9) and related sections. The credit is in addition to full deductibility of exploration expenditures but an alternative to the existing mineral exploration tax credit, and is renounced by the exploration company in favour of its shareholders. Overall these incentives attract considerable exploration funds: see Barry Barton, *Canadian Law of Mining* (LexisNexis Canada 2019) 951.

[44] Colin McClelland, 'Federal budget gives clean tech and critical minerals a $21B push' (*The Northern Miner*, 17–30 April 2023).

[45] Ontario, *Ontario's Critical Minerals Strategy 2022–2027* (March 2022) <https://www.ontario.ca/page/ontarios-critical-minerals-strategy-2022-2027-unlocking-potential-drive-economic-recovery-prosperity> accessed 2 May 2024.

[46] Québec, Ministère de l'Énergie et des Ressources naturelles, *Critical and Strategic Minerals* (2020) <https://mrnf.gouv.qc.ca/wp-content/uploads/CSMs-Brochure-for-investors.pdf> accessed 12 August 2023.

reservoirs.[47] Considering the federal and provincial strategies and associated actions together, one sees a mixture of general policy intentions and specific law changes as to natural resource management.

B. Australia

The Australian *Critical Minerals Strategy* of 2022[48] updates that of 2019 and proposes three kinds of action. The first is de-risking projects, which is basically financial support. It establishes a Critical Minerals Facility of AUD$2 billion has been established, to overcome finance gaps and get projects off the ground. A Critical Minerals Accelerator Initiative will provide grants supporting feasibility studies, design work, pilot testing, and demonstration plants. De-risking grants are also available in manufacturing and support is provided to attract international investment. The second action is to create an enabling environment, which is government R&D, regional hubs, and strengthening the ESG standards which are already seen to be a point of difference for Australia. It includes work by the Future Battery Industries Cooperative Research Centre on mineral lifecycle analysis and a battery supply chain tracing system. The third action is international partnerships, working with like-minded partner nations, to strengthen relationships and secure new sources of capital and commercial offtake agreements. One substantial partnership is a bilateral agreement with the United States.[49] Constitutional jurisdiction over minerals and mineral rights is primarily a matter for the states, so it is not surprising that the federal *Strategy* has little direct significance for mining laws.

C. United States

The basis of American federal critical minerals policy is to be found in four instruments: the Defense Production Act, Bipartisan Infrastructure Law, Inflation Reduction Act, and Executive Order 14017.[50] As in Australia, there is substantial provision for government R&D expenditure (including government geological mapping) and international cooperation agreements. However, the main policy tool is the release of government funding, whether by grants or by loans, sometimes on a large scale; for example, US$316 million to

[47] Alberta Ministry of Energy, *Renewing Alberta's Mineral Future* (2021); Mineral Resource Development Act, SA 2021 c M-16.8; Brine-hosted Mineral Resource Development Rules, Alta Reg 17/2023, and Alberta Energy Regulator, Directive 090: Brine-Hosted Mineral Resource Development, released 2 March 2023.

[48] Australia, Department of Industry, Science, Energy and Resources, *2022 Critical Minerals Strategy* (2022).

[49] Prime Minister, President of the United States of America, 'Australia-United States Climate, Critical Minerals and Clean Energy Transformation Compact: Joint Statement' (20 May 2023) <http://www.pm.gov.au> accessed 30 May 2023.

[50] White House, 'Fact sheet: Biden-Harris Administration driving U.S. battery manufacturing and good-paying jobs' (19 October 2022) <https://www.whitehouse.gov/briefing-room/statements-releases/2022/10/19/fact-sheet-biden-harris-administration-driving-u-s-battery-manufacturing-and-good-paying-jobs/> accessed 26 May 2023. Previously Executive Order 13817 (82 Fed Reg 60835, 20 December 2017) outlined a federal strategy. Executive Order 13953 of 30 September 2020. For the list of critical minerals see 'U.S. Geological Survey releases 2022 list of critical minerals' (made under the Energy Act 2020, 22 February 2022) <https://www.usgs.gov/news/national-news-release/us-geological-survey-releases-2022-list-critical-minerals> accessed 17 February 2023. On policy development, see Christina Jovanovic, 'Precious and Few: Solving Renewable Energy's Critical Minerals Problem' (2021) 9 LSU Journal of Energy Law & Resources 21.

Ascend Elements for a facility for precursor cathode materials. Most of the funding is going into processing to produce material ready for manufacturers. One that is further upstream is a grant of $50 million to Lilac Solutions for improved technology for extracting lithium from brines; another is $318 million to Talon Nickel to process nickel ore.

For natural resources law, the most interesting policy is the linkage of critical minerals to reform of the mining law.[51] American federal mining law has defied innumerable attempts to reform it, and the General Mining Law of 1872 endures largely intact,[52] so one can only marvel and admire the present Administration's willingness to tackle it. Reform objectives would include comprehensive land use planning that would manage rights to explore on lands open to mining, reporting of activities and results, royalties, and engagement with Tribal Nations.[53] Exploration companies would probably resist such reforms, but they would gain from increased clarity in permitting and increased certainly of mineral title. The mining claims of the current law were old-fashioned even in 1872, staked out with posts on the ground in claims only about 20 acres in size, and requiring an affidavit that there has already been discovered valuable mineral in place in the claim, a requirement that the courts have struggled with and stretched ever since. Patents—for full title to land and minerals—are in theory available for $5 per acre but there has been a moratorium on them for decades. No doubt reform, if it actually happens, could improve the legal regime for critical minerals, but only in the context of hard-rock minerals generally, including gold and base metals.

D. European Union

In March 2023, the European Commission proposed a regulation, the Critical Raw Materials Act, building on work it had started in 2011.[54] The EU has limited mining and processing capacity of its own, and for many minerals it is heavily reliant on imports, in some cases from a limited range of countries; for example it imports almost all of its magnesium and rare earth elements from China. The 2023 proposal is complex; it has two different lists, 'critical' raw materials, and a subset of them, 'strategic' raw materials, and the lists are to be reviewed every four years using an elaborate methodology. Criticality is evaluated by assessing supply risk (determining supply concentration, EU import reliance, input of secondary raw materials, and technical substitutability) and economic importance (determining share of use in sectors and value added, and considering economic substitutability). A material is further evaluated to see if it is also strategic, by determining its use and importance in the technologies that support the EU's green transition, digital transition,

[51] White House Fact Sheet (n 50). On this aspect at an earlier stage, see Kalen (n 5).

[52] John Leshy, *The Mining Law: A Study in Perpetual Motion* (Resources for the Future Press 1987).

[53] 'Mining Law Reform: Statement of Steve Feldgus, Deputy Assistant Secretary Land and Minerals Management, Department of the Interior, to House Natural Resources Committee Subcommittee on Energy and Mineral Resources Hearing on Reforming the Mining Law of 1872, May 12, 2002' <http://www.doi.gov/ocl/mining-law-reform> accessed 17 February 2023. Also included is a permitting action plan to improve permitting and environmental review processes for infrastructure.

[54] European Commission, 'Proposal for a Regulation of the European Parliament and of the Council establishing a framework for ensuring a secure and sustainable supply of critical raw materials and amending Regulations (EU) 168/2013, (EU) 2018/858, 2018/1724 and (EU) 2019/1020', 16 March 2023, COM(2023) 160 final, 2023/0079 (COD), with annexes. It was accompanied by a Communication, European Commission, 'A secure and sustainable supply of critical raw materials in support of the twin transition', 16 March 2023, COM(2023) 165 final.

and defence and aerospace objectives, and by projecting supply and demand for the material. Thus, for example, vanadium is a critical material but tungsten and copper are both critical and strategic. The proposal states benchmarks or targets for strategic raw materials for 2030: EU capacity to extract them reaches 10 per cent of its consumption, its processing capacity produces 40 per cent, and its recycling capacity produces 15 per cent; and that to diversify, it relies on no one foreign country for more than 65 per cent of its consumption of any strategic material.[55]

The proposed regulation includes a number of measures for monitoring stock levels and risk mitigation, with a European Critical Raw Materials Board to provide coordination; and it proposes rules to improve the circularity of use of critical raw materials and to assess the environmental footprint of materials placed on the EU market. The critical materials content of permanent magnets receives special attention. Provision is made for non-binding strategic partnerships with other like-minded nations.[56] Strategic raw materials are subject to provisions for coordinating stocks, company supply chain risk assessments, and a joint purchasing system.

Natural resources law and policy in the EU will change under special provisions for mineral exploration and project development. Member States are to produce national exploration programmes for critical raw materials.[57] Environmental and land use plans are to provide for the development of critical raw materials, and critical raw materials projects will be entitled to a 'one stop shop' form of process for the granting of permits for buildings, chemicals, grid connections, and environmental assessments and authorizations.[58] A project is even more favoured if it is determined to be a strategic project; in that case, Member States must take measures to contribute to its timely and effective implementation; it is deemed, for the purposes of environmental Directives, to be of overriding public interest or serving public health and safety; the national competent authorities responsible for environmental impact assessment procedures are subject to special time restrictions to complete their work;[59] and other procedures for granting permits are similarly restricted. The strategic project is to be treated in the most rapid way possible, and any judicial appeals or other procedures arising out of the issuance of permits are to be treated as urgent.[60] One does not need to delve deeply into EU environmental law to see that this will make significant changes and impose potentially major constraints on good environmental decision-making. How far these constraints on Member States' permit granting processes go to include their mining legislation's allocative and proprietary functions is not yet clear.[61]

In the commercial dimensions of mine projects, the proposed Regulation gives strategic projects (even projects outside the EU's borders) the benefit of efforts to accelerate investment, finance coordination, and to facilitate offtake agreements.[62] However, the definition of 'strategic project' seems to be confined to mine development and construction, and to

[55] EU Proposal (n 54) arts 1.
[56] ibid art 33; also addressed in the Communication.
[57] EU Proposal (n 54) art 18. All the critical and strategic raw materials listed are mineral in character.
[58] ibid arts 12 and 8. NB the definition of 'permit granting process' in art 2 refers to strategic projects.
[59] ibid arts 7 and 11. A proponent applies to the Commission to be recognized as a strategic project, arts 5 and 6, and the Commission exercises subsequent oversight.
[60] ibid art 9.
[61] 'Permit granting process' is widely defined in ibid art 2(19), including all relevant administrative permits.
[62] ibid arts 14, 15, and 16.

rule out exploration.[63] Relative to other critical minerals strategies, such as those of the United States and Canada, the EU's critical minerals strategy makes little use of subsidies and tax breaks; but it is striking in taking the form of legal change, even if in some parts (such as the benchmarks) it is rather unclear in its import.

E. Chile

Most recently, in April 2023, Chile announced a National Lithium Strategy, setting up a National Lithium Company to participate in the entire production cycle of the material and to operate through public–private alliances, but with the national copper companies Codelco and Enami taking the lead in the meantime, until legislation can be enacted to establish the new company.[64] For decades, lithium has been classified in Chile as a strategic mineral, so that its production is reserved to the state, and kept outside the mining law's concessions regime. Only two companies had permission to extract lithium from the country's salars (salt flats), and others were excluded. It is hoped that this new approach, state-led but partnering with private investors, will break the longstanding deadlock, while improving community participation and environmental protection. Outside the mining law, a new bidding process will be established to award private exploration contracts on salars where Codelco and Enami do not already have projects. It is taking the opportunity to enhance environmental protection, indigenous rights, and community participation, while seeking to go downstream into the production of value-added lithium products.

Chile's strategy is of course for the one mineral, but a vital one. The direction the country takes is coloured by its history of efforts to maintain national sovereignty over its copper resources. The strategy is distinctive in dealing primarily with natural resources law issues in the sense of an owner's allocation of rights to an operator company. It is a producer country's action to deal with a specific problem that has limited its ability to benefit from the buoyant market for lithium, while maintaining national sovereignty over a key resource.

F. Meeting Net Zero Needs: Common Characteristics of the Strategies

These strategies in different countries are intended, obviously, to increase mining activity, but selectively, aiming for the energy transition minerals. Market demand for these minerals is already reorienting mineral activity on a grand scale, so the strategies seek to accelerate the trend and remove bottlenecks. They are selective too in promoting activity in their home jurisdictions (or in the EU case activity that will benefit the home jurisdiction), so they are nationalistic in character, exercises of national sovereignty; in Canada they include a tightening of the foreign direct investment rules.

[63] Art 5 requires a strategic project to be one that is or will become technically feasible within a reasonable timeframe and where the expected production volume can be estimated with a sufficient level of confidence, which probably requires a full feasibility study.

[64] Government of Chile press release, 'Presidente de la República, Gabriel Boric Font, presenta Estrategia Nacional del Litio' (20 April 2023) <http://www.prensa.presidencia.cl> accessed 2 May 2024; Shawn Doyle, 'Chile announces its new National Lithium Strategy' (24 April 2023) <https://www.mccarthy.ca/en/insights/articles/chile-announces-its-new-national-lithium-strategy> accessed 2 May 2023.

The strategies have some common characteristics. Their main policy tools are fiscal; widespread subsidies in the form of grants and loans, sometimes for mine projects but more frequently downstream in mineral processing and manufacturing. Canada offers tax credits for exploration. These measures intend to build new supply chains for critical minerals, to strengthen existing ones, and to do so in the home country or in a friendly country. Public geoscience is redirected and receives new funding to focus on critical minerals, through the work of government geological surveys and institutes. This publicly-funded geological effort increases the pool of general geological knowledge of resources at a region-wide and district-wide level, and companies can use it to plan exploration programmes that will produce commercially-useful knowledge about mineral prospects. R&D and pilot projects are funded in order to improve the country's participation down the supply chain, in processing and manufacturing. In Australia and the EU, government assistance is offered with commercial aspects, in offtake agreements and finding finance. The EU goes further than others in providing for industrial coordination and joint purchasing.

Only the United States and Chile propose direct changes to their mining laws. More widespread are proposals to review laws for environmental protection, environmental assessment, social benefits, and land use zoning. Strategies generally declare a commitment to sustainability and ESG principles, but only some (eg Australia) propose strengthening them, and some, such as the EU, propose strengthening but with restrictions as well. The strategies are at their least impressive when they adopt perennial lobbying calls to cut red tape and speed up processing times. On the other hand, the EU puts substantial effort into recycling, as does Québec.

Some of the strategies are, or will be, legal in their force and character, such as that of the EU. Others, such as Australia, are expressions of government intention—cross-government action plans—without changing the law significantly or instituting a specific policy. However, their provisions are often likely to act as a framework and justification for law reform and policy development, and lawyers and policy analysts would be well advised to be familiar with them. In the meantime they may have legal significance in situations where the intentions of a government or a minister are relevant to a dispute.

IV. Effects of Critical Mineral Strategies on Natural Resources Law

At this point we can turn to consider in more detail the changes or transformations that these critical minerals strategies will bring about in natural resources law. The strategies are a new development, and they are taking legal form only in some cases, so it is too early to produce definitive answers, but a number of issues stand out. Mining law, of course, is the aspect of natural resources law most immediately on point, but environmental and social matters are directly involved, and so are recycling and circularity. There is no need here to debate the exact boundaries between the different fields of law in question. Indeed the new problems posed by the net zero transition suggest that some blurring of legal boundaries is likely. Brine-hosted lithium, for example, is not conventional hard rock mining but not really petroleum activity either. Equally, when we realize that it is important to look down materials supply chains, we may ask whether natural resources law needs to expand to find room for the concept of circularity in some manner.

A. The Structure of Mining Laws

In order to gauge the effects of these strategies on mining law, we should be aware of the main features of the mining statutes that are in place in most jurisdictions.[65] The first business of a mining statute is usually to address the ownership of minerals and mineral rights, vesting in the state being very common. From there the general pattern is for it to turn to the allocation of rights to mining operators. The relationship between the owner and the operator is the core concept or defining feature of mining law as of all natural resources law.[66] Typically the law allows different rights (permits, licences, claims, leases, concessions, etc) to be granted for prospecting and exploration and for development and production, because the different phases of the mining sequence have very different needs. Under some laws an exploration permit can be acquired as of right, without having to apply to a government agency; under others, an application must be made and the agency has a discretionary power to decide whether to issue the permit and on what terms.[67] The law generally lays down rules for the size of permits, their duration, the obligations of the permit holder to do work or carry out a programme, renewal, cancellation, and transfer to another party. For mine production permits, royalties or taxes are generally imposed. Other provisions manage land access, surface rights, and engagement with landowners, the community, and indigenous interests. Reclamation and rehabilitation requirements are imposed. Environmental assessment and permitting is sometimes part of the mining law but more frequently is carried out under its own legislation. In some countries it is common for a large project to be made the subject of a special mining agreement with the state, superseding the ordinary rules in the mining legislation.

The mining sequence has an influence over the form and operation of mining law that is sometimes overlooked. The supply chain of any mineral product does not start with mines but with the search for minerals that can be mined; minerals are not evenly distributed in the earth's crust and a great deal of effort goes into mineral exploration, to find where they might be present in concentrations big enough for an economically viable mine.[68] Exploration activity moves from low-cost wide-ranging surveys to progressively more intensive examinations of a promising location, until the point is reached where a decision can be made to build a mine and go into production. Most exploration prospects do not make it that far; they may hold too small a resource, or at too low a grade, or the resource is too expensive to extract under predicted market prices for the output. Exploration activity is therefore unpredictable and difficult to regulate.

[65] The best general overviews of the field of mining law are not always the most recent publications: J Otto and J Cordes, *The Regulation of Mineral Enterprises: A Global Perspective on Economics, Law and Policy* (Rocky Mountain Mineral Law Foundation 2002); John Southalan, *Mining Law and Policy: International Perspectives* (Federation Press 2012); Ana Elizabeth Bastida, *The Law and Governance of Mining and Minerals* (Hart Publishing 2020).

[66] Barry Barton, 'A Core Concept in Natural Resources Law; the Nexus between Owner and Operator' (2023) 41 Journal of Energy and Natural Resources Law 241.

[67] Non-discretionary allocation, often called the free entry system, is common in Canada, eg Ontario: Barton, *Canadian Mining Law* (n 43) 525. Also South Africa, Mineral and Petroleum Resources Development Act 2002 (28 of 2002) ss 2(d) and 17; see Hanri Mostert, *Mineral Law: Principles and Policies in Perspective* (Juta 2012) 82. An example of discretionary allocation is Western Australia: Mining Act 1978 (WA) ss 59, 63, and 66. Prospecting licences may also be granted, by the Mining Registrar: s 42. See Samantha Hepburn, *Mining and Energy Law* (CUP 2015) 54.

[68] Barton, *Canadian Mining Law* (n 43) 6; Southalan (n 65) 3.

Only some critical minerals strategies intend to reform their mining laws—as noted in section IIIF. Only the United States proposes reform of the mining law generally, although it is fairly clear that other actions will be taken without waiting to see if a new law is possible. In Chile the changes will address a specific matter in the holding of lithium rights by public entities. In the EU it is unclear whether Member States will be compelled to amend their mining laws as part of the permit granting process.

B. Critical Minerals Strategy Drivers for Mining Law Reform

Whether it is these jurisdictions or others intending to pursue a strategy to favour critical minerals, a mining law reform is likely to raise a number of thorny questions. One is the difficulty of providing for or regulating mineral exploration, as just noted; as well as being unpredictable, exploration is often fast-moving and small-scale. Secondly, how does a policy instrument separate critical minerals activity from other mineral activity? The Canadian critical minerals exploration credit may demonstrate what is possible with both these problems. The separation problem also appears if allocation procedures are being amended; if there is to be an improved track for the allocation of permits for critical minerals, what happens to the non-critical minerals in the permit area, can they be acquired by a second company? Under most mining laws, the grant of exploration or mining rights to a permit area includes rights to all the minerals that may be found there.

The rules for the allocation of permits will present other challenges as well. As noted above, under some mining laws a company or individual can acquire a permit without having to apply for approval, by staking the ground or designating it online. In these cases there is no governmental discretion to withhold the permit or to grant it subject to conditions. In the discretionary allocation systems, the main question may be whether the law is that the decision-maker can, or must, take the critical minerals strategy into account. The same goes for other discretionary decisions, such as approving a work programme, or extending the permit for another term. As to procedures, are critical minerals operators to have preferential processing of their applications?

The aspects of mining laws that are not so directly part of the relationship between the state as owner and the operator company may present problems that are more difficult to resolve. Should access to land and restrictions on where mineral activity takes place be eased in order to encourage critical minerals exploration and the net zero transition? Should miners' obligations to landowners be eased too? Should mine site rehabilitation and tailings dam safety rules be loosened? In truth these provisions may need strengthening rather than weakening, in face of the upheavals being already being caused by market-driven increases in critical minerals exploration and development.

The effects of increased critical minerals activity will not be evenly distributed, because target minerals are not evenly distributed in the earth's surface, and human understanding of them is not complete, so some communities will find themselves in the middle of a sudden bustle of exploration activity; a lithium rush or a cobalt rush, like a nineteenth-century gold rush. There is a degree of unpredictability about the upstream effects of critical minerals strategies, but they could be large. On a global scale the energy transition could affect many people in mine-town systems; a minimum of 33.5 million could be affected by the phase-out of coal and another 115.7 million affected if all available energy transition metals projects become operational.[69] In addition, the impact of critical minerals projects may fall especially hard on vulnerable groups; more than two-thirds of energy transition minerals projects identified in one major study are located on the lands of indigenous or peasant peoples.[70] Justice in the transition cannot be restricted to energy but must include minerals.[71]

It is very possible that these critical minerals strategies will create a new sense of urgency for access to mineral resources, and for many aspects of mining laws to be changed to reduce barriers to activity, even at a time when controls need strengthening. The effects of the net zero transition on mining law could be quite diverse.

C. Effects on Communities and the Environment

Environmental, social, and community impacts are closely related to mining law, although some would gather them into its ambit. The same can be said about recycling and the circular economy; they are at least in the penumbra of legal issues that concern mining activity. The effects of new levels of critical minerals activity on them have been noted in the literature,[72] but thus far not in relation to the formal strategy documents.

The critical minerals strategies are ambivalent about environmental and social regulation; they declare the importance of sustainability, but they also intend to expedite projects through regulatory approvals and reduce duplication (Canada) or strengthen and accelerate federal permitting and environmental reviews (United States). The EU expresses concern with the unpredictability, complexity, and, at times, excessive length of national permit granting processes, and will legally impose time limits and a 'one-stop-shop' format on them. There is nothing new in calls for speed and certainty in environmental, safety, and social controls; for decades industries have lobbied governments to cut red tape, all the while proclaiming their commitment to sustainability and ESG principles. The only things that are new are the rationale that critical minerals supply provides for these arguments, and the willingness of governments to agree to them. The net zero transition should not be turned into a lobbyist's weapon. Certainly, horror stories can be found where environmental and social regulation fails, or is done badly or slowly, but anecdotes do not justify easing the regulation that deals with the externalities that mine proponents and other industries can impose on their surroundings. Some environmental assessments take time to get right, especially if baseline data is missing; sometimes company assessments or applications are incomplete. Environmental and social protection procedures cannot necessarily be speeded up without being damaged. Equally, local opposition to a mine is not always misguided; some projects simply should not go ahead.

Some critical minerals strategies are set on constraining the hard-won environmental and social gains of the last sixty years. We must take care that the strategies do not talk up the climate change problem so as to cause other social and environmental problems, especially

[69] Kamila Svobodova and others, 'Decarbonization, Population Disruption and Resource Inventories in the Global Energy Transition' (2022) 13 Nature Communications 7674.

[70] John R Owen and others, 'Fast Track to Failure? Energy Transition Minerals and the Future of Consultation and Consent' (2022) 89 Energy Research and Social Sciences 102665.

[71] The ethical dimensions are considered by Benjamin K Sovacool and others, 'Sustainable Minerals and Metals for a Low-Carbon Future' (2020) 367(6473) Science 30.

[72] See the literature references in n 7.

when so much effort is going into legal frameworks for sustainable and responsible mining.[73] There are already many cases of conflict between renewable energy projects and environmental values, such as between wind farms and bird life or protected areas. We cannot solve one set of problems by creating another; shifting a problem around does not solve it. We must avoid such traps as we embark on policy change and law reform in the wake of the strategies.

D. Recycling and the Circular Economy

Several strategies propose action on recycling and the circular economy. Québec and the EU emphasize circular economy principles to ensure that valuable materials once extracted and used are not then discarded ('take-make-dispose'), but kept in productive use, reused, and recycled as far as possible. Critical minerals can come from 'urban mining' as well as from the ground; in circular economy terms, this is turning straight-through materials flows into loops and bending the supply chains.[74] A materials transition can be argued for, to accompany the energy transition, addressing the full supply chain.[75] The production, use, and disposal of industrial materials such as steel, plastics, aluminium, and cement account for almost a quarter of all global carbon dioxide emissions.[76] However, recovery rates are low especially for batteries and electronic waste,[77] so it is not surprising that supply from mines is still at the forefront of the policy discussion; but government funding for R&D and pilot projects should lead to improvements.

E. Planetary Boundaries and the Race for Supply

A very positive aspect of critical minerals strategies is that countries, companies, and governments are thinking hard about where materials come from, and where they go to. It is not too much to say that they are now paying more attention to the basic necessities that people need to provide for themselves and enjoy a modern standard of living. Companies are now looking further up their chains of supply than they have been used to doing, even into the early stages of the mining sequence. Market forces continue to prevail, but the major leaps forward required by the net zero transition call for a willingness to take a more active role in ascertaining where critical minerals will be obtained, and not merely sit passively, trusting that the market will provide. We can take a deliberate and systematic approach to the matter.

Much less positive is that the strategies have been put in place to win a global race for the supply of resources. Their clear purpose is to increase supply; but a fixation solely on the supply side presents problems. A country's geology may not lend itself to projects except at

[73] eg Tracy-Lynn Field, *State Governance of Mining, Development and Sustainability* (Edward Elgar 2019); Sovacool and others, 'Decarbonisation' (n 36).

[74] Jovanovic (n 50); Nihan Karali and Nihar Shah, 'Bolstering Supplies of Critical Raw Materials for Low-Carbon Technologies through Circular Economy Strategies' (2022) 88 Energy Research and Social Science 102534; Yong Geng and others, 'How to Build a Circular Economy for Rare-Earth Elements' (2023) 619 Nature 248.

[75] The World Bank acknowledges these imperatives as well: Hund and others (n 10) 16.

[76] Per-Anders Enkvist and others, 'How a "materials transition" can support the net-zero agenda', July 2022 <http://www.mckinsey.com> accessed 3 March 2023.

[77] Hund and others (n 10) 14.

great expense or at the price of unwarranted energy demands and greenhouse gas emissions. The environmental and social costs may be excessive, and in such cases, a supply fixation could bring critical minerals strategies into collision with planetary boundaries. So the demand side needs to be managed as well as the supply side. We might have to make the net zero transition with lower quantities of minerals than some of the bold forecasts have suggested, and it may well be possible to do so. The first step is technical advances that reduce the amount of critical and expensive materials required to make electrical equipment. Advances have already been made in manufacturing permanent magnets, batteries, and electrolyzers, and R&D support can probably produce more. The second step is demand-side management in the amount of energy we require from such equipment; we must be wary of forecasts that suggest that our needs for energy must increase endlessly to improve our quality of life. Critical minerals strategies must strive for efficiency in the use of minerals, while energy and climate strategies must strive for efficiency in the use of energy. The strategies should not lead us down the path of assuming that glamorous new technology is the sole solution to our climate problems. There are different ways to breach planetary boundaries, none of them good.

V. Lessons to Be Learned, and Conclusion

This chapter has explored the foreseeable effects of these newly-emerging critical minerals strategies. The strategy instruments that have emerged are sometimes rather general, but other times they are quite specific in proposing legal and policy changes. Some of their effects will be very positive, such as in facilitating the new energy technologies, in promoting circularity, and in underscoring environmental and social values. However, if mining laws are to be changed in line with the strategies, in ways that treat critical minerals exploration and development differently from other mineral activity, law reformers will encounter difficulties. Is a lithium mine to be regulated less heavily than a gold mine? Reformers may have to navigate serious tensions between the drive to accelerate critical minerals activity and the expectations of landowners and other stakeholders to protection from a minerals boom. They will also need to be alert to avoid harm to important environmental, social, and community values; the possibility of doing such harm is very visible where most of the strategies make calls to reduce delays and duplication in environmental and social regulation. The strategies cannot be implemented in a way that would undercut the widespread efforts under way to ensure that mining is sustainable and responsible. Nor should the strategies be read to offer us false assurances that we can increase the supply of minerals indefinitely, or that it is an easy matter to stay within planetary boundaries; sometimes there will be hard choices for us to make.

The critical minerals strategies that have emerged recently are a direct consequence in law and policy of the net zero transition that is necessary to address climate change. They address an essential aspect of that transition, as companies and governments struggle with the magnitude of their new needs for raw materials to supply the manufacturing of the equipment and technology required for renewables and electrification. They are a new manifestation of national sovereignty over natural resources, with a dimension of international cooperation at times, and, arguably, they represent the most far-reaching change under way, or foreseeable, in natural resources law and policy as it affects non-fuel minerals. Their emergence is recent; most of them have only appeared in the last two years, and the role that they will play is only gradually coming into view. It will be essential to engage with them as they evolve.

PART II

SECURITY AND JUSTICE RISKS IN NET ZERO TRANSITION

6

Securing the Supply of Critical Minerals for Net Zero

China's Regulatory and Policy Frameworks on Lithium

Hao Zhang

I. Introduction

The increasing global effort to drive the energy transition has led to rising demand for lithium.[1] This metal is crucial in the manufacturing of lithium-ion batteries, which are used for energy storage and electric vehicles (EVs).[2] As governments around the world push for renewable energy to achieve their clean energy targets, the role of lithium has become even more critical in making the energy transition process sustainable and affordable.[3] One country that has been at the forefront of prioritizing the security and reliability of the supply of lithium is China. China has prioritized lithium in its industrial policy agenda, given its ambition to build the world's largest EV market. This move is aimed at reducing the country's dependence on oil imports, tackling air pollution, reducing greenhouse gas (GHG) emissions from the transport sector, and upgrading the industrial and manufacturing sector through the 'Made in China 2025' national strategic initiative.[4] Securing a reliable supply of metals and minerals, particularly lithium, is fundamental to achieve these goals. The recent announcement of China's long-term climate targets, namely peaking emissions before 2030 and achieving carbon neutrality by 2060, has further consolidated China's commitment to electrifying the transportation sector.[5] Electrifying end-use, including transport, buildings, and certain industrial sectors, constitutes an essential part of the strategies to realize China's ambitious climate targets.[6]

[1] International Energy Agency (IEA), 'The Role of Critical Minerals in Clean Energy Transitions' (Part of World Energy Outlook, May 2021) <https://www.iea.org/reports/the-role-of-critical-minerals-in-clean-energy-transitions/executive-summary> (accessed 29 April 2024).

[2] ibid.

[3] Alex Scott, 'Challenging China's Dominance in the Lithium Market' (Chemical & Engineering News, October 2022) <https://www.cen.acs.org/articles/100/i38/Challenging-Chinas-dominance-lithium-market.html> (accessed 29 April 2024); Liuguo Shao and others, 'Evolution of Global Lithium Competition Network Pattern and Its Influence Factors' (2021) 74 Resources Policy 102353.

[4] Han Hao and others, 'Material Flow Analysis of Lithium in China' (2017) 51 Resources Policy 100; Na Zhou and others, 'China's Lithium Supply Chain: Security Dynamics and Policy Countermeasures' (2022) 78 Resources Policy 102866.

[5] Working Guidance for Carbon Dioxide Peaking and Carbon Neutrality in Full and Faithful Implementation of the New Development Philosophy (Central Committee of the Communist Party of China (CCCPC) and the State Council 2021) <http://www.gov.cn/zhengce/2021-10/24/content_5644613.html> (accessed 29 April 2024).

[6] Haomiao Du and Hao Zhang, 'Climate Neutrality in the EU and China: An Analysis of the Stringency of Targets and the Adaptiveness of the Relevant Legal Frameworks' (2022) 31(3) Review of European, Comparative & International Environmental Law 495.

Hao Zhang, *Securing the Supply of Critical Minerals for Net Zero* In: *Net Zero and Natural Resources Law.* Edited by: Damilola S. Olawuyi, José Juan González, Hanri Mostert, Milton Fernando Montoya, and Catherine Banet, Oxford University Press. © International Bar Association 2024. DOI: 10.1093/9780198925033.003.0006

China's leadership position in the EV market has driven the demand for lithium-ion batteries and lithium resources. China's central leadership declared the strategic importance of EVs in 2014, stating that developing the domestic EV industry is the only way that China can transform from a large automobile country to an automobile superpower.[7] In line with this ambition, the Chinese central government agencies have implemented policy support (eg subsidies) and backed Chinese firms throughout the lithium supply chain to gain comparative advantages and dominance. For instance, policy support has been the main pillar that drives the success of EVs in China, and its domestic EV market has grown to be the world's largest.[8] In 2021, China led the growth of EV sales globally, accounting for half of the increased EV sales.[9] In 2022, EV sales in China were expected to be more than in the rest of the world combined.[10] In 2020, China's State Council set a near-term target—EVs would account for 20 per cent of new car sales by 2025,[11] and commentators believe that China will likely surpass this target much in advance.[12]

However, the scarcity of lithium production and the surging demand for it due to the booming production of EVs has led to an imbalance between supply and demand across many jurisdictions, including China.[13] Although China holds the world's fourth-largest lithium resources and second-largest reserves, according to the US Geological Survey, its domestic exploitation and extraction only account for less than 10 per cent of the global mine production, making it fall far behind the major producers such as Australia, Chile, and Argentina.[14] Two main reasons underlie the lack of large-scale domestic production in China. First, China's lithium resources are scattered across provinces, with brine deposits primarily located in Qinghai and Tibet and rock-derived deposits mainly distributed in Sichuan. The vast majority of lithium resources are stored in salt lakes in Qinghai and Tibet. Still, they generally have 'inferior' quality to those found and produced in the so-called *Lithium Triangle* formed by parts of Bolivia, Chile, and Argentina.[15] Second, most of the hard-rock deposits in China are challenging to mine due to their high-altitude locations, harsh natural environment, and the lack of infrastructure in these areas.[16]

China's surging demand for lithium raw materials has led to a heavy reliance on imports. As a result, China's industrial policy for lithium has evolved over the past decade to pursue supply reliability through three essential strategies amid a global lithium rush. The strategies include expanding domestic exploitation and production, diversifying imports, and increasing China's weight and dominance over the global lithium value chain.

[7] 'Xi Jinping: Development of New Energy Vehicles is the only Way to Become a Powerful Automobile Country' (*Xinhua News*, 2014) <http://www.xinhuanet.com/politics/2014-05/24/c_1110843312.htm> (accessed 29 April 2024).

[8] IEA, 'Global EV Outlook 2022' (May 2022) <https://www.iea.blob.core.windows.net/assets/ad8fb04c-4f75-42fc-973a-6e54c8a4449a/GlobalElectricVehicleOutlook2022.pdf> (accessed 29 April 2024).

[9] ibid.

[10] Daisuke Wakabayashi and Claire Fu, 'For China's Auto Market, Electric Isn't the Future. It's the Present' (*New York Times*, 27 September 2022) <https://www.nytimes.com/2022/09/26/business/china-electric-vehicles.html> (accessed 29 April 2024).

[11] New Energy Vehicle Industry Development Plan (2021–35), State Council Order No (2020)39, 20 October 2020 (in Chinese).

[12] Wakabayashi and Fu (n 10).

[13] Shao and others (n 3); Zhou and others (n 4).

[14] National Minerals Information Center, 'Lithium Statistics and Information 2022' <https://www.pubs.usgs.gov/periodicals/mcs2022/mcs2022-lithium.pdf> (accessed 29 April 2024).

[15] Florencia Heredia and others, 'The Importance of Lithium for Achieving a Low-Carbon Future: Overview of the Lithium Extraction in the "Lithium Triangle"' (2020) 38(3) Journal of Energy & Natural Resources Law 213.

[16] Zhou and others (n 4).

The implementation of these strategies has had a significant impact on China's domestic governance and regulation. It has also influenced the energy transition process in other jurisdictions that pursue a battery-powered future while ensuring the utilization and protection of natural resources.

This chapter will examine critical lessons from China's industrial strategies and policies that promote the establishment of a lithium supply chain. Additionally, it analyses the implications of implementing such strategies and policies on the security and reliability of lithium as a critical transition mineral on a global scale. The chapter is structured as follows. After this introduction, Section II discusses China's industrial policies and the essential mechanisms contained in those policies and regulatory documents to support developing lithium supply chain strategies. Section III examines the challenges to the sustainable development of the lithium supply chain in China. Section IV highlights the need for a more sustainable, resilient, and ethical supply of lithium and its products. The importance of critical minerals like lithium in the energy transition is increasingly recognized worldwide, and the need to secure a stable supply of these minerals is becoming more urgent. However, the global supply chain for these minerals is often fragmented and lacks transparency, which creates challenges for securing supply and managing risks. Section V concludes the chapter.

II. China's Industrial Policies in Support of Lithium Supply Chain Strategies

The transition from fossil fuels to renewable energy and electrification is gaining momentum, and East Asia has emerged as a crucial region for manufacturing lithium-ion batteries. China has become the dominant player in the lithium supply chain, surpassing its competitors in the region.[17] Although China accounts for only 13 per cent of the world's lithium resources, its companies control 44 per cent of global lithium chemical production and 78 per cent of cathode production, a crucial battery manufacturing ingredient.[18] This dominance has made China the unrivalled leader in battery production, responsible for about 70 per cent of battery cell manufacturing for the EV industry.[19] Moreover, Chinese companies own around 71 per cent of the global market share for solar battery modules.[20] It is evident that China's dominance in the lithium supply chain is due to the government's incentives and support for private-sector Chinese companies.

The global race for critical materials essential for energy transition has highlighted the importance of formulating and implementing domestic policies and regulations to support the lithium supply chain and address the challenges.[21] In China, security of supply in the context of lithium development strategy entails formulating policies and establishing a regulatory framework to attract investment throughout the supply chain. The domestic

[17] Suleyman Orhun Altiparmak, 'China and Lithium Geopolitics in a Changing Global Market' (2022) Chinese Political Science Review (advance article published online).

[18] IEA, 'World Energy Outlook 2022' (October 2022) <https://www.iea.blob.core.windows.net/assets/830fe099-5530-48f2-a7c1-11f35d510983/WorldEnergyOutlook2022.pdf> (accessed 29 April 2024).

[19] IEA, 'Global EV Outlook 2022' (n 8).

[20] Arendse Huld, 'China's Lithium-Ion Battery Industry—Overcoming Supply Chain Challenges' (China Briefing, 30 November 2022) <https://www.china-briefing.com/news/chinas-lithium-ion-battery-industry-overcoming-supply-chain-challenges/> (accessed 29 April 2024).

[21] Altiparmak (n 17).

policy and regulatory framework has evolved significantly in response to the need to develop the EV industry and battery manufacturing, both of which are at the centre of China's industrial policy and climate response measures. The key components of such a policy and regulatory framework include identifying comparative advantages and weaknesses throughout the supply chain and adopting more targeted measures to safeguard the supply security of lithium raw materials, chemical products, and power batteries.

China's case provides a valuable example of understanding the content of such policies and regulations and their underlying considerations. The Chinese central government has made solid political commitments to support the establishment and dominance of the domestic lithium supply chain.[22] Estimates suggest that the Chinese central and local government has provided financial support ranging from US$60 to $100 billion over the last decade to foster the development of this domestic supply chain.[23] In China, political considerations often surpass economic objectives to support industrial development. Therefore, the government has formulated policies that convey relatively stable and long-term political commitments to support both state-owned enterprises and private companies in the lithium-related industries. These political commitments and concrete support have established a stable regulatory framework and a favourable business environment for key stakeholders and market participants.[24] This has enabled long-term investments in strategic and yet-to-emerge sectors rather than short-sighted profits.

Developing a reliable lithium supply chain is a challenging and time-consuming task. Chinese policy-makers recognized the importance of supporting the domestic EV industry in the early 2010s by providing subsidies. This support became a crucial driving force for Chinese companies to enter the upstream and midstream sectors of lithium exploration, exploitation, and processing. Policy-makers in China have also invested in capacity-building at every stage of domestic lithium-ion battery production, as well as in building the critical infrastructure necessary for the supply chain, such as lithium mining and processing facilities and battery manufacturing facilities. Additionally, they have secured lithium supplies in foreign countries through acquisitions. China's industrial policies contain specific measures to implement and realize these imperatives, which we discuss in detail in the following sections.

A. Policy Support for EV Development and Renewable Energy

Electrification of the transport sector constitutes an appealing choice to Chinese policy-makers due to three main reasons. First, China has the world's largest automotive manufacturing capacity and market, which has contributed significantly to the country's GHG emissions and also its reliance on oil imports.[25] The importance of automotive

[22] See eg National Strategic New Industry Development Plan during the 12th Five-year Period, State Council Order No (2012)28, 9 July 2012 (in Chinese).

[23] Zack Nhan, 'Challenging Chinese Dominance over Lithium Batteries—The EU and US Responses' (Institute for Security & Development, 30 May 2022) <https://www.isdp.eu/challenging-chinese-dominance-over-lithium-batteries-the-eu-and-us-responses/>(accessed 29 April 2024).

[24] ibid.

[25] Wang Tao, 'Recharging China's Electric Vehicle Policy' (Carnegie-Tsinghua Center for Global Policy, August 2013) <https://www.carnegieendowment.org/files/china_electric_vehicles.pdf> (accessed 29 April 2024); 'Guide to Chinese Climate Policy. Electric Vehicles' (SIPA Center on Global Energy Policy, Columbia University) <https://www.chineseclimatepolicy.energypolicy.columbia.edu/en/electric-vehicles> (accessed 29 April 2024).

manufacturing in China's industrial structure has often made this sector the policy target for technological innovation, upgrades, and financial support. Back in 2001, the Chinese central government announced its systematic plan to support national high-tech research and development, known as the '863 programme', through which a selected number of themes and major special projects in high-tech fields such as information technology, advanced manufacturing and automation, and energy, resource, and environment technology were considered development priorities.[26] The 863 programme identified the new energy vehicles (NEVs, classified as battery electric, hydrogen fuel cell electric, and plug-in hybrid electric vehicles) and NEV manufacturing as the major special project with national goals supported by central financial appropriations. Later on, the Ministry of Science and Technology (MOST) organized feasibility studies and established expert groups, which further clarified three sub-sectors (namely, fuel cell vehicles, hybrid vehicles, and pure EVs) and three specific areas for technology research and development (namely, power electronics controller, electric traction motor, and power battery).[27] Identifying sub-sectors and key technologies provided a foundation to kickstart the industrialization and commercialization of NEVs, with hybrid vehicles becoming the pioneers for mass production in 2008.[28]

In 2009, the Ministry of Finance (MoF) and the MOST jointly initiated large-scale pilot programmes, with thirteen cities selected to promote energy-saving and NEVs in public services through designated financial support.[29] The centrally allocated finance was provided to NEVs purchases, and local financial support mainly subsidized the construction and maintenance of supporting facilities. Five of these cities, namely Shenzhen, Shanghai, Hangzhou, Changchun, and Hefei, under the pilot programmes were then identified for subsidizing private purchases of NEVs in 2010.[30] The subsidies for private purchases provided a powerful impetus for boosting the sales of NEVs, with pure EV manufacturers benefitting significantly in terms of revenue generation and research and development (R&D). According to the subsidization scheme, a 3,000 RMB/kWh subsidy was given to NEVs that meet the relevant conditions, with maximum support of 50,000 RMB for each plug-in hybrid passenger vehicle and 60,000 RMB for each EV purchase.[31] Some local governments also adopted matching programmes to boost the central government's subsidy. For instance, Shenzhen subsidized another RMB 60,000 for EVs and RMB 30,000 for hybrid vehicles.[32] These aggressive actions to encourage NEV purchases from the central and

[26] Measures for the Administration of the National High-tech Research and Development Programme (863 Programme), Ministry of Science and Technology (MOST) Order No (2001)632, 25 December 2001, art 3 (in Chinese).

[27] MOST, Developing Electric Vehicles as the Major Scientific and Technological Project—Accelerating the Development and Industrialisation of Electric Vehicles in China, 23 December 2004 <https://www.most.gov.cn/spzl/bnyw/200604/t20060424_31702.html> (accessed 29 April 2024) (in Chinese).

[28] Products from Seven Automotive Manufacturers Listed in the Car Catalogue Published by the NDRC, NEVs Started Mass Production (*China News*, May 2008) <http://www.chinanews.com.cn/auto/cjxw/news/2008/05-09/1243908.shtml> (accessed 29 April 2024).

[29] These cities are Beijing, Shanghai, Chongqing, Changchun, Dalian, Hangzhou, Jinan, Wuhan, Shenzhen, Hefei, Changsha, Kunming, and Nanchang. Notice on Carrying out the Pilot Project of Demonstration and Promotion of Energy-Saving and New Energy Vehicles, Ministry of Finance (MOF) Order No (2009)6, 23 January 2009 (in Chinese).

[30] Notice on Launching the Pilot Programme of Subsidies for Private Purchase of NEVs, MOF Order No (2010)230, 31 May 2010 (in Chinese).

[31] ibid.

[32] Wang (n 25).

local governments sent a strong signal to the manufacturers and consumers that Chinese policy-makers are committed to supporting the proliferation of NEVs, particularly EVs. Not surprisingly, China's State Council highlighted NEVs as one of the seven strategic new industries in 2012.[33] According to the 12th Five-Year Special Plan for the Development of Electric Vehicle Technology (2011–15), battery-powered EVs stand at the centre of the technology transformation strategy, with R&D focusing on lithium-ion batteries and the core technologies required for EV manufacturing, particularly EV motors and standardization of modules for mass production of batteries.[34]

The subsidies for private purchases were renewed every two or three years, with a steady drop in subsidization amount and an increase in eligibility criteria. The Chinese central government has also adopted numerous measures to prevent subsidy cheats, with a notable discovery in 2016 that five NEV manufacturers had defrauded the central government of more than one billion RMB.[35] To decouple the growth of the EV industry from direct subsidies, the Chinese central government announced in 2021 that direct subsidies were to be completely phased out starting from 31 December 2022.[36]

B. Enhancement of Dominance over the Lithium Supply Chain

The fast growth of EV sales in China has significantly driven the demand for battery cells and the lithium chemical production essential for producing batteries. Since the identification of EV batteries as one of the strategically important areas for R&D by the 863 programme, Chinese policy-makers have directed numerous resources to facilitate the Chinese firms investing in the lithium supply chain. Given that batteries often account for nearly half of EV production costs, the policy focus essentially prioritizes government financial support for battery-based EVs to establish the domestic supply chain. In recent years, there has been a clear shift with the technological innovation of lithium batteries in China being driven more by market forces instead of policy support.[37] That being said, the current Chinese dominance over the lithium supply chain is a result of government regulatory measures that determine barriers to market entry which is essential to forge competition or eliminate it. While the upstream and downstream segments of the lithium supply chain are characterized by a relatively higher level of market dominance by a small number of firms, the suppliers at the midstream have significantly diversified and proactively developed and utilized different technologies to enhance the energy intensity and cost-effectiveness of lithium-ion batteries. Given that technological innovation at the midstream is the determining factor of improving energy intensity and cost-effectiveness of battery production, a competitive market is desirable to promote the mid- and long-term growth of lithium-ion batteries.

[33] National Strategic New Industry Development Plan during the 12th Five-year Period, State Council Order No (2012)28, 9 July 2012 (in Chinese).

[34] Notice on Issuing the '12th Five-Year' Special Plan for the Development of Electric Vehicle Technology, MOST Order No (2012)195, 27 March 2012 (in Chinese).

[35] The Ministry of Finance Exposed Five NEV Companies Defrauding more than One Billion RMB (*China News*, 9 September 2016) <https://www.news.china.com/domesticgd/10000159/20160909/23507879.html> (accessed 29 April 2024) (in Chinese).

[36] Notice on the Financial Subsidy Policy for the Promotion and Application of NEV in 2022, MOF Order No (2021)466, 31 December 2021 (in Chinese).

[37] Zhou and others (n 4).

Domestically speaking, the lithium supply chain contains a mix of state-owned enterprises and private firms, with various levels of market concentration at the upstream resources exploitation and extraction, midstream chemical production such as cathode, anode and electrolyte, and the downstream battery production).

China's upstream lithium mine development lags behind other major producer countries. In recent years, an increasing number of firms in China have entered upstream lithium processing, mainly driven by increasing demand and high profitability. In late 2022, the price of battery-grade lithium carbonate had a yearly growth of around 200 per cent, and the price is expected to increase further due to the predicted soaring demand and supply shortage after 2025.[38] Within the country, Chinese firms exploit and develop hard-rock lithium in Sichuan, Jiangxi provinces, and Xinjiang autonomous region, and brine deposits in Qinghai and Tibet.[39] Because these deposits are located in remote areas with underdeveloped infrastructure, and brine deposits take up more than 80 per cent of China's lithium reserves, which is more expensive to process due to the high magnesium content, China's domestic production of lithium raw materials is relatively small.[40] China's hard-rock mines supply most of the raw products for lithium processing, and brine deposits are yet to be fully exploited. In contrast, the major Chinese suppliers of lithium chemical materials (lithium carbonate and lithium hydroxide) rely on importing raw materials from other countries with more developed lithium mines, notably Australia and countries in the lithium triangle, due to the insufficient supply from domestic mines. This is the main reason underpinning the Chinese firms' buying spree of quality lithium assets in the significant lithium producer countries, which has raised concerns over sustainable, resilient, and ethical mining in countries with weak regulations.[41] Generally speaking, due to their first-mover advantages and the recent expansion of their lithium asset portfolio, Ganfeng Lithium, Tianqi Lithium, and Yahua Group are the leading market players.

The midstream section of the lithium supply chain is highly competitive, with low levels of market concentration.[42] Chinese companies produce all components needed for lithium batteries, actively seeking upgrades and breakthroughs in various technological aspects. Since cathode and anode materials are the core factors that determine the energy density of NEV batteries, Chinese firms carry out R&D advancements based on the current technological development.[43] For cathode production, lithium-iron phosphate (lithium ferro-phosphate—LFP) and ternary materials are being developed in parallel with their comparative advantages in energy density, safety, and cost-effectiveness.[44] Several Chinese firms specialize in developing and utilizing ternary materials, with the top five firms,

[38] Huld (n 20).

[39] Zenan Zhang and others, 'Demand Forecast of China's Lithium Mineral Resources' (2020) 29(7) China Mining Magazine 9 (in Chinese).

[40] Ibid.

[41] 'Future-Proofing the Supply of Critical Minerals for Net-Zero Emissions' (Summary report, January 2022) <https://www.unece.org/sites/default/files/2022-01/UNECE%20UK%20Critical%20Minerals%20Report%20Jan%202022.pdf>accessed 29 April 2024.

[42] Yanlong Liu, 'Development Status and Market Development Trend of China's Lithium-ion Battery Industry' (2019) 43(2) Chinese Journal of Power Sources 181 (in Chinese).

[43] ibid.

[44] Liu (n 42); Chunzheng Tian and others, 'Industrial Structure and Development Prospect of Power Lithium Battery' (2018) 42(12) Chinese Journal of Power Sources 193 (in Chinese).

including Ningbo Ronbay New Energy and Beijing Easpring Material Technology, splitting around 70 per cent of the markets (ranging from 10–15 per cent for each firm). The development trend for ternary materials is to be high nickel and cobalt-free for higher energy intensity and cost reduction. LFP production is also scattered across different firms, with leading producers located in Hunan, Guangdong, Jiangsu, and Hubei. These firms together produce around 68 per cent of the LFP production in China, with Hunan Yuneng and Shenzhen Dynanonic each accounting for 20 per cent of the market share. China's anode production has a relatively higher concentration, with the top fifteen producers in China having a market share of more than 90 per cent and more than 50 per cent by the top three producers.[45] The development trend for anode production is the application of silicon-based anode materials. Though still facing technical challenges, several Chinese firms such as Shenzhen BTR, Shanghai Shanshan, and Jiangxi Zichen have started the industrialization process.

The downstream battery production is characterized by oligopoly, where three companies Contemporary Amperex Technology Co Limited (CATL), BYD, and Gotion High Tech, exert significant control over the downstream battery manufacturing. CATL is, without doubt, the most prominent power battery producer in China, and has maintained a leading position in the downstream market since 2018. In 2020, the company's market share reached its record high (50%).[46] The fast development of China's battery manufacturing industry has benefitted significantly from the supportive policy and regulatory environment. The Action Plan for Promoting the Development of the Automotive Power Battery Industry, jointly issued by MIIT, NDRC, MOST, and MoF in 2017, systematically summarizes the critical supportive measures and assigns various responsibilities to respective central government agencies.[47] Such support includes exemption from consumption tax by eligible battery producers (whose products satisfy the national standards) and tax deduction policies explicitly designed for high-tech enterprises, technology transfer, and R&D.[48] Another critical regulatory goal is to create a level playing field conducive to fair competition within the domestic context aiming to boost R&D by leveraging private investments instead of perpetually relying on public expenditure.[49] Essential measures that underpin this regulatory goal are to continuously unify and improve the national standards on batteries (such as testing standards and product specifications) and enhance supervision of local practices to safeguard the uniform implementation of such standards nationwide (such as strictly regulating the conduct of testing agencies and third-party verifiers).[50] As a result, China's battery production capacity has significantly expanded in recent years. Accordingly, the policy and regulatory focus has shifted from leveraging private investment through public funds to enhance quality assurance, energy intensity, and cost reduction.[51]

[45] Liu (n 42).
[46] ibid.
[47] Action Plan for Promoting the Development of the Automotive Power Battery Industry, MIIT Order No (2017)29, 20 February 2017 (in Chinese).
[48] ibid.
[49] ibid part 4(2).
[50] ibid.
[51] The recent policy and regulatory documents underlying the policy shift include Standards and Specifications for Lithium-ion Battery Industry (2021 version); and Announcement of the Management Measures on Lithium-ion Battery Industry Standards (2021 version), MIIT Order No (2021)37, 10 December 2021 (in Chinese).

C. Diversification of Lithium Supply

With the consolidation of a domestic policy and regulatory framework to support the development of a lithium supply chain, Chinese policy-makers and enterprises have continuously worked to further enhance China's leading positions throughout the lithium supply chain through two essential strategies. These strategies reflect the fact that, despite China's dominant position in lithium processing and battery manufacturing, it remains overwhelmingly dependent on imports of raw materials for production. Reliance on imports and lack of adequate domestic production of lithium minerals makes the Chinese battery industry vulnerable to supply shortages and price fluctuations of raw materials, as happened in 2022.[52] To address the imbalance of supply and demand and other pressing issues that could exacerbate supply shortages (such as local protectionism and quality inconsistencies), the MIIT and SAMR released a Notice in November 2022 which put forward a set of specific measures that aim to tackle these issues.[53] Essentially, these measures underpin the first strategy that focuses on resolving the lopsided supply and demand, and enhancing regulatory oversight and the domestic infrastructure to increase lithium mining and processing.

Chinese companies have pursued a second strategy of acquiring assets overseas to ensure access to sufficient lithium supplies amidst global shortages and rising prices. While China has the largest capacity in lithium processing and refining, its domestic production falls short of meeting demand and therefore sources the bulk of raw materials overseas. Besides the goal of maximizing the output from domestic mines, Chinese companies have also been aggressively acquiring lithium-related assets in major producer countries around the world to ensure access to supplies. Beginning in 2015, an increasing number of acquisitions for upstream lithium reserves and resources has been concluded by Chinese firms, with a focus on promising development projects.[54] For example, Ganfeng Lithium and Tianqi Lithium, China's top two lithium chemical product producers, have acquired stakes in lithium mines and companies owning lithium development projects in Australia, Chile, Ireland, South America, and, more recently, Mexico. Ganfeng Lithium added the Sonora project in Mexico to its global lithium asset portfolio after purchasing a 100 per cent equity interest in Bacanora Lithium in 2022.[55] Additionally, Ganfeng also acquired Argentina-focused lithium explorer Lithea, which owns the Pozuelos and Pastos Grandes lithium salt lake assets.[56] Tianqi Lithium is the second largest shareholder of a Chilean mining company (SQM) and holds a 51 per cent share in the world's largest hard-rock lithium mine in Western Australia.[57]

[52] Zhang and others (n 39); Tian and others (n 44).

[53] Notice on Achieving the Coordinated and Stable Development of the Lithium-ion Battery Industry Supply Chain, MIIT Order No (2022) 298, 10 November 2022 (in Chinese).

[54] Kip Keen and Camille Erickson, 'China Mining, Battery Companies Sweep up Lithium Supplies in Acquisition Blitz' (S&P Global Market Intelligence, November 2021) <https://www.spglobal.com/marketintelligence/en/news-insights/latest-news-headlines/china-mining-battery-companies-sweep-up-lithium-supplies-in-acquisition-blitz-67205411> accessed 29 April 2024.

[55] Ganfeng Lithium, 'Interim Results Announcement for the Six Months Ended 30 June 2022' (Hong Kong Exchanges, August 2022) <https://www1.hkexnews.hk/listedco/listconews/sehk/2022/0830/2022083002480.pdf> accessed 29 April 2024.

[56] 'Baker McKenzie Advises Ganfeng Lithium Group on its USD 962 million Acquisition of Lithea' (Baker & McKenzie, October 2022) <https://www.bakermckenzie.com/en/newsroom/2022/10/ganfeng-lithium-group-acquisition> accessed 29 April 2024.

[57] Keen and Erickson (n 54).

In addition to the buying spree by these two market giants, other Chinese lithium raw materials producers have also gone overseas to expand their portfolio of lithium raw materials. For instance, Zijin Mining Group completed the acquisition of a Toronto-based Neo Lithium Corp., including its project Tres Quebradas in Argentina, in January 2022.[58] Another notable example is CATL's purchase of stakes in Australian Lithium miner Pilbara Minerals in 2019.[59] China's massive presence in upstream segments of the lithium supply chain reiterates the country's strategy that recognizes lithium as a key ingredient behind China's green economic transition. Chinese companies are willing to pay a premium to safeguard the security of supply in the years to come.

III. Challenges for Sustainable Development of the Lithium Supply Chain in China

Chinese dominance over the lithium supply chain has raised concerns for other countries about the security of the supply of lithium-related products.[60] However, it is only recently that the United States and the European Union (EU) have started to take steps to increase supply chain resilience through greater domestic production and more collaborative approaches.[61] The general observation of the responses adopted by the United States and the EU is that the assessment for supply security places more emphasis on identifying vulnerabilities of the lithium supply chain rather than merely focusing on the concentration of critical materials and high-capacity batteries in certain countries and jurisdictions (eg China) or technological interdependency. That being said, the United States and the EU have taken slightly different measures, with the EU prioritizing environmental, social, and governance (ESG) criteria to protect industries at home and driving fundamental changes beyond the national borders and the United States trying to limit lithium products and batteries coming from China.[62] Though no large-scale conflicts have emerged among key producer states of lithium resources (ie China and other superpowers), despite the trade war in recent years, the World Trade Organization (WTO) cases regarding China's restriction of exporting rare earth suggest that China is naturally in a position to benefit from its dominance in the supply chain.[63] The battery production capacity provides a good example. The number of planned battery plants by Chinese companies will enable them to double their current level of production by 2025.[64] With the current rate of capacity addition for

[58] Zijin Mining Group, 'Announcement in relation to Completion of Acquisition of Neo Lithium Corp.' (Hong Kong Exchanges, January 2022) <https://www1.hkexnews.hk/listedco/listconews/sehk/2022/0126/2022012600689.pdf> accessed 29 April 2024.

[59] Henry Sanderson, 'China's CATL to Buy Stake in Australian Lithium Miner Pilbara' (*Financial Times*, September 2019) <https://www.ft.com/content/b91bc53e-cf12-11e9-b018-ca4456540ea6> accessed 29 April 2024.

[60] 'FACT SHEET: Securing a Made in America Supply Chain for Critical Minerals' (The White House, 22 February 2022) <https://www.whitehouse.gov/briefing-room/statements-releases/2022/02/22/fact-sheet-securing-a-made-in-america-supply-chain-for-critical-minerals/> accessed 29 April 2024; European Parliament, 'Resilient Supply Chains in the Green Transition' (EU–US Explainer, July 2021) <https://www.europarl.europa.eu/RegData/etudes/ATAG/2021/696181/EPRS_ATA(2021)696181_EN.pdf> accessed 29 April 2024.

[61] European Parliament (n 60).

[62] Emily Burlinghaus, 'As the US Struggles to "Green" Supply Chains, New EU Battery Regulation Offers Lessons' (Atlantic Council, 11 March 2022) <https://www.atlanticcouncil.org/blogs/energysource/new-eu-battery-regulation-offers-lessons/> accessed 29 April 2024.

[63] Mark Wu, 'China's Export Restrictions and the Limits of WTO Law' (2017) 16(4) World Trade Review 673.

[64] Nhan (n 23).

battery production, a vast majority of battery manufacturing plants scheduled to enter operation by 2030 will be based in China (148 plants, compared to 11 and 21 plants in the United States and Europe, respectively).[65] Such a level of production capacity will allow the Chinese battery producers to supply batteries to more than 20 million EVs in 2026.[66]

China's dominance in the lithium supply chain and the complex geopolitical relations between China and other superpowers have shaped the potential for conflicts over the lithium supply chain. Although such conflicts are less likely to escalate to trade wars due to the highly interdependent relationships among countries throughout the supply chain, a reduced supply of lithium globally will still cause tensions that hamper global efforts towards decarbonization and green economic transition.[67] In the context of finite and limited lithium resources and the soaring demand for lithium-ion batteries, a critical regulatory question is about greater lithium supply chain sustainability, which calls for sustainable material consumption through more harmonized circularity standards and indicators such as recyclability, efficiency, environmental protection, carbon footprint, and corporate due diligence and accountability. Realizing the detrimental effects caused by lopsided lithium supply and demand, Chinese policy-makers have emphasized the importance of improving the underdeveloped system for NEV battery recycling and exploring the secondary usage of power batteries within the country.

The initial wave of NEV battery recycling rules and requirements was instituted in 2018, where battery manufacturers are given the responsibility, at least in theory, to recycle the batteries in their NEVs and to play a more proactive role in the battery recycling business.[68] The Interim Measures for the Recycling and Utilisation of Power Batteries of New Energy Vehicles ('Interim Measures'), jointly issued by MIIT and six other central government agencies, put forward stipulations that require collaboration and information-sharing among battery producers, NEV manufacturers, and recycling companies for better reuse and recycling of batteries. For instance, article 8 of the Interim Measures requires that battery manufacturers should provide technical information to disassemble batteries to NEV manufacturers promptly and provide specialized training when necessary.[69] In addition, NEV manufacturers are obliged to cooperate with recycling companies to share information on recycling outlets, numbers of recycled NEVs and batteries, and technologies related to battery disassembly for recycling purposes.[70] Although the Interim Measures paved the way for regulating the battery recycling industry, this nascent sector has been facing growing pains, including a lack of standard battery technology, lagging battery reuse, and inadequate recycling techniques and methods.[71]

To address these issues, the joint Notice released by the MIIT and SAMR in November 2022 stipulates that MIIT will take a leadership role in revising the 'Comprehensive and Standardised Technology System for Lithium-ion Batteries', which is instrumental to ensuring coordinated and sustainable development of the lithium supply and demand and

65 European Parliament (n 60).
66 Nhan (n 23).
67 Altiparmak (n 17).
68 Interim Measures for the Recycling and Utilisation of Power Batteries of New Energy Vehicles, MIIT Order No (2018) 43, 26 January 2018 (in Chinese).
69 ibid art 8.
70 ibid art 13.
71 Jian Hu and others, 'Status Quo and Suggestions for the Construction of Power Battery Standard System' (2022) 11(1) Energy Storage Science and Technology 313 (in Chinese).

establishing a digital platform to track key metrics throughout the entire battery lifecycle.[72] These preliminary yet critical steps are essential in the transition to more sustainable business models and in driving changes in greening the lithium supply chain in China, considering that Chinese firms in the mid-and downstream segments are set to continue expanding their production capacity in the coming years. However, challenges remain regarding how quickly such systems are to be established and how the recycling of batteries is to be administered. It is particularly difficult to regulate small recycling businesses, which are often cheaper than officially endorsed entities.[73] Small battery recycling businesses in China are often off the radar—they do not comply with national standards to fully recover valuable metals and often improperly dispose of waste that causes environmental harm.[74] The newest national standards published by the MIIT require that at least 85 per cent of lithium and 97 per cent of other rare earth materials from the power batteries shall be recycled.[75] The sustainable development of China's lithium supply chain requires vigorous enforcement of such standards. Since 2020, the policy direction has promoted a more standardized development of the industry and encouraged companies with financial capacity and technology to invest in battery recycling plants.[76] Nonetheless, the major stumbling block to realizing this policy goal is to control or eliminate small workshop recycling businesses. According to Li and others, there are more than 15,000 companies with battery recycling registered as part of their business scope, among which more than half are small businesses. In contrast, the Chinese government has published a list of recycling companies recognized as having the necessary capacities to recycle power batteries appropriately. Only five companies were initially appeared on the list; the list grew to eighty-eight in December 2022.[77]

The secondary usage of batteries in China is a business that has been around for a while, but government interventions and the provision of guidance for the sector's development are relatively nascent. In August 2021, MIIT and other central government agencies announced the policy document, *Measures for the Management of Ladder Utilisation of Power Batteries for New Energy Vehicles*, which requires industry stakeholders to explore the secondary usage of NEV batteries through a ladder prioritization scale.[78] Such a ladder prioritization scale means that batteries are to be reused (such as in slower and smaller EVs followed by uses in energy storage) based on a gradient approach after their normal useful life of four to six years and a gradual decrease in their energy intensity levels. The secondary usage of batteries maximizes the use and life of battery materials before they move to the recycling industry. Developing the battery reuse industry in China is an integral part of

[72] Notice on Achieving the Coordinated and Stable Development of the Lithium-ion Battery Industry Supply Chain (n 53).

[73] Wenjing Zhang, 'Discussion on the Recycling of Power Batteries of New Energy Vehicles' (2022) 5 Resources Conservation & Environmental Protection 135 (in Chinese).

[74] ibid.

[75] Interim Management Measures of the Industry Standards for the Comprehensive Utilisation of Waste Power Batteries of New Energy Vehicles (2019 Edition), MIIT Order No (2019) 59, 16 December 2019 (in Chinese).

[76] 'The Battery Recycling Policy is Implemented, and the One-stop Model that Integrates Production and Recycling has been Advocated (China Association of Automobile Association, 30 August 2021) <http://www.caam.org.cn/chn/9/cate_107/con_5234478.html> accessed 29 April 2024 (in Chinese).

[77] Hongyan Li and others, 'Development Status and Suggestions of Waste Power Battery Recycling Industry in China' (China Association of Circular Economy, 6 February 2023) <https://www.chinacace.org/news/view?id=14319> (accessed 29 April 2024) (in Chinese).

[78] Measures for the Management of Ladder Utilisation of Power Batteries for New Energy Vehicles, MIIT Order No (2021) 114, 19 August 2021 (in Chinese).

the policy imperatives to enhance resource efficiency. The 14th Five-year Plan for National Economic and Social Development aims to build a complete battery recycling system by 2025.[79] Although China claims to be the global leader in recycling lithium-ion batteries,[80] the total recycling rate (including reuse) through the official channel is reported to be around 30 per cent.[81] The fast growth of China's NEV market since the middle of 2010s will soon witness a rising number of waste power batteries pouring into the recycling and reuse sectors. If these batteries are not appropriately and adequately recycled, they will likely be improperly disposed of or recycled in small workshops, causing severe environmental damage. Despite the first-mover advantage of building the world's largest NEV market, China is now facing the pressing task of greening the lithium supply chain.

IV. Advancing Responsible Supply of Critical Minerals for Net Zero: Law and Policy Imperatives

The fast development of China's lithium-related industry results from the supportive policy and regulatory environment for lithium-related industries, notably the financial incentives for the downstream NEV industry playing an essential role in driving private investments. Over the past decade, the policy imperative to accelerate NEV development has been translated into specific policy and regulatory tools that facilitated the exponential growth of Chinese firms throughout the lithium supply chain. Chinese companies are at the forefront of the global lithium supply chain and are endeavouring to lead the innovation at a rapid pace. Improvement in lithium-ion battery technology will most likely result in greater affordability and efficiency of the EVs, which will benefit China's effort towards higher electrification and the pursuit of the carbon neutrality objective. Given that EV sales in China and other parts of the world continue to rise and the supplies of lithium raw materials tighten, prices of lithium products will likely remain high in the years to come unless the issue of lopsided supply and demand can be adequately addressed through more collaborative approaches at the global level. Considering China's dominant position in the critical aspects of the lithium supply chain, Chinese companies will continue to play an integral role in the lithium industry in the near future.

The demand-supply imbalance of lithium raw materials and related products has prompted stakeholders and institutions at national and international levels to emphasize the need for a sustainable, resilient, and ethical supply of critical transition minerals.[82] To achieve this, the following policy and regulatory imperatives are essential components of an effective supply chain: (1) establishing robust ESG standards in production is crucial to ensure shared economic benefits and minimize environmental impact; (2) upholding these standards relies heavily on transparency and traceability throughout the value chain; (3) it is imperative to accelerate the transition towards a circular economy and maximize the use of secondary resources; (4) the full potential of trade policy should be harnessed to provide

[79] Outline of the 14th Five-Year Plan (2021–2025) for National Economic and Social Development and Vision 2035 of the People's Republic of China, State Council, 12 March 2021, chapter 39, parts 1 and 2.

[80] Zachary J Baum and others, 'Lithium-ion Battery Recycling—Overview of Techniques and Trends' (2022) 7(2) American Chemical Society Energy Letter 712.

[81] Li and others (n 77).

[82] 'Future-Proofing' (n 41).

significant support for these efforts; and (5) providing clear signals to suppliers necessitates the implementation of stringent climate and sustainable development policies, alongside clear legal frameworks.[83] By focusing on these key components, a supply chain for critical transition minerals can effectively address the challenges posed by the supply-demand imbalance while promoting sustainability, resilience, and ethical practices.

A comprehensive understanding of Chinese practices, specifically their domestic policy and regulatory frameworks, is essential for effectively addressing the policy and regulatory imperatives surrounding the lithium supply chain. China's dominant position in crucial segments of the lithium supply chain highlights the need for a thorough grasp of its approach. As this chapter shows, China's policy and regulatory focus primarily centres around ensuring supply security, which involves the substantial allocation of resources and policy support to enhance the control and technological advancement of Chinese firms. It is important to avoid oversimplifying the success of China's dominance in the lithium supply chain due to the intricate nature of policy and legal details embedded in various policy and regulatory documents. However, a valuable lesson that can be gleaned from China's experience is the significance of establishing a stable and predictable policy and regulatory environment. This, coupled with targeted financial support to key industry stakeholders, proves essential for driving the development of the value chain.

The impact of China's development strategy on the sustainable, resilient, and ethical supply of critical transition minerals should not be underestimated, particularly if there is an inadequate establishment of the regulatory framework within China and in countries where lithium mines are predominantly located. This regulatory vacuum poses challenges for ensuring sustainable and responsible mining and production of lithium, necessitating responses from both domestic and international laws. Encouragingly, policy-makers in China have begun to recognize the significance of product traceability, circularity, and the promotion of battery recyclability and secondary usage. Notably, recent regulatory developments exemplify the specific policy imperative concerning the greening and sustainability of the supply chain. Acknowledging and addressing these factors makes it possible to navigate the complex landscape of the lithium supply chain and work towards achieving a more sustainable, resilient, and ethical framework. Doing so requires a comprehensive approach that accounts for regulatory frameworks both domestically and internationally.

Nonetheless, it remains a challenge whether China can green its lithium supply chain to advance the security and reliability of critical transition minerals for a net zero future. Power battery reuse and recycling are essential aspects of a sustainable development pathway for lithium-related industries. However, China's reuse and recycling markets are still nascent, with underdeveloped policy and regulatory frameworks. These challenges reflect the complexity of pursuing ambitious climate goals without global collaborations over the lithium supply chain. When it comes to the clean energy transition at the domestic level, sustainable material consumption through more harmonized circularity standards and indicators such as recyclability, efficiency, environmental protection, carbon footprint, and corporate due diligence and accountability provide the solution.

China's strategies to dominate the lithium supply chain have implications beyond its borders, including issues related to national sovereignty over natural resources. While Chinese

[83] ibid.

companies buying lithium mines overseas aim to secure supply for China's domestic processing capacity and battery demand, it has also raised concerns about other countries' sovereignty over their natural resources. Many countries rely on Chinese lithium, which could delay or constrain their energy transition initiatives if they need help to secure adequate supplies. Additionally, China's dominance in the lithium supply chain could give it significant leverage over other countries if it limits its lithium exports, impacting the global supply of lithium and the development of energy transition initiatives worldwide. To ensure a stable lithium supply, other countries need to establish collaborative mechanisms or ensure sovereignty over their natural resources. China's pursuit of dominance across the lithium supply chain highlights the need for all countries to safeguard the supply security of critical transition minerals and their products.

V. Conclusion

In the context of a world transitioning towards a low-carbon future, there will be a significant increase in the demand for critical minerals, which will consequently lead to heightened competition for these resources. To effectively address these challenges, a more coordinated approach is required to secure the supply of critical minerals. This means countries will be required to enhance their domestic policy and regulatory framework, with the objective of establishing a sustainable, resilient, and ethical supply chain for critical transition minerals.

Dealing with the existing imbalance between the supply and demand of critical minerals also calls for international collaboration and the establishment of collaborative mechanisms and partnerships. One potential solution is the proposal to create a global strategic reserve of critical minerals, aimed at mitigating risks in the supply chain and ensuring sufficient supply for the energy transition. This chapter sheds light on the Chinese policy and regulatory framework that facilitates the development of the lithium supply chain. Additionally, it emphasizes key areas that demand the attention of policy-makers, such as promoting responsible sourcing and sustainable production practices. Furthermore, the development of recycling and recovery technologies is crucial to reduce dependence on primary resources. By implementing these measures, a more stable and sustainable supply of critical minerals can be ensured while simultaneously supporting the establishment of a resilient and diversified global supply chain for these vital resources.

7

Security and Intergenerational Equity in the Net Zero Transition

Lessons from Canada

Alastair R. Lucas and Akinbobola Olukayode Olugbemi

I. Introduction

This chapter focuses on the implications of net zero for intergenerational equity in the development of natural resources. Drawing lessons from Canada, it evaluates how resource-rich countries can balance net zero ambitions with the goals of energy security and long-term sustainable energy development in a manner that advances intergenerational equity. It addresses existing and potential international and domestic law and policy tools to reconcile Canada's position among developed states as a leading global hydrocarbon producer (focused on the Alberta oil sands) and a leading advocate for net zero greenhouse gas (GHG) emissions by 2050 (net zero 2050).

There is a hydrocarbon production versus net zero 2050 emissions dilemma in Canada. Oil and gas industry GHG emissions in 2022 are 191 megatonnes (Mt), accounting for 26 per cent of total Canadian emissions, and rising.[1] Potential emissions reduction, including carbon capture, utilization, and storage (CCUS), fugitive emission reduction, particularly of methane, and an enormous shift to renewables, are expected by the industry and the provincial and federal governments to accomplish the 2050 goal. This includes shifting to a 35 per cent electric vehicle (EV) fleet by 2035 and virtually complete electric transportation, along with significant mass transit gains, by 2050.[2]

All of these imply a new overall economic model for the country that moves it away from a long-established conventional economic model centred mainly on oil and gas development and use. It contemplates at least a partially circular economy.[3] There is now ample evidence that hydrocarbon development and use is already causing severe ecosystem strain under the conventional model.[4] The perennial focus on the idea of perpetually growing GDP is gradually being replaced by ecological and related social limits measurement. At the

[1] Environment and Climate Change Canada (ECCC), 'Canada's 2030 Emissions Reduction Plan – Chapter 1: Introduction. Breakdown of Canada's GHG Emissions by Economic Sector (2019 profile)' <https://www.canada.ca/en/services/environment/weather/climatechange/climate-plan/climate-plan-overview/emissions-reduction-2030/plan/chapter-1.html> accessed 21 August 2023.

[2] ibid ch 2.

[3] See Kate Raworth, *Donut Economics: Seven Ways to Think Like a 21st-Century Economist* (Chelsea Green 2015).

[4] The sector is described in ECCC (n 1) ch 2. 'Oil and Gas' as 'a major economic contributor to the country and Canada's largest source of greenhouse gas emissions' <https://www.canada.ca/en/services/environment/weather/climatechange/climate-plan/climate-plan-overview/emissions-reduction-2030/plan/chapter-2.html#toc8> accessed 21 August 2023.

Alastair R. Lucas and Akinbobola Olukayode Olugbemi, *Security and Intergenerational Equity in the Net Zero Transition* In: *Net Zero and Natural Resources Law.* Edited by: Damilola S. Olawuyi, José Juan González, Hanri Mostert, Milton Fernando Montoya, and Catherine Banet, Oxford University Press. © International Bar Association 2024. DOI: 10.1093/9780198925033.003.0007

same time, the continued expansion of oil and gas projects raises significant questions on how to balance the net zero ambition with the quest for economic development.

However, this pressing dilemma is almost completely unacknowledged by the federal government, provincial governments, and industry. The thinking seems to be that this is a readily soluble problem. The question is whether existing or proposed statutory legal instruments aimed at achieving net zero 50 are likely to withstand constraints based on the government of Canada's conflicting commitments to continue and increase hydrocarbon production (particularly from Alberta's oil sands) during the low-carbon energy transition. The difficulty of melding sustainable development concepts of energy security and sustainability, and a low-carbon energy transition based on intergenerational equity principles requires careful examination in order to achieve a balanced response.

The oil sands in the province of Alberta are the core of the Canadian oil and gas industry. They account for 63 per cent of Canada's oil production[5] which overall ranks fourth globally.[6] There has been quick recovery from the 2020 price crash driven by COVID, and Russia–Saudi Arabia competition. Oil sands royalties and taxes have pushed Alberta into a rich budget surplus position[7] and swelled federal coffers, with oil sands producers reaching the payout point under their provincial tenure agreements when royalties increase significantly and remain at high levels into the future. The oil sands account for over 2 per cent of national GDP;[8] but they also produced at least 7.8 per cent of Canadian GHG emissions in 2010.[9] With enormous shovels and trucks and piles of sticky bitumen, for much of the public (at least outside Alberta), the oil sands industry is the very visible symbol of ominous petroleum industry GHG emissions that foster climate change. It is at the centre of a national debate about how far and how fast the federal government can go in phasing out carbon energy.[10]

There are two major factors. One is the economic value of the resources in a period of extreme economic uncertainty.[11] The other is the international GHG reduction commitments and implementing actions reviewed below that Canadian governments, particularly the federal government, have taken. There has been no shortage of federal climate promises. But these are vague and uncosted, as the fall 2020 federal election campaign showed.[12] There is increasing evidence that Canada will not be able to meet its international climate

[5] Natural Resources Canada, 'Crude Oil' <https://natural-resources.canada.ca/our-natural-resources/energy-sources-distribution/fossil-fuels/crude-oil/5849> accessed 21 August 2023.

[6] ibid.

[7] Chizu Nomiyama, 'Canada's Alberta forecasts much bigger 2022–23 budget surplus of C$13.2 bln' (Reuters, 31 August 2022) <https://www.reuters.com/article/canada-alberta-idCAO8N2ZU00M> accessed 23 August 2023.

[8] See Energy Exchange, 'Energy and Canada's GDP' (2024) (*Energy Exchange*) <https://energy-exchange.net/fuel-electricity-canadian-gdp/> accessed 21 August 2023.

[9] Government of Canada, 'Oil Sands: A strategic resource for Canada, North America and the global market: GHG Emissions' (Her Majesty the Queen in Right of Canada, 2013) (revised May 2013) <https://natural-resources.canada.ca/sites/www.nrcan.gc.ca/files/energy/pdf/eneene/pubpub/pdf/12-0614-OS-GHG%20Emissions_eu-eng.pdf> accessed 21 August 2023.

[10] See Adam Radwanski, 'Canada's new emissions targets are a big reach, even if they look relatively modest' (*The Globe and Mail*, 23 April 2021) B1 <https://www.theglobeandmail.com/business/commentary/article-canadas-new-emissions-targets-are-a-big-reach-even-if-they-look/> accessed 23 August 2023.

[11] See Konrad Yakabuski, 'Our Phony Debate about Oil Sands Won't Stop their Growth' (*The Globe and Mail*, 11 September 2021) O11 <https://www.theglobeandmail.com/opinion/article-our-phony-election-debate-over-the-oil-sands-wont-stop-their-expansion/> accessed 21 August 2023.

[12] See David Parkinson, 'Campaign climate promises undergo scientific reality checks' (*The Globe and Mail*, 16 September 2021) <https://www.theglobeandmail.com/business/commentary/article-campaign-climate-promises-undergo-scientific-reality-checks/> accessed 21 August 2023.

commitments.[13] This is on top of earlier hints, one coming from the government's own Parliamentary Budget Officer, concluding that major emission reductions will be necessary beyond the 2030 reductions that will be required under the federal Greenhouse Gas Pollution Pricing Act.[14] GDP growth will be reduced by 1.4 per cent, with the largest burden, a 10.8 per cent drop, faced by the oil and gas sector along with a 16.2 per cent reduction for the transportation sector.[15]

There is also a political factor. Western provinces have pushed back on federal climate policy, concerned about protecting their constitutional powers.[16] The new, as of 2022, Alberta premier, Danielle Smith, has promised to relitigate the Supreme Court of Canada's decision holding the federal carbon tax statute, the Greenhouse Gas Pollution Pricing Act, constitutionally valid.[17] Arguably, this has affected the stringency and timing of federal measures. World events are also relevant, including the Russian attack on Ukraine, which is buffeting national economies around the world.

What this adds up to is a classic dilemma—a policy black hole. Potential economic, environmental, and undoubtedly political harm lies in both directions—on one side cutting or limiting oil and gas production, and on the other side, doubling down on a menu of measures to reach net zero 50. In early 2024, it appears that the path to net zero 50 may inevitably lead to oil and gas industry cutbacks and the harm of the national economy. This has led to a surfeit of political vagueness and mixed messaging. There is a reluctance to recognize that the transition requires an unavoidable reduction in the production and use of fossil fuels.[18] In the short term, energy security and economics suggest that Canadian oil and gas production should be increased as markets expand.[19] Yet one study estimates that reducing oil sands emissions by 40 per cent will cost $45–65 billion through 2030, though the timing and cost for overall industry reductions are uncertain.[20] As discussed in Chapter 1 of this book, there is a need for coherence and alignment between net zero

[13] Yakabuski (n 11).

[14] Philip Bagnoli and Tim Scholz, 'Beyond Paris: Reducing Canada's GHG Emissions by 2030' (Office of the Parliamentary Budget Officer, 23 June 2021) <https://www.pbo-dpb.ca/en/publications/RP-2122-009-S--beyond-paris-reducing-canada-ghg-emissions-2030--dela-paris-reduire-emissions-gaz-effet-serre-canada-ici-2030> accessed 21 August 2023.

[15] ibid.

[16] See Meghan Potkins, 'Alberta's new premier puts Ottawa, "on notice," vows to defend provincial control of oil and gas' (*Financial Post*, 12 October 2022) <https://financialpost.com/commodities/energy/oil-gas/alberta-premier-ottawa-oil-gas> accessed 21 August 2023. Premier Smith promised to go further with an 'Alberta Sovereignty Act', authorizing Alberta to refuse to enforce federal statutes it deems to be within its jurisdiction. See Madeline Smith, 'Premier Danielle Smith at UCP AGM vows not to back away from sovereignty act' (*Edmonton Journal*, 22 October 2022) <https://edmontonjournal.com/news/politics/danielle-smith-vows-not-to-back-away-from-sovereignty-act-at-ucp-agm> accessed 21 August 2023.

[17] See *References re Greenhouse Gas Pollution Pricing Act*, 2021 SCC 11 (hereafter *References re GGPPA*). See also *Reference Re Greenhouse Gas Pollution Pricing Act*, 2019 SKCA 40; 2019 ONCA 544; 2020 ABCA 74 (provincial courts of appeal decisions regarding GGPPA constitutionality); Potkins (n 16).

[18] Jeffrey Jones, 'Energy crisis only complicating Canada's green transition' (*The Globe and Mail*, 28 April 2022) B2 <https://www.theglobeandmail.com/business/commentary/article-energy-crisis-only-complicating-canadas-green-transition/> accessed 21 August 2023.

[19] Chris Varcoe, 'Varcoe: Canada can hike oil output and decarbonize—"but at significant cost", says RBC report' (*The Calgary Herald*, 26 April 2022) A4 <https://calgaryherald.com/opinion/columnists/varcoe-canada-can-hike-oil-output-and-decarbonize-but-at-significant-cost-says-rbc-report> accessed 21 August 2023.

[20] Emma Graney, 'Cutting oil sands emissions by 40 per cent will cost billions, RBC report finds' (*The Globe and Mail*, 25 April 2022) A6, citing an April 2022 study by Royal Bank of Canada <https://www.theglobeandmail.com/business/article-cutting-oil-sands-emissions-by-40-per-cent-will-cost-billions-rbc/> accessed 21 August 2023; see also Adam Radwanski, 'Ottawa must get serious about net zero strategy: industry group' (*The Globe and Mail*, 4 June 2022) B1.

targets and decision-making on new oil sands projects. Without such regulatory coherence, it will be difficult to advance net zero and a just energy transition that promotes intergenerational equity.

This chapter assesses, with a focus on legal constraints, the elements of the Canadian federal climate plan in relation to federal and provincial energy security plans and legislation. After this introduction, Section II examines the key implications of net zero for intergenerational equity. Section III evaluates the implications of Canada's net zero plans for natural resource law and policy and the potential legal constraints that limit their potential to advance net zero and intergenerational equity. Included are existing federal carbon pricing under the Greenhouse Gas Pollution Pricing Act; the federal net zero 50 plan, particularly the Canadian Net Zero Emissions Accountability Act; the proposed federal oil and gas sector GHG emissions cap; the federal Clean Fuel Standard; and the federal Clean Electricity Plan. The constraints theme continues with a spotlight on 'faux law'—government policy, and mere announcements dressed up as law; constitutional jurisdiction uncertainties, including First Nations' rights; and energy sector emissions reduction technology. This leads to conclusions and recommendations in the final section.

II. Net Zero and Intergenerational Equity: Conceptual Context

A. Sustainability and Intergenerational Equity

Sustainability and intergenerational equity have been recognized as the fundamental values supporting the right to a healthy environment and the global quest for net zero.[21] To achieve net zero, sustainability must be 'strong', incorporating ecological principles, as opposed to notions of 'sustainable development' that contemplates an element of development as an ecological trade-off. [22]

Intergenerational equity captures future orientation—the critical need to protect future generations from present-day climate damage.[23] This runs headlong into short-term political term horizons and the rapid pace of environmental, technical, economic, and social change. Nevertheless, the idea of intergenerational equity provides a helpful perspective for addressing the energy security–net zero emissions dilemma. Intergenerational equity spotlights the needs of future generations and demands that these be balanced against present rights and economic ambitions. It is, as Edith Brown Weiss shows, applicable to climate change, a global problem.[24] In particular, it captures the future orientation and uncertainty about the relative effectiveness of the range of GHG reduction measures assessed in this chapter. The key question is: to what extent do current net zero measures in Canada advance intergenerational equity by meeting the energy security and economic needs of

[21] See Chapter 2 of this book; see also Elena Cima, 'The Right to a Healthy Environment: Reconceptualizing Human Rights in the Face of Climate Change' (2022) 31(1) RECIEL 38–49.

[22] Cima (n 21).

[23] See Otto Spijkers, 'Intergenerational Equity and the Sustainable Development Goals' (2018) 10(11) Sustainability 3836; also United Nations Secretary-General, *Intergenerational Solidarity and the Needs of Future Generations*; A/68/322; United Nations: New York, NY, USA.

[24] Edith Brown Weiss, 'Climate Change: Intergenerational Equity, and International Law' (2008) 9 Vermont Journal of Environmental Law 615.

today, without jeopardizing the rights of future generations to a safe, healthy, and sustainable environment?

B. Faux Law

Canadians are being inundated with faux climate law. A faux law is a representation that an action, statement, or expression is law when it is not. According to the Merriam-Webster Dictionary, 'faux' means: 'Not real or genuine: such as a) made to look like something else that is usually more valuable: imitation, fake (*faux* leather/fur, or a string of *faux* pearls) ... *faux* is the French word for fake, but it's a very chic fake. *Faux* marble, for example, is found in the best of homes'.[25]

Faux climate law does show concern in a broad sense. There may even be an element of current issue chic; but it is 'concern', not more specific commitment demonstrated by enforceable legal requirements, only imitation or fake as suggested by the definition. This is more closely related to policy than law.

Policy in this context means government statements of intent. These lack the fundamental characteristics of law, which is to have the capability of enforcement in substantive terms, and its creation through constitutionally supported legislative processes.[26] These characteristics are fundamental for environmental law legitimacy, even though both policy and law may be widely understood and respected. Under the rule of law, only law that is legitimate in this sense can be enforced.

One example of faux policy is a recent political statement of interest: in his National Statement to the November 2021 COP26 Summit, Prime Minister Justin Trudeau stated: 'We'll cap oil and gas sector emissions today and ensure they decrease tomorrow at a pace and scale needed to reach net zero by 2050'.[27] However, no legislative action was taken or announced beyond the still pending oil and gas sector emissions cap noted in Section III.

A second, and perhaps most audacious, faux law example is Alberta premier Danielle Smith's 'Alberta Sovereignty Act'.[28] In the 2022 UCP Party leadership vote process, Smith released an overview of an Act that:

> [w]ould affirm the authority of the legislature to refuse provincial enforcement of specific federal laws or policies that violate the jurisdictional rights of Alberta under the Constitution of Canada or Charter of Rights and Freedoms.[29]

[25] Merriam-Webster Dictionary, 'Faux' <https://www.merriam-webster.com/dictionary/faux> accessed 21 August 2023.

[26] Merriam-Webster Dictionary, 'Policy', 2b, b; 'a high-level overall plan embracing the general goals and acceptable procedures especially of a governmental body'.

[27] Prime Minister of Canada: Justin Trudeau, 'Prime Minister's remarks delivering Canada's national statement at the COP26 summit' (Glasgow, United Kingdom, 1 November 2021) <https://www.pm.gc.ca/en/news/speeches/2021/11/01/prime-ministers-remarks-delivering-canadas-national-statement-cop26-summit> accessed 21 August 2023.

[28] Anna Junker, 'Danielle Smith releases overview of proposed Alberta Sovereignty Act' *Edmonton Journal* (6 September 2022) <https://edmontonjournal.com/news/politics/danielle-smith-releases-overview-of-proposed-alberta-sovereignty-act> accessed 21 August 2023.

[29] ibid.

Later, after winning the party leadership and was about to be sworn in as premier, Smith acknowledged through an advisor that the proposed Act 'would respect Supreme Court of Canada Decisions'.[30] This bill, now enacted, nevertheless has faux features. The key implication is that the Act or its application remains constitutionally valid, even though it purports to empower the provincial legislature to authorize the provincial cabinet, in the 'public interest', to determine that a federal law is unconstitutional. The Act also authorizes a provincial response that patently intrudes on established federal jurisdiction over, for example, fisheries and interjurisdictional pipelines. Consequently, the provincial legislature thus purports to replace the courts as constitutional arbiter.[31]

Pronouncements and plans of this kind made in volatile public interest conditions are a kind of faux law that may not advance net zero and intergenerational equity.[32] This is because there may not, as in the case of an oil and gas emissions cap, be any law at all, only a promise to enact it.[33] The government action may be little more than public relations—planned legislation or future plans under a legislative process. The risk is that the action may be perceived by the public to be enforceable emission reduction requirements.

C. The Rule of Law

The rule of law is not the law itself. Rather it is a fundamental underlying societal norm that embodies a sense of normative order—of hierarchy that has been expressed in many ways. Often this is in the form of elements or core principles, such as: first, all must be treated equally, even public government and officials; and second, decisions of public bodies or officials must not be arbitrary. Yet another formulation focuses on a requirement of accountability for laws. Laws must be legislated and publicly promulgated, equally enforced, and independently adjudicated.

The former element is grounded in a substantive no arbitrariness[34] requirement, while the latter is more procedurally oriented, with a major implicit role for courts and legal processes. The Supreme Court of Canada has endorsed both the general principles of normative order idea[35] as well as the requirement that the exercise of public power must be based on a legal rule.[36] The result is fundamental for Canada's democratic order. Government requirements on citizens must be based on legal rules capable of enforcement. They must be legislated according to constitutional requirements.

[30] CBC News, 'In reversal of policy, adviser says Danielle Smith's sovereignty act would respect Supreme Court decisions' (10 October 2022) <https://www.cbc.ca/news/canada/calgary/sovereignty-act-danielle-smith-alberta-1.6612197> accessed 21 August 2023.

[31] See Martin Olsynski and Nigel Banks, 'The Amendments to Bill 1' (*ABlawg*, 12 December 2022); Smith (n 16).

[32] Oxford English Dictionary, 'Faux: Not genuine; fake or false'. Example sentence: '*their faux concern for the well-being of the voters didn't fool many*'.

[33] David V Wright, 'Bill C-12, Canadian Net zero Emissions Accountability Act: A Preliminary Review' (*ABlawg*, 23 November 2020), available online: <https://ablawg.ca/2020/11/23/bill-c-12-canadian-net-zero-emissions-accountability-act-a-preliminary-review/>.

[34] Martin Krygier, 'What is the Point of the Rule of Law' (2019) 69 Buffalo Law Review 743.

[35] *Reference Re Manitoba Language Rights* [1985] 1 SCR 721, 749.

[36] *Secession Reference* [1998] 2 SCR 217, para 71; *Provincial Judges Reference* [1997] 2 SCR 3, para 10.

This brings us to the legal consequences. Without a clear legislative basis, climate law cannot be enforced. Decisions would lack legal authority; decision-makers would lack jurisdiction, and their decisions could not be enforced.

The next section evaluates the implications of Canada's net zero plans for natural resource law and policy and the potential legal constraints that limit their potential to advance net zero and intergenerational equity.

III. Canada's Net Zero Plan and Potential Legal Constraints

A. The Federal Climate Plan

Canada's national climate plan, the 'Pan-Canadian Framework on Clean Growth and climate Change, Canada's Strengthened Climate Plan: A Healthy Environment and a Healthy Economy, Carbon Pollution, Carbon Pricing, Climate Change Resilience, Clean Technology and Jobs' was originally released in December 2020.[37] It enshrined the net zero concept in Canadian climate policy, setting a 2050 target, and explained why the Canadian Net Zero Emissions Accountability Act (CNZEAA) was introduced in Parliament on 19 November 2020. This Act is discussed in section III C below. It underlines the importance of carbon pricing, setting the stage for full implementation of the federal Greenhouse Gas Pollution Pricing Act (GGPPA).[38] In 2022, the government published the first report required under the CNZEAA, entitled '2030 Emissions Reduction Plan: Canada's Next Steps for Clean Air and a Strong Economy'.[39] This too is discussed in section III C below.

B. Carbon Pricing—the GGPPA—Federal-Provincial 'Cooperation'

The GGPPA is the cornerstone federal climate statute. It has a grand Preamble that mentions the background to global climate change, specifies Canadian commitments, addresses human and ecosystem risks, emphasizes the immediate action required, and promotes GHG pricing as a core element of necessary behavioural change. Part 1 of the GGPPA imposes a fuel charge on sellers of defined GHG producing fuels. Part 2 imposes an 'output based' pricing system on a specified group of large GHG emitters. The Act applies only to provinces that have GHG pricing legislation that the federal government considers not to be equivalent.

The constitutionality of the GGPPA was upheld by the Supreme Court of Canada under the federal national concern 'Peace, Order and Good Government' power.[40] The Court characterized the Act's main feature as 'minimum national standards of price stringency

[37] Environment and Climate Change Canada (ECCC), '2030 Emissions Reduction Plan' (July 2022) at 52 (hereafter Canada's Climate Plan).

[38] SC 2018, c 12, s 186.

[39] Canada's Climate Plan (n 37).

[40] See *References re GGPPA* (n 17). See also *Reference Re Greenhouse Gas Pollution Pricing Act*, 2019 SKCA 40; 2019 ONCA 544; 2020 ABCA 74 (provincial courts of appeal decisions regarding GGPPA constitutionality); Potkins (n 16).

for GHG emissions from designated sources', notwithstanding that the Act consists of two parts: a carbon levy, but also a levy on large carbon emitters based on production. The latter seems to be more a matter of regulation than a pure tax instrument. However, a federal–provincial cooperative mechanism has permitted 'equivalent' provincial carbon pricing legislation in most provinces, including Alberta (for large final emitters), to continue.[41]

It is also worth noting that a voluntary carbon market has been in operation for more than two decades. This may be a good fit with corporate environmental, social, and governance (ESG) initiatives.[42]

C. Canadian Net Zero Accountability Act

A significant development is the 2020 CNZEAA.[43] The Preamble makes the overall goals clear: it recites the risks posed by climate change, a global problem requiring immediate action by all Canadian governments and industry; that Canada has ratified the Paris Agreement with its 1.5-degree global temperature increase goal; that this goal requires net zero emissions; and that Canada has committed to developing a plan that will achieve net zero by 2050.

Central to the Act is the net zero emissions target that requires the Environment Minister to set a national emissions target for each 'milestone year'—2030, 2035, 2040, and 2050. An emissions reduction plan must be established, with appropriate public participation, for 2030 within six months of the Act coming into force, and for subsequent milestone years with at least five years' lead time. Plans must include emissions targets for the specific years, 'a description of the key emissions reduction measures' to achieve the plan, and a description of 'relevant sectoral strategies'.[44] It is significant that these measures are 'measures of the government of Canada', an apparent attempt to influence provincial actions.[45] Progress and assessment reports are required.[46] The latter are linked to Canadian submission of its GHG inventory reports as the Framework Convention on Climate Change requires. The Act requires ministerial reasons if targets are not met.[47]

The CNZEAA amounts to a declaration of government policy. It adds clarity and gives legislative weight to earlier government policy declarations. However, while it states that it is binding on the government,[48] this is limited to setting plans containing the specified content items. Specific quantified emissions limits are yet to be established. This shows the limits of potential judicial enforcement; and even the emission targets can be extended and amended.[49]

[41] See Government of Canada, 'How Carbon Pricing Works' https://www.canada.ca/en/environment-climate-change/services/climate-change/pricing-pollution-how-it-will-work/putting-price-on-carbon-pollution.html accessed 23 August 2023.

[42] Jeffrey Jones, 'How new proposed standards aim to bring credibility to the multibillion-dollar carbon offsets market' (*The Globe and Mail*, updated 15 August 2022) B1 <https://www.theglobeandmail.com/canada/article-carbon-offsets-credibility-market/> accessed 21 August 2023.

[43] SC 2021, c 22 (CNZEAA).

[44] ibid s 10(1).

[45] See Wright, 'Bill C-12' (n 33).

[46] See CNZEAA, ss 14–15.

[47] CNZEAA, s 16(a).

[48] CNZEAA, s 3.

[49] CNZEAA, ss 9(3), 12.

Judicial enforcement action is unlikely as shown by the Federal Court of Canada's (not the Supreme Court of Canada) decision in *Friends of the Earth v Canada*,[50] an unsuccessful 2008 action to enforce the Kyoto Protocol Implementation Act (KIPA).[51] The court reasoned that in the KPIA (and, by extension, the CNZEAA), Parliament intended only to authorize a government-managed process, not to lay down specific legally enforceable requirements. There were, said the court, 'policy-laden' considerations.[52]

Nevertheless, the CNZEAA does provide coherence for Canadian federal climate policy. It represents statutory linkage to international climate change commitments and to the Strategic Assessment on Climate Change[53] under the new federal Impact Assessment Act.[54] As noted, the Supreme Court of Canada in early 2021 upheld the federal Greenhouse Gas Pollution Pricing Act.[55]

D. Oil and Gas Sector Emissions Cap

The 2016 Alberta Oil Sands Emission Limits Act[56] is part of the Alberta Climate Leadership Plan. This Act limits combined emissions from all oil sands sites to 100 Mt annually. Currently, combined emissions are approximately 70 Mt. Consequently, the Alberta government has opted to set no current limit either by facility or industry wide. In 2017, a government Oil Sands Advisory Group recommended that the 100 Mt limit be reviewed and adjusted should emissions approach and be expected to exceed 100 Mt.

In 2022, as part of its 2030 Emissions Reduction Plan, the federal government announced that it is 'committed to cap and cut emissions from the oil and gas sector at the pace and scale needed to get to net zero by 2050'.[57] It mentioned 'collaboration with industry, provinces, indigenous partners, and civil society'. In an August 2022 discussion document, the government presented two options, namely: to establish a new cap and trade system under the Canadian Environmental Protection Act (CEPA); or modify existing Greenhouse Gas Pollution Pricing Act carbon pricing systems to create a specific oil and gas sector pricing regime.

The Options Discussion Paper notes that 'caps will not be prescribed or enforced'.[58] This may be the case should a carbon pricing approach be chosen. However, a CEPA cap and trade system involving verification issues would require caps enforceable by some means. This raises the spectre of constitutional jurisdiction discussedabove[59]

Some have argued that the federal government lacks constitutional jurisdiction to regulate oil and gas operations in provinces, which amounts to imposing operational

[50] 2008 FC 1183, [2009] 3 FCR 201, aff'd 2009 FCA 297.

[51] SC 2007, c 30 (repealed by the Harper government in 2012).

[52] See Wright (n 33).

[53] Government of Canada, 'Strategic Assessment of Climate Change, Revised October 20, 2020' (6 October 2020) <https://www.canada.ca/en/services/environment/conservation/assessments/strategic-assessments/climate-change.html> accessed 18 March 2021.

[54] See Impact Assessment Act (IAA), SC 2019, c 28, s 1.

[55] The GGPPA was held constitutionally valid by the Supreme Court of Canada. See *References re GGPPA* (n 17).

[56] SA 2016, c O-7.5.

[57] Canada's Climate Plan (n 37) 52.

[58] ibid.

[59] Section III B.

requirements on particular provincial industries.[60] However, federal legislation on national standards for GHG emissions pricing presents a sounder federal constitutional jurisdiction based on the national concern Peace, Order and Good Government power, as the Supreme Court confirmed in *References re Greenhouse Gas Pollution Pricing Act*.[61]

E. Clean Fuel Standard

Another federal Climate Plan initiative with energy sector impact, that had been in progress, emerged during the COVID pandemic. This is the Clean Fuel Standard,[62] established under the Canadian Environmental Protection Act of 1999.[63] It is intended to gradually reduce GHG emissions from fuels (gasoline, diesel, and home heating oil) by requiring suppliers to reduce the carbon intensity of fuels. Included is an investment fund to promote cleaner hydrocarbon fuels, including biofuels. A carbon market (particularly aimed at refiners) requires creation or purchase of credits representing carbon intensity reduction, with excess credits marketable in future years. Though this will not apply to the upstream oil and gas sector, it aims at price-driven carbon energy reduction.

Alberta released new, more stringent methane regulations at the provincial level that bring requirements to the level of earlier federal requirements.[64] This set the stage for a CEPA equivalency agreement,[65] which will see the provincial regulations enforced in place of the federal requirements.

Equivalency agreements have been signed with all provinces except Saskatchewan. These agreements vary somewhat, largely to address provincial action already taken.[66] They underline a fundamental federal legal challenge in designing carbon pricing legislation. The Constitution Act of 1867 gives provinces exclusive power in relation to property and civil rights in provinces, local works and undertakings, and management and sale of provincial public lands, along with the critically important ownership of provincial public lands, a core element of Canada's original constitutional design. It is on this legal basis that the oil and gas industry was established and regulated.[67]

Until 2021, it was not clear that federal jurisdiction existed to address climate change. Following a series of constitutional references by provinces to their appeal courts, the Supreme Court of Canada confirmed federal jurisdiction to enact national carbon pricing legislation as a matter of national concern based on the residual federal 'peace, order, and good government' power.[68]

[60] See Alastair Lucas and Jenette Yearsley, 'The Constitutionality of Federal Climate Change Legislation' (December 2011) 4(15) The School of Public Policy, SPP Research papers.

[61] *References re GGPPA* (n 17); see Grant Bishop, 'Oil and gas emissions cap economically, constitutionally questionable' (*The Globe and Mail*, 3 July 2022) A8.

[62] See Government of Canada, 'Canada Gazette, Part I, Volume 154, Number 51: Clean Fuel Regulations' (*Canada Gazette*, 19 December 2020) <https://gazette.gc.ca/rp-pr/p1/2020/2020-12-19/html/reg2-eng.html> accessed 18 March 2021.

[63] SC 1999, c 33 (CEPA).

[64] See Marieke Walsh and Emma Graney, 'Province toughens methane regulations' (*The Globe and Mail*, 12 May 2020).

[65] Under CEPA, s 10.

[66] See K Péloffy and others, 'Setting Expectations for Robust Equivalency Agreements in Canada' <https://climateactionnetwork.ca/wp-content/uploads/CAN-Rac-Equivalency-Paper-2019-web.pdf> accessed 18 August 2023.

[67] See Constitution Act 1867, ss 92(5), (10), (13).

[68] *References re GGPPA* (n 17).

F. Just Transition Legislation

Another strand of federal net zero climate change initiative is the promise of a 'Just Transition' Act. This is the response to public and particularly commercial concern about potential economic and social impacts of the net zero push. A just transition is described as '[an] approach to economic, environmental, and social policy that aims to create an equitable and prosperous future for workers and communities as the world builds a low-carbon economy. No worker or community can be left behind, so government climate action must be focused on those workers.'[69]

While the scope is framed in general national economic and labour terms, relief for displaced oil and gas sector workers is a central objective.

However, while a Just Transition Act appears to be the key deliverable of this initiative, for a long period there was no sign of even a draft bill. It was framed by Natural Resources Canada as simply a broad digital public consultation,[70] a vague response to the equally vague plan for actions necessary to meet the net zero by 2050 commitment. Critics ask, '[W]hatever happened to the Just Transition Act?'[71] They lamented the lack of key information as well as the volatility of international oil and gas markets and point out that market complexity makes this a task that the federal government cannot do on its own.[72] Employers and unions should be involved, they argued, not to mention provinces.[73] All of this degenerated into a fierce dispute between Alberta Premier Danielle Smith and Prime Minister Justin Trudeau. The former complains that the proposed bill is a stealth move to destroy the Alberta oil and gas industry; the federal response was that the object is a broad employment creation programme for the net zero transition, though it has conceded that the 'toxic' 'just transition' term is not appropriate.[74]

Finally on 15 June 2023, the federal government introduced Bill C-50, the Canadian Sustainable Jobs Act, in Parliament. The Act establishes a mechanism to support workers in the shift to a net zero economy, including five-year plans, a council and secretariat, and a ten-year review. Though the scope is the national economy, Premier Danielle Smith reasserted provincial constitutional rights on natural resource development and vowed that the province 'will not recognize, cooperate with or enforce any attempt to phase out the province's oil and gas industry or its workforce'.[75]

[69] Natural Resources Canada, 'Just Transition' (Government of Canada) <https://natural-resources.canada.ca/public-consultations-and-engagements/consultation-sustainable-jobs/24949> accessed 23 August 2023.

[70] See ibid.

[71] Adam Radwanski, 'Whatever Happened to Ottawa's Strategy for Oil and Gas?' (*The Globe and Mail*, 7 June 2021) B1.

[72] ibid.

[73] See Anna Zinecker and others, 'Real People, Real Change Strategies for just energy transitions' (International Institute for Sustainable Development (IISD), December 2018) 9 <https://www.iisd.org/system/files/publications/real-people-change-strategies-just-energy-transitions.pdf> accessed 21 August 2023.

[74] Chris Varcoe, 'Alberta, feds need to quit fighting like two scorpions locked in a bottle' (*The Globe and Mail*, 28 January 2023) A2; Chris Varcoe, '"Toxic" Term Just Transition is out as Ottawa Concedes Words Matter' (*The Calgary Herald*, 15 April 2023) A3.

[75] Josh Aldrich, '"Non-negotiable': While Ottawa introduces sustainable jobs act, Premier Smith stands her ground' (*The Calgary Herald*, 16 June 2023) A-1.

G. Federal Clean Electricity Plan

In August 2022, consultations were ongoing by the Canada Energy Regulator on the proposed Clean Electricity Regulations. The Alberta government fretted about whether the proposed regulations would recognize the province's unique electricity market system. Meanwhile, electricity industry officials appeared to be prepared to wait to see how the regulations initiative develops. This was little changed in early 2024.

There are two critical factors. One is that while many provinces have considerable north-south electricity export infrastructure, inter-provincial intertie powerlines are largely lacking. A second factor is that with over 80 per cent of Canadian electricity already non-emitting, based mainly on hydro-generation,[76] there is little room for emissions reduction. As Kevin Dawson, of the Alberta Electric System Operator, in a province relying mainly on fossil fuel generation noted: '[we] see trying to achieve zero physical emissions in the electric system would be extremely challenging, from both an operational and cost perspective'.[77] By comparison, approximately 20 per cent of US electricity is generated by renewables.[78]

Another part of the move to net zero 50 is federal and provincial financial support for renewable electricity development. There is considerable variation across jurisdictions concerning EV subsidies and renewable electricity generation. For EVs, a major comparative study concluded that 'more effective policies are needed to reach provincial and federal targets'.[79]

There have also been federal and provincial government moves to support renewable electricity generated by 'green' hydrogen. One potentially significant, though obviously long-term, development is an August 2020 agreement between Canada and Germany to support the development of Canadian green energy sales to Germany. Despite government and industry enthusiasm, it is unclear (with a 2026 delivery date) how quickly hydrogen production and transport facilities can be constructed and opened, even with Germany looking to replace compromised Russian gas.[80] There are also constitutional jurisdiction issues and hurdles that the implementation of net zero plans will face. These are discussed in the next section.

[76] Chris Varcoe, 'Proposals "a Great Starting Point" for Discussions' (*The Calgary Herald*, 11 August 2022) A5.

[77] Postmedia News, 'AESO reports on costs, challenges to achieving net zero power grid' (*The Calgary Herald*, 4 July 2022) A6.

[78] US Energy Information Administration (EIA), 'What is U.S. electricity generation by energy source?' (Frequently Asked Questions, updated 2 March 2023, with data from the Electric Power Monthly, February 2023) <https://www.eia.gov/tools/faqs/faq.php?id=427&t=3> accessed 21 August 2023.

[79] Sustainable Transportation Action Research Team, 'Canada's Electric Vehicle Policy Report Card' <https://sustainabletransport.ca/portfolio/canadas-electric-vehicle-policy-report-card/> accessed 28 October 2022. On 21 December 2023, the federal government announced proposed regulations to require that at least 20% of vehicles sold in Canada be zero emission by 2026, 60% by 2030, and 100% by 2035: Wendy Stueck, 'New vehicles sold must be zero emission by 2035, Ottawa says' (*The Globe and Mail*, 22 December 2022).

[80] Michael MacDonald, 'Trudeau and German Chancellor Olaf Scholz to sign hydrogen deal in Newfoundland' (*Toronto Star*, 14 August 2022).

IV. Legal Approaches on the Road to Net Zero 50

Canada's net zero ambitions and plans raise several constitutional and legal questions. This section analyses the plans, possible implementation constraints, and potential responses within the context of sustainability, interjurisdictional equity, actual legislative action, and possible implementation constraints.

A. Constitutional Jurisdiction

Did anyone in Canada think that federal and provincial natural resources and environmental jurisdiction were settled by the Supreme Court of Canada's decision in *References re Greenhouse Gas Pollution Pricing Act*?[81] The Court's majority identified the pith and substance of the federal Act as 'minimum national standards of price stringency for GHG emissions' from designated sources. In its 2021 6:3 decision, the Court held the statute valid.

In principle, expanded federal regulatory, as opposed to pricing, jurisdiction is possible. This could build on existing federal constitutional power under section 92(10)(a) of the Constitution Act 1867, in relation to approval and regulation of works and undertakings connecting two provinces. As some have argued, the federal criminal law power may also be a basis for federal authority.[82] This is raised by the federal government's two options, namely: (1) a new cap and trade system under CEPA for the oil and gas industry; and (2) a specific GGPPA carbon pricing regime for the oil and gas sector.

The subject matter of cap-and-trade legislation limited to the oil and gas sector could be characterized, in substance, as targeting an industry based largely on provincial public lands. This would be a matter in relation to provincial 'property' and 'local works and undertakings' under the Constitution Act 1867. It differs from the Supreme Court of Canada's 2021 characterization of the GGPPA as aimed at 'minimum national standards of price stringency for GHG emissions'[83] from designated sources, but not from a specific industrial sector. An oil and gas sector characterization would make it difficult to bring federal oil and gas industry emissions cap legislation within federal jurisdiction under the national concern element of the federal peace order and good government power following the Supreme Court's analysis in the 2021 Reference.

B. Electricity

On the electricity side, this expansion of federal jurisdiction might include broader powers such as direct federal planning and even powers to take ownership of electrical energy sources. Additionally, there is an open ended federal 'for the general advantage of Canada' declaratory power in section 92(10)(c). However, this power, last used in the 1960s to bring

[81] The GGPPA was held constitutionally valid by the Supreme Court of Canada: *References re GGPPA* (n 17).

[82] Peter Hogg, 'Constitutional Jurisdiction Over Greenhouse Gas Emissions' (2009) 46 Alberta Law Review 507.

[83] *References re GGPPA* (n 17); Section III B above.

grain marketing infrastructure under federal control, has not been used since and is generally considered to be constitutionally spent or perhaps no longer politically viable.[84] Moreover, provinces have jurisdiction over sites and facilities to produce electrical energy.

C. Peace, Order, and Good Government

The federal 'peace, order, and good government' residual 'national concern' power (POGG) is a more plausible possibility for federal net zero 50 jurisdiction. It is the basis for federal power over nuclear energy, though what has emerged is divided jurisdiction with untested provincial authority over electricity generated by nuclear power plants. The Supreme Court of Canada faced an analogous national concern issue concerning the federal Greenhouse Gas Pollution Pricing Act establishing minimum national standards of price stringency for GHG emissions from designated sources. In its 2021 decision, the Court held the statute valid, accepting that the statute's subject matter—'minimum national standards of price stringency for GHG emissions'—is a matter of national concern under POGG.[85]

In applying this doctrine, the Court outlined a three-step analysis. First, there must be evidence that a matter is of sufficient concern to the country as a whole; second, the matter must have a convincing degree of 'singleness, distinctiveness and indivisibility' that makes it qualitatively different from provincial matters; that there is evidence of 'provincial inability' to deal with the matter; and whether such provincial failure to fully collaborate would have serious extra provincial consequences.[86] Third, the matter must have a 'scale of impact' that renders federal intrusion on provincial autonomy, including powers over property and civil rights in provinces, reconcilable with the division of powers under the Constitution Act of 1867.

This judicial formula sets a high bar for federal national concern intrusion into exclusive provincial natural resource development and energy regulation powers. Management of electricity grids has not been the subject of international climate studies or agreements—it is a step removed from the GHG emissions it might prevent—and the seriousness of lack of interties varies considerably among provinces. '[S]ingleness, distinctiveness, and indivisibility' arguments would be difficult to build, as would convincing 'scale of impact' evidence.

Provincial property jurisdiction has a more direct role than carbon price stringency when applied to electricity grids that consist of generation and transmission facilities. Further, the Supreme Court majority in the *Reference* did not accept provincial arguments that the subject matter of the legislation properly related to exclusive provincial property and non-renewable natural resources powers under section 92A of the Constitution Act 1867.[87] This includes exclusive jurisdiction in relation to the 'development, conservation and management of sites and facilities in the province for the generation and production

[84] Constitution Act 1867, 30 & 31 Vict. c 3, ss 92(10)(c) and 91(29); see Peter Hogg, *Constitutional Law of Canada* (Carswell 2009) para 22.8.
[85] *References re GGPPA* (n 17).
[86] ibid.
[87] Constitution Act 1867, s 92A(1)(b).

of electrical energy'.[88] At first sight, this looks like strong support for exclusive provincial jurisdiction in relation to electricity grids. But section 92A is concerned fundamentally with provincial powers over energy export that are subject ultimately to paramount federal authority.[89]

D. Carbon Pricing

In the *Reference* itself, the Supreme Court focused on part 2 GGPPA, the broad-based carbon levy. Part 1, the carbon levy on large carbon emitters, was largely ignored. One reason undoubtedly was that the Act's provincial equivalency feature enabled provinces to conclude federal-provincial agreements permitting provincial emissions targets to apply to large emitters.

Some have argued that the federal criminal law power is wide enough to support climate change legislation virtually however formulated.[90] But Part 1 targets the 'output' of large carbon emitters, principally oil and gas operators. Analytically, this suggests that this subject would be characterized as regulation of GHG emissions by large provincial energy sector emitters, and allocated to provincial jurisdiction.[91]

The result is that neither federal nor provincial constitutional power is constrained by divided constitutional jurisdiction. The federal government has its constitutional law tested carbon levy, and provinces retain their oil and gas property-based regulatory jurisdiction. None have strong incentives to launch further lengthy and expensive litigation in attempts to further clarify constitutional boundaries.

E. Impact Assessment Act Constitutional Reference

Another case decided by the Supreme Court of Canada that should shed some light on the boundaries of federal and provincial jurisdiction in relation to net zero, the oil and gas industry and its climate impacts. This is the *Reference re Impact Assessment Act.*[92] The Supreme Court of Canada held that federal assessment jurisdiction purporting to underpin The *Impact Assessment Act*[93] is limited to assessment of projects concerning works or undertakings, even if within provinces, that involve impacts on recognized federal constitutional subject matters including First Nations lands, fisheries, navigation and shipping, and migratory birds.

[88] Constitution Act 1867, s 92A(1)(c).

[89] See Martin Olszynski, Nigel Bankes, and Andrew Leach, 'Alberta Court of Appeal Opines That Federal Carbon Pricing Legislation Unconstitutional' (*ABlawg*, 17 March 2020) <https://ablawg.ca/2020/03/17/alberta-court-of-appeal-strikes-down-federal-carbon-pricing-legislation-on-constitutional-grounds/> accessed 20 October 2021.

[90] Constitutional Law of Canada (n 84) s 30.7, citing *R v Hydro Quebec* [1997] 3 SCR 213.

[91] Alastair Lucas, 'The Constitutionality of Federal Climate Change Legislation', University of Calgary, School of Public Policy, Research Paper No 11-15 (10 December 2011).

[92] 2023, SCC 23 at para 98-101..

[93] SC 2019, c 28, s 1

F. First Nations' Rights and Interests

There is a strong connection between First Nations' constitutional Aboriginal and treaty rights under section 35 of the Constitution Act 1982, and environmental rights that may be recognized under the Canadian Charter of Rights and Freedoms or statutory sources. Moreover, natural resource projects that produce significant quantities of GHG emissions are typically hinterland developments likely to affect First Nations' traditional lands and cultural values. This is not to say that section 35 Aboriginal and treaty rights are the same as Charter or statute-based environmental rights. But Aboriginal or treaty rights may be dependent on a healthy environment.[94]

There is potential for Aboriginal governance rights under section 35 to give First Nations governments jurisdiction to govern natural resource development, including GHG emissions regulation within provinces. This is a possible implication of the Supreme Court of Canada's decision in *Reference re An Act respecting First Nations, Inuit and Métis children, youth and families*.[95]

On another front, the British Columbia Supreme Court has held for the first time that BC government regulatory decisions concerning the assessment of cumulative impacts by the development of natural gas and liquids in the Montney formation of Northern British Columbia infringed treaty rights to consultation.[96] The implication is that the cumulative effects of agricultural settlement and regional resource development are so pervasive that section 35 rights are violated.

In *Duncan's First Nation v Alberta*, this is precisely the issue raised by a Northern Alberta First Nation's claim that cumulative impacts authorized by Alberta infringe the First Nation's section 35 treaty rights. This action is modelled on the BC *Yahey* case, discussed earlier, which in its result, directed changes in the provincial regulatory regime.[97] If the Duncan's First Nation's case is successful, there may be a need to re-examine the processes guiding project approvals and the cumulative effect of that on Aboriginal and treaty rights.

G. Too Many Instruments?

Developing and implementing a federal climate agenda that will achieve net zero by 2050 or before is not an easy task. Pressed by reporting deadlines in its own climate accountability statute, the government has little time. Consultations on key issues, including an oil sands emission cap, EV sales targets, and a net zero national electricity grid, are just beginning. This means that the government is in the position of having to make assumptions

[94] See Lynda Collins and Meghan Murthe, 'Indigenous Environmental Rights in Canada: The Right to Conservation Implicit in Treaty and Aboriginal Rights to Hunt, Fish, and Trap' (2010) Alberta Law Review 959, 983–88.

[95] 2024 SCC 5.

[96] *Yahey v British Columbia*, 2021 BCSC 1287, 1884; see Robert Hamilton, 'Blueberry River First Nation and the Piecemeal Infringement of Treaty 8' (*Ablawg*, 20 July 2020) accessed 28 October 2022; and Robert Hamilton and Nick Ettinger, '*Yahey v BC*, and Clarification of the Standard for Treaty Infringement' (*Ablawg*, 24 September 2021) accessed 28 October 2022.

[97] Bob Weber, 'First Nation sues province over cumulative environmental effects' (*The Globe and Mail*, 7 September 2022) A6.

about the effects of policies it has not fully developed.[98] We are left with faux law. The need for federal leadership is large. Challenges include the fact that even laws already enacted quickly become dated.

However, the message now is encouraging: 'I think we can no longer afford to take four or five years to develop new regulations,' stated Environment and Climate Change Minister Steven Guilbeault.[99]

Yet even laws already enacted lack clarity. The flagship federal Greenhouse Gas Pollution Pricing Act is fundamentally about minimum national carbon price standards. But Part 1 of the Act establishes an output-based system for pricing emissions by large industrial emitters. This is still carbon pricing, but it also carries significant regulatory features involving provincial 'property and civil rights'[100] and 'local works and undertakings'[101] that are plausibly within provincial constitutional jurisdiction. The result is that these constitutional issues need to be resolved.

There is a need for continuous actual formulation of laws, and not just faux law; continuous respectful negotiations between federal and provincial governments. The approach of the two levels of government must be that of cooperation.

H. The Energy Sector and Technology Development

There is also the energy sector—particularly the oil sands producers and their voluntary 'Oil Sands Pathways to Net-zero' initiative.[102] This response to the Oil and Gas Emissions Cap includes process improvements, heavy reliance on a CCUS network, and purchase of ecology-based offset credits. Critics challenge the federal plan's timing, cost, and feasibility that assumes major government investment in largely untested CCUS plans based on slow developing scalable technologies.[103] This underlines the need for government leadership.

On the vehicle emission side, the federal government's latest commitment is all light duty vehicles to be zero emission by 2035. This would mean that by 2035, 40 per cent of vehicles on the road would be zero emission.[104] Again, critics remain sceptical.[105]

Critical minerals, key inputs for the green and digital economy, will be significant for technological development to support net zero goals. The federal government

98 Adam Radwanski, 'Ottawa has a lot to figure out on climate agenda—and little time to do it' (n 10).

99 Quoted in ibid.

100 Constitution Act 1867, s 92(13).

101 Constitution Act 1867, s 92(10).

102 See Pathways Alliance, 'Let's clear the air' <https://pathwaysalliance.ca/cleartheair/> accessed 21 August 2023; Pathways Alliance, Press Release: 'Oil Sands Pathways alliance outlines three-phase plan to achieve goal of net zero emissions' (21 October 2021) <https://pathwaysalliance.ca/pressrelease_oct21/> accessed 21 August 2023.

103 See Chris Severson-Baker, 'Federal policy must drive oil sands climate action' (*The Globe and Mail*, 4 March 2022) B4.

104 Transport Canada, 'Canada's Zero-Emission Vehicle (ZEV) sales targets' (Government of Canada, 20 June 2022) <https://tc.canada.ca/en/road-transportation/innovative-technologies/zero-emission-vehicles/canada-s-zero-emission-vehicle-zev-sales-targets> accessed 21 August 2023.

105 Mia Rabson, 'Canada still not on track to meet electric vehicle sales target despite popularity' (*Global News*, 21 April 2022) <https://globalnews.ca/news/8776540/canada-electric-vehicle-popularity-federal-sales-target/> accessed 21 August 2023.

issued a Q&A-type Consultation Paper in 2022,[106] with the comment period closing on 15 September and a strategy document released in early 2023. This builds on Canada's status as a major global mining jurisdiction, both in financial and production terms. There is significant critical minerals potential identified, with six focus minerals: lithium, graphite, nickel, cobalt, copper, and rare earths. At the same time, questions posed about 'regional infrastructure gaps' such as transportation and clean energy need to be addressed. Advancing participation by indigenous governments, organizations, and communities is highlighted.

V. Conclusions

As can be learned from Canada, advancing intergenerational equity requires attention to the economic and social implications of net zero 50. Legislative instruments must impose real enforceable legal duties, be clear and demonstrably fair, and be the product of federal–provincial cooperation.

Explicit enforceable federal legislation to support clean energy technology development is also required to achieve better coherence between net zero targets and actual outcomes. Unenforceable promises are insufficient. For example, the promised federal oil and gas sector emissions cap must be legislated and implemented. This would not only mark a definitive step in the long-running engagement with Alberta and its oil sands, but it would also send a strong message to the broader oil and gas sector that the clock continues to tick towards net zero 50. Scheduled carbon price increases under the federal GHG pricing scheme must continue.

Important steps have been taken, particularly the federal carbon tax system under the Greenhouse Gas Pollution Pricing Act (GGPPA) and the Canadian Net Zero Emissions Accountability Act with its overall plan, including five-year emission targets and specified measures. These, along with the Clean Fuel Standard and green electricity and transportation initiatives, are a good start. However, there are still key challenges that must be addressed. There is far too much unproductive federal–provincial wrangling, particularly about the federal Just Transition Act. Federal–provincial comity that showed promise a decade ago has not been renewed. Perhaps this begins with the federal acknowledgement that the 'toxic' 'just transition' term must be jettisoned. Also, there is faux law that must be reined in so the public can have a clear view of issues, difficulties, and potential roles.

Constitutional constraints on these federal initiatives have been examined. First Nations' rights and interests have a large potential to both facilitate and derail net zero 50 progress. The remedy is not better legal arguments but more respect and engagement. Federal constitutional jurisdiction over GHG emissions pricing lays down a firm, federal base. The remaining question is the nature and extent of federal regulatory jurisdiction, particularly to impose a hydrocarbon industry emissions cap.

The outstanding overall issue is the short- and long-term fate of the oil sands. This is the core of the black hole that must be negotiated. Any real low-carbon energy

[106] Government of Canada, 'Canada's Critical Minerals Strategy: From Exploration to Recycling: Powering the Green and Digital Economy for Canada and the World' (February 2023) <https://www.canada.ca/en/campaign/critical-minerals-in-canada/canadian-critical-minerals-strategy.html> accessed 24 August 2023.

transition requires the oil and gas industry to shrink and transform.[107] The federal and Alberta governments must be clear and decisive, as must industry interests. The public must understand and be involved. Without this clarity about the fate of the oil sands, the black hole will remain, and necessary emissions reduction will recede further into the future.

[107] See also the Conclusion Chapter of this book on the key transformations that are required to natural resources law to advance an orderly and coherent clean energy transition.

8

Net Zero and Energy Diversification

Lessons from Colombia

*Milton Fernando Montoya and Ana Paola Gutiérrez Rico**

I. Introduction

Colombia is focusing its efforts on achieving carbon neutrality by 2050[1] and accelerating a process of energy transition towards cleaner energies. To fulfil these aims, an analysis of the evolution of energy policy and regulations, the actions to diversify the matrix of electricity generation with renewable energy sources (RES) is presented in this chapter, without ignoring the importance of conventional sources to ensure the energy security of the country.

The subject of this chapter is relevant because it relates to security and justice risks of the net zero energy transition. This process has been gradual in Colombia because the country depends to some degree on fossil fuels. This has presented a challenge in terms of energy security and justice during the energy transition and it has been addressed, among other ways, through the diversification of the energy matrix. Energy security cannot be compromised during the energy transition process.

To accelerate the energy transition, it is essential to understand not only the renewable and non-renewable natural resources available in the country, but also the current dependency on certain resources, as well as progress and challenges regarding the incorporation of others. In this sense, there is a consensus regarding the importance of making it an irreversible, safe, and fair process, which must therefore be gradual.

In Colombia, the primary energy supply comes from the generation of clean electricity through hydroelectric power plants. In terms of electricity sources, according to the Colombian Wholesale Energy Market administrator (XM), clean sources represent 83.63 per cent of the country's energy supply. Added to other renewable energy sources such as solar (0.98%), wind (0.29%), and biomass (1.05%), it can be seen that 85.98 per cent of electricity generation corresponds to renewable energies.[2]

The result is different when we refer to the energy matrix that is made up of a set of renewable or non-renewable sources used to generate energy to meet the demand for residential use, transportation (passenger or cargo), or commerce. More than one-third of Colombia's

* We appreciate the collaboration provided by Luz Madeleine Muñoz Andrade and Ernesto Guzmán Arana, research assistants from the Mining and Energy Law Department of the University Externado of Colombia.

[1] Ministry of Environment and Sustainable Development (MESD), National Strategy for Mitigation of Short-Lived Climate Pollutants (Ministry of Environment and Sustainable Development 2020).

[2] XM, 'General Market Report. January 2023' (*XM*, 20 February 2023) <https://www.sinergox.xm.com.co/infms/_layouts/15/WopiFrame.aspx?sourcedoc={87A313A1-B438-40AA-A9BA-65DBBDD6C050}&file=00_General_Mercado_01_2023.pdf&action=default> accessed 2 March 2023.

Milton Fernando Montoya and Ana Paola Gutiérrez Rico, *Net Zero and Energy Diversification* In: *Net Zero and Natural Resources Law.* Edited by: Damilola S. Olawuyi, José Juan González, Hanri Mostert, Milton Fernando Montoya, and Catherine Banet, Oxford University Press. © International Bar Association 2024. DOI: 10.1093/9780198925033.003.0008

energy matrix comes from fossil fuels,[3] especially oil and natural gas,[4] representing about 77 per cent of the energy generation in the country.[5] Colombia's dependence on fossil fuels to generate energy presents a challenge to diversifying Colombia's energy matrix and the transition towards carbon neutrality.

Hydroelectricity, natural gas, and non-conventional renewable energy sources (sugarcane bagasse, biofuels, and firewood) account for the remaining 23 per cent of the country's primary energy supply.[6] Other renewable energy sources, such as wind and solar energy, have very limited participation in the share of variable technology in the Colombian energy matrix.[7] However, this expected to change in the coming years.[8] By 2023, eleven variable technology projects will be in operation, providing the country with approximately 1.930 MW.[9] These projects are, among others, El Campano, El Paso Solar, Cartago, San Felipe, La Loma, Windpeshi, Acacia 2 Beta I, Beta II, Alpha I, Alpha II, Camelias, and Guayepo,[10] most of which are in areas with high levels of unsatisfied basic needs.

According to the International Energy Agency (IEA), Colombia's profile is not far from the international profile of thermal consumption versus electricity consumption.[11] The IEA report analyses the data gathered by the Ministry of Mines and Energy (MME) from 1996 to 2018,[12] which shows that, of the 28.1 megatonnes (Mtoe) of thermal energy, the country consumed 5.3 Mtoe. Of what was consumed, 19 per cent was in the form of electricity.[13] The remaining 22.8 Mtoe were contributed 80 per cent by fossil fuels, of which natural gas was used to generate 18 per cent of Colombia's thermal energy, about 4.1 Mtoe per year.[14]

Colombia does not deviate much from the global trend of electrification of many of its productive sectors, including the transportation, residential, and industrial sectors.[15] In this regard, it should be noted that the speed at which this electrification process occurs is directly proportional to the capital investments by consumers and national and international investors, which does not allow for anticipating a change in the dominant position of thermal energy based on fossil fuels over electric energy in the final demand in Colombia.[16]

[3] UPME, 'Energy Demand Projection Report' (*UPME*, 2021) <https://www1.upme.gov.co/DemandayEficiencia/Paginas/Proyecciones-de-demanda.aspx> accessed 2 February 2023.

[4] Juan Benavides, Sergio Cabrales, and Martha Elena Delgado-Rojas, *Energy Transition in Colombia: Politics, the Cost of Carbon–Accelerated Neutrality and the Role of Natural Gas* (Fedesarrollo 2022).

[5] UPME, 'National Energy Plan 2020–2050' (*UPME*, 2019) <https://www1.upme.gov.co/DemandayEficiencia/Paginas/PEN.aspx> accessed 2 February 2023.

[6] ibid.

[7] Acolgen, 'Installed capacity in Colombia' (*Acolgen*, 2023) <https://www.acolgen.org.co> accessed 10 July 2023.

[8] UPME, 'National Energy Plan' (n 5).

[9] Guido Gubinelli, 'Progress and delays: The status of renewable projects coming into operation in 2023 and 2024' (*Energía Estratégica*, 16 January 2023) <https://www.energiaestrategica.com/avances-y-retrasos-el-estado-de-los-proyectos-renovables-que-entraran-en-operaciones-en-2023-y-2024/> accessed 2 February 2023.

[10] ibid.

[11] International Energy Agency (IEA), *World Energy Statistics, 2022 Edition Database Documentation* (IEA 2022).

[12] See Ministry of Mines and Energy (MME), 'Statistics 1996–2018', Colombian Electricity Information System, Bogotá, for online statistics from various editions up to 2018.

[13] ibid.

[14] ibid.

[15] Walter Cont and others, 'Ideal 2022: Energy, Water and Health for a Better Environment' (Development Bank of Latin America 2022).

[16] ibid.

The dependence on fossil fuels in the Colombian energy matrix has been one of the country's main concerns in recent decades because of the environmental, energy security, and economic issues[17] related to the importance of fossil fuels in the commercial basket, in particular, the specific weight of coal and oil in the country's exports. In the decade from 2011 to 2021, more than 67.4 per cent of the country's external sales were from the mining/energy sector.[18] According to Colombia's National Statistics Department (DANE), in 2022, the export of fuels of extractive industry products accounted for 54.6 per cent of the total free on board (FOB) value of exports for that year.[19] In response to this concern, the transition towards a more sustainable, clean, and diversified energy matrix has been a critical objective and a challenge in the country's energy policy in recent years, and different measures have been implemented to promote the adoption of renewable energies and energy efficiency.[20]

In summary, efforts to diversify the energy matrix respond to primary demand, seeking to transform it by prioritizing clean energy sources with low emissions, such as solar, wind, hydraulic, geothermal, and biomass, always keeping in mind that energy security and environmental and social sustainability are guaranteed. In this sense, it is important to call for efficient and rational energy consumption.

This chapter will address the decarbonization and zero emissions approach in the Colombian energy transition from the public policy and regulation perspective. It examines ongoing efforts in Colombia to balance net zero, the diversification of the energy matrix, and the energy security challenges, as well as the consequences of the transition policies in tax matters. Finally, it will discuss the challenges and lessons learnt from Colombia in relation to energy security.

II. Balancing Decarbonization with Energy Security and Economic Diversification: The Search for a Comprehensive Approach to Energy Transition in Fossil Fuel-Dependent Economies

The processes of decarbonization of the economy and the goals to achieve zero emissions are related, and essential aspects for the energy transition and the development of a more sustainable economy that contributes to the mitigation of the effects of climate change.[21] In countries characterized by economies with a high economic dependence on fossil fuels, the steps towards a more sustainable and low-carbon energy matrix are challenging due to the

[17] Santiago Ortega Arango, Enrique Ángel Sanint, and Andrés Jaramillo Vélez, 'Energy scenarios for Colombia in the framework of COVID 19' (EIA University, 2020) <https://www.repository.eia.edu.co/server/api/core/bitstreams/4f892ef4-b86f-4c25-a358-a0e717a6f171/content> accessed 27 August 2023.

[18] Sofía Solorzáno, 'This is how the country's exports would have been in the last decade without oil' (*La República*, 30 August 2022) <https://www.larepublica.co/economia/en-la-ultima-decada-67-de-las-exportaciones-colombianas-fueron-mineroenergeticas-3435895> accessed 10 February 2023.

[19] Government of Colombia, National Statistics Department (DANE), 'Technical Bulletin Exports (EXPO)' (DANE 2023) <https://www.dane.gov.co/index.php/estadisticas-por-tema/comercio-internacional/exportaciones> accessed 10 February 2023.

[20] H Pistonesi and others, 'Situational mapping of regional energy planning and challenges in the integration of renewable energies: towards sustainable planning for regional energy integration' (CEPAL, January 2019) <http://www.repositorio.cepal.org/bitstream/handle/11362/44937/S1900910_es.pdf?sequence=1&isAllowed=y> accessed 10 February 2023.

[21] See Philipp Thaler and Benjamin Hofmann, 'The Impossible Energy Trinity: Energy Security, Sustainability, and Sovereignty in Cross-Border Electricity Systems' (2022) 94 Political Geography 102579.

multiple factors that have to be considered. On the one hand, the environmental aspects are motivated by the protection of future generations and a better quality of life for current generations, and on the other hand, the economic aspects which entail reviewing how to ensure economic stability in the face of a change in the dynamics of energy generation, consumption, and resource generation, as well as energy security.[22] However, decarbonization and zero emission policies provide a comprehensive methodology to address these challenges.

For Colombia, a combination of different factors is proposed, some focused on technical and technological changes, but also social and economic. De-escalating the use and production of hydrocarbons must go hand in hand with an increase in the generation of renewable energies or the improvement of the efficiency of energy consumption, which are currently still backup energies. Public policy measures must also be adopted to facilitate the adoption and transition to these new energy production schemes in a gradual, irreversible, and, especially, fair way for Colombians, always considering energy security.

On the other hand, technology has made it possible to make progress in offsetting greenhouse gas (GHG) emissions by eliminating or reducing the amount of CO_2 in the atmosphere. But the challenge is not only technological and economic. The implementation of carbon capture and storage (CCS) technologies, reforestation, along with policies to avoid deforestation and reduce the use of firewood, are measures that are complemented by the implementation of sustainable agricultural practices. Carbon neutrality implies the process of achieving a net zero balance between GHG emissions and those removed from the atmosphere.[23] But it must be noted that this process cannot compromise energy security.

A comprehensive methodology must be based on the complementarity of these concepts, which becomes relevant under the transversal axis of a sustainable, safe, and fair energy transition. The processes of decarbonization of economies are essential to reduce emissions in the short and medium term in order to slow down global warming, among other effects. However, decarbonization alone will not be enough to achieve long-term climate change objectives. Achieving net zero emissions or carbon neutrality becomes an essential part of the equation to control specifically those emissions that cannot normally be reduced through decarbonization processes in different sectors, such as emissions from livestock and other agro-industrial sectors.[24]

Although the processes related to decarbonization are normally focused on sectors such as power generation, industry, and transportation, measures should be implemented to reduce emissions in other sectors, such as the adoption of alternative energy sources and sustainable agricultural practices. In addition, it is necessary to address the construction of public policies aimed at achieving zero emissions surrounding domestic harvesting, by abandoning the use of fuels, such as firewood, for example, an element that is still commonly used in several territories in Colombia by several people as a fuel for cooking, heating, or electricity production.[25]

[22] ibid. See also Chapter 1 of this book.

[23] ibid.

[24] Government of Colombia, 'Colombia's E2050 long-term climate strategy for complying with the Paris Agreement' (Government of Colombia, 2021) <https://www.unfccc.int/sites/default/files/resource/COL_LTS_Nov2021.pdf> accessed 20 April 2023.

[25] DANE, 'Methodological indicator sheet. Environmental satellite account. National accounts and synthesis directorate. Per capita consumption of firewood' (DANE) <https://www.dane.gov.co/files/investigaciones/pib/ambientales/cuentas_ambientales/indicadores/cuenta-ambiental-y-economica-de-flujos-del-bosque/Consumo-per-capita-de-lena/consumo-per-capita-de-lena.pdf> accessed 20 April 2023.

The design and implementation of a comprehensive methodology to achieving a sustainable, safe, and fair energy transition, especially in economies highly dependent on fossil fuels, must have, among other necessary elements, energy security, the decarbonization of productive devices, and zero emissions.[26] The implementation of such strategies must respond to the strategic combination of these two factors. Considering these notions for an energy transition process will allow the establishment of more ambitious objectives and goals at the economic, political, and technological levels and will also generate a greater degree of certainty for the fulfilment of the goals imposed by governments. Thus, the strategic and combined use of these concepts is designed to address the challenges of climate change and reduce GHG emissions in a comprehensive manner without compromising energy security.

Furthermore, what is called a sustainable, safe, and just energy transition is a series of processes that should include not only the adoption of clean technologies, but also the implementation of solid regulatory frameworks and adequate policies to foster systemic change. A just energy transition should advance the diversification of the energy matrix, promote measures aimed at energy efficiency, energy security, and thus promote academic research and development of technologies that convert economies into sustainable models and facilitate the participation of all stakeholders in the public and private sectors, as well as mixed-economy companies.[27] This is essential to address all the socio-economic aspects of the energy transition, which are fundamental to the analysis presented in this document, such as changes in the reallocation of jobs in traditional sectors to emerging sectors, changes in fiscal aspects that help reduce economic dependence on fossil fuels, and energy security, which are some of the consequences of transition policies for the national energy matrix.

The implications of a sustainable, safe, and fair energy transition move away from being a purely technical process and become a multidisciplinary process where disciplines such as law and economics, among others, play an important role. Furthermore, if we consider energy as a transversal axis for development, the transition has important socio-economic implications, which implies that this type of process has a significant impact on society at all levels, both globally and locally.

The processes related to decarbonization and zero emissions are not unrelated to the socio-economic impacts concerning the energy transition when seeking the transformation of sectors such as hydrocarbons and mining. There is a transition in labour needs, that is, there will be a real migration of work areas. This shift to new labour areas must be accompanied by the implementation of a series of policies and programmes for training and labour reallocation to ensure a fair transition for those who are affected, generating processes and opportunities for training and job retraining.

From a global analysis, decarbonization and zero emissions also have a regional impact that will be qualified considering the greater or lesser dependence that a country or region has on the fossil fuel industry and mining.[28] Although there should be a principle of

[26] See Aleh Cherp and Jessica Jewell, 'The Concept of Energy Security: Beyond the Four As' (2014) 75 Energy Policy 415–21.

[27] See Chapter 2 of this book. See also the UNESCO, 'Declaration of Ethical Principles in relation to Climate Change' (Paris 13 November 2017) <https://www.en.unesco.org/themes/ethics-science-and-technology/ethical-principles> accessed 27 August 2023.

[28] See Chapters 18 and 19 of this book.

co-responsibility among all the countries of the world, this responsibility should be directly proportional to the damage generated by each country's emissions. The design and development of methodologies and strategies for sustainable regional development aimed at energy security and the effective and efficient diversification of the energy matrix, and the creation and adjustment of new sectors related to the new fields of work that the energy transition will bring with it, are of great importance. Major infrastructure works, research and development, new companies, and ventures in areas that are not dependent on fossil fuels and that can leverage the fiscal transformation will be required in this type of process.

In Colombia, the last two governments—for the periods 2010 to 2018 and from 2018 to 2022[29]—established, through different instruments of public policy,[30] a series of objectives and goals for the promotion of renewable energy in the country. The most notable is the goal of reaching 10 per cent participation of non-conventional renewable energy sources (FNCER) in the energy matrix by 2022 and the goal of reducing GHG emissions by 20 per cent by 2030, compared to 2010 levels.[31]

Regarding the concern about reducing the percentage of GHG emissions, Colombia currently contributes approximately 0.37 per cent, which is equivalent to 180,008.18 Gigagrams (Gg) of total GHGs emitted in the world, equivalent to approximately 49 gigatonnes (GT).[32] Therefore, although the percentage of the country's emissions is not perhaps as high as the percentages reported by other countries, Colombia is one of the twenty countries most affected by natural phenomena such 'El Niño' or 'La Niña', which generate periods of extreme drought or flooding. In this sense, it is stated that when Colombia is identified as a country victim of climate change and tends to be more affected by these natural phenomena that are recurrent and predictable, their consequences can be unpredictable and irresistible.[33]

As a result, the country has developed a series of incentives and programmes to promote auctions, financing, and tax exemptions for renewable energy projects to advance the electrification of the economy, starting with particular sectors such as transport.[34]

The Law 607 of 2001[35] was dedicated to promoting the rational and efficient use of energy and the use of alternative energies. It lists some of them, such as solar, wind, biomass,

[29] Led by presidents Juan Manuel Santos and Ivan Duque, respectively.

[30] 'By means of which provisions are issued for the energy transition, the revitalization of the energy market, the economic reactivation of the country and other provisions', among others. Republic of Colombia, Department of National Planning, CONPES 4075 of 2022 (30 March 2022) <https://www.colaboracion.dnp.gov.co/CDT/Conpes/Económicos/4075.pdf> accessed 27 August 2023; and Republic of Colombia, Energy Transition Law, Law 2099 of 2021 (10 July 2021).

[31] Carlos Robles Algarin and Omar Rodríguez Álvarez, 'An overview of renewable energy in the world, Latin America and Colombia' (2018) 39(10) Spaces <https://www.revistaespacios.com/a18v39n34/18393410.html> accessed 5 February 2023.

[32] Republic of Colombia, Ministry of the Environment and Sustainable Development (IDEAM), 'Background on the National Inventory of Greenhouse Gases' (*IDEAM*, 2022) <http://www.cambioclimatico.gov.co/gases-de-efecto-invernadero> accessed 5 February 2023.

[33] Jose Vicente Zapata and Ana Paola Gutiérrez, *Legal Regime for Climate Change and Renewable Energy* (Externado de Colombia University 2022).

[34] María Silvina Eirin and others, 'Study on energy policies for the promotion of renewable energies in support of electromobility' Ciudades Inclusivas, Sostenibles e Inteligentes (CISI) (CEPAL, 2022).

[35] Congress of the Republic of Colombia, 'Bill: "Which encourages the rational and efficient use of energy, promotes the use of alternative energies and establishes other provisions"' (Congress of the Republic of Colombia, 2001) <http://www.secretariasenado.gov.co/senado/basedoc/ley_0697_2001.html> accessed 10 February 2023.

geothermal energy, and small hydro-energy developments (does not exceed the equivalent of 10 MW). Also, the standard includes the definition and differentiation between conventional and non-conventional energies. Furthermore, Law 1715 of 2014[36] established the initial framework within Colombian public policy to promote alternative energies or non-conventional sources of renewable energy such as biomass, small hydroelectric projects, wind, geothermal, solar, seas, and green and blue hydrogen. This was complemented by an auction policy and the so-called Energy Transition Law (Law 2099 of 2021) that modernized the current legislation.[37]

In a country with a medium/low income, such as Colombia and the majority of South American countries, energy is a fundamental vector for the development and well-being of the population in general, and it is essential to overcome social gaps and reduce poverty indices.[38] In Colombia, close to 1,800,000 households still cook with firewood, which increases not only deforestation but also respiratory diseases.[39]

Considering all of the above, Colombia has made efforts to establish a network of laws and regulations aimed at addressing the wide range of energy security challenges that it faces in the energy transition. These include the quest for diversification of the energy matrix, promoting broad public participation for a just energy transition, and reducing its perennial dependence on fossil fuels that play a vital role in securing energy provision in contexts of natural phenomenon such as extreme drought or flooding that affect the energy generation. The next section examines the context of Colombia's efforts to balance net zero, economic diversification, and energy security in carbon-intensive sub-sectors of the natural resource industry.

III. Balancing Net Zero, Energy Diversification, and Energy Security: The Colombian Context

Advancing net zero and clean energy transition in Colombia will require significant reductions in current levels of GHG emissions across the entire value chain of its natural resource sector. This section discusses the key contributors to GHG emissions in Colombia's natural resource sector.

[36] Congress of the Republic of Colombia, 'Bill: "Whereby the integration of non-conventional renewable energies to the National Energy System is regulated"' (Congress of the Republic of Colombia, 2014) <http://www.secretariasenado.gov.co/senado/basedoc/ley_1715_2014.html> accessed 10 February 2023.

[37] Congress of the Republic of Colombia, 'Bill: "Whereby provisions are issued for the energy transition, the dynamization of the energy market, the economic reactivation of the country and other provisions are issued"' (Congress of the Republic of Colombia, 2021) <http://www.secretariasenado.gov.co/senado/basedoc/ley_2099_2021.html> accessed 10 February 2023.

[38] Juan Manuel Monroy, Juan Carlos Ramirez Jaramillo, and Jairo Nunez Mendez, *Dynamics of Poverty in Colombia in the XXI Century* (ECLAC, 2022) <https://www.cepal.org/es/publicaciones/47796-dinamica-la-pobreza-colombia-siglo-xxi> accessed 10 February 2022.

[39] Naturgas, 'More than 1.5 million households in Colombia still cook with firewood. Natural gas is key to the plan to change this reality' (Naturgas, 15 August 2023) <https://www.naturgas.com.co/mas-de-15-millones-de-hogares-en-colombia-todavia-cocinan-con-lena-el-gas-natural-es-clave-en-el-plan-para-cambiar-esta-realidad/> accessed 16 August 2023.

A. Electricity Sector

When evaluating the electricity matrix and its contribution to GHG emissions, especially CO_2, a point of discussion is the true percentage of participation in emissions by the electricity sector.[40] Although it is true that 20.31 million tonnes of CO_2 equivalent of electricity and heat emissions are reported, according to the Colombian electricity market manager XM, the electricity sector's emissions were 9.4 million tonnes in 2021. The remaining 10.91 million tonnes refer to heat production. In highlighting that electricity generation currently comes from 85.98 per cent renewable energy (83.63% hydroelectric), it turns out that the electricity sector contributes and is responsible for less than 5 per cent of emissions in the country.[41] This does not mean that progress should not be made in the goal of reducing this percentage of participation. So, projected solutions are moving in two ways: one focuses on reducing emissions, and the other is focused on reducing the use of coal to produce electricity.

The CO_2 emissions produced by coal contribute significantly to the electricity sector's emissions.[42] However, the phase-out should be gradual, and a transition period must be considered, which will depend on factors such as the reliability of the electricity sector and the speed of implementation of generation projects with clean sources. In this scenario, although there is a roadmap for the elimination of coal as a raw material for power generation, mainly in thermoelectric plants, it is considered that the transition period should be approximately ten years.[43] This represents the interrelationship between climate neutrality programmes and energy security because, through the diversification of the energy matrix and the transition to clean sources by building projects, if these projects have issues in their construction, such as citizen participation, and environmental and regulatory issues, energy security might be affected.

Furthermore, to increase electricity production based on other sources considered cleaner, gas should not be ruled out as an environmentally cleaner energy source compared to other fossil fuels, increasing the hydro, solar, and wind generation matrix. Although it is often assumed that the answer must include photovoltaic or wind systems, as will be demonstrated in the next section, electricity is only one part of the equation. It should be pointed out here that energy diversification is the challenge and the answer to energy security, not to depend on only one source.

In terms of CO_2 emissions, in Colombia, thermal power plants that use natural gas and coal are the main emitters of GHGs in the Colombian electricity sector.[44] But, as anticipated,

[40] United Nations Environment Program (UNEP), 'Emissions Gap Report 2022: The Closing Window—Climate crisis calls for rapid transformation of societies' (UNEP, 27 October 2022) <https://www.unep.org/emissions-gap-report-2022> accessed 10 February 2023.

[41] XM (n 2).

[42] Ministry of Mines and Energy (MME), 'Coal mining in Colombia. Transforming the future of the industry' (MME, 2021) <https://www.minenergia.gov.co/static/mineriaco/src/document/documento%20carbon.pdf> accessed 10 July 2023.

[43] Unidad de Planeación Minero-Energética (UPME), 'Indicative Plan for the Expansion of Energy Generation and Transmission 2020–2034. Reference Expansion Plan Generation: Transmission 2020–2034' (UPME, 2021) <http://www.upme.gov.co/Docs/Plan_Expansion/2020/Volumen1_Plan_Expansion_Generacion_Transmision_2020_2034_Final.pdf> accessed 27 August 2023.

[44] Jaime Arias Restrepo and Laura Stefania Varela, 'Clean Energy and Its Social Access in Colombia Sustainable Development Goals (SDG)' in Luis Ferney Moreno (ed) and Carlos Villanueva (coord), *Ibero-American Energy Law Yearbook-Volume II: Regulation of the Energy Transition* (Externado of Colombia University 2020).

it's only one part of the equation in the total number of GHG emissions. In 2021, 11 per cent of the emissions correspond to the transportation sector, 52 per cent correspond to activities related to land, the agro-industrial sector, crops, and livestock, 21 per cent correspond to the industrial and services sector, the mining-energy sector has a participation of 12 per cent, and the remaining 4 per cent is distributed between activities such as treatment and disposal of industrial wastewater and residences.[45] It is evident then that since the problem of CO_2 emissions in Colombia does not originate only in the electricity sector, nor can the solution be achieved with the commitment of a single sector either, since this is only one factor to be taken into account in the framework of this problem. Therefore, this is another challenge related to climate neutrality that might impact energy security.

The use of fuel fossil fuels such as coal and oil has been substantially reduced over the past century due to the greater availability and simplicity of natural gas production, compared to other gas production processes such as biogas. The natural gas industry, consequently, has become a bastion and support for the production of goods and services such as electricity, fertilizers, steel, food, and essential human activities such as mobility, cooking, and heating.[46] For this reason, taking into account the availability of the resource, as well as all the ongoing efforts to promote its massive use, natural gas is seen as a safer and more environmentally friendly option that could impact energy security despite associated challenges.

Based on the foregoing, and without ignoring the potential of hydroelectricity, natural gas should continue to be exploited, while the development of non-conventional renewable generation projects should be increased by more than 70 per cent. Such diversification of the energy mix could by 2034 result in an electricity generation matrix that has a percentage of approximately 45 per cent generation of solar and wind in onshore and offshore plants, as well as advancing by leaps and bounds as required, the elimination of firewood consumption.[47]

In summary, there is a clear interrelationship between climate neutrality programmes and energy security, and there are challenges related to climate neutrality that could impact energy security, such as those mentioned above.

B. Contribution of the Mining Sector to CO_2 Emissions and Coal Exports

With respect to the mining sector, it should be noted that Colombia's mineral production includes coal (thermal, metallurgical, and anthracite), emeralds, nickel ore, iron, copper, precious metals such as gold, silver, and platinum, and materials for mining construction. According to the information reported by the National Mining Agency (ANM), coal represents 54 per cent of exports, followed by gold and precious metals with 37 per cent, ferronickel with 6 per cent, and emeralds with 1 per cent.[48]

[45] Asociación Nacional de Empresarios de Colombia (ANDI), 'A low carbon footprint: the new competitiveness' (ANDI 2022) < https://www.andi.com.co/Uploads/01_Cartilla%20CO2%20Andi_Español%20N11.pdf> accessed 27 August 2023.

[46] Promigas, 'Report of the Natural gas sector' (Promigas, 2022) <https://www.promigas.com/InformeSectorGas2022/Paginas/default.aspx> accessed 27 August 2023.

[47] UPME, Plan for the Expansion of Energy Generation and Transmission (n 43).

[48] National Mining Agency (ANM), 'Colombia has unlimited export potential to international markets': President of ANM' (ANM, 21 April 2021) <https://www.anm.gov.co/?q=colombia-tiene-un-potencial-de-exportacion-ilimitado-hacia-los-mercados-internacionales#:~:text=de%20la%20ANM-,"Colombia%20ti

As indicated by the Colombian Mining Association (ACM)[49] in 2022, mining had a record value in exports, increasing by 52 per cent compared to the value of 2021, representing up to US$20.387 million. Thus, the contribution of exports at the national level during that year was 36 per cent product of coal, gold, coke, and nickel.[50] Colombia currently has one of the largest open-pit coal mines in the world, which has made it the world's leading exporter of thermal coal. In 2022, Colombia exported more than 46 million tonnes of coal, and this represents between 15 to 20 per cent of the country's mining GDP and between 1.5 to 2 per cent of the national GDP.[51] It was estimated that in 2023 coal would reduce its share in terms of production from a historical production of 90 million tonnes per year to a production calculated between 68 and 70 million tonnes per year, and the operations of other minerals such as gold, nickel, and copper.

Coal has historically been an important source of carbon dioxide emissions, but, as previously mentioned, it is not the only source of energy or the activity that generates the most emissions. Although deforestation happens to be the activity that contributes the most to the emissions of GHGs in Colombia each year, about 2 per cent of the country's total CO_2 emissions are related to coal mining activity.[52]

On this path, the mining sector in Colombia has been undergoing a transformation process to reduce its GHG emissions and adopt practices that allow the country's productive apparatus to adapt, based on a long-term climate strategy.[53] This reduces the risks associated with climate change, making the industry work with sustainability criteria and the consequences these policies could have on energy security.[54] Among the goals to which the country has committed, the most significant is aimed at reducing the country's GHG emissions by 51 per cent by 2030, compared to the emission levels reported in 2010.[55] Thus, it is expected that, as a result of the transformation processes in the mining sector, it will contribute to this effort and to the achievement of the proposed goals without compromising energy security.

Thermal coal is Colombia's main mining export and is an important source of economic activity and tax revenues, especially in the regions of Cesar and La Guajira. The demand for thermal coal in Colombia will have a direct territorial impact on these regions, both of

ene%20un%20potencial%20de%20exportación%20ilimitado%20hacia%20los%20mercados,Business%202020%20del%20Banco%20Mundial> accessed 10 February 2023.

[49] Colombian Mining Association (ACM), 'Mining exports reach record in 2022' (*ACM Blog*, 20 February 2023, updated) <https://www.acmineria.com.co/blog-minero-14/> accessed 25 February 2023.

[50] DANE, 'Exports Information June 2023' (DANE, 2023) <https://www.dane.gov.co/index.php/estadisticas-por-tema/comercio-internacional/exportaciones> accessed 25 February 2023.

[51] Amanda Vargas Prieto and Javier García Estévez, 'The Impact of the Mining-Energy Sector on the Social Development of the Regions: In the Case of Catatumbo, Colombia' in Hugo Fernando Guerrero and others (eds), *Studies on Environment and Sustainability: A View from Colombia* (Universidad Santo Tomás.2018).

[52] ANDI, 'A low carbon footprint' (n 45).

[53] Daniela Aguilar, Milton Fernando Montoya, and Luz Madeleine Muñoz Andrade, 'The Mining and Energy Industry in Colombia: A 30-Year Overview' (2022) 40(4) Journal of Energy & Natural Resources Law <https://www.tandfonline.com/doi/full/10.1080/02646811.2022.2128000> accessed 10 February 2023.

[54] Republic of Colombia, 'Colombia's long-term climate strategy E2050 to comply with the Paris Agreement' (Republic of Colombia, 2021) < https://unfccc.int/sites/default/files/resource/COL_LTS_Nov2021.pdf> accessed 10 February 2023.

[55] Asociación Ambiente y Sociedad, 'Greenhouse gas reductions in Colombia: report on the mining and energy and transportation sectors, 2020–2022' (Asociación Ambiente y Sociedad, 2022) <https://www.ambienteysociedad.org.co/wp-content/uploads/2022/11/Reducciones-de-gases-de-efecto-invernadero-en-Colombia-2.pdf> accessed 14 February 2023.

which are highly dependent on the coal industry, as 38 per cent and 35 per cent of the GDP of these regions, respectively, is generated by mining, and is also an important source of direct and indirect employment.[56]

In addition, global demand for thermal coal has declined in recent years due to growing concern about climate change and the adoption of stricter policies on the use of fossil fuels.[57] However, the figures reported in 2022 highlight Colombia as one of the five countries with the highest exports of coal with low ash content and low sulphur dioxide emissions and with one of the largest proven reserves of anthracite coal and bituminous coal in Latin America.[58]

The situation is explained by the need to diversify global supply sources, worldwide, due to the rapid recovery of the Chinese economy, the conflict between Russia and Ukraine, and the consequences for various European countries, in addition to the fact that both the United States and China have increased their coal imports in the short term. This was reflected in higher coal prices in sales to China, Japan, countries of the former Soviet Union, and Europe. Additionally, the country did not assume any commitment at COP26 and COP27 regarding coal production. The commitments undertaken are to reduce CO_2 emissions by 51 per cent by 2030, combat deforestation, and achieve carbon neutrality by 2050.

In any case, the Colombian mining sector has faced challenges in the commercialization of its coal production, which has had serious implications for the profitability of mining companies as well as for their tax contributions and the national and regional economy of those regions and municipalities with mining activity.[59] In line with the rest of the productive sectors, the goals established by the Colombian government, and the commercial and fiscal situation of products derived from mining, mining companies have begun to explore more sustainable alternatives for their production processes, such as the production of coal with low GHG emissions and investment in new technologies in renewable energies.[60]

There is a commitment not only from the Colombian government but also from the mining industry to meet goals. These commitments can be met by leveraging a series of public policies to encourage the adoption of cleaner technologies in the mining sector and promote economic diversification in mining regions,[61] which, as a direct effect, will reduce the sector's share of emissions and have an impact on business and research strategies. For example, the impact can be seen through the analysis of the transition feasibility of the

[56] Silvio López and Fernando Patzy, *Thermal Coal in Colombia: implications for the economy of La Guajira and Cesar* (Natural Resource Governance Institute (NGRI) 2021).

[57] Paola Yanguas Parra and others, 'The decline of coal and the need for a just transition in Colombia' (Stockholm Environment Institute, 2021) < https://www.sei.org/wp-content/uploads/2021/12/21121-ortiz-arond-reporte-transiciones-justas-la-guajira-y-cesar.pdf> accessed 14 February 2023.

[58] ANM (n 48).

[59] Yanguas Parra and others (n 57).

[60] Astrid Martínez and Martha Delgado-Rojas, 'The challenges of the Ecopetrol group and the country in the face of the energy transition' (Fedesarrollo, 2021) < https://www.repository.fedesarrollo.org.co/bitstream/handle/11445/4256/Repor_Noviembre_2021_Martínez_et_al..pdf?sequence=1&isAllowed=y> accessed 15 March 2023.

[61] Juan Sebastián Simbaqueba and Mario Freddy Martínez, 'Economic diversification at the national level and in extractive territories in Colombia: policies during the super cycle, current situation and proposals' (Foro Nacional por Colombia, 2019) < https://redextractivas.org/catalogo/boletines/la-diversificacion-economica-a-nivel-nacional-y-en-territorios-extractivos-en-colombia-politicas-durante-el-superciclo-situacion-actual-y-propuestas/> accessed 15 March 2023.

thermal coal industry for the production of blue hydrogen in Colombia through the gasification of coal.

Analysing the production of hydrogen from coal and the possibilities of carbon capture, storage, and use in these projects could provide an efficient solution to reducing emissions, decarbonizing the economy, and transforming the Colombian mining sector, and it can also contribute to energy security.[62] Currently, coal mined in Colombia is not only used for thermal power generation.[63] Of the exports, 1.9 million tonnes are from the metallurgical sector and 4.4 million tonnes from the coke industry.[64] This makes coal a source for industry and the generation of another type of energy, cleaner in terms of GHG emissions.[65]

It should also be noted that coal plays a very important role not only in the social and economic aspects of its production, but also in the Colombian energy matrix. As noted earlier, Colombian coal is used for thermal power generation, providing energy security to the Colombian energy matrix in the context of natural phenomena that could affect the main source of energy production—hydroelectric power plants.

Other sources that provide energy security to the Colombian energy matrix are: (1) oil, which is important because of its exports and fiscal revenues it provides, but also its supply and satisfaction of energy needs in the same context of coal; and (2) hydrocarbons, especially gas which provides reliable energy generation. This is explained by the high dependence on hydric resources where there are climatic variables and phenomena that could affect supply and, therefore, energy security. This is where the resources of the extractive industries come in to supply and guarantee energy security.

IV. Legal Approaches to the Challenges: Progress and Lessons Learned

This section evaluates emerging net zero and clean energy transition legislation and policies aimed at promoting diversification and decarbonization in Colombia's natural resource sector. It reflects on progress made and the challenges that remain.

A. Policy and Regulation to Reduce Co_2 Emissions and Advance Carbon Neutrality

The reduction of GHG emissions for the coming decades poses challenges in the fields of innovation and technology to find possible solutions that contribute to achieving carbon neutrality. In Colombia, to reduce CO_2 emissions, it is necessary to move towards carbon neutrality, considering the country's fiscal dependence on the resources from the mining-energy sector, for which it is necessary to implement a series of policies and regulations to promote the adoption of sustainable practices in all sectors of the economy.[66]

62 Fenalcarbón, 'The Colombian coal chain' (*Portafolio*, 13 March 2023) <https://www.portafolio.co/contenido-patrocinado/la-cadena-del-carbon-colombiano-579835> accessed 15 March 2023.

63 ibid 60.

64 ibid.

65 ibid.

66 Diana Vela-Almeida, Mauricio León, and José Luis Lewinsohn, *Sustainability Indicators in Metal Mining* (CEPAL, 2021).

Through Law 164 of 1994, Law 629 of 2000, and Law 1844 of 2017, the United Nations Framework Convention on Climate Change was ratified, and the Kyoto Protocol and the Paris Agreement were approved, respectively.[67] Law 2169 of 2021, known as the Climate Action Law, creates minimum measures in the short, medium, and long term that are expected to allow the country to achieve carbon neutrality by 2050.[68] Resolution 40807 of 2018 adopts the Comprehensive Management Plan of Sectoral Climate Change (PIGCCS) of the energy mining sector.[69]

Regarding the regulations that promote the incorporation of renewable energies, there are Law 697 of 2001,[70] Law 1715 of 2014[71] on the incorporation of non-conventional sources of renewable energies, Law on Electric Mobility 1964 of 2019,[72] Law 2099 of 2021[73] on energy transition, and Law 2128 of 2021[74] through which the supply, continuity, reliability, and coverage of fuel gas in Colombia is promoted.

Some relevant resolutions are Resolution 41286 of 2016,[75] Program for the Rational Use of Energy (PROURE), Resolution 849 of 2022,[76] which establish the guidelines for the formulation and implementation of Comprehensive Territorial Climate Change Management

[67] Congress of the Republic of Colombia, 'Bill: "Approving the 'United Nations Framework Convention on Climate Change', adopted in New York on May 9, 1992,"' (Congress of the Republic of Colombia, 1994) <http://www.secretariasenado.gov.co/senado/basedoc/ley_0164_1994.html> accessed 10 February 2023.

Congress of the Republic of Colombia, 'Bill: "Approving the 'Kyoto Protocol to the United Nations Framework Convention on Climate Change', done in Kyoto on December 11, 1997"' (Congress of the Republic of Colombia, 2000) <https://www.minambiente.gov.co/wp-content/uploads/2022/01/2.-Ley-629-de-2000.pdf> accessed 10 February 2023.

Congress of the Republic of Colombia, 'Bill: "Approving the 'Paris Agreement', adopted on December 12, 2015, in Paris, France"' (Congress of the Republic of Colombia, 2017) <http://www.secretariasenado.gov.co/senado/basedoc/ley_1844_2017.html> accessed 10 February 2023.

[68] Congress of the Republic of Colombia, 'Bill: "Whereby the low carbon development of the country is promoted through the establishment of minimum goals and measures in terms of carbon neutrality and climate resilience and other provisions are enacted."' (Congress of the Republic of Colombia, 2021) <http://www.secretariasenado.gov.co/senado/basedoc/ley_2169_2021.html> accessed 10 February 2023.

[69] Ministry of Mines and Energy, 'Resolution: "adopting the integrated climate change management plan for the mining and energy sector—PIGCC"' (Ministry of Mines and Energy, 2018) <https://www.pigccme.minenergia.gov.co/public/assets/files/1_res_40807_2018.pdf> accessed 10 February 2023.

[70] Congress of the Republic of Colombia, 'Bill: "Which encourages the rational and efficient use of energy, promotes the use of alternative energies and establishes other provisions"' (Congress of the Republic of Colombia, 2001) (n 35).

[71] Congress of the Republic of Colombia, 'Bill: "Whereby the integration of non-conventional renewable energies to the National Energy System is regulated"' (n 37).

[72] Congress of the Republic of Colombia, 'Bill: "Whereby the use of electric vehicles is promoted in Colombia and other provisions are issued"' (Congress of the Republic of Colombia, 2019) <http://www.secretariasenado.gov.co/senado/basedoc/ley_1964_2019.html> accessed 10 February 2023.

[73] Congress of the Republic of Colombia, 'Bill: "Whereby provisions are issued for the energy transition, the dynamization of the energy market, the economic reactivation of the country and other provisions are issued"' (n 38).

[74] Congress of the Republic of Colombia, 'Bill: "Whereby it promotes the supply, continuity, reliability and coverage of fuel gas in the country"' (Congress of the Republic of Colombia, 2021) <http://www.secretariasenado.gov.co/senado/basedoc/ley_2128_2021.html> accessed 10 February 2023.

[75] Ministry of Mines and Energy, 'Resolution: "Whereby the Indicative Action Plan 2017–2022 is adopted for the development of the Rational and Efficient Energy Use Program (Proure), which defines indicative energy efficiency objectives and goals, sectorial actions and measures and base strategies for the fulfillment of goals, and other provisions are adopted in this regard"' (Ministry of Mines and Energy, 2016) <https://www.cancilleria.gov.co/sites/default/files/Normograma/docs/resolucion_minminas_41286_2016.htm> accessed 10 February 2023.

[76] Ministry of Environment and Sustainable Development, 'Resolution: "Whereby the Guide for the formulation and implementation of the Integrated Territorial Climate Change Management Plans—PIGCCT is established"' (Ministry of Environment and Sustainable Development, 2022) <https://www.minambiente.gov.co/wp-content/uploads/2022/08/Resolución-0849-de-2022.pdf> accessed 10 February 2023.

Plans—PIGCCT and Resolution 0552 of 2022,[77] which implement the operation of the Study Commission for the Promotion and Development of Carbon Markets in Colombia. As background, there are the development plans for the periods between 2010 to 2014, 2014 to 2018, and 2018 to 2022, and at the time of writing, there is the bill of the national development plan (NDP) from 2022 to 2026, 'Colombia world power of life'.[78]

Additionally, the 2050 Strategy is a state policy that has served to guide actions in the country, but also in the territories and by sectors for the fulfilment of the proposed goals based on long-term sectoral and territorial planning to build a climate-resilient future in Colombia, while constituting a long-term planning exercise.[79]

Regarding the Draft Law of the National Development Plan,[80] this establishes that in order to comply with the objective of productive transformation and internationalization and climate action: for which it is proposed to use the financial surpluses of coal and oil to make an energy transition that leads the country towards a green economy, add 2,000 MW of capacity based on non-conventional sources of renewable energy, reduce deforestation, promote sustainable mobility, and diversify exports to reduce the dependence that currently exists on those reported by the energy mining sector, without compromising energy security.

In accordance with the country's main obligations to reduce GHG emissions and adopt measures to adapt to the adverse effects of climate change, progress has been made in terms of public policies and regulations. However, there is a need for greater regulatory coherence in the design and implementation of such regulations. A regulatory improvement methodology that is reflected in an adequate regulatory impact analysis and promotes innovation that allows not only for the energy transition to renewable sources but also the transition from economic dependence on fossil fuels will be essential. This process should balance an irreversible but gradual transition, in which public policy does not affect the energy supply.

Some of the regulatory challenges that Colombia faces to achieve carbon neutrality by 2050 include: first, the challenge related to environmental regulation. Based on an adequate regulatory inventory of GHG-intensive sources, coherent and integrated regulation must be established to advance the Comprehensive Sectoral Climate Change Management Plan (PIGCCS) of the mining-energy sector, and in the creation and implementation of other sectoral management plans, such as in the transportation sector.[81]

A second challenge is related to carbon taxes and fees, which should be focused on incentivizing the reduction of emissions and the adoption of more sustainable practices in their production processes. However, it is cautious with this type of measure since such practices

[77] Ministry of Environment and Sustainable Development, 'Resolution: "Implementing the operation of the Study Commission for the Promotion and Development of Carbon Markets in Colombia"' (Ministry of Environment and Sustainable Development, 2022) <https://www.minambiente.gov.co/wp-content/uploads/2022/05/Resolucion-0552-de-2022.pdf> accessed 10 February 2023.

[78] Senate of the Republic of Colombia, 'Bill: "Whereby the national development plan 2022–2026 'Colombia world power of life' is issued"' (Congress of the Republic of Colombia 2023) <https://www.senado.gov.co/index.php/documentos/senado-prensa/6892-proyecto-de-ley-pnd-2022-2026-articulado/file> accessed 10 February 2023.

[79] The Ministry of Environment and Sustainable Development (MESD), the National Planning Department (DNP), and the Foreign Ministry, with the support of the government of France, lead the strategy formulation process and follow the guidelines defined in the Roadmap approved by the Intersectoral Commission on Climate Change (CICC) (September 2019).

[80] Senate (n 79).

[81] Economic Commission for Latin America and the Caribbean (ECLAC), 'Science, technology and innovation: cooperation, integration and regional challenges' (ECLAC, 2022).

must respond to a methodological study of the sector and do not provide incentives to pay for pollution, on the contrary, they discourage contamination.[82]

Third, it is important to promote sustainable agriculture because 52 per cent of the emissions in Colombia correspond to activities related to land, the agro-industrial sector, crops, and livestock. Therefore, it is necessary to reduce these emissions, and sustainable agricultural practices, such as organic farming and agroforestry, should be encouraged,[83] always bearing in mind the characteristics of the territory.

Fourth, it is crucial to promote sustainable transport because 11 per cent of emissions relate to the transport sector, which makes this sector a significant contributor to GHG emissions. Sustainable transport practices must be regulated, such as the use of electric vehicles (EVs) and bicycles and the electrification of public transport.[84]

Fifth, it must be considered that fostering highly productive alternative industries makes a progressive change, but one that will surely allow us to reduce and change the financial dependence of the mining-energy sector.[85] Companies must be able to assume the tax burden that is currently assumed by the mining and energy sector.

Sixth, it is essential to promote the industrial factor around reforestation and ecosystem restoration to encourage the generation of industry and to generate business models in reforestation and environmental restoration processes.

Seventh, a system of environmental labelling for products and services must be established. An essential aspect of an environmental labelling system of a good or service is to fulfil its communicative function that it is representative of the user of the good and service, that is, the consumer.[86] Eight, it is necessary to establish and monitor long-term GHG emission reduction targets in accordance with international agreements.

Finally, it is necessary to strengthen the existing regulation that allows the coexistence of sources and advances in different low-carbon environmentally sustainable technologies (ESTs). For example, it is important to strengthen investments in green hydrogen, biofuels, and other technological innovations that allow for an orderly transition. In addition to advancing net zero and clean energy transition, new ESTs can also advance several aspects of energy security, such as: (1) meeting the growing energy needs of society; (2) ensuring supply and greater reliability and resilience of energy networks and systems; (3) reducing dependence on energy imports from countries with scarce hydrocarbon resources; (4) advancing a circular economy through the integrated management and recovery of domestic, livestock, or agricultural organic waste for energy generation; and (5) reducing

[82] Carlos Esteban Aristizábal Alzate and Jose Luis González Manosalva, 'Carbon Taxation in Colombia: A Tax Mechanism Against Climate Change' (2019) 22(52) Economic Semester <https://www.doi.org/10.22395/seec.v22n52a8> accessed 10 March 2023.

[83] Food and Agriculture Organisation of the United Nations (FAO), 'Towards sustainable and resilient agriculture in Latin America and the Caribbean: Analysis of seven successful transformation trajectories' (FAO, 2021) <https://www.fao.org/americas/priorities/sustainable-and-resilient-agriculture/panorama-2021/en/> accessed 27 August 2023.

[84] Fabian Maximilian Kreuzer and Gordon Wilmsmeier, 'Energy efficiency and mobility in Latin America and the Caribbean: A roadmap for sustainability' (CEPAL, 2014) < https://repositorio.cepal.org/server/api/core/bitstreams/089ed98f-ceaf-440b-a54a-96ad29fb584f/content> accessed 27 August 2023.

[85] ANDI, 'Strategy for a new industrialization II: Colombia, a country of opportunities' (ANDI, 2017) <https://www.andi.com.co/Uploads/estrategia-para-una-nueva-industrializacion-ii.pdf> accessed 15 March 2023.

[86] María Jesús Agost Torres, 'Representativeness of environmental labelling according to their design features' (24th International Congress on Project Management and Engineering, 10 July 2020) <http://www.dspace.aeipro.com/xmlui/bitstream/handle/123456789/2483/AT03-058_20.pdf?sequence=1&isAllowed=y> accessed 15 March 2023.

GHG emissions from the energy and natural resources sector through a progressive use of greener fuels with zero or low-carbon intensity, among other aspects.[87] These factors show the need for research and clean technology entrepreneurship as an essential bedrock for advancing the clean energy transition.

The issues described in this chapter illustrate the need for an integrated approach that leverages decarbonization and clean energy transition as a tool for economic diversification and energy security.[88] For countries such as Colombia, which are dependent on mining-energy activities, the road to carbon neutrality must take advantage of the structural advantages to reduce emissions, promote energy and economic diversification, while also transforming tax regimes to improve revenue generation needed to finance the transition process.

B. Transition or Transformation Process in Tax Matters

Currently, the mining-energy sector is significant in the country's trade basket; minerals and energy account for about 40 per cent of total exports, more than 30 per cent of foreign investment, 15 per cent of tax revenues, and 25 per cent of investment in the country's regions.[89]

If this scenario continues, efforts should not only focus on accelerating the energy transition but also on ensuring a fiscal transition. Substitute the tax benefits and those obtained via royalties generated in the hydrocarbon or mining value chain phases, mainly those of production and export. The government must seek a more sustainable economy with less dependence on fossil fuels,[90] which implies a gradual substitution.

This issue is related to the energy transition and the process of diversifying the energy matrix. There are security challenges associated with reducing the dependence on oil, gas, and coal, which now provide energy security as a backup for electricity generation in Colombia. Hence, the consequences of the transition policies for the national energy matrix and energy transition should be addressed, considering the importance of these sources in fiscal matters of the country.

First, or in parallel, a plan for the transition or transformation in fiscal and budgetary matters must be established; it must be implemented as stated, among other things to: (1) establish the replacement of resources from royalties from the sectors of mines and hydrocarbons; (2) strengthen other productive industries;[91] and (3) generate new exports.

This process implies a change, which does not necessarily translate into the instant dismantling of the mining-energy sector. On the contrary, both the energy and fiscal transition must be gradual, safe, and irreversible without compromising energy security, one of the biggest challenges. In this order of ideas and considering the importance of the transition processes, both energy and fiscal, it is considered that, in the case of Colombia with

[87] Promigas (n 46).

[88] Oscar Cetrángolo and Belén Fonteñez, 'Opportunities for a more sustainable and low-carbon post-pandemic recovery in Argentina: environmental fiscal policy' (CEPAL, 2022).

[89] Editorial La República, 'First you have to talk about the fiscal transition' (*La República*, 23 January 2023) <https://www.larepublica.co/opinion/editorial/primero-hay-que-hablar-de-la-transicion-fiscal-3526881> accessed 10 February 2023.

[90] José I Casar, 'Notes from the reading of the book by Ramón Carlos Torres: The hour of the energy transition' Reseña (2 February 2023) Economy UNAM 20 (58) 171–75 <http://www.revistaeconomia.unam.mx/index.php/ecu/article/view/771/706> accessed 27 August 2023.

[91] *La República* (n 89).

its developing economy, transition should start from the stability provided by the mining-energy industry and gradually migrate to the preponderance of other industries such as tourism, banking, or the development of software and hardware to name a few.

Accelerating the energy transition and fiscal transformation has a cost that, as previously indicated, must be leveraged by the hydrocarbon and mining sectors, and their contributions to the Colombian economy. On the other hand, a policy that suspends the activity of exploration and/or exploitation of gas, oil, and/or coal precipitously and that does not respond to a gradual process not only risks energy security analysed from the perspective of self-sufficiency and energy sovereignty.

A policy that abandons an available resource on which the country currently continues to depend, represents a high risk to the country's fiscal sustainability, in terms of its development and its economic growth,[92] in addition to influencing foreign investment and annulling the process of orderly fiscal transition and compromising energy security through a reliable supply of energy, considering the resources that the country has. The consolidation of a new productive sector not only needs resources but also requires confidence from investors and legal certainty, messages that go against this type of policy.

This transition process or fiscal migration should promote investment diversification, not only to renewable energies such as solar and wind energy but also to other productive sectors that can fiscally substitute revenues originating from mining, oil, and gas. Diversification of investments can help to reduce dependence on hydrocarbons and mining and promote a more sustainable economy.[93] Public policies must be structured so as to encourage investment in the different sectors, accompanied by tax incentives and subsidies that can help promote the fiscal transition.

The tax revenue model of the mining-energy industry in countries like Colombia is used for a multiplicity of social, infrastructure, and development projects, among others. This source of resources for the state in an eventual decarbonization process must be replaced or substituted by one or more other sectors that assume this tax burden, but during the transition, taxes and fees on the use of fossil fuels can be implemented so that energy security is not compromised.[94] This is aimed, on the one hand, at discouraging the use of fuels and, on the other, at replacing direct taxes for the exploration and exploitation of hydrocarbons and mining.

In addressing this issue, there are a few factors to consider, such as the reliability of hydrocarbons and coal in the energy-generation process and promoting efficiency and energy security through incentives that help to improve the non-profit energy system. Only generation from consumption, as well as consolidating energy efficiency processes[95] and other initiatives that tend to generate efficiency in the electrical system, can generate a reduction in energy demand and have the indirect result of favouring fiscal transition processes.

Another factor to consider for the tax transition is that related to education and public awareness. Education programmes and awareness campaigns can help to create a sense of support and social responsibility towards the fiscal transition.

[92] Ibid.

[93] Aron Atteridge and Claudia Strambo, 'Seven principles for a just transition towards a low carbon economy' (Stockholm Environment Institute (SEI], 2021).

[94] Carlos Fernando Alkaid Castro Hernández and others, 'Elasticities of Fossil Fuels in Mexico' (2022) 19(57) Economy UNAM <http://www.revistaeconomia.unam.mx/index.php/ecu/article/view/746> accessed 27 August 2023.

[95] Gloria Alicia Fuentes Roldán, 'Energy security during the transition to low carbon energy production: the case of Mexico' (National University of Remote Education Spain 2020).

This section provided some insights into the tax consequences of transition policies in the energy matrix to achieve carbon neutrality. It noted that the transition should consider fossil fuels' reliability in the energy matrix, providing energy security. It should be done without substituting the revenues obtained via royalties for the exploitation of the mining sector.

V. Conclusion

Fossil fuel-dependent economies face a number of energy security challenges and decisions in their efforts to reduce dependence on carbon-intensive natural resources such as oil and coal, achieve economic diversification, and advance a just and inclusive energy transition. The economic dependence of states such as Colombia on the income from the mining and hydrocarbon sector is a variable that must be considered in the energy transition equation and the decarbonization of the economy. Otherwise, the social and economic development of the country would be affected.

Colombia is moving forward in the energy transition process by diversifying its energy matrix and increasing the incorporation of non-conventional renewable energy sources for electricity generation. However, a structural change in the energy generation model of countries such as Colombia requires a holistic and coherent regulatory process that leverages the energy transition to advance progress on other sustainability issues such as the environment and a circular economy, fiscal reforms to tax and royalties, sustainable agriculture, sustainable transport, alternative industries, the emissions trading system, clean technology entrepreneurship, promotion of an industrial factor around reforestation, ecosystem restoration, nature-based solutions, and an environmental labelling system, as well as establishing and enforcing clear GHG reduction objectives across the entire natural resource sector value chain.

The use of so-called green gases, or low-carbon intensity, as well as natural gas and green hydrogen, will play crucial roles during the energy transition. Using cleaner fuels, such as natural gas or green hydrogen, which have low or zero emissions, can help to speed up the transition process and ensure energy security.

Finally, a progressive and fair fiscal transition process must be guaranteed. The substitution of fossil fuels for low-emission fuels, which generate a lower carbon footprint, is a variable that must be accompanied by the incorporation of non-conventional sources of renewable energy. It must be accompanied by the consolidation of innovative business models related to energy. The substitution of fiscal resources, and the generation of sources of income for social development and infrastructure, must be considered.

In the equation of energy transition in the path of net zero vs energy diversification in a country highly dependent on fossil fuels, many factors should be considered. This chapter has addressed the regulation and policies adopted that aim to diversify the Colombian energy matrix and achieve carbon neutrality, as well as their consequences. The key is to diversify the energy matrix so that the country is not dependent on only one source. However, there are many options to consider, since some of these resources may not always be available due to different reasons, like political or natural phenomena.

The energy transition and net zero policies cannot compromise a country's energy security and supply. It must consider its resources and capacity to carry out the transition, diversifying the energy matrix in a gradual but irreversible way. A just and inclusive energy transition should guarantee among other things, energy security, energy efficiency, foreign investment, legal certainty, and fiscal security.

9

Extractive Justice and the Net Zero Transition

Some African Perspectives

Hanri Mostert and Lindsay Taylah Moses

I. Introduction

To transition from fossil fuel-based energy sources to renewable energy and its required storage, the world will need more than 3 billion tonnes of minerals.[1] As discussed in Chapter 1 of this book, a five-fold rise in production is expected for 'energy transition minerals' (ETMs), that are essential to the production of renewable energy technologies, such as solar panels, wind turbines, and electric vehicles (EVs).[2] The demand for common base metals needed for energy generation, transmission, and storage will rise concomitantly.[3] Unavoidably, such an increase in demand will strain mineral governance systems, especially in resource-rich but economically poor states.[4] The history of colonization has taught us that such states become vulnerable to transgressions of their resource sovereignty,[5] especially where governance systems are already weak, as so often is the case. [6] To avoid inadvertently falling victim to the adverse human rights impacts of net zero emissions goals, African states must consider how governance of strategic mineral resources may position them best in a global renewable energy supply chain.

Drawing lessons from Zambia and South Africa, this chapter considers how countries can balance, through their regulatory frameworks, the opportunities presented by the rising demand for ETMs with the negative socio-environmental impacts and energy- and resource-intensive aspects of mining. The selected case studies, Zambia and South Africa, are African countries that meet at least two criteria: First, they are likely, based on their geology, to experience increased pressure on the extraction of their resources for the energy transition. Second, they have a custodial resource-holding model.[7] Of the various models of

[1] International Energy Agency (IEA), 'The Role of Critical Minerals in Clean Energy Transitions' (IEA, 2021) <https://www.iea.org/reports/the-role-of-critical-minerals-in-clean-energy-transitions> accessed 30 June 2023.

[2] See also Jagaban Drexhage and others, 'The Growing Role of Minerals and Metals for a Low Carbon Future' (World Bank 2017) <https://documents1.worldbank.org/curated/en/207371500386458722/pdf/117581-WP-P159838-PUBLIC-ClimateSmartMiningJuly.pdf> accessed 13 May 2023, 58.

[3] IEA, 'The Role of Critical Minerals' (n 1) 46.

[4] Ali Saleem and others, 'Mineral Supply for Sustainable Development Requires Resource Governance' (2017) 543 Nature 367.

[5] Walter Rodney, *How Europe Underdeveloped Africa* (Howard UP 1981) 164–73; Stephen Ocheni and Basil C Nwakho, 'Analysis of Colonialism and its Impact in Africa' (2012) 8(3) Cross-Cultural Communication 46.

[6] Clare Church and Alec Crawford. 'Minerals and the Metals for the Energy Transition: Exploring the Conflict Implications for Mineral-Rich, Fragile States' in Manfred Hafner and Simone Tagliapietra (eds), *The Geopolitics of the Global Energy Transition* (Lecture Notes in Energy Book Series No 73) (Springer 2020) 299.

[7] Hanri Mostert, 'Custodial Resource Holding as an Expression of Constitutional and Economic Intent' in Nico Steytler and Charles M Fombad (eds), *Constitutions, Constitutionalism and the Economy in Africa* (OUP 2022) 241–87.

Hanri Mostert and Lindsay Taylah Moses, *Extractive Justice and the Net Zero Transition* In: *Net Zero and Natural Resources Law*.
Edited by: Damilola S. Olawuyi, José Juan González, Hanri Mostert, Milton Fernando Montoya, and Catherine Banet, Oxford University Press. DOI: 10.1093/9780198925033.003.0009

resource holding prevalent in the African context,[8] custodial resource holding is the most promising in terms of responding to the increase in demand for ETMs. This model has been incorporated into several African countries' mining laws over the past thirty years.[9] As a mechanism to assert resource sovereignty, it has enough flexibility to allow just and sustainable extraction of ETMs, even as demand rises.

The following section examines the key indicators of just resource extraction and the sustainable mineral extraction for the just energy transition. Case study identification follows, based on the attributes mentioned above. The chosen jurisdictions' rule sets for engaging with the net zero goal are then evaluated. From this we collect insights for concluding suggestions as to how laws may be adapted or amended to bolster their states' ability to cater for just resource extraction and responsible supply chains in the net zero age.

II. Just Resource Extraction and the Energy Transition: Key Pillars

To understand how the pressures upon ETMs can be managed better, one must engage with the relationship between resource sovereignty and resource holding: the assertion of states' rights to control their natural resources, and the models that help guide how those resources are used, managed, and distributed. These are two key concepts discussed (in B) below. Then, the discussion proceeds (in C) to explain extractive justice as a theoretical context within which to engage with the challenges that new demands for ETMs place on resource sovereignty and resource holding. First, though, the discussion begins with the concept of ETMs in Africa.

A. Energy Transition Minerals

The energy transition and its concomitant technological advancement are directing the extraction of minerals in several ways: For one, the transition to renewable energy technologies has brought about a shift in the demand for specific minerals (eg lithium and cobalt, among others).[10] It is causing increased exploration and extraction of ETMs globally, even in regions that are not traditionally major mineral producers. Simultaneously, research endeavours to find alternative resources.[11] Further, the energy transition is casting new light on the importance of responsible and sustainable sourcing of minerals: environmental impacts, social factors, and human rights receive more attention in the extraction and processing of minerals, to promote the establishment of ethical and transparent supply chains.[12]

As a significant source of ETMs, Africa plays a vital role in relevant global supply chains.[13] The continent is rich in several minerals known to be critical to these technologies,[14]

[8] ibid.

[9] ibid 251.

[10] See Chapters 5 and 6 in this book.

[11] eg Storm WD Gourley, Tyler Or, and Zhongwei Chen, 'Breaking Free from Cobalt Reliance in Lithium-Ion Batteries' (2020) 23(9) 101505 iScience 1, 9.

[12] Marie-Theres Kügerl, Michael Hitch, and Katharina Gugerell, 'Responsible Sourcing for Energy Transitions: Discussing Academic Narratives of Responsible Sourcing Through the Lens of Natural Resources Justice' (2023) 326 Part B 116711 Journal of Environmental Management 1, 11. See also Chapter 11 of this book.

[13] Clara Galeazzi and others, 'Africa's Resource Export Opportunities and the Global Energy Transition' Live Wire Series (World Bank Group, 2020) < http://hdl.handle.net/10986/34946> accessed on 13 May 2004, 1–10.

[14] United States Geological Survey (USGS), *Mineral Commodity Summaries* 2022, 'Table 4 – Salient Critical Mineral Statistics 2021' 18.

including copper,[15] cobalt,[16] lithium,[17] rare earth elements,[18] platinum group metals (PGMs),[19] and manganese.[20] Their prevalence provides an opportunity for African states to reshape their participation in global markets and supply chains. But the extraction of such resources must be approached with care and wisdom. Extracting and processing these minerals will have socio-environmental impacts[21] and hence African states must participate in shaping the discourse and decisions around sourcing, beneficiation, and cost mitigation.[22]

B. Resource Sovereignty and Custodial Resource Holding

Endorsed by a series of post-Second World War United Nations General Assembly Resolutions, resource sovereignty is seen as a protective shield, keeping a state's natural resources from being exploited by foreign corporations or governments.[23] As discussed in Chapter 3 of this book, a state's sovereignty of mineral resources manifests, among others, in its ability to permit mining operations in its territory, both inland and in its offshore exclusive economic zone.[24] A further manifestation of resource sovereignty is in a state's ability to impose conditions controlling the method and rate of extraction, and in its exercising of decision-making powers to allocate the costs and benefits arising from mineral resource extraction appropriately within its polity.[25]

After the end of the colonial era, African states could shape their resource holding in ways that could serve the principle of resource sovereignty and affirm their ability to control extraction and use of resources to their nations' interests, intent on realizing socio-economic rights.[26] Hence there arose various models of resource holding which placed the state at centre stage, be it as owner or sole controller of mineral resources.[27] In particular, mining law reforms over the past thirty years began casting the state in the role of caretaker, steward, or custodian of mineral resources.[28]

[15] Copper (used in wind turbines and solar panels) is a crucially useful electrical conductor. Zambia is the largest copper producer in Africa. Copper deposits also prevalent in the Democratic Republic of Congo (DRC), South Africa, Namibia, and Botswana.

[16] For rechargeable batteries (especially in EVs). The DRC produces 70% of the world's cobalt. Further significant deposits prevalent in Zambia, Morocco, South Africa, and Uganda.

[17] For batteries and energy storage systems. Deposits in i.a. Zimbabwe, Namibia, Uganda and the DRC.

[18] For wind turbines, electric motors, and energy-efficient lighting. Significant sources include Namibia, South Africa, Madagascar, Mozambique, Egypt, Uganda, and Zambia.

[19] For hydrogen fuel cells. South Africa and Zimbabwe have rich deposits.

[20] For batteries in EVs. South Africa is the world's largest producer of manganese (and ferrochrome). Manganese is also prevalent in Gabon, Ghana, Burkina Faso, and Côte d'Ivoire.

[21] David P Edwards and others, 'Mining and the African Environment' (2013) 7 Conservation Letters 302.

[22] Susan Nakanwagi, 'Just Criticality: A Justice Framework for Critical Minerals Value Chains' (DPhil Thesis, University of Dundee, 2022).

[23] See Chapter 3 of this book. Also Ricardo Pereira and Orla Gough, 'Permanent Sovereignty Over Natural Resources in the 21st Century: Natural Resource Governance and the Right to Self-Determination of Indigenous Peoples Under International Law' (2013) 14(2) Melbourne Journal of International Law 1, 3.

[24] Jeremy Walker and Matthew Johnson, 'On Mineral Sovereignty: Towards a Political Theory of Geological Power' (2018) 45 Energy Research & Social Science 56, 57.

[25] Margaret Moore, 'Natural Resources, Territorial Right, and Global Distributive Justice' (2012) 40(1) Political Theory 84.

[26] Victoria R Nalule, *Mining and the Law in Africa: Exploring the Social and Environmental Impacts* (1st edn, Palgrave Pivot Cham 2019) 16.

[27] Mostert (n 7) 241–87.

[28] African Union, *African Mining Vision* (2009) < https://au.int/sites/default/files/documents/30995-doc-africa_mining_vision_english_1.pdf> accessed on 13 May 2024; Stephen E Kesler and Adam C Simon, 'Custodianship of Global Mineral Resources' in David Alderton and Scott A Elias (eds), *Encyclopedia of Geology* (Academic Press Oxford 2021) 621, 622.

This 'custodial resource holding model' (or 'custodial model' for short) can be useful as the energy transition continues to press the global agenda for strategic resources, because it offers a modality capable of accounting for all stakeholder interests.[29] States subscribing to the custodial model typically seek further-reaching beneficial outcomes to extractive projects, beyond simply awarding and administering authorizations to mine.[30] They assert their positions through constitutional, legislative, and regulatory means,[31] in which they attempt to manage environmental degradation and sanction human rights infringements,[32] as well as promote benefit-sharing, for example through local content requirements such as mandatory procurement of local labour and technologies.[33] The custodianship model expects of the state attributes of foresight, prudency, transparency, and accountability in how resources are governed.[34] It places a duty on the state to act and regulate in its people's best interests, regardless of who owns the mineral resource.[35] It also places clear expectations on the nature of the state's custodial duty, along the same lines as fiduciary obligations.[36] As such, it holds considerable promise in protecting Africa's mineral resources from further, unjust post-colonial exploitation, while promoting African countries' global participation as equal partners in the energy transition. As a new future for African mineral resource management, however, the custodial model must subscribe to the tenets of a just extractive regime (or 'extractive justice' for short).

C. The Tenets of Extractive Justice

Resource custodianship requires that the inevitably complex, polycentric interests at play in mineral extraction be dealt with through a value-based approach, informed by considerations of justice,[37] that can converse with the discourse referring to the 'just' energy transition.[38] This means, for one, that there must be rules ensuring benefit to those worst off

[29] Mostert (n 7) 241–87.

[30] Kesler and Simon (n 28) 622.

[31] A commitment to custodial resource holding can usually be found in a state's constitutional protective mechanisms and declarations specifically regarding property and the environment. It can also be seen in how licences or authorizations to mine are formulated or interpreted by the courts (eg Namibian Constitution, s 100 was interpreted as establishing a custodial model in *Rostock CC and Another v Van Biljon* [2011] NAHC 259, paras 8–10. Further Mostert (n 7) 241–87.

[32] Often evidenced in the compulsory provision of an environmental management plan detailing environmental damage mitigation, proof of community or civil society consultation, and resettlement of nearby landowners and lawful occupants who may be adversely impacted prior to a mining licence application submission. See Chapter 11 of this book.

[33] See eg Zambia's Mines and Minerals Development Act 11 of 2015 (MMDA), s 20: 'Preference for Zambian products, contractors and services and employment of citizens'.

[34] Hendrik Schmidt, 'The Legal Meaning of State Custodianship in the Context of the Mineral and Petroleum Resources Development Act 28 of 2002 (PhD, University of Cape Town 2023) 154–66.

[35] ibid 60–72 and 154–66.

[36] ibid 145ff.

[37] Hanri Mostert and H van Niekerk, 'Disadvantage, Fairness, and Power Crises in Africa' in Y Omorogbe and A Ordor (eds), *Ending Africa's Energy Deficit and the Law: Achieving Sustainable Energy for All in Africa* in Yinka Omorogbe and Ada Ordor (eds), *Ending Africa's Energy Deficit and the Law: Achieving Sustainable Energy for All in Africa* (OUP 2018) 45–70.

[38] eg Iñigo del Guayo and others (eds), *Energy Law and Energy Justice* (OUP 2020) Part III Procedural Justice, Community Participation, and Restorative Justice, 67–178 ; Raphael Heffron, 'Applying Energy Justice into the Energy Transition' (2022) Renewable and Sustainable Energy Reviews 1.

in the system. Also, the costs (and the burdens of dealing with those costs) must be shared equally.[39] We may refer to this as 'distributive justice'.

A justice-based approach to resource management, secondly, also demands the implementation of restorative practices to mitigate the negative consequences of mining while providing economic incentives through secondary activities and more complex enterprises.[40] We may see these as outcomes of 'restorative justice'.

However, a fair distribution of material goods—evening out socio-economic inequality—is not enough. Hence, thirdly, to distribute power and wealth equitably, recognition of a social group's 'culture or way of life, the dignity of their status as persons, and the inviolability of their physical integrity'[41] is crucial. We may refer to this as 'recognition justice'.

Recognition, restoration, and distribution need sound processes that drive decision-making. This is the 'procedural justice' aspect.[42] It is about the quality of treatment a person or a group can expect in their dealings with the state. Procedural justice thrives in conditions that foster impartiality, access to, and fairness of, decision-making.[43]

In a post-colonial context, and in the face of the existential threat posed by the transgression of Earth's planetary boundaries that render the energy transition critical, the consideration of cross-border consequences of net zero ambitions and efforts are also crucial for resource management. Nakanwagi[44] and Bastida[45] have both engaged with this element already, explaining it as 'cosmopolitan justice'.

A value-driven approach that places justice at the heart of custodial resource holding, thus would offer at least five tenets to address concerns of the Global South, and particular Africa, in negotiating the wheres, whats, and hows of extracting ETMs: distribution, recognition, process, restoration, and cosmopolitanism. Adhering to these tenets will make extraction of ETMs more 'just'. In the following section, we use these tenets to evaluate the state of play in Zambia and South Africa.

III. Just Extraction for Net Zero: Opportunities and Challenges in the Laws of South Africa and Zambia

Regulatory and governance frameworks need to ensure that the demand for ETMs is met without exacerbating the negative socio-environmental and human rights impacts and the energy- and resource-intensive aspects of mining. Our discussion of Zambia and South Africa's legal frameworks below highlights two points: First, that just extraction of ETMs can

[39] Najma Mohamed and Gaylor Montmasson-Clair, 'Applying a Normative Framework to Assess the Just Transition to a Net Zero Carbon Society in South Africa' in Nqobile Xaba and Saliem Fakir (eds), *A Just Transition to a Low Carbon Future in South Africa* (MISTRA 2022) ch 3, 58, 61; Sufyan Droubi, Raphael J Heffron, and Darren McCauley, 'A Critical Review of Energy Democracy: A Failure to Deliver Justice?' (2022) Energy Research & Social Science 2.

[40] Nakanwagi (n 22) 29, 147.

[41] Translator's Introduction to Axel Honneth, *The Struggle for Recognition: The Moral Grammar of Social Conflict* (MIT Press 1996) x.

[42] See eg Lawrence B Solum, 'Procedural Justice' (November 2004) 78 Southern California Law Review 181.

[43] Robert S Summers 'Evaluating and Improving Legal Processes—A Plea for "Process Values"' (1974) 60 Cornell Law Review 1, 21.

[44] Nakanwagi (n 22) 230–33.

[45] Ana Elizabeth Bastida, *The Law and Mining of Minerals: A Global Perspective* (Hart Publishing 2020) 30. See also Raphael J Heffron, 'The Role of Justice in Developing Critical Minerals' (2020) 7(3) The Extractive Industries and Society 855.

be facilitated well if states adopt a custodial resource holding model. Second, that extractive justice manifests already in the way in which custodial resource states' regulatory frameworks are designed. This does not mean, however, that there is no room for improvement.

A. Custodial Resource Holding as Primer for Extractive Justice

To evaluate how custodial resource holding advances or limits extractive justice in relation to ETMs, this chapter singles out South Africa and Zambia for further analysis. They already have custodial models of resource holding and are likely to experience increased pressure to extract, due to existing geological reserves that can feed the rising global demand for net zero technologies.[46] The subsections below set out the basic legal context in which custodial resource holding operates for each of South Africa and Zambia. Looking at opportunities and challenges in the contexts and laws of these countries lays the foundation for a closer examination of the ways in which these jurisdictions' frameworks reflect the tenets of extractive justice in the next part of the chapter.

1. South Africa

South Africa has an explicit custodial resource-holding model.[47] Its mineral resource sector is well positioned to benefit from the energy transition, given the country's significant deposits of many key minerals used in renewable energy technologies. Endowed with rich deposits of platinum group metals (PGMs), essential to fuel cell dynamism of hydrogen electrolyzers,[48] South Africa is the largest global producer of platinum and palladium.[49] It also has the largest manganese reserves in Africa and is the leading chromium producer globally, holding 40 per cent of the world's total chromium reserves,[50] and substantial reserves of other critical minerals such as some rare earth elements. It is the third largest global vanadium producer.[51] Even so, its mineral resource sector faces several challenges, including regulatory uncertainty, labour disputes, and a lack of investment in infrastructure and technology.[52]

Although still heavily reliant on coal-fired power,[53] South Africa is developing policies and regulations to support the sustainable development of its mineral resource sector. Its 2019 Integrated Resource Plan outlines a path towards a more diversified and sustainable energy mix.[54] The government has also made some tentative commitments to support the development of renewable energy and clean technology industries.[55]

[46] eg grid electrification, energy storage, carbon capture, and wind energy technology. IEA, *World Energy Outlook Report: The Role of Critical World Energy Outlook Special Report Minerals in Clean Energy Transitions* (revised version 2022) 26.

[47] Mineral and Petroleum Resource Development Act 28 of 2002 (MPRDA), ss 2 and 3.

[48] IEA, *Report: Critical Minerals 2022* (n 46) 111.

[49] United States Government, Department of the Interior: U.S. Geological Survey '2017–2019 Minerals Yearbook: South Africa' <https://www.pubs.usgs.gov/myb/vol3/2017-18/myb3-2017-18-south-africa.pdf> accessed 22 June 2023.

[50] USGS (n 14) 18.

[51] I Robinson, 'The Globalization of the South African Mining Industry' (2016) 116(8) Journal of the Southern African Institute of Mining and Metallurgy 769.

[52] Cyril Ramaphosa/Presidency of the Government of South Africa, *Media Statement* (7 February 2023) Investing in African Mining Indaba, 2023, Cape Town International Convention Centre.

[53] Victoria R Nalule, 'Transitioning to a Low Carbon Economy: Is Africa Ready to Bid Farewell to Fossil Fuels?' in Geoffrey Wood and Keith Baker (eds) *The Palgrave Handbook of Managing Fossil Fuels and Energy Transitions* (Palgrave Macmillan 2020) 261–86.

[54] GN 1359 of 2019—*Integrated Resource Plan* (IRP2019)—October 2019 <https://www.energy.gov.za/irp/2019/IRP-2019.pdf> accessed 22 June 2023.

[55] Cyril Ramaphosa/Presidency of the Government of South Africa, 'South Africa's Just Energy Transition Investment Plan', Media Statement (4 November 2022) Virtual Meeting of the Presidential Climate Commission

2. Zambia

Zambian mineral resources are considered 'property of the public' vested in the President, but its governing frameworks are implicitly custodial, being infused with language of popular benefit and fiduciarity.[56] For instance, there is reference to the prudent use, development, and conservation of mineral resources considering the 'need of present and future generations'. There are also express commitments to the values of socio-economic development, safety, health and environmental protection in the extraction and development of mineral resources, and requirements that deal with wastefulness and sustainable development, citizens' right to equitable access and benefit from mineral resource development, and local community development.[57]

Zambia has significant mineral reserves, especially of copper[58] but also cobalt.[59] Nevertheless, its mineral resource sector is currently challenged in several ways. It lacks, for instance, investment to update its old infrastructure and outdated technology,[60] which means it is not optimally equipped to extract minerals efficiently and sustainably. Even so, state ambitions extend to partaking in and influencing global ETM value chains.[61] Zambia's mineral resource sector is also not well diversified: its economy depends heavily on copper and thus is vulnerable to copper price fluctuations.[62] Additionally, Zambia is facing environmental and social challenges, as its mining industry contributes significantly to greenhouse gas (GHG) emissions, and there are concerns about the impact of mining activities on local communities and the environment.[63] Such challenges could limit Zambia's ability to meet the growing demand for minerals that will be needed to support the energy transition.

B. Extractive Justice in the Laws of Zambia and South Africa: Manifestations and Misses

Having outlined the context and challenges for both Zambia and South Africa above, this section now turns to interrogate some elements of these countries' legal frameworks that must ensure just extraction of ETMs in a net zero era. By highlighting the way in which the five identified tenets of extractive justice manifest (or are absent from) the legal frameworks,

(PCC); Presidency of the Government of South Africa, 'Confronting the Energy Crisis: An Action Plan to End Loadshedding', Media Release (25 July 2022) 9 <https://www.presidency.gov.za/content/confronting-energy-crisis-actions-end-load-shedding-and-achieve-energy-security> accessed 23 June 2023.

[56] MMDA, ss 3, 4.

[57] ibid.

[58] J Sikamo, A Mwanza, and C Mweemba, 'Copper Mining in Zambia—History and Future' (2016) 116(6) The Journal of the Southern African Institute of Mining and Metallurgy 491, 492ff.

[59] EC Savinova and others, 'Will Global Cobalt Supply Meet Demand? The Geological, Mineral Processing, Production and Geographic Risk Profile of Cobalt' (2023) 190 Resources, Conservation and Recycling 1, 4.

[60] Rita Kesselring, 'The Electricity Crisis in Zambia: Blackouts and Social Stratification in New Mining Towns.' (2017) 30 Energy Research & Social Science 94; Michael Baxter and others, 'Zambia Mining Investment and Governance Review' (World Bank, 2016) < https://pubdocs.worldbank.org/en/370251463440936494/MInGov-Zambia-report-160512-FINAL.pdf> accessed on 13 May 2024, 1, 3, 24.

[61] Paul Chanda Kabuswe/Member of National Assembly of Zambia, 'Ministerial Statement by the Minister of Mines and Minerals Development on the Government Position and Strategy for the Mining Sector' (Media Statement, 6 October 2021) < https://www.parliament.gov.zm/node/9807> accessed 13 May 2024.

[62] Accounts for over 70% of the country's export earnings; see Republic of Zambia Minister of Commerce, Trade and Industry, '*Annual Report latest 2021*' at 42; Sikamo (n 58) 491–96.

[63] A Muimba-Kankolongo and others, 'Impacts of Trace Metals Pollution of Water, Food Crops, and Ambient Air on Population Health in Zambia and the DR Congo' (2022) Journal of Environmental and Public Health 1, 2.

this section evaluates Zambia and South Africa's readiness for just extraction of ETMs. We mention examples of legal regulation in both jurisdictions to demonstrate how the ideal of just extraction is manifested or missed.

1. Procedure and Recognition

Prerequisites for eligibility and approval of extractive rights are opportune instances for states holding resources under custodianship to ensure procedural justice. Recognition justice, in addition, manifests in how the various stakeholders involved in negotiating resource extraction engage with each other. Procedure and recognition are discussed together here, as the recognition of stakeholder voices can form an integral part of a process which is perceived fair.

Publicly accessible, observable, and transparent processes that guide state decision-making in the awarding of licences allow procedural justice to thrive.[64] The fairness of the process, real or perceived, through which the state exercises its authority and makes decisions, such as allowing natural resource extraction, influences public behaviour (such as compliance or protest).[65] Procedural justice can hence yield cooperation, compliance, and long-term trust among stakeholders.[66] These stakeholders include, inter alia, government authorities, applicant mining companies, mining communities, and others engaged in negotiating benefit distribution and harm mitigation strategies of a particular extractive project.[67] Consultation obligations, especially of historically marginalized stakeholders, are also indicative of recognition justice.[68] This is illustrated by the examples of South Africa and Zambia.

South Africa's licensing procedure includes mechanisms which increase public participation and involvement, and foster transparency and accountability.[69] A prime example of these mechanisms is found in the procedures applicable to applications for rights/licences to mine. South Africa's Mineral and Petroleum Resources Development Act (MPRDA) lays down the application and granting requirements for prospecting rights,[70] mining rights,[71] and mining permits.[72] The provisions contain the formalities, imperatives for consultation with landowners, lawful occupiers, and interested and affected parties, as well as the conditions and time-frames for granting such rights. There are further provisions dealing with the sequencing and prioritizing of applications received, and the treatment of competing applications.[73] No distinction is made between different types of minerals.

[64] Tom R Tyler, 'What Is Procedural Justice-Criteria Used by Citizens to Assess the Fairness of Legal Procedures?' (1988) 22 Law & Society Review103; Rick L Lawrence, Steven E Daniels, and George H Stankey, 'Procedural Justice and Public Involvement in Natural Resource Decision Making' (1997) 10 Society & Natural Resources 577, 587.

[65] Tom R Tyler, 'Procedural Justice, Legitimacy, and the Effective Rule of Law' (2003) 30 Crime and Justice 283, 284.

[66] ibid 283–357.

[67] Lila Barrera-Hernández and others (eds), *Sharing the Costs and Benefits of Energy and Resource Activity: Legal Change and Impact on Communities* (OUP 2016) 1–21.

[68] Colonialism was marked by the injustice of historical and cultural misrecognition, non-recognition, disrespect, and neglect. Nancy Fraser, 'Social Justice in the Age of Identity Politics: Redistribution, Recognition, and Participation' (1999) 1 Culture and Economy After the Cultural Turn 25.

[69] Promotion of Access to Information Act 2 of 2000; Mineral and Petroleum Resource Development Regulations GN R420 GG 43172 on 27 March 2020 (hereafter MPRD Regs), Addition of Regulation 46C, 'Guideline for Consultation with Communities and Interested and Affected Parties' <http://www.dmr.gov.za/Portals/0/consultation_guideline.pdf> accessed 31 May 2023 (hereafter DMR Consultation Guidelines).

[70] MPRDA, ss 16 and 17.

[71] MPRDA, ss 22 and 23.

[72] MPRDA, ss 27.

[73] MPRDA, s 9.

For current purposes, the requirements around the submission of a Social and Labour Plan (SLP)[74] and an Environmental Impact Assessment (EIA) in the context of mining rights are particularly interesting. The SLP is a state-sanctioned social, environmental, and economic accountability mechanism that attunes to the needs of communities and affected persons in that potential right holders must provide comprehensive plans for socio-economic risk mitigation. The EIA is a mechanism used to evaluate the potential environmental effects of a proposed project or development. It is a systematic and comprehensive analysis that identifies, predicts, and evaluates the likely environmental consequences of a project. Together, these two mechanisms form a bridge between procedural and recognition justice, which may be key to creating the responsiveness that the regulatory framework needs to meet the demands of the energy transition when it comes to ETMs.

The EIA requires an Environmental Management Plan (EMP), or an Environmental Management Programme (EMPr) to be included in the application for mining rights.[75] EIAs require public participation.[76] The SLP and EMP must be submitted for approval and made publicly accessible in English plus another regionally dominant language.[77] The accountability that the SLP and EMP mechanisms offer is amplified by the requirement that right holders must submit annual reports detailing their compliance with their approved SLP and EMP. For SLPs, right holders must also engage in three meetings annually, with mine communities and interested and affected persons of the prospective project to provide updates on SLP compliance.[78] SLPs may be reviewed every five years, provided there is consultation with mine communities and interested and affected persons.[79] Right holders wishing to amend their EMPr, add new information, or change objectives must invite comments from interested and affected parties on proposed changes.[80]

These obligations to publish SLPs and EMPs and consult in the creation and amendment thereof create transparency and ensure information is accessible. They also imbue the process with the element of recognition justice, by requiring consultation.[81] The obligation to regularly review the SLP, in collaboration with affected persons, allows meaningful engagement (see further in section 2 that follows). Practical measures (such as language considerations) further make procedural involvement accessible.[82]

South Africa explicitly recognizes how colonial injustices of its past have contributed to systematic neglect of a host of persons and communities and created social inequity in its mining sector.[83] The MPRDA responsively includes various points of mandatory notification and consultation by right holders.[84] For instance, landowning traditional and

[74] MPRDA, s 25(2)(f); GNR.527 of 23 April 2004: MPRD Regs, s 46 *Contents of Social and Labour Plan.*

[75] MPRDA, s 24; National Environmental Management Act, 107 of 1998 (NEMA), s 24N.

[76] NEMA Public Participation Guideline in terms of. the National Environmental Management Act, 1998 Environmental Impact Assessment Regulations (NEMA PPG) <https://www.dffe.gov.za/sites/default/files/docs/publicparticipationguideline_intermsofnemaEIAregulations.pdf> accessed 22 June 2023.

[77] MPRD Regs, Addition of Regulation 46C.

[78] ibid. Amendment of Regulation 45.

[79] ibid. Amendment of Regulation 45, Addition of Regulation 46B.

[80] NEMA PPG (n 76) 7.

[81] Anri Heyns, 'Mining Community Development in South Africa: A Critical Consideration of How the Law and Development Approach the Concept "Community"' (2019) Law and Development Review 96.

[82] MPRD Regs 2020 (n 77) Addition of Regulation 46C.

[83] MPRDA Preamble.

[84] MPRDA, s 5A(c) – 21 days' notice before mining/prospecting begins; s 10 – consultation with interested/affected parties; s 16(4)(b) – application for prospecting right; s 22(4)(b) – application for mining right; s 27(5)(a) – application for mining permit; Amendment to the MPRD Regs – see definition of 'meaningful consultation'.

indigenous communities impacted by extractive activities, who practise customary law, are legally recognized stakeholders able to engage in revenue negotiations effectively in South Africa.[85] In fact, communities who own land communally under African customary law, are the only landowners whose consent must be sought prior to exploration or extractive activities.[86] What complicates matters is that attributing a particular set of people with the descriptor 'community' in the South African legislative context has often been difficult. As it is by no means easy to determine who forms part of the community and thus must be consulted and have their concerns considered,[87] objectives may become disjointed.

For Zambia, as for South Africa, environmental management planning presents opportunities for recognition and procedural justice. When applying for a licence, the applicant must also make a capital investment forecast and an undertaking for management of the environment in the mining area.[88] These mandatory accompanying attachments to the mining licence application leave room for public involvement, particularly as part of the Environmental Management Plan.[89]

Zambia's environmental management is guided by principles of public collaboration and inclusion.[90] Zambian citizens are entitled to take part in the decision-making of public officials where decisions affect the environment.[91] The responsibility for informing citizens when such decisions will be made, and how one can be involved, rest with the authoritative body making that decision. Obligations on the licence holder include, for example, maintaining accurate technical records, geological reports and surveys, and prescribed financial records.[92] These records, however, are only available for authorized officers to inspect, and not the wider public or concerned, interested, and affected parties.

Consent is a further consideration where land use is affected by the proposed mining activities. Mineral licence holders and right holders have no automatic right to use the land or surface area and thus may not exercise their rights to mine without the written consent of 'landowners, lawful occupiers, chiefs/traditional authorities'.[93] Consent must be given prior to any extractive operation commencement. [94] Zambia's Mining Licensing Committee must consider if the applicant needs to seek consent for any proposed mining area.[95] Further, where a customary community withholds consent for minerals right holders to access the land and exercise their rights, it is considered a dispute which the Director of Mining Cadastre may direct to arbitration.[96] Access agreements can also be mobilized by landowning communities to influence how mineral rights are exercised.[97]

[85] DMR Consultation Guidelines (n 69).

[86] Interim Protection of Informal Land Rights Act 1996 (IPILRA), s 2; affirmed in *Baleni and Others v Minister of Mineral Resources and Others* 2019 2 SA 453 (GP).

[87] Heyns (n 81) 95.

[88] MMDA, s 32(2).

[89] MMDA, s 32(2)(e).

[90] Environmental Management Act 12 of 2011 (EMA), s 6(f): "the people shall be involved in the development of policies, plans and programmes for environmental management;" (g): "the citizens shall have access to environmental information to enable the citizen make informed personal choices which encourages improved performance by industry and the Government."

[91] ibid s 91: '(1) The public have the right to be informed of the intention of public authorities to make decisions affecting the environment and of available opportunities to participate in such decisions. (2) The public shall have the right to participate in decisions concerning the formulation of environmental policies, strategies, plans and programmes and to participate in the preparation of laws and regulations relating to the environment.'

[92] MMDA, s 35.

[93] MMDA, s 52(1).

[94] ibid.

[95] MMDA, s 31(1)(d).

[96] MMDA, s 56(1)(b).

[97] MMDA, ss 53, 54.

The Zambian and South African laws take different approaches to ensure fair procedures, but both suffer some shortcomings. Despite the provisions envisaging consultation, for instance, the Zambian framework could benefit from clarification of the link between process and recognition. For instance, the primary provision on licensing contains no explicit obligations on applicants to consult or involve the public or interested and affected parties.[98] And although the South African process is more overtly committed to participatory decision-making to award rights, its implementation still leaves much more to be desired. For instance, the processes of aligning the content of the SLP with that of the relevant municipalities' Integrated Development Plans (IDPs) draw criticism because the mining companies are called on too late in the IDP negotiation process to allow them to make a meaningful contribution to development in their locality.[99]

In both jurisdictions, however, there is legislative awareness of the importance of a reliable process. Better measures of transparency may foster more accountable practices in the awarding of rights to mine or prospect, but only if the processes facilitate timeous and meaningful consultation. Otherwise the process, and the consultative elements thereof, may become a meaningless exercise in box-ticking.

2. Distribution and Restoration

An essential marker of resource custodianship is using the central control of the state to ensure benefits are distributed to serve the people.[100] A further marker of custodianship is found in restorative justice: implementing restorative practices to mitigate the negative consequences of mining, while providing economic incentives through secondary activities and more complex enterprises. Restorative justice and distributive justice are intertwined social, economic, and environmental dimensions of just extraction. They serve the goals of sustainable development by offering modes for operationalizing a justice-led extractive legal framework. Under both restorative and distributive justice, the adverse effects of mining are acknowledged, those who are the subject of the harm are acknowledged and informed of this harm, harm mitigation strategies are created, harm-doers are responsible for mitigation, and enforcement bodies ensure there is compliance in mitigation.[101] The sections below offer two examples: (a) local content provisions as a manifestation of distributive justice, and (b) mine closure requirements as an aspect of restorative justice.

a) Local Content Provisions as Distributive Justice

A framework ensuring just distribution of benefits must contain provisions and procedures outlining specific long-term, sustainable benefits which will accrue to the most adversely affected stakeholders in the project lifecycle.[102] Numerous benefits may stem from extractive projects, because of their large profit potential. Distributive justice is observable in guiding principles, local content provisions, benefits optimisation clauses, and royalties and revenues management. [103] Here we focus on local content provisions to illustrate how distribution justice manifests in the legal frameworks of Zambia and South Africa.

[98] MMDA, s 30.

[99] Personal conversation with a local government representative during an intergovernmental workshop hosted by the DST/NRF SARChI Research Chair: Mineral Law in Africa, 21 August 2018 (Law Faculty Research Ethics Committee, *Clearance Process Report for L0096-2018: 'Coordinating Mineral Regulation and Compliance across Different Organs of State'* (24 July 2018)).

[100] Kesler and Simon (n 28) 621, 628.

[101] Bastida (n 45) 89.

[102] Nakanwagi (n 22) 236–37.

[103] ibid 219.

The Zambian legal framework provides guiding principles applicable to all mining activities, including the development of local communities in surrounding areas, and sustainable natural resource use which benefits all Zambian citizens.[104] The legal framework empowers 'target citizens'[105] to own, manage, control and exploiting economic resources as a means to overcome income inequalities in the country.[106] Mining and minerals processing right holders must further give preference to Zambian products, contractors, and services and employment of citizens with relevant skills and qualifications throughout operations, and when purchasing products, installing infrastructure, or decommissioning facilities. [107] The MMDA also attaches obligations of skills and knowledge transfer on right holders throughout their extractive operations.[108] Applicants for large-scale mining licences must append undertakings for local business development and proposals for employment and training in their mining application, which are then considered conditions of the licence when it is granted.[109]

Similarly comprehensive local content requirements are found in the South African legislative framework, driven by explicit goals of redress, empowerment, and socio-economic transformation.[110] All mining activity must comply with the country's broad-based black economic empowerment (BBBEE) framework.[111] Various incentives, such as government contracts and licences, are offered to entities that demonstrate a high level of compliance with BBBEE in key areas. These areas of compliance include ownership of productive assets, management control, skills development, and human resources, equitable representation at all levels, enterprise/supplier development, and socio-economic development.[112] Right holders are further required to contribute levies to a skills development set-up for the mine workers' benefit.[113]

Broader local content provisions like these are important benefits capturing mechanisms for the ETM supply chains, especially for countries like Zambia and South Africa that engage in raw materials export. Prioritizing skills and knowledge transfer will become especially important for countries wishing to partake in the ETM supply chain and eventually

[104] In particular, Zambia's Citizen Economic Empowerment Act 9 of 2006 (CEE Act) and the Zambia Development Agency Act 17 of 2022. The CEE Act is incorporated by reference into the MMDA; See also MMDA, s 4: 'The following principles shall apply to the mining and development of minerals—(f) development of local communities in areas surrounding the mining area based on prioritisation of community needs, health and safety'; EMA, s 6: Principles governing environmental management (i) 'the environment . . . shall be used sustainably in order to achieve poverty reduction and socio-economic development;' and (l) 'the sharing of benefits arising from the use of the resources shall be promoted and facilitated'.

[105] CEE Act, s 2. Defined as 'a citizen who is or has been marginalized or disadvantaged and whose access to economic resources and development capacity has been constrained due to various factors including race, sex, educational background, status and disability'.

[106] CEE Act, s 2. 'Economic empowerment' is defined as 'an integrated broad-based and multi-faceted strategy aimed at substantially increasing meaningful participation of targeted citizens, citizen empowered companies, citizen influenced companies and citizen owned companies in the economy and decrease income inequalities'.

[107] MMDA, s 20(1) and (2).

[108] MMDA, s 20(2): 'A holder of a mining right or mineral processing licence shall, in the course of operations—(b) conduct training programmes for the transfer of technical and managerial skills to Zambians.'

[109] MMDA, s 35(1)(*d*)(i) and (ii).

[110] MPRDA, s 2.

[111] MPRDA, s 100; Employment Equity Act 55 of 1998; Broad-Based Socio-Economic Empowerment Charter for the Mining and Minerals Industry 2018 GN1002 GG 41934 of 27 September 2018 (hereafter Mining Charter 2018); Mining Charter 2018 Implementation Guidelines GN 1399 GG 42122 of 19 December 2018.

[112] Broad Based Black Economic Empowerment Act 53 of 2003; Broad Based Black Economic Empowerment Amendment Act 46 of 2013.

[113] Skills Development Act 97 of 1998; Skills Development Levies Act 9 of 1999.

become influential.[114] In both Zambia and South Africa, far-reaching legislative provision for fair distribution of resources are already in place. They may in principle be harnessed in authorizing the extraction of ETMs.

b) Mine Closures and Restorative Justice

The potency of restorative justice lies in the environmental protective provisions regulating land restoration and mine closure. We take a brief look at mine closures here to illustrate the prevalence of restorative justice in the legal frameworks of Zambia and South Africa.

Copper-rich Zambia, like coal-rich South Africa, faces risks of unsustainable mining practices causing irreparable harm. These kinds of mining activity produce waste and tailings which could be especially detrimental to soil qualities, food production, subsistence livelihoods, and opportunities of alternative land use.[115] In particular, abandoned mines are a threat to the health and safety of persons. When these mines lie fallow and are not rehabilitated, they pose risks ranging from pollution of ground and surface water, to fostering illegal mining activity and its concomitant social ills.[116]

Applicable environmental management principles in South Africa foreground sustainable development.[117] All rights granted under the MPRDA require environmental authorization, upfront, before the mining (or other) rights can be granted. [118] The applicants must also provide, at the outset, a Mine Closure Plan.[119] During the mine's lifetime, the mine company must contribute to a rehabilitation fund.[120] At the other end of the process, at the mine's life end, the law requires right holders to attain a closure certificate.[121] The mine's owners must then ascertain how much it will cost, determine the conditions that will allow it to be sustainably closed, provide a closure plan, and then allow the environmental authority to review and see whether a mine is fit for closure.[122] The closure certificate can only be issued if the environment has been rehabilitated. Unfortunately, however, this is easier said than done. South Africa is reported to have around 6,000 abandoned mine shafts, with almost none of them rehabilitated.[123] In 2007, the Department of Mineral Resources and Energy estimated the cost of rehabilitating these mines at R100 billion.[124] Very little has been done in the ensuing seventeen years to tackle this imperative.

[114] Mian Ajmal and Yohanes Kristianto, 'Knowledge Sharing in Supply Chain' (2010) 1(4) International Journal of Strategic Decision Sciences 44.

[115] Chipasha Mulenga, 'Soil Governance and the Control of Mining Pollution in Zambia' (2022) 6 Soil Security 1, 2.

[116] Elvis Fosso-Kankeu, A Manyatshe, and F B Waanders, 'Mobility Potential of Metals in Acid Mine Drainage Occurring in the Highveld Area of Mpumalanga Province in South Africa: Implication of Sediments and Efflorescent Crusts' (2017) 119 International Biodeterioration & Biodegradation 661.

[117] NEMA, s 24R substituted by s 8 of Act 25 of 2014.

[118] MPRDA, ss 38A and 38B. Approved EMPs are considered environmental authorization.

[119] NEMA, ss 24R and 24N; National Environmental Management Act: Regulations: Financial Provision for Prospecting, Exploration, Mining or Production Operations GNR1147 GG 39425 of 20 November 2015, Appendix 4 (hereafter Financial Provision Regs).

[120] NEMA, s 24P.

[121] MPRDA, s 43.

[122] NEMA, s 24P(3); Financial Provision Regs (n 119) Appendix 3.

[123] Human Rights Watch Report, '*The Forever Mines, Perpetual Rights Risks from Unrehabilitated Coal Mines in South Africa*' (Human Rights Watch, July 2022) < https://www.hrw.org/report/2022/07/05/forever-mines/perpetual-rights-risks-unrehabilitated-coal-mines-south-africa#:~:text=(Johannesburg%2C%20July%205%2C%202022,in%20a%20report%20released%20today.> accessed 13 May 2024.

[124] ibid.

The Zambian mining legislative framework provides precautionary environmental protection through its licensing regime. All mining activities must be undertaken in compliance with applicable Environment Plans[125] (EPs), which are considered conditions of any large-scale mining licence granted and which must adhere to specifications and practices established by national standards and guidelines.[126] These are preceded by Environmental Project Briefs (EPBs) and EIAs undertaken by the Environmental Management Agency.[127] Throughout operations, licence holders are required to submit reports on environmental compliance, and the quantity of sources of ore, discharge, or tailings.[128] However, there is no overt obligation under Zambian law to obtain a closure plan. Still, licence holders may also be required to submit additional reports, records, or information,[129] which leaves some room for achieving the same functionality as a closure plan.

Although Zambian environmental protective mechanisms are not as comprehensive as South Africa's, there are some provisions dealing with mine closure. For example, closure is only possible once application is made for abandonment.[130] Mine abandonment is possible, provided a mining right holder includes a certificate of closure and the abandonment is approved by the Director of Mining Cadastre (DMC). Within three months of mining operations ceasing, the DMC must be informed by the right holder of any details of any 'potentially hazardous substances' that are in the area and the DMC must then consult with the Director of Mines Safety (DMS).[131] The DMS may make an order for safe substance removal based on the information given.[132] There is scope for rehabilitative obligations to be attached to these certificates by Zambian authorities. The Director-General of Environmental Management may also make a site restoration order, provided there was a breach of waste management licences issued.[133] Right holders are strictly liable for the cost of reinstatement, rehabilitation, or clean-up measures where mining operations or processing causes harm.[134] However, Zambian authorities have not been enforcing environmental rehabilitation strictly, which has resulted in the end recipients of pollution (surrounding communities) suffering most. It also left government with the expensive task of rehabilitation.[135]

Critical levels of pollution have already wreaked socio-environmental havoc in Zambian communities to the point of major project partnerships having to step in to rehabilitate land and address hazardous waste build-up.[136]

Explicit rehabilitative plans and obligations on right holders, from the state (as custodian of the people and their land and biodiversity), prior to the issuing of any abandonment or closure certificates would benefit Zambia. This would also realize the goal of infusing Zambia's mining activities and mineral development with the guiding principles

[125] MMDA, s 25(4)(b).

[126] MMDA, s 25(1)(d).

[127] MMDA s 41(a); EMA s 29(1).

[128] EMA, s 35.

[129] MMDA, ss 41, 81(1)(c).

[130] MMDA, Sch I, Form XVII 'Application for abandonment certificate'.

[131] MMDA, s 74(2).

[132] MMDA, s 743)(c).

[133] EMA, s 60.

[134] MMDA, s 87.

[135] World Bank, 'Zambia—Mining and Environmental Remediation and Improvement Project' (led by CM Ingoe and SU Renner) P154683 <https://www.projects.worldbank.org/en/projects-operations/project-detail/P154683> accessed 22 June 2023.

[136] ibid.

of environmental protection, sustainable development, conservation, prudence, and foresight and preservation of future generations' needs.[137]

Looking at the situation of mine closure and rehabilitation, both jurisdictions have laws in place that should support restorative justice. However, the follow-through on these laws seems weak. Lack of implementation pertaining to closure and rehabilitation of mines and failure to ensure the protection of the environment are not in the interests of the people of South Africa and Zambia. In this regard, their custodial holding models have not yet lived up to expectations.

3. Cosmopolitanism

There is no such thing as a resource-'independent' country: not in the developing world, nor in the developed world.[138] Cosmopolitan justice acknowledges that the choices and behaviours in one part of our global system may have an effect on altogether different parts, even different regions.[139] The demand and supply of critical minerals in global value chains demonstrate this well,[140] even though the relationship at present still has the Global North demanding, and the Global South supplying.

Cosmopolitan justice focuses on the cross-border consequences and interests affected by decisions and behaviours.[141] Hitherto, the industrialized economies of the mineral-consuming Global North countries have driven trends in the extraction of ETMs. Their interests compel them to focus on the economic and industrial importance of such minerals, and the risk of supply shortages or breakdowns. They are less interested in the concerns pertinent to the developing countries of the Global South, which are far more varied and multiple, and relate to social, ecological, spatial, policy, political, technological, and economic issues.[142]

Given the lopsidedness of North–South relations[143] in the demand and supply of minerals, critical mineral-rich countries like Zambia and South Africa need imperatives guiding how these minerals can be extracted and who will carry the costs and enjoy the benefits of such extraction. Taking into account the other aforementioned tenets of process, recognition, restoration, and distribution, we posit that manifesting cosmopolitan justice in the extraction and supply chains of ETMs will necessitate further inquiry into the following: (1) integrating indigenous/traditional communities in the ETM value chain; (2) the effect of the political landscape on extraction of existing resources; and (3) the socio-cultural influences on communities surrounding ETM mining operations.

For now, Zambia and South Africa's regulatory frameworks can be assessed for how well they respond to global supply chain demands. The current trend to subscribe to 'responsible sourcing' practices, for instance, is primarily driven by policy shifts in the Global

[137] MMDA, s 4(a), (c), (d); EMA, s 6; Constitution of Zambia Act 1 of 2016, Preamble.

[138] Simon Caney, 'Global Interdependence and Distributive Justice' (2005) 31(2) Review of International Studies 389; Hanri Mostert, Cheri-Leigh Young, and Julie L Hassman, 'Towards Extractive Justice: Europe, Africa and the Pressures of Resource Dependency' (2019) 26(2) South African Journal of International Affairs 233, 236; Bastida (n 45) 179.

[139] Bastida (n 45) 7–11.

[140] Nakanwagi (n 22) 231.

[141] ibid; see also Heffron (n 45).

[142] Nakanwagi (n 22) 231.

[143] Mostert (n 138) 235; Bastida (n 45) 179.

North,[144] without sufficient thought dedicated to how exclusionary and dismissive practices will affect the poorest of the poor, and the most vulnerable members of the mine host communities.[145]

Standards of sustainability in mining should consider international benchmarks, but be infused with domestic realities. For example, poverty is often a motivation for, and precedes, artisanal mining.[146] Artisanal mining provides an easily accessible livelihood.[147] However, Global North supply chain policies, such as those excluding artisanally sourced mineral products from the value chains, are bound to affect poverty in the Global South. The yields from artisanal mining may often fail the benchmarks of responsible sourcing, yet policy shifts excluding such yields from permissible sourcing may well deprive the most vulnerable from their only remaining sources of power and income.[148] Since mining is an important poverty reduction strategy,[149] holistic and region-specific resource management is required.

South Africa is an example of a state that criminalizes those engaged in many Artisanal and Small-scale Mining (ASM) activities, on the basis of extractive methods, nationality, or licensing.[150] ASM is not thoroughly regulated in the law, and hence such activity in South Africa, taking place without authorizations to mine, is treated as illegal.[151] Moreover, unregulated ASM is often associated with gangsterism, money laundering schemes, trafficking, smuggling, tax evasion, and lost revenue.[152] Such illegal activity, undertaken alongside unauthorized mining, is perceived as a threat to the state's economy and overall sustainable development ideals.[153]

An alternative framing is offered by host states like Zambia, who bring artisanal miners and mining products into the realm of domestic mineral regulation and revenue streams, decriminalizing attempts to secure livelihoods. Their approach may be better placed to bring ASM into the global value chain.[154] However, while these states may promote legitimating artisanal mining activity, the bureaucracy and associated costs of business legitimization are formal employment barriers and thresholds into legalization of artisanal mining.[155]

[144] Consolidated text: Regulation (EU) 2017/821 of the European Parliament and of the Council of 17 May 2017 laying down supply chain due diligence obligations for Union importers of tin, tantalum and tungsten, their ores, and gold originating from conflict-affected and high-risk areas.

[145] Nakanwagi (n 22) 220.

[146] Rebecca L Pein, 'The "Formalisation Dilemma" of Artisanal and Small-Scale Mining: An Analysis with Reference to the Democratic Republic of the Congo' (PhD, UCT, 2022) 3–4.

[147] Wayne Malinga, 'From an Agro-Based to a Mineral Resources-Dependent Economy: A Critical Review of the Contribution of Mineral Resources to the Economic Development of Zimbabwe' (2018) 48(1) Forum for Development Studies 71, 84.

[148] Willemien du Plessis, 'Women, Mining and the Law' (2016) 37 Obiter 652.

[149] Nicole M Smith and others, 'Human Health and Safety in Artisanal and Small-Scale Mining: An Integrated Approach to Risk Mitigation' (2016) 129 Journal of Cleaner Production 43.

[150] Pein (n 146) 23.

[151] MPRDA, ss 5, 98(a); Mineral and Petroleum Resources Development Act 28 of 2002 Publication of the Artisanal and Small Scale-Mining Policy 2022 for Implementation GN 1938 GG 46124 of 30 March 2022 at Item 11 'Governments Policy Stance on Illegal Mining'.

[152] Richard Chelin and Naomi Tite, 'SA must dig deeper for a solution to illegal mining' (Institute for Security Studies, 25 June 2019) <https://www.issafrica.org/iss-today/sa-must-dig-deeper-for-a-solution-to-illegal-mining> accessed 22 June 2023.

[153] Pein (n 146) 161.

[154] Gavin Hilson and others, 'Artisanal and Small-Scale Mining (ASM) in Sub-Saharan Africa: Re-Conceptualizing Formalization and "Illegal" Activity' (2017) 83 Geoforum 80. Also discussion on the Zambian ASM model which is taxation-based in Gavin Hilson, 'The "Zambia Model": A Blueprint for Formalizing Artisanal and Small-Scale Mining in Sub-Saharan Africa?' (2020) 68 Resources Policy 101765.

[155] MPRDA, s 27.

Artisanal and small-scale miners need institutional support to enable them to meet domestic legal obligations, and in turn to access a wider global market.[156] Global North states can also engage in cosmopolitan and distributive justice through recognizing the interdependent relationship with Global South host nations, and the effects and outcomes that can stem from extractive projects and regulation.[157]

IV. Conclusion

The energy transition may shift understanding of what types of minerals are critical or strategic for the future of humankind and indeed the entire planet, but it should not perpetuate or entrench patterns of unfair and skewed distribution of the costs and benefits of extractive activity. However, without adherence to the mentioned tenets of extractive justice, the transition to a low-carbon future will do exactly that. In Africa especially, ridden by its colonial legacies, it is essential to ensure that the regulatory frameworks are committed to the eradication of injustice. This also applies to laws and policies that must facilitate the energy transition generally and the extraction of energy transition minerals specifically.

Undoubtedly, many of the systems that now exist will need to be overhauled to prioritize the net zero goals. Such overhaul must be mindful of the imperatives of social equity and inclusiveness, as the ideal regulatory framework is being fashioned.[158] A custodial resource holding model may in law offer a means to appoint the state as a responsible resource management institution, which in turn provides a site of accountability.[159] Bolstering accountability is especially important for African states' mineral governance, given that corruption often plagues the mineral sectors in resource-abundant states with inefficient infrastructure and poor regulatory institutions.[160]

Looking at South Africa and Zambia's regulatory frameworks and their readiness for a new age of mining for the energy transition has yielded several lessons. First, meaningful participation of all stakeholders in decision-making will be key in making the energy transition 'just'. Countries that are experiencing hikes in the extraction of ETMs would be well advised to put in place (or improve existing) strategies, including capacity development and training support, to empower and increase the involvement of the disenfranchised in governing natural resources.[161] Second, even if the ideals of distribution and restoration are expressed in law, the absence of political will or state infrastructure to ensure enforcement and implementation will render the best-laid plans meaningless. Finally, North–South relations may remain lopsided if a justice-based matrix is not embraced to redefine resource (inter)dependency around the world.

[156] Laura-Anne Wilson, 'Unshackling South African Artisanal Miners: Considering Burkina Faso's Legislative Provisions as a Guideline for Legalisation and Regulation' (LLM Dissertation, UCT, 2018) 79.

[157] Mostert (n 138) 233–50.

[158] Foreword to United Nations, 'Theme Report on Enabling SDGs Through Inclusive, Just Energy Transitions' (2021) VI.

[159] Werner Scholtz, 'Custodial Sovereignty: Reconciling Sovereignty and Global Environmental Challenges Amongst the Vestiges of Colonialism' in Koen De Feyter (ed), *Globalization and Common Responsibilities of States* (1st edn, Routledge 2013) 336–37.

[160] J Grant, W Compaoré, and Matthew Mitchell (eds), *New Approaches to the Governance of Natural Resources: Insights from Africa* (Springer 2014) 6.

[161] United Nations Development Programme, 'Environmental Justice—Comparative Experiences in Legal Empowerment' (UNDP, June 2014) 5 <https://www.undp.org/sites/g/files/zskgke326/files/publications/Environmental-Justice-Comparative-Experiences.pdf> accessed 22 June 2023.

10

Gender Justice and Net Zero Energy Transition

Perspectives from the United Kingdom and Sub-Saharan Africa

Adenike Adebukola Akinsemolu and Walters Nsoh

I. Introduction

This chapter examines gender-based vulnerabilities and risks in the net zero transition and how natural resources law and policy can address those barriers. It identifies law and policy measures to mitigate gender issues associated with the energy transition and to enhance gender justice in the global net zero energy transition.

As discussed in Chapter 2 of this book, just transition aims to ensure the fair, inclusive, and equitable implementation of clean energy transition policies and programmes in a manner that upholds the human rights of impacted peoples and communities and ensures that no one is left behind.[1] Gender justice therefore emphasizes the elimination of gender-based inequalities in the design and implementation of net zero and clean energy transition programmes.[2] For several decades, international law instruments—ranging from the Universal Declaration of Human Rights of 1948 (UDHR), the Convention on the Elimination of Discrimination Against Women (CEDAW), Goal 5 of the Sustainable Development Goals (SDGs) of 2015, to the Paris Agreement and the Gender Action Plan (GAP) under the United Nations Framework Convention on Climate Change (UNFCCC), amongst others—have emphasized the need to respect, protect, and fulfil the rights of women to equality and non-discrimination in climate action and development efforts.[3] However, as this chapter illustrates, policy approaches aimed at implementing net zero and clean energy transition fail to coherently address gender-based exclusions and environmental injustice in many parts of Africa.[4] In many countries, men remain better placed to

[1] See also United Nations Working Group on Business and Human Rights (UN WGBHR), *Extractive Sector, Just Transition and Human Rights* (2023) UN General Assembly Report.

[2] Jenny Lieu and others, 'Three Sides to Every Story: Gender Perspectives in Energy Transition Pathways in Canada, Kenya and Spain' (2020) 68 Energy Research & Social Science 101550; see also Sohna Ngum and Luisa Kim, *Powering a Gender-Just Energy Transition* (March 2023) <https://www.gggi.org/wp-content/uploads/2023/03/GGGI_GGKP_Gender_Report.pdf> accessed 19 August 2023.

[3] UN Women, 'Realizing women's rights to land and other productive resources', 2nd edn <https://www.unwomen.org/en/digital-library/publications/2020/10/realizing-womens-rights-to-land-and-other-productive-resources-2nd-edition> accessed 19 August 2023; also UN General Assembly, *Transforming Our World: the 2030 Agenda for Sustainable Development*, 21 October 2015, A/RES/70/1.

[4] Franziska Muller and others, 'Assessing African Energy Transitions: Renewable Energy Policies, Energy Justice, and SDG 7' (2021) <https://www.cogitatiopress.com/politicsandgovernance/article/view/3615> accessed 19 August 2023; see also Elisabeta Smaranda Olarinde and Hilary Okoeguale, 'Energy Transition and the Role of Women: Advancing Gender-Aware Transition in the Natural Gas Industry' in Damilola S Olawuyi and Eduardo G Pereira (eds), *The Palgrave Handbook of Natural Gas and Global Energy Transitions* (Springer International Publishing 2022).

Adenike Adebukola Akinsemolu and Walters Nsoh, *Gender Justice and Net Zero Energy Transition* In: *Net Zero and Natural Resources Law.*
Edited by: Damilola S. Olawuyi, José Juan González, Hanri Mostert, Milton Fernando Montoya, and Catherine Banet,
Oxford University Press. © International Bar Association 2024. DOI: 10.1093/9780198925033.003.0010

benefit from new technologies, programmes, and economic opportunities associated with the clean energy transition.[5]

Additionally, the workforce in the energy sector, which is driving the adoption of clean energy remains male-dominated in many parts of the world, which limits the involvement of women in clean energy transition decisions.[6] The limited involvement of women in making the decisions and policies that drive the transition to green energy has two adverse impacts on women vis-à-vis clean energy. First, the resulting net zero policies ignore women's energy needs, which differ from the energy needs of their male counterparts, yielding clean energy solutions that benefit both genders disproportionately.[7] Second, government policies aimed at ameliorating the socio-economic impacts of clean energy transition focus on fuels and products used by men, excluding household energy needs. In many countries, women are the main users of energy in households, which typically make up a significant percentage of energy usage globally.[8] Policies that exclude women from different stages of formulation and decision-making therefore yield clean energy solutions that are not gender-just. While the need for net zero is clear and incontrovertible, domestic laws and policies on net zero will need to be better aligned with international legal principles on gender justice.[9]

Drawing on lessons from South Africa, Kenya, Malawi, and Nigeria, frontier natural resources jurisdictions in Africa with publicly accessible net zero and clean energy transition policies, this chapter examines progress made, and the challenges that remain in developing and implementing gender-just energy transition policies in the natural resources sector. It then examines how recent progress in the United Kingdom in integrating gender justice in net zero policies may inform reform in the surveyed African countries. While gender gaps remain in the United Kingdom's natural resources sector, recent efforts to advance gender mainstreaming in energy transition programmes provide salient lessons on innovative approaches for advancing gender justice. In addition to the similarity of legal cultures between the United Kingdom and the surveyed countries, the United Kingdom was one of the earliest countries to enact climate change legislation, which also makes it an ideal case study in terms of accumulated implementation experience from a significant natural resources hub.[10]

After this introduction, Section II explores the links between the net zero transitions and gender justice. Section III evaluates net zero and clean energy policies in the surveyed countries and identifies gender justice gaps in their design and implementation. Section IV

[5] International Labour Organization (ILO), *Just Transition: An Essential Pathway to Achieving Gender Equality and Social Justice* (ILO 2022) 1–10; Nitya Rao and others, 'Gendered Vulnerabilities to Climate Change: Insights from the Semi-Arid Regions of Africa and Asia' (2019) 11(1) Climate and Development 14–26.

[6] See eg African Development Bank, 'Women's Economic Empowerment in Oil and Gas Industries in Africa' (AFDB, 2016), stating that in African extractive industries, 'while benefits accrue mostly to men in the form of employment and compensation, the costs (e.g. family or social disruption, environmental degradation) fall most heavily on women'.

[7] Marula Tsagkari, 'The Need for Gender-based Approach in the Assessment of Local Energy Projects' (2022) 68 Energy for Sustainable Development 40-49.

[8] Phil Grünewald and Marina Diakonova, 'Societal Differences, Activities, and Performance: Examining the Role of Gender in Electricity Demand in the United Kingdom'(2020) 69 Energy Research & Social Science 101719.

[9] ILO (n 5).

[10] Climate Change Committee, 'The UK Climate Change Act' (CCC Insights Briefings 1, October 2020I) <https://www.theccc.org.uk/wp-content/uploads/2020/10/CCC-Insights-Briefing-1-The-UK-Climate-Change-Act.pdf> accessed 19 August 2023.

highlights the need for gender-inclusive net zero policies that promote gender justice and involve everyone in their formulation, implementation, and evaluation. Section V is the concluding section.

II. Gender and Net Zero: Linkages and Pillars of Gender-Just Net Zero Transition

Advancing a gender-just energy transition and equitable access to energy resources requires the design and implementation of net zero and climate policies that advance tenets of gender justice. Three key elements of gender justice are identified in the literature as relevant in the evaluation of the policies that are driving the net zero transition.[11]

The first element of an effective gender justice framework is the need to ensure equality in the composition of the workforce that develops, implements, and evaluates net zero policies.[12] The composition of these groups typically reflects the composition of the labour force in the energy sector. Globally, employment in energy sectors and energy-related projects is male-dominated.[13] While the proportions of men to women in the industry vary by project, country, and region, the underrepresentation of women in the sector is universal and limits their involvement in all aspects of the net zero transition, from policy formulation to the realization of the positive benefits of the policies.[14]

The second element of gender justice is the consideration of the needs of different genders in the design of the policies and frameworks that guide clean energy transition projects and other net zero initiatives. Men and women have different energy needs due to their historical and traditional social roles.[15] Disparities in their involvement in the formulation of net zero policies, frameworks, and projects yield gender-blind energy policies that deny women equal access to clean energy and subsequent secondary benefits such as improved quality of life and entrepreneurship opportunities.[16] Unfortunately, social norms have long denied some population groups, particularly women in the Global South, from enjoying access to energy and the inherent limitations in their rights to the utilization of the resource are being replicated in the transition to clean energy.[17] According to a United Nations (UN) report, women in Africa and Asia are particularly vulnerable to the impacts of environmental disasters due to skewed power relations and inequitable cultural and social norms.[18] The limited access of women to resources in these regions are often replicated across all areas including access to energy, such that they often have the lowest access to

[11] Ngum and Kim (n 2); Tsagkari (n 7).
[12] ibid.
[13] Bipasha Baruah, 'Renewable Inequity? Women's Employment in Clean Energy in Industrialized, Emerging, and Developing Economies' (2016) 41(1) Natural Resources Forum 18–29.
[14] ibid.
[15] ibid; see also ILO (n 5).
[16] Phil Grünewald and Marina Diakonova (n 8).
[17] See Lola Okolosie, 'Beyond "Talking" and "Owning" Intersectionality' (2014) 108(1) Feminist Review 90–96; Johanna Bond, 'International Intersectionality: A Theoretical and Pragmatic Exploration of Women's International Human Rights Violations' (2003) 52(1) Emory Law Journal 71–186, 76.
[18] Christian Nellemann, Ritu Verma, and Lawrence Hislop (eds), 'Women at the Frontline of Climate Change: Gender Risks and Hopes: A Rapid Response Assessment' (United Nations Environment Programme, GRID-Arendal, ICIMOD, Center for International Climate and Environmental Research, Oslo, 2011) 6.

electricity and clean cooking energy.[19] Such systemic inadequate access to energy resources may persist through the transition to greener energy unless policies and frameworks that are guiding the transition reflect the need to guarantee equal access for all to clean energy.

The third element is the establishment of vulnerability assessments and responses to limit the inequitable outcomes of net zero projects. Energy justice begins with a clear acknowledgement and measurement of distributive, recognitional, and procedural injustices, which are caused by policies that are not inclusive.[20] This requires gathering transparent data on how net zero policies are impacting men and women, and how many women benefit directly from economic opportunities in clear energy sectors, such as renewable energy, ecosystem protection, or restoration programmes. Lack of statistical data and vulnerability assessments result in broadly framed energy programmes that fail to protect women from adverse outcomes such as the loss of income and shelter when communities are displaced to pave way for green energy projects.[21]

International legal instruments relating to gender justice recognize the foregoing pillars as pivotal to the development and adoption of gender-just net zero policies.

A. International Law Requirements on Gender Justice in Net Zero Energy Transition

The international legal frameworks on gender justice are found in the international legal instruments relating to climate change and clean energy transition. The Paris Agreement expressly recognizes the need for all Parties to 'respect, promote and consider their respective obligations on human rights' when taking action to address climate change, including by ensuring gender equality, empowerment of women and intergenerational equity.[22] Article 7(5) of the Paris Agreement states that all parties must adopt a gender-responsive approach to climate change.[23] The gender justice focus of article 7 of the Paris Agreement is reinforced by article 11's requirement that capacity-building initiatives related to climate change should be gender-inclusive. Together, these provisions impose a legal obligation on Parties to the Paris Agreement to place gender justice squarely at the heart of net zero and clean energy transition policies in response to the climate emergency. Similar provisions regarding gender inclusion are also enshrined in the United Nations Framework Convention on Climate Change (UNFCCC). For instance, the expanded Lima Work Programme on Gender (LWPG) and its GAP (decision 13/CP.25), which builds on the prior LWPG (decisions 18/CP.20 and 21/CP.22) and the first GAP (decision 3/CP.23), are the key decisions regarding gender under the UNFCCC.[24] The COP 18 Gender Decision also mandates

[19] Tsitsi Matekaire and Tara Carey, 'Malawi: Climate Change Is Putting Women & Girls in Malawi at Greater Risk of Sexual Violence' (Inter Press Service, 1 August 2022) <https://www.allafrica.com/stories/202208010467.html> accessed 10 October 2022.

[20] ibid 27.

[21] Damilola Olawuyi, 'Gender, Indigeneity and the Search for Environmental Justice in Post-Colonial Africa' in Carmen Gonzalez, Sara Seck, and Sumudu Attapatu (eds), *Cambridge Handbook of Environment Justice and Sustainable Development* (CUP 2021).

[22] Paris Agreement to the United Nations Framework Convention on Climate Change, 12 December 2015, TIAS No. 16-1104, Preamble, also arts 2.2 and 4.1.

[23] ibid art 7.5.

[24] UNFCCC, 'Gender and Climate Change Brief for the Adaptation Committee' <https://www.unfccc.int/sites/default/files/resource/Brief_Gender%20in%20the%20work%20of%20the%20AC.pdf> accessed 19 August 2023.

COP 22 to evaluate progress towards gender parity by UNFCCC Parties and other establishments under the Kyoto Protocol and the Convention.[25]

Other than the UNFCCC, the Paris Agreement, and the Kyoto Protocol, several international instruments also reference the need for gender justice in development efforts. Though not legally binding, article 2 UDHR provides for the entitlement to all rights of all persons without discrimination based on gender and sex. Also, article 7 provides equality before the law to all persons without discrimination.[26] The second pact on gender equality safeguarding is the CEDAW.[27] Women's rights to equality are recognized in article 26 of the International Convention on Civil and Political Rights (ICCPR). The provision indicates that the application of the laws should be equal to all persons without discrimination.[28] Also, the International Convention on Economic and Social-Cultural Rights (ICESCR) requires state parties to commit to realizing the rights set thereof without any form of discrimination on differences such as sex. Though not legally binding, the United Nations Guiding Principles (UNGPs) on Business and Human Rights also place a responsibility on states and business enterprises to address business-related abuses and gender-based exclusions faced by women in key sectors, including the natural resources sector.[29]

Lastly, the SDGs are a set of good international policies advocating for women's rights to equal treatment. SDG 5 aims at a universal end to gender discrimination against women in all parts of the world.[30] Furthermore, though not legally binding, articles 10 and 11 UNESCO Declaration of Ethical Principles in Relation to Climate Change, require all efforts to achieve net zero energy transitions to consider the needs of vulnerable groups, including women, and provide education and information on climate change to everyone irrespective of gender.[31]

B. Regional Instruments

In addition to the international instruments that address gender justice issues in the context of energy transition, there are also regional documents that contain general provisions on the rights to equality and non-discrimination. The African Charter on Human and People's Rights (ACHPR) has equality rights in multiple provisions.[32] Article 1, for instance, guarantees universal rights and freedoms to all persons without discrimination

[25] International Institute for Sustainable Development (IISD), 'The COP 18 Gender Decision—A Step Towards Gender Equality in the Climate Regime' (2013) para 3 <http://www.sdg.iisd.org/commentary/guest-articles/the-cop-18-gender-decision-a-step-towards-gender-equality-in-the-climate-regime/> accessed 19 August 2023.

[26] ibid 38.

[27] Convention on Elimination of All Forms of Discrimination Against Women (CEDAW) 1979.

[28] International Covenant on Civil and Political Rights (ICCPR) 1966.

[29] See Principles 3, 7, 12, 20 of 'Guiding Principles on Business and Human Rights: Implementing the United Nations "Protect, Respect and Remedy" Framework' (UNGPs) <http://www.ohchr.org/documents/publications/guidingprinciplesbusinesshr_en.pdf> accessed 19 August 2023.

[30] United Nations, GA Res 70/1, Transforming Our World: The 2030 Agenda for Sustainable Development (25 September 2015) <https://sdgs.un.org/2030agenda> accessed 12 August 2023.

[31] UNESCO, 'Declaration of Ethical Principles in Relation to Climate Change' (2017). See also para 21 of the ILO 'Declaration on Just Transition' ILC.111/Record No.7A, which calls on governments to 'formulate, implement, monitor and evaluate gender responsive, inclusive, integrated and coherent just transition frameworks'.

[32] Organization of African Unity (OAU), 'African Charter on Human and Peoples' Rights (Banjul Charter)' (27 June 1981, entered into force 21 October 1986) CAB/LEG/67/3 rev 5, 21 ILM 58 (1982) <https://www.refworld.org/docid/3ae6b3630.html> accessed 19 August 2023.

in their enjoyment. Article 22(1) protects the equality rights of all persons concerning the enjoyment of economic, social, and cultural rights.[33] Similarly, the Maputo Protocol to the ACHPR aims to safeguard equality, justice, and non-discrimination for African women. Among its core provisions are those relating to access to justice, equality before the law, the right of women to participate, and socio-economic rights, among others.[34] Though not legally binding, the African Union's 2012 Resolution on a Human Rights-Based Approach to Natural Resources, amongst other things, calls on governments to 'ensure independent social and human rights impact assessments that guarantee . . . women, indigenous and customary people's rights' across the natural resources industry. There are several other regional and sub-regional efforts by African governments that demand environmental and human rights safeguards by investors and business enterprises in Africa's extractive industries to ensure meaningful and inclusive participation of women in decision-making.[35]

Despite the wide range of international legal instruments on the need for gender justice in climate change governance and clean energy transition efforts, a number of legal and institutional barriers continue to limit their application in Sub-Saharan African countries. The next section provides a survey of the barriers to gender justice in net zero efforts in Sub-Saharan Africa.

III. Gender Gaps in Net Zero Policies: Survey of Legal Barriers and Limitations in Select Sub-Saharan African Countries

Africa is one of the most vulnerable continents as far as climate change impact is concerned.[36] Net zero energy transition in Sub-Saharan African countries has therefore focused primarily on updating national laws and policies to advance climate change mitigation and adaptation. Despite these efforts, however, a wide range of legal and institutional gaps continue to limit the advancement of gender justice.

A. Lack of Specific Laws on Net Zero and Lack of Specific Mention of Gender in Natural Resources Laws

Despite being signatories to various international pacts on climate change, there is still a lack of specific laws on net zero and climate change in many Sub-Saharan African countries with the exception of a few.[37] For example, South Africa has various national policies

[33] ibid 43.

[34] African Union (AU), 'Protocol to the African Charter on Human and Peoples' Rights on the Rights of Women in Africa' (Maputo Protocol Text, 11 July 2003) <https://www.refworld.org/docid/3f4b139d4.html> accessed 19 August 2023.

[35] See the ECOW-GEN, *ECOWAS Policy for Gender Mainstreaming in Energy Access* (4 June 2017); see also the declarations of the Pan African Parliament, and the 2009 African Mining Vision; see also D Olawuyi, 'Increasing Relevance of Right-Based Approaches to Resource Governance in Africa: Shifting from Regional Aspiration to Local Realization' (2015) 11 McGill International Journal of Sustainable Development Law & Policy 113.

[36] United Nations Environment Programme (UNEP), 'Responding to Climate Change' (*United Nations Environment Programme*, n.d.) <https://www.unep.org/regions/africa/regional-initiatives/responding-climate-change> accessed 14 May 2024.

[37] See eg Nigeria: Climate Change Act 2021; Kenya: Climate Change Act 2016. See generally the 'Climate Change Law of the World', London School of Economics and Political Science <https://www.climate-laws.org> accessed 19 August 2023.

addressing decarbonization and energy justice, such as the National Development Policy for 2030, the National Climate Change Response of 2011, the Nationally Determined Contribution Policy of 2021, and the recent Framework for Just Transition in South Africa of 2022.[38] On the whole, these policies focus on ensuring equal access to electricity through renewable sources, affordability, and sustainability in all parts of South Africa but are lacking the legislative backing in the form of specific laws to ensure that the pursuit of equal access to electricity is consistent with net zero ambitions.

A specific law on net zero, with clear and comprehensive provisions on gender justice, would give legislative backing to the targets, plans, and policies designed to support the transition to net zero. It would also make enforcement of such policies possible, especially in domestic courts.[39] For example, Nigeria has national law that aims to assist in the realization of just net zero energy transition. The Climate Change Act 2021 elaborates a National Climate Change Action Plan in Nigeria every five years[40] and directs that the federal government, under their environmental and national planning ministries, must employ carbon budgeting.[41] This is a laudable step, but like South Africa and Malawi, the mitigation of gender vulnerabilities associated with energy transition is still left to policy instruments rather than legally binding and enforceable laws on clean energy transition and net zero. While such policy documents contain reference to gender justice and women empowerment in climate action and policies, they are not legally binding legislation, which often poses challenges when it comes to demanding their enforcement.[42] Accordingly, despite having clear gender inclusivity policies, gender gaps persist in the country's net zero policies and domestic energy laws.[43]

Kenya is one of the few Sub-Saharan African countries to have taken real steps towards achieving gender justice in clean energy transition and net zero through specific laws. The Energy Act 2019 forms the basis of the net zero energy transition. Part IV of this legislation focuses on renewable energy sources in Kenya and provides proper structures for regulating, enforcing, and considering renewable sources into the national grid.[44] This is in addition to the Climate Change Act 2016, which was the first piece of climate change legislation in Africa to contain express language on gender mainstreaming in all aspects of climate change responses. The Act establishes the National Climate Change Council and provides that its membership must adhere to the two-thirds gender rule.[45] The Kenyan Constitution also has a substantive constitutional provision on equality and non-discrimination of all persons based on gender with article 27(3) according both men and women the right to equal treatment, consisting of rights to equal opportunities in political, economic, and cultural spheres. Policy frameworks aimed at just energy transition in Kenya also include the Kenya National Electrification Strategy, the Vision 2030, the National Gender and Equality Commission Act, and the National Policy on Gender and Development which include clear

[38] ibid.

[39] UNEP, 'Responding to Climate Change' (n 36) 50.

[40] Frank Eze, *Policy Thrusts for Net-Zero Carbon Emission in Nigeria* (2021), DOI: 10.13140/RG.2.2.19636.58242, accessed 19 August 2023.

[41] Climate Change Act 2021, s 19(1)(a).

[42] Olawuyi, 'Gender, Indigeneity and the Search for Environmental Justice' (n 21).

[43] ibid.

[44] Government of the Republic of Kenya, Energy Act No 1 of 2019 (14 March 2019), Part IV.

[45] Climate Change Act 2016, 11, ss 5–7. <http://kenyalaw.org:8181/exist/rest//db/kenyalex/Kenya/Legislation/English/Acts%20and%20Regulations/C/Climate%20Change%20Act%20-%20No.%2011%20of%202016/docs/ClimateChangeAct11of2016.pdf> accessed 12 May 2024.

provisions that aim to provide equal opportunities for women in the clean energy transition.[46] Kenya's Vision 2030 also highlights gender mainstreaming in the promotion and development of green energy for vulnerable communities and groups.[47] Finally, in 2019, Kenya released its Gender in Energy Policy, the first of such gender-focused energy policies in Africa, which expressly recognizes the need for gender-equal approaches in the country's energy transformation process.[48]

However, as laudable as the legislative and policy efforts are, lack of concerted implementation remains a key barrier to gender justice in net zero efforts in Kenya.[49] In addition to legislation and policies, African countries will need to dismantle systemic barriers to active female engagement and participation in energy decision-making, barriers which continue to limit equitable access to energy resources, as well as gender inclusion in the design and implementation of net zero policies.[50]

B. Lack of Coherent Implementation Strategies on Gender Justice

As seen with Kenya, and across much of Sub-Saharan Africa, there is no shortage of national policies that express the aim of mainstreaming gender into clean energy transition. However, what is missing are clear action plans and strategies to enforce and ensure coherent implementation of such policies across the natural resources industry value chain.[51] This means that across many African countries, while the intention is there to implement net zero projects in an inclusive manner, in practice, several projects have been implemented without compliance with such policy prescriptions. The disconnect between policy ambitions and actual compliance, which some studies describe as 'policy evaporation', means that the implementation of net zero and energy transition policies across Africa remain gender blind.[52]

For example, in South Africa although women in the country are participating in the transition to zero energy, compared to men, they face biases stemming from gaps in net zero policies that fail to enforce gender justice in clean energy projects and technologies. For instance, an all-female company in Cape Town is supporting the transition through the production of 20,000 solar panels every month.[53] As consumers, women in South Africa

[46] Kenya National Gender Policy 2021–25 <https://www.home.creaw.org/wp-content/uploads/2022/03/Isiolo-County-Gender-policy-Abridged-f2_compressed.pdf> accessed 19 August 2023.

[47] Government of the Republic of Kenya, Kenya Vision 2030, 'Social Pillar | Kenya Vision 2030' (Updated 2022) <http://www.vision2030.go.ke/social-pillar/> accessed 11 October 2022; also Government of the Republic of Kenya, 'Sector Plan for Gender Youth and Vulnerable Groups 2013–2017' (2013) ii <https://www.vision2030.go.ke/wp-content/uploads/2018/05/SECTOR-PLAN-FOR-GENDER-YOUTH-AND-VULNERABLE-GROUPS-2013-2017.pdf> accessed 19 August 2023.

[48] Energia, 'Kenyan Ministry of Energy Launches First National Gender Policy in the Energy Sector' (11 November 2019) <https://www.energia.org/kenyan-ministry-of-energy-launches-first-national-gender-policy-in-the-energy-sector-ever/> accessed 19 August 2023.

[49] Emmaqulate Kemunto, 'Gender-Responsive Transition' (8 March 2022) <https://www.kcspog.org/2022/03/08/gender-responsive-energy-transition/> accessed 19 August 2023.

[50] ibid.

[51] ibid.

[52] Gill Allwood, 'Gender Mainstreaming and Policy Coherence for Development: Unintended Gender Consequences and EU Policy' (2013) 39(2) Women's Studies International Forum,42–52; also Lieu (n 2).

[53] Nasi Hako, 'New 15MW women-led solar assembly plant launched in Cape Town' (2023) <https://www.esi-africa.com/renewable-energy/solar/new-15mw-women-led-solar-assembly-plant-launched-in-cape-town/> accessed 19 August 2023.

are reducing the country's carbon emissions by adopting biomass stoves in their kitchens. Currently, about 33 per cent of households in the country have switched from charcoal and wood to biomass briquettes.[54] However, several other projects exclude women from training and engagement in the development of clean energy products and access to credit facilities to enable them to acquire products such as solar technology.[55]

Similarly, in Kenya, gender inclusivity features mainly in the consultation of women at the inception stages of clean energy transition projects. However, in many instances, follow-up measures are required to ensure that the expressed needs and priorities of female groups are reflected in the outcomes and implementation of such projects.[56] For instance, Kenya recently installed the Lake Turkana Wind Farm project with 365 turbines that generate 850kW of electric power transmitted to the national grid.[57] Gender was a key consideration in its planning, implementation, and definition of its desired outcomes. Women in the community were consulted through their self-help groups as some of the project's stakeholders, their energy sources and needs were studied extensively, and women were employed for some of the project's construction work.[58] Such projects have significantly increased rural electrification and massive carbon emission reductions in Kenya, with 8.6 million out of the country's 12 million households currently connected to electricity.[59] Over 30 per cent of these households are headed by women. However, although Kenya is taking positive steps towards gender inclusivity in clean energy projects, project implementation does not always reflect gender mainstreaming.[60] Furthermore, lack of clear, comprehensive, and reliable data on how many women have access to clean energy benefits of such projects, compared to men, makes it difficult to properly evaluate the success or otherwise of gender mainstreaming efforts.[61] A good example is the countrywide rural electrification project, which failed to include domestic water collection solutions that would have saved women 1.5 hours walking daily.[62] Consequently, despite having extensive policies and laws that seek to prioritize equal rights and non-discrimination of women in access to energy resources, including clean energy projects, gender injustice concerns in energy access remain.[63]

Like South Africa and Kenya, gender justice in net zero energy transition projects in Nigeria is also undermined by the lack of a coherent national action plan and strategy to

[54] Whitney Pailman and others, 'Experiences with Improved Cookstoves in Southern Africa' (2018) 29(4) Journal of Energy in Southern Africa 29.

[55] Khayaat Fakier, 'Women and Renewable Energy in a South African Community: Exploring Energy Poverty and Environmental Racism' (2018) 19(5) Journal of International Women's Studies 165–76.

[56] Kemunto (n 49).

[57] African Development Bank, 'Lake Turkana Wind Power Project: The Largest Wind Farm Project in Africa' (African Development Bank, *Building Today, a Better Africa Tomorrow*, 2015). <https://www.afdb.org/en/projects-and-operations/selected-projects/lake-turkana-wind-power-project-the-largest-wind-farm-project-in-africa-143>.

[58] Lake Turkana Wind Power Project, 'Environmental and Social Impact Assessment Study Report' (2009). <https://www3.dfc.gov/Environment/EIA/laketurkanawind/ESIA%20wind%20farm%20site_2009.pdf>.

[59] Xinhua, 'Kenya Connects 8.6 million Households to Electricity' (*The East African*, 2022).

[60] Lieu (n 2); Kemunto (n 49).

[61] Lieu (n 2); Kemunto (n 49). See also Food and Agricultural Organization (FAO), 'The community land rights of women and youth in Turkana County, Kenya' (March 2017) <https://www.fao.org/3/i7037en/i7037en.pdf> accessed 19 August 2023.

[62] Energia, 'Gender in the Transition to Sustainable Energy for All: From Evidence to Inclusive Policies' (Energia, 2019) < https://www.energia.org/assets/2019/04/Gender-in-the-transition-to-sustainable-energy-for-all_-From-evidence-to-inclusive-policies_FINAL.pdf>

[63] Kemunto (n 49); FAO (n 61).

enforce gender justice in clean energy transition and net zero projects and policies. The mismatch between government policies on gender equality and actual outcomes in the Nigerian natural resources industry in terms of female participation is so huge that it has been described as a men's club.[64] Gender inequality in Nigeria's energy transition is exacerbated by the same preexisting patterns of the lack of vulnerability assessment and information on the roles of, and opportunities available to, women in the natural resources industry value chain.[65] As Olawuyi and Olaniyan note, the NCDMB, as well as other regulators, have yet to pay sufficient attention to studying, analysing, and unpacking patterns of opportunity and wealth (non-)creation for women in the natural resources industry.[66] The number of local content opportunities, such as jobs, financing, procurement contracts, and training, provided for girls and women in the Nigeriaare hardly measured, assessed, or documented in a clear and transparent manner. Such lack of gender vulnerability assessment across the industry means that clean energy transition programmes are built on a foundation of weak consideration of the critical linkages between gender justice energy security, and overall sustainable development.[67]

African countries will need to align targets and aspirations on gender justice and just energy transition with implementation in practice. This requires a careful assessment of barriers to the enforcement and implementation of gender policies across the entire natural resources value chain, and taking active steps to dismantle such barriers.

C. Resource and Capacity Issues

In addition to the lack of coherent enforcement of national action plans and strategies, achieving gender justice in energy transition projects is also undermined by issues of capacity (human and financial).[68] Estimates indicate that 'only 7% of total private equity and venture funding in emerging markets is targeted towards female-led businesses and, similarly, just 3% of philanthropic environmental funding supports girls' and women's environmental activism'.[69] Women-led clean energy initiatives across Africa still face challenges in accessing loans, financial resources and technologies needed to start energy ventures.[70]

[64] See BBC News, 'Nigeria's Growing Number of Female Oil Bosses' (*BBC News*, 11 September 2014) <https://www.bbc.com/news/business-29127436> accessed 19 August 2023; A Ademuson, 'Women Domination and Oppression in Nigerian Society: Implications for Sustainable Development' (2016) 19 African Journal for the Psychological Studies of Social Issues 24.

[65] Damilola S Olawuyi and Ayobami J Olaniyan, 'Local Content and the Sustainable Development of Oil and Gas Resources in Nigeria' in D Olawuyi (ed), *Local Content and Sustainable Development in Global Energy Markets* (CUP 2021).

[66] ibid.

[67] ibid; also Ademuson (n 64).

[68] Allwood (n 52).

[69] UNEP, 'Gender, climate and finance: How financing female-led businesses can lead the way to a net-zero future for people and the planet' (21 December 2022) <https://www.unepfi.org/themes/climate-change/gender-climate-and-finance-how-financing-female-led-businesses-can-lead-the-way-to-a-net-zero-future-for-people-and-the-planet/> accessed 19 August 2023.

[70] Jumana Farouky and Justus Wanzala, 'Failed by Banks, Kenyan Women in Clean Energy Embrace Crowdfunding' (The New Humanitarian, 2018) < https://deeply.thenewhumanitarian.org/womensadvancement/articles/2018/04/03/failed-by-banks-kenyan-women-in-clean-energy-embrace-crowdfunding> accessed 10 May 2024; also Roz Price, 'Access to climate finance by women and marginalised groups in the Global South' (2021) K4D Helpdesk Report 1004, *Institute of Development Studies*, 4 <https://opendocs.ids.ac.uk/opendocs/bitstream/handle/20.500.12413/16622/1004_Access_to_climate_finance_by _women_and_marginalised_groups.pdf?sequence=1&isAllowed=y> accessed 19 August 2023.

To advance gender justice in the clean energy transition, there is a need for increased solidarity and collaboration amongst governments, the private sector, and financial institutions to provide dedicated financial services and programmes to advance women-led eco-ventures.[71]

Issues of capacity can be addressed through setting and adhering to strict gender-inclusive policies, including promoting women-focused capacity development, knowledge-sharing, and empowerment initiatives.[72] Initiatives such as the Solar Sister partnership,[73] supporting female entrepreneurs with businesses that promote green energy,[74] and having women in leadership positions,[75] can also go a long way to address issues of capacity. Gender-just policies must focus on empowering women, in terms of resources and capacity, to effectively engage as active participants in developing and implementing clean energy solutions.[76]

In summary, the above challenges demonstrate that while African states are taking some steps to ensure that energy transition is gender-just, there is a need for greater regulatory coherence aimed at integrating gender justice into all aspects of natural resources governance, including the design and implementation of net zero and clean energy transition programmes. The next section examines ongoing innovations in the United Kingdom aimed at aligning and integrating gender justice in net zero and clean energy transition programmes.

IV. Towards Gender-Just Net Zero Policies: Some Lessons from the United Kingdom

As can be learned from the United Kingdom, to promote regulatory coherence in the design and implementation of gender-just net zero programmes, clear and comprehensive legislation on climate change that establishes mandatory obligations for all stakeholders is necessary. Furthermore, there is a need for tailored programmes that assess and address gender-based vulnerabilities and impacts in the design and implementation of net zero policies and programmes.[77] Such programmes will need to empower and provide a level playing field for women to play active roles both in decision-making on net zero, as well as in accessing opportunities and financing on clean energy transition.[78]

[71] UNEP, 'Gender, climate and finance' (n 69).

[72] InfraCo Africa, 'JCM Power: The 20MW Golomoti Solar PV and Battery Energy Storage Project has Successfully Entered Commercial Operations' (2022). < https://infracoafrica.com/the-20mw-golomoti-solar-pv-and-battery-energy-storage-project-has-successfully-entered-commercial-operations/> accessed 19 August 2023.

[73] Solar Sister (2018) <https://www.solarsister.org/> accessed 19 August 2023.

[74] Emily Bellis, 'Malawi's "Shining Mothers"' will accelerate energy access in rural communities' (*Solar-Aid*, 2021) < https://solar-aid.org/news/malawis-shining-mothers-will-accelerate-energy-access-in-rural-communities/> accessed 10 May 2024.

[75] J Swanson, 'Women in Energy: Anita Nana Okuribido' (*USEA | United States Energy Association*, 11 November 2020) <https://usea.org/article/women-energy-anita-nana-okuribido> accessed 11 October 2022.

[76] Monica Maduekwe and others, 'Gender Equity and Mainstreaming in Renewable Energy Policies—Empowering Women in the Energy Value Chain in the Economic Community of West African States (ECOWAS)' (2019) 6 Current Sustainable Renewable Energy Reports 13-21.

[77] 'Women and the Net Zero economy: A briefing on changes in garment, agriculture and energy supply chains' (WOW Helpdesk Guidance Note No 3, April 2021). <https://assets.publishing.service.gov.uk/media/60868074d3bf7f012fa75e31/Guidance3-Women--Net-Zero-Economy-Briefing1.pdf> accessed 1 May 2024.

[78] ibid.

The United Kingdom's net zero efforts are underpinned by the Climate Change Act 2008, which provides a clear legal basis for the United Kingdom's approach to tackling and responding to climate change. While there is no clear mention of gender in the Act, a 2009 impact assessment of the law showed that it would have no adverse impact on gender equality.[79] This assessment is supported by the United Kingdom's Equality Act 2010, which addresses several discrimination laws while placing obligations on public authorities.[80]

With respect to net zero, pursuant to the Climate Change Act, in 2019, the UK government set a net zero target of 100 per cent GHG reduction by 2050 compared with 1990 levels.[81] In 2021, the United Kingdom released a net zero strategy which, inter alia, references the need for a just transition.[82] Despite legal debates and challenges on the design of the net zero strategy, it remains an important bedrock of the United Kingdom's clean energy transition.[83] The gender justice aspect of the just transition is specifically elaborated in the United Kingdom government's 2022 submission to the UNFCCC on the 'gender-differentiated impacts of climate change' which recognizes 'gender-differentiated impacts of climate change, as well as the critical role that women and girls have to play as agents of change in climate action'.[84] The submission outlines efforts by the United Kingdom to achieve gender equality in climate change initiatives and net zero energy transition.[85] It identifies measures aimed at protecting women from climate vulnerabilities related to health, education, gender-based violence, and economic empowerment. These measures include climate finance, locally-led climate action, education, and women's economic empowerment that aim to empower women as change agents in promoting gender equality.[86] The set gender action plan also aims to facilitate meaningful and equal participation of women in leadership at all policy levels on climate change.

Under section 14 of the Climate Change Act 2008, the UK government has a duty to submit to Parliament its plans for adapting to the risks of climate change. Accordingly, in its recent net zero strategy, submitted to Parliament, there is a clear commitment to gender equity in all areas of energy transition to net zero.[87] Amongst other things, this strategy aims to shift to green energy through the Green Jobs Group aimed at revolutionizing the industry towards a green economy that promotes diversity, including gender. For example,

[79] Government of the United Kingdom, Department of Energy and Climate Change (DECC), 'Climate Change Act 2008 Impact Assessment' (2009) <https://www.legislation.gov.uk/ukia/2009/70/pdfs/ukia_20090070_en.pdf> accessed 19 August 2023.

[80] UNFCCC, 'United Kingdom of Great Britain and Northern Ireland's Nationally Determined Contribution' 17 <https://www.unfccc.int/sites/default/files/NDC/2022-09/UK%20NDC%20ICTU%202022.pdf> accessed 19 August 2023.

[81] See the Government of the United Kingdom, 'Climate Change Act 2008 (2050 Target Amendment) Order 2019'. <https://www.legislation.gov.uk/uksi/2019/1056/introduction/made > accessed 1 May 2024.

[82] Government of the United Kingdom, 'Net Zero Strategy: Build Back Greener' (October 2021) <https://www.gov.uk/government/publications/net-zero-strategy> accessed 19 August 2023.

[83] See *R (oao Friends of the Earth) v Secretary of State for Business Energy and Industrial Strategy*, High Court of Justice of England and Wales, EWHC 1841, 18 July 2022 (United Kingdom of Great Britain and Northern Ireland), in which the court found that the UK government had failed to comply with its legal duties under the Climate Change Act 2008 in the design and approval of its net zero strategy.

[84] Government of the United Kingdom, 'The United Kingdom of Great Britain and Northern Ireland's Submission to the United Nations Framework Convention on Climate Change on the Gender-Differentiated Impacts of Climate Change, the Role of Women as Agents of Change and Opportunities for Women' (Government of the United Kingdom, 2022) < https://www4.unfccc.int/sites/SubmissionsStaging/Documents/202205051542---Gender-differentiated%20impacts%20of%20climate%20change.pdf> accessed 10 May 2024.

[85] ibid.

[86] ibid.

[87] UK government, 'Net Zero Strategy' (n 82).

across the areas of innovation for net zero, namely: investment; jobs, skills, and industries; government action; local climate action; empowering the public and businesses; and international leadership and collaboration, the United Kingdom has expressed its commitment to the UNFCCC GAP and increased gender representation.[88] This is an important commitment and shows how clear specific laws backed by a clear strategy can ensure that gender justice is reflected through the various areas of the net zero transition.

As part of its commitment to international leadership in this area, in 2021, the United Kingdom government also joined the International Energy Agency (IEA) Gender Advisory Council as a move towards gender diversity in the entire energy sector.[89] Further, the government committed itself to a Declaration Supporting the Just Transition Internationally, with the objective to facilitate an all-inclusive net zero energy transition that is gender-just.[90]

The initiatives in the United Kingdom have been progressively more successful compared to those in the surveyed Sub-Saharan African countries. First, unlike in many parts of Africa where climate change laws are only just emerging, the United Kingdom, as one of the first few countries in the world to enact climate change legislation, has had many years of linking its climate change legislation with guidelines and policies in several sectors, including the natural resources sector. Such rule linkage and regulatory coherence has enhanced awareness, education, and capacity building on climate change, net zero; and the integration of gender equality into climate action.[91]

Second, while resource constraints and lack of committed funding for gender justice programmes remain a challenge in the surveyed African countries, the United Kingdom has taken active steps to provide capacity development and support for industry-led initiatives aimed at addressing gender gaps in the clean energy transition.[92] Furthermore, tailored investment in expanding science, technology, engineering, and maths (STEM) skills for women across the United Kingdom is a good practice that aims to reduce education, training, and capacity gaps between women and men, especially women from underprivileged backgrounds.[93] Such empowerment programmes can significantly reduce employment inequalities and increase women's involvement in the net zero sector.[94]

Third, despite progress on gender justice in the clean energy transition, the United Kingdom energy and natural resources industry still has a long way to go in achieving gender justice, especially with respect to bridging the huge pay gap between men and women and increasing women's representation in board level appointments in the sector.[95] However, the United Kingdom's focus on regular gender vulnerability assessments, data gathering, and reporting of progress made and challenges that remain is an essential

[88] ibid 206–96.

[89] Government of the United Kingdom, 'United Kingdom of Great Britain and Northern Ireland's Nationally Determined Contribution' (2022) <https://assets.publishing.service.gov.uk/government/uploads/system/uploads/attachment_data/file/1109430/NDC_ICTU_MASTER_VERSION_20PT_tables.pdf> accessed 19 August 2023.

[90] ibid 90.

[91] eg Clean Energy Ministerial (CEM), 'Clean Energy Education and Empowerment Initiative' <https://www.cleanenergyministerial.org/content/uploads/2022/03/c3e-fact-sheet-june-2019.pdf> accessed 19 August 2023.

[92] eg POWERful women <https://powerfulwomen.org.uk/> accessed 19 August 2023.

[93] UK Government, 'Net Zero Strategy' (n 82) 11–12.

[94] UNICEF, 'Mapping Gender Equality in STEM from School to Work' (20 November 2020) <https://www.unicef.org/globalinsight/stories/mapping-gender-equality-stem-school-work> accessed 19 August 2023.

[95] 'Exclusive: How big is the gender pay gap in the energy industry in Britain and who are the worst offenders?' (*Energy Monitor*, 13 April 2022) <https://www.energymonitor.ai/policy/just-transition/exclusive-how-big-is-the-gender-pay-gap-in-the-energy-industry-in-britain-and-who-are-the-worst-offenders/> accessed 19 August 2023.

foundation for gender justice that remains lacking in the surveyed African countries.[96] The assessment of gender justice and gender-based vulnerabilities in net zero and clean energy transition must be prioritized in African countries, bearing in mind the vital importance of information in designing responsive, efficient, and coherent policies.[97] As can be learned from the United Kingdom, simply having the legislation and policies in place does not necessarily mean that they will be sufficient in addressing systemic barriers to gender justice, especially in the context of the fast-changing pace of the energy transition. There is, therefore, a need for gender-focused human rights due diligence, gender vulnerability assessments, data gathering, and monitoring as part of the design and implementation of clean energy transition programmes.[98]

V. Conclusion

A just and inclusive net zero energy transition is unachievable unless underlying root causes of gender-based exclusions in the natural resources sector are addressed. Despite the increased introduction of gender mainstreaming policies in many countries, especially Sub-Saharan Africa, lack of coherent implementation remains a key concern. Gender injustice in the design and implementation of net zero and clean energy transition programmes are exacerbated by a lack of legally binding legislation or policy frameworks on climate change and net zero, with clear gender justice requirements. Furthermore, systemic challenges such as historical exclusion from senior management and decision-making roles, limited training, and limited access to resources for women-led clean energy initiatives continue to widen the gap in gender justice ambitions and practical realization. While some efforts have been made to support a just net zero energy transition in the surveyed African countries, much still needs to be done in terms of effective enforcement, empowerment, and capacity development to drive coherent implementation of those laws and policies in a gender-just manner.

Despite challenges that remain, the United Kingdom's approach to mainstreaming gender justice in net zero efforts provides lessons on how natural resource regulators in Africa can address gender vulnerabilities of net zero policies across the natural resources value chain. First, a comprehensive needs assessment should be written into net zero policy, requiring all clean energy projects to consider the energy needs of every member of the communities they target. Since energy needs vary by gender, a comprehensive needs assessment would ensure that all net zero-related projects and technologies yield outcomes that meet the needs of all beneficiaries. These should be underpinned by specific laws on net zero and specific mention of gender equity in other natural resources laws. Clear and

[96] UK government, 'Net Zero Strategy' (n 82) 11–12; UKAID and WOW, 'Women and the Net Zero Economy: A Briefing on Changes in Garment, Agriculture and Energy Supply Chains' (WOW Helpdesk Guidance Note No. 3, 2021) < https://assets.publishing.service.gov.uk/media/60868074d3bf7f012fa75e31/Guidance3-Women--Net-Zero-Economy-Briefing1.pdf> accessed 10 May 2024.

[97] Myria Allen and Christopher Craig, 'Rethinking Corporate Social Responsibility in the Age of Climate Change: A Communication Perspective' (2016) 1 International Journal of Corporate Social Responsibility1.

[98] Marie Crawley and Louise O'Meara, *The Gender Proofing Handbook: An Initiative of Six County Development Boards* (Dublin: NDP Gender Equality Unit, DJELR, 2002) 1–5; F Mackay and K Bilton, Equality Proofing Procedures in Drafting Legislation: International Comparisons (Edinburgh: Scottish Executive Central Research Unit, 2001) 5–8.

coherent legislation and strategies on gender justice, can enhance regulatory coherence and enforcement. The development of such laws should be accompanied by a clear assessment of the impacts of such laws on gender equality as in the United Kingdom's approach.

Second, while there is a consensus that climate change governance and gender issues are integral, rather than optional,[99] laws on their own are unlikely to deliver the gender equity for women in net zero energy transition initiatives. There is a need for clear national action plans and strategies to ensure that gender considerations are consistently and coherently applied throughout the lifecycle of net zero energy transition projects. Regular vulnerability assessment and reporting can help all stakeholders to monitor progress made and the challenges that remain.

Third, tailored financing and gender-focused capacity development programmes are required to promote women's participation across all aspects of the natural resources value chain, including in clean energy transition. As Okoroafor notes, there cannot be a 'just' transition if women's voices are not considered in the net zero transition.[100] Laws and policies can secure women's access to energy resources by requiring financial institutions to maintain gender equality in their credit portfolio by funding female entrepreneurs in the clean energy sector. Such laws could also incentivize the institutions to provide training, market linkages, and other facilitation services to women-owned or -led green energy projects. This can go a long way to addressing some of the capacity issues.

The problem of inadequate representation of women leaders in energy boards, senior management positions, and technical roles in the clean energy sector could be addressed from its source through investment in STEM education for women. The impact of this reform may take a few years to be realized but it will increase the number of women acting in different capacities in the energy sector. Finally, to deter irresponsible investment and practices that promote gender-based exclusions in the clean energy sector, countries will also need to penalize entities and initiatives that shut out women or yield outcomes that place an unfair burden on women and other vulnerable members of society.

[99] Karen Morrow, 'Tackling Climate Change and Gender Justice—Integral; Not Optional' (2021) 11(1) Climate Justice in the Anthropocene 207.

[100] Felix Douglas, 'African Women for Energy Transition Advocate for Green Hydrogen—Energy Focus Report' (*Energy Focus Reports*, 2022) <https://www.energyfocusreport.com/african-women-for-energy-transition-advocate-for-green-hydrogen/> accessed 11 October 2022.

11

Net Zero, Human Rights, and ESG Risk Management

Damilola S. Olawuyi and Elena I. Athwal

I. Introduction

This chapter examines how new and emerging forms of environmental, social, and governance (ESG) risks associated with net zero energy transitions are transforming natural resources law and policy. It discusses the drivers and dimensions of transition-related ESG risks, the barriers to the effective regulation and governance of transition-related ESG risks, and the natural resources law and policy innovations and strategies required to address such barriers effectively.

Over the last several decades, the concept of due diligence in natural resources investments has focused mainly on investigating the economic, legal, fiscal, and factual circumstances of an asset, proposed transaction, activity, or project to avoid legal risks.[1] Broadly framed, legal risks refer to the risk of financial, reputational, or investment loss, legal liability, or dispute settlement; costs to a company or institution that may arise from a defective commercial arrangement or transaction.[2] In transactional contexts, natural resources law practitioners would typically engage in in-depth title reviews, corporate and commercial searches, and a review of potential litigation and regulatory fines that may result in legal risks in a possible acquisition of an asset.

However, the rapid transformation of natural resources law in response to the ongoing net zero and clean energy transition has seen a strategic shift in the concept of risk in transactional contexts to include justice risks.[3] Justice risks in this context refers simply to risks relating to human rights violations in the design and implementation of net zero and energy transition programmes. As discussed in Chapter 1 of this book, despite the importance of the rapidly emerging net zero and clean energy transition programmes, they have also been linked with complex human rights violations in many countries.[4] Such concerns include land grabs, forced displacements, modern slavery, gender injustice, and environmental pollution, especially in indigenous communities and conflict-affected regions.[5]

[1] Damilola Olawuyi, 'Legal Strategies and Tools for Mitigating Legal Risks Associated with Oil and Gas Investments in Africa' (2015) 39(3) OPEC Energy Review 247.

[2] ibid.

[3] See Raphael Heffron and others, 'The Identification and Impact of Justice Risks to Commercial Risks in the Energy Sector: Post COVID-19 and for the Energy Transition' (2021) 39(4) Journal of Energy & Natural Resources Law 439; also World Economic Forum, 'Nature Risk Rising: Why the Crisis Engulfing Nature Matters for Business and the Economy' (WEF, January 2020).

[4] See United Nations Working Group on Business and Human Rights (UN WGBHR), *Extractive Sector, Just Transition and Human Rights* (2023) UN General Assembly Report stating that 'the energy transition cannot replicate or create new forms of human rights and environmental abuses, including corruption and conflict risks'.

[5] See Australian Clean Energy Council, 'Addressing Modern Slavery in the Clean Energy Sector' <https://www.cleanenergycouncil.org.au/resources/resources-hub/addressing-modern-slavery-in-the-clean-energy-sector> accessed 27 August 2023.

Damilola S. Olawuyi and Elena I. Athwal, *Net Zero, Human Rights, and ESG Risk Management* In: *Net Zero and Natural Resources Law*.
Edited by: Damilola S. Olawuyi, José Juan González, Hanri Mostert, Milton Fernando Montoya, and Catherine Banet,
Oxford University Press. © International Bar Association 2024. DOI: 10.1093/9780198925033.003.0011

Secondly, increased demand for transition minerals due to net zero requirements have also been linked with complex human rights violations, especially in conflict affected regions.[6] For instance, recent reports show that in the Democratic Republic of Congo (DRC), children as young as seven years old work in dangerous artisanal cobalt mines.[7] The DRC accounts for more than half (60%) of the global supply of cobalt, an essential transition mineral needed to manufacture batteries for electric vehicles, solar, wind, and other renewable energy infrastructure.[8] As net zero policies and projects ramp up in scale and ambition, global demand for cobalt, and other transition minerals, is projected to increase significantly.[9] This dramatic increase in demand may further exacerbate human rights violations in mining contexts across the world, especially in Global South countries such as the DRC, where the legal and institutional framework on human rights is currently weak.[10] These concerns have accentuated discussions on the need for sound ESG governance in the natural resource sector to advance a just transition.

ESG refers to the wide range of environmental, social, and governance factors which, together with human rights impacts, should be considered by responsible operators and investors in order to minimize legal and justice risks, while maximizing strong financial, sustainable, and ethical outcomes.[11] The ESG concept therefore aims to promote coherence in addressing the adverse impacts of resource development activities on peoples, communities, and societies to achieve long-term sustainable outcomes.[12] For example, several resolutions, declarations, and expert reports, such as the 'Guiding Principles on Business and Human Rights: Implementing the United Nations 'Protect, Respect and Remedy' Framework' (the UNGPs), have emerged, which state that business enterprises, including those in the extractive and energy sectors, have a responsibility to respect, protect, and fulfil human rights when undertaking climate change and net zero programmes.[13] As a

[6] Amnesty International, 'Amnesty challenges industry leaders to clean up their batteries' <https://www.amnesty.org/en/latest/press-release/2019/03/amnesty-challenges-industry-leaders-to-clean-up-their-batteries/> accessed 27 August 2023.

[7] Amnesty International, 'Democratic Republic of Congo: "This is what we die for": Human rights abuses in the Democratic Republic of the Congo power the global trade in cobalt' (2016) < https://www.amnesty.org/en/documents/afr62/3183/2016/en/> accessed 12 May 2024; see also UN WGBHR; and UN Security Council Resolution on the Democratic Republic of Congo, Resolution 1952 (2010), which calls on all companies purchasing, processing and consuming minerals in the DRC to apply and implement rights-based due diligence standards.

[8] ibid.

[9] UN WGBHR (n 4).

[10] See Robin Goad, 'New Cobalt Supply Central to Growing Electric Vehicle Market' Canadian Mining Journal (January 2019), <https://s1.q4cdn.com/337451660/files/doc_downloads/in-the-media/190101-Ca-nadian-Mining-Journal-Cobalt-Commentary.pdf [https://perma.cc/HJA4-2H9K> accessed 05 May 2024, stating that regardless of its history of poor human rights record, corruption, instability, and environmental concerns, the DRC will continue to be the world's largest producer of cobalt.

[11] See UN Global Compact, 'Who Cares Wins: Connecting Financial Markets to a Changing World' (2004) 3–4 <https://documents1.worldbank.org/curated/en/280911488968799581/pdf/113237-WP-WhoCaresWins-2004.pdf> accessed 12 May 2024; Riccardo Boffo and Robert Patalano, 'ESG Investing: Practices, Progress and Challenges' (OECD 2020) <https://www.oecd.org/finance/ESG-Investing-Practices-Progress-Challenges.pdf> accessed 12 May 2024.

[12] Boffo and Patalano, ibid.

[13] United Nations, 'Guiding Principles on Business and Human Rights: Implementing the United Nations "Protect, Respect and Remedy" Framework' (UNGPs) <https://www.ohchr.org/documents/publications/guidingprinciplesbusinesshr_en.pdf> accessed 27 August 2023; see also UN WGBHR (n 4), stating that 'the energy transition cannot replicate or create new forms of human rights and environmental abuses, including corruption and conflict risks'.

result, domestic laws, national action plans, and extractive sector guidelines that emphasize the responsibility of investors to address human rights impacts across their entire value chain, through robust ESG standards are also on the rise.[14] For example, France's Duty of Vigilance Law, the European Union (EU)'s Due Diligence Law, the German Supply Chain Act, and the United Kingdom's Modern Slavery Act, amongst others, all emphasize the need to respect, protect, and fulfil all human rights when investing in mining and energy sectors.[15] Close to thirty countries have already adopted National Action Plans on Business and Human Rights, which enshrine the need for human rights due diligence and impact assessments in the natural resources sector.[16]

The rapid transformations in natural resources law in light of the energy transition require a fresh understanding of the guiding principles for managing ESG risks in natural resource investments, especially in net zero transition efforts. For example, more than 2,000 climate change disputes have arisen in thirty-eight countries on the direct and indirect impacts of climate change and decarbonization efforts.[17] In addition to disputes over how the introduction of such new ESG regulations and standards by states may constitute a breach of contract, other claims include the potential breach of stabilization provisions by government measures to reduce or phase out extractive operations, and how the introduction of incentive regimes for renewables energy may be a violation of international trade law requirements on non-discrimination.[18] Therefore, there is a strong business case, in terms of cost, reputation, and effectiveness, for stakeholders in the natural resources sector to comprehensively understand and manage the wide range of ESG-related risks.

The five sections of this chapter unpack regulatory and governance strategies to address ESG risks associated with net zero transition. After this introduction, Section II explores the drivers and dimensions of transition-related ESG risks. Section III examines gaps in the current response to ESG risk management both from the regulatory and enterprise standpoints. It offers examples of how lack of regulatory clarity and inconsistent reporting on ESG, absence of climate change laws, lack of institutional coordination, and weak capacity of corporate governance structures to spot and address ESG risks in a timely manner are escalating transition-related risks, especially in resource-dependent regions and countries, such as the Middle East and North Africa (MENA) region. Section IV discusses good governance strategies, especially how regulatory clarity, institutional effectiveness, corporate accountability, structural process change, and product upgrades can significantly reduce the social, financial, and sustainable development cost of ESG risks. Section V is the concluding section.

[14] See also Damilola Olawuyi, 'Corporate Accountability for the Natural Environment and Climate Change' in Ilias Bantekas and MA Stein (eds), *Cambridge Companion to Business and Human Rights* (CUP 2021).

[15] Damilola Olawuyi and Oyeniyi Abe, *Business and Human Rights Law and Practice in Africa* (Edward Elgar 2022) 1–15.

[16] ibid.

[17] Joana Setzer and Catherine Higham, 'Global Trends in Climate Change Litigation: 2023 Snapshot' <https://www.lse.ac.uk/granthaminstitute/wp-content/uploads/2023/06/Global_trends_in_climate_change_litigation_2023_snapshot.pdf> accessed 27 August 2023; see also United Nations Environment Program (UNEP), 'The UNEP Global Climate Litigation Report: 2020 Status Review' (UNEP 2020) 8–10.

[18] See Chapters 2 and 4 of this book. See also Sven Volkmer and Taylor Gillespie, 'Energy Transition and Investor-State Disputes' (White & Case, 8 April 2022).

II. Drivers and Scope of the ESG Concept

A. History and Meaning of the ESG Concept

Traditionally, in many countries, separate sets of laws, rules, and institutions apply to ESG issues.[19] However, recent studies have increasingly underlined the ESG framework as a tool for coherent, holistic, and integrated planning to address crosscutting adverse environment, social, governance, and human rights impacts of investments in key economic sectors, in a manner that avoids overlap, constraints, and trade-offs.[20]

The ESG concept became popularized when a United Nations (UN) report published in 2004 called for 'better inclusion of environmental, social and corporate governance (ESG) factors in investment decisions' to achieve integrated and coherent consideration of all adverse impacts of an investment or project.[21] The ESG concept would later emerge as one of the six guiding elements of the UN Principles for Responsible Investment (UNPRI), a voluntary initiative launched by the UN in 2005, which calls on investors to 'incorporate ESG issues into investment analysis and decision-making processes'.[22] The three ESG pillars are also integrated into the UN 2030 Agenda for Sustainable Development which sets a wide range of economic, social, and environmental targets to be attained by the year 2030.[23] Furthermore, the Organisation for Economic Co-operation and Development (OECD) has transformed the ESG concept into key guidelines for sustainable investing practices.[24]

The environmental pillar (*planet*) in ESG emphasizes the protection of natural capital (ie land, air, water, minerals, etc) from degradation and pollution.[25] This includes eliminating greenhouse gas (GHG) emissions to achieve net zero, reducing all forms of environmental pollution in production processes, and utilizing green supply chains in the procurement of goods and services for natural resource development activities.[26] The social pillar (*people*) emphasizes the need to address social exclusions and human rights violations that may result from natural resource development activities and projects.[27] This includes addressing concerns of child labour and modern slavery in minefields, promoting local content, inclusivity, and community relations, consumer protection, gender justice, land justice, fair and

[19] Damilola Olawuyi, 'Increasing Relevance of Right-Based Approaches to Resource Governance in Africa: Shifting from Regional Aspiration to Local Realization' (2015) 11 McGill International Journal of Sustainable Development Law and Policy 113.

[20] Harriet Agnew, Adrienne Klasa, and Simon Mundy, 'How ESG Investing Came to a Reckoning' (*The Financial Times*, 6 June 2022); Beate Sjåfjell and Benjamin J Richardson, *Company Law and Sustainability: Legal Barriers and Opportunities* (CUP 2015) 1–34.

[21] See UN Global Compact, 'Who Cares Wins: Connecting Financial Markets to a Changing World' (2004) 3–4.

[22] UNPRI, 'What Are the Principles of Responsible Investment?' <https://www.unpri.org/about-us/what-are-the-principles-for-responsible-investment> accessed 27 August 2023.

[23] United Nations, 'Transforming our world: the 2030 Agenda for Sustainable Development', UNGA Res 70/1 (25 September 2015).

[24] Boffo and Patalano (n 11).

[25] United Nations Environment Programme (UNEP), 'Nature Risk Profile: A methodology for profiling nature related dependencies and impacts' (UNEP, 2023).

[26] Damilola Olawuyi and Elena Athwal, 'ESG Considerations for Midstream and Downstream Oil and Gas' in Eduardo Pereira, Kim Talus, and Vera de Gyarfas (eds), *Encyclopaedia of Midstream and Downstream Oil and Gas* (Globe Law and Business Ltd 2022).

[27] Boffo and Patalano (n 11); see also Franklin Templeton, 'Build Back Better: COVID-19 Brings the "S" From ESG Into Focus' (2020) <https://www.franklintempleton.ch/articles/blogs/build-back-better-esg-focus> accessed 12 May 2024.

equitable wages for local labour populations in business operations, and eradicating fraud, corruption, illicit financial flows, and resource theft, especially in conflict-affected regions.[28] The governance pillar (*process*) emphasizes the need for institutional frameworks, such as audit committees and sustainability-focused boards, that promote transparency, accountability, and full compliance with applicable laws and best practices in business operations.[29] This includes structural process change to ensure proactive, reliable, and accessible sustainability disclosure and climate-related reporting concerning all aspects of ESG management. The ESG concept is, therefore, about integration, that is, integrating or harmonizing institutions, information-sharing, policy and investment decision-making relating to the ESG impacts of a natural resource activity through a coordinated or holistic approach.

The rapid ascendancy of ESG risk management in natural resource investments over the last decade is due to five key drivers. First is the rise of rights-based approaches to development in all economic sectors, including the natural resources and extractives industry.[30] A wide range of international instruments have increasingly recognized the human right to a clean, healthy, and sustainable environment as a fundamental right.[31] Similarly, at the regional level, the need for investors and stakeholders in the natural resource sector to consider, anticipate, and prevent human rights implications of natural resources projects on the enjoyment of a satisfactory environment was recognized in the African Union's 2012 Resolution on a Human Rights-Based Approach to Natural Resources Governance (2012 Resolution).[32] The 2012 Resolution harmonizes and builds on previous efforts by African governments that demand social and environmental safeguards by investors and business enterprises in Africa's extractive industries.[33] Similarly, the 2011 OECD Guidelines for Multinational Enterprises (OECD Guidelines) elaborate on the need for responsible business conduct by addressing all ESG risks in investment and planning.[34]

A second and related driver is the growing consensus that business enterprises, such as those in the natural resources sector, have a prominent role to play in addressing the growing adverse social, environmental, and economic impacts of development.[35] The UNGPs, as well as other declarations and reports, have clarified that business enterprises have a responsibility to respect, protect, and fulfil human rights in their operations and

[28] See Principles 10, 11, and 16 of the International Law Commission's *Principles on Protection of the Environment in relation to Armed Conflicts* <https://legal.un.org/ilc/texts/instruments/english/draft_articles/8_7_2022.pdf> accessed 10 August 2023; also Reg Fowler, 'Corporate Social Responsibility and Joint Venture Governance—The Forgotten Issues' (2021) 14(5) The Journal of World Energy Law & Business 297.

[29] Olawuyi and Athwal, 'ESG Considerations' (n 26); also D de Felice, 'Business and Human Rights Indicators to Measure the Corporate Responsibility to Respect: Challenges and Opportunities' (2015) 37(2) Human Rights Quarterly 511.

[30] United Nations Human Rights Council (UN HRC), 'Promotion and protection of all human rights, civil, political, economic, social and cultural rights, including the right to development' (6 October 2021) UN Doc A/HRC/48/L.23/Rev.1; see also UN Doc A/HRC/45/17 of 6 October 2020, UN Doc A/HRC/45/30 of 7 October 2020, and UN Doc A/HRC/46/7 of 23 March 2021.

[31] See United Nations General Assembly (UNGA) (26 July 2022) UN Doc A/76/L.75.

[32] The African Commission on Human and Peoples' Rights (African Commission), 'Resolution on a Human Rights-Based Approach to Natural Resources Governance', 51st Session (2 May 2012) ACHPR/Res.224(LI)2012; see also *the Resolution on Business and Human Rights in Africa* – ACHPR/Res.550 (LXXIV) 2023, noting that businesses are paramount in achieving all of Agenda 2063 goals and aspirations.

[33] Olawuyi, 'Rights-Based Approaches' (n 19) 113–58.

[34] OECD, *OECD Guidelines for Multinational Enterprises* (OECD 2011) 1–10.

[35] Olawuyi and Athwal, 'ESG Considerations' (n 26) 5–6.

investments.[36] As many more countries adopt National Action Plans on Business and Human Rights, the obligation of business enterprises to adopt sound ESG programmes and plans that reduce adverse human rights impacts in their natural resource operations and investments will remain a crucial aspect of natural resources law and policy.[37]

A third driver is the growing effort by countries worldwide to address the problem of climate change. As signatories to the Paris Agreement and the United Nations Framework Convention on Climate Change, several countries have already committed, in their nationally determined contributions (NDCs), to contribute to net zero.[38] Such commitments have led to a rise in regional and national policies that require natural resources investors to disclose ongoing efforts to reduce GHG emissions and address ESG risks across their entire value chain.[39] For example, the 2007 Arab Ministerial Declaration on Climate Change contains regional aspirations by all ministers responsible for environment and climate change in the oil and gas-rich Arab region to include 'policies to deal with climate change issues in all sectors within national and regional policies for sustainable development'.[40] Furthermore, the Paris Agreement recognizes that parties should 'when taking action to address climate change, respect, promote and consider their respective obligations on human rights'.[41] By forging an explicit link between climate action and human rights, the Paris Agreement reinforces the need for countries to ensure that all climate projects and investments within their jurisdictions, including projects conducted by or in partnership with private enterprises, integrate ESG considerations.

Fourthly, with the rise of business and human rights norms, business enterprises themselves increasingly recognize the important roles they can play in advancing responsible net zero investments in a just, inclusive, and rights-based manner that eliminates ESG risks,[42] for example a coalition of governments and business enterprises came together in 2023 to adopt a comprehensive agreement that calls on all signatories to integrate human rights into energy transition efforts.[43] Similarly, in 2013 more than 500 businesses under the aegis of the Coalition for Environmentally Responsible Economies (CERES) adopted the CERES Principles, which encourage companies to prioritize and support a just and equitable transition.[44] Moreover, at the 21st Meeting of the Conference of the Parties (COP) to

[36] UNGPs (n 13); see Pillar II, paras 17–21.

[37] Damilola Olawuyi, *Climate Change Law and Policy in the Middle East and North Africa Region* (Routledge 2022) 1–10.

[38] UNFCCC, Paris Agreement under the United Nations Framework Convention on Climate Change, Conference of the Parties Twenty-first Session Paris, 30 November to 11 December 2015, UN Doc FCCC/CP/2015/L.9, arts 2(1), 4, 6, and 7.

[39] Layla El-Wafi, *ESG Developments in the MENA and GCC Region: Look Back 2021/Look Ahead 2022* <https://www.tamimi.com/law-update-articles/esg-developments-in-the-mena-and-gcc-region-look-back-2021-look-ahead-2022/> accessed 27 August 2023; also Olawuyi, 'Corporate Accountability (n 14).

[40] Arab Ministerial Declaration on Climate Change, adopted by the Council of Arab Ministers responsible for the Environment (6 December 2007) UN Doc E/ESCWA/SDPD/2012/Technical Paper 2.

[41] See Preamble, UNFCCC, Paris Agreement (n 38).

[42] Karlheinz Spitz, John Trudinger, and Matthew Orr, *Environmental Social Governance: Managing Risk and Expectations* (CRC Press 2022) 12.

[43] International Responsible Business Conduct Agreement for the Renewable Energy Sector, 'Integrating sustainability and human rights in the energy transition' <https://www.imvoconvenanten.nl/-/media/imvo/files/hernieuwbare-energie/convenant_hernieuwbare_energie_engels.pdf?la=en&hash=A2A7D070969D49FFCF53239F91258369> accessed 27 August 2023.

[44] Coalition for Environmental Responsible Economies (CERES), 'CERES Introduces the CERES Roadmap 2030: A 10-year action plan for sustainable business leadership' (6 October 2020) <https://www.ceres.org/resources/news/ceres-introduces-the-ceres-roadmap-2030-a-10-year-action-plan-for-sustainable-business-leadership> accessed 12 May 2024; also CERES Principles <https://www.iisd.org/business/tools/principles_ceres.aspx> accessed 27 August 2023.

the UNFCCC, several leading business enterprises signed the Paris Pledge for Action, to 'play their part to support the objectives of the Paris Agreement'.[45] A similar initiative is the Equator Principles (EP), a voluntary set of standards adopted by over eighty commercial banks worldwide to ensure that investments and projects that violate environmental and social goals will not be funded.[46] Comparably, the Report of the Task Force on Climate-related Financial Disclosures emphasizes the need for companies, banks, and investors to transparently monitor and disclose climate-related risks and opportunities across their entire operations.[47] Though several of the foregoing efforts are voluntary and not legally binding, they have played important roles in raising awareness of what responsible corporations can do to limit environmental harm and damage that threaten fundamental human rights.

Fifthly, the importance of systemic and coordinated approaches that limit ESG risks has assumed greater significance and urgency with the adoption of the United Nations' 2030 Agenda for Sustainable Development.[48] SDG 17 underscores the need for enhanced partnerships—globally, regionally, and nationally—on the environment, human rights, trade, investment, shared governance, and other issues in order to advance collective action on all of the SDGs.[49] Since the adoption of the SDGs, business enterprises have increasingly aligned enterprise-wide risk management and investment decision-making efforts with the seventeen SDGs.[50] For example, the Mining Principles released by the International Council on Mining and Metals (ICMM) aim to advance all aspects of the SDGs in mineral development.[51] Also, in June 2022, the ICMM added Diversity, Equity and Inclusion (DEI) to include additional actions towards gender equity and the elimination of harassment and discrimination from the workplace in mining activities.[52] Furthermore, IPIECA (formerly the International Petroleum Industry Environmental Conservation Association) has released similar guidelines and principles which aim to advance ESG in petroleum activities.[53] These industry-led efforts are driving a growing integration of ESG requirements in natural resource contracts and bidding requirements.[54]

Despite debates surrounding the practical implementation of the ESG concept, the expectation that natural resource stakeholders should appropriately investigate, assess, and price ESG risks which may arise in transactional contexts has become an essential part of

[45] The Paris Pledge for Action (2015) <https://www.corporateleadersgroup.com/reports-evidence-and-insights/news-items/lappel-de-paris-paris-pledge-for-action> accessed 27 August 2023.

[46] The Equator Principles, 'Equator Principles -EP4' (July 2020) < https://equator-principles.com/app/uploads/The-Equator-Principles_EP4_July2020.pdf> accessed 12 May 2024.

[47] Task Force on Climate-related Financial Disclosures, 'Recommendations of the Task Force on Climate-related Financial Disclosures' (2017) <https://assets.bbhub.io/company/sites/60/2021/10/FINAL-2017-TCFD-Report.pdf> accessed 12 May 2024.

[48] UN 2030 Agenda (n 23).

[49] Andreas Rechkemmer and Damilola Olawuyi, 'SDG17: Strengthen the Means of Implementation and Revitalize the Global Partnership for Sustainable Development' in Ilias Bantekas and Francesco Seatzu, *The UN Sustainable Development Goals: A Commentary* (OUP 2023) 1247–1323.

[50] See eg Qatar Petroleum, Sustainability Report (2018) 28–29 <https://www.qatarenergy.qa/en/MediaCenter/Publications/QP%202018%20Sustainability%20Report.pdf> accessed 27 August 2023. See also TotalEnergies, 'Our Sustainability Approach' <https://totalenergies.com/sustainability/our-approach> accessed 27 August 2023.

[51] International Council on Mining and Metals (ICMM), 'Mining Principles: Performance Expectations: Strengthening DEI in ICMM Mining Principles' (15 June 2022) <https://www.icmm.com/en-gb/our-principles/mining-principles/mining-principles> accessed 27 August 2023.

[52] ibid.

[53] IPIECA, 'Engaging with the UNFCCC and IPCC' <https://www.ipieca.org/work/climate/engaging-with-unfccc-and-ipcc> accessed 27 August 2023.

[54] See Chapter 4 of this book.

natural resource law.[55] The next section examines the nature and dimensions of ESG risks that are emerging in the natural resources industry in view of the rapid legal developments on ESG.

B. Dimensions of Net Zero-Related ESG Risks

The net zero transition raises direct and indirect ESG risks that should be coherently anticipated and managed in natural resource planning, investment, and decision-making.[56] *Direct ESG risks* may result from the failure of licensees to comply with emission reduction, pollution control, local content, corporate disclosure, business and human rights, and other ESG-related standards stipulated in legislation and industry guidelines. Anticipating and addressing direct risks, therefore, requires a strong culture of complying with applicable laws relating to net zero as stipulated in the country where the investment is taking place.

Indirect ESG risks, on the other hand, relate to new structural, transitional, and disclosure-related ESG requirements, especially in light of the ongoing low-carbon energy transition that may significantly increase transaction or compliance costs.[57]

The three core aspects of indirect risks are discussed below:

1. Structural Risks

As discussed in Chapter 13 of this book, legal requirements relating to net zero buildings, energy efficiency, and climate-smart infrastructure are on the rise. Structural risks, therefore, relate to risks and costs associated with the potential disruptions to an investor's activities or clean energy transition programmes due to the physical impacts of climate change or complying with net zero infrastructure standards.

Apart from climate-induced water scarcity, flooding, and fatal heat waves, climate change could have wide-ranging effects on pipelines, electricity networks, and other physical and associated infrastructure required for advancing energy security during the transition.[58] This includes the potential failure of facilities, reduced life expectancy of buildings, and increased operational and maintenance expenditure of electricity, water, and aviation infrastructure, amongst others, as a result of climate change impacts.[59]

To advance energy security during the transition, there is a need for increased investment in climate-smart infrastructure, that is, buildings, structures, and systems that reduce GHG emissions and improve society's ability to adapt to, and cope with, the risks posed by climate change.[60] Furthermore, in the transactional context, it is necessary to consider whether a target entity operates, or if its raw materials are sourced, in areas prone to flooding or at risk of rising sea levels and if such risks may result in disruptions to infrastructure and

[55] UN Global Impact (n 9). For the debates, see Sjåfjell and Richardson (n 20) 1–34.

[56] This section builds upon discussions in Olawuyi and Athwal, 'ESG Considerations' (n 26).

[57] See UNEP (n 25); also Terje Aven and Bodil S Krohn, 'A New Perspective on How to Understand, Assess and Manage Risk and the Unforeseen' (2014) 121 Reliability Engineering & System Safety 1.

[58] See Chapter 15 of this book.

[59] Jeannette Sieber, 'Impacts of, and Adaptation Options to, Extreme Weather Events and Climate Change Concerning Thermal Power Plants' 121 Climatic Change (2013) 55.

[60] Olawuyi, *Climate Change Law and Policy* (n 37).

supply chains. Addressing structural risks therefore requires integrating resilience planning and resource efficiency into the entire natural resource value chain to reduce disruptions.[61]

2. Transition Risks

Transition risks relate to new or more stringent ESG standards and requirements that are arising from the ongoing net zero and clean energy transition plans and programmes worldwide. As discussed in Chapter 3 of this book, as more countries and corporations adopt net zero plans, natural resource investors will increasingly have to deal with limited access to financing, loss of anticipated revenue, oil price volatility, stringent low-carbon technology and efficiency standards, and 'leaving it in the ground' obligations. All of these factors may reduce the availability of financing needed for new or existing energy access projects.[62] In addition, it would be critical to assess the extent of capital required to maintain compliance with ESG requirements, in order to factor them into the negotiation of natural resource contracts in a net zero era. Natural resource contracts would also have to be aligned with just transition requirements, including gender justice, local content, and free prior informed consent of local communities, amongst others, to avoid the risk of litigation and regulatory fines.[63]

3. Disclosure Risks

Disclosure risks relate to requirements to transparently measure and disclose climate opportunities and risks, as well as progress made with net zero and sustainability programmes. The need for climate-related disclosure is increasingly recognized by many countries and energy multinational corporations, such as ExxonMobil.[64] One of the key risk points is the need to ensure timely, transparent, and accurate disclosure to avoid greenwashing, which refers to deliberate disinformation, or misleading or unsubstantiated claims or reporting of a company's ESG programmes.[65] For example, a recent Australian Competition and Consumer Commission report expressed concern that about 57 per cent of environmental and net zero claims made by businesses represent 'greenwashing'.[66] In response, several regions and countries have introduced legislation that imposes regulatory sanctions and fines on companies that provide misleading environmental claims.[67] For example, pursuant to the Australian Competition and Consumer Act 2010, the Australian Competition and

[61] See Catherine Banet and others (eds), *Resilience in Energy, Infrastructure, and Natural Resources Law: Examining Legal Pathways for Sustainability in Times of Disruption* (OUP 2022).

[62] See Chapter 3 of this book.

[63] See Chapter 2 of this book.

[64] CERES, 'ExxonMobil Investors Make History with Majority Vote on Climate Risk Disclosure' (31 May 2017) <https://iasj.org/exxonmobil-investors-make-history-majority-vote-climate-risk-disclosure-ceres-press-release/> accessed 14 May 2024.

[65] United Nations, 'Zero tolerance for greenwashing, Guterres says at report launch' (10 November 2022) <https://www.un.org/en/delegate/'zero-tolerance-greenwashing'-guterres-says-report-launch> accessed 27 August 2023; Al Attiyah Foundation, 'Guidebook on ESG: Contributing to Knowledge and Insights on the Emerging Concepts of ESG Best Practices' <https://www.abhafoundation.org/media-uploads/reports/Guidebook_on_ESG_by_The_Al-Attiyah_Foundation.pdf> accessed 27 August 2023.

[66] Australian Competition and Consumer Commission, 'ACCC "greenwashing" internet sweep unearths widespread concerning claims' (2 March 2023) <https://www.accc.gov.au/media-release/accc-greenwashing-internet-sweep-unearths-widespread-concerning-claims> accessed 12 May 2024.

[67] See the UK government, 'Guidance: Making environmental claims on goods and services' (20 September 2021) <https://www.gov.uk/government/publications/green-claims-code-making-environmental-claims/environmental-claims-on-goods-and-services> accessed 12 May 2024.

Consumer Commission have issued fines of up to AUS$6 Million for greenwashing.[68] In the United States, the Federal Trade Commission Act outlaws fraudulent or deceptive environmental marketing and the Federal Trade Commission (FTC) has released guidelines aimed at greenwashing.[69] The FTC has also charged and imposed fines on a number of companies for greenwashing.[70] Similarly, the US Securities and Exchange Commission (SEC) recently levied a US$1.5 million fine to the fund management arm of BNY Mellon for allegedly providing misleading information on ESG investments.[71]

As indicated in Table 11.1, a wide range of practical considerations can enable natural resource operators to better anticipate and address salient human rights and ESG issues that may result in the most severe adverse impacts across their ensure natural resource value chains.[72] Failure to address such direct and indirect risks in transactional contexts could effectively lead to significant financial, reputational, and litigation risks for entities in the natural resource sector. Legislation penalizing misleading environmental claims necessitates accurate, transparent reporting from natural resource operators, including thorough due diligence when negotiating contracts, ensuring compliance with climate disclosure requirements, and verifying the veracity of public statements about net zero efforts.

Only a portion of the foregoing risks can be identified and addressed through traditional due diligence and title review processes. This accentuates the need for human rights due diligence and proactive risk management approaches that anticipate and minimize a wide range of technical and operational risks in light of the fundamental transformations in the natural resource sector. Yet, as the next section demonstrates, piecemeal and uncoordinated approaches to the legislation and enforcement of ESG standards have not provided the necessary regulatory clarity to drive industry coherence.

III. The Search for Coherence in ESG Implementation and Enforcement

While the aim of the ESG framework is clear, several gaps from regulatory and enterprise governance standpoints still need to be clarified and addressed to better streamline the guiding principles of natural resources law and policy relating to ESG risk management, especially in the context of net zero transition efforts.

[68] See 'Nurofen fine over misleading claims in Australia increased to £3.5 million' (*The Telegraph*, 16 December 2016) <https://www.telegraph.co.uk/business/2016/12/16/nurofen-fine-misleading-claims-australia-increased-35-million/> accessed 27 August 2023.

[69] See the Federal Trade Commission (FTC) Act 15 USC 45(a), s 5; also the FTC Guides for the Use of Environmental Marketing Claims clarifies the nature of environmental marketing claims that are unfair, deceptive, and therefore illegal within the provisions of s 5.

[70] Jennifer Elks, 'FTC Cracking Down on Misleading, Unsubstantiated Biodegradability Claims' <https://sustainablebrands.com/read/marketing-and-comms/ftc-cracking-down-on-misleading-unsubstantiated-biodegradability-claims> accessed 27 August 2023.

[71] ibid. See also 'Environmental NGO wins greenwashing lawsuit against TotalEnergies' <https://www.cleanenergywire.org/news/environmental-ngo-wins-greenwashing-lawsuit-against-totalenergies> accessed 27 August 2023.

[72] On the importance of saliency assessment, see the UN Guiding Principles Reporting Framework, 'Salient Human Rights Issues' <https://www.ungpreporting.org/resources/salient-human-rights-issues/> assessed 12 November 2023.

Table 11.1 Risks and ESG considerations

ESG risks	Key considerations
Direct Direct ESG risks may result from the failure of licensees to comply with legal obligations in applicable legislation that require operators to proactively anticipate, mitigate, and redress all sources of environmental pollution, social exclusion, and lack of transparency in their activities and projects, especially in local communities where they operate.	○ Are there possibilities of flooding, air and water pollution, some levels of noise in the project construction and operational phase, mass displacements of people from their homes, traditional lands and forests, loss of access to drinking water, loss of arable farmlands, risks of spillage or explosions? ○ Who is likely to be impacted? ○ Has their free, prior, informed consent been obtained prior to the approval and commencement of the project? ○ Are there programmes in place to address human rights risks (especially those relating to land, and clean and healthy environment) and promote local content, supplier development, and empowerment?
Indirect risks refer to associated *structural, transitional, and disclosure-related* uncertainties and risks that may result from ESG standards and obligations, especially in light of the ongoing low-carbon energy transition.	○ Key considerations and questions below
Structural Ongoing transition to low-carbon energy systems require net zero buildings and climate-smart infrastructure. Failure to comply with net zero infrastructure standards may result in potential disruptions to an investor's activities or clean energy transition programmes and may attract regulatory fines or sanctions.	○ Does the business operate, or are its raw materials sourced, in areas prone to flooding or at risk of rising sea levels? ○ What assets may be impacted by climate change and other environmental hazards? ○ Are the investor's buildings and infrastructure compliant with latest net zero, water and energy efficiency, and climate-smart infrastructure regulations or requirements? ○ Any additional costs to comply with such net zero infrastructure requirements?
Transition Ongoing transitions to low-carbon energy systems may result in new regulatory standards that may fundamentally change business structure, limit the availability of financing for non-renewable assets, or raise the cost of compliance.	○ Will the resource activity or project be required to make significant capital expenditures to obtain or maintain compliance with land use, zoning, or other regulations? ○ Will ongoing or planned low-carbon technologies and projects of the target (such as renewable energy projects) affect human rights, especially with respect to land and property rights? ○ Are there short-, medium-, and long-term plans in place to transition from GHG-intensive energy sources and to attain clean energy and zero carbon? ○ Is there a framework in place for respect for human rights relating to water, environment, and food in such energy transition programmes?

(*continued*)

Table 11.1 Continued

ESG risks	Key considerations
Disclosures Emerging requirements to transparently measure and report climate-related risks and opportunities, as well as progress made with net zero and sustainability programmes. Failure to disclose net zero programmes in a timely, transparent, and accurate manner may result in legal risks, including risks relating to greenwashing.	○ How are climate-related risks and opportunities likely to impact the business's current and future financial position as reflected in its income statement, cash flow statement, and balance sheet? ○ Has the business complied with ESG, sustainability or climate disclosure requirements, or have they made public statements or disclosures concerning GHG emissions, net zero plans and programmes risk that may in any way be considered misleading? ○ Are the sustainability and energy transition reports timely, accurate, and easy to access in terms of language and readability?

Source: Authors' compilation

A. Lack of Regulatory Clarity on ESG Standards, Reporting, and Rating

Natural resources laws and policies in many parts of the world include the requirement for licence holders to measure and report on their sustainability and climate programmes. Corporate reporting on ESG can have great relevance and utility to various stakeholders in that it may provide a greater level of transparency as to the level of compliance with applicable ESG standards.[73] ESG reporting can provide a means for natural resource operators to respect, protect, and fulfil access to information (ATI) right, a right enshrined in several core international human rights instruments.[74]

However, methodological factors such as a lack of regulatory clarity on what such reports should contain, fraudulent practices in reporting, and a lack of accuracy and consistency in reporting and rating of ESG performance continue to limit the informational and transformational values of ESG reports.[75] This gap is often related to the lack of specific mention of ESG or human rights measurement or reporting in natural resource legislation in many countries despite the evidence of human rights risks in natural resource activities.[76] The lack of regulatory clarity makes it difficult for stakeholders in the natural resource sector to properly understand and evaluate which entity is performing better in terms of ESG compliance.[77]

Furthermore, as firms worldwide have embraced sustainability reporting, several ESG reporting standards and frameworks have been developed and adopted such that

[73] UNCTAD, 'Disclosure of the Impact of Corporations on Society: Current Trends and Issues' (2004) <https://unctad.org/system/files/official-document/iteteb20037_en.pdf> accessed 18 August 2023.

[74] See Report of the Special Rapporteur, 'Promotion and Protection of the Right to Freedom of Opinion and Expression' (28 January 1998) UN Doc E/CN.4/1998/40, para 1.

[75] Petrina McDaniel and others, 'Lack of Uniformity in ESG Ratings System Poses Risks, Opportunities' (16 May 2022) < https://news.bloomberglaw.com/esg/lack-of-uniformity-in-esg-ratings-system-poses-risks-opportunities> accessed 12 May 2024.

[76] Damilola Olawuyi, 'Energy (and Human Rights) for All: Addressing Human Rights Risks in Energy Access Projects' in Raya Salter and others (eds), *Energy Justice: US and International Perspectives* (Edward Elgar 2018).

[77] Petrina McDaniel and others (n 75). See also Damilola Olawuyi, 'Climate Justice and Corporate Responsibility: Taking Human Rights Seriously in Climate Actions and Projects' (2016) 34(1) Journal of Energy & Natural Resources Law 27.

it requires sifting through a maze of what represents the international best practice on corporate reporting. The most widely adopted frameworks include the Global Reporting Initiative (GRI), Sustainability Reporting Framework,[78] the International Integrated Reporting Council (IIRC),[79] and the Sustainability Accounting Standards Board.[80] Financial regulatory institutions, such as the United Kingdom's Financial Reporting Council, have also released guidelines aimed at creating a stronger reporting framework.[81] Similarly, the European Commission has put forward proposals for regulating greenwashing and promoting coherence in net zero disclosures.[82] Furthermore, in 2024, the US Securities and Exchange Commission issued new rules on standardizing climate-related disclosures in the United States.[83] While these efforts can help streamline ESG requirements, there is also a need for international standard-setting under the international climate change framework to promote a common language and multijurisdictional methodology on ESG reporting.

Furthermore, for ESG reporting to be useful for stakeholders, national authorities should establish clear legislative guidelines for its scope and content, mandating companies to adopt simplified, accessible standards. Reports should be transparently released in formats and languages that all stakeholders, especially local communities, can easily understand and utilize.

B. Limited or Inadequate Climate Change and BHR Laws

Another key challenge is the uneven pace of regulation on climate change and business and human rights (BHR) in many parts of the world, which has not fostered a coherent and industry-wide understanding of ESG requirements in the natural resource sector. While national visions and strategies on net zero are increasing worldwide, several countries, especially in the Global South, are yet to enact specific or comprehensive laws to achieve those targets and deadlines.[84] For example, while the Qatar National Vision 2030 expressly identifies climate change mitigation and adaptation as a national priority, clear, specific,

[78] See Global Reporting Initiative (GRI), 'GRI Sustainability Reporting Framework' <http://www.globalreporting.org/standards/reporting-frameworkoverview/Pages/default.aspx> accessed 27 August 2023.

[79] The International Integrated Reporting Council (IIRC) was formed in August 2010 with the objective of creating a globally accepted framework for corporate reporting.

[80] The Sustainability Accounting Standards Board (SASB)'s sustainability accounting standard provides a framework for assessing the key systemic sustainability issues in key sectors.

[81] 'Audit watchdog to overhaul UK corporate governance code: FRC lays out plans to make boards more accountable for fraud and company finances' (*Financial Times*, 12 July 2022).

[82] See the European Commission's proposed Directive on Green Claims (22 March 2023) <https://eur-lex.europa.eu/legal-content/EN/TXT/PDF/?uri=CELEX:52023PC0166> accessed 27 August 2023; also European Commission, 'Finance: Sustainability-related disclosure in the financial services sector and Regulation on sustainability-related disclosure in the financial services sector' <https://finance.ec.europa.eu/sustainable-finance/disclosures/sustainability-related-disclosure-financial-services-sector_en> accessed 27 August 2023.

[83] Securities and Exchange Commission, 'The Enhancement and Standardization of Climate-Related Disclosures for Investors' (Effective on May 28, 2024) 89 FR 21668 <https://www.sec.gov/files/rules/final/2024/33-11275.pdf> accessed 12 May 2024. See also Qatar Stock Exchange, 'Guidance on ESG Reporting' <https://www.qe.com.qa/documents/20181/726774/Guidance_ESG_Reporting/62aac132-0e46-f419-08d7-fedd3958530b> accessed 12 May 2024

[84] eg Kenya enacted the Climate Change Act on May 2016, while Nigeria enacted the Climate Change Act 2021 on 17 November 2021, in conformity with the Paris Agreement on climate change. For other efforts across the Global South, see Grantham Research Institute on Climate Change and the Environment, *The Climate Change Laws of the World Database* <https://www.climate-laws.org> accessed 27 August 2023.

and comprehensive legislation on climate-change proofing is still in the works.[85] Several other oil and gas-rich countries in the Middle East and Africa are yet to enact legislation on climate change and net zero, which makes it more complex for investors to understand ESG requirements in those contexts.[86] Similarly, several countries are yet to enact legislation or develop National Action Plans (NAPs) on BHR to clarify what responsible investors must do to advance the 'S' in ESG. For example, only three African countries (Kenya, Uganda, and Nigeria) have NAPs on business and human rights, with the pace of implementation even in those countries remaining slow.[87]

Effective domestic laws and regulations are crucial in promoting ESG and net zero goals within the natural resource industry, especially to mandate climate change and human rights considerations in project planning and decision-making. Legal frameworks must clarify climate technologies, human rights due diligence (HRDD) requirements, and rights-based operational standards, net zero building and efficiency standards, renewable technologies, project registration, certification, and monitoring procedures that responsible natural resource investors must comply with.

Climate change laws play a significant role in addressing the human rights impacts of climate action on marginalized communities. They can mitigate ESG risks by ensuring inclusive decision-making processes. In addition to having clear and comprehensive NAPs on business and human rights, climate change laws should also require prospective project licensees to conduct human rights impact assessments and due diligence, integrating human rights concerns into net zero project planning and execution.

C. Limited Institutional Coordination

Effective management of ESG risks in natural resource investments necessitates coordinated multistakeholder participation from various institutions like national oil or mining companies and ministries for energy, construction, finance, and interior. Despite the common ESG risks in net zero projects, a lack of inter-ministerial coordination often hinders an integrated view of net zero policies' effectiveness, requiring enhanced institutional coordination for inclusive laws and policies that minimize ESG risks.[88] For example, lack of institutional coordination in the design and implementation of climate change and net zero policies has been described as a key hindrance to coherence in the MENA region.[89] Problems of limited institutional coordination also remains a hindrance to just energy transition and the fulfilment of human rights in net zero efforts in several parts of the world.[90]

[85] ibid. See also Damilola Olawuyi and Elena Athwal, 'Law and Governance Innovations on Sustainability in Qatar' in Logan Cochrane and Reem-Al Habibi (eds), *Sustainable Qatar* (Springer 2022) 37–54.

[86] *Climate Change Laws of the World Database* (n 84).

[87] United Nations, 'National Action Plan on Business and Human Rights' <https://www.ohchr.org/en/special-procedures/wg-business/national-action-plans-business-and-human-rights> accessed 27 August 2023.

[88] Damilola Olawuyi, 'Sustainable Development and the Water-Energy-Food Nexus: Legal Challenges and Emerging Solutions' (2020) 103(1) Journal of Environmental Science & Policy 1–9.

[89] Riyad Fahkri, Laila Dalaa, and Saad Belkasmi, 'Enhancing the Effectiveness of National and Regional Institutions in Addressing Climate Change in the MENA Region: Lessons from Morocco and the Maghreb' in Damilola Olawuyi, *Climate Change Law and Policy in the MENA Region* (Routledge 2021) 109–18.

[90] See UN WGBHR (n 4).

To improve institutional coordination, pragmatic and standardized approaches that foster cooperation and minimize role duplication are essential.[91] It is crucial to perform cross-sector analysis of key institutions, their coherence, potential conflicts or duplication, and the availability of shared platforms for knowledge-sharing and cooperation. These efforts, complemented by open knowledge-sharing systems, and an institution-wide approach to human rights compliance can foster more coherent and synergistic planning that promote better ESG outcomes.

D. Inadequate Capacity and Resources to Spot and Address ESG Risks in a Timely Manner

Institutional capacity of corporate boards, regulators, management, and field operators to effectively anticipate and address ESG risks remains a key challenge in many parts of the world.[92] The success of any ESG strategy relies heavily on operational teams' knowledge of environmental compliance, pollution management, human rights safeguards, and community relations, highlighting the need to bridge the gap between ESG compliance intentions and actual investment performance. It is equally essential to empower national authorities and monitoring entities with the skills, resources, and tools necessary for enforcing ESG standards.

Due to a lack of training, equipment, and data-gathering technologies, many natural resource stakeholders, including regulators, struggle to monitor compliance with ESG standards and process ESG-related data transparently, undermining public trust and policy efficacy. For example, recent studies indicate that only about 12 per cent of publicly listed companies in the MENA region monitor or disclose ESG data, including those relating to net zero and GHG emissions.[93] Similarly in Nigeria, studies have highlighted how, due to a lack of training, equipment, and tools, environmental and human rights institutions are unable to monitor compliance with ESG standards.[94] Furthermore, the lack of statistical and data-gathering technologies and tools means that regulators in a number of countries simply lack the capabilities to transparently collate, evaluate, and process ESG-related data in a manner that can instill public confidence and policy effectiveness.[95] Addressing capacity and resource constraints is crucial for developing and implementing natural resources laws and policies that yield strong ESG outcomes.

The next section discusses good governance and decision-making techniques through which state and non-state actors in the natural resource sector can better evaluate and address ESG risks in a net zero era.

[91] ibid.

[92] PWC Insights, 'Six key challenges for financial institutions to deal with ESG risks compliance and long-term value creation' <https://www.pwc.nl/en/insights-and-publications/services-and-industries/financial-sector/six-key-challenges-for-financial-institutions-to-deal-with-ESG-risks.html> accessed 27 August 2023.

[93] Patricia Torres, 'Insights: Maximising the potential of ESG investing in the MENA region' (Gulf Business, 9 February 2023) <https://gulfbusiness.com/potential-of-esg-investing-in-mena/> accessed 27 August 2023.

[94] Damilola Olawuyi and Zibima Tubondenyefa, 'Review of the Environmental Guidelines and Standards for the Petroleum Industry in Nigeria (EGASPIN)' (Institute for Oil, Gas, Energy, Environment and Sustainable Development, 2019) 1–25.

[95] Afe Babalola and Damilola Olawuyi, 'Overcoming Regulatory Failure in the Design and Implementation of Gas Flaring Policies: The Potential and Promise of an Energy Justice Approach' (2022) 14(11) Sustainability 6800.

IV. Good Governance and Decision-Making Strategies for Managing ESG Risks in Resource Investments

Dynamic legal innovation is required in the design, enforcement, and implementation of natural resources law and policy to ensure coherent and comprehensive management of ESG risks in natural resource investments, including clean energy projects. ESG implementation requires a smart mix of regulatory and governance strategies that enhance the abilities of national authorities, business enterprises, and other natural resource stakeholders to effectively anticipate, address, and report on ESG risks. On the part of national authorities, regulatory clarity and institutional coordination will be required to provide a clearer regulatory framework for ESG risk identification and reporting. On the part of business enterprises, process and product change will be required in order to improve ESG compliance. For example, updating procurement processes to ensure that suppliers and subcontractors address all adverse social and environmental impacts will be essential. Similarly, product upgrades such as sustainable packaging and production processes that significantly reduce the social, financial, and sustainability cost of activities will be important. For example, by addressing issues of child labour, modern slavery, and other human rights violations in the extraction of transition minerals, the public will have greater confidence that the transition process will progress in a just, inclusive, and right-based manner.

To comprehensively address ESG risks in the natural resource sector, three key steps are essential. First is the need for governments and industry regulators to develop clear NAPs and industry-specific guidelines that clarify ESG priority areas and what responsible investors should do to promote responsible, just, and rights-based net zero transition efforts in the natural resource industry. As demonstrated in this chapter, the drivers of ESG risks are interlinked and cannot be effectively addressed in isolation. The intertwined nature of ESG risk drivers necessitates clear NAPs and industry-specific guidelines that elucidate ESG priorities and investor responsibilities for a responsible and rights-based net zero transition in the natural resource sector. Developing these plans requires cross-sector analysis of ESG risk factors in transition-related investments and the creation of integrated response programmes across diverse domains. Infusing human rights safeguards into natural resource legislation, such as mandatory human rights impact assessments (HRIAs) and due diligence for obtaining licences, allows for early assessment and management of ESG risks. Legal frameworks should integrate HRIA into environmental impact assessment legislation, enabling local communities to demand action when projects increase local vulnerabilities or affect human rights and ensuring considerations for vulnerable groups like women and children. NAPs can also help identify and rectify conflicts or overlaps across various sectors and institutions, promoting consistent and coherent programmes for evaluating and monitoring ESG projects.

Second is the need for clear and comprehensive laws on climate change and net zero. The lack of standardization in ESG investing and reporting is directly linked to the lack of clear regulatory standards on net zero and the reporting of ESG efforts.[96] Clear, comprehensive climate change laws are vital to place project planners under an obligation to

[96] United Nations, 'Climate Action: Credibility and Accountability of Net-Zero Emissions Commitments of Non-State Entities' (2022) <https://www.un.org/en/climatechange/high-level-expert-group> accessed 27 August 2023.

integrate human rights into natural resource investments and projects. Such legislation can standardize key measures for project design and approval, including permitting, licensing, efficiency standards, and financing options, as well as standardize ESG reporting to prevent greenwashing and promote transparent, accessible, and timely reporting. This legislative clarity enables efficient evaluation of net zero programmes and progress-tracking based on set timelines. Such legislation should also clarify the roles and responsibilities of different government entities and institutions to avoid role duplication and promote greater synergy across the environment, human rights, social development, and justice institutions.

Third is the need for natural resource investors and operators to incorporate ESG considerations in all aspects of project planning and risk management. Aligning corporate governance and internal risk management policies with evolving ESG risk perceptions is crucial for businesses and regulators. A five-step approach focusing on risk identification, control methodology, risk focal points, information dissemination, and monitoring facilitates the integration of ESG considerations into natural resource investments.[97] Starting with material risk identification, natural resource operators need to implement comprehensive HRDD to assess potential ESG risks before initiating investments or project activities.[98] Upon identifying actual or potential adverse ESG risks, an integrated, multidisciplinary management approach becomes necessary for addressing these risks across the entire value chain, leveraging various mitigation techniques.[99] Appointing a diverse risk management committee as a focal point for risk identification, collection, reporting, and staff instruction on risk management strategies is also essential.[100] Furthermore, a robust feedback mechanism ensures stakeholder engagement throughout the risk control process. The next essential step involves proactive, transparent disclosure of ESG mitigation plans and efforts. Periodic climate or sustainability reports that disclose efforts to address ESG risks are essential for public understanding of potential ESG impacts and mitigation measures, requiring these reports to be timely, accurate, and accessible.[101] Lastly, effective monitoring tracks the success of ESG risk anticipation and response measures, using high-quality statistical data and maintaining alertness to new risks. Tailored training programmes on climate change, due diligence, and risk mitigation should be embedded into business value chains and cultures, ensuring staff remain updated on ESG risk management strategies.

V. Conclusion

The expectation that natural resource investors and stakeholders should appropriately identify, assess, disclose, and manage ESG risks has become an essential part of natural resources law and policy. Even when domestic laws are silent on these issues, the increasing regulation across the world on human rights due diligence and import bans on minerals sourced with child labour, unfair labour conditions, or inhumane working conditions

[97] Allison Herren Lee, 'Climate, ESG, and the Board of Directors: "You cannot direct the wind, but you can adjust your sails"' (2022) 40(2) Journal of Energy & Natural Resources Law 275.

[98] See UN WGBHR (n 4).

[99] Olawuyi, 'Corporate Accountability' (n 14).

[100] ibid. See also Keiko Kamioka and Eileen Cronin, 'Enterprise Risk Management: Approaches and Uses in the United Nations System Organization' JUI/REP/2020/5 <https://www.unjiu.org/sites/www.unjiu.org/files/jiu_rep_2020_5_english.pdf> accessed 12 May 2024.

[101] Olawuyi, 'Corporate Accountability' (n 14).

may result in financial loss, protracted litigation, as well as reputational damage. Natural resource investors and operators can avoid costly legal risks to their operations by incorporating direct and indirect ESG factors into the design, approval, financing, implementation, and reporting of natural resource investment, especially transition-related projects. Understanding ESG risks through a coherent planning and decision-making process can help natural resource operators to understand how their operations may result in adverse sustainability outcomes and how to develop responsive and coherent risk management processes.

As for the role of lawyers representing companies and investors in transition-related natural resource investments, it is important to emphasize the significance of early human rights due diligence when providing counsel. The growing insistence of courts and tribunals on the rights to information, public participation, and benefit-sharing for those persons potentially affected by energy transition projects and the extraction of transition minerals should lead lawyers to advise their clients of the wisdom of early compliance with human rights requirements in such investments and projects. Through comprehensive HRDD and HRIAs, natural resource investors can coherently address all ESG risk points commonly encountered in a transactional context.

Furthermore, national authorities can benefit from establishing clear and comprehensive regulatory frameworks that provide clarity on the ESG obligations of operators. Adopting coherent and comprehensive ESG guidelines, which safeguard environmental and human rights principles, can accelerate the implementation of net zero investments and projects in a just, inclusive, and rights-based manner that leaves no one behind. Such legislation can also clarify how stakeholders can effectively measure, verify, and report ESG progress in a transparent and accessible manner.

12

Net Zero and Environmental Impact Assessments

The Baseline Bar in the United States

Nadia B. Ahmad

I. Introduction

This chapter analyses the need for standardized and more rigorous environmental impact assessment (EIA) processes and legal environmental baseline limits as key requirements for accelerating a net zero energy future while addressing environmental impacts.

The current global energy landscape relies heavily on the extraction and consumption of fossil fuels, a reliance which contributes to greenhouse gas (GHG) emissions and exacerbates the climate crisis. To achieve a net zero energy future, it is imperative to transition away from fossil fuels and embrace renewable and sustainable energy sources. One critical aspect of this transition is the implementation of standardized and rigorous EIA processes. EIAs are essential tools that evaluate the potential environmental consequences of proposed projects, such as energy infrastructure developments, before they are approved and implemented. These assessments help identify and mitigate the adverse effects on ecosystems, biodiversity, air quality, water resources, and local communities. However, the current EIAs often fall short in adequately addressing the environmental impacts associated with energy projects. They may lack comprehensive methodologies, overlook crucial factors, or fail to consider long-term consequences. This inadequacy undermines the effectiveness of regulatory measures and compromises the sustainability goals for a net zero transition.

The road to sustainability for the planet's people and natural ecosystems does not include rampant extractivism.[1] More than 80 per cent of the world's known hydrocarbon reserves must remain in the ground to avoid runaway climate change.[2] A 2021 study have found that, to have a 50 per cent chance to stay within a 1.5 °C carbon budget by 2050, the quantity of fossil fuels that must be left in the ground regionally and globally is roughly 60 per cent of oil and fossil methane gas and 90 per cent of coal must remain unextracted.[3] While the numbers may vary, the collective momentum of the 'Leave it in

[1] James Rothwell, Rob Crilly, and Emily Gosden, 'Paris Climate Change Deal—Ministers Adopt Historic Agreement to Keep Global Warming "Well below" 2C' (*The Telegraph*, 12 December 2015) <https://www.telegraph.co.uk/news/earth/paris-climate-change-conference/12047133/Final-text-of-climate-deal-to-be-released-imminently.html> accessed 10 June 2023; United Nations (UN), 'As Humanity's Environment Footprint Becomes Increasingly Unsustainable, Global Leaders Recommit to Joint Climate Action, at Opening of Stockholm Summit' (2 June 2022) <https://www.press.un.org/en/2022/envdev2046.doc.htm> accessed 10 June 2023.

[2] Christophe McGlade and Paul Ekins, 'The Geographical Distribution of Fossil Fuels Unused When Limiting Global Warming to 2 °C' (2015) 517 Nature 187.

[3] Dan Welsby and others, 'Unextractable Fossil Fuels in a 1.5 °C World' (2021) 597 Nature 230.

Nadia B. Ahmad, *Net Zero and Environmental Impact Assessments* In: *Net Zero and Natural Resources Law*. Edited by: Damilola S. Olawuyi, José Juan González, Hanri Mostert, Milton Fernando Montoya, and Catherine Banet, Oxford University Press.
 DOI: 10.1093/9780198925033.003.0012

the Ground' movement is not being matched by the legal mechanism to limit fossil fuel extraction. This chapter challenges the dominant paradigm as to why the 'no action' alternative provision of the US law of National Environmental Policy Act is used more as a tool of assessment to move a project forward than as a tool of prohibition to halt a project and its deleterious environmental impacts.[4] To strengthen the 'no action' alternative, this chapter recommends a more detailed analysis to conserve delicate environmental spaces and alleviate the phenomenon of environmental racism. Increased detail and specificity would establish what this chapter refers to as 'the baseline bar', the point at which environmental, social, and economic metrics for a proposed federal agency action lead to a recommendation of 'no action'. The baseline bar can be achieved through NEPA's 'no action' alternative as well as through other environmental laws, including the Clean Water Act, the Clean Air Act, the Endangered Species Act, amongst others. The baseline bar would operate to halt project development once specific metrics are not satisfied or delay them so they become economically unfeasible. Manifestations of the baseline bar have led up to the earlier rejection of extractive industry projects, such as Alaska's Pebble Mine and TransCanada's Keystone XL Pipeline. Yet these projects and many other hydrocarbon and mining enterprises, including the Willow Project in Alaska, now face rebirth.[5] Adherence to NEPA's procedural requirements could delay or inhibit such projects. The lack of a baseline bar is evident in the water crisis in Flint, Michigan. Further, this analysis of the baseline bar will work towards understanding the next wave of environmental lawsuits and dispute resolution.

To advance net zero, there is a need for more stringent environmental due diligence and impact assessment process that screen out unsustainable investments and projects, especially in the natural resource sector. With increased energy consumption, soaring population growth, and more intense land use impacts, a more robust 'no action' alternative is key in the analysis for considering the environmental impact statement (EIS) on whether or not the project should go forward. This chapter proceeds in six sections. Section II will provide an overview of the EIS processes and discuss the problem of the lack of uniformity embedded in these processes. Section III will clarify ways of incorporating this proposal for a baseline bar to create more robust environmental impact statements through case studies and legal decisions for a net zero future. This section will analyse the unique dimensions of environmental, social, and economic metrics for the assessment process. Section IV reconciles the 'no action' alternative with existing laws and illustrates the normative implications of the baseline bar and the more robust analysis of the 'no action' alternative. Section V offers policy recommendations on the coherent implementation of the baseline bar approach to EIAs in a net zero era.

[4] See 40 CFR § 1502.14(d) (2016). Lance N McCold and James W Saulsbury, 'Defining the No-Action Alternative for National Environmental Policy Act Analyses of Continuing Actions' (1998) 18 Environmental Impact Assessment Review 15.

[5] Oliver Milman, Nina Lakhani, and Maanvi Singh, 'Biden Approves Controversial Willow Oil Drilling Project in Alaska' <https://www.theguardian.com/us-news/2023/mar/13/alaska-willow-project-approved-oil-gas-biden> accessed 14 March 2023.

II. The Environmental Impact Assessment Process in Natural Resource Projects

EIAs are vital tools for analysing potential environmental impacts of proposed projects, particularly in the natural resource sector. They support informed decision-making, helping to mitigate detrimental effects and drive sustainable resource use. EIAs are crucial for achieving net zero emissions by identifying, quantifying, and mitigating the impacts of carbon-intensive industries. However, implementation gaps often undermine EIA effectiveness. These include the lack of clear, quantifiable impact metrics and the insufficient consideration of the 'no action' alternative. The baseline bar model addresses these gaps by establishing specific impact metrics and strengthening the role of the 'no action' alternative, leading to more robust EIAs that support a net zero future. In the United States, NEPA mandates EIAs for federally funded projects. Despite its pivotal role, the implementation of NEPA faces similar gaps, emphasizing the need for a more stringent approach, like the baseline bar, in EIA processes.

What is unsettling about NEPA is that it does not impose an independent requirement for the federal agency to set a 'legal' environmental baseline. The establishment of a 'baseline is not an independent legal requirement, but rather, a practical requirement in environmental analysis often employed to identify the environmental consequences of a proposed agency action'.[6] Consider the baseline bar through the lens of trade and economics. As a starting point, the baseline bar is the status quo to maintain the existing environmental equilibrium. The lack of legal baseline leaves only undefined environmental, social, and economic metrics that lead to a degree of uncertainty, unreliability, and inconclusiveness.

As this chapter demonstrates, the separate baseline benchmark bars—social, environmental, and economic—are necessary for establishing and maintaining equilibrium both for trade and environmental protection. As such, considering the 'no action' alternative as a baseline bar is the unrelenting ambition for species survival as well as air, water, and soil quality controls. The unimpeded extractivist capitalism model has taken a detrimental toll on the natural world. The baseline bar would be an affirmative negation to unsustainable economic growth in line with the existing NEPA regulations and other environmental mandates. These environmental laws are tools and legal mechanisms to provide protection for life, air, water, and land when economics is a driving motivation. This tussle between nature and commercial activity has taken place most rapidly since the dawn of the Industrial Revolution. The twenty-first century has yielded new technologies to expand capitalist extractivism to make drilling and mining processes more efficient and increase access to hard-to-reach resources. The new technologies have decreased geological barriers for extraction. Increased security forces have lessened political and social impediments. Having a baseline bar to halt projects would force the deployment of renewable energy technologies and require an appreciation for zero-growth economic strategies.

Certain human populations are more vulnerable to environmental degradation, including marginalized communities in low-income areas and people of colour. These communities

[6] *American Rivers et al v Federal Energy Regulatory Commission et al* [2000] United States Court of Appeals (9th Circuit) No 98-70084.

are more likely to be impacted by the disastrous impact of negative environmental externalities. Environmental racism considers how people of colour and low-income households are more likely to be in the vicinity of pollution sources and away from clean water, air, and soil.[7] The location of marginalized communities near sources of pollution springs from racist government policies.[8] Environmental racism does not capture the environmental inequalities created on the basis of class. The term 'environmental injustice' more adequately accounts for the marginalization of communities on the basis of class as well as race.[9]

The absence of a legal environmental baseline limits incentives for industry operators to adequately account for environmental inequalities in the EIS process. The United States provides a government mechanism for the formation of EIA reports.[10] These environmental problems present a legal predicament. What is problematic about the EIS process is the lack of standardization in these regulations. While the implementation of a legal baseline may be more difficult to achieve, I additionally propose a more robust analysis of the 'no action' alternative. This more robust analysis of the 'no action' alternative would be in line with previous Council of Environmental Quality (CEQ) guidelines.[11] Changes in White House leadership in 2017 and 2021 have led to mixed prioritization of previous efforts at climate change adaptation and consideration of environmental justice impacts. As such, a deeper analysis of the 'no action' alternative can provide environmental and land conservation activists additional NEPA claims to legally contested extraction projects.

In an EIA, the 'no action' alternative assesses the implications of not implementing a proposed project, essentially maintaining the status quo. This evaluation is a critical component of NEPA in the United States, serving as a baseline for comparing potential environmental impacts of proposed actions. In the context of natural resources law and achieving net zero emissions, this approach guides decision-makers to consider if a proposed project, such as new mining or infrastructure, is necessary or if more sustainable alternatives exist, encouraging the pursuit of low-carbon or carbon-neutral alternatives, supporting the transition towards a net zero future. The 'no action' alternative does not mean 'nothing happens'.[12] In the context of achieving a net zero future, the no action alternative can be a powerful tool, allowing decision-makers to carefully consider whether a project or action

[7] Bryce Covert, 'Race Best Predicts Whether You Live Near Pollution' <https://www.thenation.com/article/archive/race-best-predicts-whether-you-live-near-pollution/> accessed 10 June 2023. Lisa Song, 'At Flint Debate, Clinton and Sanders Avoid Talk of Environmental Racism' (*Inside Climate News*, 8 March 2016) <https://www.insideclimatenews.org/news/08032016/environmental-justice-racism-flint-water-crisis-hillary-clinton-bernie-sanders-debate-climate-change/> accessed 10 June 2023.

[8] Javacia Harris Bowser, 'Understanding Environmental Racism and How It Can Make People Sick' (*Good Housekeeping*, 14 March 2023) <https://www.goodhousekeeping.com/health/a43097513/what-is-environmental-racism/> accessed 10 June 2023.

[9] Luke Cole and Sheila Foster, *From the Ground Up: Environmental Racism and the Rise of the Environmental Justice Movement* (NYU Press 2000) <https://www.nyupress.org/9780814715376/from-the-ground-up> accessed 10 June 2023.

[10] Robert D Bullard and Glenn S Johnson, 'Environmentalism and Public Policy: Environmental Justice: Grassroots Activism and Its Impact on Public Policy Decision Making' (2000) 56 Journal of Social Issues 555.

[11] 'Final Guidance for Federal Departments and Agencies on Consideration of Greenhouse Gas Emissions and the Effects of Climate Change in National Environmental Policy Act Reviews' (2016) Federal Register <https://www.federalregister.gov/documents/2016/08/05/2016-18620/final-guidance-for-federal-departments-and-agencies-on-consideration-of-greenhouse-gas-emissions-and> accessed 10 June 2023.

[12] 'What Is the No Action Alternative?' (*US Army Corps of Engineers, Northwestern Division*, 16 March 2019) <https://www.nwd.usace.army.mil/Media/News-Stories/Article/1849987/what-is-the-no-action-alternative/https%3A%2F%2Fwww.nwd.usace.army.mil%2FMedia%2FNews-Stories%2FArticle%2F1849987%2Fwhat-is-the-no-action-alternative%2F> accessed 10 June 2023.

is necessary, and whether there are alternative approaches that could achieve the desired goals without significant environmental impacts. By evaluating the no action alternative, policy-makers can explore strategies that prioritize sustainability, reduce GHG emissions, and promote a transition to a net zero carbon economy.

III. NEPA and the EIA Process in the United States

> '[T]o waste, to destroy, our natural resources, to skin and exhaust the land instead of using it so as to increase its usefulness, will result in undermining in the days of our children the very prosperity which we ought by right to hand down to them amplified and developed.'
>
> Theodore Roosevelt[13]

NEPA, which was signed into law on 1 January 1970, required federal agencies to calculate the environmental effects of their proposed actions before issuing a decision.[14] The range of actions covered by NEPA is broad and covers permit applications, federal land management actions, and highways and other publicly-owned facilities.[15] Using the NEPA process, agencies evaluate the environmental and related social and economic effects of their proposed actions.[16] Agencies offer means for public review and comment on those evaluations.

A. Environmental Impact Statement as a Procedural Mechanism

In the realm of environmental law, benchmarking also occurs in the preparation of impact statements which assess the feasibility of a project. More environmental data should be generated and used in making agency determinations as information is power. More so, access to information is power. Sidney Shapiro and Rena Steinzor proposed a plan for establishing positive metrics that could offer a valuable tool to promote agency accountability.[17] Alyson Flournoy suggested that metrics could serve as shorthand for determining the quality and quantity of natural resources in her proposal for a new statute—the National Environmental Legacy Act—'to define in concrete terms the environmental legacy we wish to leave to future generations and provide a mechanism to ensure that we preserve that legacy'.[18] I propose that having a more precise measure of water quality, air quality, soil impacts, and climate change impacts in the 'no action' alternative of NEPA would provide a clearer rendition of the actual 'big picture' of a project. Doing so would enable marginalized

[13] Theodore Roosevelt, 'December 3, 1907: Seventh Annual Message' (*University of Virginia Presidential Speeches*, 20 October 2016) <https://www.millercenter.org/the-presidency/presidential-speeches/december-3-1907-seventh-annual-message> accessed 10 June 2023.

[14] 42 USC § 4332 (2012).

[15] 42 USC § 4321 (2012).

[16] 42 USC § 4332 (2012).

[17] Sidney A Shapiro and Rena I Steinzor, 'Capture, Accountability, and Regulatory Metrics' (2008) 86 Texas Law Review 1769.

[18] Alyson C Flournoy, 'The Case for the National Environmental Legacy Act' in Alyson C Flournoy and David M Driesen (eds), *Beyond Environmental Law: Policy Proposals for a Better Environmental Future* (CUP 2010) <https://www.cambridge.org/core/books/beyond-environmental-law/case-for-the-national-environmental-legacy-act/98C6237BBE14665F14B234F1789C91AA> accessed 10 June 2023.

groups, environmental activists, and communities collectively to have improved administrative regimes and increased access to information. Vigorous argument exists over the nature of the state's obligations to future generations.[19]

NEPA's federal mandate includes statutory responsibilities of 'fulfill[ing] the responsibilities of each generation as trustee of the environment for succeeding generations,' 'assur[ing] for all Americans safe, healthful, productive, and esthetically and culturally pleasing surroundings,' and 'attain[ing] the widest range of beneficial uses of the environment without degradation, risk to health or safety, or other undesirable and unintended consequences.'[20] The rules also specifically provide an assurance of safe and healthy surroundings for all Americans.[21] Since NEPA litigation has been ongoing since the statute was passed in 1969, most questions about the Act's requirements may seem to have been settled.[22] Expanded federal activity, complex systems, and higher public awareness of NEPA's mandates have increased the importance of its procedural requirements.

The Supreme Court recognized that NEPA articulates 'a broad national commitment to protecting and promoting environmental quality.'[23] After NEPA's passage, the House congressional committee with jurisdiction over NEPA described the law 'as revolutionary in intent and designed to steer this Nation on a course of environmental management.'[24] The detailed EIS must describe (1) 'the environmental impacts of the alternatives including the proposed action'; (2) 'any adverse effects that cannot be avoided should the proposed action be implemented'; (3) 'the relationship between short-term uses of the environment and the maintenance and enhancement of long-term productivity'; and (4) 'any irreversible or irretrievable commitments of resources which would be involved in the proposal should it be implemented.'[25] In interpreting NEPA, the CEQ crafted regulations to ensure 'environmental information is available to public officials and citizens before decisions are made and before actions are taken.'[26] Various provisions demonstrate that NEPA seeks to create an open and collaborative process.[27]

B. The NEPA Mandate as Action Forcing

The action-forcing procedural requirements are necessary for NEPA compliance. Those factors are the environmental impact, adverse environmental effects, and the alternatives to the proposed action. NEPA requires that a wide range of environmental effects[28] be evaluated under 40 CFR § 1502.16, including: *direct effects*—effects that 'are caused by

[19] RI Sikora and Brian Barry (eds) *Obligations to Future Generations* (White Horse Press 2012) <https://www.jstor.org/stable/j.ctv289dvx3> accessed 10 June 2023.

[20] Mason Baker, 'What Does It Mean to Comply with NEPA: An Investigation into Whether NEPA Should Have Procedural or Substantive Force' (2011) 31 Utah Environmental Law Review 241 (quoting 42 USC § 4331 (2000)).

[21] 42 USC § 4331(b)(2) (2012).

[22] Baker (n 20).

[23] *Robertson v Methow Valley Citizens Council*, 490 US 332, 348 (1989) (citing 42 USC § 4331).

[24] Sam Kalen, 'The Devolution of NEPA: How the APA Transformed the Nation's Environmental Policy' 33 (citing Comm. On Merch. Marine & Fisheries, Administration of the National Environmental Policy Act, HR Rep 92–316, at 1 (1971)).

[25] 22 CFR § 216.6his(5) (2016).

[26] 40 CFR § 1500.1(b) (2016).

[27] 40 CFR § 1501.6 (2016)

[28] Effects, whether direct, indirect, or cumulative, fall into various topical categories. 40 CFR § 1508.8 (2016).

the action and occur at the same time and place';[29] *indirect effects*—effects that 'are caused by the action and are later in time or farther removed in distance, but are still reasonably foreseeable';[30] *cumulative impacts*—'the impact on the environment which results from the incremental impact of the action when added to other past, present, and reasonably foreseeable future actions regardless of what agency (federal or non-federal) or person undertakes such other actions'.[31] Executive power causes agency action to 'make achieving environmental justice part of its mission by identifying and addressing, as appropriate, disproportionately high and adverse human health or environmental effects of its programs, policies, and activities on minority populations and low-income populations in the United States and its territories'.[32] The EPA has this goal for all communities and people across the country.[33] Actualizing environmental justice would lead to the same protections from environmental and health hazards for all people and access to the decision-making process to have a healthy environment.[34]

C. Full Spectrum of Reasonable Alternatives

CEQ guidance is vast, but notes that where 'a very large number of alternatives' are present, the federal agency must 'only consider a "reasonable number" but they must cover the full spectrum of alternatives'.[35] Environmental impact statements need to consider climate change and GHGs in their environmental analysis. The purpose of requiring a side-by-side comparison of reasonable alternatives is to 'sharply defin[e] the issues and provid[e] a clear basis for choice among options by the decisionmaker and the public'.[36] As the project purpose is narrowed, the range of alternatives also gets narrowed, often resulting in the rejection of environmental-friendly alternatives.[37] In light of *Department of Transportation v Public Citizen*,[38] it is important for plaintiffs challenging an EA/EIS to affirmatively propose alternatives ignored by the agency. Failure to make specific recommendations could be fatal to a plaintiff's case.

D. The 'No Action' Alternative

Section 1502.14(d) of the Code of Federal Regulations (CFR) provides the mandate for the EIS to 'include the alternative of no action'.[39] At its core, the 'no action' alternative analysis

[29] 40 CFR § 1508.8(a) (2016).
[30] 40 CFR § 1508.8(b) (2016).
[31] 40 CFR § 1508.7 (2016).
[32] Exec Order No 12,898, 59 Fed Reg 7629, 1-101 (11 February 1994).
[33] OEJECR US EPA, 'Learn About Environmental Justice' (13 February 2015) <https://www.epa.gov/environmentaljustice/learn-about-environmental-justice> accessed 10 June 2023.
[34] ibid.
[35] Daniel R Mandelker, *NEPA Law and Litigation* (Clark Boardman Callaghan 1992) Section 10:09[4]. George Coggins and Robert Glicksman, *Public Natural Resources Law* (2nd edn, Thomson Reuters 2016) <https://www.store.legal.thomsonreuters.com/law-products/Treatises/Public-Natural-Resources-Law-2d-Environmental-Law-Series/p/100027670> accessed 10 June 2023.
[36] 40 CFR § 1502.14 (2016).
[37] In *Simmons v U.S. Army Corps of Engineers*, 120 F.3d 664, 667 (7th Cir 1997).
[38] 541 US 752 (2004).
[39] 40 CFR § 1502.14(d) (2016).

provides a baseline for decision-makers to gauge the environmental impacts of a project.[40] The CEQ regulations mandate agencies consider the effects of taking 'no action' at all.[41] 'The no action alternative may be thought of in terms of continuing with the present course of action until that action is changed.'[42] 'NEPA does not impose an independent requirement that the agency set a "legal" environmental baseline.'[43] However, 'the discussion of alternatives in an EIS must compare the beneficial and adverse effects of the alternatives considered against a no action status quo alternative. . . . Further, the baseline must be consistent throughout the analysis in the EIS.'[44]

The next section will address how benchmarks for the baseline bar can be created in line with a more robust analysis of the 'no action' alternative. While the same metrics cannot be applied to all situations, certain commercial activities, including mining, fossil fuel extraction, timber harvesting, and pipeline projects should face more scrutiny given the land use impact and potential for toxic waste.

IV. The Baseline Bar as a Legal Approach

Historically, the reasonable alternatives, particularly the 'no action' alternative, were perceived as essential to the EIS mandate.[45] While agency personnel were concerned about the number of alternatives required, the alternatives themselves were not fully scrutinized.[46] Bear explains the rationale for this growing aversion to alternatives, noting '[o]ne line of thought holds that alternatives simply take too much time and elimination of them will further streamline the environmental review process.'[47] The second reason, she explains, is 'that requiring alternatives identification and analysis is antithetical to collaboration.'[48] At the same time, the courts have pushed back on requirements to limit the number of alternatives and the sufficiency of the detail included in the specific alternatives. The 'no action' alternative has specifically been evaluated as discussed in this section.

A. The Environmental Baseline: Case Study of Alaska's Pebble Mine and Water Quality

This subsection offers a case study, focusing on the Pebble Mine project in Alaska. The Pebble Mine project, if permitted, would have been one of the world's largest open-pit mines. However, its location in the Bristol Bay watershed, one of Alaska's most productive salmon fisheries, posed significant environmental concerns. These concerns were central

[40] ibid 17-271–17-272 (citing *Biodiversity Conservation All. v U.S. Forest Serv.*, 765 F.3d 1264, 1268–70 (10th Cir 2014)).
[41] *Native Ecosystems Council v U.S. Forest Serv.*, 428 F.3d 1233, 1235, 1245–46 (9th Cir. 2005).
[42] Coggins and Glicksman (n 35).
[43] ibid.
[44] ibid.
[45] Dinah Bear, 'Some Modest Suggestions for Improving Implementation of the National Environmental Policy Act' (2003) 43 Natural Resources Journal 931.
[46] ibid.
[47] ibid.
[48] ibid.

to the decision to halt the project. This case study aims to demonstrate the importance and effectiveness of incorporating a baseline bar approach in the EIS analysis process, showing how legal benchmarks for water quality and considerations related to local biodiversity influenced the decision to stop the project. Although a NEPA review wasn't fully completed for this project, the case nonetheless highlights how the interplay of environmental, social, and economic metrics can be crucial in such decisions. This case study underscores the importance of transparent and inclusive decision-making processes, demonstrating that public participation is critical in environmental decision-making and should be facilitated at both state and federal levels. The limited opportunities for public comments during the decision-making process of the Pebble Mine project serve as an example of the need for improvement in this area.

The Pebble Mine project was 'a copper-gold-molybdenum porphyry deposit in the advanced exploration stage'[49] and the second-largest deposit of its kind in the world.[50] The project is located on state land in the Bristol Bay Region of southwest Alaska.[51] The project was placed on hold by the Pebble Limited Partnership (PLP) following a federal decision to halt the project.[52] In the Bristol Bay watershed, the project is at 'the headwaters of one of the most productive salmon fisheries in Alaska'.[53] Even though 'the company claims that development of the mine can be done . . . to protect the aquatic ecosystem, that possibility is unlikely'.[54] This section will examine how legal benchmarks for water quality swayed the decision to stop the extraction project. This failed venture provides an opportunity to show how the establishment of a baseline bar can be used with greater uniformity and specificity for EIS analysis. The ecological and biodiversity concerns of the region were factored into the economic metrics of the impact of the proposed mining project on Alaska's fishing industries.

Sockeye salmon measure 18 to 31 inches in length and weigh 4 to 15 pounds and are located in the headwaters near the proposed Pebble Mine.[55] Through a study, the mining company estimated that the Pebble Mine project could support 15,000 American jobs and contribute more than $2.4 billion annually to US GDP over several decades.[56] An additional concern with the Pebble Mine project was the issue of public participation in the decision-making process. States lack democratic and transparent environmental decision-making. Meanwhile, on the federal level, the call for public comments allows a short period of time, which may not afford opportunity to all who are interested to offer comment.

[49] Alaska Department of Natural Resources, 'Pebble Project' <https://www.dnr.alaska.gov/mlw/mining/large-mines/pebble/> accessed 10 June 2023.

[50] Bluemink Elizabeth, 'Pebble's Value Keeps Growing' (*Anchorage Daily News*, 29 September 2016) <https://www.adn.com/alaska-news/article/pebbles-value-keeps-growing/2008/02/26/> accessed 10 June 2023.

[51] Alaska Department of Natural Resources (n 49).

[52] ibid.

[53] 'Northern Alaska Environmental Center' (*Northern Alaska Environmental Center*) <https://www.northern.org/> accessed 10 June 2023.

[54] ibid.

[55] Alaska Department of Fish and Game, 'Sockeye Salmon Species Profile' <http://www.adfg.alaska.gov/index.cfm?adfg=sockeyesalmon.main> accessed 10 June 2023.

[56] IHS, 'The Economic and Employment Contributions of a Conceptual Pebble Mine to the Alaska and United States Economies' <https://www.northerndynastyminerals.com/site/assets/files/4333/study.pdf> accessed 10 June 2023.

1. Clean Water Initiatives and Opposition to Pebble Mine

Opposition to Pebble Mine began in 2005 with concerns regarding salmon in Bristol Bay.[57] Following failed attempts at the state level, mine opponents turned to the US federal government.[58] Pebble Mine protestors tried to certify the first Clean Water Initiative in early 2007.[59] Alaska's Attorney General rejected it, stating it was an appropriation, interfering with the legislature's 'power to allocate [various types of] resources amongst competing uses'.[60] In this way, the Attorney General rejected additional regulations.[61] A second Clean Water Initiative met a similar fate.[62] Finally, a third Clean Water Initiative was sent to the Lieutenant Governor in October 2007, and was certified because it only disallowed harmful discharge of waste and pollutants instead of all waste or pollutants.[63] While the desired outcome has been achieved temporarily for environmental protection, the greater problem is the steep path to blocking the permitting process. Three separate attempts were made at the state level before the Environmental Protection Agency (EPA) stepped in on the federal level to ensure environmental protection.

2. Future Permitting and Review Processes

The Pebble Mine review process was the first time since the Clean Water Act that the EPA had exercised its authority without a permit application.[64] Mine proponents argue that special interest groups urged the Obama administration to ignore NEPA and rush a decision on a copper mine in Alaska in an attempt to 'subvert and evade NEPA'.[65] Arguments in favour of the mine fail to see how the weakness of the rule being justified on the basis of the Clean Water Act review instead of NEPA is inconsequential because the outcome under NEPA or Clean Water Act would be the same. The phenomenon of the baseline bar was evident based on the conglomeration of scientific environmental expertise. Salmon is 'the lifeblood of the region, supporting valuable fish-related economic activity ($1.5 billion annually and 14,000 jobs), Alaska Native subsistence culture, and a vast array of wildlife'.[66] Brett Miller questions the water-energy contradictions of the

[57] Timothy J Mullins, 'The Clean Water Initiatives and the Proper Balance Between the Right to Ballot Initiatives and the Prohibition on Appropriations' 26 Alaska Law Review 135–70 (2009) <https://scholarship.law.duke.edu/alr/vol26/iss1/4>.

[58] Kimberley A Strassel, 'The Greens' Back Door at the EPA' (*Wall Street Journal*, 14 May 2015) <http://www.wsj.com/articles/the-greens-back-door-at-the-epa-1431645574> accessed 10 June 2023.

[59] See *Op. Alaska Att'y Gen., Review of 07WATR Initiative Application*, 663-07-0179, 2007 Alas. AG LEXIS 10, 1 (21 June 2007) <https://law.alaska.gov/pdf/opinions/opinions_2007/07-016_663070179.pdf>

[60] ibid *28–35.

[61] ibid *37.

[62] *Op. Alaska Att'y Gen., Review of 07WTR2 Initiative Application*, 663-07-0179, 2007 Alas. AG LEXIS 25, *8–36 (27 September 2007).

[63] *Op. Alaska Att'y Gen., Review of 07WTR3 Initiative Application*, 663-07-0179, 2007 Alas. AG LEXIS 26, *30–31 (17 October 2007).

[64] Carline Simson, 'EPA Pebble Mine Review Wasn't Fair, Report Suggests' (*Law360*, 6 October 2015) <https://www.law360.com/articles/711421/epa-pebble-mine-review-wasn-t-fair-report-suggests> accessed 10 June 2023.

[65] John Shively, 'Will Team Obama Ignore the Rule of Law and Preemptively Veto Pebble Mine?' (*Fox News*, 9 March 2015) <https://www.foxnews.com/opinion/will-team-obama-ignore-the-rule-of-law-and-preemptively-veto-pebble-mine> accessed 10 June 2023.

[66] Taryn Kiekow Heimer and Joel Reynolds, 'The EPA Should Stop the Pebble Mine By Prohibiting or Restricting Discharges Associated with Large-Scale Mining in the Bristol Bay Watershed' (*NRDC*, 28 January 2015) <https://www.nrdc.org/resources/epa-should-stop-pebble-mine-prohibiting-or-restricting-discharges-associated-large-scale> accessed 10 June 2023.

regulatory impact of the Pebble Mine decision on renewable energy's dependence on non-renewable copper.[67]

The basis of the proposed determination was effects of fishery areas from construction and routine operation of Pebble Mine; loss of anadromous fish streams; loss of tributaries, wetlands, lakes, and ponds; and the downstream flow alteration.[68] Mine tailings would impact the water quality in the region most dramatically, but impacts to land, air, and terrestrial animals would also be significant.[69] The EPA's action did not sidestep NEPA, but worked in harmony with the Clean Water Act and existing federal guidelines. Whether a project is thwarted due to NEPA litigation or permitting process is a matter of due process, but having a Clean Water Act determination does not undermine the NEPA processes, rather, it complements them.

B. The Social Baseline: Costs, Caveats, and Complaints

The acrimonious disputes involving the Keystone XL Pipeline and the Pebble Mine project impacted rights of American Indians to their land. American Indian tribes were at the forefront of both efforts to thwart the projects. An analysis of the baseline bar accounts for formulations of social metrics. Native American tribes often have deep cultural and historical connections to the land. Recognizing their rights means acknowledging their traditional ecological knowledge and their role as stewards of the environment. This can lead to better conservation practices and sustainable land management, which are essential for achieving a net zero future. The rights of indigenous groups should be factored into determination decisions on the permitting process.[70] This subsection will look at the interplay between the rights of stakeholders in project development, focusing on indigenous populations. I argue that the 'no action' alternative of NEPA should address concerns of indigenous populations, not only with respect to environmental impacts and land use, but should more fully account for cultural heritage and stakeholder consent. 'When TransCanada filed its application to expand its cross-border oil pipeline operations in the fall of 2008, it triggered a unique federal approval process and a national dialogue on climate and energy policy.'[71]

A Joint Policy Statement on Principles and Guidelines on Indigenous and Traditional Peoples and Protected Areas stated their 'rights should be respected in relation to the lands, territories, waters, coastal seas and other resources which they traditionally own or otherwise occupy or use, and which fall within protected areas'.[72] International environmental law norms are implicated in the pipeline siting cases, including in the United States, which historically has sought to ignore international law.[73] The doctrine of free,

[67] Brett A Miller, 'Embracing the Water-Energy Contradiction: The Pebble Mine Conflict and Regulatory Implications Associated with Renewable Energy's Dependence on Non-Renewable Copper' (2016) 19 Water Law Review 213.

[68] ibid 4-1–4-57.

[69] Lori Howk, 'Pebble Mine Report' (*Wild Salmon Center*) <https://www.wildsalmoncenter.org/resources/pebble-mine-report-main-page/> accessed 10 June 2023.

[70] Uma Outka, 'Environmental Justice Issues in Sustainable Development: Environmental Justice in the Renewable Energy Transition' (2012) 19 Journal of Environmental and Sustainability Law 60.

[71] Sam Kalen, 'Thirst for Oil and the Keystone XL Pipeline' (2012) 46 Creighton Law Review 1.

[72] Javier Beltrán, 'Indigenous and Traditional Peoples and Protected Areas' (2000) <https://www.iucn.org/resources/publication/indigenous-and-traditional-peoples-and-protected-areas> accessed 10 June 2023.

[73] *Mary and Carrie Dann v United States* [2002] Inter-American Commission on Human Rights 5, 75/02.

prior, and informed consent (FPIC) is crucial in the context of energy siting.[74] Indigenous people's FPIC right has gained traction in the area of international human rights and the Convention on Biological Diversity (CBD).[75] International standards lean towards consultation of the affected peoples when any development project is either within their lands and territories or that affects traditionally used resources.[76]

The President of the Rosebud Sioux Indian Tribe has threatened that his tribe will close its reservation borders to the Keystone XL Pipeline, describing authorization of any permit of the pipeline as 'an act of war against our people'.[77] Whether the Rosebud Sioux Tribe in South Dakota can inevitably prevent the Keystone XL Pipeline or future pipelines from permitting, construction, and operation rests on the environmental impacts of the project. President Barack Obama preempted any further action on the Keystone XL in 2015.[78] While TransCanada Corp. does not plan 'for the pipeline to cross any tribal land, some [American Indians] fear the project could infringe on their rights'.[79] 'Various executive orders, laws and treaties require federal officials to consult with [American Indian] tribes about decisions that could affect them.'[80] Despite the tribal trust responsibility, the federal government has a poor record of tribal consultation, which effectively denies American Indians 'their right to make decisions that affect their land'.[81]

In reanalysing the pipeline application, NEPA is sufficient as a legal mechanism to deny the project. What would strengthen NEPA would be consideration of social impacts of the project in the discussion of the 'no action' alternative. Social, cultural, and spiritual impacts to indigenous groups and others are rather imprecise to measure. NEPA's establishment of a comprehensive environmental review process for all major federal actions reflects the self-evident principle that compliance must precede actual implementation of any action. 'NEPA procedures must insure that environmental information is available to public officials and citizens *before* decisions are made and *before* actions are taken.'[82] The statute also requires discussion of 'any irreversible and irretrievable commitments of resources which would be involved in the proposed action should it be implemented'[83]—indicating Congress's intent that full environmental review occur before a decision to act is made and, of course, before the action itself is implemented. Courts have adopted this phrase—'irreversible and irretrievable commitment of resources'—to strike down attempts to comply with NEPA that come only after the agency has already made such a commitment.[84]

[74] Brant McGee (ed), 'The Community Referendum: Participatory Democracy and the Right to Free, Prior and Informed Consent to Development' (2009) 27 Berkeley Journal of International Law 570.

[75] Fergus MacKay, 'Indigenous People's Right to Free, Prior and Informed Consent and the World Bank's Extractive Industries Review' (2004) 4 Sustainable Development Law & Policy <https://www.digitalcommons.wcl.american.edu/sdlp/vol4/iss2/12>.

[76] Tara Ward, 'The Right to Free, Prior, and Informed Consent: Indigenous Peoples' Participation Rights within International Law' (2011) 10 Northwestern Journal of Human Rights 54.

[77] Mark Hefflinger, 'Rosebud Sioux Tribe: House Vote in Favor of Keystone XL Pipeline an Act of War' (*Bold Nebraska*, 15 November 2014) <https://www.boldnebraska.org/rosebud-sioux-tribe-house-vote-in-favor-of-keystone-xl-pipeline-an-act-of-war/> accessed 10 June 2023.

[78] Elise Labott Berman Dan, 'Obama Rejects Keystone XL Pipeline' (*CNN*, 6 November 2015) <https://www.cnn.com/2015/11/06/politics/keystone-xl-pipeline-decision-rejection-kerry/index.html> accessed 10 June 2023.

[79] Timothy Cama and Megan R Wilson, *Tribes Say No to Keystone* (Hill, 14 April 2015) <http://www.thehill.com/policy/energy-environment/238691-tribes-say-no-to-keystone>accessed 10 June 2023.

[80] ibid.

[81] Andrea Giampoli, 'The "New Beginning": Private Cause of Action Under the International Oil Pipeline Permitting System' (2013)14 Rutgers Race & Law Review, Note, 155, 174–78.

[82] 40 CFR § 1500.1(b) (2016) (emphasis added).

[83] 42 USC § 4332(2)(C)(v) (2012).

[84] See *Metcalf v Daley*, 214 F.3d 1135, 1143 (9th Cir. 2000).

Supreme Court precedent, however, indicates that preliminary injunctive relief should not be automatically granted on a presumption of irreparable harm in environmental cases.[85] Parties alleging violations of NEPA must be prepared to seek injunctions or stays pending appeal of adverse rulings. Failure to obtain an injunction or stay may allow the disputed action to proceed to completion, thereby mooting the underlying challenge.[86]

V. Implementing the Base line Approach: Policy Recommendations

Considering the backdrop of ambitious net zero goals, clean energy transition, and natural resource conservation, the baseline bar approach becomes even more critical. In the context of the Willow Project, for instance, integrating a baseline bar approach would entail a thorough assessment of the project's potential impacts on the local ecosystem, wildlife, and climate against defined environmental, social, and economic metrics. Environmental activists have opposed President Biden's approval of the Willow Project, a significant oil and gas drilling project in Alaska, due to its climate and wildlife impacts.[87] The Willow Project would permit the development of up to 30,000 acres of land in the National Petroleum Reserve-Alaska (NPRA), a region that is home to numerous significant wildlife species, such as caribou, wolves, and bears. The endeavour is also anticipated to emit up to 600,000 metric tons of GHGs annually, contributing to global warming.[88] The Willow Project, according to environmental groups, is a significant setback for President Biden's climate agenda.[89] Ben Jealous, Executive Director of the Sierra Club has said, 'This project has the potential to entirely undo the clean energy progress we've made, lock us into fossil fuel drilling for another 30 years, and threaten the communities and wildlife who rely on these Alaskan landscapes.'[90] The Biden administration has defended the Willow Project on the grounds that it will generate employment and stimulate the Alaskan economy.[91] The administration has also stated that strict environmental regulations will apply to the endeavour. However, environmental groups have expressed doubt that the project can be implemented in a manner that safeguards the environment.[92] They have also pointed out that the Willow Project is unnecessary to satisfy the energy needs of the United States. The Willow Project is still in its early phases of development and has become a significant flashpoint in the climate change and energy policy debate.

[85] See *Amoco Prod. Co. v Vill. of Gambell*, 480 US 531, 544–46 (1987).

[86] See *One Thousand Friends of Iowa v Mineta*, 364 F.3d 890, 893–94 (8th Cir. 2004) (holding that a NEPA claim was moot because the completion of construction projects prevented the existence of a case or controversy for the court to resolve).

[87] Ella Nilsen, 'Biden Administration Approves Controversial Willow Oil Project in Alaska, Which Has Galvanized Online Activism' (*CNN*, 13 March 2023) <https://www.cnn.com/2023/03/13/politics/willow-project-alaska-oil-biden-approval-climate/index.html> accessed 14 March 2023.

[88] 'Why the Willow Project Is a Bad Idea' (*NRDC*, 30 March 2023) <https://www.nrdc.org/stories/why-willow-project-bad-idea> accessed 10 June 2023.

[89] 'Alaska's Willow Oil Project Is Controversial. Here's Why' (*AP NEWS*, 13 March 2023) <https://www.apnews.com/article/alaska-oil-drilling-biden-environment-climate-c39147c8ae1797aab9cb27219bf92675> accessed 10 June 2023.

[90] Ben Jealous, 'Big Oil's Willow Project Just Got Approved, But Our Work Isn't Over' <https://www.sierraclub.org/articles/2023/03/big-oil-s-willow-project-just-got-approved-our-work-isn-t-over> accessed 10 June 2023.

[91] Lisa Friedman, 'Biden Administration Expected to Move Ahead on a Major Oil Project in Alaska' (*The New York Times*, 11 March 2023) <https://www.nytimes.com/2023/03/10/climate/biden-willow-oil-alaska.html> accessed 10 June 2023.

[92] Nilsen (n 87).

The 'no action' alternative would then be weighed in light of these metrics, providing a clear picture of the potential long-term consequences of not proceeding with the project. The projected GHG emissions from the Willow Project is a significant factor that might be compared against the nation's broader net zero targets. The question would not be merely about the project's compliance with environmental regulations but whether it aligns with the country's long-term climate goals. This underscores the necessity of integrating the baseline bar approach in EIA processes as it ensures that the true costs—both environmental and social—are taken into account and compared against the long-term sustainability goals of a nation.

Academics and activists are often dissatisfied with particular aspects of environmental law. A common criticism is that environmental laws frequently allow projects to proceed despite their potential negative environmental effects.[93] This is sometimes ascribed to regulatory frameworks that impose conditions rather than prohibiting harmful activities outright. Critics argue that these conditions may not be sufficient to mitigate the environmental impacts effectively, allowing projects to proceed without adequate safeguards. Some environmental laws may not adequately address the matter of project necessity. In other words, these laws may place a greater emphasis on regulating the environmental impacts of a project than on determining whether the project is genuinely necessary or whether viable alternatives with fewer environmental impacts exist. This move can result in the approval of environmentally damaging projects solely on the basis that they meet regulatory requirements, without a comprehensive evaluation of their necessity or the exploration of alternatives. These criticisms demonstrate the need for ongoing refinement and development of environmental laws and regulations.

A baseline bar is a conceptual framework that is similar to the #DenyThePermit call for permits related to the siting of environmentally harmful facilities.[94] While blackletter environmental law does not recognize such a baseline bar, its conceptualization is essential for the 'Leave it in the Ground' advocates—vital on account of the conspicuous deficiency of updated environmental regulations. New environmental laws have not been enacted since a flurry of activism spawned the passage of numerous environmental laws in the 1970s and early 1980s. This understanding of environmental activities is reflected in NEPA. Comprehensive environmental laws sought to regulate commercial activity to harmonize with nature.[95] 'When stakeholders and constituencies realized the environmental harms of commercial activity, they sought to protect natural resources and enact environmental laws and regulations.'[96] The United States was a party to the 2015 climate change accord in

[93] Jorge Vinuales and Mercure Jean-François, 'Reframing Environmental Law from "Optimising" False Certainties to "Steering" under True Certainty' (2021) Economics of Energy Innovation and System Transition Working Papers <https://www.eeist.co.uk/wp-content/uploads/CEENRG_2021_01.pdf>.

[94] Kiana Courtney, '#DenyThePermit? A Call for Cumulative Impacts Legislation by Frontline Communities' (*Environmental Law & Policy Center*, 8 December 2021) <https://www.elpc.org/blog/deny-the-permit-a-call-for-cumulative-impacts-legislation-by-frontline-communities/> accessed 10 June 2023.

[95] Nadia Ahmad, 'Meta-Regulation for Environmental Monitoring and Corporate Sustainability Reporting' in Lez Rayman-Bacchus and Philip Walsh (eds), *Corporate Responsibility and Sustainable Development: Exploring the Nexus of Private and Public Interests* (Routledge 2016) <https://www.routledge.com/Corporate-Responsibility-and-Sustainable-Development-Exploring-the-nexus/Rayman-Bacchus-Walsh/p/book/9781138304208> accessed 10 June 2023.

[96] ibid.

Paris, withdrew, and then rejoined.[97] Meanwhile, the federal government continues to lease public lands and water for fossil fuel extraction.[98] The administration of President Donald Trump sought to deconstruct public land management policies to encourage a national energy plan promoting hydrocarbon extraction activities and reforms to reduce the amount of land managed by the federal government through mechanisms for land transfers to individual states.[99] President Joe Biden faces immense opposition in his efforts to block the development of the gold and copper mine in Alaska in 2023, but has used it as a centrepiece of his environmental record.[100] In the face of such seismic policy shifts in energy infrastructure projects, NEPA regulations carry a greater burden for protecting environmental systems.

A baseline bar and thorough 'no action' alternative are both necessary for a net zero future. A baseline bar sets environmental boundaries to ensure that projects meet strict requirements that favour land preservation and ecosystem protection, which are crucial for sustainability. The 'no action' option is part of the EIA process, which evaluates project need and alternatives. This reconfiguration drives decision-makers to analyse environmental implications and consider net zero emission strategies. These approaches in the NEPA impact statement protocols allow environmental supporters to sue developments that breach environmental standards. They might reject environmental projects to promote sustainability and protect future generations. The baseline bar approach requires environmental, social, and economic metrics that meet sustainability goals. These tools must be integrated into EIA regulation, which requires all EISs to assess proposed actions against baseline conditions. Every EIS must include detailed forecasts for each option, including 'no action'.

The EIA procedure should elevate the 'no action' alternative to a real choice rather than a formality. Public hearings, consultations, and internet platforms are needed to increase public engagement and openness in the EIA. These EIA rules must be strictly followed, including the minimal norm. This shift requires judicial oversight and punishment, making it a useful tool for sustainable development and environmental protection. Effectively implementing these strategies will be a driver for tackling economic growth, environmental degradation, and achieving a future without net carbon emissions.

VI. Conclusion

The struggle for achieving sustainable and reliable energy sources and establishing sustainable energy infrastructure will lead to increased conflicts for natural resources in the coming decades as with the Willow Project. The baseline bar is important for a complete and final future of rejecting projects that may undermine net zero and the clean energy transition, such as the already stayed projects involving Alaska's Pebble Mine and the Keystone XL

[97] Elian Peltier and Somini Sengupta, 'U.S. Formally Rejoins the Paris Climate Accord' (*The New York Times*, 19 February 2021) <https://www.nytimes.com/2021/02/19/world/us-rejoins-paris-climate-accord.html> accessed 10 June 2023.

[98] Nilsen (n 87).

[99] Bobby Magill, 'U.S. Public Lands Open for Oil Development?' (*KQED Science*, 29 November 2016) <https://www.ww2.kqed.org/science/2016/11/29/u-s-public-lands-open-for-oil-development/>accessed 10 June 2023.

[100] Liz Ruskin Media Alaska Public, 'In Rose Garden Address, Biden Celebrates with Alaskans Opposed to Pebble Mine' (*Alaska Public Media*, 11 May 2023) <https://www.alaskapublic.org/2023/05/11/in-rose-garden-address-biden-celebrates-with-alaskans-opposed-to-pebble-mine/> accessed 10 June 2023.

Pipeline. These projects and others face rebirth. For example, after the halt of the Keystone XL Pipeline, the proposed Dakota Access Pipeline crossing native burial grounds also received significant resistance, leading up to the denial of the US Army Corps of Engineers of a critical easement.[101]

The balancing of natural resource constraints leads to greater land preservation if the baseline bar is configured and brought into practice. Having a specific, more robust 'no action' alternative in the environmental impact assessment will be critical for achieving greater coherence between net zero targets and actual progress in terms of decarbonization and energy security.

[101] Nadia Ahmad, 'Trust or Bust: Complications with Tribal Trust Obligations and Environmental Sovereignty' (2017) 41 Vermont Law Review 799.

13

Resource Efficiency and Net Zero Buildings

LeRoy Paddock

I. Introduction: The Net Zero Buildings Imperative

This chapter examines ongoing transformations in natural resources law aimed at promoting net zero infrastructure development. It examines how the development and implementation of laws and policies for net zero buildings can advance low-carbon energy transition in key sectors.

The construction and operation of buildings have a dramatic impact on natural resources from the production of building materials to the use of fossil fuels in heating and cooking, and the use of electricity for lighting, cooling, and other functions.[1] One of the most important impacts of building energy use is its impact on climate change. Heating, cooling, and other energy use associated with buildings account for about 40 per cent of all energy use in both the United States[2] and worldwide.[3] Global CO_2 emissions from buildings have increased by 50 per cent over the period from 1990 to 2019.[4] With buildings responsible for over 21 per cent of global greenhouse gas (GHG) emissions and over 31 per cent of global CO_2 emissions, substantial reductions of GHG attributable to buildings must be an important element of climate mitigation strategies. However, buildings also have a major impact on the generation of other pollutants. In the United States the building sector is responsible for 76 per cent of electricity use and 40 per cent of all primary energy use.[5] The emphasis on efficiency and renewable energy that is a key part of the net zero buildings transition has important implications for natural resources protection by substantially reducing a wide range of impacts associated with fossil fuel energy production, including water pollution and land disturbance associated with coal mining; volatile organic emissions (VOCs) associated with natural gas production (about 10% of all VOC emissions);

[1] See Mark Levine, Diana Ürge-Vorsatz and others, 'Residential and Commercial Buildings' in Intergovernmental Panel on Climate Change, *Climate Change 2007 Synthesis Report* (CUP 2007) 389–90 <https://www.ipcc.ch/site/assets/uploads/2018/02/ar4-wg3-chapter6-1.pdf> accessed 1 May 2023, for a 2007 assessment of the importance of the buildings sector in addressing climate change.

[2] US Energy Information Agency, 'How much energy is consumed in residential and commercial buildings in the United States?' <http://www.eia.gov/tools/faqs/faq.cfm?id=86&t=1> accessed 30 April 2023.

[3] United Nations Environment Programme (UNEP), 'Buildings and Climate Change: Summary for Decision-Makers' (2009) 3 <https://www.cakex.org/sites/default/files/documents/buildings_and_climate_change.pdf> accessed 30 April 2023; Architecture 2030, 'The Built Environment' <https://architecture2030.org/why-the-building-sector/#:~:text=The%20built%20environment%20generates%2040%25%20of%20annual%20global%20CO2%20emissions> accessed 30 April 2023; Luisa F Cabeza and others, 'Buildings' in Preyadarshi R Shukla and others (eds), *Climate Change 2022: Mitigation of Climate Change: Working Group III Contribution to the Sixth Assessment Report of the Intergovernmental Panel on Climate Change*, 955 <https://www.ipcc.ch/report/ar6/wg3/downloads/report/IPCC_AR6_WGIII_FullReport.pdf> accessed 1 May 2023.

[4] Cabeza and others (n 3).

[5] US Department of Energy, 'Quadrennial Technology Review', ch 5 (introduction) <https://www.energy.gov/sites/default/files/2017/03/f34/qtr-2015-chapter5.pdf> accessed 29 June 2023.

LeRoy Paddock, *Resource Efficiency and Net Zero Buildings* In: *Net Zero and Natural Resources Law.* Edited by: Damilola S. Olawuyi, José Juan González, Hanri Mostert, Milton Fernando Montoya, and Catherine Banet, Oxford University Press. © International Bar Association 2024. DOI: 10.1093/9780198925033.003.0013

and particulate matter (pm) (about 40% of all pm2.5), and a substantial portion of sulphur dioxide, nitrogen oxide, and heavy metal pollution associated with fossil-based electricity generation.[6] The challenge of addressing building GHG emissions is likely to grow with building floor area expected to rise by 75 per cent from 2020 to 2050, 80 per cent of which will be in emerging markets and developing economies.[7] The International Energy Agency (IEA) observed in its Net Zero by 2050 roadmap for the energy sector that '[a]chieving net zero in the building sector is a particularly steep challenge' since 'decarbonisation of energy use in the sector requires almost all existing buildings to undergo a single in-depth retrofit by 2050, and new construction to meet stringent efficiency standards.[8]

Importantly, buildings constructed today are likely to still be in use well beyond 2050, the date targeted for reducing GHG emissions to a level that would avoid serious climate change. Based on 2013 census data, the median year houses in the United States were built was 1976, and the largest percentage of residences is between thirty-five and sixty-four years old.[9] The life expectancy of commercial buildings ranges from just over fifty years for wood buildings to more than eighty-seven years for concrete buildings.[10] Between 85 and 95 per cent of the buildings in use today will still be in use in 2050.[11] Refurbishing and extending the useful life of existing buildings will present an important opportunity to reduce carbon emission by retrofitting them to include much more efficient energy systems, by adding sources of renewable energy, and by rehabilitating buildings that might otherwise be demolished, avoiding much of the embodied carbon that would occur with new construction.[12] Rates of building rehabilitation will need to more than double from just over 1 per cent to about 2.5 per cent to meet 2050 goals.[13] Given these facts, global climate goals cannot be achieved without dramatic and prompt reduction in both operational and embodied carbon emissions associated with buildings. The concept of net zero buildings is seen as key to accomplishing the goal with some jurisdictions already requiring new buildings to be at least near net zero[14] and other jurisdictions already prohibiting the use of natural gas in new buildings.[15]

[6] International Energy Agency (IEA), 'World Energy Outlook—2016 Special Report Energy and Air Pollution' 266 <https://iea.blob.core.windows.net/assets/6b75c4ae-e633-4fa0-9569-b28e226e6103/WorldEnergyOutlookSpecialReport2016EnergyandAirPollution.pdf> accessed 29 June 2023.

[7] International Energy Agency (IEA), 'Net Zero by 2050: A Roadmap for the Global Energy Sector' (May 2021) 142 <https://iea.blob.core.windows.net/assets/deebef5d-0c34-4539-9d0c-10b13d840027etZeroby2050-ARoadmapfortheGlobalEnergySector_CORR.pdf> accessed 1 May 2023.

[8] ibid 143.

[9] US Census Bureau, '2013 Housing Profile: United States. American Housing Survey Fact Sheets' (May 2015) <http://www2.census.gov/programs-surveys/ahs/2013/factsheets/ahs13-1_UnitedStates.pdf> accessed 1 May 2023.

[10] Jennifer O'Connor, 'Survey on actual service lives for North American buildings' (October 2004) 1, 5 <http://cwc.ca/wp-content/uploads/2013/12/DurabilityService_Life_E.pdf> accessed 1 May 2023.

[11] European Environmental Agency (EEA), 'Building renovation: where circular economy and climate meet' <https://www.eea.europa.eu/publications/building-renovation-where-circular-economy> accessed 1 May 2023.

[12] ibid.

[13] European Council, 'A Renovation Wave for Europe—greening our buildings, creating jobs, improving lives' (14 October 2020) 2–3 <https://eur-lex.europa.eu/resource.html?uri=cellar:0638aa1d-0f02-11eb-bc07-01aa75ed71a1.0003.02/DOC_1&format=PDF> accessed 2 May 2023.

[14] National Law Review, 'Every New Building in the Netherlands Must Be (Almost) Carbon Neutral by January 1, 2021' <https://www.natlawreview.com/article/every-new-building-netherlands-must-be-almost-energy-neutral-starting-jan-1-2021≥ accessed 1 May 2023.

[15] New York became the first state to ban the use of natural gas in new buildings beginning for buildings under seven stories in 2026. See Anna Phillips, 'New York passes first-in-nation law to ban natural gas and other fossil fuels' (*Washington Post*, 3 May2023) <https://www.washingtonpost.com/climate-environment/2023/05/03/

Much of the technology needed to achieve net zero buildings is available today including heat pumps, energy-efficient appliances, and material-efficient building designs and materials.[16] Utilizing the best technology available today could lower energy demands by 61 per cent for residential buildings and 78 per cent for commercial buildings.[17] Unfortunately, the United Nations (UN) has reported that despite an increase in energy efficiency, total carbon emissions from buildings increased in 2020 by 5 per cent over the previous year and 2 per cent over pre-pandemic levels in 2019, setting an all-time high of 10GtCO2.[18] And, according to the IEA, 'floor area in the buildings sector worldwide is expected to increase 75% between 2020 and 2050, of which 80% is in emerging markets and developing economies'.[19]

A great deal more needs to be done to reduce the impact of building construction and operation on climate change and other natural resources concerns related to fossil fuel use. Creating a legal and policy framework that supports the rapid implementation of both new and renovated net zero buildings is increasingly seen as a critical element of international climate policy. Section II of the chapter looks at how net zero buildings is defined and some of the key issues related to the concept. Section III distinguishes between operational and embodied carbon and Section IV addresses the challenges in achieving net zero buildings. Section V examines the development of net zero buildings laws and Section VI discusses private sector net zero building initiatives. Section VII sets out pathways for achieving the goal of net zero buildings.

II. Defining Net Zero Buildings

The European Union (EU) uses the phrase 'zero emissions buildings'. The EU's 2021 proposed Directive on the energy performance of buildings defines a 'zero emissions building' as a building with a 'very high energy performance, where the very low amount of energy still required is fully covered by energy from renewable sources generated on-site . . . , from

newyork-gas-ban-climate-change/> accessed 3 May 2023. Several cities in the United States have adopted similar bans. However, the bans are controversial, with twenty states adopting laws prohibiting cities from adopting fossil fuel bans. Ella Nilson, 'Cities tried to cut natural gas from new homes. The GOP and gas lobby preemptively quashed their efforts' (*CNN*, 17 February 2022) <https://www.cnn.com/2022/02/17/politics/natural-gas-ban-preemptive-laws-gop-climate/index.html> accessed 3 May 2023. The US 9th Circuit Court of Appeals recently held that a natural gas ban adopted by the city of Berkeley, California is preempted by the Energy Policy and Conservation Act (EPCA or the 'Act') (42 USC §§ 6291 et seq) which prohibits states from setting appliance standards once a federal energy conservation standard becomes effective for a covered product. *California Restaurant Association v City of Berkeley*, No 21-16278 (17 April 2023). While the case invalidated, within the Circuit's jurisdiction, natural gas bans for new buildings based on the approach Berkeley took in restricting natural gas use, other approaches such as zoning laws or building codes that do not encroach on federal appliance standards may still be viable.

[16] EIA, 'Buildings' (n 8) 142.

[17] US Department of Energy, 'Chapter 5: Increasing Efficiency of Building Systems and Technologies' (September 2015) 155–56 <https://www.energy.gov/articles/chapter-5-increasing-efficiency-buildings-systems-and-technologies> accessed 2 May 2023.

[18] United Nations Environment Programme (UNEP), '2022 Global Status Report for Buildings and Construction: Towards a Zero-emission, Efficient and Resilient Building and Construction Sector' (2022) xv <https://www.unep.org/resources/publication/2022-global-status-report-buildings-and-construction> accessed 2 May 2023.

[19] International Energy Agency (IEA), 'Net Zero by 2050' 141 (May 2021).

a renewable energy community . . . or from a district heating and cooling system'.[20] This definition allows the use of off-site renewable energy.

Several other definitions have been used to describe the concept, including zero energy buildings (ZEBs)[21] developed by the US Department of Energy (DOE) which emphasizes on-site generation of renewable energy. There is also the zero-carbon-ready building created by the IEA that adds a focus on embodied carbon. [22] While the definitions vary, the focus of all the definitions is on achieving substantial reductions in the carbon contribution and other resource impacts of buildings through more efficient use of energy, switching to renewable energy sources, and conservation of natural resources through extending the useful life of buildings.

Like the transition to renewable energy generation and to electric vehicles (EVs), the transition to net zero buildings involves critical societal issues. Recognizing this fact, the UN's International Panel on Climate Change (IPCC) has suggested that a 'sufficiency, efficiency, and renewables' (SER) framework must underpin the net zero buildings effort. SER involves three key concepts—'sufficiency' which addresses avoiding the need for energy and materials by better utilizing existing assets including sharing building use in multifamily settings, 'efficiency' in the use of both energy and materials, and 'renewables'.[23] The 'sufficiency' element of the SER framework emphasizes distributional equity by pointing out that shelter is an essential pre-condition for human wellbeing that defines the minimum level of housing that should be available for all.[24] Sufficiency also reflects the importance of Sustainable Development Goal (SDG) 7 in that adequate and affordable renewable energy must be available for all in order to achieve building net zero goals.[25] Increasing availability of affordable, efficient, and renewably powered buildings contribute to meeting the solidarity principle that is a central theme of this book.

Achieving the goal of net zero buildings will require major changes in line with the SER approach including (1) avoiding energy use and conserving natural resources where possible including building more multifamily housing and repurposing buildings rather than demolishing buildings that could be reused (applying the sufficiency principle); (2) improving the energy efficiency of all buildings (applying an efficiency first principle); (3) expanding generation of renewable energy emphasizing on-site generation of renewable energy to avoid damage to the environment caused by fossil fuel energy generation;

[20] European Union (EU), 'Proposal for a Directive of the European Parliament and the Council on the energy performance of buildings (recast)' 2021/0426.

[21] The DOE defines a zero energy building (ZEB) as an 'energy-efficient building where, on a source energy basis, the actual annual delivered energy is less than or equal to the on-site renewable exported energy'. In addition, the definition requires that '[w]hen energy is consumed on-site, the conversion to source energy must account for the energy consumed in the extraction, processing and transport of primary fuels such as coal, oil and natural gas; energy losses in thermal combustion in power generation plants; and energy losses in transmission and distribution to the building site'. Kent Peterson and others, 'A Common Definition of Zero Energy Buildings' (US Department of Energy, September 2015) 7 <https://www.energy.gov/eere/buildings/articles/common-definition-zero-energy-buildings#:~:text=Generally%20speaking%2C%20a%20zero%20energy,campuses%2C%20portfolios%2C%20and%20communities> accessed 20 May 2023. ZEBs are expected to use 'all cost-effective measures to reduce energy usage through energy efficiency'. ibid 1.

[22] IEA, 'Roadmap' (n 8) 144.

[23] Cabeza and others (n 3) 957–58.

[24] ibid.

[25] United Nations (UN), Department of Economic and Social Affairs, Sustainable Development, 'Ensure access to affordable, reliable, sustainable and modern energy for all' <https://sdgs.un.org/goals/goal7> accessed 1 May 2023.

(4) fuel switching from natural gas for heating, hot water, and cooking to electricity in most cases (electrification at least doubles by 2050[26] and green forms of gas such as hydrogen fuel cells become available), also avoiding generation of GHG and VOCs; (5) substantially reducing the carbon embedded in the production of building materials (embodied carbon—see Section III); and (6) behavioural changes such as reducing demand for energy and switching to non-carbon fuel sources for functions such as cooking and heating.[27]

Building codes will need to play a major role in this effort. As the IEA has observed, 'Building energy codes covering new and existing buildings are the fundamental policy instrument to drive such changes. Building energy codes currently exist or are under development in only 75 countries, and codes in around 40 of these countries are mandatory for both the residential and services sub-sectors.'[28] However, achieving 'the net zero goals for 2050 will require mandatory zero-carbon-ready building energy codes for all new buildings ... to be in place by 2030 and retrofits need to meet the same code requirements by 2050.'[29]

III. Operational and Embodied Carbon

An important distinction that is commonly found in the net zero discussion is between *operational* carbon emissions that focus on carbon emissions from the energy used to heat, cool, or provide other services to maintain a building[30] and *embodied* carbon. 'Embodied carbon'[31] is the carbon emissions that result from the production of building materials, transporting the materials to building sites, operating construction equipment, and building demolition and disposal of building materials.[32] Of the total energy consumed in a building's lifecycle, embodied energy accounts for between 10 and 38 per cent of total energy use for conventional buildings and between 9 and 46 per cent for more energy-efficient buildings.[33]

Embodied carbon may account for up to one quarter of the carbon emissions from buildings.[34] The Architecture 2030 programme sets out steps that can be taken to limit embodied carbon—'*reuse*, including renovating existing buildings, using recycled materials, and

[26] IEA, 'Roadmap' (n 8) 142.

[27] ibid 67–69, 141–42.

[28] ibid 144.

[29] ibid 143.

[30] Aysegül D Dilsez and others, 'Embodied versus Operational Energy in Residential and Commercial Buildings: Where Should We Focus?' (2019) J. Phys.: Conf. Ser. 1343 012178 <https://iopscience.iop.org/article/10.1088/1742-6596/1343/1/012178/pdf> accessed 2 May 2023.

[31] Eduardo Souza, 'Embodied Energy in Building Materials: What It Is and How to Calculate It' (*ArchDaily*, 26 September 2021) <https://www.archdaily.com/931249/embodied-energy-in-building-materials-what-it-is-and-how-to-calculate-it> accessed 1 May 2023. Cement production alone accounts for 5–7% of global emissions with one ton of cement production releasing 900 kilogrammes of carbon into the atmosphere. In 2012, iron and steel accounted for 31% of industrial carbon emissions. Gia Mora, 'How to Measure Embodied Energy in Buildings, Treehugger' (5 July 2022) <https://www.treehugger.com/embodied-energy-in-building-materials-5441578> accessed 1 May 2023.

[32] Søren E Lutken and Harry Wretlind, 'City Based Carbon Budgets for Construction' (United Nations Environment Programme Working Paper No 13, 2016) 3 <https://unepccc.org/publications/city-based-carbon-budgets-for-buildings/> accessed 1 May 2023.

[33] Cassandra L Thiel and others, 'A Materials Life Cycle Assessment of a Net-Zero Energy Building' (2013) 6 Energies 1125, 1127 <http://www.mdpi.com/1996-1073/6/2/1125/htm> accessed 1 May 2023.

[34] Rebecca Esau and others, 'Reducing Embodied Carbon in Buildings' (Rocky Mountain Institute, 2021) <https://rmi.org/insight/reducing-embodied-carbon-in-buildings/> accessed 2 May 2023.

designing for deconstruction; *reduce*, including material optimization and the specification of low to zero carbon materials; and *sequester*, including the design of carbon sequestering sites and the use of carbon sequestering materials'.[35] In the United States, the Inflation Reduction Act of 2022[36] included $3.3 billion for the Government Services Administration (GSA) (the owner or lessee of US government buildings) to invest in federal buildings with low-carbon materials as well as emerging and sustainable technologies.[37] To advance zero energy buildings, the DOE's Green Proving Ground programme recently released a Request for Information (RFI) that seeks input from industry on leading-edge technologies that help reduce GHG emissions of commercial buildings, improve grid resiliency, and have significant potential for equitable and broad adoption in the US marketplace.[38]

Renovations and circular economy[39] approaches are also an important part of achieving needed carbon reductions. In Europe, building renovation rates need to double from 1 per cent to 2 per cent each year to meet net zero goals.[40] In addition, the EU has taken steps to encourage a circular economy approach to buildings that can substantially reduce carbon emissions. The European Commission's proposal to revise the Construction Products Regulation (2022) will increase environmental and climate performance of construction products by requiring that the design and manufacture of construction products are state of the art, making them more durable, repairable, recyclable, and easier to re-manufacture.[41] Among the key circular economy steps are extending the life span of buildings, reducing the need for materials, and developing a new generation of lower-carbon building materials.[42]

IV. Key Challenges in the Transition to Net Zero Buildings

Implementing net zero policies and laws is a challenging process for several reasons. First, net zero buildings may have a higher initial cost even though they may have lower

[35] Architecture 2030, 'Actions for a zero carbon built environment: Embodied carbon' <https://architecture2030.org/embodied-carbon-actions/> accessed 20 May 2023.

[36] US Environmental Protection Agency, 'Inflation Reduction Act' <https://www.epa.gov/inflation-reduction-act/inflation-reduction-act-programs-fight-climate-change-reducing-embodied> accessed 2 May 2023.

[37] US General Services Administration, 'GSA, DOE Issue RFI for Technologies for Net-Zero Carbon Buildings' (11 October 2022) <https://www.gsa.gov/about-us/newsroom/news-releases/gsa-doe-issue-rfi-for-technologies-for-netzero-carbon-buildings-10112022> accessed 2 May 2023.

[38] ibid.

[39] The concept of circular economy seeks to minimize the use of materials in the first instance. Circular economy approaches to materials use then encourage products to be designed in a way that promotes repurposing and reuse, and ultimately designs that facilitate disassembly to maximize the use value of materials and minimize the impact of the products on the environment. See UNCTAD, 'Circular Economy' <https://unctad.org/topic/trade-and-environment/circular-economy#:~:text=A%20circular%20economy%20entails%20markets,economy%20or%20used%20more%20efficiently> accessed 2 May 2023. Circular economy concepts such as minimizing waste created in producing building materials, repurposing buildings, and deconstructing buildings at the end of their life are important aspects of reducing embodied carbon in buildings. The EU adopted a circular economy plan in 2020. See European Commission, 'Circular Economy Action Plan' <https://environment.ec.europa.eu/strategy/circular-economy-action-plan_en> accessed 2 May 2023.

[40] European Council, 'Council approves conclusions on an EU renovations wave' (11 June 2021) <https://www.consilium.europa.eu/en/press/press-releases/2021/06/11/council-approves-conclusions-on-an-eu-renovation-wave/?utm_source=dsms-auto&utm_medium=email&utm_campaign=Council+approves+conclusions+on+an+EU+renovation+wave> accessed 2 May 2023.

[41] European Parliament, 'Revision of the Construction Products Regulation' 1–2 <https://www.europarl.europa.eu/RegData/etudes/BRIE/2022/739243/EPRS_BRI(2022)739243_EN.pdf> accessed 2 May 2023.

[42] ibid.

operational costs over the lifecycle of the building, especially when the net zero calculation includes materials with lower embodied carbon. One study indicates that the initial cost premium for net zero buildings can range from 5 to 19 per cent.[43] Other studies have indicated the cost premium for net zero residential buildings is about 7 to 8 per cent, although the perception among many is that the cost is higher.[44] Concerns about higher initial costs can increase resistance to net zero laws and policies among many industry actors. Higher initial costs may also have important equity implications, especially as net zero programmes extend to residential buildings as is increasingly the case. Laws and policies may need to include new financing mechanisms that make the initial investments in net zero buildings more affordable or tax incentives that help subsidize some of the investments, especially during the early years when the new technology is scaling up. This may be especially true for residential buildings in underserved areas where housing affordability is a critical issue.[45]

Second, net zero programmes will require phasing out of fossil fuels such as natural gas which has been the principal source for heating, hot water, and cooking in many countries for several years. Resistance to phasing out natural gas is already evident among fossil fuel producers and supporting organizations, among some conservative politicians, and among many individuals who have a strong attachment to using natural gas for cooking.[46] Addressing the sociological challenges to the lifestyle changes that net zero may create will be important for the success of the idea.

Reducing embodied carbon also presents major challenges in the way steel, concrete, and aluminum are produced to reduce embodied carbon, changes in building codes and fire codes that will allow wider use of wood in higher rise buildings, switching heavy construction equipment from diesel to electric power, building more multifamily housing units, and the adoption of new circular economy approaches to reusing and deconstructing building at the end of their initial useful life. The cement and concrete industry has confronted this challenge adopting a net zero plan for 2050 that emphasizes the role of low-carbon concrete in constructing affordable housing.[47]

Perhaps the most important challenge in achieving net zero in buildings is the timely phase-out of fossil energy. While many buildings may be able to achieve net zero using efficiency measures and onsite renewable generation, the goal of achieving net zero for all buildings by 2050 likely will require high levels of grid-connected renewables. The phase-in/phase-out timing is important to avoid excessive mid-term carbon emissions. However, the natural gas phase-out is not a simple process. Natural gas is used in buildings for three primary purposes: space heating, water heating, and cooking. The most recent data for

[43] District Department of the Environment, 'Net Zero and living Building Challenge Financial Study: A Cost Comparison Report for Buildings in the District of Columbia' <https://newbuildings.org/wp-content/uploads/2015/11/ZNECostComparisonBuildingsDC1.pdf> accessed 2 May 2023.

[44] See Alisa Peterson, Michael Gartman, and Jacob Garvidae, 'The Economics of Zero-Energy Homes' (Rocky Mountain Institute, 2019) 7 <https://rmi.org/insight/economics-of-zero-energy-homes/> accessed 2 May 2023.

[45] Kelly Vaughn, 'Social Equity, Affordable Housing, and the Net-Zero Energy Opportunity' (Rocky Mountain Institute, 19 May 2018) <https://rmi.org/social-equity-affordable-housing-and-the-net-zero-energy-opportunity/> accessed 2 May 2023.

[46] See Pew, 'Natural Gas Bans are New Front in Effort to Curb Emissions' (6 January 2022) <https://www.pewtrusts.org/en/research-and-analysis/blogs/stateline/2022/01/06/natural-gas-bans-are-new-front-in-effort-to-curb-emissions> accessed 20 May 2023.

[47] Global Cement and Concrete Association (GCCA), 'Concrete Future: The GCCA 2050 Cement and Concrete Roadmap for Net Zero Concrete', 48 <https://mail.google.com/mail/u/0/#search/dolawuyi%40hbku.edu.qa?projector=1> accessed 29 June 2023.

all building types and sizes across the United States showed that annual consumption of natural gas for space heating was 1,307 billion cubic feet (bcf).[48] Natural gas overshadows electricity as a primary space-heating energy source by 1,240 bcf to 51 bcf.[49] Natural gas-fired power generation increased 19 per cent in 2015 and growth is expected to continue.[50] Near-term switching of space heating, water heating, and cooking from natural gas to electricity is likely to mean that the electricity is provided by a significant amount of coal or gas-fired generation. Thus, it is important for policy-makers and builders to develop a strategy for simultaneously phasing out fossil fuel use in space heating, cooking, and water heating while facilitating the expansion of grid-based renewables to allow electrification of these functions so that the switchover progresses at the same time the grid is being decarbonized. This switch alone will create a 20 per cent decrease in total building final energy use, reducing final energy use even as floor space increases.[51] Fuel-switching on the scale needed to achieve a net zero energy goal is a long-term project that will require coherent and concerted efforts to accomplish.[52]

V. The Emerging Law of Net Zero Buildings

A. European Union

In the EU, the 'Fit for 55' programme calls for a mix of tools to reduce GHG emissions by 55 per cent by 2030.[53] The buildings portion of Fit by 55 mandates that new government buildings be net zero by 2028 and all new buildings be net zero by 2030.[54] It also requires all existing buildings to be net zero by 2050.[55] 'The new ETS [emissions trading system] creates economic incentives for building decarbonisation and generates revenues for public support, targeted in particular to support vulnerable households. The revised Energy Performance of Buildings Directive addresses non-economic barriers to renovation. It creates an enabling framework that provides financial support to renovation without directly mobilizing the required funding.'[56] For example, 'National building renovation plans will pay attention to monitoring the reduction of people affected by energy poverty and of population living in inadequate housing (eg, leaking walls or roofs) or with inadequate

[48] See US Energy Information Agency, 'Commercial Buildings Energy Consumption Survey' Table E8 (May 2016) <https://www.eia.gov/consumption/commercial/data/2012/c&e/cfm/e8.cfm> accessed 2 May 2023.

[49] ibid.

[50] See Victoria Zaretskaya, 'Many natural gas-fired power plants under construction are near major shale plays' (US Energy Information Administration, 19 May 2016) <http://www.eia.gov/todayinenergy/detail.cfm?id=26312> accessed 2 May 2023.

[51] James H Williams, Benjamin Haley, and Ryan Jones, 'Policy Implications of Deep Decarbonization in the United States' (Deep Decarbonization Policy Project 2015) 22 <https://irp.cdn-website.com/be6d1d56/files/uploaded/2015-report-on-policy-implications.pdf> accessed 2 May 2023.

[52] Major infrastructure investments in natural gas transmission and distribution lines as well as natural gas power-generating facilities have lifespans of forty years or more. Accordingly, a decision is needed in the short term about current and future construction of natural gas facilities and infrastructure. The longer decisions about the fate of natural gas usage are delayed, the more infrastructure will be built making the issue of compensation for stranded assets more significant.

[53] European Commission, '"Fit for 55": delivering the EU's 2030 Climate Target on the way to climate neutrality' (2021).

[54] ibid.

[55] ibid.

[56] ibid 2.

thermal comfort conditions. The plans will present an overview of national policies and measures empowering and protecting vulnerable households, alleviating energy poverty and ensuring housing affordability.'[57]

The proposal encourages all Member States to set minimum energy performance standards (MEPS) for all buildings but would make these MEPS mandatory across the EU for the 'worst performing' buildings.[58] The proposal makes it clear that zero-emission buildings should become the standard for new buildings, the level to be attained by a deep renovation as of 2030, and the vision for the entire building stock in 2050.

B. United States

In the Energy Security Act of 2007,[59] Congress set a goal of zero net energy[60] use for all new commercial buildings by 2030 and for half of the existing commercial building stock by 2040.[61] In 2021 President Biden signed an Executive Order (EO) requiring a government net zero emissions building portfolio by 2045, including a 50 per cent emissions reduction by 2032.[62] The EO also set a goal of zero emissions from federal procurement, including a Buy Clean policy to promote use of construction materials with lower embodied emissions.[63] As noted above, the Inflation Reduction Act[64] of 2022 provided the Government Service Administration (GSA) $3.4 billion to acquire construction materials with lower embodied carbon, and to accelerate GSA's high performance green building programme to support a federal net zero footprint.[65] The 2021 American Recovery and Reinvestment Act also provided billions of dollars to support energy efficiency programmes that contribute to net zero efforts. Among these efforts is the Net-Zero Energy Commercial Buildings Initiative, a collaborative effort with the private sector.[66]

California and New York have been climate leaders in the United States and that leadership is reflected in their focus on net zero buildings. California developed the nation's first green building standard in 2007 with the adoption of the California Green

[57] ibid 3.

[58] ibid 9.

[59] Energy Independence and Security Act, 42 USC § 17001 (2007).

[60] While the DOE ZEB definition does not allow the use of off-site renewable energy to offset on-site energy use, it does recognize another type of ZEB that can utilize renewable energy credits to achieve zero energy status—the REC-ZEB. DOE has also created a third form—the Renewable Energy Certificate-Zero Energy Building (REC-ZEB). The premise is that '[m]ulti-story *buildings* that occupy entire lots located in dense urban areas, or *buildings*, such as hospitals with high process loads, may not be able to balance *annual delivered energy* with *on-site renewable energy* simply because the site is not large enough to accommodate all the *on-site renewable energy* required.' Peterson and others (n 21). The REC-ZEB is defined as '[a]n energy-efficient building where, on a *source energy* basis, the actual *annual delivered energy* is less than or equal to the on-site renewable *exported energy* plus acquired *Renewable Energy Certificates* (RECs).' US Environmental Protection Agency, 'Renewable Energy Certificates (RECs)' <https://www.epa.gov/greenpower/renewable-energy-certificates-recs> accessed 2 May 2023.

[61] Energy Independence and Security Act of 2007, 42 USC § 17082.

[62] EO 14057, 'Catalyzing Clean Energy Industries and Jobs Through Federal Sustainability' (8 December 2021).

[63] ibid section 102(v).

[64] Inflation Reduction Act of 2022, 136 Stat. 1818.

[65] US General Services Administration, 'Inflation Reduction Act' <https://www.gsa.gov/governmentwide-initiatives/inflation-reduction-act> accessed 2 May 2023.

[66] Amanda Kolson Hurley, 'An Architect's Guide to the American Recovery and Reinvestment Act' (*Architect*, 31 July 2009) <https://www.architectmagazine.com/design/buildings/an-architects-guide-to-the-american-recovery-and-reinvestment-act_o> accessed 2 May 2023.

Buildings Code (CalGreen).[67] The Act required all new state buildings that began design after 2017 to be net zero and half of existing state buildings to be net zero by 2025.[68] Its 2019 energy efficiency standards[69] require the installation of solar panels on new and remodelled single-family and low-rise residential buildings while its 2022 standards[70] encourage the use of heat pumps for heating and hot water, driving the phase-out of natural gas.

New York State's draft Climate Action Plan notes that New York City's 'Local Law 154 of 2021 sets carbon dioxide (CO_2) emission limits that effectively prohibit fossil fuel combustion equipment for heating, hot water, and most appliances in new construction, beginning in 2024 for lower-rise residential buildings, and by 2027 for commercial and large multifamily housing. The Plan suggests that the state should adopt comparable codes, applicable to all municipalities, to prohibit fossil fuel combustion systems and fossil fuel combustion equipment in new construction.'[71] The Plan also suggests the adoption of building energy use disclosure and benchmarking requirements.[72] The Scoping Plan anticipates the adoption of zero emission codes that support requiring zero emission new construction for low-rise residential buildings by 2025 and for commercial buildings by 2028.[73] Finally, the Scoping Plan calls for shifting substantial public funding to support building and rehabilitation of housing focusing on affordable and public housing, and on disadvantaged communities.[74] The proposal has drawn the support of an environmental committee of the New York Bar Association.[75]

C. Other Jurisdictions

Several other countries have enacted ambitious net zero policies. In the Netherlands, new buildings were required to be 'almost energy neutral' by 1 January 2021. Government buildings had already been required to meet this standard.[76] Canada has adopted a new building code through its National Research Council that will require new buildings to be net zero by 2030 utilizing either on-site or off-site renewable energy. The United Kingdom issued a 'call for evidence' related to preparation of a net zero building standard that includes issues

[67] California Department of Government Service, 'CalGreen' <https://www.dgs.ca.gov/BSC/CALGreen> accessed 2 May 2023.

[68] California Department of General Services, 'Zero Net Energy (ZNE)' <https://www.energy.ca.gov/programs-and-topics/programs/building-energy-efficiency-standards/2022-building-energy-efficiency> accessed 2 May 2023.

[69] Cal Code Title 24, parts 6 and 11.

[70] California Energy Commission, '2022 Building Energy Efficiency Standards' <https://www.energy.ca.gov/programs-and-topics/programs/building-energy-efficiency-standards/2022-building-energy-efficiency> accessed 2 May 2023.

[71] New York State, 'Scoping Plan' (December 2022) 185 <https://climate.ny.gov/resources/scoping-plan/> accessed 2 May 2023.

[72] ibid 190.

[73] ibid Executive Summary 14.

[74] ibid.

[75] New York State Bar Association Environmental & Energy Law Section, 'Comments on the Draft Scoping Plan Prepared by the New York State Climate Action Council' (28 June 2022).

[76] Marijn Bodelier and Jan Herfkens, 'Every New Building in the Netherlands Must Be (Almost) Energy Neutral Starting January 1, 2021' (xxxx) XI(6) Natural Law Review <https://www.natlawreview.com/article/every-new-building-netherlands-must-be-almost-energy-neutral-starting-jan-1-2021> accessed 2 May 2023.

related to embodied carbon.[77] Australia has created a carbon offset standard for buildings that requires carbon emissions to be calculated, the emissions to be reduced, and any remaining carbon emissions to be offset.[78] In April 2022, Japan adopted a net zero programme that requires a 46 per cent reduction in emissions by 2030 as compared to 2013 emissions and requires by 2025 that all residential and non-residential buildings conform to the country's Energy Conservation Standard.[79] In Indonesia, the International Energy Agency has noted that a pathway for the implementation of zero carbon-ready building (ZCRB) energy codes is established in the mid-2020s.... Building energy codes ramp up in stringency from 2030 and reach ZCRB levels by the mid-2030s.[80]

MENA countries have not yet adopted codes that specifically address net zero for buildings even though several of the countries have committed to overall net zero GHG emissions by 2050 or 2060,[81] and have introduced energy efficiency programmes and adopted rating systems for buildings.[82] Very ambitious 'new city' projects in Qatar, UAE, and Saudi Arabia are being built as net zero projects.[83] Similarly, South Africa has yet to require net zero buildings but Cape Town, Durban, Johannesburg, and Tshwane, participants in the C40 Cities climate programme, committed to net zero standards in 2018 through C40's Net Carbon Buildings Accelerator[84] to achieve net zero carbon new buildings by 2030 and for all buildings by 2050.[85]

VI. Private Sector Net Zero Buildings Initiatives

The consulting firm KPMG has observed that '[a]s governments look ahead to their net-zero commitment deadlines, decarbonization legislation is becoming more prominent—a trend that is only likely to accelerate. This puts pressure on companies to develop plans and, equally important, disclose their performance . . . '.[86] In addition to growing government

[77] UK Net Zero Carbon Buildings Standard, 'Call for Evidence' (2023) <https://www.nzcbuildings.co.uk/_files/ugd/6ea7ba_7dc5e7812784430db1d9bfb308760751.pdf> accessed 2 May 2023.

[78] World Green Buildings Council, 'Australian Government Launches Net Zero Building Standard with WGBC' <https://worldgbc.org/article/australian-government-launches-net-zero-building-standard-with-gbca/> accessed 2 May 2023.

[79] See Re-Think Tokyo, 'Energy Conservation Architecture to be mandatory for Japan real estate from 2025' (25 April 2022) <https://www.rethinktokyo.com/news/2022/04/25/energy-conservation-architecture-be-mandatory-japan-real-estate-2025/1650839788> accessed 2 May 2025.

[80] International Energy Agency, 'An Energy Sector Roadmap to Net Zero Emissions in Indonesia' 127 (September 2022).

[81] Lena Kurkowska, 'Is the Gulf's real estate ready for a net-zero challenge?' (*Cityscape*, 17 August 2022) <https://www.cityscape-intelligence.com/sustainable-design/gulfs-real-estate-ready-net-zero-challenge> accessed 2 May 2023.

[82] See Damilola Olawuyi, *Environmental Law in Arabic States* (OUP 2022) 142–44.

[83] Elif Selin Calif, 'Four special projects in the MENA region leading the way to NET-ZERO 2050'(*Middle East Monitor*, 4 August 2022) <https://www.middleeastmonitor.com/20220804-four-special-projects-in-the-mena-region-leading-the-way-to-net-zero-2050/> accessed 2 May 2023.

[84] C40 Cities, 'Net Zero Carbon Buildings Accelerator' <https://www.c40.org/accelerators/net-zero-carbon-buildings/> accessed 2 May 2023.

[85] C40 Cities, 'C40 Cities South Africa Buildings Programme' <https://www.c40.org/what-we-do/scaling-up-climate-action/energy-and-buildings/c40-cities-south-africa-buildings-programme/> accessed 2 May 2023. The South Africa Green Building Council has announced a net zero building certification programme as part of the World Green Building Council's 'Advancing Net Zero' programme, the goal of which is to achieve net zero for all buildings by 2050. World Green Building Council, 'Green Building Council South Africa launches net zero building certification' <https://worldgbc.org/article/green-building-council-south-africa-launches-net-zero-building-certification/> accessed 2 May 2023.

[86] KPMG, 'Net-zero commitments: Where's the plan?' <https://kpmg.com/kw/en/home/insights/2021/11/net-zero-commitments-where-the-plan.html> accessed 2 May 2023.

action on net zero, private sector net zero building initiatives are being driven by several factors including a recognition of the climate change threats to businesses, corporate social responsibility initiatives, and demand from customers for building environments that help achieve the goals of the Paris Accords. The World Green Building Council's Net Zero Carbon Buildings Commitment is one example of such an initiative. The Commitment requires that, by 2030, 'existing buildings reduce their energy consumption and eliminate emissions from energy and refrigerants removing fossil fuel use as fast as practicable' and 'where necessary compensate for residual emissions'.[87] Under the Commitment, existing buildings eliminate fossil fuel use as soon as possible and new buildings and major renovations 'are built to be highly efficient, powered by renewables, with a maximum reduction in embodied carbon and compensation for all upfront residual emissions'.[88] At least 140 businesses and organizations, twenty-nine cities, and six states and regions have signed the Commitment, including major enterprises like IBM.[89]

The world's largest manager of commercial property, CRBE, has committed to achieving net zero carbon for its portfolio by 2040.[90] In several countries there has been strong market demand for those who construct commercial buildings to meet increasingly strong green building standards established by such organizations as Green Building Councils and the US Energy Star Buildings programme. This same phenomenon has now extended to zero energy/zero carbon buildings including the embodied energy aspects of new buildings and the refurbishing and extending the life of existing buildings. One industry survey of real estate professionals found that 65 per cent of their organizations had made net zero pledges.[91]

The 'Architecture 2030' challenge of the American Institute of Architects (AIA) envisions all new buildings and major renovations being carbon neutral by 2030.[92] To address the need to eliminate embodied carbon, Architecture 2030 has also launched the 'Carbon Smart Materials Palette' that identifies high impact building materials and provides strategies for reducing emissions.[93]

VII. The Path to Net Zero Buildings

Reaching the goal of net zero buildings is yet another of the major climate challenges the planet faces, but just as with carbon-free electricity, the phase-out of internal combustion engines, and other major climate challenges, the path is becoming more apparent.

[87] World Green Building Council, 'The Net Zero Carbon Buildings Commitment' <https://worldgbc.org/thecommitment/> accessed 2 May 2023.

[88] ibid.

[89] ibid; see also IBM, 'The Net Zero Carbon Commitment explained' <https://ibm.com/blogs/internet-of-things/net-zero-carbon-buildings-commitment-explained/> accessed 3 May 2023.

[90] CBRE, 'CRBE Commits to Net Zero by 2040' (20 September 2021) <https://www.cbre.com/press-releases/cbre-commits-to-net-zero-by-2040> accessed 3 May 2023.

[91] CBRE, 'Net-zero carbon goals, employee experience drive increased focus on ESG' (2 December 2022) <https://www.cbre.com/insights/briefs/net-zero-carbon-goals-employee-experience-drive-increased-focus-on-esg> accessed 3 May 2023.

[92] Architecture 2030, 'The 2030 Challenge: All new buildings, developments, and major renovations shall be carbon-neutral by 2030' <http://architecture2030.org/2030_challenges/2030-challenge/> accessed 3 May 2023.

[93] Architecture 2030, 'Carbon Smart Materials Palette: An immediately applicable, high-impact pathway to embodied carbon reductions in the built environment' <https://materialspalette.org> accessed 3 May 2023.

Reducing GHG emissions through rapid expansion in the number of net zero buildings will require significant governmental action, coupled with complementary private sector initiatives and supportive changes in public values (namely, embracing electrification of buildings and the phase-out of natural gas for most building applications). No single legal or policy tool is likely to be sufficient or appropriate on its own in a particular country, but a menu of options is now available.[94]

A. Governments

1. Leading the Way

Governments, often one of the largest owners and occupiers of buildings in a country, should start with their own building stock now, setting aggressive net zero goals for both new and existing buildings, rapidly phasing out the use of fossil fuels in their buildings, requiring the use of highly energy-efficient equipment in new and rehabilitated buildings, and extending the life of buildings whenever possible, as several governments have already done. Through the procurement process, governments can drive changes in the level of embodied carbon in building materials by specifying low carbon materials,[95] requiring the use low carbon emitting construction equipment, and contracting for rehabilitation or de-construction of buildings rather than demolition whenever feasible. Finally, governments can help accelerate net zero buildings by establishing clear net zero building goals for both new and renovated buildings to provide a clear roadmap for other actions by government and the private sector.

2. Regulatory Steps

Governments will need to play a strong regulatory role to reach the goal of net zero buildings by 2050. There are several tools governments can use to drive net zero buildings and in most cases governments will need to utilize several of the tools. By putting a price on carbon through either cap-and-trade systems or carbon taxes that apply broadly to carbon use in buildings, including embodied carbon as suggested by the Global Cement and Concrete Association,[96] governments can stimulate significant carbon reduction.

Governments will need to adopt advanced energy and building codes such as the IEA's zero carbon-ready code or the CalGreen code based on an efficiency-first principle that require the use of energy-efficient equipment and more energy-efficient new and rehabilitated structures. They will also need to reexamine building and fire codes to allow the use of lower carbon materials to be considered in building construction and to facilitate the phase-out of fossil fuel use in buildings. Governments could also require buildings to meet specific energy use outcomes such as the 'energy efficiency coefficient' in the Netherlands that sets a minimum energy performance level for buildings.[97] Governments could also

[94] See Lee Paddock and Caitlin McCoy, 'New Buildings' in Michael B Gerrard and John C Dernbach, *Legal Pathways to Deep Decarbonization in the United States* (Environmental Law Institute 2019) ch 12, for a detailed discussion of approaches to decarbonizing buildings in the United States.

[95] GCCA (n 47) 19.

[96] ibid.

[97] International Energy Agency (IEA), 'Energy performance for Buildings (EPG)' <https://www.iea.org/policies/8709-energy-performance-standards-for-buildings-epg> accessed 20 May 2023.

incentivize private investment by allowing owners of net zero buildings to charge an energy efficiency fee that reflects the prorated additional building cost of achieving net zero status for the building but also reflects the energy savings from efficiency improvements such as the Dutch Energieprestatievergoeding system.[98] Governments could also adopt mandatory energy efficiency retrofit laws at the time of sale, and mandate annual or time-of-sale energy use disclosure requirements for larger buildings such as those adopted by many cities in the United States[99] to ensure new owners can purchase highly efficient buildings.

Governments will need to establish clear timelines for the build-out of renewable energy generation and provide financial support for building the infrastructure needed for a rapid transition to renewable energy to ensure sufficient renewable energy is accessible as fossil fuel use in buildings is phased out. They will need to revise public utility regulations to permit wide use of distributed renewable energy production including microgrids and to ensure grid-based renewables remain affordable. They will also have to ensure that local zoning laws do not unduly restrict on-site renewable energy generation.

Finally, governments can play an important role in advancing net zero buildings by including both operational and embodied carbon in environmental impact assessments (EIAs) of significant government initiated, permitted, or funded building projects.

3. Government Non-regulatory Steps

Governments will also need to play an important non-regulatory role in achieving net zero buildings by 2050. Governments can assist in the net zero transition by conducting research and sharing information on low-carbon building materials and assessing and certifying energy-efficient equipment as is done through the US 'Energy Star' programme.[100] Governments will need to consider new financial support mechanisms that can address the potential higher front end construction costs of net zero buildings and the cost of net zero retrofits so that net zero residential buildings are affordable and so that net zero developments in lower income areas do not result in making housing in these areas unaffordable. Governments should also support the construction of more multifamily housing to reduce the amount of embodied carbon in building materials. Further, they should provide tax incentives to support wider adoption of energy-efficient technologies like heat pumps as was done through the Inflation Reduction Act in the United States. In addition, governments should support educational programmes that prepare the workforce that will be needed to construct net zero buildings and public education campaigns that help the public understand the need to move to net zero buildings to support the sociological changes that will help support net zero efforts.

B. Private Initiatives

The private sector has increasingly assumed a more active role in pursuing environmental goals that are not required by law. Companies are pursuing environmental goals for a

[98] See <https://www-rijksoverheid-nl.translate.goog/onderwerpen/energie-thuis/vraag-en-antwoord/energieprestatievergoeding-epv-bij-huurwoningen-op-warmtenet?_x_tr_sl=nl&_x_tr_tl=en&_x_tr_hl=en&_x_tr_pto=sc> accessed 20 May 2023 (translated).

[99] Consortium for building Energy Innovation, 'Benchmarking and Disclosure' <http://www.cbei.psu.edu/benchmarking-and-disclosure/index.html> accessed 20 May 2023.

[100] See <https://www.energystar.gov≥accessed 20 May 2023.

wide range of reasons including building and protecting their reputation, saving money, responding to individual customer demands, addressing green supply chain standards of business customers, government green procurement requirements, liability mitigation, and other reasons. The commercial buildings market provides a good example of this situation. The US Green Building Council reports that 'Between January 2017 and December 2021, over 36,835 projects earned its Leadership in Environment and Energy Design (LEED) certification, covering 4.63 billion gross square feet of space' and that '[i]n the first three quarters of 2022 (January through September), over 5,000 additional projects were certified'.[101]

The private sector has a very important role to play in accelerating net zero buildings. Steps that private sector architects, builders, building owners, and tenants can take include, consistent with the American Institute for Architecture's 2030 Challenge, committing to building only ZEBs by no later than 2030[102] and taking full lifecycle costs and the impacts of embodied carbon into account when deciding on the energy efficiency and building materials options for buildings. The private sector can also specify that energy for new buildings must be derived from renewable energy sources through on-site generation, the use of power purchase agreements for off-site renewable energy, or the purchase of certified Renewable Energy Certificates, and encourage trade associations and other organizations involved in training building professionals to provide training opportunities for architects, developers, and builders on constructing net zero buildings.

VIII. Conclusion

Dramatically reducing the operational and embodied carbon footprint of buildings in order to preserve natural resources and to reduce GHGs and other environmental pollutants, soon (since buildings have a long lifetime) is an essential aspect of achieving global net zero goals. This effort has important implications for two of the key themes of this book, security and solidarity: security because of the potential impact of electrification of buildings through dramatic expansion of renewable energy sources and solidarity by assuring net zero buildings and renewable energy sources are affordable for everyone. The transition must be coherently managed to ensure that an adequate supply of renewable energy is available as fossil fuels are phased out of use in buildings. In addition, careful attention must be paid to the availability and affordability of building for all as well as access to renewable energy by all. This is likely to require a new financing mechanism that can offset any higher initial costs associated with net zero buildings. It also requires attention to the sufficiency principle advanced by the IPCC which seeks more focus on providing 'sufficient' buildings for more people through approaches such as broader use of multifamily housing.

The transition also has important implications for many areas of natural resources law and practice given the major social changes needed to achieve net zero buildings by 2050. These practice areas include planning and zoning, land use, local governmental law,

[101] US Green Building Council, 'LEED data trends from the last five years' <https://www.usgbc.org/articles/leed-data-trends-past-five-years> accessed 3 May 2023.

[102] Specifically, new buildings should be fully electric and use only renewable energy, whether generated on-site or off-site.

procurement, construction law, environmental law, and energy law, among others. To succeed, the transition will also require a nexus governance approach to promote regulatory coherence across these wide range of areas.[103] Thoughtful education, capacity development, and awareness programmes for members of the public on the reasons for and implications of the regulatory changes required by net zero is also essential.

Moving rapidly to net zero buildings is one of the critical areas of decarbonization that must be pursued to stabilize the global climate. Even without major technology changes it is a goal that can be achieved. The pathways are becoming clearer and countries and many businesses have begun aggressively moving along those pathways.

[103] See the concluding chapter of this book for a detailed discussion of the nexus governance approach to net zero transition.

14

Hydrogen and the Net Zero Transition

Hugo Meyer van den Berg

I. Introduction

As discussed in Chapter 1 of this book, innovative technology solutions are required to achieve a just and orderly net zero and clean energy transition that does not worsen energy insecurity. This chapter examines hydrogen as a potential energy source for advancing net zero, as well as energy security during the transition. It discusses the legal barriers to introducing green hydrogen in the energy mix before discussing the policy considerations that may guide in addressing these barriers.

On 26 May 2023, the Namibian Government Hyphen Hydrogen Energy (Pty) Ltd signed a Feasibility and Implementation Agreement to develop, implement, and operate sub-Saharan Africa's largest (and only fully vertically integrated) green hydrogen project.[1] Shortly afterwards, on 20 June 2023, neighbouring South Africa concluded a Heads of Agreement with the governments of Netherlands and Denmark to launch a new 'SA-H2 Fund'. [2] This fund aims to facilitate and accelerate the development of a green hydrogen sector and circular economy in South Africa. These two recent developments in Southern Africa follow worldwide momentum in developing and adopting policies aimed at green hydrogen. For example, in 2017, Japan was the first to release its Basic Hydrogen Strategy.[3] Australia released its National Hydrogen Strategy in November 2019, which envisions 'a clean, innovative, safe and competitive hydrogen industry' benefitting all Australians.[4] In July 2020, the US Department of Energy's Office of Fossil Energy released its hydrogen strategy,[5] followed on 5 June 2023 by its Clean Hydrogen Strategy and Roadmap.[6] Also in 2020, the European Union (EU) released the EU Hydrogen Strategy for a Climate-Neutral

[1] Hyphen Hydrogen Energy (Pty) Ltd, 'The Government of the Republic of Namibia and Hyphen Hydrogen Energy Sign US$10 billion Green Hydrogen Project Agreement at Official Ceremony' (*Hyphen Hydrogen Energy (Pty) Ltd*, 26 May 2023) <https://www.hyphenafrica.com/news/the-government-of-the-republic-of-namibia-and-hyphen-hydrogen-energy-sign-us10-billion-green-hydrogen-project-agreement-at-official-ceremony/> accessed 24 June 2023.

[2] The Development Bank of Southern Africa, 'Unveiling the 'SA-H2 Fund': South Africa's Dedicated Green Hydrogen Fund' (*DBSA*, 20 June 2023) <https://www.dbsa.org/press-releases/unveiling-sa-h2-fund-south-africas-dedicated-green-hydrogen-fund> accessed 24 June 2023.

[3] Reuters, 'Japan to invest $107 billion in hydrogen supply over 15 years' (*Reuters*, 6 June 2023) <https://www.reuters.com/business/energy/japan-invest-107-bln-hydrogen-supply-over-15-years-2023-06-06/> accessed 25 June 2023.

[4] Australian Government: Department of Climate Change, Energy, the Environment and Water, 'Australia's National Hydrogen Strategy' (Australian Government, 2019) <https://www.dcceew.gov.au/energy/publications/australias-national-hydrogen-strategy> accessed 24 June 2023.

[5] US Department of Energy, 'Hydrogen Strategy: Enabling a Low-Carbon Economy' (*Office of Fossil Energy*, July 2020) <https://www.energy.gov/sites/prod/files/2020/07/f76/USDOE_FE_Hydrogen_Strategy_July2020.pdf> accessed 26 June 2023.

[6] US Department of Agriculture, 'U.S. National Clean Hydrogen Strategy and Roadmap' (US Department of Agriculture, 2023) <https://www.hydrogen.energy.gov/pdfs/us-national-clean-hydrogen-strategy-roadmap.pdf> accessed 26 June 2023.

Hugo Meyer van den Berg, *Hydrogen and the Net Zero Transition* In: *Net Zero and Natural Resources Law.* Edited by: Damilola S. Olawuyi, José Juan González, Hanri Mostert, Milton Fernando Montoya, and Catherine Banet, Oxford University Press. © International Bar Association 2024. DOI: 10.1093/9780198925033.003.0014

Europe, recognizing hydrogen as 'a key priority to achieve the European Green Deal and Europe's clean energy transition'.[7] These are just some examples—at least forty-five countries have developed or are developing green hydrogen policies.[8]

The current momentum that hydrogen is experiencing comes at a critical time in the energy transition. Faced with the mammoth challenge of climate change and the significant contribution of the energy sector to greenhouse gas (GHG) emissions, the climate crisis and the simultaneous combatting of climate change are central policy drivers of the green hydrogen revolution in many jurisdictions. These policy drivers must be seen against the backdrop of the urgent need to balance other critical policy issues: the quest for the security of energy supply and the diversification of energy sources during the net zero transition.[9] While interest in hydrogen is usually linked with climate change policies, hydrogen can play a significant role in energy security, energy access, energy justice, local air pollution control, and economic development.[10]

Many countries are exploring ways to fast-track the transition from reliance on fossil fuels to cleaner energy in pursuit of their domestic net zero goals. But, as discussed in Chapter 1 of this book, there are significant obstacles in this transition. While great strides have been made with renewable energy and the cleaning of electricity—which accounts for around 20 per cent of global energy use—some sectors are still heavily reliant on fossil fuels. Transportation, industry, power and buildings, and heating sectors still depend on fossil fuels, and some countries are pursuing renewable energy for the electrification of numerous end-use processes.[11] Other sectors, typically called hard-to-abate or hard-to-decarbonize sectors, cannot be electrified and are still dependent on fossil fuels as their primary energy source. Steelmaking, chemical high-temperature industrial heat, and transport (aviation, shipping, and long-distance and long-haul road transport) are examples of these hard-to-abate sectors.[12] The reality is, the world is still very much reliant on fossil fuels—a significant contributor to CO_2 emissions.[13]

Within the pursuit of diversification of energy sources and combatting climate change, hydrogen has emerged as a potential primary solution to release the energy sector from the grip of fossil fuels. In fact, the Intergovernmental Panel on Climate Change (IPCC), in its recent Synthesis Report of the IPCC Sixth Assessment Report (AR6),[14] discusses several options to reduce industrial emissions and recommends, amongst others, for light industry

[7] European Commission, 'Communication from the Commission to the European Parliament, the Council, the European Economic and Social Committee and the Committee of the Regions' (European Commission, 08 July 2020) <https://www.eur-lex.europa.eu/legal-content/EN/TXT/PDF/?uri=CELEX:52020DC0301> accessed 27 May 2023.

[8] World Economic Forum (WEF), 'What's stopping the world from using more green hydrogen?' (World Economic Forum, 10 August 2022) <https://www.weforum.org/agenda/2022/08/green-hydrogen-climate-change-energy/?DAG=3&gclid=CjwKCAjwkeqkBhAnEiwA5U-uM1chPD_OpDAIxJUR5v8Q0vbr-eUJ1Lw2AqlxsMnsjp2PsXo-p-1TphoCEwgQAvD_BwE> accessed 28 June 2023.

[9] Philipp Thaler and Benjamin Hofmann, 'The Impossible Energy Trinity: Energy Security, Sustainability, and Sovereignty in Cross-Border Electricity Systems' (2022) 94 Political Geography 102579.

[10] International Energy Agency (IEA), *The Future of Hydrogen: Seizing Today's Opportunities* (IEA 2019) 23–24. See also Kevin Joseph Dillman and Jukka Taneli Heinonen, 'A 'Just' Hydrogen Economy: A Normative Energy Justice Assessment of the Hydrogen Economy' (2022) 167 Renewable and Sustainable Energy Reviews 112648.

[11] Alexandra M Oliveira, Rebecca R Beswick, and Yushan Yan, 'A Green Hydrogen Economy for a Renewable Energy Society' (2021) 33 COCE 1, 1.

[12] IEA (n 10) 23.

[13] Oliveira, Beswick, and Yan (n 11).

[14] Intergovernmental Panel on Climate Change (IPCC), 'Synthesis Report of the IPCC Sixth Assessment Report (AR6)' (IPCC, March 2023) <https://www.ipcc.ch/report/ar6/syr/downloads/report/IPCC_AR6_SYR_LongerReport.pdf> accessed 23 July 2023.

and manufacturing to advance net zero, to resort to available abatement technologies, electrification, and switching to low- and zero-GHG emitting fuels, such as hydrogen, ammonia, and bio-based and other synthetic fuels.[15]

Despite the optimism about the role of green hydrogen in the net zero transition, several policy and legal challenges will need to be addressed. While the hydrogen market has existed for several decades, green hydrogen as a clean energy source is nascent, and the regulation thereof still needs to be developed. Countries intending to pursue green hydrogen production and distribution face various challenging questions. Since green hydrogen production, distribution, and use is still an emerging sector, most regulatory frameworks do not cater for it specifically, and it is uncertain to what extent it can be facilitated under existing frameworks.

This chapter first looks at what hydrogen is before discussing its potential role in pursuing net zero. It also examines hydrogen production and application and identifies substantial challenges that introducing green hydrogen in the energy mix faces. Finally, it considers how policy measures may address some of these challenges.

II. Hydrogen in Context

Hydrogen is the simplest,[16] most abundant element in the universe and the first element on the periodic table of elements.[17] Hydrogen gas—the gas with the lowest density of all gases—liquifies at -253°C (-423°F) and, while in a gaseous state, is odourless, colourless, and non-toxic.[18] It can only be found on earth as part of chemical compositions,[19] such as hydrocarbons and water, and not naturally by itself.[20] In its pure form (dihydrogen or H_2), however, it has several physical properties which make it useful for energy purposes.[21] Hydrogen is highly reactive when it comes into contact with oxygen—a reaction which releases significant energy.[22] Pure hydrogen does not contain any carbon atoms and therefore emits no CO_2 when it combusts or is burned (either to produce heat or electricity, or both).[23] This aspect of hydrogen—a carbon-free fuel—makes hydrogen particularly appealing in the battle against climate change.[24]

[15] ibid.

[16] One hydrogen atom consists of a single proton orbited by a single electron. See Alverà de Marco, *The Hydrogen Revolution: A Blueprint for the Future of Clean Energy* (Hodder and Stoughton Ltd 2021) 67.

[17] ibid. See also Ruven Fleming and Joshua Fershee, 'The "Hydrogen Economy" in the United States and the European Union: Regulating Innovation to Combat Climate Change' in Donald Zillman and others (eds), *Innovations in Energy Law and Technology: Dynamic Solutions for Energy Transitions* (OUP 2018) 153.

[18] John Armstrong, *The Future of Energy: Hydrogen: Hope or Hype? Hydrogen in the Future Energy System* (Amazon 2021) 25.

[19] Hydrogen's single electron is highly reactive and attaches easily to other elements. See de Marco (n 16) 79.

[20] Luis Ferney, Moreno Castillo, and Daniela Aguilar, 'Hydrogen in the Energy and Mobility Sectors in Colombia and in the International Context: Projects, Public Policy, and Regulatory Framework' (2021) 28 International Law Students Association Journal of International & Comparative Law 405, 407.

[21] European Investment Bank (EIB), *Unlocking the Hydrogen Economy—Stimulating Investment Across the Hydrogen Value Chain: Investor Perspectives on Risks, Challenges and the Role of the Public Sector* (European Investment Bank 2022) 7.

[22] Armstrong (n 18) 25. The reaction of hydrogen with oxygen can be catastrophic, as happened with the Hindenburg disaster.

[23] Fleming and Fershee (n 17) 153; EIB (n 21); Tommaso Capurso and others, 'Perspectives of the Role of Hydrogen in the 21st Century Energy Transition' (2022) 251 Energy Convestion and Management 1, 2.

[24] ibid.

Despite the reactive nature of hydrogen, it has traditionally not been pursued for its potential as an energy source. The rise of fossil fuels as the predominant energy source resulted in hydrogen never enjoying any limelight as an energy source.[25] Unlike hydrogen, which does not exist naturally by itself on earth, fossil fuels are freely available, thus making it difficult for hydrogen to present worthwhile competition to fossil fuels as an energy source.[26]

Hydrogen is, however, popular for various other purposes, and the hydrogen industry is already well established.[27] The most significant demand for hydrogen comes from the chemicals sector (as a feedstock for producing chemicals such as methanol and ammonia)[28] and the refining sector (hydrocracking[29] and desulphurization of fuels).[30] Producers of iron and steel, glass, speciality and bulk chemicals and electronics also rely on hydrogen.[31]

In 2020, industry demand for hydrogen was 87.1Mt; in 2021, demand reached 94Mt (with associated emissions exceeding 900MT CO_2).[32] The main challenge of hydrogen lies in the fact that it does not occur naturally on the earth, but only as part of compounds. To utilize hydrogen, it must be extracted (or separated) from the compound. Extracting hydrogen from compounds requires significant energy input. Currently, demand for hydrogen is being met predominantly by fossil fuel-based hydrogen production, with steam-methane reforming (or SMR) as the most common hydrogen production method.[33] This form of production leaves a significant carbon footprint. Other methods of producing hydrogen include oil and coal gasification and (to a much lesser extent) via electrolysis.[34] Hydrogen can be produced with different processes and energy sources. A colour coding (mainly grey, blue, turquoise, and green hydrogen) is used to differentiate between hydrogen produced in different ways. For example, grey hydrogen refers to hydrogen produced from methane or coal through SMR or gasification—this type of production results in significant CO_2 emissions. Blue hydrogen refers to hydrogen produced also produced from methane or coal through SMR or gasification, but combined with carbon capture and storage. With this type of production, CO_2 emissions are substantially reduced, but not eliminated. Turquoise hydrogen refers to hydrogen produced from methane through pyrolysis. Finally, green hydrogen refers to hydrogen produced from renewable energy through electrolysis.[35]

[25] de Marco (n 16) 77.

[26] ibid 79.

[27] IRENA, *Hydrogen from Renewable Power: Technology Outlook for the Energy Transition* (IRENA 2018) 13.

[28] The agricultural sector is the biggest consumer of ammonia globally, as around 85% of global ammonia production is used for fertilizers. IRENA, *Green Hydrogen for Industry: A Guide to Policymaking* (IRENA 2022) 18. See also IEA, *Global Hydrogen Review* (IEA 2022) 29.

[29] Hydrocracking is the process where hydrogen is used to upgrade heavy residual oils into higher-value oil products. IEA, *The Future of Hydrogen* (n 10) 92.

[30] IRENA, *Hydrogen from Renewable Power* (n 27) 13; IRENA, *Green Hydrogen* (n 28) 16; IEA, *Global Hydrogen* (n 28) 22.

[31] Michel Noussan and others, 'The Role of Green and Blue Hydrogen in the Energy Transition—A Technological and Geopolitical Perspective' (2021) 13 Sustainability 1, 1; National Engineering Policy Centre (NEPC), *The Role of Hydrogen in a Net Zero Energy System* (National Engineering Policy Centre 2022) 10; Gavin Fitch, Michael Barbero, and Kimberly Wasylenchuk, 'Hydrogen Roadmap: Policy, Regulation, and Prospect for Future Development in Alberta' (2022) 60 Alberta Law Review 435, 437; IRENA, 'Hydrogen from Renewable Power' (n 27) 13.

[32] IRENA, *Green Hydrogen* (n 28) 16; IEA, *Global Hydrogen* (n 28) 5, 71.

[33] Over 95% of current hydrogen production is based on fossil fuels. IRENA, *Hydrogen from Renewable Power* 13 (n 27). See also IEA, *Global Hydrogen* (n 28) 71.

[34] IRENA, *Hydrogen from Renewable Power* 13 (n 27).

[35] IRENA, *Green Hydrogen* (n 28) 8.

III. Green Hydrogen's Role in Advancing Net Zero

Hydrogen can be the missing link in the energy transition[36] and a vital option to realize net zero GHG emissions commitments.[37] If renewable energy is used to produce hydrogen, the resulting green hydrogen can provide energy to hard-to-abate sectors. In other words, green hydrogen can act as an energy carrier that facilitates energy transport from one place to another in a usable form.[38] The potential of hydrogen as an energy carrier has been known for decades, but this potential has been overshadowed by the barriers it faces. For green hydrogen to play a significant role in pursuing net zero, it must be tackled on two fronts.[39] First, cleaning up the production methods for hydrogen by moving towards a goal of green hydrogen and, secondly, promoting green hydrogen's utility as an energy carrier. The green hydrogen value chain (production to consumption) consists of many elements interlinked with the broader energy sector, and each aspect faces specific barriers and challenges.[40] For this contribution, the focus is only on hydrogen production and hydrogen as an energy carrier.

A. Green Hydrogen Production

Above, it is mentioned that the bulk of hydrogen in demand today is produced as grey hydrogen. In other words, it is produced from fossil fuels and still has a high carbon footprint. Blue hydrogen is produced when combined with carbon capture and storage, which results in far less CO_2 emissions, but has other challenges (and still results in some CO_2 emissions).

Hydrogen was first generated using electrolysis in the nineteenth century, but due to the high costs involved, it was abandoned in favour of hydrogen generation by way of processes based on fossil fuels.[41] With the decrease in renewable energy costs, the opportunity for producing green hydrogen is growing. Where green hydrogen is produced from renewable energy through electrolysis, there are no CO_2 emissions. Electrolysis is an electrochemical process where pure water is split into hydrogen and oxygen using an electrolyzer.[42] Three main electrolysis systems are available: alkaline electrolysis, proton exchange membrane electrolysis, and solid oxide electrolysis.[43] The technology for alkaline electrolyzers is mature, as it has been used for almost a century in industry.[44] Nickel, steel, and aluminium are key metal inputs used in alkaline electrolyzers, and the cost of the metals represents around 3.5 per cent of the total electrolyzer costs.[45] Proton exchange membrane electrolyzers are gaining popularity for their flexibility and smaller carbon footprint.[46] However, since these

[36] IRENA, *Hydrogen from Renewable Power* (n 27) 7.
[37] IEA, *Global Hydrogen* (n 28) 12.
[38] EIA, 'Hydrogen explained' (EIA, 2023) <https://www.eia.gov/energyexplained/hydrogen/> accessed 11 June 2023.
[39] IEA, *The Future of Hydrogen* (n 10) 17. See also Dillman and Heinonen (n10).
[40] IRENA, *Green Hydrogen* (n 28) 8.
[41] Noussan and others (n 31) 1, 3–4.
[42] IEA, *The Future of Hydrogen* (n 10) 42.
[43] Simeon Shiweda Hamukoshi and others, 'An Overview of the Socio-Economic Impacts of the Green Hydrogen Value Chain in Southern Africa' (2022) 33 Journal of Energy in Southern Africa 12, 14.
[44] IRENA, *Hydrogen from Renewable Power* (n 27) 19.
[45] IEA, *World Energy Outlook* (IEA 2022) 170.
[46] IRENA, *Hydrogen from Renewable Power* (n 27) 19.

electrolyzers use platinum and iridium as electrode catalysts, the metal costs represent around 12 per cent of the total electrolyzer cost.[47] Solid oxide electrolyzers are emerging technologies and have yet to be commercialized. They use ceramics as the electrolyte and have low material costs overall, but operate at high temperatures as they use steam as a heat source.[48]

The only by-product of green hydrogen production is water. It does, however, require significant renewable energy to power the electrolyzer. Since green hydrogen can be produced anywhere globally, areas with potentially prominent renewable energy capacity are being sought for possible green hydrogen projects. This then requires a significant expansion of renewable energy capacity.[49] But a key benefit of green hydrogen is its ability to store renewable energy when it is unavailable.[50]

Implementing a green hydrogen economy will require, amongst other things, research, development, and innovation, a significant reduction in electrolyzer costs, proper infrastructure, and an increase in demand for hydrogen products. This will take time, so interim, low-carbon options should also be pursued, such as expanding blue hydrogen production. This will increase hydrogen production generally and increase the hydrogen demand side and investment interest.[51] Blue hydrogen can also assist in decarbonizing existing hydrogen production, and it is suggested that blue hydrogen be used to clean up existing hydrogen production projects in parallel with the introduction of green hydrogen production projects.

B. Green Hydrogen Applications

Hydrogen in its pure form can be used as an energy carrier, or it can be used as an industrial raw material. Combined with other inputs, it can produce hydrogen-based fuels and feedstocks.[52] It is envisaged that hydrogen, as an energy carrier, can play a significant role in the energy transition by providing energy to sectors that are otherwise hard to decarbonize through electrification. Like electricity, hydrogen is not an energy source but an energy carrier.[53] Hydrogen is, however, a chemical energy carrier, which makes it more attractive than electricity. Chemical energy can be stored and transported stably for long periods and may be burnt at high temperatures.[54]

While renewable energy has made significant inroads in greening various sectors, some sectors cannot be decarbonized by electrification, whether from renewable energy or otherwise. These include industry, transport, and building sectors, where hydrogen can be implemented, and can therefore be crucial in decarbonization, while also having the potential to reduce emissions in the power sector.

[47] IEA, *World Energy Outlook* (n 45) 170.
[48] IEA, *The Future of Hydrogen* (n 10) 44.
[49] NEPC (n 31) 22.
[50] ibid 23.
[51] OECD, *Innovation and Industrial Policies for Green Hydrogen* (OECD Publishing 2022) 47.
[52] IEA, *The Future of Hydrogen* (n 10) 33.
[53] EIA (n 38).
[54] IEA, *The Future of Hydrogen* (n 10) 33; Daniel J Fiorino, *The Clean Energy Transition: Policies and Politics for a Zero-Carbon World* (Polity 2022) 171.

1. Industry

Hydrogen can be used in the chemical industry to produce ammonia, methanol, and other chemicals.[55] It is already an essential component of these chemicals, primarily grey hydrogen.[56] The potential impact of green hydrogen on emissions in the chemical feedstock industry is often overlooked.[57] However, introducing green hydrogen will require little modification; only the production method needs to change to water electrolysis.[58] It is anticipated that there will be rapid growth in the production of low-emission ammonia from now to around 2030 if the envisaged projects are realized.[59] Anticipated projects for low-emission methanol are still at an early stage.[60]

In the refining sector—which currently relies mainly on fossil fuel-based hydrogen—replacing that grey hydrogen with green hydrogen presents relatively low technical challenges, as it does not amount to a fuel switch but rather a like-for-like substitution.[61] The number of plants using electrolyzers is slowly increasing, and it is expected that the energy crisis, coupled with the Ukrainian invasion by Russia, may accelerate the use of blue and green hydrogen in refining.[62]

Green hydrogen can also be used in producing green steel. Currently, steel is produced either by blast furnace-basic oxygen furnace (BF-BOF) to produce primary steel, electric arc furnace (EAF) to produce secondary steel from scraps, or, in the absence of steel scrap, direct reduction of iron (DRI) to feed the EAF.[63] The BF-BOF route is carbon intensive, while the DRI-EAF route—which typically uses syngas—is more energy efficient, although traditional DRI still relies on fossil fuels.[64] The latter, however, only accounts for 5 per cent of current steel production. In 2020, the DRI-EAF route consumed approximately 4.3Mt of hydrogen. In a blast furnace, hydrogen is an auxiliary reducing agent, while it can potentially be a primary reducing agent in the DRI process.[65] Plans for several commercial-scale DRI plants—mainly in Europe—have been announced, and it is expected that DRI using hydrogen technology will be commercially available earlier than initially anticipated.[66]

Because of the high-grade heat produced by hydrogen combustion, hydrogen can also be used in industries[67] that require high-temperature heat (above 400°C).[68] Fossil fuels or combustible by-products are currently used to provide around 95 per cent of high-temperature heat. Electricity can also be used for high-temperature heat, but this option is not feasible as electrification of high-grade heating requires capital for redesigning industrial equipment. Using hydrogen for high-temperature heat is much less invasive.[69]

[55] IRENA, *Green Hydrogen* (n 28) 18.
[56] IEA, *Global Hydrogen* (n 28) 30.
[57] Oliveira, Beswick, and Yan (n 11) 1, 3.
[58] IRENA, *Green Hydrogen* (n 28) 18.
[59] IEA, *Global Hydrogen* (n 28) 31.
[60] ibid 33.
[61] ibid 24.
[62] ibid.
[63] IRENA, *Green Hydrogen* (n 28) 19.
[64] A mixture of carbon monoxide and hydrogen to reduce iron ore chemically for steelmaking is employed in conventional DRI technology. IEA, *Global Hydrogen* (n 28) 37.
[65] IRENA, *Green Hydrogen* (n 28) 21.
[66] IEA, *Global Hydrogen* (n 28) 15.
[67] Production of iron and steel, chemicals, and cement. IRENA, *Green Hydrogen* (n 28) 22.
[68] ibid 21.
[69] ibid 22.

2. Transport

Hydrogen contains more energy per unit of mass than gasoline or natural gas. It is thus attractive as a transport fuel. It is, however, the lightest element and therefore has a low energy density per unit of volume.[70] From 2020 to 2021, hydrogen demand in road transport increased by approximately 60 per cent.[71] In the transport sector, hydrogen is used mainly in road vehicles. The deployment of fuel cell electric vehicles (FCEV) has significantly increased over the last few years. FCEVs consume pure hydrogen and oxygen and release only water vapour.[72] While most are passenger vehicles, fuel-cell heavy-duty trucks have also recently been put into operation.[73] Hydrogen can also be a solution to decarbonizing diesel rail lines since battery-electric trains are not feasible due to the distances, and electrification is difficult. In August 2022, the first hydrogen fuel cell train fleet was deployed in Germany, and other countries are experimenting with hydrogen-fuelled passenger trains.[74]

In addition to transport by rail, hydrogen demand in other non-road transport areas (mining, shipping, and aviation) is also taking off.[75] Hydrogen can contribute significantly to decarbonizing the aviation sector by using hydrogen fuel cells and sustainable aviation fuels (partly based on hydrogen).[76] It is envisaged that, by 2050, 40 per cent of all aircrafts will be powered by hydrogen and the other 60 per cent by sustainable aviation fuels. Hydrogen-derived fuels (like ammonia) are also likely to be adopted to decarbonize the maritime sector.[77]

3. Buildings

Hydrogen's role in buildings is negligible at this stage. However, in the light of their net zero commitments, many countries are banning fossil fuel use in new buildings. Introducing hydrogen technologies in buildings will be challenging, given the more efficient, low-carbon alternatives such as electricity, district heat, and distributed renewables.[78] There are, however, ongoing projects investigating the possibility of introducing hydrogen applications in buildings with existing natural gas infrastructure, either for blending hydrogen with natural gas or using pure hydrogen, especially where energy use is hard to decarbonize.[79] Indirect use of hydrogen in buildings through district heat networks is also being pursued.[80]

4. Power Sector

There is increasing interest in using hydrogen and ammonia in the power sector. According to the IEA, technologies for electricity generation that can rely on hydrogen are already commercially available.[81] Reciprocating gas engines can already handle gases with a hydrogen content of up to 70 per cent, and engines handling solely hydrogen may be

[70] IEA, *The Future of Hydrogen* (n 10) 34.
[71] IEA, *Global Hydrogen* (n 28) 40.
[72] Oliveira, Beswick, and Yan (n 11) 1, 3.
[73] IEA, *Global Hydrogen* (n 28) 14.
[74] ibid 40.
[75] ibid 49–55.
[76] NEPC (n 31) 13.
[77] ibid.
[78] Oliveira, Beswick, and Yan (n 11) 1, 4.
[79] IEA, *Global Hydrogen* (n 28) 57.
[80] ibid 61.
[81] ibid 64.

commercially available in the coming years. Gas turbines can operate on hydrogen-rich gases, and hydrogen use in fuel cells is promising.[82]

One of the most prominent landmarks in combatting carbon emissions has been the introduction of renewable energy, particularly wind and solar power. But the challenge with renewable energy continues to be its intermittent nature, as the available wind and solar power depends on the availability of wind and the sun. Hydrogen can also be key in addressing this challenge, as hydrogen and electricity are complementary in the energy transition.[83] For example, with power-to-gas technology, excess electricity is converted to hydrogen, which is used in the gas grid or stored and later reconverted to electricity.[84] During periods of low electricity demand, green hydrogen can therefore be produced for energy storage (either as a gas or a liquid) and reconverted to electricity via fuel cells during periods of high electricity demand, which may improve grid resilience and energy security.[85] Since hydrogen can be stored for longer periods than batteries, it is valuable for integrating variable renewables into electricity grids.[86]

Green hydrogen can, therefore, play a significant role in decarbonizing key sectors in pursuit of net zero. But several legal challenges need to be addressed to unlock the full potential of green hydrogen.

IV. Minding the Gap: Addressing Legal Barriers to Introducing Green Hydrogen in the Energy Mix

A drastic shift from fossil fuels is required to reach net zero and keep up with interim targets set by countries. But transitioning from fossil fuels is a gradual process that requires various policies and measures to inform the transition.[87] Green hydrogen can play a vital role in this energy transition, but producing green hydrogen and expanding its application face significant legal and other challenges, with one of the major barriers being a need for sufficient policy ambition across the entire green hydrogen value chain.[88] A lack of adequate policy ambition translates into a lack of proper regulatory frameworks for hydrogen exploitation, which poses a challenge to hydrogen production, developing hydrogen infrastructure, and promoting hydrogen applications. Furthermore, for green hydrogen to play any significant role in a country's net zero goal and reaching interim targets, decarbonization should not only be a policy objective, but implementation strategies should also be identified, which many current hydrogen policies currently lack.[89]

Governments play a crucial role in helping hydrogen reach its potential[90] and can do so by adopting appropriate policy measures supporting green hydrogen. Significant momentum is currently being experienced globally in developing and adopting green hydrogen policies. But policies must address all the legal challenges faced in all three critical components

[82] ibid; NEPC (n 31) 12.
[83] IRENA, *Hydrogen from Renewable Power* 15 (n 27).
[84] Fleming and Fershee (n 17) 139.
[85] NEPC (n 31) 11; Fleming and Fershee (n 17) 150.
[86] Fiorino (n 54) 172.
[87] IRENA, *Green Hydrogen* (n 28) 11.
[88] ibid 25; IEA, *The Future of Hydrogen* (n 10) 27.
[89] Wenting Cheng and Sora Lee, 'How Green Are the National Hydrogen Strategies' (2022) 14 Sustainability 1, 3.
[90] IEA, *The Future of Hydrogen* (n 10) 30.

of green hydrogen: production, infrastructure, and applications. These policies and strategies also need to be implemented through well-crafted legislative measures that not only give effect thereto, but ensure that achieving policy objectives is possible and that progress is measurable. However, notwithstanding the increase globally in green hydrogen policies and strategies, there is still a regulatory gap in most jurisdictions regarding green hydrogen, which poses a material barrier to investment. Policies are not being implemented through legal frameworks for green hydrogen, or implementation is piecemeal or just very slow.

The legislative measures introduced to accommodate green hydrogen within a country's energy mix must be aligned with other policy objectives, such as those relating to socio-economic development, environment, and other industries. Legislative measures must address the entire value chain of green hydrogen, from production to end-user consumption. Policy considerations as the basis for legislative reforms are divided into categories for this contribution: hydrogen production (supply), infrastructure, and hydrogen applications (demand). Other essential policy considerations not addressed here may relate to promoting research and development and international trade and cooperation. Below, the key challenges and policy considerations are discussed, as well as suggestions on improving legal frameworks for green hydrogen.

A. Hydrogen Production

The production of green hydrogen is capital-intensive and far more expensive than grey hydrogen. The more mature fossil-based processes are cheaper than green production processes.[91] This has a knock-on effect on the cost of the green products produced and will make competition of green products with traditionally produced products difficult.[92] For green hydrogen to be competitive, it needs to reach cost parity with grey hydrogen as far as production is concerned.[93] The high capital requirements of green hydrogen projects make financing a critical consideration.[94] Dedicated renewable energy sources would also be required to meet hydrogen demand.[95] A decrease in the cost of production of green hydrogen is promising for the role the hydrogen can play in decarbonizing hard-to-abate sectors.[96] However, it is not only the production costs that pose a challenge, but also conversion, transport, and storage costs.[97]

Green hydrogen policies need to set clear targets from the outset and should be clear on the role of government support. Government support encouraging investment in green hydrogen can take many forms and should also be aimed at reducing investor risks. Some government policies may envisage direct state involvement in hydrogen projects through equity stake,[98] joint ventures, public–private partnerships,[99] or other forms of involvement.

[91] IRENA, *Green Hydrogen* (n 28) 23.
[92] ibid.
[93] IRENA, *Green Hydrogen Supply: A Guide to Policymaking* (IRENA 2021) 15.
[94] ibid 16.
[95] IRENA, *Green Hydrogen* (n 28) 25.
[96] ibid 11.
[97] IRENA, *Green Hydrogen Supply* (n 93) 17–18.
[98] Namibia, eg, envisages an optional equity stake in its hydrogen projects, similar to its existing petroleum projects.
[99] eg the European Clean Hydrogen Alliance, which envisages a collaboration between public authorities, industry, and civil society. See Ruven Fleming, 'Green Hydrogen Developments in the EU: Cross-border

Many countries already have state-involvement measures in other sectors, such as petroleum and mining, with established track records of effectiveness.

Governments may also consider introducing measures to support investments through direct financial support or fiscal incentives. Direct financial support can be using grants and loans. Germany, for example, has dedicated US$2.4 billion to partnerships with countries where hydrogen production can occur. France has also committed US$8.3 billion by 2030 to its national hydrogen strategy, while the Australian Renewable Energy Agency announced a funding round of approximately US$42 million for green hydrogen (targeting electrolyzers).[100]

Governments may also pursue fiscal incentives to promote hydrogen production. Fiscal investment policies aimed at reducing the costs in relation to electrolyzer investment will decrease production costs and enhance the business case for a hydrogen project.[101] Fiscal incentives can also be more comprehensive by providing favourable tax rates or tax rebates for companies involved in hydrogen production, deductible project expenses, import relief, and other fiscal relief and incentives. Incentives must be supported by appropriate standards and certification schemes linked with the type of hydrogen produced. Guarantees of Origin (GoOs) will play a vital role in ensuring the future hydrogen economy's sustainability and promotion.[102] Apposite carbon pricing would also provide revenue while contributing to cost-efficient decarbonization.[103] A proper certification scheme enhances traceability and transparency and comforts buyers on the hydrogen's origin.[104] Adopting and implementing a certification scheme will also show that a country is serious about promoting green hydrogen specifically, not just hydrogen generally.

Policies envisaging a ban or mandated phasing out of technologies based on fossil fuels (such as blast furnaces in steelmaking and SMR in grey hydrogen production) should be considered to loosen the grip of fossil fuel-based processes in the industrial space.[105] Another possibility is whitelisting decarbonized technologies or blacklisting fossil fuel-based technologies[106] or introducing penalties for fossil fuels (eg through carbon pricing or coal phasing-out timelines).[107] Policy measures to create a demand for green hydrogen production will also stimulate and encourage investment, such as introducing green hydrogen quotas in the industrial sector.[108] The challenge with introducing penalties is that this will discourage investment in fossil fuel industries, which remains a crucial industry for many countries and an emerging industry in others (such as Namibia).[109] But countries serious about relying on green hydrogen in pursuit of net zero need to be clear on their position regarding fossil fuels and fossil fuel-based technologies. This is particularly important for

Cooperation between Germany and the Netherlands' in Martha M Roggenkamp and Catherine Banet (eds), *European Energy Law Report XIV* (Intersentia 2021) 275.

[100] IRENA, *Green Hydrogen Supply* (n 93) 28.
[101] ibid.
[102] Lena Tholen and others, 'The Green Hydrogen Puzzle: Towards a German Policy Framework for Industry' (2021) 13 Sustainability 1, 4.
[103] OECD (n 51) 45.
[104] Cheng and Lee (n 89) 1, 5.
[105] WEF (n 8).
[106] ibid.
[107] Cheng and Lee (n 89) 1, 4.
[108] WEF (n 8).
[109] Cheng and Lee (n 89) 1, 4.

countries with developed or emerging petroleum industries[110] or countries using CCS technologies.[111]

Green hydrogen production may also be stimulated through policies ensuring a sufficient renewable energy supply. It is estimated that around 3000 GW of renewable energy is needed by 2050 for large-scale green hydrogen to be possible and cost-effective.[112] A significant decrease in the cost of renewable energy is therefore required. Countries with low renewable energy capacity should consider obtaining green hydrogen from countries with better renewables that can produce green hydrogen cheaper.[113] Countries with significant renewable energy capacity should promote these sectors.

Many countries (particularly in Africa) do not clearly define or regulate renewable energy; instead, renewable energy is often an 'add-in' of other sectors (such as electricity) without a proper regulatory framework for renewable energy specifically. For purposes of integration of green hydrogen in a country's energy mix, a clear and comprehensive framework governing renewable energy is essential; a lack of comprehensive regulation of renewable energy will be a deterrent to investment in green hydrogen as well.[114]

Legislative frameworks regulating green hydrogen production need to be drafted with investment and financing as key considerations. Other considerations include the discouraging of fossil fuel-based products and processes. This, however, requires a delicate balancing of government policy priorities, especially in countries with an established or emerging petroleum industry.

In general, legal frameworks in respect of green hydrogen should be investor-attractive. To achieve this, they should reduce risk and uncertainty.[115] Investors also require a clear legal framework that eliminates unnecessary regulatory barriers. Regulatory frameworks should leave no doubt as to the licences and permits required for hydrogen projects.[116] Some countries adopt ambitious hydrogen strategies without hydrogen-specific regulatory frameworks. As a result, it is unclear where a hydrogen project will fit within the country's existing energy regulations and what licensing requirements will be triggered. Some countries with established gas frameworks may want to provide for hydrogen under this framework, while others may include it under general energy regulations or electricity frameworks.[117] Whatever the case may be, investors need to have certainty about the licensing and other regulatory requirements and obligations of a proposed hydrogen project.

[110] Namibia, eg, is currently in an interesting position. Earlier this year, it signed a facility and implementation agreement for the development, implementation, and operation of sub-Saharan Africa's largest (and only fully vertically integrated) green hydrogen project. During the last couple of years, however, significant discoveries of offshore oil have also been made, thus breathing life into Namibia's hitherto insignificant petroleum industry. So, at this point Namibia is poised to become a key player in Africa as far as green hydrogen is concerned, but also possibly a significant player in the petroleum industry. Both industries will play major roles in achieving socio-economic development goals, but they will conflict on other objectives. How this will be managed is yet to be seen. Namibia is one of the countries that committed to the Glasgow Breakthroughs of COP26.

[111] Cheng and Lee (n 89) 1, 4.

[112] OECD (n 51) 44–45.

[113] Agora, *12 Insights on Hydrogen* (Agora Energiewende 2021) 39.

[114] Katundu Imasiku and others, 'A Policy Review of Green Hydrogen Economy in Southern Africa' (2021) 13 Sustainability 1, 2.

[115] OECD (n 51) 46.

[116] Imasiku and others (n 114) 1, 11.

[117] In Namibia, eg, a specific regulation in the form of a proposed Synthetic Fuels Act is envisaged as the existing energy framework does not cater for hydrogen at all.

Green hydrogen projects require investment with government cooperation. Therefore, legislative frameworks should be clear as to the role government will play in green hydrogen projects. Legislative frameworks should also provide for financial support and fiscal incentives aimed at promoting and supporting investment in green hydrogen projects, together with appropriate certification schemes. These provisions should be unambiguous and transparent to promote public confidence.

Legislative frameworks should also encourage research and development to reduce electrolyzer costs and improve technologies.[118] Technological breakthroughs are essential for the green hydrogen industry, and the regulatory frameworks should accommodate current and future technologies. Laws should not be designed technology-specific but rather technology-neutral to ensure their longevity.[119]

Legal frameworks for hydrogen production should adopt health and safety measures that cater specifically for hydrogen—from production to storage, transport, and application. Existing health and safety measures should either be amended or bespoke measures introduced for the hydrogen industry. This should all take place against the backdrop of country's overall alignment of its net zero commitments to accommodate hydrogen.

B. Hydrogen Infrastructure

The lack of dedicated infrastructure for transport, storage, and end-user consumption of green hydrogen is also a critical barrier to integrating green hydrogen into the energy mix. Proper hydrogen storage may ensure a steady supply and increase overall green hydrogen costs.[120] But storage also comes at an increased cost and depends on the availability of storage locations. As far as infrastructure for transport is concerned, given its low-energy density, hydrogen transportation is costly, although it is still cheaper than transporting renewable energy.[121] Existing natural gas infrastructure may be repurposed for green hydrogen as many regions (such as Africa) do not have such structures.[122] Introducing green hydrogen in specific sectors (like steelmaking) will also require a complete technological shift.

Hydrogen can be produced on-site by end-users, although large-scale production and distribution will be more cost effective.[123] This, however, requires proper infrastructure for transport and storage.[124] Policies supporting hydrogen infrastructure may be aimed at repurposing existing grids or supporting new grid construction.[125] In Germany, for example, transmission system operators are looking at repurposing 5900 km of pipeline to hydrogen and introducing only 100 km of new pipeline.[126] As more countries move from traditional gas to carbon-free alternatives, the available infrastructure could be well-suited for hydrogen

118 OECD (n 51) 16.
119 Cheng and Lee (n 89) 1, 5.
120 IRENA, *Green Hydrogen* (n 28) 23.
121 OECD (n 51) 18.
122 IRENA, *Green Hydrogen* (n 28) 13.
123 OECD (n 51) 38.
124 Tholen and others (n 102) 1, 5.
125 See also Oleh Chechel and others, 'Reform of State Regulation of Production and Transportation of Hydrogen on the Territory of European States in the Context of EU Positive Practice' (2022) 117 Eastern European Journal of Enterprise Technologies 78, 83.
126 IRENA, *Green Hydrogen* (n 28) 43.

transport.[127] Policies aimed at infrastructure may also include measures supporting seasonal storage[128] and policies aimed at facilitating capital flows for network expansion and repurposing.[129] In Namibia, the government's green hydrogen and derivatives strategy envisages establishing a common-use infrastructure for the first large-scale hydrogen projects aimed at de-risking projects and accelerating the scale-up of green hydrogen production.[130]

Policy-makers should identify solutions supporting the seasonal storage of green hydrogen. This can be by means of ensuring that the power system has a minimum level of seasonal storage capacity for demand during off-peak periods or by introducing a feed-in tariff or premium scheme compensating producers who produce during prolonged low variable renewable energy periods.[131] Given the uncertainty and intermittent nature of renewable energy, hydrogen and electricity can be utilized together to store and convert energy between them.[132]

Where injection and storage of hydrogen in geological formations is envisaged, this must be aligned with other national policies and regulatory measures, such as those dealing with environment, ownership, and safety.[133] Existing laws and policies can be relied on in many jurisdictions—especially those with established carbon capture and storage activities.[134] But for other jurisdictions, it may require completely new laws to accommodate hydrogen storage.[135]

Integrating green hydrogen into a country's energy mix requires clear and transparent laws governing renewable energy. In addition, laws should also be developed dealing in detail with hydrogen storage and transport. Where existing infrastructure is in place, laws should address the repurposing of this infrastructure for hydrogen purposes. The transport and storage of hydrogen has critical implications for health, safety, and the environment. The storage and transportation of green hydrogen and the laws regulating this need to be aligned with environmental and health and safety laws.

C. Hydrogen Applications

Another barrier is the need for more demand and value recognition for green products, especially in the light of the cheaper, fossil fuel-based alternatives.[136] There is no existing green hydrogen market. Without targets or incentives promoting green hydrogen products, demand for green hydrogen is limited.[137] Developing comprehensive legal frameworks for hydrogen production and infrastructure without also focusing on the promotion of

[127] Fleming (n 99) 268.
[128] IRENA, *Green Hydrogen Supply* (n 93) 43.
[129] ibid 45.
[130] NIPDB, 'Green Hydrogen Strategy: Namibia Green Hydrogen & Derivatives Strategy' (NIPDB, 16 December 2022) <https://www.nipdb.com/download/green-hydrogen-strategy/> accessed 24 June 2023.
[131] IRENA, *Green Hydrogen Supply* (n 93) 45; Oliveira, Beswick, and Yan (n 11) 1, 5.
[132] Oliveira, Beswick, and Yan (n 11) 1, 5.
[133] IRENA, *Green Hydrogen Supply* (n 93) 45.
[134] ibid.
[135] In Namibia, eg, none of the existing laws will provide for adequate control over hydrogen storage and transportation.
[136] IRENA, *Green Hydrogen* (n 28) 28.
[137] ibid 13.

hydrogen applications may negatively impact the overall objective of promoting a hydrogen economy.

A lack of demand may also hamper infrastructure development.[138] Policy considerations should also seek to implement incentives for the consumption of material produced using green hydrogen to ensure that these goods can compete with material produced through reliance on fossil fuels.[139] Applying taxes and levies to grey hydrogen can assist with levelling the playing field and ensuring that green hydrogen becomes competitive. This may also be achieved by offering tariffs or price premiums to purchase green hydrogen.[140] Further, demand for goods created using green hydrogen may be increased using quotas.[141] This will require substantial amendments to fiscal legislation.

When designing policies for green hydrogen applications, the focus should be on hard-to-abate applications rather than applications where more efficient and economical means are available or low-priority applications. For example, Japan's Basic Hydrogen Strategy—the first to focus on hydrogen—is criticized for focusing on 'bad ideas' for green hydrogen applications.[142] The Strategy is set to be revised to restructure its goals.[143] The argument is that policies and legislative measures designed to promote hydrogen applications should focus applications where cheaper, readily available alternatives are not possible.

Social acceptance of green hydrogen is critical to the adoption of hydrogen applications.[144] Social acceptance is more forthcoming where clear and transparent just transition policies and frameworks are in place to ensure in order, inclusive, and orderly green hydrogen production and applications.[145] This is particularly true in countries (especially in Africa) where major foreign-driven and foreign-financed projects are often met with scepticism and allegations of corruption, social exclusion, and inequity.[146]

Hydrogen projects and applications must be promoted and implemented within a clear and transparent regulatory framework that enhances energy justice and leaves no one behind.[147] A just hydrogen economy will increase social acceptance for hydrogen applications, especially in local communities.[148] Legislative frameworks for hydrogen applications should focus on hard-to-abate applications. Tariffs and price premiums can be introduced in the regulatory framework to encourage use of green hydrogen. Legislative measures may also be introduced to discourage use of products derived from, or using, grey hydrogen by providing for taxes and levies.

138 IRENA, *Green Hydrogen Supply* (n 93) 21.
139 IRENA, *Green Hydrogen* (n 28) 25.
140 IRENA, *Green Hydrogen Supply* (n 93) 34.
141 Tholen and others (n 102) 1, 5; WEF (n 8).
142 Renewable Energy Institute, *Re-examining Japan's Hydrogen Strategy: Moving Beyond the 'Hydrogen Society' Fantasy* (Renewable Energy Institute 2022) 4.
143 Leigh Collins, '"A complete failure" | Japan's "fantasy" hydrogen strategy does nothing for decarbonisation: study' (*Hydrogeninsight*, 4 October 2022) <https://www.hydrogeninsight.com/policy/a-complete-failure-japans-fantasy-hydrogen-strategy-does-nothing-for-decarbonisation-study/2-1-1326788> accessed 28 June 2023.
144 Arturo Vallejos-Romero and others, 'Green Hydrogen and Social Sciences: Issues, Problems, and Future Challenges' (2023) 15 Sustainability 1, 12.
145 See Dillman and Heinonen (n.10). See also Chapter 2 of this book on elements of a just transition.
146 Afe Babalola and Damilola Olawuyi, 'Overcoming Regulatory Failure in the Design and Implementation of Gas Flaring Policies: The Potential and Promise of an Energy Justice Approach' (2022) 14 Sustainability 1, 4.
147 Dillman and Heinonen (n.10).
148 Vallejos-Romero and others (n 144) 1, 11–12.

V. Conclusion

Low to zero carbon hydrogen production can play a vital role in the energy transition in pursuit of net zero, especially in sectors that are hard to decarbonize by electrification. According to the IEA, if the envisaged blue and grey hydrogen projects are realized, the annual production of low-emission hydrogen may reach more than 24Mt of hydrogen by 2030.[149] Green hydrogen is therefore central to the goal of achieving zero carbon emissions by 2050. Given green hydrogen's small role in the energy mix, drastic intervention is required to unlock its potential. This will happen over time, and interim measures should be employed to reduce carbon emissions while building the green hydrogen economy. Blue hydrogen can help support the transition to a complete green hydrogen economy if blue hydrogen technology is deployed to clean up existing hydrogen production.[150]

The introduction of green hydrogen in the energy mix faces various legal challenges in addition to costs, infrastructure, and demand. The continuous reliance on the availability of cheaper fossil fuel-based alternatives amplifies these challenges. The challenges can be addressed by coherent and integrated policy measures for hydrogen production, infrastructure, and applications.[151] Many countries across the world have already adopted hydrogen-specific policies or are developing these policies. Hydrogen's role in a country's energy mix should be established within long-term energy strategies and translated into appropriate legislative measures.[152]

When drafting policies, policy-makers must be cognizant of the barriers to introducing green hydrogen in the energy mix and address these barriers at every level of the hydrogen value chain. Generally, policy measures should be investor-sensitive and incentivize all value chain aspects. Various fiscal and related incentives may be introduced at each stage in the value chain to encourage investment and stimulate demand. Measures can also be introduced to discourage the use of products produced by fossil fuel technologies or promote the use of products produced by green hydrogen technologies. Policy-makers must, however, ensure that policy frameworks reduce risk and uncertainty and are aligned with policy provisions for other industries directly and indirectly affected by hydrogen production, transport, and application.

Policies must be translated into appropriate regulatory frameworks for green hydrogen. This may involve amending existing frameworks (such as those regulating gas or electricity) or introducing hydrogen-specific frameworks. The proposed route must already be anticipated at policy revel to provide certainty. Key for the regulatory frameworks is having a proper definition of green hydrogen, supported by the necessary certification schemes. A proper regulatory regime for renewable energy is also essential to promote investment in green hydrogen. Legislative frameworks must also establish certainty on the licencing and permitting requirements for hydrogen projects and the necessary environment, health, and safety provisions to accommodate hydrogen. Regulatory frameworks should also provide for the regulation of hydrogen transport and storage.

[149] IEA, *Global Hydrogen* (n 28) 72.
[150] Fiorino (n 54) 171.
[151] See Chapter 22 of this book on the guiding principles of promoting coherence in natural resources law in a net zero era.
[152] See also Imasiku and others (n 114) 1, 14.

To stimulate the demand for green hydrogen—and thus increase interest in investment in hydrogen production—regulatory frameworks should promote green hydrogen applications. This can be done either by implementing measuring rewarding the use of green hydrogen, or measures penalizing the use of grey hydrogen or fossil fuels, or both. An increase in end-user demand for green hydrogen will not only increase investment interest, but also promote research and development in hydrogen production technologies.

15

How Net Zero Goals Impact Electricity Systems and Supply Security

An Analysis of the EU Legal Framework

Martha M. Roggenkamp

I. Introduction

Net zero goals affect all economic sectors that make use of fossil fuels, including the energy sector. The need to reduce greenhouse gas (GHG) emissions to reach international and national net zero goals can be achieved in different ways, for example by replacing the production and use of fossil fuels with renewable energy sources (RES). The Ukraine war has also demonstrated that substituting fossil fuels for renewables is essential to guarantee energy supply security and even energy sovereignty in the European Union (EU).[1] This process of decarbonization will especially impact the electricity sector as most cables have been designed to connect thermal power stations to end-consumers and not to meet the requirements of RES production and supply. Although the process of energy transition and decarbonization of the network-bound electricity sector is a worldwide phenomenon, this chapter focuses on the developments in the EU as the EU provides a good example of the challenges resulting from such transition and how the law addresses these challenges. This chapter will thus explore the impact of the rapid increase of RES on the electricity system in the EU and in particular how large volumes of RES can be fed into the grid and, at the same time, guarantee end-consumers' energy security through an uninterrupted supply of reliable and sustainable energy supply.

In the EU, this process is taking place in a liberalized energy market where market parties and network operators may have differing and sometimes opposing interests. Traditionally, the electricity chain consists of one (sometimes more) national transmission grid and several regional distribution grids. In general, large production facilities were connected to the transmission grid and most consumers to the regional grid, with some exceptions for some very large consumers that were connected to the transmission grid. Prior to market liberalization the transmission and/or distribution grids were part of production and/or distribution companies, that is, vertically integrated. This enabled a close coordination with production and supply of electricity. Market liberalization, however, drastically changed this approach. In order to provide market parties (producers as well as consumers) with freedom of choice and to ensure that grid operators are not abusing their monopoly

[1] European Council, 'The time is now: The EU needs a genuine Energy Union' <https://www.consilium.europa.eu/en/european-council/president/news/2022/10/10/20221005-pec-newsletter-energy-union/> accessed 27 August 2023

Martha M. Roggenkamp, *How Net Zero Goals Impact Electricity Systems and Supply Security* In: *Net Zero and Natural Resources Law*. Edited by: Damilola S. Olawuyi, José Juan González, Hanri Mostert, Milton Fernando Montoya, and Catherine Banet, Oxford University Press. © International Bar Association 2024. DOI: 10.1093/9780198925033.003.0015

position, transmission and distribution grids have to be operated independently from production and supply activities.[2] How such unbundling is achieved differs per jurisdiction. Market liberalization and the freedom of choice resulting therefrom also enabled new companies to enter the energy production market and existing producers to choose RES as their primary fuel, both on a large and small scale. Connecting these RES generators to the electricity grid poses some challenges as system operators need to ensure grid reliability and supply security.

The challenges the EU transmission system operators (TSOs) and distribution system operators (DSOs) currently face due to the gradually increasing levels of RES production and consumption include: (1) a possible imbalance between consumption and supply and thus a risk of black-outs or brown-outs, and (2) a lack of grid capacity and thus the possibility of congestion. These challenges all involve a mismatch between production and network capacity or production and consumption. This chapter addresses these legal challenges posed by such rapid increase of renewable energy sources to the current unbundled transmission and distribution system in the EU. It examines the legal instruments on EU level governing system balancing, congestion management, grid investments, and alternative grid solutions enabling renewable electricity to reach end-consumers.

This chapter is organized as follows. After this introduction (Section I), it will discuss the concept of balancing and some legal mechanisms to address imbalances resulting from increasing volumes of renewables (Section II). Thereafter, it will analyse the legal framework governing the allocation of (insufficient) grid capacity, including congestion management and grid expansions (Section III). Next, the chapter will present some alternative grid configurations relating to large offshore (wind energy) projects and local energy supply projects (Section IV). This will be followed by a conclusion (Section V).

II. Network Balancing and Energy Security

A. The Concept of Balancing

One of the specific features of the electricity system is that the grid must be balanced at all times, which means that the volumes of electricity fed into the grid have to match the volumes extracted from the grid. In other words, electricity production and consumption must be equal at all times. The balance is measured through the frequency of the electricity being transported via the grid, which is set at 50 Hz in Europe.[3] If the frequency increases or decreases too much, that is, more electricity is extracted from the system than planned beforehand (or vice versa), a situation of imbalances may occur and this may result in a brown-out (partial outages) or black-out (complete shut-down) of the entire system and thus endanger supply security.[4]

[2] See, for a more in-depth analysis of EU energy market liberalization, Hans Vedder and others, 'EU Energy Law' in Martha M Roggenkamp and others (eds), *Energy Law in Europe— National, European and International Regulation* (3rd edn, OUP 2016) ch IV.

[3] GRIDRADAR, 'Real-time behaviour of power frequency' <https://www.gridradar.net/en/mains-frequency> accessed 27 August 2023.

[4] F Elskamp, 'RES and the Impact on Security of Supply and Dispatching' in Martha M Roggenkamp and others (eds), *Energy Law, Climate Change and Environmental Law* (Edward Elgar 2021) 380–81.

Prior to market liberalization, system balancing was relatively simple as electricity companies were vertically integrated and information about production, consumption, and network capacity could easily be shared. It was thus relatively straightforward to plan for and maintain network frequency. With the liberalization process and the subsequent separation ('unbundling') between production and supply on the one hand, and network operations on the other, TSOs and DSOs cannot directly control production nor influence any planned consumption. Therefore, a mechanism was needed to ensure a continuous adjustment of electricity production and consumption, even in case of forecasting errors and/or technical disturbances. This is referred to as balancing.

Given the central role of the TSOs in the entire energy system, they are obliged, if necessary, to intervene in order to ensure the equilibrium between production and consumption. To achieve this, TSOs need to receive each day from all grid- connected parties a schedule of estimated production and consumption levels. Grid- connected parties that are acknowledged and registered as such by TSOs are referred to as Balancing Responsible Parties (BRPs). Small (household) consumers are exempted as BRPs; instead their supply companies have to inform the TSOs of the estimated consumption levels on the basis of aggregated usage data. These data are increasingly collected via smart meters and other smart ICT technologies.[5] The energy programmes (the accepted schedules) provided by the BRPs are binding and form the legal basis to settle any imbalances for which the BRPs are financially liable. Apart from this, TSOs need to act when they detect the grid is not in balance. Such intervention entails that the TSO needs to buy electricity from some designated suppliers for balancing purposes.

B. EU Legal Framework Governing Balancing

1. Legal B asis

Although balancing is essential for electricity system operations, rules at EU level were developed relatively late. The first Electricity Directives[6] (E-Directives) did not refer to balancing at all. Although the 2009 E-Directive required that balancing rules and charges for possible imbalances have to be objective, transparent, and non-discriminatory,[7] a definition is included for the first time in Regulation 914/2019 on the internal electricity market, which defines 'balancing' as: 'all actions and processes, in all timelines, through which transmission system operators ensure, in an ongoing manner, maintenance of the system frequency within a predefined stability range and compliance with the amount of reserves needed with respect to the required quality . . . .'[8] In parallel, the 2019 E-Directive introduced the concept of 'balancing markets' as it includes in the definition of 'electricity markets' also those markets relevant for balancing and ancillary services.[9]

[5] Lea Diestelmeier, 'A Legal Framework for Smart Grids' in Martha M Roggenkamp and others (eds), *Energy Law, Climate Change and the Environment* (Edward Elgar 2021) 645– 55.

[6] Directive 96/92/EC of 19 December 1996 concerning common rules for the internal electricity market was replaced by Directive 2003/54/EC, which again was repealed by Directive 2009/72/EC, OJ L 211 (hereafter 2009 E-Directive). In 2019, this D irective was replaced by Directive 2019/944, OJ L 158 (hereafter 2019 E-Directive).

[7] 2009 E-Directive, art 15, para 7.

[8] Regulation (EU) 2019/943 on the internal electricity market (recast) [2019] OJ L158/54, art 2(10) (hereafter 2019 E-Regulation).

[9] 2019 E-Directive, art 2(45).

Further rules on balancing and balancing markets are included in EU network codes and guidelines drafted by the European Network of TSOs for Electricity (ENTSO-E).[10] These network codes and guidelines have been adopted as EU Regulations and are thus directly applicable to all Member States. Relevant for guaranteeing operational security and balancing are: the System Operations Guidelines, which aim at safeguarding operational security and power supply frequency of the interconnected system,[11] and the Balancing Guidelines, which provide a set of technical, operational, and market rules to govern the functioning of electricity balancing markets.[12]

2. Balancing Services and Markets

Given the interconnectivity of the national transmission systems, an imbalance in one M ember S tate can directly impact the entire EU system. A famous example is the EU-wide supply interruption of 2006 when the German TSO E.ON Netz had to switch off an extra-high voltage cable across the river Ems in Northern Germany to enable a cruise ship to pass safely underneath. In combination with other circumstances (diverging wind energy forecasts), an interconnection line further south in Germany tripped due to overloading, which resulted into a cascade of line trips throughout Europe and caused a black out in several EU countries, including Italy.[13] The evaluation reports showed, amongst others, a lack of coordination amongst TSOs and that TSOs could not sufficiently control or monitor the behaviour of decentralized generators. It also called for an appropriate legal framework.[14]

In order to avoid similar incidents, several TSOs developed in 2008 on a voluntary basis some Regional Security Coordination Initiatives (RSCI), which were renamed to Regional Security Coordinators (RSCs) in 2009. Although the 2017 System Operation Guideline requires these RSCs to perform some specific coordination tasks, a clear legal basis is included in the 2019 E-Regulation, which explicitly requires the establishment of Regional Coordination Centres (RCC), replacing the RSCs. These RCCs (as their predecessors) are shareholding companies in which TSOs hold all shares.[15] Their objective is to identify risks of operational security and identify the most efficient remedial action. For this purpose they share data on the available capacity for the following day (so-called 'D-1 activities') and perform coordinated security analyses.[16] The RCCs present these

[10] Regulation 714/2009 on conditions for access to the network for cross-border exchanges in electricity obliged the TSOs to cooperate through ENTSO-E and mandated ENTSO-E to draft network codes, arts 4–11.

[11] Regulation (EU) 2017/1485 establishing a guideline on electricity transmission system operation, OJ L220 (hereafter System Operations Guideline).

[12] Regulation (EU) 2017/2195 establishing a guideline on electricity balancing, OJ L 312 (hereafter Balancing Guideline).

[13] See also Bundesnetzagentur für Elektrizität, Gas, Telekommunikation, Post und Eisenbahnen, 'Report by the Federal Network Agency for Electricity, Gas, Telecommunications, Post and Railways on the disturbance in the German and European Power System on the 4th of November 2006' (Bundesnetzagentur, February 2007) <https://www.bundesnetzagentur.de/SharedDocs/Downloads/EN/Areas/ElectricityGas/Special%20 Topics/Blackout2005/BerichtEnglischeVersionId9347pdf.pdf?__blob=publicationFile&v=4> accessed 22 August 2023.

[14] European Regulators Group of Electricity and Gas (ERGEG) as summarized i n ibid 17 .

[15] The first RSCIs were Coreso (Coordination of Electrical System Operators operating in the Central Western European region) and TSCNet (TSO Security Cooperation operating in Central and South Eastern Europe) and were followed by other initiatives. <https://www.docstore.entsoe.eu/major-projects/RSC/Pages/default.aspx and https://www.coreso.eu/about-us/our-history/ and https://www.coreso.eu/about-us/our-history/> accessed 25 August 2023.

[16] 2019 E-Regulation, art 35. The five core services are listed in 2019 E-Regulation, art 27.

analyses to the TSOs who then need to decide whether or not to implement the RCCs' recommendations.

As the TSOs are responsible for grid balancing, they may request producers to decrease or increase electricity production (delivering frequency containment or frequency restoration reserves), or consumers to change their consumption (controlled interruptions of or disconnections from the power supply).[17] Since 2019, balancing services are offered by balancing service providers (BSPs), that is, those parties connected to the grid who are willing to offer balancing services.[18] These include large consumers and large adjustable combustion units but potentially also storage facilities. These BSPs will offer their capacities on the balancing market, indicating when their services will be available and at what price. The TSO then selects the capacity it considers necessary. Likewise, the BRPs will submit to the TSOs their schedules (expected electricity production and/or consumption) per unit of time. If BRPs fail to stick to their schedule, the TSO activates the necessary balancing energy bids as provided by BSPs on the balancing market and BRPs have to pay for the (imbalance) costs caused to the system according to the prices established on the balancing market.[19] In practice, the regional balancing markets differ.[20] These differences may relate to product definitions, methodologies, procurement procedures, and imbalance settlement mechanisms.[21] Attempts are made to harmonize these balancing markets[22] and to lower balancing costs by, amongst others, enabling TSOs to share reserves and organize joint procurements.[23]

TSOs will increasingly make use of balancing products offered by BRPs connected to the distribution grid. This requires some coordination between TSOs and DSOs. The Balancing Guideline requires DSOs, TSOs, BSPs, and BRPs to 'cooperate in order to ensure efficient and effective balancing' and DSOs to 'provide, in due time, all necessary information in order to perform the imbalance settlement to the connecting TSO'.[24] In addition, the System Operation Guideline provides for the exchange of data between TSOs and DSOs, essentially requiring DSOs to provide all relevant data they have (with regard to distribution grid-connected facilities) to the TSO.[25] Member States apply this data- sharing obligation in different ways and there are no clear rules indicating whether either the TSO or the DSO has priority to use a flexibility resource connected to the distribution.

C. Renewables and System Operations

A major increase of RES is needed to meet the earlier-mentioned net zero goals. In practice, the type of RES will vary between Member States and depend on their availability. Obviously,

17 i bid.

18 These BSPs have been introduced in 2019 E-Regulation, art 2(12).

19 RAC Van der Veen and RA Hakvoort, 'The Electricity Balancing Market: Exploring t he Design Challenge' (2016) 43 Utilities Policy 187 .

20 See, for a specific example, Astrid Skjønborg Brunt, 'The New Nordic Balancing Model' in Martha M Roggenkamp and Catherine Banet (eds), *European Energy Law Report XIV* (Intersentia 2021) 149– 69.

21 T Schittekatte, V Reif, and L Meeusim Schittekatte, V Reif, and L Meeus, 'The EU Electricity Network Codes' (2020) Florence School of Regulation 64.

22 i bid 80, 88.

23 ENTSO-E, Balancing Report 2020, 4.

24 Balancing Guideline, at 15.

25 System Operation Guideline, Part II, title II, chapters 3 and 5.

the use of hydropower is restricted to mountainous areas and is also relatively predictable. This is less the case with electricity from solar and wind. Production facilities making use of the latter can be connected to the distribution grid and developed by small (household) consumers or by large customers who install solar panels or a wind turbine on their property. These so-called prosumers are feeding electricity into the grid if production exceeds their demand and extract from the grid, if necessary. Only large producers and prosumers are BRPs (see S ection II.A). Irrespective of these producers' size, there may be an issue of imbalance given the intermittency (and unpredictability) of solar and wind energy. Additionally, the growth in the number of decentralized generators will have an impact on distribution systems as back-feeding (reversing the direction of power flow) will become more common, and the electricity loads that distribution grids need to process will thus increase.[26] This requires some new or alternative regulatory approaches as will be discussed below.

1. Pooling M echanisms

As discussed above, each BRP needs to present daily production and/or consumption schedules. Large wind and solar electricity producers will face a challenge given the intermittency of the primary energy source. By contrast to 'traditional' generators, wind and solar producers may thus be confronted with incorrect schedules and thus with considerable imbalance costs (see Section II.A). One of the means to avoid such a situation is to make use of a pooling system, which means that a BRP transfers its balancing responsibility to another BRP with the idea that a pooling of resources (e g renewables with gas-fired power stations) will level out any imbalances and thus limit imbalance costs.[27] A different type of pooling applies to small (household) consumers as they are exempted from providing such daily schedules because their supply company is acting as the BRP. Hence, these supply companies are also acting as some sort of pooling service.

The 2019 E-Directive introduces a new concept: aggregators. This D irective defines 'aggregation' as 'a function performed by a natural or legal person who combines multiple customer loads or generated electricity for sale, purchase or auction in any electricity market'[28] and an 'aggregator' as 'a market participant engaged in aggregation who is not affiliated to the customer's supplier'.[29] It seems that a supply company can act as an aggregator but only if he is not also acting as supplier for the same customer. In addition, others can become independent aggregators as long as the aggregated products can be offered or purchased on an electricity market and thus also on the balancing markets (as discussed Section IIA2).[30] In order to do so, the D irective facilitates the use of aggregation contracts. Final customers do not need permission from their supplier to conclude such contracts.[31] Since aggregators can combine multiple loads, they are also in the position to combine loads from a range of renewables and other flexibility resources like battery storage and thus reduce potential imbalances.[32]

[26] Elskamp (n 4) 378.

[27] See eg PVNED, 'Imbalance and imbalance pooling' (2023) <https://www.pvned.eu/en/imbalance-and-imbalance-pooling/> accessed 22 August 2023.

[28] 2019 E-Directive, art 2(18).

[29] 2019 E-Directive, art 2(19).

[30] 2019 E-Directive, arts 31(8), 32(3).

[31] 2019 E-Directive, art 13.

[32] See also S Kercher and P Arboleya, 'The Key Role o f Aggregators in the Energy Transition Under t he Latest European Regulatory Framework' (2022) 134 International Journal of Electrical Power and Energy Systems 107361 <https://www.sciencedirect.com/science/article/pii/S0142061521006001> accessed 23 August 2023.

2. Managing Grid Input

Another way to avoid imbalance is to manage the volumes of electricity injected into the grid. For this purpose, use can be made of Demand Response (DR) or energy storage. These two mechanisms are not directly RES-related but will become extremely relevant as they will enable grid balancing and can be offered on the balancing market.

The possibility to influence electricity demand via interruptible supply contracts is not new. Such contracts were also used before energy market liberalization, albeit only involving large consumers.[33] Currently DR is defined as 'the change of electricity load by final customers from their normal or current consumption patterns in response to market signals, . . . or in response to the acceptance of the final customer's bid to sell demand reduction or increase at a price in an organized market . . . '.[34] Hence, DR now involves all final customers (including small customers) and all customers can provide DR services. The price of such DR services will be set by the electricity (and balancing) markets.[35]

New, however, is the use of energy storage. Until recently the general belief was that electricity cannot be stored. This is changing and currently many storage options are being considered, such as pumped hydro and battery storage.[36] If more electricity is produced than can be consumed, temporary storage is an option in order to avoid imbalance. Such storage can also be used as an ancillary service. To facilitate energy storage, the 2019 E-Directive contain s a provision on energy storage.[37] Although storage will be a relevant balancing tool, the 2019 E-Directive, in essence, prohibits DSOs and TSOs from owning and operating storage assets.[38] It considers energy storage a commercial activity that should be owned and operated by market parties (including small consumers) and not by system operators.[39] System operators will, however, be able to procure storage services if needed.[40] Storage can be traded on the balancing market as an ancillary service.[41]

III. Grid Capacity

Closely connected to the issue of balancing, is available grid capacity. Whereas 'traditional' large thermal power plants are connected to the transmission system, RES-projects can be connected to the transmission as well as the distribution grid. In practice RES-projects may vary from small-scale projects (e g one or more solar panels or wind turbines on a property) to large-scale projects (e g large on- or offshore wind parks or solar parks). By contrast to most small RES-projects, large renewable production units like offshore wind parks or

[33] The vertical integrated Dutch company NV SEP, eg , applied interruptible contracts to reduce demand. The financial compensation was higher the closer to the moment demand had to be reduced.

[34] 2019 E-Directive, art 2(20).

[35] 2019 E- Regulation, arts 3(e), (g), (j), (m) and 6(1) (a), (c) .

[36] M van Leeuwen and M Roggenkamp, 'Regulating Electricity Storage in the European Union: How to Balance Technical and Legal Innovation' in D Zillman and others (eds), *Innovation in Energy Law and Technology—Dynamic Solutions for Energy Transition* (OUP 2018) 154 – 71.

[37] 2019 E-Directive, art 2(57).

[38] 2019 E-Directive, arts 36 and 54.

[39] 2019 E-Directive, arts 15, 2(11)(c), and 16.

[40] 2019 E-Directive, arts 32(1) and 40(1)(d).

[41] See, for a discussion on the role of storage on local flexibility markets, R Mauger and MM Roggenkamp, 'Balancing Local Grids', Smart Island Energy Systems (SMILE), Deliverable D7.4, for the European Commission, European Climate, Infrastructure and Environment Executive Agency (CINEA) <https://www.h2020smile.eu/wp-content/uploads/2021/12/D7.4_SMILE_final_rev0.pdf> accessed 23 August 2023.

solar parks in rural areas will be situated far from energy consumers. Hence, existing transmission and distribution systems increasingly lack available capacity to transport the electricity produced. In case of insufficient capacity, the existing grid may become congested as the request for transport capacity outweighs the available capacity. One straightforward solution would be to expand network capacity, but this is costly and time consuming. Although necessary in the long term, in the short term, system operators have to make use of other solutions such as limiting the number of grid connections and/or making use of congestion management procedures. Both are primarily governed by EU network codes and guidelines.

A. Grid Connection and System Access

The EU liberalized electricity market is based on the principle of non-discriminatory third-party access (TPA) to the electricity transmission and/or distribution system . In practice, a distinction needs to be made between system access and grid connection. Both will be discussed below.

1. Non-Discriminatory System Access

Currently all customers—small (household) consumers and large (industrial) consumers—are entitled to choose their supplier and thus require non-discriminatory grid access.[42] To enable this, all system operators are required to provide system users with the information they need for efficient system access and refrain from discriminating between system users.[43] Although the principle of non-discrimination is fundamental to EU market liberalization, it does not mean that all system users need to be treated equally. It is possible to distinguish between classes of system users and treat these classes differently. Different treatment is not, however, allowed within the same class of system users.[44] Until 2018, renewable electricity producers were considered as a specific class of system users and given '*guaranteed access*' or even '*priority access*' to the grid.[45] With the entry into force of the 2018 Renewable Energy Directive,[46] RES-based electricity is increasingly treated similarly to 'conventional' electricity although the D irective still acknowledges that priority dispatch may apply to electricity from RES.[47] The term 'dispatch' refers to the situation where energy producers decide when and how much electricity they will feed into the grid. In a liberalized market, dispatching is a market-based activity and as a result the available energy sources will be ranked according to a merit order based on price signals. As RES have very low marginal costs, they will often be first in the merit order. Member States are entitled to require DSOs, when dispatching generating installations, to give priority to installations

[42] Until 1 July 2007, TPA was only required for categories of eligible customers and excluded small (household) consumers.

[43] 2019 E-Directive, art 6.

[44] See further Hannah Kruimer, *The Non-Discrimination Obligation o f Energy Network Operators: European Rules and Regulatory Practice* (Intersentia 2014) 203.

[45] Directive 2001/77/EC on the promotion of use of renewable energy sources and article 16 of Directive 2009/28/EC, replacing Directive 2001/7/EC, art 7.

[46] Directive 2018/2001/EU on the promotion of the use of energy from renewable sources (recast), OJ L 328/82 (hereafter 2018 Renewable Energy Directive).

[47] See 2018 Renewable Energy Directive, Recital 60.

using RES.[48] These producers can nevertheless be faced with another exemption to the general rule of TPA and that is the lack of available grid capacity as EU law provides that a lack of capacity is a reason for system operators to refuse third parties grid access but only if properly substantiated and based on objective and technically and economically justified criteria.[49] Moreover, system operators need to take into account existing public service obligations such as supply security. This entails that small (household) customers in general always will be given system access.[50]

2. Grid C onnection

The extent to which customers have system access does obviously depend on the question whether they have a connection to the grid. The European Court of Justice (ECJ) ruled in 2007 that the obligation to provide system users TPA does not involve a general right to be connected to the grid. The court stressed in the case of *Julius Sabatauskas and Others* that the term 'access' refers to the right to use the electricity system and should be distinguished from the term 'connection' that corresponds to a physical connection to the system.[51] The term 'access' therefore applies to the ability to have energy 'transported' through networks, which requires that network capacities are available and can technically facilitate transportation, including the necessary system services required for this. The term 'connection' corresponds to the physical connection to the grid and is a matter of subsidiarity as long as the general access to the system is ensured. Member States thus have the possibility to govern the way in which system users are connected to the grid as long as the process is based on objective and non-discriminatory criteria. In other words, the principle of non-discriminatory grid access does not allow customers to choose, at their own discretion, how and to which system—transmission or distribution system—they wish to be connected to.

Meanwhile the EU has introduced additional provisions on grid connections in two network codes. First, the Generators Connection Code contains requirements for grid connections of four different categories of generators (types A-D), based on the maximum capacity of the generators and their connection voltage level.[52] Each generator needs to take into account these standards when connecting to the grid. Next, and of specific importance for the decarbonization process, is the Demand Connection Code,[53] which governs the connection of demand response facilities to the transmission and distribution system. By facilitating the connection of a wide range of demand facilities and thus demand response options (see Section II. C.2), it aims at easing the integration of solar and wind energy to the system. Both Connection Codes present a wide range of harmonized technical standards to ensure that the electricity system will be able to face unexpected disturbances in real time due to unexpected supply of volumes from RES or changes in demand. Together these C odes aim at increasing system and operational security whilst enabling the integration of the large volumes of RES into the electricity system.[54]

[48] 2019 E-Directive, art 31, para 4.

[49] 2019 E-Directive, art 6, para 2.

[50] See also 2019 E-Directive, art 9, para 2.

[51] C-239/07 *Julius Sabatauskas and Others* [2007] ECR II-7523, para 42.

[52] Regulation (EU) 2016/631 establishing a network code on requirements of grid connection of generators OJ L 112/1 (hereafter Generators Connection Code).

[53] Regulation (EU) 2016/1388 of 17 August 2016 establishing a Network Code on Demand Connection [2016] OJ L 223/10 (hereafter Demand Connection Code).

[54] Both C odes are in the process of being amended in order to facilitate new developments such as e-mobility, storage, and energy communities. See <https://www.acer.europa.eu/news-and-events/news/acer-consults-updating-grid-connection-network-codes-cover-e-mobility-and-storage> accessed 23 August 2023.

Although Member States are entitled to limit the number of connections to the system, these Connection Codes are relevant for controlling the number and type of grid connections and are a means to avoid an oversupply on the system. In case of oversupply, there is the possibility of congestion. If so, the network operators need to turn to other solutions and possibly curtail the volumes injected, including electricity from RES. This may involve a regime of congestion management as will be discussed below.

B. Congestion Management

Grid congestion occurs if the grid is unable to ensure the free flow of electricity due to grid capacity constraints. Supply security may be affected if a grid is overloaded and unable to transport additional electricity flows. Although this seems straightforward, one can distinguish between contractual and physical congestion. Contractual congestion aris es if the guaranteed volumes of electricity contracted with the system operator outweigh the capacity of the grid. Physical congestion, however, refers to a situation where the level of demand for actual deliveries exceeds the technical capacity of the grid at some point in time.[55] Whereas physical congestion may result in a system shut down, this is not necessarily the case with contractual congestion as system users often decide not to use all contracted transport capacity. As contractual congestion mainly appears at the local (distribution) level, it is presently governed by national law. EU law is focu sing on the constraints within the integrated electricity transmission system.

Traditionally, national transmission systems have sufficient transport capacity available as they are designed to supply all end-consumers within their jurisdiction. Although incidental congestion may occur, problems arise when grids are structurally congested. In the EU such bottlenecks are often found at interconnectors,[56] which generally were developed before market liberalization in order to guarantee supply security rather than market integration. Electricity Regulations have been governing the development and use of interconnectors since 2003.[57] In order to deal with scarce (interconnector) capacity, the EU introduced the concept of bidding zones, which are defined as 'the largest geographical area within which market participants are able to exchange energy without capacity allocation'.[58] Within each bidding zone, there is an unlimited exchange of electricity. With some exceptions,[59] the geographical areas of these bidding zones are equivalent to the territory of Member States and the operating areas of national TSOs.[60] Although there is a free flow of electricity within each bidding zone, trade between bidding zones is usually restricted due to a lack of capacity. Market parties who wish to buy or sell electricity in another bidding zone will thus face capacity constraints, that is, congestion, which is a situation in which all

[55] Regulation 2015/1222 establishing a guideline on capacity allocation and congestion management, OJ L 197/24 (hereafter CACM Guideline).

[56] 2019 E-Regulation, art 2(1) defines an interconnector as 'cross-border transmission lines connecting the national transmission systems of two Member States'.

[57] Regulation 1228/2003 as amended by Regulation 714/2009, and replaced by Regulation 2019/943.

[58] Regulation (EU) No 543/2013 on submission and publication of data in electricity markets and amending Annex I to Regulation (EC) No 714/2009, OJ L 163/1, art 2.

[59] Italy, Denmark, Norway, and Sweden.

[60] See, for a more elaborate analysis of these bidding zones, Leonardo Meeus, *The Evolution of Electricity Markets in Europe* (Edward Elgar 2020).

requests from market participants to trade between network areas (bidding zones) cannot be accommodated because they would significantly affect the physical flows on network elements which cannot accommodate those flows.[61] In order to ensure sufficient trading capacity, all TSOs are now required to allocate 70 per cent of the physical interconnector capacity to the market for cross-zonal trading before 2026.[62] The EU Agency for the Cooperation of Energy Regulators (ACER)[63] concluded in its 2023 annual target report that the 70 per cent target had been met on most borders making use of DC current, but that improvements we re needed on borders with AC networks.[64]

As a general rule, capacity between bidding zones has to be allocated to market parties via a system of explicit (capacity only) auctions or implicit (capacity and electricity) auctions and be awarded to the highest bidder.[65] For this purpose, TSOs have to assess the maximum capacity that can be made available to market participants.[66] In case of physical congestion, EU law provides for some remedial actions. Countertrading can, for example, be applied by TSOs to relieve physical congestion.[67] This entails that TSOs can buy energy in a congested area and sell the energy in a congestion-free area. Alternatively use can be made of re-dispatch, which alters the generation, load pattern, or both, in order to change physical flows in the electricity system and relieve a physical congestion or otherwise ensure system security.[68] Transactions curtailment is an option of last resort and can only be used in emergency situations, namely where a TSO must act promptly and re-dispatching or countertrading is not possible.[69]

Increasing levels of RES enter the market. Bearing in mind supply security needs, lower levels of electricity generation from wind energy in Northern Europe can be compensated by additional solar power generated in Southern Europe. This would require more coordination between bidding zones. Hence, the importance of the 70 per cent target as this will facilitate cross-zonal electricity flows. The goal to achieve 300 GW offshore wind energy by 2050 also has a direct impact on the development of cross-zonal connections and thus the 70 per cent target (see S ection IV. A).[70] Besides, many Member States are now facing internal congestion at the level of TSOs and DSOs due to the rapidly increasing levels of RES. As EU law does not apply, national laws need to remediate internal congestion. Such national measures may include re-dispatch to mitigate internal congestion or a decision to postpone the connection of large renewable plants of demand sources to the grid. These measures apply pending initiatives to expand the existing grid.

[61] 2019 E-Regulation, art 2(4).

[62] 2019 E-Regulation, art 16, para 8.

[63] Regulation (EC) No 713/2009 establishes ACER. It is an independent legal entity consisting of representatives of the national energy regulatory authorities of EU M ember S tates.

[64] The full report is available at <https://www.acer.europa.eu/Publications/ACER%20MACZT%20Report%202021.pdf> accessed 22 August 2023 (hereafter ACER Annual Target Report).

[65] CACM Guideline.

[66] CACM Guidelines, art 16 and 2019 E-Regulation, arts 15, 20.

[67] See definition in 2019 E-Regulation, art 2(26).

[68] See J Rumpf, 'Congestion Displacement in European Electricity Transmission Systems— Finally Getting a Grip o n It? Revised Safeguards in the Clean Energy Package and the European Network Codes' (2020) 4 Journal of Energy & Natural Resources Law 409– 36.

[69] 2019 E-Regulation, art 16, para 2. According to ACER the curtailment of renewable energy sources should not rise above 5 per cent: (n 60) 58.

[70] See also ACER Annual Target Report (n 6 4).

C. Grid Expansion

Expanding the grid to increase network capacity requires major investments and is time consuming. As a general rule, regulated network tariffs—that is, the tariff set or approved by the national regulatory authority (NRA)—need to cover the costs of investments and national authorization procedures tend to be lengthy and cumbersome.[71] In fact, there is limited EU law applicable to the development of electricity systems. However, gradually, some legal mechanisms have been introduced that impact grid investments and the EU de carbonization process. These include the concept of network development plans and trans-European energy networks.

1. Network Development Plans

Since 2009 all TSOs and DSOs are required to develop national and/or regional electricity network development plans (NDP).[72] They have to submit to their NRA at least every two years an NDP which presents for a period of five to ten years the investments needed for the development of the transmission and distribution grid. These NDPs are thus fundamental to identify where grid investments are needed.

When drafting these NDPs, the NRAs have to consult all relevant stakeholders and publish the result of the consultation process.[73] Whereas DSOs prepare the NDPs in consultation with the TSO(s) and all relevant network users only, a more detailed process applies to TSOs.[74] After having consulted all relevant stakeholders, including network users, TSOs have to submit a ten-year network development plan (TYNDP) based on existing and forecasted supply and demand. This plan has to show the main transmission infrastructure that needs to be built or upgraded over the next ten years, the decided and planned investments for the next three years, as well as the time frame for these investments. The NRAs have to examine whether the TYNDP covers all investment needs identified during the consultation process and whether they are consistent with the non-binding EU -wide TYNDP. In case of doubts regarding the consistency with the EU -wide network development plan, the NRA shall consult ACER and may require the TSO to amend its TYNDP.[75] Last but not least, NRAs will monitor and evaluate the implementation of the TYNDP and if a TSO is not investing according to the plan, and there are no overriding reasons beyond its control, the NRA may (1) require the TSO to execute the planned investments, or (2) organize a tender procedure open to any investors for these investment, or (3) oblige the TSO to accept a capital increase to finance the necessary investments and allow independent investors to participate in the capital.[76]

These NDPs need to consider the net zero goals. DSOs are, for example, required to take into account the connection of new generation capacity, including production from RES, as well as technical possibilities to avoid network expansion such as energy storage facilities.[77] Additionally , TYNDPs have to consider the de carbonization of the electricity

[71] See Vedder and others (n 2).
[72] 2019 E-Directive, arts 32, paras 3, 4, and 51.
[73] i bid.
[74] 2019 E-Directive, art 51.
[75] 2019 E-Directive, art 51, para 5.
[76] 2019 E-Directive, art 51, paras 5, 7, and 8.
[77] 2019 E-Directive, art 32, para 3.

transmission systems as NRAs are obliged to examine the impact on the grid of the national energy and climate plans, which show how Member States will achieve their climate and renewable energy goals.[78]

2. Trans-European Energy Networks and Projects of Common Interest

The decarbonization process will require significant investments in new networks and in upgrading networks by integrating devices like energy storage and IT facilities (e g smart grids[79]). The EU may assist this process if the infrastructure falls under the umbrella of trans-European networks for energy (TEN-E).[80] For this purpose it needs to be (1) considered as a project of common interest (PCI) and (2) part of one of the 'priority corridors and areas of TEN-E'. Specially designated Regional Groups select every two years, on the basis of some general and specific criteria, those projects that can be included in an E U list of PCI-projects (Union list).[81] Each of the selected PCIs will need to draft an implementation plan, which includes a timetable for feasibility studies and the award of necessary permits and authorizations.[82]

As a general rule, all costs for developing, constructing, and operating PCI-projects need to be borne by the users of the infrastructure, but certain projects may be granted some EU financial support. For this purpose, the 2013 TEN-E Regulation introduces a cost–benefit analysis, which needs to be included in the above-mentioned TYNDPs. Although the requirements for financial support may differ per Regional Group, some support can be granted if the developers can demonstrate a lack of commercial viability and that the project will provide significant positive externalities, like supply security, solidarity, and innovation.[83] The fifth PCI-list published by the European Commission includes some important infrastructure to achieve the EUs net zero goals, for example smart grids, pumped-hydroelectricity storage projects, and the North Sea grid.[84]

IV. Alternative Grid Configurations

The decarbonization process has also led to the development of alternative grid configurations. The reason is usually a lack of available cable connections near the sites of RES. Typical examples are the establishment of large offshore wind parks that need to be connected to shore, and onshore RES-projects requiring alternative grid solutions due to, inter alia, congested distribution systems. These alternative grids are a prerequisite to enable RES to reach the market and ensure supply security. From a legal perspective, these developments require new or a re-assessment of existing regulatory approaches.

[78] 2019 E-Directive, art 51, para 5. Pursuant to Regulation 2018/1999 of 11 December 2018 on the Governance of the Energy Union and Climate Action [OJ 2018 L 328/1], art 3, all Member States need to submit to the European Commission an integrated national energy and climate plan indicating how they will meet their renewable energy and climate goals.

[79] Regulation (EU) No 2013/347 on guidelines for Trans-European Energy Infrastructure, OJ L 115/39, art 2(7) (hereafter TEN-E Guideline) provides a definition of a smart grid. See Diestelmeier (n 5).

[80] Treaty on the Functioning of the European Union (TFEU), a rt s 170–1 72 .

[81] TEN-E Guideline, art 4.

[82] TEN-E Guideline, art 5.

[83] TEN-E Guideline, art 11 ff.

[84] Regulation (EU) 2022/564 OJ L 109/14 of November 2021 amends Regulation (EU) 347/2013 and contains the most recent Union list of PCIs.

A. Offshore Electricity Grid

Since the turn of the century, many coastal states have been developing offshore wind energy, especially in the North Sea area. The most important reason for this is the need to meet the steadily increasing RES-goals (culminating into the 2050 net zero goal) in combination with limited possibilities to meet these targets onshore due to, inter alia, public opposition, but also the need to ensure supply security. Coastal states that are entitled to, and have claimed, an Exclusive Economic Zone (EEZ) have functional jurisdiction regarding the production and use of offshore wind energy. Consequently, all North Sea states are regulating offshore wind energy. In line with these powers, EU law also applies offshore.[85] Relevant for offshore wind energy and EU market integration are the 2019 E-Directive and E-Regulations, and the 2018 Renewable Energy Directive with regard to permitting and support schemes (and thus state aid requirements).

Albeit not based on a dedicated EU D irective, national permitting regimes have been restructured and harmonized. National laws of the North Sea states currently require governments to pre-select suitable offshore areas, which then will be tendered or auctioned on a competitive basis, and possibly subsidized.[86] The regimes governing the construction and use of the park-to-shore cables have also changed. Instead of considering the cable as part of the offshore wind park (i e production), coastal states now treat the cable as a separate object, that is, an offshore transmission cable. This reduces, on the one hand, the costs of wind park developers and thus the need for financial support, but on the other hand, provides a challenge for both parties involved as the construction of the cable and the wind park must take place in parallel. Completing the cable before the wind park, and/or vice versa, will result in a loss for one of the parties, and possibly a claim for damages. Different approaches apply. Whereas Belgium, Denmark, Germany, and the Netherlands require the national TSOs to connect the offshore wind park in the EEZ and thus to expand the onshore transmission grid offshore, the United Kingdom has a different approach as the offshore connections are developed and/or exploited by private parties on the basis of a tender. These British park-to-shore cables are operated by Offshore Transmission Owners (OFTO) and financed by private parties.[87]

Meanwhile, increasingly, wind parks are developed further from shore as suitable nearby locations already are in use or are deemed unsuitable. For reasons of costs and spatial restrictions, attempts are made to limit the number of park-to-shore cables. Gradually wind parks are therefore connected to an offshore converter station from where one transmission cable transports the electricity to shore.[88] These converter stations are part of the grid (like transformer stations) and thus operated by the TSO. Attempts are also made to build artificial offshore energy islands in order to facilitate the interconnection of several offshore cable systems (by acting as some sort of converter station).[89] Another alternative

[85] HK Müller, *A Legal Framework for a Transnational Offshore Grid in the North Sea* (Intersentia 2015) 21–93.

[86] Whereas, before, some coastal states also used a regime of 'first come, first served'. M Roggenkamp and L Diestelmeier, 'EU Climate Law and Energy Network Regulation' in E Woerdman and others (eds), *Essential EU Climate Law* (2nd edn, 2022) 219– 25.

[87] i bid; and CT Nieuwenhout, *Regulating Offshore Electricity Infrastructure in the North Sea: Towards a New Legal Framework* (PhD, Groningen, 16 November 2020) <http://www.rug.nl/research/portal/nl/publications/regulating-offshore-electricity-infrastructure-in-the-north-sea> accessed 23 August 2023.

[88] See examples in Germany, the Netherlands, and Belgium.

[89] JJ Waverijn, 'Artificial Islands under UNCLOS: Room for " New Beasts" ?' in R Fleming and others (eds), *A Force of Energy— Essays in Energy Law in Honour of Professor Martha Roggenkamp* (University of Groningen Press 2022) 103– 20.

is to connect offshore wind parks to interconnectors. Although recital 66 of the 2019 E-Regulation refers to 'offshore hybrid assets' as a possibility to transport offshore wind energy to shore via a connection to interconnectors, there is no insight (yet) in the appropriate legal framework. As discussed above, an important obstacle is to combine the 70 per cent capacity target applying to interconnectors, with the need of offshore wind park developers to ensure an uninterrupted transport of electricity to shore.[90]

B. Local Grids

Also onshore, and primarily on the local level, the increase of renewable electricity production has led, and will lead, to alternative cable connections. Others besides DSOs may be interested in developing such alternatives. Current EU law identifies three options: closed distribution systems (CDS), direct lines, and energy communities.

Whereas a direct line is defined as a line linking (1) an isolated generation site with an isolated customer or (2) a producer with a supply undertaking in order to supply directly their own premises, subsidiaries, and customers,[91] a CDS consists of a system that distributes electricity within a geographical confined industrial or commercial area such as airports, hospitals, and camping sites.[92] Although both can be developed and operated by parties other than existing DSOs, and are exempted from rules regarding unbundling and regulated TPA, they need to apply non-discriminatory and transparent authorization criteria (including negotiated TPA). The extent to which and how EU Member States have transposed the provisions governing direct lines and CDS in their national law, varies.[93] Notably, the number of CDS and direct lines is increasing as large renewable electricity producers (e g large onshore solar parks) have difficulties in getting a connection to the grid due to ongoing congestion. An alternative is to build a cable to a nearby large consumer (e g camping site).[94] So far, direct cables or CDS are not set to supply small (household) customers due to public service obligations[95] and/or the limitation that only licensed suppliers are entitled to supply households with electricity.

Recently, a possible alternative is being offered via the concept of Citizen Energy Communities (CEC) and Renewable Energy Communities (REC).[96] RECs are generally considered as a sub-category of CECs.[97] Both communities need to be established as a legal entity, based on voluntary participation and controlled by its members or shareholders (e g natural persons, local authorities, or small enterprises). Albeit they can engage in the generation, distribution, supply, consumption, aggregation, and storage of electricity, these activities should achieve environmental, economic ,or social benefits for the communities'

[90] CT Nieuwenhout, 'Dividing the Sea into Small Bidding Zones? The Legal Challenges of Connecting Offshore Wind Farms t o Multiple Countries' (2022) Journal of Energy & Natural Resources Law 314 .

[91] 2019 E-Directive, arts 2(41) and 21.

[92] 2019 E-Directive, Recital 66 and art 38.

[93] See for these differences also the national chapters in Martha M Roggenkamp and others (eds), *Energy Law in Europe—National, European and International Regulation* (3rd edn, OUP 2016) .

[94] <https://www.solarmagazine.nl/nieuws-zonne-energie/i22507/solarfields-en-solar-proactive-gaan-zelf-zonneparken-aansluiten-op-hoogspanningsnet> accessed 23 August 2023.

[95] 2019 E-Directive, art 9.

[96] 2019 E-Directive, arts 2(11), 16; 2018 Renewables Directive, arts 2(16), 22.

[97] M Jasiak, 'Energy Communities in the EU: Challenges for the Implementation of the EU Legal Framework' in M Roggenkamp and C Banet (eds), *European Energy Law Report XIV* (Intersentia 2021) 197–218 .

participants or the local area where they operate. Notably, CECs may 'own, establish, purchase or lease distribution networks and autonomously manage them'.[98] CECs may contract a DSO or TSO to operate the grid on their behalf, but Member States may also grant CECs a right similar to a CDS or a direct line.[99] If so, these networks can potentially supply electricity from RES to small household consumers.

V. Conclusion

RES will be essential to meet the EU's net zero goals but also to ensure supply security following declining levels of fossil fuels. The Ukraine war has clearly demonstrated the need for the EU to become less dependent on fossil fuels. The EU considers energy independence as an essential pillar of EU sovereignty. This goal must be achieved within the framework of creating an internal and liberaliz ed energy market. As the growing levels of RES especially have an impact on the network-bound electricity system, this chapter has focu sed on three challenges relating to safe and reliable system operations. First, the challenge of grid balancing in relation to the intermittency of RES. Secondly, the challenge of connecting RES-projects in case of insufficient grid capacity. Finally, there is a need for alternative grid solutions due to the location of the RES-projects. Although these challenges are different in scope, they are closely connected as they all have an EU dimension and are relevant for ensuring supply security. Network balancing is a prerequisite for supply security. In order to keep the system at a 50 Hertz frequency, consumption and production need to be balanced. Experiences have shown that increasing levels of (intermittent) RES and a lack of balancing procedures could easily lead to supply interruptions. Although the EU has been slow in regulating balancing, it is now facilitating this process. It has issued a legal framework (1) identifying the relevant parties (i e TSOs, BRPs, and BSPs) and procedures, (2) establishing (regional) balancing markets where balancing products can be traded, and (3) introducing new market parties like aggregators and storage operators that can offer flexibility. Future challenges involve the need to (1) further harmoniz e (regional) balancing markets and (2) consider the role of DSOs in network balancing.

The increasing levels of RES also have a direct impact on the available network capacity especially as RES-projects often are located away from thermal power projects and connections are needed where insufficient network capacity is available. The EU has issued a guideline governing capacity allocation and, if needed, congestion management. For this purpose, it applies the concept of bidding zones and the assumption that there is free flow of electricity within each bidding zone and congestion is a matter of cross-zonal bottlenecks only. However, many Member States are increasingly facing internal congestion and are not able to meet all requests to connect to the grid additional RES. Although EU law provides that, if needed, existing bidding zones can be amended, this may in practice lead to an increase in the number of bidding zones and thus administrative burdens. The rapid increase of RES resulting in internal congestion and Member States applying diverging national remedies may negatively impact energy market integration. There may thus be a need for new EU solutions. Scarce capacity can also be resolved by expanding the grid,

98 2019 E-Directive, art 16, para 4.
99 Jasiak (n 97) 213– 14.

which is time consuming and requires high investments. Applicable EU law is limited to (1) requiring system operators to draft NDPs and subsequently identify investment needs, and to (2) co-financing of some CPI-projects. Permitting is a matter of national sovereignty. The EU has thus limited powers to enforce grid expansion. Investments are also needed to develop alternative grid configurations such as the offshore electricity grid and transport systems within local energy communities. Both are relevant to accommodate RES-projects but require a reorientation of the existing legal framework and potentially introduce a new type of operator in addition to the traditional TSOs and DSOs.

Currently, TSOs and DSOs are key players in the EU electricity market. The increasing use of RES to meet the net zero goals has a direct impact on these networks. Given the challenges ahead, it may be necessary to assess the potential of others to transport electricity and via different systems. The interest in developing energy communities and direct lines seems to indicate such a trend. Another alternative yet to be explored is the use of electric vehicles as an alternative method to transport electricity. If electric vehicles become an alternative to using networks, the electricity sector is no longer purely network-bound and this would provide a new approach to energy and natural resources law and the need to balance energy market integration, energy supply security, and net zero goals.

PART III

BUILDING SOLIDARITY FOR NET ZERO: LESSONS LEARNED AND FUTURE DIRECTIONS

16

The Role of Regional Emissions Trading Systems in the Achievement of a Net Zero Energy Economy

Íñigo del Guayo and José Antonio Redondo Torres

I. Introduction

Natural resources laws and regulations dealing with climate change, include provisions based on either command-and-control (CAC) regulation theory, climate change nudges or market-based approaches (MBAs).[1] The first are based on the following premise: individuals are rational and if certain behaviours are sanctioned, certain actions incompatible with the achievement of climate objectives will be avoided. Despite their notable expansion, CACs generally represent inflexible and expensive mechanisms.[2] 'A climate nudge is any intentional modification of the choice architecture that aims to alter citizen behaviour towards climate-friendly actions while maintaining their earlier alternatives.'[3] Climate nudges can also be defined as relatively new tools that aim to encourage decision-making or the development of actions that are more beneficial for the environment by citizens, inspired by the knowledge of cognitive psychology and behavioural economics and without resorting to the rigour of the CACs. Unlike CACs, climate change nudges are often less expensive and easier to manage. Finally, MBAs, which are incentive-based mechanisms, provide flexibility for achieving pollution control. The role of MBAs in environmental matters has been growing gradually since 1968, the year in which the emissions trading systems (ETSs) were designed.

Within an ETS, a cap is set on the total amount of certain greenhouse gases (GHGs) that can be emitted by the operators covered by the system. Within the cap, operators buy or receive emissions allowances, which they can trade with one another as needed. By limiting the total number of allowances available, the system ensures they have a value. Price signals incentivize emission reductions and promote investment in low-carbon technologies, while trading brings flexibility that ensures emissions are cut where it costs the least to do so.[4]

[1] Georgios Dimitropoulos and Almas Lokhandwala, 'Addressing Climate Change in the MENA Region through Regulatory Design: Instrument Choice Questions' in Damilola Olawuyi (ed), *Climate Change Law and Policy in the Middle East and North Africa Region* (Routledge 2022) 65–68.

[2] ibid.

[3] Helea Siipi and Polaris Koi, 'The Ethics of Climate Nudges: Central Issues for Applying Choice Architecture Interventions to Climate Policy' (2022) 13(2) European Journal of Risk Regulation 218–35.

[4] European Commission, 'A cap and trade system' <https://climate.ec.europa.eu/eu-action/eu-emissions-trading-system-eu-ets_en#a-cap-and-trade-system> accessed 20 August 2023.

Íñigo del Guayo and José Antonio Redondo Torres, *The Role of Regional Emissions Trading Systems in the Achievement of a Net Zero Energy Economy* In: *Net Zero and Natural Resources Law.* Edited by: Damilola S. Olawuyi, José Juan González, Hanri Mostert, Milton Fernando Montoya, and Catherine Banet, Oxford University Press.
DOI: 10.1093/9780198925033.003.0016

In efforts to accelerate decarbonization and net zero in the natural resource industry, emissions trading has been identified as one of the main instruments (of a market nature), to reduce the emission of carbon dioxide (CO_2) and other GHGs, across the three sub-industries (production, networks, and retail) and in the petroleum and mining subsectors of the industry.[5] The use of the market as an environmental protection technique responds to an elementary logic: pollution is a negative externality or market failure that the ordinary market alone cannot solve. Technical correction of the market can lead to an efficient and profitable way of dealing with the aforementioned externalities.[6] Likewise, it makes it possible to alleviate the inefficiency, hypertrophy, and shortages of other environmental regulations, such as sectorization, bureaucratization, and excessive interventionism. In addition, ETSs promote the development of low-carbon technologies. The European Commission has taken this approach for years.[7] Despite the growing relevance of MBAs in the net zero era, MBAs also present drawbacks, such as high administrative costs, the need for mature markets, and a high institutional capacity.[8] The use of market instruments to achieve a net zero economy clearly reflects an underlying solidarity principle. True markets are the maximal expression of solidarity among their members, since the supply of goods by some members of the market satisfy their needs at a cost (and a price) which reflects preferences and expectations of consumers. In the case of the European Union (EU) ETS, solidarity pushes emitters to make an effort to limit and/or reduce emissions. For a number of reasons, which are discussed in this chapter, there is a need for transparent and efficient public monitoring of the system, to keep CO_2 prices within certain upper and lower limits, with such monitoring being guided by the principle of solidarity.

While it is true that the MBAs, and more specifically the ETSs, could play a decisive role today in advancing net zero and, therefore, their implementation would be relevant in all regions of the world, it is necessary to combine the use of ETSs with other measures that significantly reduce GHG emissions (such as measures the set forth above). The exclusive reliance on carbon pricing (within which emissions trading is included) suffers from five drawbacks, which limit its ability to accelerate a deep decarbonization of the economy. First, carbon pricing frames climate change as a market failure rather than as a fundamental systemic problem. Second, it places particular weight on efficiency as opposed to effectiveness. Third, it tends to stimulate the optimization of existing systems rather than their transformation. Fourth, it suggests a universal, instead of context-sensitive, policy approach. Fifth, geopolitical realities may hinder its transparent monitoring and application.[9]

The joint application of the ETSs with other regulatory instruments can bring various cross-sectoral solidarity and coherence benefits. First, more certainty regarding the costs of pollution control can be achieved through the setting of taxes. Some argue that the choice between an ETS and a carbon tax depends on the political preferences and circumstances

[5] See Chapter 1 of this book; also Jingxiao Zhang and others, 'Investigating the Role of Emissions Trading Policy to Reduce Emissions and Improve the Efficiency of Industrial Green Innovation' (2021) 6(4) Journal of Management Science and Engineering 377.

[6] Jingxiao Zhang and others (n 5).

[7] See European Commission, 'Green Paper on market-based instruments for environment and related policy purposes' (2007) 140 final COM 3.

[8] Giorgios Dimitropoulos and Almas Lokhandwala (n 1); Jingxiao Zhang and others (n 5).

[9] Gorgios Dimitropoulos and Almas Lokhandwala (n 1); Jingxiao Zhang and others (n 5).

of each jurisdiction, although it acknowledges that they are not mutually exclusive measures.[10] In fact, several jurisdictions use them jointly and others have implemented a carbon tax as a step prior to the establishment of an ETS.[11] Second, overcoming technological failures in the market can happen through financial support for research and development (R&D). Third, an increase in behavioural responses can be attained by providing information through eco-labelling.[12]

This chapter argues, therefore, that a pragmatic mix of measures can ensure greater coherence and progress towards climate goals than using the ETS technique in isolation. Certainly, administrative costs are likely to rise with the joint use of several measures, which may negatively affect profitability. As demonstrated in this chapter, it is important, therefore, to consider administrative costs when examining the appropriate combination of measures. This chapter reviews various existing emissions trading systems in different parts of the world, the gaps to the coherent implementation to advance net zero objectives, and the reforms that are being carried out in the EU, from which several lessons are drawn in order to advance the efficiency of ETS.

After this introduction (Section I), which includes a definition of an ETS, and its placement relative to a wider framework of solidarity within the natural resources sector, Section II addresses the nature, scope, and range of some of the existing ETSs. Section III analyses the EU ETS within the framework of net zero targets, which mainly implies an analysis of the European Climate Law and the measures included in the 'Fit for 55' package. Section IV examines recent legal reforms of the EU ETS in the context of the 'Fit for 55'. Section V offers a conclusion, with some lessons to be learned from the EU ETS by other emissions trading systems.

II. Nature, Scope, and Overview of Some of the Existing Emissions Trading Systems

The purpose of this section is to clarify what we mean by an 'emission trading system', or ETS, by identifying some of the main existing instruments. In 2023, almost one third of the global population lives under an ETS in force, making up 55 per cent of global GDP. Seventeen per cent of global greenhouse gas (GHG) emissions are covered by an ETS. [13] Last, there are twenty-eight ETSs in force, eight are under development and twelve jurisdictions are considering the role an ETS can play in their climate change policy mix.[14] The

[10] Alexander Ezenagu, 'Carbon Taxation as a Tool for Sustainable Development in the MENA Region: Potentials and Future Directions' in Damilola Olawuyi (ed) *Climate Change Law and Policy in the Middle East and North Africa Region* (Routledge 2022) 187–204.

[11] See, further, ICAP, 'Emissions Trading and Carbon Tax: Two Instruments, One Goal' (ICAP, 2021). See https://icapcarbonaction.com/en/publications/emission-trading-and-carbon-tax-two-instruments-one-goal-brief-9#:~:text=Dec%2014%2C%202023-,Emission%20Trading%20and%20Carbon%20Tax%3A%20Two,%2C%20One%20Goal%20(Brief%209)&text=ETS%20works%20by%20capping%20the,for%20every%20tonne%20they%20emit.

[12] European Environment Agency (EEA), 'Using the market for cost-effective environmental policy: market-based instruments in Europe' 2006 (1) 12. "EEA report" (https://ieep.eu/publications/using-the-market-for-cost-effective-environmental-policy-eea-report-2006/).

[13] ICAP, 'Emissions Trading Worldwide: Status Report 2023' (ICAP 2023) 28–29.

[14] ibid.

data reflected here are sufficiently expressive of the current importance of emissions trading at a global level. The main existing systems and their most recent developments are briefly described below (the EU ETS and its reform will be analysed in Section III).[15]

Set up in 2021, the British system encompasses around 1,000 facilities across the energy, industrial, and domestic aviation sectors.[16] The default allocation method is auction, although free allocations are also used, to a lesser extent, for competitiveness reasons, and to minimize the risk of carbon leakage. In March 2022, the United Kingdom launched a consultation on reforming the UK ETS. In August 2022, an initial response was published, outlining changes to be implemented from 2023. These included covering emissions from flights departing the United Kingdom for Switzerland, amending free allocation in 2022 to reflect activity level changes in 2020 caused by the COVID-19 pandemic, and minor amendments to Measurement, Reporting, and Verification (MRV) of Carbon Credits provisions. A full response to the consultation was expected in 2023. The UK government launched another consultation in spring 2023 to explore policies that could potentially mitigate future risk of carbon leakage.[17]

Launched in 2021, the Chinese National ETS is already the largest ETS in the world. It has been under development since 2013, with several pilot markets located in Chinese provinces and cities.[18] These pilot markets will continue to operate in parallel and will gradually be incorporated into the national market as it expands its sectoral coverage. Despite suffering the drawbacks of any new market, the system has successfully completed its first cycle of compliance. For the coming years, it is intended to restrict the number of allocations to maintain reasonable supply and demand levels, introduce auctions, expand market coverage, strengthen supervision, introduce new products and accelerate innovation with a view to creating a more complex market, among other initiatives.[19]

In operation since 2012, the California Cap-and-Trade Program currently covers 75 per cent of the GHG emissions of the State of California and the approximately 400 facilities attached to its energy, industrial, transport, and building sectors. Rights are assigned via auctions, free of charge, or free with consignment. The Californian ETS is implemented under the authority of the California Air Resources Board (CARB). In May 2022, CARB presented its 'Draft 2022 Scoping Plan Update'.[20] The new Plan identifies a technologically feasible and cost-effective pathway to achieve carbon neutrality by 2045. After continued public consultation over the summer, the 'Final 2022 Scoping Plan' published in November 2022 projected a 48 per cent reduction of emissions below 1990 levels in 2030.[21] The Final Plan was adopted in December 2022. CARB would report to the state legislature by the end

[15] For the selection of the main ETSs, we have taken into consideration ICAP (n 11) 38.

[16] UK government, 'UK Emissions Trading Scheme' <https://www.gov.uk/government/collections/uk-emissions-trading-scheme-uk-ets-technical-guidance-and-tools> accessed 20 August 2023.

[17] ICAP (n 11) 72.

[18] Hao Zhang, 'Emissions Trading and China: Learning by Doing and Implications for Policy Making' (2013) 28(7) Australian Environment Review 690; and Hao Zhang and Ping Xu, 'Designing Regulation for China's Emission-Trading Pilot Programs Through Trial and Error: An Effective Approach?' (2017) 7(2–3) Climate Law 125.

[19] Anatole Boute and Hao Zhang, 'Fixing the Emissions Trading Scheme: Carbon Price Stability in the EU and China' (2019) 25(3) European Law Journal 333; Jin Li and others, 'The First Compliance Cycle of China's National Emissions Trading Scheme: Insights and Implications' (2022) 1(1) Carbon Neutrality 9 (art 34).

[20] See the Californian Draft 2022 Scoping Plan Update <https://ww2.arb.ca.gov/sites/default/files/2022-05/2022-draft-sp.pdf> accessed 20 August 2023.

[21] ibid.

of 2023 on any potential programme changes to help achieve the accelerated 2030-target and carbon neutrality no later than 2045.[22]

Launched in 2015 as East Asia's first nationwide mandatory ETS, the Korean ETS covers around 74 per cent of South Korea's national GHG emissions and 684 emitters in the power, industrial, buildings, waste, transport, and domestic aviation sectors. At least 10 per cent of allowances must be auctioned. Since August 2022, a consultation procedure has been taking place. The first set of changes was announced in 1 November the same yeart, and these include increasing incentives to reduce emissions and facilitate low-carbon investment by issuing more free allowances to the top 10 per cent most efficient covered entities per sector, as well as to those which implement new energy efficiency measures. Second, the modifications encourage trading and mitigate price volatility by opening up the ETS to more financial firms and increasing the current Korean Allowance Unit (KAU) holding limit. Third, the changes help in facilitating the conversion of international offset credits to Korean Credit Units (KCUs). Fourth, the changes will begin strengthening the MRV system. Fifth, the modifications provide increasing support for small businesses and new entrants.[23]

In operation since 2008, the New Zealand ETS stands out for its broad sectoral coverage. Auctions started two years ago, with the free allocation method being used only for emissions-intensive and trade-exposed activities and based on output and intensity-based benchmarks. In 2022, the New Zealand government continued to make incremental improvements to the operation of the system. Changes which came into effect for the forestry sector in 2023 included a shift to averaging accounting and a new 'permanent forest' category. Decisions were taken to tighten the eligibility and accounting rules for industrial allocation, while consultations on an improved market governance framework are ongoing. The cost containment reserve (CCR) was triggered during the first two quarterly auctions and the full reserve quantity was released. In May 2022, the Climate Emergency Response Fund (CERF) was established to administer the New Zealand ETS revenues with an initial funding of NZ$4.5 billion (US$2.9 billion). Over the last year, the government and agricultural sector stakeholders have consulted on a carbon-pricing mechanism for biogenic emissions from agriculture. A decision on the mechanism was taken in early 2023.[24]

Notwithstanding the importance of establishing new ETSs,[25] in our opinion the possibility of linking ETSs with one another should not be underestimated. This option offers several potential benefits, including reducing the cost of cutting emissions, enabling participants in one system to use units from another system for compliance purposes, increasing market liquidity, making the carbon price more stable, levelling the international playing field by harmonizing carbon prices across jurisdictions, and supporting global cooperation on climate change. However, experience shows that linking ETSs can take several years.[26] It also shows that ETS linkages can be vulnerable to political changes.[27]

22 ICAP, 'Emissions Trading Worldwide: Status Report 2023' (2023) 79 (n 11)

23 ibid 173.

24 ibid 166.

25 eg we should celebrate the fact that Nigeria has become the first African country to move decisively towards establishing a national ETS. See further ICAP, 'Status Report 2023' (n 11) 131.

26 Negotiations for the merger between the EU ETS and the Swiss ETS started in 2010. A merger agreement was signed in November 2017 and became operational in January 2020.

27 eg following Australia's 2013 national elections, the linking plan between EU ETS and the Australian ETS was abandoned as the new Australian government decided to repeal the whole ETS legislation.

To consider linking ETSs, however, well-functioning domestic ETSs are needed in the first place, and establishing a well-functioning ETS requires a non-trivial institutional effort.

To overcome all these obstacles, new institutional models could be developed. For example, protocols that ensure a minimum degree of design homogeneity among ETSs and regulate linking and de-linking processes in some detail, could be very helpful. This would be particularly important to facilitate a hypothetical future linking between UK ETS and EU ETS, an option that has been frequently discussed after Brexit.[28] In any case, there are those who think that such a union should, in theory, be simple, since the rules of the UK ETS reflect those of its European counterpart.[29]

III. The EU Emissions Trading System within the Framework of Net Zero Targets

A. The Regulatory and Energy Policy Framework of the EU ETS

Before analysing the EU ETS and its forthcoming reform, we must briefly refer to the existing EU regulatory and energy policy framework with a direct or indirect impact on the EU ETS, and, particularly, the climate change policies and laws.

1. The European Climate Law

The European Climate Law (ECL)[30] aims to comply with the long-term objective regarding the global average temperature, stipulated in article 2(1)(a) of the Paris Agreement, as well as advance the global commitment to adapt to climate change, provided for in article 7. To this end, the EU has set the objective of internal climate neutrality before 2050. It reads as follows:

> Union-wide greenhouse gas emissions and removals regulated in Union law shall be balanced within the Union at the latest by 2050, thus reducing emissions to net zero by that date, and the Union shall aim to achieve negative emissions thereafter.[31]

To strengthen the fulfilment of this purpose, the ECL adopts some guidelines in the form of 'intermediate climate objectives'.[32] The reduction of net GHGs by 2030 by at least 55 per cent compared to 1990 levels is now raised to the level of legal obligation. Although

[28] Stefano F Verde and Simone Borghesi, 'The International Dimension of the EU Emissions Trading System: Bringing the Pieces Together' (2022) 83(1) Environmental and Resource Economics 34, 41.

[29] Bernadett Papp, 'La historia alcista del mercado europeo de emisiones' ('The Bullish Story of the EU ETS') (2021) 66 Cuadernos de Energía 39.

[30] Regulation 2021/1119 of the European Parliament and of the Council of 30 June 2021 establishing the framework for achieving climate neutrality and amending Regulations 401/2009 and 2018/1999 (9 July 2021) OJ L 243.

[31] European Commission, Regulation (EU) 2021/1119 of the European Parliament and of the Council of 30 June 2021 establishing the framework for achieving climate neutrality and amending Regulations (EC) No 401/2009 and (EU) 2018/1999 ('European Climate Law') (published 9 July 2021 and entered into force on 29 July 2021), art 2 (1) (ECL). The passing of the ECL has given rise to several inconsistencies within energy governance in the EU: see Leigh Hancher, 'EU Energy Governance-Moving Targets and Flexible Ambitions between Opacity and Opportunism?' (2022) 41 Yearbook of European Law 166.

[32] ECL, art 4.

the EU is increasing its ambition, some studies of equitable mitigation efforts suggest that, for the EU climate policy to be compatible with the long-term objective stipulated in the Paris Agreement, it would be necessary to reduce GHG emissions by 86 per cent by 2030 and reach the climate neutrality between 2036 and 2040. Therefore, it would probably have been preferable to enshrine in the ECL at least a 60 per cent reduction by 2030, an objective which the European Parliament called for during the negotiations. Second is the revision of the European energy and climate regulations. The last intermediate climate objective consists of setting a new emissions reduction goal for 2040. To this end, the European Commission must submit a legislative proposal to amend the ECL Regulation, within six months after the issue of the first global assessment stipulated in article 14 of the Paris Agreement. The first global balance was reached at COP28 in 2023, therefore, by mid-2024 at the latest, the EU will already have a new emissions reduction target for 2040.[33]

2. The 'Fit for 55' Package and Measures Included: Legal Challenges

By mandate of the ECL,[34] in July 2021, the EU adopted a set of proposals aimed at reviewing European energy and climate regulations and establishing new legislative initiatives, with a view to complying with the net GHG emissions reduction target set for the current decade. This is how the 'Fit for 55' package was born, and its ultimate goals are as follows: ensure an equitable and socially fair transition, maintain and strengthen the innovation and competitiveness of EU industry while ensuring a level playing field vis-à-vis economic operators from third countries, and sustain the Union's leading position in the global fight against climate change.[35]

Together with the Carbon Border Adjustment Mechanism (CBAM) (which is discussed in Section IV), the 'Fit for 55' package updates the Member State emissions reduction targets in line with the 2030 climate target plan. The 2018 Effort Sharing Regulation, as amended in 2023,[36] increases the EU-level GHG emissions reduction target for 2030 from 29 per cent to 40 per cent (compared with 2005), in the sectors concerned. It sets binding national objectives for each year in sectors not covered by the EU ETS or by the Regulation on Land Use, Land Use Change and Forestry.[37] This sector is responsible for CO_2 emissions

[33] Climate Home News, 'EU to push for fossil fuel phaseout "well ahead of 2050" at Cop28' (12 July 2023) <https://climatechangenews.com/2023/07/12/eu-fossil-fuel-phaseout-2050-cop28/> accessed 20 August 2023.

[34] ECL, art 4(1), (2).

[35] Information about measures included within the Fit for 55 programme is taken from Council of the European Union, 'Fit for 55', European Green Deal <https://www.consilium.europa.eu/en/policies/green-deal/fit-for-55-the-eu-plan-for-a-green-transition/> accessed 20 August 2023.

[36] Regulation 2018/842 of the European Parliament and of the Council of 30 May 2018 on binding annual greenhouse gas emission reductions by Member States from 2021 to 2030 contributing to climate action to meet commitments under the Paris Agreement and amending Regulation 525/2013 (OJ L 156 of 19 June 2018). It has recently been amended: Regulation (EU) 2023/857 of the European Parliament and of the Council of 19 April 2023 amending Regulation (EU) 2018/842 on binding annual greenhouse gas emission reductions by Member States from 2021 to 2030 contributing to climate action to meet commitments under the Paris Agreement, and Regulation (EU) 2018/1999 (Text with EEA relevance) (OJ L 111 of 26 April 2023).

[37] Regulation 2018/841 of the European Parliament and of the Council of 30 May 2018 on the inclusion of greenhouse gas emissions and removals from land use, land use change and forestry in the 2030 climate and energy framework, and amending Regulation 525/2013 and Decision 529/2013/EU (19 June 2018) OJ L 156. It has recently been amended: Regulation (EU) 2023/839 of the European Parliament and of the Council of 19 April 2023 amending Regulation (EU) 2018/841 as regards the scope, simplifying the reporting and compliance rules, and setting out the targets of the Member States for 2030, and Regulation (EU) 2018/1999 as regards improvement in monitoring, reporting, tracking of progress and review (Text with EEA relevance) (21 April 2023) OJ 107 L.

and its absorption from the atmosphere. New rules set an increased EU-level target of at least 310 million tonnes of CO_2 equivalent net removals of GHGs for 2030, with binding national targets for each Member State.

The legal problems involved are varied and serious. In situations of instability and volatility of international natural gas prices, such as the EU has recently experienced, Member States are tempted to increase and/or favour the use of polluting technologies (such as coal or natural gas itself). This increase is accompanied by government measures that cushion the effect on consumers, relying on exceptions to the prohibition of state aid, authorized by the European Commission. So, support for consumers in times of high prices is given at the expense of the fight against polluting emissions. Thus, the objectives of these standards are not really met.

Cars and vans account for 15 per cent of the total of carbon dioxide emissions in the EU. In 2023, the EU introduced progressive EU-wide emissions reduction targets for cars and vans for 2030 and beyond. This last goal makes it impossible to sell new passenger cars and vans with internal combustion engines from 2035 in the EU.[38] The EU gave the green light to the new legislation, which establishes a ban on the sale of new gasoline and diesel cars (and vans) from 2035, after Germany lifted its veto by winning an exception for synthetic fuels. The so-called 'e-fuels' will allow the survival of the internal combustion engine. Germany has led a group of countries critical of how the legislation came about.

There are proposals to reduce methane emissions in the energy sector,[39] which . which faces the challenge of achieving at the same time the reduction of electricity obtained from coal and nuclear energy and leading the production of electricity by means of natural gas to its highest peaks in several countries.

There are also proposals to reduce emissions in the transport sector (terrestrial, maritime, and aerial), where the aim is to bring about a 90 per cent reduction in GHG emissions.[40] A Regulation of the European Parliament and of the Council on the deployment of alternative fuels infrastructure and repealing Directive 2019/94/EU, ensuring that the public has access to a sufficient infrastructure network for recharging or refuelling road vehicles or ships with alternative fuels, has already been adopted.[41] Legal obstacles for the actual lowering of emissions in the transport sector relate to the existence of a multiplicity of regulatory levels. Traffic is the responsibility of the central state, but also of other sub-state entities, such as regions and municipalities. Without a coordinated effort from all

[38] Regulation (EU) 2023/851 of the European Parliament and of the Council of 19 April 2023 amending Regulation (EU) 2019/631 as regards strengthening the CO_2 emission performance standards for new passenger cars and new light commercial vehicles in line with the Union's increased climate ambition (Text with EEA relevance) (25 April 2023) OJ L 110.

[39] Proposal for a Regulation of the European Parliament and od the Council on methane emissions reduction in the energy sector and amending Regulation (EU) 2019/942, COM (2021) 805 final/2, 2021/0423 (COD), Brussels, 3 March 2022.

[40] See Council of the European Union, '"Fit for 55" package: Council adopts its position on three texts relating to the transport sector' (2 June 2022) <https://www.consilium.europa.eu/en/press/press-releases/2022/06/02/fit-for-55-package-council-adopts-its-position-on-three-texts-relating-to-the-transport-sector/> accessed 20 August 2023.

[41] The Regulation was adopted in July 2023, but has not been published at the time of writing (7 August 2023). See Iñigo del Guayo and others, 'The Future Regulation on the Development of Alternative Fuels Infrastructure, within the "Fit for 55" Package' (2022) 20(1) OGEL Energy Law Journal 1.

three levels, the new regulations will not do much good. Thus, it is necessary for all municipalities, at least the large ones, to establish a zero-emission zone, so that the circulation of polluting vehicles in city centres is excluded. Similarly, municipal urban planning will have to adapt to these European regulations. If the local development plan does not include alternative fuel facilities, then the targets will not be met.

Other initiatives within the 'Fit for 55' package are concerned with: (1) the increase of the use of renewable sources, by means of a revision of the 2018 Directive on Renewable Energy Sources;[42] (2) the increase of energy efficiency by means of a revision of the Energy Efficiency Directive;[43] (3) the increase of the efficiency of buildings by means of a revision of the Energy Efficiency of Buildings Directive;[44] (4) a revision of the Council Directive on the Taxation of Energy Products and Electricity;[45] and (5) the shift from natural gas to renewable and low-carbon gases (green hydrogen) and boost their uptake in the EU by 2030 and beyond. The package consists of a Regulation and a Directive.

B. The EU Emissions Trading System

1. Origin and Aims of the EU Emissions Trading System

Increasing the ambition of the EU ETS is one of measures of the 'Fit for 55' package. The EU ETS finds its starting point in the Kyoto Protocol (1997), which established for the first time legally binding emissions reduction or limitation targets for thirty-seven industrialized countries. The aforementioned Protocol also established three 'Flexibility Mechanisms' to facilitate the achievement of the commitments stipulated within it: the Clean Development Mechanism (CDM), the Joint Application Mechanism (JAM), and Emissions Trading (ETS). In March 2000, the European Commission adopted a 'green paper' with some initial notions of what would end up being the EU ETS. It was finally created through Directive 2003/87/EC of the European Parliament and of the Council of 13 October 2003 establishing a system for GHG emissions allowances trading within the EU, and amending Council Directive 96/61/EC,[46] and launched in 2005. Since then, its importance within European climate policy has progressively grown so that it has become the cornerstone of the EU's policy to combat climate change and its key tool for reducing GHG emissions cost-effectively. Several reforms of the EU ETS have been made in 2023, which are analysed in Section IV. As proof of its importance, the following data should be noted: the EU ETS has managed to reduce EU emissions by 41 per cent since it came into operation; it covers approximately 40 per cent of the total CO_2 emissions of the EU; and more than 10,000 facilities are subject to the system.

[42] Directive 2018/2001 of the European Parliament and of the Council of 11 December 2018 on the promotion of the use of energy from renewable sources (21 December 2018) OJ L 328.

[43] Directive 2012/27/EU of the European Parliament and of the Council of 25 October 2012 on energy efficiency, amending Directives nº 2009/125/EC and 2010/30/EU and repealing Directives 2004/8/EC and 2006/32/EC (14 November 2012) OJ L 315.

[44] Directive 2010/31/EU of the European Parliament and of the Council of 19 May 2010 on the energy performance of buildings (18 June 2010) OJ L 153.

[45] Council Directive 2003/96/EC of 27 October 2003 restructuring the Community framework for the taxation of energy products and electricity (31 October 2003) OJ L 283.

[46] Council Directive 2003/87/EC (25 October 2003) OJ L 275.

Regarding the objectives of the EU ETS, we must look at the doctrine established by the Court of Justice of the EU (CJEU).[47] The CJEU takes into account article 1 and Recital 5 of the EU ETS Directive, and states that the EU legislator seeks to create a market that encourages the reduction of emissions. It also tries to minimize the impact of emissions on economic development and employment, thus evidencing that the primary objective of the EU ETS is environmental and, the second, related to that, is economic. This conclusion must be considered equally applicable to any ETS, since despite the fact that the economic component plays a very relevant role due to the market's own operations, emissions trading is still a carbon-pricing instrument and, therefore, it intends not only to create 'rights to pollute', but rather to apply the 'polluter pays' principle.

C. The Basics of the EU Emissions Trading System

The EU ETS works based on the so-called 'cap-and-trade' principle. The latter consists in the fact that the EU establishes a maximum limit of permitted emissions and, under this reference parameter, 'emission rights' are created and are distributed among the countries integrated into the system (EU countries, Iceland, Liechtenstein, and Norway). The states, in turn, award emission rights to the facilities that need them for their industrial or commercial activities. These operators can acquire the rights via free allocation or by auction. Once assigned, exchange is possible, that is, companies that have more emissions rights than they need to justify their emissions, can sell them to other more polluting companies. Under this supply and demand adjustment, a market is established whose ultimate goal is encouraging the saving of emissions (polluting costs money, not polluting can bring benefits).

The cap guarantees that the emissions rights have a value, the price signal promotes the reduction of emissions and investment in low-carbon technologies. The promotion of low-carbon technologies will be possible to the extent that the EU ETS is efficient and provides a high enough price so that regulated facilities perceive it as less expensive to implement energy efficiency initiatives or use less polluting fuels than to acquire more emission rights. The trading of emissions provides the flexibility to ensure emissions are cut where it costs less to do so. The cap is being reduced annually, which means a smaller allocation of rights and, therefore, the facilities must issue less or acquire a greater amount of rights. This causes greater demand and less supply, which affects the market price, increasing it.

Regarding allocations, auctions are the ideal mechanism; however, free allocations are planned for sectors in which the auction method is still in its infancy. In this way, the aim is to avoid 'carbon leakage', that is, ensuring that the cost for certain facilities is not excessive and, consequently, that they can be competitive outside the EU where equivalent environmental costs are not established or there is less ambitious climate legislation. However, free assignments have some drawbacks. For example, it is known that they affect low-carbon technological innovation (particularly in the early years of the EU ETS, where free allocations prevailed, as it was a pilot phase). In addition, while this practice may be justified from the point of view of industrial policy, it runs counter to the 'polluter pays' principle underlying environmental policy-making in the EU.

[47] Decisions of 7 November 2007, *Germany v Commission* T-374/04 n 124; 23 September 2009, *Poland v Commission*, T-183/07; 29 March 2012, *Commission v Poland*, C-504/09; *Commission v Estonia*, C-505/09, among others.

From another perspective, regulated companies must account for their emissions by justifying a number of emissions rights equal to or greater than the emissions generated. If this is not done, sanctions are imposed.

With regard to the legal nature of emission rights, although the EU ETS Directive does not define it, the CJEU has done so occasionally. For example, it stated that emission rights are assimilated for tax purposes to assignments and concessions of copyrights, patents, licences, and trademarks, always in accordance with EU law and without prejudice to the qualifications used by the Member States in their transposing regulations (subjective rights, incorporeal rights, etc).

D. The Carbon Price in the EU ETS

The reform in phase IV and the establishment of the Market Stability Reserve (MSR) mechanism addressed the problem of excessively low prices during the early phases. Likewise, the high natural gas prices and the new EU emissions reduction target for 2030 have indirectly contributed in recent years to the rise in the price of carbon. In this way, the price has not stopped increasing since 2018, reaching 100 euros/tonne for the first time in February 2023, which is a historic milestone in the EU's fight against climate change, since polluting costs more and more. Due to this remarkable increase in price, some even argue that, after a decade of worrying about low allowance prices, the EU may soon find itself struggling with a carbon price that spirals out of control.[48]

However, in the generation of electricity, fossil fuel thermal power plants face, among other things, the cost of the emission rights necessary for production, which tends to be high, since when using highly polluting technologies, more emission rights are necessary. For this reason, when formulating their offer prices, these generators include in their opportunity cost that income that they give up for not selling the emission rights in the market, which gives rise to higher matching prices, the higher the price of carbon.

Given that consideration is currently being given to extending the coverage of the system to, among other sectors, the maritime sector, a higher fuel price is forecast and, consequently, an exponential increase in the price of carbon. No one disputes the progress that the new measures will make in achieving the EU's emission reduction targets, however, passing on costs to customers remains a critical point. New initiatives such as the Social Climate Fund are welcome, to protect the most vulnerable households from the additional costs of expanding the sectoral coverage of the EU ETS.

IV. Recent Legal Reforms of the EU Emissions Trading System in the Context of the 'Fit for 55' Plan: Lessons Learned

The core issue of the legislative reform of the EU ETS passed in 2023, is that the achievement of the EU's emission reduction target for 2030 must imply a reduction in the emissions

48 See Reyer Gerlagh and others, 'Shifting Concerns for the EU ETS: Are Carbon Prices Becoming too High?' (2022) 17(5) Environmental Research Letters 5.

of the sectors covered by the EU ETS of 62 per cent compared to 2005.[49] This ambition has been translated into several sectors. There are several lessons to be learned from the EU ETS by other emissions trading systems.

In the maritime transport sector, starting from January 2024, the EU ETS has been extended to cover CO_2 emissions from all large ships (of 5,000 gross tonnage and above) entering EU harbours, irrespective of their flags.[50] The ETS covers 50 per cent of emissions from maritime routes starting or ending outside of the EU. The reforms allow the third country to decide on appropriate action for the remaining share of emissions. This raises the question as to whether the 'Common but Differentiated Responsibilities and Respective Capabilities' principle of international law is fulfilled.[51] The EU ETS will also cover 100 per cent of emissions in maritime routes between two EU harbours.[52] The first lessons to be learned are the need for a gradual approach (since the inclusion of vessels and/or products within the EU ETS has been introduced progressively) and the need to cooperate with countries outside the EU ETS.

There are also some reforms in the aviation sector. While the EU ETS will continue to apply for intra-European flights (including departing flights to the United Kingdom and Switzerland), the Carbon Offsetting and Reduction Scheme for International Aviation (CORSIA) will apply to extra-European flights to and from third countries participating in CORSIA.[53] This differentiation will lead to a complicated co-existence of measures and to relatively high administrative burdens for both participating airlines and for administering authorities. The baseline for offsetting with CORSIA credits is set at 85 per cent of the 2019 emissions level. A revision of the baseline will take place in 2026. Airlines oppose these reforms, since the review in 2026 may extend the EU ETS to all flights into and out of the EU after 2026, unless CORSIA is 'positively evaluated'. This hijacks CORSIA, as well as creating potential competitive distortions to the market.[54] Free allocations will be phased out in order to use auctions exclusively by 2026. It is assumed that auctions are the best allocation system, but this will depend on how those auctions are arranged.

As discussed in Chapter 17 of this book, the CBAM was created to be applied in conjunction with the EU ETS. The objective of this mechanism is to face the risk of carbon leakage and avoid the EU's efforts to reduce emissions being diminished by an increase in emissions outside Europe, because of the relocation of production, or the increase in imports

[49] Directive 2023/959 of the European Parliament and of the Council of 10 May 2023 amending Directive 2003/87/EC establishing a system for greenhouse gas emission allowance trading within the Union and Decision 2015/1814 concerning the establishment and operation of a market stability reserve for the Union greenhouse gas emission trading system (OJ L 130 of 16 May 2023), Recital 30.

[50] CH_4 (methane) and N_2O (nitrous oxide) emissions will also be covered, but only as from 2026.

[51] Lavanja Rajamani, 'The Principle of Common but Differentiated Responsibilities and Respective Capabilities in the International Climate Change Regime' in Rosemary Lyster and Robert Verchick (eds), *Research Handbook on Climate Disaster Law* (Edward Elgar Publishing 2018) 46–60.

[52] Regulation 2023/957 of the European Parliament and of the Council of 10 May 2023 amending Regulation 2015/757 in order to provide for the inclusion of maritime transport activities in the EU Emissions Trading System and for the monitoring, reporting and verification of emissions of additional greenhouse gases and emissions from additional ship types (16 May 2023) OJ L 130. The reform is built on a system of monitoring, reporting, and verification of CO_2 emissions from maritime transport, introduced in 2009 and amended in 2015: Regulation 2015/757 of the European Parliament and of the Council of 29 April 2015 on the monitoring, reporting and verification of carbon dioxide emissions from maritime transport, and amending Directive 2009/16/EC (19 May 2015) OJ L 123.

[53] Directive 2023/958 of the European Parliament and of the Council of 10 May 2023 amending Directive 2003/87/EC as regards aviation's contribution to the Union's economy-wide emission reduction target and the appropriate implementation of a global market-based measure (16 May 2023) OJ L 130.

[54] See IATA, 'EU ETS reform destabilizes international consensus for aviation carbon reductions' Europe Region Blog (18 April 2023) <https://www.iata.org/en/about/worldwide/europe/blog/eu-ets-reform-destabilizes-international-consensus-for-aviation-carbon-reductions/> accessed 20 August 2023.

of more carbon-intensive products.[55] The CBAM will be phased in gradually, in parallel to a phasing out of the free allowances, once this takes effect under the revised EU ETS for the sectors concerned.[56] Free allowances for sectors covered by the CBAM will be phased out between 2026 and 2034. The main problems of this instrument relate to international law. Third states involved (those states that, according to the EU, are not making a sufficient effort to reduce their emissions) may feel discriminated against by companies in the EU, especially if they are not given the opportunity to demonstrate that they comply with the standards of the EU. Additionally, there are peripheral regions of the EU that may need electricity from those third countries and, when the markets offer very high prices, perhaps they can offer cheaper energy, even if it has not been produced with the same degree of sustainability as the energy of the Member States of the EU. These problems should have been resolved by 2023, but it remains to be seen if the system works in times of turmoil.[57]

One lesson to be learned from the maritime, aviation, and the CBAM sectors is the need for international cooperation (in the case of the EU, with third countries and other regions). If the ETS is to work, and in order to avoid duplication and unfair trade conditions, cooperation mechanisms must be set up among various ETS.

A specific and independent ETS, starting in 2027, has been created in the EU for emissions from buildings, road transport, and other sectors (essentially small industry), since decarbonization is not easy in those fields (this is the so-called ETS2, created by the reform of the ETS Directive, in 2023, within its Chapter IV). Monitoring and reporting will start earlier, in 2025. If this new ETS is to be successful, it will be necessary to align many other disparate laws, comprising regulations at national, regional, and/or municipal levels. The EU ETS does not exist in isolation of a vast number of other laws. We may pick three examples. First, laws governing traffic on roads at various territorial levels, whether national, regional, or municipal laws. Second, laws related to town and country planning, since the location of new installations related to the reduction of CO_2 must be included (such as installations to recharge electric vehicles). Third, laws related to the production of new cars or new fuels. Success of this ETS2 is dependent on a parallel reform of those laws. The law governing the ETS must be flexible, in the sense that governments must be empowered to delay the entering into force of some provisions, which are dependent on the international prices of some energy resources (namely, oil and gas). The new ETS2 may also impose too high a regulatory burden on small- and medium-sized companies, which, in turn, may necessitate a more generalized system of governmental subsidies to those companies. This then has the effect of endangering competition within the EU internal market.

A Social Climate Fund is established from 2026 to 2032 which will be at the disposal of Member States to finance measures to support vulnerable households, micro-enterprises, and transport users, and to help them cope with the impact of rising prices for buildings, road transport, and other sectors, as a result of the new ETS.[58] This is another lesson: governments setting up an ETS must take measures to help small consumers, particularly when the price of CO_2 is high.

[55] See Chapter 17 of this book.
[56] ibid.
[57] Regulation 2023/956 of the European Parliament and of the Council of 10 May 2023 establishing a carbon border adjustment mechanism (16 May 2023) OJ L 130.
[58] Regulation 2023/955 of the European Parliament and of the Council of 10 May 2023 establishing a Social Climate Fund and amending Regulation 2021/1060 (OJ L 130 of 16 May 2023).

V. Conclusion

The ETS is currently conceived as a regulatory mechanism to implement the reduction of emissions and, therefore, to achieve a net zero economy. The use of the market as an environmental protection tool is grounded in CO_2 pollution (together with other GHGs), as a negative externality. The existence of externalities, such as environmental ones, is the basis for regulation, on the ground of public interest. Whereas externalities, the costs of transactions, and the lack of proper information, lead to the emergence of *social regulation*, natural monopolies lead to the exercise of *economic regulation*.[59] Regulation aims to correct markets. In the case of ETS, they respect markets while fostering low-carbon technologies and a reduction in emissions. Insofar as the main responsible industry for the emission of CO_2 is the energy industry (where there is a clear component of a natural monopoly), then the ETS becomes a mixture of social and economic regulation. This technique is most convenient in the context of a research about the principle of solidarity in the industry of natural resources, in relation with the achievement of a net-zero economy. One may think that markets are spaces open to abuse from companies exercising their market power over vulnerable consumers but, in fact, true markets express solidarity between suppliers and consumers.

The EU ETS has become the cornerstone of the EU's policy to combat climate change and its key tool for reducing GHG emissions cost-effectively. The EU regulatory and energy policy framework, with a direct or indirect impact on the EU ETS, is basically made up of the ECL, the 'Fit for 55' package, and the measures it encompasses, as well as other community financing instruments. The EU ETS is currently being revised in order to align it with the 'intermediate climate target' enshrined in the ECL consisting of the reduction of net GHG emissions by at least 55 per cent compared to 1990 levels. To this end, five legislative acts have been formally adopted with a cross-sectoral approach.

However, emissions trading is not the only instrument for the reduction of GHG emissions and its effectiveness must be seen in combination with another set of regulatory instruments. In this regard, the EU ETS offers some lessons for other emissions trading systems. One of those lessons is the need for successive reforms aimed at maintaining the price of CO_2 above certain levels. As a regulatory option, the implementation of an emissions trading regime requires constant monitoring of its operation because a balance must be maintained over time. The balance is between prices of permitted CO_2 emission being high enough to encourage decarbonization, but not so high that electricity prices become unaffordable for most consumers. As an externality, the price of CO_2 must be internalized in the price of electricity. If it is high, it will cause high electricity prices, creating a problem for many consumers. If the price is low, there is inadequate incentive to reduce emissions; and if the price is very low, the emissions trading system may break down altogether. The EU ETS is designed in such a way that electricity producers should find it cheaper not to emit CO_2 rather than buy credits to emit more CO_2. This means that, as has happened in the EU, the effectiveness and efficiency of the system must be periodically reviewed, and measures adopted to avoid the collapse of the price per ton of CO_2. Therefore, it is a system that finds itself between Scylla and Charybdis.

[59] Anthony I Ogus, *Regulation. Legal Form and Economic Theory* (OUP 1994).

17

Promoting Solidarity for Net Zero

The Potential and Limitations of the EU Carbon Border Adjustment Mechanism

Louis de Fontenelle and Elodie Annamayer

I. Introduction

This chapter evaluates the potential of border carbon adjustment (BCA) as an instrument choice for promoting international solidarity for net zero. Drawing lessons from the implementation of the carbon border adjustment mechanism (CBAM) in the European Union (EU), it evaluates the key opportunities and challenges associated with BCA, and the legal innovations required to enhance their effective design and implementation to advance net zero and the clean energy transition.

As discussed in Chapter 1 of this book, the success of advancing carbon neutrality will depend on international solidarity, especially preventing the risk of carbon leakage in the net zero transition process. Carbon leakage occurs 'when companies in certain industrial sectors or subsectors relocate their production to other countries or when imports from these countries substitute equivalent products that are less intensive in terms of greenhouse gas emissions because of the costs associated with climate change policies'.[1] Carbon pricing schemes have risen across the world as potential tools to address the risk of carbon leakage and to advance the clean energy transition.[2] A recent World Bank report, 2023, identifies seventy-three carbon pricing schemes that have emerged worldwide.[3] It highlights a wide range of carbon pricing models, of which two main systems stand out: the carbon tax and the emissions trading scheme (ETS).[4] The report also found that the share of global emissions covered by carbon pricing schemes has risen from 7 per cent to around 23 per cent over the past decade.[5]

EU law is not devoid of mechanisms to limit the risk of carbon leakage and to foster regional cooperation on net zero. There are at least two. The first is the EU ETS, which allows certain companies to receive emission reduction allowances so as not to weaken competition with producers in third countries.[6] There are also financial measures to offset

[1] Regulation (EU) 2023/956 of the European Parliament and of the Council establishing a carbon border adjustment mechanism [2023] OJ L 130, § 9 (hereafter EU Carbon border adjustment mechanism Regulation 2023).

[2] Michael A Mehling and Robert A Ritz, 'From Theory to Practice: Determining Emissions in Traded Goods Under a Border Carbon Adjustment' (2023) 39(1) Oxford Review of Economic Policy 123.

[3] World Bank, *State and Trends of Carbon Pricing 2023* <https://openknowledge.worldbank.org/handle/10986/39796> accessed 18 August 2023.

[4] ibid.

[5] ibid.

[6] See Chapter 16 of this book. See also Directive 2003/87/EC of the European Parliament and of the Council establishing a scheme for greenhouse gas emission allowance trading within the Community and amending Council Directive 96/61/EC [2003] OJ L 275 (hereafter EU Scheme for greenhouse gas emission allowance trading Directive 2003).

Louis de Fontenelle and Elodie Annamayer, *Promoting Solidarity for Net Zero* In: *Net Zero and Natural Resources Law.* Edited by: Damilola S. Olawuyi, José Juan González, Hanri Mostert, Milton Fernando Montoya, and Catherine Banet, Oxford University Press. © International Bar Association 2024. DOI: 10.1093/9780198925033.003.0017

the cost of indirect emissions due to the increase in electricity prices associated with the application of the EU ETS.[7] The EU has recently established a carbon border adjustment mechanism (hereafter EU's CBAM) to fill the blind spot of the old systems by focusing on imports of products that emit greenhouse gases (GHGs).[8] The adoption of the EU's CBAM was possible because the EU institutions themselves had to make compromises to avoid potential political tensions and legal difficulties in its relations with third countries.[9] These compromises stem from three major political and legal difficulties, namely the complex administrative control of their implementation; the risk of incompatibility with World Trade Organization (WTO) rules; and the avoidance of any form of 'protectionism.'[10] The ultimate aim of the EU CBAM therefore is to advance net zero by cutting down GHG emissions and to prevent the risk of carbon leakage.[11]

In principle, the introduction of the CBAM is useful, as it aims to both level the playing field in the marketplace and combat global warming. However, its design and implementation must ensure the CBAM is not a discriminatory measure (ie a disguised restriction on international trade), and that it is a tool for decarbonizing industries and not a disguised tool for European protectionism, leading to situations of discrimination or unjustified restrictions. With this in mind, the system should be based on solidarity, a value that must be integrated into legal instruments at both EU and international level, and thus shape a new social contract linking the market economy and environmental protection.[12] International law traditionally distinguishes between the law of coexistence and the law of cooperation.[13] The former aims to establish rules and mechanisms to avoid conflict, but in doing so it presupposes conflict and, in a sense, institutes it. The second law aims at agreement, participation in a common project, a common vision, the general interest of all states. For the time being, however, the CBAM mechanism looks more like an instrument likely to generate conflict. It will therefore be necessary to establish rules of coexistence at international level.

For example, solidarity could be demonstrated by setting a universal carbon price.[14] As international trade law stands, this remains hypothetical. From an economic point of view, setting this harmonized carbon price remains one of the difficulties.[15] This is what EU's CBAM is all about. Border carbon adjustment measures, if not designed in a spirit of solidarity, could be perceived as protectionist measures that undermine international trade. CBAM is not a tool for economic protection, but for balancing the conditions of economic

[7] See in particular the European Commission's recent decision to validate a French aid scheme for 'les entreprises exposées à un risque significatif de fuite carbone visant à compenser les hausses de prix de l'électricité résultant de l'inclusion des coûts des émissions de gaz à effet de serre imputables' to the ETS
European Commission Decision Compensation des coûts des émissions indirectes en France pour la période 2021–2030 [2022] OJEC C/013/2023 C(2022) 8907 final.

[8] EU Carbon border adjustment mechanism Regulation 2023 (n 1).

[9] IMF/OECD, *Tax policy and climate change: IMF/OECD report for the G20 finance ministers and central bank governers*, Italy, April 2021. <https://www.oecd.org/tax/tax-policy/imf-oecd-g20-report-tax-policy-and-climate-change.htm>.

[10] ibid.

[11] Alice Pirlot, 'Carbon Border Adjustment Measures: A Straightforward Multi-Purpose Climate Change Instrument?' (2022) 34(1) Journal of Environmental Law 25; Erik Haites and others, 'Contribution of Carbon Pricing to Meeting a Mid-Century Net Zero Target' (2023) Climate Policy (24)1.

[12] See Chapter 1 of this book on the definition and importance of solidarity for net zero.

[13] Wolfgang Friedmann, 'Droit de la coexistence et droit de la coopération. Quelques observations sur la structure changeante du droit international' [1970] 1 Revue Belge de Droit International 1.

[14] Christian Gollier, 'Le prix du risque climatique et le prix du carbone' (2019) 1(133) Revue d'économie financière 171.

[15] ibid.

competition with a view to protecting the environment in a spirit of solidarity and collective commitment to combating climate change. For this reason, the introduction of carbon adjustment measures at borders should not only be considered from an internal and regional perspective, but consideration should also be given to their international implications and the necessary support from companies and third countries for the success of CBAM. Solidarity must permeate the whole of the general economy, its design, and its application.

The question is: are BCA mechanisms appropriate for promoting international solidarity for net zero? Focusing on the EU's CBAM system, this chapter evaluates the key opportunities and challenges associated with BCA, and the legal innovations required to enhance the effective design and implementation of BCA mechanisms. After this introduction, Section II provides a comprehensive overview of the existing literature on the CBA in general and the EU CBAM in particular. It also explains how it works. Section III presents the EU's CBAM as an act of compromise that cannot avoid certain legal weaknesses. These legal weaknesses could compromise the solidarity at the heart of the system itself. From this point of view, Section IV will show that solidarity should be even more present if the EU's CBAM is to be an instrument at the service of a net zero greenhouse gas emissions. Section V concludes by opening up new perspectives should other states or economic regions be tempted to adopt their own BCA, in a spirit of international solidarity.

II. BCA as an Instrument Choice for Net Zero

A. The Concept of Border Carbon Adjustment (BCA)

The EU's CBAM is a type of BCA. Until the recent adoption of the EU's CBAM, BCAs were hypothetical public policies modelled in the scientific literature, in particular by economists.[16] A BCA is defined as 'a measure applied to traded products that seeks to make their prices in destination markets reflect the costs they would have incurred had they been regulated under the destination market's greenhouse gas emission regime'.[17] In other words, within a legal system corresponding to a territorial perimeter of economic activity that applies a carbon price (eg through GHG emission allowance systems), it's designed to force economic operators outside that legal system to submit to equivalent conditions for controlling their GHG emissions, by applying a surcharge to imported goods whose production is not subject to a carbon price (or is subject to a low carbon price).

BCA is a legal and economic instrument set up in regional or national systems in order to move towards a net zero society. In this respect, the BCA is an instrument that leads to the creation of new economic relationships because it structurally integrates the issue of carbon emissions and thus the fight against global warming. It is the foundation of a new

[16] Jiarui Zhong and Jianson Pei, 'Carbon Border Adjustment Mechanism: A Systematic Literature Review of the Latest Developments' (2023) Climate Policy DOI: 10.1080/14693062.2023.2190074.

[17] Aaron Cosbey and others, 'A Guide for the Concerned: Guidance on the Elaboration and Implementation of Border Carbon Adjustment' (International Institute for Sustainable Development, 2012) <www.iisd.org/library/guide-concernedguidance-elaboration-and-implementation-border-carbon-adjustment> accessed 12 August 2023.

low-carbon economic model based on a new way of using natural resources, whether renewable or not. In this way, it provides a structuring dimension that, in turn, re-qualifies the way in which human activities appropriate the environment and physically use natural resources.

Scientific studies on the concept of BCAs have highlighted their potential impact on environmental policy and the reduction of GHG emissions worldwide. In this respect, a recent publication summarizes the theoretical benefits of BCAs: they reduce carbon leakage (1), they maintain the competitiveness of companies (2), and they improve the cost-effectiveness (in terms of reducing global emissions) of the unilateral actions that led to their introduction.[18] The aim is to encourage other countries or economic regions to introduce carbon pricing mechanisms or take action to mitigate climate change.[19] However, legal and political obstacles could reduce their effectiveness. The main difficulties relate to compliance with WTO rules and international governance in the fight against climate change. We will explore this in this chapter, using the EU CBAM as an example.[20]

B. The EU's CBAM

The EU CBAM is part of the EU's policy to achieve climate neutrality by 2050, with targets set on the basis of the Paris Agreement.[21] The intention to introduce a CBAM dates back to the Green Deal[22] and was explicitly mentioned in the 'Fit for 55' legislative package.[23] The introduction of this measure falls within the scope of the EU's environmental powers as described in article 191 of the Treaty on the Functioning of the European Union (TFEU). Although the EU does not have an explicit climate change competence, it has nonetheless, on the basis of article 191 TFEU, established an ambitious and proactive climate policy in its European legislation.[24] The EU's CBAM system is part of this climate policy, which has already given rise to market-based approaches, such as the EU ETS. Directive 2003/87/EC introduced harmonized pricing of GHG emissions for energy-intensive sectors and sub-sectors.

With the introduction of the CBAM, the EU institutions are attempting to use unilateral legislation to regulate an extraterritorial situation affecting trade. This normative strategy is not new per se. However, there has been an increase in the use of unilateral measures and legislation to resolve global crises (health, environment, climate) and geopolitical

[18] Christoph Böhringer and others, 'Potential Impacts and Challenges of Border Carbon Adjustments' (2022) Nature Climate Change 12, 22–29.

[19] Michael Keen, Ian Parry, and James Roaf, 'Border Carbon Adjustments: Rationale, Design and Impact' (2022) 43 Fiscal Studies 209.

[20] ibid; Böhringer and others (n 18).

[21] Council Decision (EU) 2016/1841 on the conclusion, on behalf of the European Union, of the Paris Agreement adopted under the United Nations Framework Convention on Climate Change [2016] OJ L 282.

[22] Communication from the Commission to the European Parliament, the European Council, the Council, the European Economic and Social Committee and the Committee of the Regions, The European Green Deal [2019] COM/2019/640 final (hereafter Green Deal Communication 2019).

[23] Communication from the Commission to the European Parliament, the Council, the European Economic and Social Committee and the Committee of the Regions 'Fit for 55': delivering the EU's 2030 Climate Target on the way to climate neutrality [2021] COM/2021/550 final.

[24] Regulation (EU) 2021/1119 of the European Parliament and of the Council of 30 June 2021 establishing the framework for achieving climate neutrality and amending Regulations (EC) 401/2009 and (EU) 2018/1999 ('European Climate Law') [2021] OJ L 243.

conflicts. From this point of view, the EU is counting on a backlash from certain regions or third countries, which could be tempted to reproduce and implement a carbon adjustment system at their borders.

Since the introduction of the EU ETS, the legal system governing international trade in which the CBAM will operate has evolved. Since the 2000s, and particularly since the failure of the Doha Round of negotiations in 2005, the multilateral system of trade relations has been in 'crisis'.[25] It is no longer privileged. This is partly due to the behaviour of certain world powers, such as the United States,[26] which are increasingly adopting unilateral measures to redefine trade relations.[27] In this context, it would have been difficult a priori to resolve the situation of border carbon pricing through a multilateral treaty. Moreover, the European CBAM regulation will operate in an increasingly integrated normative space which, in addition to WTO law, includes all the bilateral agreements concluded by the EU with its trading partners.

While the EU's CBAM has some original features that will be examined in this chapter, other border carbon adjustment mechanisms are already in place at the state level, such as in the United States, or at the sub-state level, such as in California.[28] The success of the EU's CBAM could revive discussions and encourage certain countries or economic regions to adopt a border carbon adjustment system. In any case, the European CBAM will inevitably have an impact on the economies of third countries, which is why it is an international instrument. It raises crucial questions about solidarity between states and international companies. For these reasons, this is a sensitive issue, which explains why it has taken so long to put the EU's CBAM in place.[29] The first proposals for a CBAM date back to 1991, before the Rio Summit in 1992. But they failed.

The project was finally relaunched much later, as part of the 2019 Green Deal. On this occasion, the European Commission announced in a communication its intention to set up a border carbon adjustment mechanism by 2021 to avoid the risk of carbon leakage.[30] The creation of the CBAM was finally ratified on 10 May 2023. This was made possible only because there was a strong political will.[31] The measure just introduced by the EU is a powerful act that will have an impact on international trade relations and will impose equality between companies through the force of law and an economic mechanism.

The EU's CBAM is based on a regulatory mechanism linked to the system of GHG emission allowances (known in the EU as the ETS system), the purpose of which is to oblige importers to purchase so-called CBAM certificates[32] in order to import certain goods into the customs territory of the Union. The aim of this system is clear and simple: to prevent

[25] Andréa Hammann, 'La "crise" du multilatéralisme commercial' (2018) 64 Annuaire français de droit international 691.

[26] ibid.

[27] Robin Denys-Sacha, *Actes unilatéraux des États et formation du droit international* (LGDJ 2022).

[28] Michael Mehling and others, 'Designing Border Carbon Adjustments for Enhanced Climate Action' (2019) 113(3) American Journal of International Law 433 doi:10.1017/ajil.2019.22.

[29] Pascal Lamy, Geneviève Pons, and Pierre Leturcq, *Verdir la politique commerciale de l'UE, Une proposition d'ajustement carbone aux frontières de l'Union Européenne* (Europe Jacques Delors, Thinking Europe, policy paper, 2020) <https://institutdelors.eu/wp-content/uploads/2020/06/PP-200603-Verdirlecommerce3_Lamy-Pons-Leturcq_FR.pdf> accessed 12 August 2023.

[30] Green Deal Communication 2019, 2.1.1.

[31] <https://www.politico.eu/article/europe-climate-change-carbon-leakage/> accessed 23 March 2021.

[32] The CBAM certificate is defined as 'a certificate in electronic format corresponding to one tonne of CO2e of embedded emissions in goods', EU Carbon border adjustment mechanism Regulation 2023 (n 1) art 3.

the risk of carbon leakage outside the EU and to equalize the carbon price for imported and EU products. In other words, the aim is to avoid discrimination between European and imported products, thus creating the conditions for a level playing field between operators in a context of respect for the fight against global warming. In addition, if a market for allowances has been created, this is not the logic the EU legislator wants to follow for CBAM allowances.

The EU's CBAM model, which is based on the importer's responsibility, imposes new regulatory and administrative obligations and constraints on the importer. The system will be based on the purchase and surrender of CBAM allowances, and even buy-backs if there is a surplus of CBAM allowances after surrender. All these operations will be carried out through a common platform, a registry, managed by the European Commission. Authorized CBAM-declaring importers will be able to purchase CBAM allowances from the competent authorities through this registry. Each year, CBAM registrants must surrender the number of CBAM allowances in relation to the emissions reported and verified for the previous calendar year. Where appropriate, registrants may request a reduction in the number of allowances to be surrendered if the imported goods originate from a country that is already subject to carbon pricing.[33]

The EU CBAM is designed to work in conjunction with the EU ETS.[34] The EU legislator aims to achieve equivalence between the import rules for CBAM goods and products subject to the ETS. The general idea is to level the playing field in terms of carbon emissions. However, the CBAM and EU ETS mechanisms each have their own logic. From this perspective, the CBAM will not set quantitative limits on imports and will not impose quantitative restrictions on trade flows. In contrast, the ETS operates on the basis of a cap on GHG emissions. What's more, the CBAM is designed to apply to products imported into the EU's customs territory, while the EU ETS applies indiscriminately to all industries in the EU.

Setting the price of CBAM certificates shows the originality of the CBAM mechanism in that it is likely to have an impact on the EU's foreign trade policy. In order to achieve an equivalent price for carbon between imported goods and EU products, the EU legislator wants to ensure that the price of CBAM certificates follows the trend of the price of allowances under the ETS, which are themselves set on the basis of an auction.[35] Too large a difference in price levels between CBAM allowances and EU ETS prices could encourage the risk of carbon leakage and thus weaken the incentive to decarbonize imported goods. Achieving price equivalence is a complex process because the two systems are based on different rationales. The price of allowances varies according to supply and demand in the market.

Since the beginning of the debate on the CBAM, the question of its compatibility with WTO law, that is, the GATT agreements, has been raised, including by EU institutions.[36] For this reason, much of the academic literature has examined the compatibility of carbon pricing mechanisms[37] and precisely the EU's CBAM[38] with WTO law.

[33] See EU Carbon border adjustment mechanism Regulation 2023 (n 1) arts 20–24.

[34] See Chapter 16 of this book.

[35] The value of the price is expressed in euros per tonne of CO_2 emitted.

[36] European Parliament Resolution towards a WTO-compatible EU carbon border adjustment mechanism [2021] (2020/2043(INI)) (hereafter Carbon border adjustment mechanism Resolution 2021).

[37] Haites and others (n 5).

[38] Raphaël Kempf, *L'OMC face aux changements climatiques* (Pedone 2009); Jennifer A Hillman, 'Changing Climate for Carbon Taxes: Who's Afraid of the WTO?' (Climate & Energy Policy Paper Series, 2013) <https://scholarship.law.georgetown.edu/facpub/2030/>; Stéphanie Monjon and Philippe Quirion, 'A Border Adjustment for the EU ETS: Reconciling WTO Rules and Capacity to Tackle Carbon Leakage' (2011) 11 Climate Policy 1212.

The risk of carbon leakage has been on the minds of European policy-makers since 2008.[39] Some of the academic literature has shown that there is little or no evidence to date that the EU ETS has caused carbon leakage.[40] Indeed, a recent economic study suggests that the EU's CBAM would be a more effective instrument for reducing carbon leakage than the free allowance method within the EU ETS.[41]

Finally, the numerous attempts to introduce a 'carbon tax' at EU level have led some scholars to reflect on the EU's role in the governance and regulation of the global economy in the fight against climate change.[42] Since the Commission's 2011 proposal to introduce a CBAM, studies have highlighted the potential impact of its application on the EU's trading partners (major world powers and least developed countries). Indeed, one study concluded that the gradual implementation of the CBAM is likely to have a significant impact on the industries in China that export most to the EU, such as the aluminium sector. The risk of a 'green paradox' has, therefore, not been ruled out for this example.[43] Another study concluded that the application of the CBAM is likely to generate disparities between countries and for certain sub-regional levels.[44] Other scientific studies have highlighted the negative impact of the CBAM system on the least developed countries.[45] For example, some African and Eastern European countries depend on exports of products that will be subject to CBAM. Depending on the scenarios studied, the impact of applying CBAM in these countries could be a loss of jobs, a loss of export-related income, or even a loss of tax revenue.[46] These studies analysed the effectiveness of additional measures (exemptions, redistribution through investment or subsidies of revenues generated by the sale of CBAM to LDCs) that could have been proposed as part of the implementation of CBAM to reduce these negative externalities.

III. Implementing BCA in the Context of Net Zero: Legal Barriers and Limitations

For a BCA to effectively advance solidarity, a shift from a logic of conflict to one of cooperation is essential. To ensure the exchange of knowledge, information, and joint monitoring

[39] The risk of carbon leakage was raised at the European Council of 13 and 14 March 2008. These discussions took place at the end of the first phase of the ETS I. They envisaged changes to the operation of the ETS to address the risk of carbon leakage <https://www.consilium.europa.eu/uedocs/cms_data/docs/pressdata/fr/ec/99435.pdf> May 20, 2008

[40] See, among others, Helene Naegele and Aleksandar Zaklan, 'Does the EU ETS Cause Carbon Leakage in European Manufacturing ?' (2019) 93 Journal of Environmental Economics and Management 125.

[41] Cecilia Bellora and Lionel Fontagné, 'EU in Search of a Carbon Border Adjustment Mechanism' (2023) 123 Energy Economics 106673.

[42] Robert Y Shum, 'Decarbonizing Contending Industries: Policy Design and the EU's CBAM' (2023) Climate Policy.

[43] Lin Boqiang and Zhao Hengsong, 'Evaluating Current Effects of Upcoming EU Carbon Border Adjustment Mechanism: Evidence from China's Futures Market' (2023) 177 Energy Policy 113573.

[44] Jiarui Zhong and Jiansuo Pei, 'Beggar Thy Neighbor? On the Competitiveness and Welfare Impacts of the EU's Proposed Carbon Border Adjustment Mechanism' (2022) 162 Energy Policy 112802.

[45] Laima Eicke and others, 'Pulling up the Carbon Ladder? Decarbonization, Dependence, and Third-Country Risks from the European Carbon Border Adjustment Mechanism' (2021) 80 Energy Research & Social Science 102240; Guilherme Magacho and others, 'Impacts du CBAM sur les partenaires commerciaux de l'UE: conséquences pour les pays en développement' (AFD Research Papers, 2022) 1–20 <https://www.cairn-int.info/journal-afd-research-papers-2022-238-page-1.htm> accessed 18 August 2023.

[46] Magacho and others (n 45).

that is at the heart of BCA, the logic of solidarity must be integrated in its design and implementation.

However, the drafting of the European CBAM Regulation was based on a logic of conflict and led to compromises between the EU institutions, which continue to limit its effective implementation. The implementation of CBAM is based on complex procedures involving a large number of actors (industry, national administrations, European Commission).

A. Conflict within the EU

The risks of conflict associated with the definition of the principles and procedures for the implementation of the CBAM first became apparent between the EU institutions themselves during the discussions that preceded the adoption of Regulation 2023/956 and then, to some extent, between the EU institutions and the Member States.

The difficulty of reaching agreement between the EU institutions was illustrated by the intensity and acrimony of the debate on the proposed European Regulation establishing the CBAM. It was the European Parliament that started the hostilities with a resolution in 2021, even before the European Commission had communicated its draft legislative act.[47] In particular, the European Parliament set out the details of how the future CBAM would be made compatible with WTO law. Since 14 July 2021, the date on which the proposal for a European Regulation was adopted by the European Commission, it took almost two years of discussions and divergent positions between the EU institutions for the CBAM mechanism to be finally approved. In the meantime, a conciliation procedure was made possible. On 13 December 2002, the EU institutions adopted a plan to reach a provisional agreement on the general philosophy of the CBAM.[48]

Regulation 2023/956 is a compromise text which may be amended if its objectives cannot be effectively achieved. There have been various points of discussion, but at least two of them deserve special attention. First is the issue of defining the scope of the CBAM, that is, the products covered by the instrument. The products are listed in Annex I of the European Regulation.[49] Initially, the EU institutions agreed on those with the highest GHG emissions (1), those with the highest risk of carbon leakage (2), and those that do not entail a significant increase in administrative burden for national authorities and importers (3). Specifically, these are the goods with the highest GHG emissions in the cement, iron and steel, aluminium, fertilizers, electricity, and hydrogen sectors. The December 2022 agreement made it possible to include hydrogen in this list. The aim is to anticipate a plausible increase in hydrogen imports into the EU. The CBAM also applies to indirect emissions, subject to certain conditions. These indirect emissions are those resulting from the generation of electricity used in the production of goods covered by the CBAM. Initially, they should only affect a limited number of goods listed in Annex II of the European Regulation. Changes to the scope of the CBAM are therefore expected in the medium term. Before the end of the transitional period for the implementation of the CBAM, the European

[47] Carbon border adjustment mechanism Resolution 2021 (n 36).

[48] EU <https://www.consilium.europa.eu/fr/press/press-releases/2022/12/13/eu-climate-action-provisional-agreement-reached-on-carbon-border-adjustment-mechanism-cbam/> accessed 12 August 2023.

[49] EU Carbon border adjustment mechanism Regulation 2023 (n 1).

Commission is expected to determine the extent to which the scope can be extended to other products that present risks of carbon leakage, and then to all products covered by the ETS by 2030.[50]

On the authority responsible for implementing and supervising the CBAM: while the European Commission favoured implementation by national administrations, the European Parliament proposed the creation of a 'CBAM Authority', thus paving the way for the centralization of CBAM supervision procedures.[51] The Council deviated somewhat from the European Commission's model by proposing to centralize only the register of CBAM declarants and importers, which the Commission would have been responsible for monitoring. The EU legislator opted instead for the first solution. A control system based on decentralized arrangements, under the responsibility of the national administrations, will ultimately be organized. It is on this point that the differences between the EU institutions are most striking. This is perfectly logical, since everyone will agree that the control of the CBAM is the central element of credibility.

The conflicts between the European institutions that arose during the drafting of the CBAM lead us to make two observations. The first is that it took a united front to push through the CBAM mechanism. The second is that this reveals a fundamental difficulty with the system. This relates to the way it is designed, and is based on two aspects: the intensity of control to be chosen, and the amount of credibility to be given to importers.

B. Conflict with Companies Currently Benefitting from Free Quotas

Allowance allocation is actually based on three methods: free allocation, auctioning, and a secondary market where allowances are traded between industries. The idea was to prevent industries from relocating to countries that do not have an emissions trading system. The free allocation of allowances was a solution for companies most exposed to the negative effects of the EU ETS, thus preventing carbon leakage.[52]

Since 2013, the allocation of allowances in the EU ETS has been based on a different logic. It was decided that the allocation of allowances on the basis of auctioning would be introduced gradually and replace free allocation in the medium term. Some industrial sectors are exclusively subject to auctioning. This has been the case for electricity generation since 2013. In this case, the risk of carbon leakage is minimized because competition on the international market remains low.[53] Industries in this sector can therefore pass on the cost of carbon. However, free allocation has been maintained for certain energy-intensive sectors. These were sectors where the risk of carbon leakage was considered real. Companies in these sectors continued to face strong competition in international markets from competitors not subject to the same carbon pricing requirements (this was particularly true for aviation and industry).[54]

[50] ibid.

[51] European Parliament Amendments to the proposal for a regulation of the European Parliament and of the Council establishing a border carbon adjustment mechanism [2022] COM(2021)0564, C9-0328/2021, 2021/0214(COD), P9_TA(2022)0248 (hereafter EU Border carbon adjustment mechanism Amendments 2022).

[52] See Chapter 20 of this book.

[53] Edwin Woerdmam, Martha Roggenkamp, and Marijn Holwerd, *Essential EU Climate Law* (2nd edn, Edward Elgar Publishing 2021).

[54] ibid.

The CBAM will gradually reduce their usefulness as it is designed to restore a level playing field between European and non-EU industries by subjecting companies to common rules on carbon charges. Nevertheless, the gradual phasing out of free allocation will be a source of tension and there could be questions as to its relevance. Of course, this replacement must be gradual. For this reason, it was already decided that the transition period and the full entry into force of the CBAM would be modelled on the gradual phasing out of allowances allocated free of charge under the ETS. Directive 2023/959 applies a reduction factor to the allocation of free allowances in line with the introduction of the CBAM. The aim is to gradually reduce the rate, with the final phase-out of allowances in 2034.[55]

C. Conflict with the Consumer

It is rather surprising that the final consumer has not been considered, or has only been considered as secondary, in the discussions on the CBAM measure. Yet it is they who will bear the cost of the introduction of the CBAM measure, both through the risk of higher prices for goods or services imported from outside the EU and through the reduction in free allowances, which will inevitably have an impact on prices for the final consumer.[56] At the same time, this price increase will have the effect of highlighting the negative externalities of producing certain goods and services abroad and may therefore encourage consumers to change their behaviour and consumption patterns. However, it is not certain that consumers will understand the reasons for this and will instead see a reduction in their purchasing power. In the name of a just transition, the question of how to distribute the revenues from the sale of CBAMs becomes crucial. The most promising option was to use a climate fund to help the least developed countries with their energy transition.[57]

Similarly, it would be desirable for part of the revenue to be allocated to the newly established Social Climate Fund.[58] Established for a period from 2026 to 2032, it will provide 'financial support to Member States for measures and investments included in their Social Climate Plans'. The fund will benefit 'households, micro-enterprises and transport users, which are vulnerable and particularly affected by the inclusion of greenhouse gas emissions from buildings and road transport within the scope of Directive 2003/87/EC, in particular households in energy poverty or households in transport poverty'. This anticipates the increase in carbon costs for consumers associated with the extension of the ETS to the road transport and buildings sectors. It is envisaged that the Fund will be financed by revenues from the current ETS, followed by revenues from ETS II for road transport and buildings.

[55] The proposed figures are as follows: 97.5% in 2026, 95% in 2027, 90% in 2028, 77.5% in 2029, 51.5% in 2030, 39% in 2031, 26.5% in 2032, and 14% in 2033. See EU Carbon border adjustment mechanism Regulation 2023 (n 1).

[56] High Council for the Climate, *Annual report, 2022* (2022) 129, <https://www.hautconseilclimat.fr/en/publications/>

[57] Sigit Perdana and Marc Vielle, 'Making the EU Carbon Border Adjustment Mechanism acceptable and climate friendly for least developed countries' (2022) 170(November) Energy Policy 113245.

[58] Regulation (EU) 2023/955 of the European Parliament and of the Council establishing a Social Climate Fund and amending Regulation (EU) 2021/1060 [2023] OJ L 130 (hereafter EU Social Climate Fund Regulation 2021).

D. Conflicts with Foreign Industrial and Commercial Companies and States

The adoption of the EU's CBAM raises the potential risk of conflict with WTO legislation. Of course, a clear and definitive answer as to its compatibility with the provisions of the WTO agreements can only be given if the matter is referred to the WTO judge. Here are the main points raised.

Several conflicts of legal qualification with WTO agreements are anticipated: with the Agreement on Subsidies and Countervailing Measures on the notion of prohibited subsidies (Article 3 and Annex I)[59] and with the General Agreement on Tariffs and Trade (GATT). The legal qualification chosen for CBAM is a political and legal choice.[60] CBAM is a regulatory measure, not a tax. The European Regulation, based on article 192(1) TFEU, allows the European Parliament and the Council to adopt, in accordance with the ordinary legislative procedure, acts relating to environmental policy, one of the objectives of which is 'to promote measures at international level to deal with regional or worldwide environmental problems, and in particular to combat climate change'.[61] This legal qualification makes it possible to circumvent a political obstacle. By making CBAM a tax, the European Regulation would have had to be adopted on the basis of a special legislative procedure requiring unanimity in the Council (art 192(2)). The adoption of such a divisive measure between Member States on this legal basis would probably have been doomed to failure.

However, this political choice has its weaknesses when it comes to the legal classification of CBAM under WTO law. As a result, doubts about its legal status have consequences for the analysis of its compatibility with WTO law. To summarize the positions taken by legal scholars,[62] it is not certain that the CBAM can fall within the scope of article II:2(a) GATT, which allows the parties involved to 'impose at any time on the importation of a product: (a) a charge equivalent to an internal tax imposed in accordance with paragraph 2 of Article III on a like domestic product or on a good which has been incorporated into the imported product'. There are different interpretations of what constitutes an 'internal tax' under WTO law, and whether CBAM could affect a product that has been incorporated into the imported article within the meaning of WTO law. Subject to reservations, CBAM could also be understood as a measure of a regulatory nature within the meaning of article 3 GATT, that is, 'laws, regulations and requirements affecting the sale, offering for sale, purchase, transport, distribution and use of such products in the domestic market'.

The analysis is based on three clauses: the first clause, contained in article 1, concerning General Most-Favoured-Nation Treatment which stipulates that 'any advantage, favour, privilege or immunity granted by any contracting party to any product originating in or destined for any other country shall be accorded immediately and unconditionally to the like product originating in or destined for the territories of all other contracting parties'. From an analytical point of view, this clause ensures that a Member cannot introduce a measure that discriminates against one or more trading partners without extending it to all other WTO Members. The Regulation provides for exemptions according to the carbon tariffs applied in other countries (art 9). This could conflict with article 1, as it

[59] Keen, Parry, and Roaf (n 19).

[60] Sabrina Robert, 'Un mécanisme d'ajustement carbone aux frontières compatible avec le droit de l'OMC: une gageure' (2022) 7(1) European Papers 239.

[61] Treaty on the Functioning of the European Union (TFEU) 2008/C 115/01.

[62] ibid.

would mean applying different measures to products from countries considered to have climate ambitions close to those of the EU, compared to products from third countries with lower climate ambitions. In other words, there can be no discrimination between 'like products' as defined in article 1. The analysis of the similarity of products in order to assess the conformity of measures with the GATT agreements is also contained in article 3 on national treatment in respect of internal taxation and regulation. In particular, this article provides that '[t]he products of the territory of any contracting party imported into the territory of any other contracting party shall not be subject, directly or indirectly, to internal taxes or other internal charges of any kind in excess of those applied, directly or indirectly, to like domestic products'. However, with few exceptions in the case law,[63] judges have adopted a strict interpretation of similarity, which has led some commentators to say that it could contravene these first two clauses and thus be qualified as a discriminatory measure.[64]

If the WTO judge were to uphold this qualification against the CBAM, it would have to meet the conditions set out in article XX in order to survive. This clause sets out the exceptions to the rules of WTO law that allow states to adopt restrictive measures on international trade in order to preserve certain imperatives considered to be in the general interest. Some of these requirements include the following: necessary to protect human, animal or plant life or health (paragraph b of GATT article XX) relating to the conservation of exhaustible natural resources if such measures are made effective in conjunction with restrictions on domestic production or consumption (paragraph g of GATT article XX). However, the same clause states that: 'Subject to the requirement that such measures are not applied in a manner which would constitute a means of arbitrary or unjustifiable discrimination between countries where the same conditions prevail, or a disguised restriction on international trade, nothing in this Agreement shall be construed to prevent the adoption or enforcement by any contracting party of measures.' In other words, the assessment of the justification of the CBAM under article XX will depend very much on the conditions under which it is applied in practice. In order to ensure that the measures are justified and do not reveal arbitrary choices on the part of the competent authorities, it will be necessary to consider and compare the situations in third countries and in the EU. This should lead the European authorities to adapt certain CBAM procedures to the situation in each of these third countries.[65]

Finally, the question that arises from these three clauses is the discriminatory nature of the measure, its intention, and its practice. This tension in the implementation of the CBAM reveals the fragility of international law. The CBAM is not designed as an instrument of cooperation, but as an element of commercial conflict, established on the idea of forcing other states to respect the rules of economic competition based on respect for the climate. The conflicts in the legal characterization and interpretation of the CBAM in relation to WTO law only serve to confirm that the latter does not appear to be adapted to today's climate issues, as the European Parliament has pointed out. In its Resolution 2021, it stresses the urgent need to 'pursue a comprehensive reform of the WTO, enabling it to

[63] Robert (n 60).

[64] Geneviève Dufour and Valériane Thool, 'Le projet de mécanisme européen d'ajustement carbone aux frontières: passe-t-il le test du droit de l'OMC?' in Olivier Bichsel, Oliver Delas, and Mulry Mondélice (eds), *L'Union européenne, puissance globale dans les relations internationales et translatantiques* (Bruylant 2023) 513.

[65] ibid.

guarantee fair trade, while at the same time combating global warming'.[66] In any case, the legal provisions of the GATT agreements could be constructively interpreted by the WTO judge, should the matter be referred to him or her. The WTO judge's 'evolving' interpretation[67] has already opened up the GATT agreements to non-trade considerations such as environmental protection and sustainable development objectives.[68]

IV. Legal Approaches for Addressing the Challenges: Lessons Learned

Although not explicitly mentioned in Regulation 2023/956, solidarity is an issue that is inextricably linked to the construction of the border carbon adjustment mechanism and its application. It permeates its operation in several ways. Each of the parties involved is expected to show solidarity. Firstly, the EU legislator bases the effectiveness of the system on a large degree of autonomy granted to manufacturers to certify that their export activities comply with the CBAM requirements, under the supervision of the competent authorities. Secondly, national administrations are the main authorities responsible for ensuring that the CBAM is properly applied. National authorities will therefore be trusted to ensure that manufacturers comply with European requirements and even to penalize fraudulent behaviour. Finally, the creation of the Social Fund for Climate Change is a system that combines solidarity between the EU institutions and the Member States. Its general objective is indeed to 'contribute to a socially fair transition towards climate neutrality by addressing the social impacts of the inclusion of greenhouse gas emissions from buildings and road transport within the scope of Directive 2003/87/EC'.[69]

Solidarity can be found on three levels, and there could be lessons to be learned. Firstly, the question of the allocation of the revenue generated by the CBAM needs to be addressed. The establishment of a European mechanism implies that the revenue should be earmarked for something that is considered to be of common benefit to all Member States. For the time being, the idea is to earmark the revenue to the budget's own resources in order to support climate policy and achieve the objectives of the Green Deal.[70] This logic was confirmed in the next generation of the EU's recovery instrument, adopted in response to the COVID-19 crisis. A proposal for a Council Regulation has also been tabled for 2022.[71] Another idea put forward by the European Parliament, which raises a strong issue of cooperation, was based on allocating part of the revenue to the least developed countries for manufacturing.[72] Regulation 2023/956 does not fully resolve this issue. However, the Preamble states that 'The Union is working towards introducing a new own resource based on the revenues generated by the sale of CBAM certificates'. It is also clear from the Preamble that this revenue

[66] Carbon border adjustment mechanism Resolution 2021 (n 39).

[67] Gabrielle Marceau, 'L'interprétation évolutive par le juge OMC: Sophisme ou nécessité' (2018) 122(1) Revue Générale de Droit International Public 23.

[68] Gabrielle Marceau and Clément Marquet, 'La jurisprudence de l'OMC et la recherche d'un équilibre entre développement économique et considérations non-commerciales: le cas de l'environnement' (2017) 30(2) Quebec Journal of International Law 119.

[69] EU Social Climate Fund Regulation 2021 (n 58) art 3

[70] Carbon border adjustment mechanism Resolution 2021 (n 36).

[71] Proposal for a Council Regulation on the methods and procedure for making available own resources based on the Emissions Trading System, the Carbon Border Adjustment Mechanism and reallocated profits and on the measures to meet cash requirements [2022] COM(2022) 101 final, 2022/0071(NLE).

[72] EU Border carbon adjustment mechanism Amendments 2022 (n 51).

could eventually be used to support climate change adaptation and mitigation policies in low- and middle-income third countries.[73]

The second issue is the development of administrative cooperation so as not to undermine or weaken the operation of the CBAM and its objectives (avoiding the risk of carbon leakage). This is a crucial issue on which a decent practical chance of success depends. Good European administrative cooperation will be needed to ensure that there are no differences in approach between EU Member States. This is why the European Parliament proposed the creation of a CBAM Authority. Its main task would have been to prevent, detect, and punish any circumvention—abuse or fraud—in coordination with the customs authorities.[74] The solution finally adopted was to centralize certain control tasks and missions (such as those relating to circumvention practices in art 27) within the European Commission. These include helping and exchanging information with the national authorities responsible for implementing the CBAM system.[75] The Commission is also responsible for monitoring the register of CBAM certificates (art 14). The third is to ensure economic and legal certainty for importers, since the gradual introduction of the CBAM will have an impact on supply costs. European Regulation 2023/956 therefore provides for a transitional period with a comprehensive timetable.[76]

The EU's CBAM therefore remains a major challenge for external trade policy. This can be seen on two levels. Cooperation is essential to ensure that control measures are appropriate and accepted by third countries. The European Regulation does not immediately introduce specific provisions to address the impact of the application of the CBAM on least developed countries (LDCs). One option in particular that is being considered is to provide financial assistance to help LDCs decarbonize their industries.[77] In this context, the Preamble of Regulation 2023/956 refers to the study on the introduction of 'a new own resource based on the revenues generated by the sale of CBAM certificates'.[78]

Some commentators see the CBAM instrument as a first step towards the development of a global climate club to deepen international solidarity on net zero.[79] Similarly, the European Parliament has put forward the idea of creating an international forum to ensure continuity between the EU's trading partners by promoting better comparison and coordination between the carbon pricing measures adopted by different countries in order to combat carbon leakage.[80] This institutional approach is also mentioned in the Preamble of the Regulation.[81]

Finally, cooperation with industry is essential to prevent carbon leakage and fraudulent behaviour. One of the underlying objectives of the CBAM is to encourage third-country

[73] EU Carbon border adjustment mechanism Regulation 2023 (n 1) para 74.

[74] EU Border carbon adjustment mechanism Amendments 2022 (n 51).

[75] EU Carbon border adjustment mechanism Regulation 2023 (n 1) art 12.

[76] The timetable is as follows: October 2023 – Application of the Regulation begins, with the start of the transitional period during which importers will make declarations (1); 2026 – Application of the CBAM mechanism and coexistence with the allocation of free allowances under the ETS EU system (2); Directive 2023/959 completes this transitional period by providing for the definitive abolition of free allocation in 2034 (3).

[77] EU Carbon border adjustment mechanism Regulation 2023 (n 1) para 72.

[78] ibid para 74.

[79] Simone Tagliapietra and Guntram B Wolff, 'Conditions Are Ideal for a New Climate Club' (2021) 158 Energy Policy 112527; David G Tarr and others, 'Why Carbon Border Adjustment Mechanisms Will Not Save the Planet but a Climate Club and Subsidies for Transformative Green Technologies May' (2023) 122 Energy Economics 106695.

[80] EU Border carbon adjustment mechanism Amendments 2022 (n 51).

[81] EU Carbon border adjustment mechanism Regulation 2023 (n 1) para 73.

producers to use cleaner technologies. Of course, mechanisms need to be put in place to monitor circumvention practices by stakeholders. To this end, a new article 27 defines and identifies circumvention practices that could be subject to sanctions.

V. Conclusion

To be an effective tool for advancing net zero ambitions, BCA would ideally involve a logic of cooperation, or at least rules of coexistence, with a more general idea of international solidarity in the face of climate change. This can be seen on two levels. First, that of the EU's effectiveness in implementing the CBAM. If the CBAM is to be presented to the outside world in a way that is binding on third-country operators and convincing to the EU's trading partners, there must be agreement within the EU (the greater this agreement, the more effective the CBAM mechanism will be). At the very least, this will require close cooperation between national administrations and a European administration. At best, it would be a model where the European institution itself intervenes in the application of the CBAM. As with the state aid regime, the Commission could have the power to monitor the application of the CBAM rules. From a practical point of view, hybridization would perhaps have been a first step towards direct management, creating synergies at national level and gradually creating an independent body with increasing powers of control and data collection.

The problem in international trade law today is that the CBAM system is designed to be WTO-compliant without any thought being given to overhauling the WTO system. International law, through treaties, should provide for a CBAM system with global operating rules. The idea of establishing a world economy and a world law would be the most appropriate, pending the ultimate stage, which could be a GHG trading system. Again, this would require a step-by-step approach: first, setting up information exchange networks between the EU administration and the EU's third country trading partners, then establishing an international text, perhaps by revising the WTO rules through a new round of GATT negotiations, or perhaps one day introducing an ETS at international level.

In any case, BCA is a first step towards raising the question of multilateralism, in general, to deal with the new competitive situation, which means structurally integrating the fight against global warming and environmental protection. It results from a new normative strategy based on unilateral actions and legislation that incorporate specific values of solidarity, sharing, and use of natural resources that will have an impact beyond the state or regional international organization. The aim is to indirectly redefine human societies' use of natural resources through public policies and regional regulations, thereby laying the foundations for a new international society that is carbon-neutral and, perhaps, based on solidarity.

18

Regional Free Trade Agreements and Net Zero Transitions

Lessons from the US, Mexico, and Canada Free Trade Agreement

José Juan González and Ana María Pacheco Ruiz

I. Intr oduction

This chapter examines the need for regional solidarity in defining a regional roadmap for transitioning to a zero emissions economy, in compliance with the commitments of the Paris Agreement, without distorting free competition. Drawing lessons from the United States, Mexico, and Canada Trade Agreement (USMCA),[1] it evaluates the role of regional free trade agreements, with clear and comprehensive natural resource and environmental provisions, as an instrument for decarbonizing natural resource supply value chains and advancing regional solidarity for net zero.

The United States, Mexico, and Canada comprise one of the world's most dynamic trading blocs. Still, at the same time, the North American region is one of the most significant contributors to climate change.[2] In 2021, the United States ranked second in CO_2 emissions with 4,752,079 tonnes of CO_2, Canada ranked eleventh with 563,538 tons, and Mexico ranked fifteenth with 418,348 tons of CO_2.[3] In the North American region, each person emits twice as much carbon dioxide as in Europe, more than five times that of Asia and more than thirteen times that of Africa.[4] Notwithstanding, per capita emissions are many times higher in Canada and the United States than in Mexico.[5]

Due to the North American region being one of the significant contributors to climate change, its response to achieving the net zero for 2050 goal is vital. Besides, following the principle of climate solidarity,[6] the region is committed to defining a regional roadmap to transit to net zero emissions for contributing to sustainable development and guaranteeing

[1] Office of the United States Trade Representative, 'Agreement between the United States of America, the United Mexican States, and Canada 7/1/20 Text' <https://www.ustr.gov/trade-agreements/free-trade-agreements/united-states-mexico-canada-agreement/agreement-between> accessed 25 August 2023 (hereafter USMCA).

[2] Hannah Ritchie, 'Who Has Contributed Most to Global CO2 Emissions?' (*Our World in Data*, 1 October 2019) <https://ourworldindata.org/contributed-most-global-co2> accessed 30 May 2023.

[3] 'Emisiones de CO2 2021' (Datosmacro.com 2022) <https://www.datosmacro.expansion.com/energia-y-medio-ambiente/emisiones-co2> accessed 28 February 2023.

[4] Commission for Environmental Cooperation, 'The North American Mosaic: An overview of critical environmental issues' (CEC.ORG (n.d.)) <http://www.cec.org/files/documents/publications/985-north-american-mosaic-overview-key-environmental-issues-en.pdf> accessed 21 February 2023.

[5] ibid.

[6] Giacomo Bazzani, 'Climate Solidarity: A Framework and Research Agenda for Low-Carbon Behavior' (2023) Sociological Forum. P.355

José Juan González and Ana María Pacheco Ruiz, *Regional Free Trade Agreements and Net Zero Transitions* In: *Net Zero and Natural Resources Law*. Edited by: Damilola S. Olawuyi, José Juan González, Hanri Mostert, Milton Fernando Montoya, and Catherine Banet, Oxford University Press.
 DOI: 10.1093/9780198925033.003.0018

access to affordable, reliable, sustainable, and modern energy for all, as the Sustainable Development Goals (SDGs) postulate. This roadmap must rely on the principle of climate solidarity; the solidarity of the region with the rest of the world; solidarity among the three members of the USMCA; and solidarity at the national level with the less fortunate people who suffer the effects of climate change.[7]

The first attempt to define a regional policy for decarbonizing natural resource supply value chains and advancing regional solidarity for net zero was made in 2016, just one year after the adoption of the Paris Agreement.[8] That year, the United States, Mexico, and Canada agreed to the 'North American Climate, Clean Energy, and Environment Partnership Action Plan' (the Plan) to deal with climate change.

However, the Plan delivered few results due to the changes in the United States and Mexico's climate change public policies in those years.[9] The failure of this Plan revealed how important the principle of solidarity is to achieve the goal of net zero emissions between three countries that have different energy policies and that are commercially integrated through a trade agreement that does not provide a clear basis for the definition of a road map that allows reaching that goal.

In 2018, the renegotiation of the North American Free Trade Agreement (NAFTA) opened a new possibility to define a regional policy for decarbonizing natural resource supply value chains and advancing regional solidarity for net zero. Although the new treaty resulting from the negotiations does not include specific provisions on climate change, it is possible to argue that it provides the foundations to endorse a regional net zero policy.

There is no lack of studies on the legal and regulatory framework driving the transition to a zero-emission economy at the level of national jurisdictions. However, no significant studies focus on regional solidarity for net zero. Specifically, in the case of the North American region, bibliographical references are scarce.[10] This chapter will contribute to the analysis of the USMCA as an instrument for decarbonizing natural resource supply value chains and advancing regional solidarity for net zero.

In that context, this chapter proposes a roadmap for promoting regional solidarity for net zero through regional trade agreements that allow countries to move towards a net zero emissions economy, contribute to sustainable development, and guarantees access to affordable, reliable, sustainable, and modern energy for all.

To achieve this goal, this chapter is divided into five sections. After this introduction, Section II discusses national net zero emissions policies, legislation, and initiatives in the

[7] José Juan González Márquez, *El T-MEC y La Protección Del Medio Ambiente* (1st edn, Tirant lo Blanch 2022) 22.

[8] The White House: Office of the Press Secretary, 'North American Climate, Clean Energy, and Environment Partnership Action Plan' (29 June 2016) <https://www.obamawhitehouse.archives.gov/the-press-office/2016/06/29/north-american-climate-clean-energy-and-environment-partnership-action#:~:text=Strive%20to%20achieve%20a%20goal,goal%20being%20in%20accordance%20with> accessed 23 May 2023.

[9] Jesús Francisco Ramírez Bañuelos, 'El Tratado Entre México, Estados Unidos y Canadá Como Instrumento Complementario al Acuerdo de París En La Lucha Contra El Cambio Climático' (2022) 7 Derecho global. Estudios sobre derecho y justicia.

[10] The only studies touching on this subject appear to be: Simone Lucatello, 'Mexico's "Catch-22": The Implications of Being a Trade and Climate Partner of the United States and the European Union' (IDOS Discussion Paper 11/2022) (German Institute of Development and Sustainability (IDOS)) <https://www.doi.org/10.23661/idp11.2022> accessed 25 August 2023; and James Bacchus, 'Using the USMCA for Climate Action', *USMCA forward 2022. United States, Mexico, and Canada. Building a more competitive, inclusive, and sustainable North American economy* (Global Economy and Development at Brookings 2022) <efaidnbmnnnibpcajpcglclefindmkaj/https://clips.cato.org/sites/default/files/Bacchus_brookings_usmca.pdf> accessed 3 may 2024.

context of the North American region. Section III surveys barriers and limitations for the USMCA to be the instrument of solidarity for net zero in the North American area. It also examines the USMCA's opportunities and challenges in achieving this goal. Section IV proposes the legal approach for addressing these challenges and opportunities. Finally, Section V provides some conclusions.

II. National Net Zero Emissions Policies, Legislation, and Initiatives

As mentioned in Chapter 1 of this book, a net zero emissions economy means two things. First, reducing to the minimum possible anthropogenic greenhouse gas (GHG) emissions,[11] and second, removing any residual atmospheric emissions through natural or artificial removal measures.[12] The net zero emissions paradigm has a foundation in several instruments of soft international law: The Paris Agreement (2015), the 2030 Agenda (2015), and the Net Zero Initiative (2022).[13]

Thus, achieving the global net zero emissions goal requires innovative policies and measures, including net zero targets in legislation.[14] Adopting the Paris Agreement gave impetus to the issuing of new legislation to provide a legal framework for national plans and programmes on net zero emissions. By enshrining in legislation commitments adopted in the Paris Agreement, nation-estates give such obligations the character of hard law.

By 2021, the US Library of Congress identified thirty-nine jurisdictions worldwide with a net zero emissions or climate neutrality goal enshrined in legislation. The list includes Canada and the United States, but Mexico still needs to adopt legislation containing a net zero emissions goal.[15]

However, as will be analysed later in this chapter, harmonizing national plans and laws among the North American region's three countries is fundamental for the proper functioning of the regional economic integration model postulated by the USMCA.

This section briefly analyses the legislative changes and plans passed by the three commercial partners in response to achieving a net zero emission of GHGs that cause climate change and evaluates the differences between the three jurisdictions.

A. Canada

Canada has taken several significant steps towards a net zero emissions economy. For instance, in March 2022, it released its climate plan, 'The 2030 Emissions Reduction Plan'

[11] Canadian Institute for Climate Choices, 'Canada's Net Zero Future' (Canadian Climate Institute, 27 July 2022) <https://www.climateinstitute.ca/reports/canadas-net-zero-future/> accessed 27 April 2023.

[12] According to the David Suzuki Foundation, achieving zero emissions requires shifting technologies and energy systems that do not produce greenhouse gas (GHG) emissions. Stephen Thomas and Tom Green, *Shifting Power Zero-Emissions Electricity Across Canada by 2035* (David Suzuki Foundation 2022).

[13] This initiative was launched by the United States during the 2022 COP27 hosted in Egypt, inviting governments to lead and achieve net zero emissions from national government operations by 2050. Eighteen countries joined the United States in this new initiative.

[14] Fabiano de Andrade Correa de and Christina Voigt, 'The Paris Agreement and Net Zero Emissions: What Role for the Land-SEC' (2021) Carbon & Climate Law Review <https://www.cclr.lexxion.eu/article/CCLR/2021/1/3> accessed 1 March 2023.

[15] The Law Library of Congress, 'Global Legal Research Directorate', 2021 LL File No 2021-020617 LRA-D-PUB-002566.

(ERP).[16] This Plan provides a detailed sector-by-sector roadmap identifying the measures and strategies needed for Canada to reach its 2030 emissions target. It also put in place building blocks to achieving net zero emissions by 2050. Finally, as part of Canada's Plan, the government has launched the US$8 billion net zero Accelerator Fund to help large emitters reduce their emissions.[17]

In 2022, the leaders of the Group of Seven (G7) (Canada, France, Germany, Italy, Japan, United Kingdom, and the United States) issued the 2022 G7 communiqué. It includes a commitment for countries to submit a net zero emissions-aligned Long-Term Strategy to the United Nations Framework Convention on Climate Change (UNFCCC). Canada complied with this commitment by producing the 'Exploring Approaches for Canada's Transition to Net Zero Emissions' document.[18] This document summarizes Canada's ambition to achieve net zero emissions by 2050 and to decarbonize the economy.[19] According to the document, the actions to reach the goal of zero emissions in 2050 include, among others, electrification of end-use applications and clean electricity generation, energy efficiency and demand-side management, reduction of non-carbon dioxide GHGs such as methane and hydrofluorocarbons, and sequestration from Canada's forests and lands.[20]

New legislation passed by the Canadian Congress supports the 2030 Emissions Reduction Plan and net zero emissions-aligned Long-Term Strategy. In June 2021, Congress passed the Canadian Net Zero Emissions Accountability Act.[21] The Act codifies setting national emissions reduction targets every five years and introduces planning and reporting mechanisms to achieve those targets up to 2050. According to an official report, the Canadian Net Zero Emissions Accountability Act enshrines in legislation the government of Canada's commitment to achieve net zero GHG emissions by 2050. It provides a framework of accountability and transparency to deliver on it.

Analysis of this piece of legislation reveals three relevant aspects:[22] (1) the Act establishes the obligation to set five-year national emission reduction targets and develop credible, science-based emission reduction plans to achieve each target; (2) the Act establishes Canada's Nationally Determined Contribution (NDC),[23] setting up Canada's 2030 GHG emissions target under the Paris Agreement to reduce emissions 40 to 45 per cent below

[16] Government of Canada, '2030 Emissions Reduction Plan: Clean Air, Strong Economy' (Canada.ca, 12 July 2022) <https://www.canada.ca/en/services/environment/weather/climatechange/climate-plan/climate-plan-overview/emissions-reduction-2030.html> accessed 23 May 2023.

[17] Government of Canada, 'Net Zero Emissions by 2050' (Canada.ca, 27 January 2023) <https://www.canada.ca/en/services/environment/weather/climatechange/climate-plan/net-zero-emissions-2050.html> accessed 28 February 2023.

[18] Environment and Climate Change Canada, 'Exploring Approaches for Canada's Transition to Net Zero Emissions Canada's Long-Term Strategy Submission to the United Nations Framework Convention on Climate Change' (2 November 2022) 1.

[19] ibid 4.

[20] ibid 7.

[21] Alastair Lucas and Iñigo Del Guayo, 'Extreme Natural Event Impacts on the Energy Sector and its Regulation: Canada and North America' in Catherine Banet and others (eds), *Resilience in Energy, Infrastructure and Natural Resources Law: Examining legal pathways for sustainability in times of disruption* (1st edn, OUP 2022).

[22] Canadian government, 'Canadian Net Zero Emissions Accountability Act' (Canada.ca, 29 March 2022) <https://www.canada.ca/en/services/environment/weather/climatechange/climate-plan/net-zero-emissions-2050/canadian-net-zero-emissions-accountability-act.html> accessed 14 April 2023.

[23] According to Nava Escudero, countries are obliged to submit their nationally determined contributions (NDCs) under the Paris Agreement, but their commitments are voluntary. Cesar Nava Escudero, 'El Acuerdo De París. Predominio Del Soft Law en el Régimen Climático' (2016) XLIX Boletín Mexicano de Derecho Comparado 99. However, these commitments become mandatory by including the NDC in national law.

2005 levels by 2030; and (3) the Act also establishes the obligation to set national emission reduction targets for 2035, 2040, and 2045, ten years in advance.[24]

B. The United States

The United States has also begun to move towards a net zero emission economy. Since Joe Biden assumed the presidency, he has set out to regain world leadership in the fight against climate change. In 2021, the United States took several steps in that direction: it re-joined the Paris Agreement; set an ambitious NDC to reduce net GHG emissions by 50 to 52 per cent in 2030; and, like Canada, it launched its '2021 Long-Term Strategy', which lays out how the United States can reach its goal of net zero emissions no later than 2050.[25] According to the US 2021 Long-term Strategy, viable routes to net zero involve five key transformations: decarbonize electricity, electrify end-uses and switch to other clean fuels, cut energy waste, reduce methane and other non-CO_2 emissions, and scale up CO_2 removal.[26]

In addition to the above, on 8 December 2021, President Biden signed the 'Executive Order on Catalyzing Clean Energy Industries and Jobs Through Federal Sustainability' (Executive Order (EO) 14057).[27] The EO 14057 affirms that: 'It is therefore the policy of my Administration for the Federal Government to lead by example in order to achieve a carbon pollution-free electricity sector by 2035 and net-zero emissions economy-wide by no later than 2050.'[28] The EO 14057 directs the federal government to use its procurement power to limit GHG emissions. It requires the heads of principal agencies to develop and implement annual Sustainability Plans based on yearly guidance provided by the Council on Environmental Quality (CEQ).[29]

The EO focuses on five primary goals: (1) 100 per cent carbon pollution-free electricity (CFE) by 2030, at least half of which will be locally supplied clean energy to meet 24/7 demand; (2) 100 per cent zero-emission vehicle (ZEV) acquisitions by 2035, including 100 per cent zero-emission light-duty vehicle acquisitions by 2027; (3) net zero emissions from federal procurement no later than 2050, including a Buy Clean policy to promote the use of construction materials with lower embodied emissions; (4) a net zero emissions building portfolio by 2045, including a 50 per cent emissions reduction by 2032; and (5) net zero emissions from overall federal operations by 2050, including a 65 per cent reduction by 2030.

In addition to the actions above, during the last two years, the US Congress has passed several laws related to decarbonization: the Energy Law of 2020, the Infrastructure Investment and Employment Law of 2021, the CHIPS and Science Law of 2022, and the Law of Reduction of Inflation of 2022 (IRA).[30] The Energy Law is framework

[24] Despite all these advances, in Chapter 7 of this book, the authors argue that Canada will not meet its net zero emissions targets by 2050.

[25] US Department of State and the US Executive Office of the President, 'The Long-Term Strategy of the United States: Pathways to Net-Zero Greenhouse Gas Emissions by 2050' (Washington DC, November 2021).

[26] ibid.

[27] Joe Biden Jr, 'Executive Order on Catalyzing Clean Energy Industries and Jobs through Federal Sustainability' (The White House, 8 December 2021) <https://www.whitehouse.gov/briefing-room/presidential-actions/2021/12/08/executive-order-on-catalyzing-clean-energy-industries-and-jobs-through-federal-sustainability/> accessed 23 May 2023.

[28] ibid Section 101.

[29] ibid Section 402.

[30] Although the IRA was passed in 2022, most of its provisions became effective on 1 June 2023.

legislation designed to modernize US energy policies to foster innovation on technologies critical to energy, national security, and environmental protection across the board.[31] The Infrastructure Investment and Employment Law is an Act to authorize funds for federal-aid highways, highway safety programmes, transit programmes, and other purposes.[32] The CHIPS and Science Law provides roughly US$280 billion in new funding to boost domestic research and manufacturing of semiconductors in the United States.[33]

However, the most crucial action Congress has taken on clean energy and climate change in the history of the United States is passing IRA.[34] IRA is not just a law regarding carbon emissions; it 'directs new federal spending toward reducing carbon emissions, lowering healthcare costs, funding the Internal Revenue Service, and improving taxpayer compliance'.[35] In the specific field of climate change, it offers funding, programmes, and incentives to accelerate the transition to a clean energy economy. It is likely to drive the significant deployment of new clean electricity resources.[36] A US Senate document notes, 'The IRA aims to make a historic down payment on deficit reduction to fight inflation, invest in domestic energy production and manufacturing, and reduce carbon emissions 40 per cent by 2030.'[37]

According to the IRA, the US government will allocate nearly US$400 million to low-cost energy investments for families and small businesses.[38] The central part of this amount in energy and climate funding is in the form of tax credits. Corporations are the biggest recipient, with an estimated US$216 billion worth of tax credits. These are designated to catalyse private investment in clean energy, transport, and manufacturing. Many of the tax incentives in the bill are direct pay, meaning that an entity can claim the total amount even if its tax liability is less than the credit.[39]

Under the IRA, companies that emit GHGs forgo subsidies that would otherwise boost their bottom line. This is intended to encourage industries that use fossil fuels to reduce emissions by installing carbon removal technologies or building new natural gas plants with direct air capture.

[31] The Energy Law, s 7002 requires that the executive branch designate a list of critical minerals and update that list every three years and that the United States Geological Survey (USGS) conduct domestic resource assessments of essential minerals and make that information publicly available.

[32] The Act was initially a US$547–715 billion infrastructure package that included provisions related to federal-aid highway, transit, highway safety, motor carrier, research, hazardous materials, and rail programmes of the Department of Transportation.

[33] The CHIPS and Science Act combines two bipartisan bills: the Endless Frontier Act, designed to boost investment in domestic high-tech research and the CHIPS for America Act, designed to bring semiconductor manufacturing back to the United States. The Act is aimed at competing with China.

[34] The White House, 'Inflation Reduction Act Guidebook' (The White House, 3 April 2023) <https://www.whitehouse.gov/cleanenergy/inflation-reduction-act-guidebook/> accessed 28 April 2023.

[35] Adi Kumar and others, 'The Inflation Reduction Act: Here's What's in It' (McKinsey & Company, 24 October 2022) <http://www.mckinsey.com/industries/public-and-social-sector/our-insights/the-inflation-reduction-act-heres-whats-in-it> accessed 23 May 2023.

[36] See Environmental Protection Agency (EPA), 'The Inflation Reduction Act' <https://www.epa.gov/green-power-markets/inflation-reduction-act> accessed 28 April 2023.

[37] US Senate, 'Summary: The Inflation Reduction Act of 2022' (US Senate) <https://www.democrats.senate.gov/imo/media/doc/inflation_reduction_act_one_page_summary.pdf> accessed 23 April 2023.

[38] The IRA includes provisions covering healthcare, taxation, and climate.

[39] Adi Kumar and others, 'The Inflation Reduction Act: Here's What's in it' (McKinsey & Company, 24 October 2022) <https://www.mckinsey.com/industries/public-and-social-sector/our-insights/the-inflation-reduction-act-heres-whats-in-it> accessed 2 May 2023.

Finally, the IRA is a big deal for the climate economy; it provides US$27 billion in funds for competitive grants to finance GHG reduction projects. The funds will go to state, local, and tribal governments and non-profits, with more than US$15 million targeting low-income and disadvantaged communities.[40]

C. Mexico

Unlike in the cases of Canada and the United States, the Mexican government's policies on climate change have so far been ambiguous. Although it has signed the main international instruments on the matter, Mexico is the only member of the North American region that has yet to announce any plans to reach net zero emissions.[41] Nor does it have a net zero target. Moreover, Mexico is also the only member of the Group of Twenty (G20) that has yet to announce a plan to achieve net zero emissions by 2050.

After signing the North American Climate, Clean Energy, and Environment Partnership Statement with Canada and the United States in 2016,[42] Mexico announced several commitments to transitioning to a net zero emissions economy.[43] Nevertheless, there still needs to be a comprehensive plan articulating all these commitments and legislation giving them a mandatory character.

For example, during COP 26, Mexico adopted the Glasgow Agreement to Transition to a Zero-Emission Cars Initiative. This Agreement, signed by at least 100 entities, including governments, companies, cities, regions, and automobile manufacturers, establishes the elimination of internal combustion vehicles by 2035 in specific markets and for the entire world in 2040. Although Mexico was one of the countries that joined this initiative, such a document is not mandatory.

In addition, in its 2020 NDC, Mexico committed to further reduce its GHG emissions by 22 per cent by 2030. In 2022, during COP 27, the Mexican government increased its commitment to reduce GHG emissions by 2030 from 22 to 35 per cent. However, Mexico has yet to commit to the net zero emissions goal by 2050.[44] Neither has the Mexican government allocated budgetary resources to finance compliance with its climate commitments. Instead, it has given nearly US$11 billion towards the construction of a new refinery.[45]

[40] Alex Liun Betty Jiang, Maheep Mandloi and others (30 November 2022) *US Inflation Reduction Act: A catalyst for climate action,* Credit Suisse. Accessed 29 August 2023.

[41] Mexico's economy uses carbon intensively, and moving towards net zero emissions will require profound structural transformations and substantial investment. Alejandro Limón Portillo and Adrián García Gómez, 'Cambio Climático y Acuerdo de París: Implicaciones' (CIEP, 23 November 2022) <https://www.ciep.mx/cambio-climatico-y-acuerdo-de-paris-implicaciones/> accessed 28 August 2023.

[42] This statement aims to ensure a 'competitive, low-carbon and sustainable' North America and aims to achieve 50 per cent clean power generation by 2025.

[43] SDG Knowledge Hub, 'Canada, US, Mexico Forge North American Climate, Clean Energy' IISD (SDG Knowledge Hub, 30 June 2016) <https://www.sdg.iisd.org/news/canada-us-mexico-forge-north-american-climate-clean-energy-and-environment-partnership/> accessed 2 May 2023.

[44] The new Mexican climate change commitments mean: (1) doubling the country's clean energy generation capacity in the next eight years; (2) 2 million additional hectares of Protected Natural Areas; (3) a reforestation process of 1.5 million hectares; and (4) accelerating the adoption of electromobility and energy efficiency in Mexico.

[45] E Efe, 'Amlo Reconoce Aumento Del 46% En Costo de Refinería Dos Bocas' (*El Financiero*, 8 October 2022) <https://www.elfinanciero.com.mx/nacional/2022/10/08/amlo-reconoce-aumento-del-46-en-costo-de-dos-bocas/> accessed 23 May 2023.

In the legal field, Mexico needs to make more progress. Mexican laws related to climate change and energy transition predate the signing of the Paris Agreement. The Climate Change Law passed in 2012, and the Energy Transition Laws, approved in 2015, are the only pieces of legislation that provide the basis for emission reduction goals and the replacement of fossil fuels with clean energies. However, these laws do not refer to the pursuit of net zero emissions for 2050, and the emission reduction commitments indicated in them are only accepted conditionally.

The Climate Change Law states in the first part of its Second Transitory article that Mexico assumes the no binding objective or aspirational goal of reducing by 2020, 30 per cent of emissions concerning the baseline, as well as a 50 per cent reduction in emissions by 2050 about those emitted in the year 2000.[46] However, the second part of this provision indicates that Mexico can only achieve these goals if an international organism provides financial and technological support from developed to developing countries, including Mexico.[47]

On the other hand, according to the same legal provision, Mexico undertakes to unconditionally reduce by 22 per cent its GHG emissions and 51 per cent of its black carbon emissions by the year 2030 for the baseline. This commitment, assumed as an NDC, implies reaching a maximum of national emissions by 2026; and decoupling GHG emissions from economic growth. The intensity of emissions per unit of gross domestic product (GDP) will be reduced by about 40 per cent between 2013 and 2030.

The 22 per cent reduction in GHG emissions will be achieved through the commitment of the different participating sectors under the following goals: transportation, 18 per cent; electricity generation, 31 per cent; residential and commercial, 18 per cent; oil and gas, 14 per cent; industry, 5 per cent; agriculture and livestock, 8 per cent; and waste, 28 per cent.[48]

Apart from the Climate Change Law, the Energy Transition Law states in its third transitory provision that: 'The Ministry of Energy will set as a goal a minimum participation of clean energies in electric power generation of 25 per cent for the year 2018, 30 per cent for 2021 and 35 per cent by 2024'.[49] Nevertheless, this legislation does not rule out any legal instrument aimed at achieving such goals.

However, not everything is negative, Mexico is currently piloting an emissions trading system (ETS). In this regard, on 10 January 2019, the Mexican government published the Executive Agreement establishing the preliminary bases of the Emissions Trading System Test programme that complies with article 94 of the General Law on Climate Change.[50]

According to the bases, the ETS comprises two phases; the first stage, known as the Test Programme of the Emissions Trading System, which will allow participants to observe the behaviour of an emissions market, and the second stage, known as the Operational Phase, that will enter into force at the end of the transition phase of the Test Programme.

[46] ibid.

[47] Therefore, Mexico assumes these commitments conditionally. ibid.

[48] Second transitional article of the Climate Change Law (n 46).

[49] Mexico, Energy Transition Law <https://www.climate-laws.org/documents/energy-transition-law_5613?id=energy-transition-law_320e> accessed 28 August 2023.

[50] SEGOB: Diario Oficial de la Federación (10 January 2019) (ACUERDO por el que se establecen las bases preliminares del Programa de Prueba del Sistema de Comercio de Emisiones) <https://www.dof.gob.mx/nota_detalle.php?codigo=5573934&fecha=01/10/2019#gsc.tab=0> accessed 2 March 2023.

By the 2018 reform of the General Law on Climate Change, and as established in the Annex of the Bases, the Test Programme, without economic effects for the participating sectors, will be valid for thirty-six months, thus it ended in December 2022. The pilot phase of the Test Programme ran from 1 January 2020 to 31 December 2021. The transition phase of the Test Programme towards the Operational Phase started on 1 January and concluded on 31 December 2022.[51] This mechanism has the potential to contribute to a significant reduction in GHG emissions in Mexico.

Finally, at the local level, the government of Mexico City issued a Local Climate Action Strategy in 2021.[52] According to this Strategy, Mexico City commits to contributing to the global effort to limit the increase of the Earth's average temperature below 1.5°C and, with it, to significantly reduce the risks that climate change poses to ecosystems, people, and their means of life, especially priority care groups.

From the brief analysis developed in this section, it is argued that the main difference between the climate change policy of the Mexican government and that of its commercial partners is that while they have enshrined in their legislation the goal of zero emissions for 2050 and have established the mechanisms to achieve this goal, Mexican legislation is unclear in this regard and public policy seems run counter to that postulated by the Paris Agreement. However, while Canada and the United States are making progress in advancing the net zero ambition, Mexico has committed to the Paris Agreement, the 2030 Agenda and the Net Zero Initiative, but it is still moving mainly in the zone of soft law. There is a need for Mexico to enshrine in clear and comprehensive legislation its net zero goal for 2050, that complies with global ambitions on net zero, and without distorting the proper functioning of the USMCA.

The USMCA could be the instrument that motivates Mexico to harmonize its law and policy with its two commercial partners and to advance net zero. With this agreement, Mexico, the United States, and Canada would form the largest clean energy market in the world. Otherwise, Mexico will lose the opportunity to decarbonize its energy sector. The next section discusses the opportunities and challenges of promoting regional solidarity for net zero through regional trade agreements.

III. Promoting Solidarity for Net Zero in North America through Regional Trade Agreements: Barriers and Limitations

The attempt to build a roadmap to define a regional policy through a North American Climate, Clean Energy, and Environment Partnership Action Plan faced various obstacles that prevented the achievement of its objectives. Notwithstanding, the USMCA establishes an institutional framework that, in principle, regulates the trade of goods and services as well as investments between the three countries, but which, by incorporating concerns for

[51] Lilia Alonso, 'Sistemas De Comercio De Emisiones En México' (Plumas al debate, 5 July 2022) <https://www.energiaadebate.com/sistemas-de-comercio-de-emisiones-en-mexico/#:~:text=Energ%C3%ADa%20a%20Debate%20es%20un,ciudadan%C3%ADa%20informada%20en%20asuntos%20energ%C3%A9ticos> accessed 2 March 2023.

[52] Gobierno de la Ciudad de México, 'Estrategia Local de Acción Climática 2021–50' (2021) Secretaria de Medio Ambiente. < efaidnbmnnnibpcajpcglclefindmkaj/http://www.data.sedema.cdmx.gob.mx/cambioclimaticocdmx/images/biblioteca_cc/PACCM-y-ELAC_uv.pdf> accessed 3 May 2024 p10

the protection of the environment in its 24th chapter, can also be the instrument for decarbonizing natural resource supply value chains and advancing regional solidarity for net zero.[53]

The discussion on the relationship between international trade and the environment arose in the last century with the debate on the NAFTA, especially at the end of the negotiations.[54] These discussions led to incorporating some environmental provisions into the Treaty and signing a Side Agreement on Environmental Matters as conditions for its ratification by the United States and Canada.

An essential part of the literature supports the idea that to avoid unfair competition, the globalization of international trade drives towards the standardization of environmental policies between trading partners.[55] In this sense, the results of trade integration among USMCA members should include a regional climate policy definition. The following subsection discusses this issue in detail.

In November 2018, the governments of the United States, the United Mexican States, and Canada concluded a new Trade Agreement (USMCA) that replaced NAFTA 1994.[56]

Unlike the NAFTA, the USMCA includes a specific chapter on environmental protection.[57] Although, for political reasons,[58] the USMCA chapter contains provisions regarding protecting the ozone layer[59] and air quality,[60] it does not refer to the climate change paradigm. Nevertheless, its preambular provisions and various sections of the ecological chapter provide enough basis to make regional free trade compatible with the fulfilment of Goal 7 of the UN SDGs and the emissions reduction commitments adopted in the Paris Agreement and promote regional solidarity for net zero.

In the preamble of USMCA, the three partners committed to promoting high levels of environmental protection, including through effective enforcement by each Party of its environmental laws and enhanced environmental cooperation, and further the aims of sustainable development. Similarly, Chapter 24 USMCA includes twenty-six environmental protection provisions.[61]

In that sense, article 24.8 USMCA refers in a general way to Multilateral Environmental Agreements (MEAs). This provision has three parts. In the first part, the signatory parties recognize the importance of these agreements for protecting the environment, especially as a response to the international community to global or regional environmental problems. In the second, the signatory parties affirm their commitment to implement the MEAs to which they are a party, which applies to the Paris Agreement. Finally, in the last part, the

[53] Bacchus (n 10).

[54] Lucatello (n 10).

[55] González Márquez (n 7) 19–29.

[56] The USMCA is a free trade agreement between Canada, the United States, and Mexico that resulted from the renegotiation of NAFTA proposed by the United States. After several months of negotiations, the parties signed it on 30 November 2018, at a side event to that year's G20 Summit in Buenos Aires, Argentina. Unlike the NAFTA, the USMCA does not have a specific chapter on energy. However, different parts of the Agreement contain rules applicable to this sector and revolve around national treatment and free competition, so they also promote regional energy integration. See USMCA (n 1).

[57] Bashar H Malkawi and Shakeel Kazmi, 'Dissecting and Unpacking the USMCA Environmental Provisions: Game-Changer for Green Governance?' (*Jurist*, 5 June 2020) <https://www.jurist.org/commentary/2020/06/malkawi-kazmi-usmca-environment/> accessed 23 May 2023.

[58] USMCA (n 1) Chapter 24, 24-1.

[59] USMCA (n 1) art 24.9, 24-6.

[60] USMCA (n 1) art 24.11, 24-9.

[61] González Márquez (n 7) 164–85.

signatory parties commit to consult and cooperate, as appropriate, concerning matters related to trade and the MEAs.

Therefore, although the USMCA does not have the main objective of governing regional environmental policy, it provides elements that would support a regional initiative for the transition towards decarbonization. Notwithstanding the opportunities the USMCA offers to the region's countries to define a roadmap towards decarbonization within the framework of the principle of solidarity, a number of limitations and obstacles that may arise are examined in the next section.

A. Limitations and Obstacles

Leveraging the USMCA as an instrument for decarbonizing natural resource supply value chains and advancing regional solidarity for net zero faces several limitations and obstacles. First, since Chapter 24 USMCA does not include any principle on climate and energy policies, this trade agreement does not favour adopting a regional strategy to achieve the net zero goal. However, as discussed on subseccion B of this section, that conclusion may only partially be accurate.

Second, some provisions of the Treaty appear to favour nationalism to the detriment of commercial integration at the regional level. Indeed, unlike in the case of the European Union (EU), according to article 24.4 USMCA, no supranational authority is recognized in the North American region. The application of national laws corresponds to each country. In addition, according to article 24.3, each party to the USMCA has the sovereign right to establish its levels of environmental protection and priorities and establish, adopt, or modify its environmental laws and policies.

Third, according to article 24.1.3 USMCA, promoting trade or investment by weakening or reducing the protection granted in their respective environmental laws is inappropriate. Therefore, a party to the USMCA may not waive or otherwise derogate from, or offer to waive, the protection afforded in ecological regulations to encourage trade or investment between the parties.

Consequently, in line with the USMCA, each country in the North American region could move at its own pace, making it difficult to consolidate a regional market and define a regional climate change policy.

There are also several contextual obstacles that may hinder the USMCA's effective function as an instrument for decarbonizing natural resource supply value chains and advancing regional solidarity for net zero. First, the USMCA is only a trade agreement and does not have environmental protection as an objective. Hence, supporters of globalization could assume that this agreement postulates free trade even at the cost of environmental degradation.

Second, the structure of each of the three countries' energy sectors has substantial differences. For instance, the differences in the legal systems that govern each country may hinder the harmonization of energy policies among them.

Third, the current Mexican energy policies do not sufficiently emphasize achieving net zero emissions by 2050, which may limit the prospects of Mexico supporting a regional net zero policy. The relaxation in the application of environmental legislation by the Mexican government in the case of public mega-projects exempted from essential authorizations such as Environmental Impact Assessments (EIAs) also point to a lack of emphasis on net zero by Mexico which may not provide a foundation for regional net zero policies.[62]

However, despite these limitations and obstacles, the USMCA could play an essential role in decarbonizing the Mexican economy and consolidating regional climate solidarity.

B. Opportunities and Challenges within the USMCA

The transition towards a net zero emissions economy is not a concern in the USMCA.[63] However, to the extent that the United States and Canada have already defined their commitment to this universal aspiration, the Mexican government must move in the same direction. Otherwise, the Mexican climate policy would violate the trilateral trade agreement.

In the same vein, Mexico's more relaxed ecological regulations could be used as a mechanism to attract investment to the territory of that country or vice versa; environmental regulations could create non-tariff barriers to give an advantage to Mexican industries and distort free trade in the region.

Mexico is already facing a trade dispute with the United States and Canada due to the application of its national energy policy illustrates such arguments.[64] The trade dispute in which the United States and Canada accuse Mexico of violating the USMCA originates in the energy policies applied by the Mexican government as of 2018.[65] Among other issues that, according to both trading partners, are contrary to the Treaty, we can mention the refusal of Mexico to grant renewable energy generation permits to companies from Canada and the United States; the modification of the dispatch rules that prioritize access to the network of fossil energies produced by the Mexican public company CFE; and the requirement that only Canadian and US companies comply with the obligation that the diesel they sell be ultra-low in sulphur, while the public company PEMEX is exempt from that obligation.[66]

[62] The President of Mexico issued a decree exempting all environmental permits for projects promoted by the government, including the Mayan train, the trans-isthmus train, and the Dos Bocas refinery. These projects have significant negative impacts on the environment and were exempted from complying with environmental regulations. Presidencia de la República, *Acuerdo por el que se instruye a las dependencias y Entidades de la Administración Pública federal a realizar las acciones que se indican, en relación con los proyectos y obras del gobierno de México considerados de Interés Público y seguridad nacional, Así Como prioritarios y estratégicos para el Desarrollo Nacional, Diario Oficial de la Federación* (2021) <https://www.dof.gob.mx/nota_detalle.php?codigo=5635985&fecha=22%2F11%2F2021#gsc.tab=0> accessed 26 May 2023.

[63] Under art 2, the USMCA has the following objectives: (1) eliminate trade barriers and facilitate the cross-border movement of goods and services between the territories of the parties; (2) promote conditions of fair competition in the free trade area; (3) increase substantially investment opportunities in the territories of the parties; (4) provide adequate and effective protection and enforcement of intellectual property rights in each party's territory; (5) create effective procedures for the implementation and application of this Agreement, for its joint administration and the resolution of disputes; and (6) establish a framework for further trilateral, regional, and multilateral cooperation to expand and enhance the benefits of this Agreement.

[64] Under arts 31.2 and 31.4 USMCA, the United States requests consultations with Mexico concerning various measures of Mexico that favour its state-owned electrical utility, Comisión Federal de Electricidad (CFE), and petroleum company, Petróleos Mexicanos (Pemex), and negatively impact US companies operating in Mexico and US-produced energy. These measures appear to breach Mexico's commitments under the USMCA. See the document at: <https://www.ustr.gov/sites/default/files/US%20Cons%20Req%20Mexico%20energy_072022.pdf> accessed 23 May 2023.

[65] Luis Estrada, 'Explanation of Mexico's Energy Sector Dispute under USMCA' (Conecta National News Desk, 29 July 2022) <https://www.conecta.tec.mx/en/news/national/education/explanation-mexicos-energy-sector-dispute-under-usmca> accessed 28 August 2023.

[66] 'United States Requests Consultations Under the USMCA Over Mexico's Energy Policies' <https://www.ustr.gov/about-us/policy-offices/press-office/press-releases/2022/july/united-states-requests-consultations-under-usmca-over-mexicos-energy-policies> accessed 28 August 2023.

The accusation, on the part of the United States and Canada against Mexico, for which there was a request for consultations, asserted that Mexico was not only in violation of the USMCA, but also in violation of the environmental commitments assumed under the Paris Agreement, the 2030 Agenda, and the Net Zero Initiative.[67]

Under the dispute resolution rules established by the USMCA, the conflicting parties have exhausted the consultation stage and have yet to reach an agreement. The next step is forming a Panel for which no specific term is defined in the Treaty. The solution adopted in this Panel will establish a significant precedent about the importance of the USMCA as an instrument to enforce the environmental obligations of the parties, but also the role that it can play in the decarbonization of natural resource supply value chains and advancing regional solidarity for net zero.[68]

All the factors mentioned above cast doubt on the viability of the North American region in meeting the goals of sustainable development, the Paris commitments, and the plans for the transition to a net zero emissions economy. However, if a Commercial Panel decides to force Mexico to modify its energy policy in the specific case of the issues referred to in the request for consultations mentioned above, the USMCA would function as a mechanism to standardize national energy regulations of Mexico with those of Canada and the United States and, in that sense, act as a booster towards a regional climate policy.

Conversely, the USMCA offers opportunities to define a regional net zero emissions policy but poses challenges that the parties must address. The greatest of these challenges is determining the proper interpretation of Chapter 8 USMCA. Chapter 8 recognizes the ownership of the Mexican State over hydrocarbons.[69] The Mexican government has interpreted this provision to mean that the country's government can define its energy policy even though this is contrary to the commitments assumed in the international treatises, which brings the principle of national sovereignty into conflict with the principle of solidarity. Under these circumstances, defining a regional policy of zero emissions would be impossible.

IV. Advancing Regional Solidarity for Net Zero: Legal Approaches to Addressing the Challenges

As can be gleaned from the North American experience, lack of a clear regional strategy and legal framework on net zero may hinder effective regional solidarity and cooperation needed for a net zero economy. The roadmap towards a North American regional net zero economy is tied to the fate of the USMCA that governs trade and investment between the three North American countries. Therefore, although the legal gap generated by the absence of a legal framework on energy and climate change can be covered through the interpretation of other provisions of the Treaty, as happened in the case of the Environmental Side Agreement of the NAFTA, the signing of a parallel agreement to the USMCA regarding the decarbonization of the economy would be the best route to follow.

67 Ramírez Bañuelos (n 9).

68 Chapter 31 USMCA.

69 Chapter 8 USMCA states that 'In the case of Mexico, and without prejudice to their rights and remedies available under this Agreement, the United States and Canada recognise that (a) Mexico reserves its sovereign right to amend its Constitution and its laws internal; and (b) Mexico has direct, inalienable and imprescriptible ownership of all hydrocarbons in the subsoil of the national territory, including the continental shelf and the exclusive economic zone located outside the territorial sea and adjacent to it, in strata or deposits, regardless of their physical conditions by the Political Constitution of the United Mexican States.'

As is well known, world trade is primarily governed today by the rules of the General Agreement on Tariffs and Trade (GATT) and its complementary agreements. The USMCA has its foundation in such a general agreement. Therefore, to interpret trade accordingly, it is necessary to refer to the provisions of the GATT.

Under article XX GATT and the Agreement on Technical Barriers, no GATT member is permitted to use its environmental laws in a manner that constitutes a disguised restriction on trade or investment between the signatory parties. This rule permits two exceptions: protecting the health and life of people, animals, and plants; and conserving non-renewable natural resources.[70]

Therefore, the United States and Canada can restrict investments and trade in goods or services of Mexican origin when they fail to comply with the environmental protection levels established by those two countries' governments. Sometimes, however, these restrictions have been used as artificial barriers to international trade, as happened in the famous 'tuna-dolphin' case;[71] in other cases, the mere possibility that they can be imposed has helped raise the levels of environmental protection in countries with weak legislation.

In this sense, applying the rules of a trade agreement can promote the harmonization of environmental legislation. Also in this sense, despite the USMCA's limitations in terms of climate change, this Agreement can be an essential instrument for decarbonizing natural resource supply value chains and advancing regional solidarity for net zero. The proposed mechanism to achieve this goal could be the signature by the parties to a side agreement on net zero emissions.

This proposed side agreement must define minimum guidelines that allow for the standardizing of commitments assumed by each of the three countries in their nationally determined contributions and long-term strategies. It also has to design the rules for a regional market of carbon credits and establish economic mechanisms that strengthen natural sinks and reservoirs. The Agreement must rely on the principle of climate solidarity, solidarity between the region and the rest of the world, solidarity between the three trading partners and solidarity with the most vulnerable groups within each country of the area. Although Mexico is one of the strongest economies in the world,[72] it needs financial and technological assistance from its trading partners to decarbonize its value chains. The United States and Canada can support decarbonization in the southern countries through the Mexican electricity networks and oil and gas pipelines. With this, the North American region could become a world leader on the path towards zero emissions by 2050, and contribute to achieving the principles contained in the SDGs.

V. Conclusion

Advancing regional solidarity for net zero requires a regional strategy and legal framework, with clear and comprehensive natural resource and environmental provisions on net zero, that promote regional knowledge-sharing, trade cooperation, and collective regional action.

[70] See sections b and g of art XX GATT.

[71] World Trade Organization (WTO), 'Mexico Etc versus US: "Tuna-Dolphin"' (World Trade Organization) <https://www.wto.org/english/tratop_e/envir_e/edis04_e.htm> accessed 28 August 2023.

[72] Mexico ranks 14th among the strongest economies in the world. See the World Bank, 'Mexico' <https://www.worldbank.org/en/country/mexico/overview> accessed 28 August 2023.

As can be seen from the North American experience, while Canada and the United States have taken significant steps towards decarbonizing natural resource supply value chains and advancing regional solidarity for net zero, Mexico would appear to be moving in the opposite direction, which complicates any prospect for building a regional net zero policy. Although, in the past, the region's countries have tried to formulate a regional strategy, that effort was unsuccessful. However, the USMCA offers an institutional framework to create a path towards decarbonizing the North American Free Trade Area. The disparity between Mexico's environmental policies and those of its trading partners not only distorts the functioning of the free trade zone but also stands in the way of a regional zero emissions policy. The recent request for consultations filed by the United States and Canada against Mexico for considering that some of its energy policies violate the USMCA rules illustrates this distortion.

Given that in the USMCA system, there is no supranational authority that defines the basic guidelines that should guide national policies, and given the soft law nature of the most relevant provisions of the Paris Agreement, the 2030 Agenda, and the Net Zero Initiative, there is a need for a clear and innovative roadmap to drive regional solidarity. A way forward for decarbonizing natural resource supply value chains and advancing regional solidarity for net zero in the North American region could be the signing of a side agreement to the USMCA on zero emissions. Such an agreement must rely on the principle of climate solidarity as discussed in Chapter 2 of this book, by simplifying the exchange of technologies, best practices, and resources needed to accelerate the clean energy transition at a coherent pace across the three countries.

19

Mitigating Damages in Net Zero Energy Transitions through Investment Treaty and Market Reforms

Anatole Boute and Sara Soini

I. Introduction

This chapter examines how international solidarity and cooperation on the reform of investment treaties relating to the utilization of non-renewable natural resources, and the regulation of energy markets, could help mitigate the wide range of sovereignty, security, and justice risks of net zero and the clean energy transition.

The net zero transition in the energy sector requires keeping fossil energy resources in the ground and closing down existing fossil-based power plants.[1] In its Net Zero Roadmap for the Global Energy Sector, the International Energy Agency (IEA) considers that, from 2021, there shall be 'no new unabated coal plants approved for development [and] no new oil and gas fields approved for development; no new coal mines or mine extensions'.[2] Unabated coal-fired power plants shall be phased out in advanced economies by 2030, and elsewhere by 2040.

As discussed in Chapter 1 of this book, a number of states have already imposed a ban on non-renewable natural resource projects such as the use of coal for power generation, although some states decided to postpone the closure of their coal-fired power plants in response to the disruption of Russian gas supplies to Europe in 2022. In parallel, certain governments have decided to halt exploration and production of oil and gas, cancelling existing oil and gas exploration and production licences.[3] Although necessary

[1] This chapter partly builds on Sara Soini and Anatole Boute, 'Coal Phase Out and Investment Law: Navigating the Arbitration Barrier through Market Forces' in Graham Butler and others (eds), *The EU Law of Investment: Past, Present, and Future* (Hart Publishing/Bloomsbury 2023) (forthcoming), Anatole Boute and Francine Hug, 'Coal Phase Out and Foreign Investment Protection: Tackling China's Global Carbon Footprint' (2024) Georgetown Environmental Law Review (forthcoming), and Anatole Boute, 'Investor Compensation for Oil and Gas Phase Out Decisions: Aligning Valuation Methods to Decarbonization' (2023) 23 Climate Policy 1087-1100; and benefitted from research funding by the HK Research Grants Council Project, General Research Fund project number 14609122.

[2] International Energy Agency (IEA), *Net Zero by 2050* (OECD, 2021) 20 <http://www.iea.org/reports/net-zero-by-2050> (all online sources last accessed on 30 May 2023). On the need 'to retire a large number of existing coal power plants early' to transition to net zero energy systems, see also, eg Paola A Yanguas Parra and others, 'Global and Regional Coal Phase-Out Requirements of the Paris Agreement: Insights from the IPCC Special Report on 1.5°C' (Climate Analytics, 2019) 22 <https://www.climateanalytics.org/media/report_coal_phase_out_2019.pdf>; Benjamin M Kefford and others, 'The Early Retirement Challenge for Fossil Fuel Power Plants in Deep Decarbonisation Scenarios' (2018) 119 Energy Policy 294.

[3] Felix Todd, 'Italy Oil and Gas Ban on Exploration Could Spark Legal Action, Says Analyst' (*NS Energy*, 6 March 2019) <https://www.nsenergybusiness.com/news/italy-oil-gas-ban/>; Agence France-Presse, 'France Bans Fracking and Oil Extraction In All of Its Territories' (*The Guardian*, 20 December 2017) <https://www.theguardian.com/environment/2017/dec/20/france-bans-fracking-and-oil-extraction-in-all-of-its-territories>; Jillian Ambrose, 'Denmark to End New Oil and Gas Exploration in North Sea' (*The Guardian*, 2020) <https://

Anatole Boute and Sara Soini, *Mitigating Damages in Net Zero Energy Transitions through Investment Treaty and Market Reforms* In: *Net Zero and Natural Resources Law.* Edited by: Damilola S. Olawuyi, José Juan González, Hanri Mostert, Milton Fernando Montoya, and Catherine Banet, Oxford University Press. © International Bar Association 2024. DOI: 10.1093/9780198925033.003.0019

for climate change mitigation purposes, decisions to cancel oil and gas licences to keep these resources in the ground and closing down fossil-based thermal power plants can conflict with states' obligations under international investment treaties, possibly resulting in damages to be paid to fossil investors. A central concern is whether states can 'discourage all further investments into fossil fuel', without violating their international obligations towards investors.[4] Banning the use and production of fossil fuels creates possible tensions with international investment protection, as fossil investments become so-called 'stranded assets' raising a wide range of justice concerns discussed in Chapter 3 of this book.[5] This chapter examines the threat that investment arbitration poses to such bans (or phase-out decisions) and critically discusses the need for reforms, based on international cooperation and solidarity, to mitigate the risk of damages associated with these decisions.

The constraints that investment arbitration imposes on states' right to implement ambitious environmental measures to transition to net zero energy systems are an increasingly sensitive issue, as highlighted by the criticism of international investment law. For instance, the European Parliament is 'alarmed by the thousands of existing Member State BITs which still protect fossil fuel investments' and the 'increasing number of legal proceedings before investment tribunals]that[target environmental measures'.[6] Similarly, according to the Intergovernmental Panel on Climate Change (IPCC), international investment agreements have 'constrain[ed] the latitude of host countries in adopting environmental policies'.[7] This criticism follows an increasingly important body of literature on the negative impact of international investment law on climate change mitigation, including the right of states to keep fossil energies in the ground and close down fossil-based power plants.[8] For instance, in their 2022 analysis of 'legal and financial risks associated with limiting oil and gas production', Tienhaara and others estimated that 'global

www.theguardian.com/business/2020/dec/04/denmark-to-end-new-oil-and-gas-exploration-in-north-sea>; Sophie Hirsh, 'Portugal Is No Longer Extracting Fossil Fuels After Canceling Two Remaining Contracts' (*Green Matters*, 24 September 2020) <https://www.greenmatters.com/p/portugal-fossil-fuel-contracts>.

[4] European Union (EU), *EU Text Proposal for the Modernization of the Energy Charter Treaty (ECT)* (2020) <https://trade.ec.europa.eu/doclib/docs/2020/may/tradoc_158754.pdf>.

[5] See also International Renewable Energy Agency (IRENA), 'Stranded Assets and Renewables: How the Energy Transition Affects the Value of Energy Reserves, Buildings and Capital Stock' (IRENA, 2017) 21 <https://www.irena.org/-/media/Files/IRENA/Agency/Publication/2017/Jul/IRENA_REmap_Stranded_assets_and_renewables_2017.pdf>, defining stranded assets in the power generation sector 'as fossil fuel power plants that call for closure before the end of their anticipated technical lifetimes'.

[6] European Parliament Resolution of 23 June 2022 on the Future of EU International Investment Policy (2021/2176(INI)) <https://www.europarl.europa.eu/doceo/document/TA-9-2022-0268_EN.html>. See also European Parliament Resolution of 24 November 2022 on the Outcome of the Modernization of the Energy Charter Treaty (2022/2934(RSP)) https://www.europarl.europa.eu/doceo/document/TA-9-2022-0421_EN.html ('at least 150 investment arbitration cases have been instituted under the ECT, one third of which relate to fossil fuel investments').

[7] Jim Skea and others, 'Climate Change 2022: Mitigation of Climate Change' (Intergovernmental Panel on Climate Change, 2022) <https://www.report.ipcc.ch/ar6/wg3/IPCC_AR6_WGIII_Full_Report.pdf>.

[8] Kyla Tienhaara and Lorenzo Cotula, 'Raising the Cost of Climate Action? Investor-state Dispute Settlement and Compensation for Stranded Fossil Fuel Assets' (International Institute for Environment and Development, 2020) <https://www.pubs.iied.org/17660iied>. According to van Asselt, 'the normative guidance from international investment law seems to hinder a transition away from fossil fuel production to achieve climate goals'. Harro van Asselt, 'Governing Fossil Fuel Production in the Age Of Climate Disruption: Towards an International Law of "Leaving it in the Ground"' (2021) 100 Earth System Governance 118.

action on climate change could generate upward of $340 billion in legal claims from oil and gas investors'.[9]

In the spirit of international solidarity and cooperation, states have sought to address these concerns by modernizing investment treaties to align them with the pressing necessity to adopt ambitious environmental measures and decarbonize energy systems. However, as illustrated by the criticism expressed against the modernization of the Energy Charter Treaty (ECT) and existing arbitral practice concerning environmental carve-outs, it is a complex task to balance international investment protection with states' right to close down fossil assets. The following analysis first introduces the risk of international liability and damages for ambitious net zero energy transition measures, before discussing how international cooperation on the reform of investment treaties impacting the utilization of non-renewable natural resources, and the regulation of energy markets, could help mitigate these risks.

II. Liability and Damages for Net Zero Policies

A. Liability

Natural resource investors affected by a ban on the production of fossil fuels or a prohibition on their use could challenge these decisions before international arbitration, for example under the expropriation and fair and equitable treatment standards.[10] Foreign investors in coal-fired power generation and fossil production have already initiated arbitration disputes against states' decisions requiring the closure of their assets.

Most notably, the German energy company RWE challenged the legality of the Dutch coal phase-out decision based on the ECT, arguing that its 'investments have been indirectly expropriated by the Coal Ban Law'.[11] By expressly 'forbidding to generate electricity in a production plant using coal', the Netherlands 'prohibited the very essence of Eemshaven's business activity (i.e. electricity generation by burning coal), depriving Claimants of the use of their aforementioned investments and destroying their value. Neither the permit nor the plant, its operating company or shares therein have any use or value for Claimants without the ability to burn coal.'[12]

The US coal company Westmoreland challenged the decision of the provincial government of Alberta (Canada) to phase out coal-fired power plants in the province by 2030

[9] Kyla Tienhaara and others, 'Investor-state Disputes Threaten the Global Green Energy Transition' (2022) 376 Science 701. More generally, see Kyla Tienhaara, *The Expropriation of Environmental Governance: Protecting Foreign Investors at the Expense of Public Policy* (CUP 2009) 3, arguing that 'It is evident that arbitrators have *expropriated* certain fundamental aspects of environmental governance from states. As a result, environmental regulation has become riskier, more expansive and less democratic, especially in developing countries.'

[10] eg it was foreseen that the Dutch coal utility-owners would resist closing their plants without compensation, 'given that they are still generating positive cash flows'. Gerard Wynn, 'The Dutch Coal Mistake' (IEEFA, 2016) 3 <https://www.ieefa.org/wp-content/uploads/2016/11/The-Dutch-Coal-Mistake_November-2016.pdf>.

[11] *RWE v Netherlands*, ICSID Case No ARB/21/4, Request for Arbitration (20 January 2021) <https://www.italaw.com/cases/9156>.

[12] ibid.

based on the investment regime of the North American Free Trade Agreement (NAFTA). The company alleged that it did not receive any 'compensation for damages caused by the accelerated Alberta coal phase-out, including stranded capital, loss of revenues, and accelerated costs of reclamation, the process of rehabilitating the land after coal mining operations have ceased'.[13]

Based on the ECT, the British company Rockhopper Exploration Plc brought arbitration proceedings against the decision by Italy to ban the exploration and exploitation of oil and gas within twelve miles of the Italian coastline. For the investor, the 'decision to deny Rockhopper Italia's Production Concession Application amounts to an expropriatory measure. With this decision, Rockhopper Italia no longer enjoyed the right—nor even the legitimate expectation—that it would be awarded the Production Concession to exploit the Ombrina Mare Field.'[14]

The RWE case before the ECT was discontinued.[15] In *Westmoreland v Canada*, the tribunal refused jurisdiction based on temporal grounds, but noted that 'given the increasing awareness of the negative environmental and human health impacts of coal combustion to produce electricity, governments around the world have increasingly been committed to reducing emissions from coal-fired electricity generation'.[16]

In *Rockhopper v Italy*, the tribunal accepted that the claimants had a right to be granted a production concession and that Italy's ban expropriated the claimants' investment by taking away this right.[17] More specifically, 'the Claimants went, in one fell swoop, from a position where they had rights to a valuable production concession which would actually lead, under Italian law, to such production concession, to essentially nothing at all. . . . There was, factually speaking, an immediate and complete deprivation of the Claimants' investment.'[18]

These decisions have further fuelled the criticism against the ECT, and investment law more generally, as obstacle to the net zero transition.[19]

B. Damages

With few exceptions (eg the 1977 *Texaco* decision in which the Libyan government was directed to restore Texaco's rights after the nationalization of its concession),[20] tribunals have generally refrained from ordering the restitution in kind of an investment in the production of fossil fuels as this would contradict the state's permanent

[13] *Westmoreland Mining Holdings, LLC v Canada*, ICSID Case No UNCT/20/3 <https://www.italaw.com/cases/7002>.

[14] *Rockhopper Italia S.p.A., Rockhopper Mediterranean Ltd, and Rockhopper Exploration Plc v Italian Republic*, ICSID Case No ARB/17/14, Final Award (23 August 2022) (hereafter *Rockhopper*) <https://www.italaw.com/cases/5788>.

[15] See *RWE AG and RWE Eemshaven Holding II BV v Kingdom of the Netherlands*, ICSID Case No ARB/21/4 <https://www.italaw.com/cases/9156>.

[16] *Westmoreland Mining Holdings, LLC v Canada*, Final Award (31 January 2022), para 73.

[17] *Rockhopper* (n 14) paras 193–94.

[18] ibid para 194.

[19] 'Outrage as Italy Ordered to Pay Out Millions to Oil Investor Over Energy Charter Treaty Claim' (Press Release, Climate Action Network, 2022) <https://caneurope.org/outrage-as-italy-ordered-to-pay-out-millions-to-oil-investor-over-energy-charter-treaty-claim/>.

[20] *Texaco Overseas Petroleum Company and California Asiatic Oil Company v Libya*, Award on the Merits (19 January 1977) (1979) 53 International Law Reports 389.

sovereignty. According to the *BP v Libya* decision, 'in matters of essentially economic significance', the principal remedy under international law is financial compensation.[21] The physical reinstatement of the investor into the position it occupied before nationalization is only relevant as a possible reference point for the calculation of the amount of damages.

In *Libyan American Oil Company (LIAMCO) v Libya*, the tribunal recognized Libya's sovereignty over oil and its right to nationalize oil assets, but awarded compensation to the investor including 'equitable compensation' for the loss of its concession rights.[22] In the *American Independent Oil Company (Aminoil) v Kuwait* decision, the majority of the tribunal accepted that the expropriation was lawful but nonetheless integrated lost profits in its valuation of damages.[23]

Arbitration tribunals commonly use the Discounted Cash Flow (DCF) method to calculate damages in cases concerning the expropriation of fossil fuel production assets.[24] In particular, tribunals determine future revenues based on the volume and production profile of the projects and forecasted oil prices, adjusted to costs and discount rate.[25] For instance, in *ConocoPhillips Petrozuata, ConocoPhillips Hamaca and ConocoPhillips Gulf of Paria v Venezuela*, the tribunal determined the estimated production volumes over a period of about twenty years, taking into account the actual production profile, the possible use of new extraction techniques, and the possibility of repairing and adding wells. As for the price of oil, the tribunal used actual sales prices for production prior to the award, and average market prices for 2020 with an increase of 1.2 per cent per year for future production.[26] In *Venezuela Holdings, B.V., et al v Venezuela*, the tribunal held that nationalization was lawful, as Venezuela made the investors proposals for compensation.[27] For one oil production asset, the tribunal limited compensation to the documented value of the claimants' actual investment. As the project was at an early stage of development when it was expropriated, using the DCF method would have been inappropriate.[28] For another asset,

[21] *BP Exploration Company Limited v Libya*, Award (10 October 1973) (1979) 53 International Law Reports 297, 375.

[22] *Libyan American Oil Company (Liamco) v Government of the Libyan Arab Republic* (1982) 62 International Law Reports 141.

[23] *American Independent Oil Company (Aminoil) v Kuwait*, Award (24 March 1982), (1982) 21 ILM 976.

[24] Darrell Chodorow, Florin Dorobantu, and Fernando Bañez, 'Quantum in Oil and Gas and Mining Disputes' (2022) Global Arbitration Review <https://globalarbitrationreview.com/guide/the-guide-damages-in-international-arbitration/5th-edition/article/quantum-in-oil-and-gas-and-mining-disputes>. On damages calculation more generally, see eg I Marboe, *Calculation of Compensation and Damages in International Investment Law* (OUP 2017).

[25] *ConocoPhillips Petrozuata, ConocoPhillips Hamaca and ConocoPhillips Gulf of Paria v Venezuela*, ICSID Case No ARB/07/30, Award (8 March 2019) <https://www.italaw.com/cases/321>. On the breach of the expropriation standard by Venezuela, see *ConocoPhillips Petrozuata, ConocoPhillips Hamaca and ConocoPhillips Gulf of Paria v Venezuela*, ICSID Case No ARB/07/30, Decision on Jurisdiction and Merits (3 September 2013) <https://www.italaw.com/cases/321>.

[26] Gregg Coughlin, 'ICSID Tribunal Awards Conocophillips USD 8.7 Billion Plus Interest in Dispute with Venezuela' (*Investment Treaty News*, 23 April 2019) <https://www.iisd.org/itn/en/2019/04/23/icsid-tribunal-awards-conocophillips-usd-8-7-billion-plus-interest-dispute-venezuela-gregg-coughlin/>.

[27] *Venezuela Holdings, B.V., et al (case formerly known as Mobil Corporation, Venezuela Holdings, B.V., et al) v Bolivarian Republic of Venezuela*, ICSID Case No ARB/07/27, Award (9 October 2014) <https://www.italaw.com/cases/713>.

[28] Matthew Weiniger QC and Florencia Villaggi, 'Exxon Mobil is Awarded US$1.6 Billion in ICSID Claim Against Venezuela—to Be Set off Against Award in Parallel Contractual Arbitration' (Herbert Smith Freehills, 16 October 2014) <https://www.hsfnotes.com/arbitration/2014/10/16/exxon-mobil-is-awarded-us1-6-billion-in-icsid-claim-against-venezuela-to-be-set-off-against-award-in-parallel-contractual-arbitration/>.

the tribunal assessed the net revenues expected to be generated until September 2035 in accordance with the DCF method. In determining the expected production volume after expropriation, the tribunal relied on past production levels, and rejected the claimants' plans of production expansion that still required authorization.

The DCF method has also been used in cases concerning electricity production. For instance, in *Total v Argentina*, the tribunal ruled that Argentina breached the fair and equitable treatment standard by keeping electricity prices below the investor's operating costs,[29] and assessed damages by 'comparing the "actual scenario" (the present value of future cash flows/earnings taking into account the impact that Argentina's measures in breach of the BIT have had on Total's investments) and the "but-for" counterfactual scenario (in the absence of breaches)'.[30] To estimate the cash flows that the investment would have obtained under the 'but-for scenario' and ultimately determine the generators' 'but-for value', the tribunal took into account the specific prices that the investor would have obtained without the changes made to the pricing regime, the quantity of electricity that the generators would have dispatched, figures for but-for revenues, which are obtained by applying the prices to the quantities, and discounting to obtain the but-for fair market value of the generators.[31] If tribunals decide that coal phase-out decisions amount to an expropriation or unfair and inequitable treatment, damages are likely to be calculated following a similar DCF approach. The high damages resulting from the application of this valuation method to fossil investors could dissuade states from requiring the closure of their fossil fuel and carbon-intensive assets.[32]

C. Environmental Considerations in Damages Decisions

Integrating environmental considerations into the assessment of environmental measures under the substantive investment protection standards and in the calculation of damages is a contentious issue. Tribunals have recognized the 'police powers' of the host states and thus their right to regulate in the public interest, including environmental protection.[33] The right of host states to regulate can justify state measures even if these measures may jeopardize the economic viability of an investment.[34] However, '[t]here must be a reasonable relationship of proportionality between the charge or weight imposed on the foreign investor

[29] See eg Anatole Boute, 'Challenging the Re-regulation of Liberalized Electricity Prices under Investment Arbitration' (2011) 32 Energy Law Journal 497.

[30] *Total S.A. v Argentina*, ICSID Case No ARB/04/1, Award (27 November 2013) <https://www.italaw.com/cases/1105>.

[31] ibid para 141.

[32] Kyla Tienhaara and others, 'Investor-state Dispute Settlement: Obstructing a Just Energy Transition' (2022) Climate Policy 10.1080/14693062.2022.2153102.

[33] *Saluka Investments BV v The Czech Republic*, UNCITRAL, Partial Award (17 March 2006), para 255; *Methanex Corporation v the United States*, UNCITRAL, Award (7 August 2005), part IV, Chapter D, para 7 ('[a]s a matter of general international law, a non-discriminatory regulation for a public purpose, which is enacted in accordance with due process and, which affects, inter alios, a foreign investor or investment is not deemed expropriatory and compensable unless specific commitments had been given by the regulating government to the then putative foreign investor contemplating investment that the government would refrain from such regulation'). See also Walid Ben Hamida, 'La prise en compte de l'intérêt général et des impératifs de développement dans le droit des investissements' (2008) 135 Journal du Droit International: Clunet 999.

[34] *Marvin Roy Feldman Karpa v United Mexican States*, ICSID Case No ARB(AF)/99/1, Award on Merits (16 December 2002), para 112 <https://www.italaw.com/cases/435>.

and the aim sought to be realized by any expropriatory measure'.[35] As argued by Wälde and Kolo, 'in the extreme case of complete and indefinite destruction of the economic value of property by otherwise fully legitimate regulation, and if individuals are required by regulation to make a special sacrifice in terms of their proprietary rights for the benefit of the society at large, compensation is also owed'.[36]

With regard to the integration of environmental considerations into the assessment of damages due for expropriations, certain tribunals have accepted a reduction in damages by taking into account the host state's international obligations to implement certain conservation measures.[37] However, other arbitral tribunals have refused to reduce damages based on the environmental purpose of the measures taken. In *Santa Elena v Costa Rica*, a case concerning the expropriation of land to expand a natural park, the tribunal stated that:

> While an expropriation or taking for environmental reasons may be classified as a taking for a public purpose, and thus may be legitimate, the fact that the Property was taken for this reason does not affect either the nature or the measure of the compensation to be paid for the taking. That is, the purpose of protecting the environment for which the Property was taken does not alter the legal character of the taking for which adequate compensation must be paid. The international source of the obligation to protect the environment makes no difference. Expropriatory environmental measures—no matter how laudable and beneficial to society as a whole—are, in this respect, similar to any other expropriatory measures that a state may take in order to implement its policies: where property is expropriated, even for environmental purposes, whether domestic or international, the state's obligation to pay compensation remains.[38]

To summarize, arbitral tribunals could find phase-out decisions to amount to expropriation if they consider that these measures destroyed the economic value of the investment. The calculation of damages, for example based on the DCF method, that by far exceed the initial investment cost of these fossil assets has exacerbated the criticism of international investment law as an obstacle to the net zero transition.[39]

III. Mitigating Damages for Net Zero Policies through International Cooperation

As discussed in Chapter 1 of this book, international cooperation and solidarity are essential to facilitate the implementation of strategies to transition away from fossil fuels. According to the Production Gap Report:

[35] *Tecnicas Medioambientales Tecmed S.A. v The United Mexican States*, ICSID Case No ARB(AF)/00/2, Award (29 May 2003), para 122 <https://www.italaw.com/cases/1105>. See also *LG&E Energy Corp., LG&E Capital Corp., and LG&E International, Inc. v Argentine Republic*, ICSID Case No ARB/02/1, Decision on Liability (3 October 2006), para 195 <https://www.italaw.com/cases/621>; and *Azurix Corp v Argentine Republic*, ICSID Case No ARB/01/12, Award (14 July 2006), paras 311–12 <https://www.italaw.com/cases/118>.

[36] See eg Thomas Wälde and Abba Kolo, 'Environmental Regulation, Investment Protection and "Regulatory Taking" in International Law' (2001) 50 International and Comparative Law Quarterly 811, 846.

[37] *Southern Pacific Properties (Middle East) Limited v Arab Republic of Egypt*, ICSID Case No ARB/84/3, Award (20 May 1992) <https://www.italaw.com/cases/3300>.

[38] *Compañia del Desarrollo de Santa Elena S.A. v Republic of Costa Rica*, ICSID Case No ARB/96/1, Final Award (17 February 2000), paras 71–72 <https://www.italaw.com/cases/3413>.

[39] See eg European Parliament Resolution of 24 November 2022 on the Outcome of the Modernization of the Energy Charter Treaty (2022/2934(RSP)). See also Climate Action Network, 2022 (n 19).

> [I]nternational cooperation can support a more effective and equitable transition away from fossil fuels. Through international processes such as the UNFCCC [United Nations Framework Convention on Climate Change], governments can enhance transparency and ambition by communicating plans to align their fossil fuel production and climate goals, including through their NDCs [Nationally Determined Contributions] and long-term low emissions development strategies under the Paris Agreement. . . . Through international cooperation, countries can also seek to ensure that declines in fossil fuel production are distributed as equitably as possible, while minimizing the risks of disruption and maximizing the participation of affected stakeholders.[40]

In the same vein, Piggot and others argue that 'international cooperation can strengthen the effectiveness of supply-side approaches to limit fossil fuel production'.[41] In particular, international cooperation can increase the confidence of states that others are taking action, reduce the risk of carbon leakage, and 'send an important signal to policymakers, investors, companies, consumers and civil society, that the world is moving beyond a fossil fuel economy'.[42]

Similarly, international cooperation and solidarity to modernize investment law is needed to address the obstacles posed by investment treaties to the closure of fossil assets. These reforms can consist in environmental carve-outs, climate-friendly damages methods, and the use of market-based approaches to the phasing out of fossil investments.

A. Environmental Carve-outs and Phase-out Decisions

International cooperation on the conclusion of new investment treaties and the modernization of existing agreements has resulted in the inclusion of safeguards aimed at protecting states' right to adopt environmental protection measures. For instance, treaties can clarify that:

> Except in rare circumstances, such as when a measure or series of measures is so severe in the light of its purpose that it cannot be reasonably viewed as having been adopted in good faith, non-discriminatory measures by a Party that are designed and applied to protect legitimate public welfare objectives, for example health, safety and the protection of the environment, do not constitute indirect expropriation.[43]

Furthermore, treaties can include environmental exceptions, similar to the general exception of the General Agreement on Trade and Tariffs (GATT). For instance, article 2201(3) of the Canada–Colombia Free Trade Agreement (FTA) provides that:

> subject to the requirement that such measures are not applied in a manner that constitute arbitrary or unjustifiable discrimination between investment or between investors, or a

[40] SEI, IISD, ODI, E3G, and UNEP, 'The Production Gap Report 2021' <http://www.productiongap.org/2021report>.

[41] Georgia Piggot and others, 'Curbing Fossil Fuel Supply to Achieve Climate Goals' (2020) 20 Climate Policy 881.

[42] ibid.

[43] See eg Free Trade Agreement between Canada and the Republic of Colombia (signed 21 November 2008, entered into force 15 August 2011) (Canada–Colombia FTA), annex 811(2)(b).

disguised restriction on international trade or investment, nothing in this Agreement shall be construed to prevent a Party from adopting or enforcing measures necessary:

(a) To protect human, animal or plant life or health, which the Parties understand to include environmental measures necessary to protect human, animal or plant life and health;
(b) To ensure compliance with laws and regulations that are not inconsistent with this Agreement; or
(c) For the conservation of living or non-living exhaustible natural resources.[44]

However, there is a risk of narrow interpretation of these provisions. In *Eco Oro v Colombia*, the tribunal held (by majority) that Colombia's decision to prohibit mining activities in an environmentally sensitive area did not amount to an indirect expropriation as it constituted a legitimate and good faith exercise of police powers.[45] However, the tribunal ruled (by majority) that Colombia breached the minimum standard of treatment (MST) and decided that the environmental exception did not stand in the way of damages. More specifically, the tribunal construed the environmental exception (ie art 2201(3) Canada–Colombia FTA) 'such that whilst a State may adopt or enforce a measure pursuant to the stated objectives in Article 2201(3) without finding itself in breach of the FTA, this does not prevent an investor claiming under Chapter Eight that such a measure entitles it to the payment of compensation.'[46]

The *Eco Oro* decision showed that 'the deliberate inclusion by treaty drafters of express treaty language to balance States' environmental obligations with the rights of foreign investors does not appear to have brought the desired clarity or outcomes. The majority's finding on MST and on the duty to pay compensation circumvented the stated intention of the treaty parties to protect State discretion in environmental matters and exclude the duty to pay compensation in the exercise of such discretion.'[47] Similarly, there is a risk that the inclusion of an environmental exception in investment treaties would not suffice to shield host states against the risk of important damages to investors for decarbonization measures in the net zero energy transition. Considering the risk of narrow interpretation of environmental exceptions, it is necessary to draft environmental exceptions in a way that specifically excludes the obligation to pay compensation for phase-out decisions.[48]

B. Carving out Fossil Assets from Investment Protection

Besides reinforcing states' right to regulate, negotiations on the modernization of the ECT resulted in a 'flexibility mechanism' that would allow contracting parties 'to exclude

[44] ibid art 2201.

[45] *Eco Oro Minerals Corp v Republic of Colombia*, ICSID Case No ARB/16/41, Decision on Jurisdiction, Liability and Directions on Quantum (9 September 2021), paras 629–99 <https://www.italaw.com/cases/6320>.

[46] ibid para 830.

[47] Robert Garden, 'Eco Oro v Colombia: The Brave New World of Environmental Exceptions' (2023) 38 ICSID Review—Foreign Investment Law Journal 17, 24.

[48] See eg ibid 23, arguing that 'certain solutions that may be offered by treaty drafters may include expressly stipulating in treaties, such as in the Morocco Model Bilateral Investment Treaty, that an exception excludes the duty to pay compensation if it applies, or even expressly providing in interpretative language that a tribunal shall find the exception applies if seized with a dispute'. See also the proposal by Joshua Paine and Elizabeth Sheargold, 'A Climate Change Carve-Out for Investment Treaties' (2023) 26 Journal of International Economic Law 285.

investment protection for fossil fuels in their territories, considering their individual energy security and climate goals'.[49] In host states that would activate this flexibility mechanism, the carve-out of fossil fuel-related investments from investment protection under the ECT would apply to 'existing investments after 10 years from the entry into force of the relevant provisions and for new investments made after 15 August 2023 as of that date with limited exceptions'. Thus, after ten years, states hosting foreign investments in fossil fuel could phase out these investments without risking arbitration proceedings under the ECT.

For the EU and an increasing number of its Member States, this carve-out mechanism was not satisfactory. In its Resolution of 23 June 2022 on the Future of EU International Investment Policy, the Parliament had called upon the Commission and the Member States 'to ensure consistency between IIAs and the European Green Deal, ... by excluding from treaty protection investments in fossil fuels'.[50] However, the continued protection of existing fossil fuel investments for ten more years after the entry into force of the modernized ECT was seen as insufficient to align the Treaty to the EU carbon neutrality targets.[51] Instead, the ECT should 'immediately prohibit fossil fuel investors from suing contracting parties for pursuing policies to phase out fossil fuels in line with their commitments under the Paris Agreement'.[52] However, as a result of failure to find such consensus among the contracting parties at the Energy Charter Conference meeting of 22 November 2022, the modernization package was not adopted and ultimately taken off the agenda, leaving the unmodernized ECT to apply. In response, the EU Commission proposes, as 'the only available solution', a Council decision withdrawing the EU from the ECT, as 'the protection granted to fossil fuels ... does not fit with EU objectives as defined in the European Green Deal, the REPowerEU Plan or the Climate Law'.[53]

C. Climate-Friendly Damages Methods

The modernization of the ECT did not include the alignment of damages calculation methods to decarbonization. For instance, the European Parliament 'regret[ted] that the modernised ECT fails to address the critical issue of valuation techniques, enabling awards of compensation that vastly outweigh the amounts invested' and 'note[d] that these methods are highly controversial owing to their very wide margin of discretion and reliance on highly complex and inherently speculative assumptions'.[54]

[49] Decision of the Energy Charter Conference, Public Communication Explaining the Main Changes Contained in the Agreement in Principle, Doc CCDEC 2022(24 June 2022) <https://www.energycharter.org/fileadmin/DocumentsMedia/CCDECS/2022/CCDEC202210.pdf>.

[50] European Parliament Resolution of 23 June 2022 on the Future of EU International Investment Policy (2021/2176(INI)) <https://www.europarl.europa.eu/doceo/document/TA-9-2022-0268_EN.html>.

[51] See eg European Parliament Resolution of 24 November 2022 on the Outcome of the Modernization of the Energy Charter Treaty (2022/2934(RSP)), expressing concern that the ten-year period by which all investments in fossil fuels will no longer be protected if the parties activate the carve-out, 'is at odds with current knowledge on the speed of fossil fuel phase-out needed to limit global warming to 1.5°C above pre-industrial levels and that it will undermine the EU's climate objectives'.

[52] ibid.

[53] European Commission Proposal of 7 July 2023 on the withdrawal of the Union from the Energy Charter Treaty (2023/0273 (NLE)).

[54] ibid.

Reforms of international investment treaties can help align damages calculations to the net zero transition.[55] In particular, modernized investment treaties should require tribunals, in their damages calculation, to take into account the contribution of a state measure to the achievement by the state of its decarbonization commitments under the Paris Agreement.[56] This reform would avoid tribunals ignoring the environmental nature of a phase-out decision, as has been the case in previous damages decisions.[57] Furthermore, states can reform their investment treaties to explicitly require tribunals to take into account the polluter-pays principle in their damages calculation.[58]

Modernized damages provisions could also require tribunals to factor in the discount rate the significant regulatory and market risks that fossil assets face in the net zero transition. The net zero transition requires ambitious regulatory measures, for example phase-out decisions, carbon pricing, emission limits, and technology requirements, that are likely to severely impact on the use and production of fossil fuels. Besides a drop in the price of oil as a result of the decarbonization of the energy supply,[59] the increased competitiveness of renewable energy is expected to gradually push coal power out of the market and thus undermine its future profitability.

D. Market-Based Phase-out

Besides reforming investment treaties, states can implement regulatory reforms to gradually phase out fossil assets through market forces.[60] The EU for instance relies on market instruments to move away from fossil fuels in the electricity sector and phase out coal power. In addition to the impact of strict emission standards on the decommissioning of older coal-fired power plants,[61] the tightening of the cap under the Emissions Trading System and the

[55] Anatole Boute, 'Investor Compensation for Oil and Gas Phase Out Decisions: Aligning Damages with Decarbonization' (2023) 23 Climate Policy 1087–1100.

[56] It must be noted that, according to European Parliament Resolution of 24 November 2022 on the Outcome of the Modernization of the Energy Charter Treaty (2022/2934(RSP)) 'proposed changes to provisions on damages awards would have little impact, as arbitrators tend to interpret the concept of 'loss' very broadly, including expected future profits'.

[57] See eg *Santa Elena v Costa Rica* (n 38). For an analysis of the relevant arbitral practice, see Jorge E Viñuales, *Foreign Investment and the Environment in International Law* (CUP 2012).

[58] See eg Kyla Tienhaara, Lise Johnson, and Michael Burger, 'Valuing Fossil Fuel Assets in an Era of Climate Disruption' (*Investment Treaty News*, 20 June 2020) <https://www.iisd.org/itn/en/2020/06/20/valuing-fossil-fuel-assets-in-an-era-of-climate-disruption/> proposing to adjust damages calculation by using the 'social cost of carbon'.

[59] IEA (n 2).

[60] See Chapters 16 and 17 of this book. See also Anatole Boute, 'Phasing Out Coal Through Electricity Market Regulation' (2022) 59 Common Market Law Review 1007.

[61] Directive 2001/80/EC on the limitation of emissions of certain pollutants into the air from large combustion plants [2001] OJ L 309/1, replaced by Directive 2010/75/EU on industrial emissions (integrated pollution prevention and control) [2010] OJ L 334/17. On the impact of these emission standards on the closure of coal power in the EU, see eg Gerrit Rentier and others, 'Varieties of Coal-Fired Power Phase-Out Across Europe' (2019) 132 Energy Policy 623; Hannah Schindler, 'Managing the phase-out of Coal—A comparison of Actions in G20 countries' (Climate Transparency, 2019) 5 <https://www.climate-transparency.org/wp-content/uploads/2019/05/Managing-the-phase-out-of-coal-DIGITAL.pdf>; Sylvie Cornot-Gandolphe, 'The European Coal Market: Will Coal Survive the EC's Energy and Climate Policies' (Institut français des relations internationals, 2012) 35 <https://www.ifri.org/sites/default/files/atoms/files/noteenergiescornotgandolphe.pdf>; Maciej M Sokołowski, 'Burning out Coal Power Plants with the Industrial Emissions Directive' (2018) 11 Journal of World Energy Law & Business 260, 260.

introduction of a Market Stability Reserve increase the cost of fossil-based electricity generation, gradually pushing these facilities out of the market.

Under the 2019 Electricity Directive and Regulation, market forces are supposed to drive the exit of fossil generators from the market, and thus lead to their eventual decommissioning.[62] Furthermore, by adding low-carbon production capacity to the system, the EU Renewable Energy Directive indirectly contributes to undermining the profitability of fossil-based assets.[63] The Renewable Energy Directive explicitly encourages the deployment of renewable energy for heating and cooling, and electricity supply, to replace fossil fuels.[64] The EU market-based approach was effective in facilitating the market exit of coal power until the 2021–2022 energy crisis.[65] In 2020, Europe was 'phasing out coal sooner than initially expected'.[66]

The market-based approach to the phasing out of fossil-based assets thus provides a less intrusive alternative to regulatory phase-out decisions, limiting the risk of breaching international investment protection standards.[67] By reducing the profitability of fossil assets, market-based reforms can also contribute to limiting damages due in case of regulatory phase-out. As fossil assets are expected to be gradually driven out of the market, tribunals must factor in a drop in their future cash flows and possibly a shorter operating lifetime.

IV. Reforming Natural Resources Law and Policy to Mitigate Investment Risks: Recommendations

International cooperation and solidarity are required to better align international investment treaties with global objectives on net zero and the clean energy transition. First, the urgency to phase out fossil fuels must be reflected in the limitations set on their protection by excluding all fossil investments from the international investment protection regime. Second, through environmental carve-outs, modernized investment treaties should explicitly recognize the right of states to adopt phase-out decisions, and specifically exempt them from the obligation to pay compensation for these decisions. These reforms are needed to

[62] See eg Directive (EU) 2019/944 on common rules for the internal market in electricity [2019] OJ L 158/125 (EMD), art 3: Member States shall ensure that 'no undue barriers exist within the internal market for electricity as regards market entry, operation and exit'; and Regulation (EU) 2019/943 of the European Parliament and of the Council of 5 June 2019 on the internal market for electricity [2019] OJ L 158/54 (EMR), art 3(n).

[63] Directive (EU) 2018/2001 on the promotion of the use of energy from renewable sources [2018] OJ L 328/82 (RED II), Recital 14.

[64] RED II, art 15(6). The Commission defines 'technology lock-in' as 'where the approach focused on energy efficiency only triggers fossil fuel technologies being replaced by more efficient but still fossil fuel solutions'. European Commission, Proposal for a Directive on the promotion of the use of energy from renewable sources (recast) COM(2016) 767 final/2, 15.

[65] Johanna Lehne and others, 'The EU ETS: From Cornerstone to Catalyst—The Role of Carbon Pricing in Driving Green Innovation' (E3G and Jacques Delors Institute, 2021) 10 <https://institutdelors.eu/wp-content/uploads/dlm_uploads/2021/04/JDI-E3G-paper_innovation-in-the-ETS_final.pdf>.

[66] European Commission Communication, 'An EU-wide assessment of national energy and climate plans', 17 September 2020, COM(2020)564 final, 14 and 26.

[67] Soini and Boute (n 1); Boute (n 60) 1007.

address the risk of investor compensation for the phasing out of fossil assets before the end of their economic life.

Moreover, the high regulatory and market risks that fossil investments face in the transition to net zero emissions must be reflected in the valuation of these assets according to the DCF method commonly used in energy cases. Investment treaty provisions setting out the compensation methods should be modernized to explicitly include environmental considerations, including by requiring tribunals to (1) factor in the contribution of a state measure to the achievement by the state of its decarbonization commitments, (2) take into account the polluter-pays principle, and (3) factor in the discount rate of the regulatory and market risks that fossil assets are currently facing in the net zero transition.

In parallel, market-based reforms, aimed at reducing the profitability of fossil assets, should be adopted in the energy sector in order to reduce the possible damages due when fossil assets are required to close down. As renewable energy becomes increasingly competitive and gradually pushes traditional energy sources out of the market, the damages due to fossil investments must be reduced to reflect the fundamental market and regulatory changes that characterize the decarbonization of energy systems. Such reforms, apart from promoting renewable energies, include, for example, removing any remaining fossil fuel subsidies, price distortions, and barriers to exit.[68]

V. Conclusion

In light of the risk of damages claims initiated by investors in case of the forced closure of their fossil assets, international investment law is increasingly criticized as an obstacle to the net zero energy transition. As coal power plants have to be closed by 2030 in developed economies and 2040 elsewhere, and fossil fuels have to remain in the ground, the net zero transition requires safeguarding states' right to adopt ambitious phase-out decisions without payment of significant damages to investors. In the spirit of international cooperation and solidarity, reforms of international investment treaties are needed to mitigate the risks that investment arbitration poses for states that adopt and implement ambitious decarbonization measures in the net zero energy transition.

As pointed out by the critics of the modernized ECT, a fossil carve-out must apply as soon as possible. Another aspect that was not taken into account in the modernization of the ECT was the integration of environmental considerations into the calculation of damages, which could have helped reduce the damages risks for states adopting ambitious decarbonization measures.

In addition to investment-treaty reforms, certain market-based reforms in the energy sector can contribute to reducing the damages due in case fossil assets are required to close down. Investment-treaty and market-based reforms can help states limit the

[68] Soini and Boute (n 1).

risk of damages due for closing down fossil assets and keeping their fossil fuels in the ground, without terminating or withdrawing from investment treaties that have a role to play in de-risking the clean energy investments needed to transition to net zero emissions.[69]

[69] See Chapters 16, 17, and 18 of this book; also Anatole Boute, 'Combating Climate Change through Investment Arbitration' (2011) 35 Fordham International Law Journal 613; Anatole Boute, 'Energy Justice in Times of Crisis: Protection of Consumers and Market-based Renewable Energy Investments' (2023) 26 Journal of International Economic Law 770. See also Markus Gehring and Marios Tokas, 'Synergies and Approaches to Climate Change in International Investment Agreements' (2022) 23 The Journal of World Investment & Trade 778, 808; though note Kyla Tienhaara, 'Regulatory Chill in a Warming World' (2018) 7 Transnational Environmental Law 229.

20

Power Politics

American Law and the Challenges of Promoting Solidarity for Net Zero

Donald Zillman and Anthony Moffa

I. Introduction

The United States has a significant role to play in promoting global solidarity for net zero and the clean energy transition. As indicated in Chapter 1 of this book, several of the justice, security, and sovereignty challenges to net zero cannot be addressed in isolation. Natural resources law therefore emphasizes the continued importance of, and need for, solidarity and cooperation in advancing clean energy transition at domestic, regional, and global levels. Furthermore, current geopolitics suggests that other countries, particularly in Europe, take cues from US energy policy.[1] Russia's attempted invasion of Ukraine has only accelerated that dynamic of policy transfusion. How, and how fast, societies transition to renewable sources of energy are vital policy questions with a wide range of answers. How the United States responds to those queries unfortunately depends on much more than scientific and economic realities.

The choices made by the US government will be shaped by the American legal structure and, perhaps even more so, by the American political process. The last half dozen years have been marked by unprecedented division in American political leadership with climate change being among the issues dividing the two major political parties—Democrats and Republicans.[2] This chapter introduces readers unfamiliar with American law, government, and politics to those subjects. It highlights the role lawyers, as dealmaking law-makers and practitioners, play in designing, advancing, and implementing the net zero initiatives that have broken through, and will break through, the political logjam.

The chapter focuses on the national (federal) government as the most prominent hope for effective net zero law and policy in the United States. However, it is not the only influential body that will define the United States' role in net zero and climate change decisions. State (eg California and Texas) and local (eg New York City, Miami) governments have important governmental roles to play,[3] as do small and large private businesses and the wide

[1] See Luke Murphy. 'Winning the global green race: lessons for the UK from the US' Inflation Reduction Act' Institute for Public Policy Research (IPPR) (*JSTOR*, 2023) <http://www.jstor.org/stable/resrep48469> accessed 7 August 2023; Carlos Pascual, 'The new geopolitics of energy' The Center on Global Energy Policy (CGEP) (Columbia University School of International and Public Affairs (SIPA), 2015).

[2] Drew Desilver, 'The polarization in today's Congress has roots that go back decades' (Pew Research Center, 10 March 2022) <https://www.perma.cc/2N9W-U4JZ> (describing 'a Pew Research Center analysis [which] finds that, on average, Democrats and Republicans are farther apart ideologically today than at any time in the past 50 years').

[3] See generally Anthony Moffa, 'Uniform Climate Control' (2020) 54 University of Richmond Law Review 993.

Donald Zillman and Anthony Moffa, *Power Politics* In: *Net Zero and Natural Resources Law.* Edited by: Damilola S. Olawuyi, José Juan González, Hanri Mostert, Milton Fernando Montoya, and Catherine Banet, Oxford University Press.
 DOI: 10.1093/9780198925033.003.0020

variety of private non-governmental organizations (NGOs).[4] We limit our examination here to the national government of the United States, recognizing its primary or exclusive role in such matters as international relations, regulation of business and environmental matters between states, and the funding of massive expenses to address many net zero and climate change issues.

The hyper-partisan political environment from which net zero policy must emerge is not unique to the United States. Thus, the lessons of the US policy-making process can and must be heeded by governments across the world. If any meaningful net zero energy transition is to take place on a global scale, it will require solidarity between vastly different political parties, ideologies, governance structures, and cultures. Focus needs to shift from bickering over areas of disagreement across a wide variety of issues to searching for areas of consensus on the most urgent issue—climate change. As the US experience has revealed, possibilities exist for meaningful steps towards net zero that enjoy widespread popular support and look like consensus. This chapter attempts to demonstrate how that policy came to be, how it functions (at least in its infancy), and how other countries might learn from the US experience.

The chapter proceeds in four remaining sections. Section II begins by defining the sources of American law that affect, directly and indirectly, net zero policies in the United States. Following that table setting, the chapter examines how polarized politics have infected the law-making process and made straightforward net zero policy challenging to enact. Section III provides a brief, but useful, guide to the laws and regulations that emerged as a result of abandonment of, and attempts at, consensus-building. The final section (Section IV) extrapolates some lessons learned for national and international lawmakers trying to address the urgent need to advance net zero with solidarity between with feuding political factions.

II. Sources of American Law on Net Zero

A. The US Constitution

The US Constitution defines American national government and the people and institutions that control efforts to reach net zero. The Constitution was drafted in 1787, shortly after the Revolutionary War had gained American independence from Great Britain. It both structured a national government and placed limits on that national government that preserved rights of states (formerly colonies) and individual citizens.

The first three articles of the Constitution establish a national government. Article I places '[a]ll legislative Powers' in a Congress composed of a Senate and a House of Representatives.[5] Each state is given two Senators elected for six-year terms and a number of Representatives determined by the population of the state.[6] Representatives are elected for two-year terms.[7]

4 See generally Anthony Moffa, 'Private Environmental Nudges' (2022) 127 Dickinson Law Review 361.
5 US Constitution, art I.
6 ibid.
7 ibid.

Federal legislation requires the approval of both houses and the agreement of the President.[8] If the President does not approve proposed legislation, two-thirds of both houses can reject the presidential veto and enact the law.[9]

Article II of the Constitution vests the 'executive Power' in a 'President of the United States' elected for a four-year term.[10] Of particular importance to international agreements on climate, including net zero, Section 2 specifies the duties of the President to include 'making treaties with consent of Congress' and '[taking] Care that the Laws be faithfully executed'.[11]

Article III creates and defines the 'Judicial Power' of the United States.[12] The power 'shall be vested in one supreme Court, and in such inferior courts as the Congress many from time to time ordain and establish'.[13] Unlike the President and members of Congress, the federal judges have no fixed term of service. They shall hold their position 'during good Behavior'.[14] In practice, this provides lifetime tenure for a federal judge or justice. Crucial to implementation of environmental law and treaties, the federal courts are vested with jurisdiction over cases arising 'under the Constitution, the Laws of the United States, and treaties'.[15]

The three articles and subsequent amendments structure a government with checks and balances against one branch exercising excessive powers.

B. Legislation

For the last 160 years the American political structure has been shaped by two political parties, the Republicans and the Democrats. Since 1953, seven Republicans and six Democrats have served as President with neither party controlling for more than twelve consecutive years.[16] In recent decades the Senate and House of Representatives have regularly alternated majorities between the two parties. As noted above, all three of these governmental power centres—Senate, House, and Presidency—have a role to play in federal law-making. When a piece of legislation has House and Senate majority approval, it then arrives at the President's desk for signing into law. These federal laws define more precisely the landscape of permissible conduct for businesses, including utilities, and private citizens. These laws impose taxes and create subsidies. They delegate power to government agencies to regulate.

Federal laws relevant to net zero efforts date back to the original efforts to bring electricity to citizens across the nation in the early twentieth century. For instance, the Federal Power Act (FPA),[17] enacted in 1920, set up the system of governance of the transmission and sale of electric power. That system is integral to the energy transition away from fossil

[8] ibid.
[9] ibid.
[10] US Constitution, art II.
[11] ibid.
[12] US Constitution, art III.
[13] ibid.
[14] ibid.
[15] ibid.
[16] See Amy Tikkanen, 'Presidents of the United States' in *Encyclopedia Britannica* (Online) <https://www.britannica.com/topic/presidency-of-the-United-States-of-America/Presidents-of-the-United-States> accessed 7 August 2023.
[17] 16 US Code §§ 791 et seq.

fuel generation. Much more recently, the Energy Policy Act of 2005[18] made important changes regarding how energy is produced, including amending and repealing some outdated earlier statutes like the Public Utility Holding Company Act of 1935. As laid out in much greater detail in Section III.D, the recently enacted Inflation Reduction Act includes a number of provisions intended to facilitate the transition to clean energy. Nonetheless, the legislation that ultimately garners enough support to pass both houses of Congress encompasses an increasingly narrow sphere of consensus.

Things have changed in the five or so decades since that bipartisan era of environmental protection, making the environment an increasingly polarizing partisan issue. This change has been most acute over the last ten to fifteen years, and most starkly felt in the last two presidential administrations (Trump and Biden). This chapter will focus, therefore, on the urgent need for consensus-building and solidarity across the political spectrum. It will highlight the type of legislation that can and has become law in such an environment and why and how more can be done.

C. Regulatory and Executive Action

In the United States, legislation rarely settles all the details of complicated policy matters, such as energy and environmental protection. Instead, the laws enacted by Congress (and signed by the President) empower agencies to regulate particular industries, pollutants, etc. These agencies are, for the most part, run by administrators appointed by the President. Thus, politics influences their actions as well and building broad consensus around policy choices can be vitally important to a particular programme's success. It was not always this way. In the 1970s a Republican President—Richard Nixon—signed the countries' seminal environmental laws, establishing the Environmental Protection Agency (EPA) and empowering it to reign in polluting industries via regulation.[19] That task was initially conceived and understood as a technical and scientific undertaking, outside the reach of politics and the whims of popular opinion. In the years since, the reality has been much different and a general pattern has emerged. Broadly speaking, Democratic control yields more regulatory and tax incentive programmes for green energy projects, while Republican control resists policies that shift away from fossil fuels. Often, Democratic control leads to increased regulation of emissions, while Republican control leads to deregulation.

In the last decade or so, climate change policy, including efforts towards net zero and promotion of renewable energy more generally, has become beholden to partisan politics. The answer to what the United States, and consequently lawyers licensed to practise in that country, can and will do to advance towards net zero depends, in significant part, on the political party in power of each of the co-equal branches of government described above.

[18] 42 US Code § 15801.

[19] See Richard J Lazarus, 'The Greening of America and the Graying of United States Environmental Law: Reflections on Environmental Law's First Three Decades in the United States' (2001) 20 Virginia Environmental Law Journal 75, 77–82 (describing the first generation of US environmental laws and the way they resulted from a political era where 'both Democrats in Congress and Republicans in the White House sought to demonstrate their environmental credentials to enhance their competing aspirations for national office').

III. Political Challenges to Solidarity for Net Zero

The recent political history of the United States reveals just how significantly polarization now impacts the ability to enact meaningful policy, especially as it relates to net zero. The differences of opinion, and of outcomes, highlighted in this section demonstrate the urgent necessity for more consensus-building and solidarity in the face of a common enemy—climate change.

A. The Election of 2016 and President Donald J Trump

In 2016 the presidential election featured two 'first ever' candidates, who could not have drawn a sharper contrast on almost every relevant issue, including energy policy. The Democrats nominated Hillary Clinton, the first woman to be the candidate for President of one of the major parties. The Democrats highlighted Clinton's experience as the spouse of former President Bill Clinton and as Secretary of State for President Barack Obama and elected US Senator from New York.[20] Clinton pledged to promote laws and policies that would cut greenhouse gas (GHG) emissions 30 per cent by 2025 and more than 80 per cent by 2050—in other words, make real progress towards a net zero energy future. The Republicans nominated Donald Trump, the first presidential candidate with no prior governmental experience in state or national office or service in the US military.[21] The Trump campaign highlighted Trump's private sector career as a New York City real estate developer and a television show host.[22] It also highlighted Trump's views as a sceptic of government and an 'outsider' to the Washington, DC establishment.[23] One of those views included a promise to continue to promote coal as America's energy fuel, a significant step in the opposite direction of net zero energy production.[24]

When the votes were counted, Clinton won the majority of individual votes.[25] Trump won a majority of the Electoral College votes selected by voters in the individual states according to the Constitution.[26] Trump won narrow victories in half a dozen 'swing states' and became the 45th President of the United States. Hillary Clinton conceded her defeat.[27]

What followed was an administration that sharply divided America. Trump's inaugural address in January 2017 made little effort to draw the nation together. He was strongly

[20] See 'Hillary's vision for America' (Office of Hillary Rodham Clinton), 2016, <https://www.hillaryclinton.com/issues/> accessed 7 August 2023.

[21] See Bill Yenne, *The Complete Book of U.S. Presidents* (4th edn, Chartwell Books 2021).

[22] See Benjamin C Waterhouse, 'Donald Trump: Campaigns and Elections' (University of Virginia Miller Center), 11 April 2017 <https://www.millercenter.org/president/trump/campaigns-and-elections> accessed 14 May 2024.

[23] ibid.

[24] Justin Worland, 'Why Trump's Promise to Save the Coal Industry Does More Damage Than Good' (*Time*, 12 August 2016) <https://www.time.com/4447586/trump-coal-industry-energy/>.

[25] See '2016 Presidential Election Results' (*New York Times*, 9 August 2017) <https://www.nytimes.com/elections/2016/results/president> accessed 7 August 2023.

[26] ibid.

[27] See Hillary Clinton, 'Hillary Clinton's Concession Speech for the 2016 Presidential Election' (9 November 2016) <https://www.time.com/4564480/read-hillary-clintons-concession-speech-full-transcript/> accessed 7 August 2023.

critical of his predecessor, Democrat Barack Obama, and intensely disturbed by the state of America in 2017.[28]

Despite having a majority in both the Senate and House of Representatives, Trump appeared to have only limited interest in advancing a legislative agenda or in consensus-building with Democrats, on energy policy or anything even remotely related. His major statutory achievement was a significant tax reduction that favoured large businesses and wealthy individuals.[29]

President Trump's 'America first' policies meant that he actively rebuffed international commitments to reduce fossil fuel consumption and combat climate change. He famously announced the withdrawal of the United States from the Paris Climate Agreement within his first six months in office, declaring, 'I was elected to represent the citizens of Pittsburgh, not Paris'.[30] Because the Agreement included a provision prohibiting withdrawal until three years after it came into force *and* required a one-year waiting period after notification of withdrawal,[31] the United States did not formally give notice of withdraw until 2019 with an effective date of 2020.[32]

Domestically, President Trump's administration made concerted efforts to direct the country *away* from a net zero future and towards continued dependence on fossil fuels. The EPA replaced previously promulgated rules targeting GHG emissions from power plants (the so-called 'Clean Power Plan (CPP)') with much less ambitious rules emphasizing costs (the so-called 'Affordable Clean Energy Rule (ACE)').[33] Expert modelling projected that national CO_2 emissions would be higher under the ACE than the CPP, with the former only slightly reducing CO_2 emissions from a no-policy scenario.[34] The EPA justified this backwards decision by claiming that the Clean Air Act did not authorize the agency to act as aggressively to combat GHG emissions as it did in the CPP.[35] The DC Circuit disagreed and ultimately struck down the ACE.[36]

[28] See Donald J Trump, '2017 Donald Trump inauguration speech' (20 January 2017) <https://www.politico.com/story/2017/01/full-text-donald-trump-inauguration-speech-transcript-233907> accessed 7 August 2023.

[29] See Tax Cuts and Jobs Act of 2017 (USA) (2017) Pub L 115–97.

[30] Pittsburgh Post Gazette, 'I was elected to represent the citizens of Pittsburgh not Paris' (1 June 2017) <https://www.post-gazette.com/news/politics-nation/2017/06/01/I-was-elected-to-represent-the-citizens-of-Pittsburgh-not-Paris-Trump-to-pull-U-S-out-of-Paris-climate-agreement/stories/201706010198> accessed 7 August 2023.

[31] Article 28 of the Paris Agreement provides that: '1) At any time after three years from the date on which this Agreement has entered into force for a Party, that Party may withdraw from this Agreement by giving written notification to the Depositary. . . . 2) Any such withdrawal shall take effect upon expiry of one year from the date of receipt by the Depositary of the notification of withdrawal, or on such later date as may be specified in the notification of withdrawal.' United Nations Framework Convention on Climate Change (UNFCCC), 'On the Possibility to Withdraw from the Paris Agreement: A Short Overview' (14 June 2017) <https://www.unfccc.int/news/on-the-possibility-to-withdraw-from-the-paris-agreement-a-short-overview> accessed 14 May 2024

[32] Michael Pompeo, 'On the U.S. Withdrawal from the Paris Agreement' US Department of State Press Statement (4 November 2019) <https://www.2017-2021.state.gov/on-the-u-s-withdrawal-from-the-paris-agreement/index.html> accessed 7 August 2023.

[33] US Environmental Protection Agency (EPA), Final Rule 'Repeal of the Clean Power Plan; Emission Guidelines for Greenhouse Gas Emissions from Existing Electric Utility Generating Units; Revisions to Emission Guidelines Implementing Regulations' (*US Federal Register*, 8 July 2019) <https://www.federalregister.gov/d/2019-13507> accessed 7 August 2023.

[34] Amelia T Keyes and others, 'The Affordable Clean Energy Rule and the Impact of Emissions Rebound on Carbon Dioxide and Criteria Air Pollutant Emissions' (2019) 14 Environmental Research Letters 044018. National CO_2 emissions are projected to be slightly lower under the ACE compared to no policy, and higher compared to the CPP, in all modelled years but 2050.

[35] EPA, 'Repeal of the Clean Power Plan' (n 33).

[36] *American Lung Association v Environmental Protection Agency* [2021] DC Cir, No 19-1140.

President Trump's administration, through the EPA and the Department of Transportation, also cut Corporate Average Fuel Economy (CAFE) standards for new automobiles[37] in an attempt to slow the transition to electric vehicles (a necessary shift on the path to net zero).[38] Major car manufacturers, many of which were on track to meet the Obama-era standards thanks to investments in research and development, did not ask for or forcefully support the change.[39]

President Trump's exercises of executive powers showed his views of relations with long-standing American allies. His relations with foreign governments asserted support for Russia's Vladimir Putin[40] and North Korea's Kim Jong Un[41] and scepticism about traditional North Atlantic Treaty Organization (NATO) and other allies' policies.[42] German Chancellor Angela Merkel observed that European nations could no longer rely on American leadership in international affairs,[43] including global efforts to address climate change.[44]

President Trump's election, governing decisions, and diplomatic efforts marked major shifts in how the United States made policy and law. Consensus, or even the appearance of bipartisanship, lost importance. Instead of identifying common enemies of society or the planet (eg climate change), politicians identified the enemy as opposing politicians and their supporters. The result for solidarity on domestic energy policy proved disastrous—existing areas of disagreement were highlighted and conflicts escalated. On the world stage, the United States stepped back from a position where it might have brought parties together and moved global energy policy back towards an isolationist model.

B. The Decoupling of Science from Regulatory Policy

In the past, there existed at least some political solidarity when confronted with stark scientific realities, particularly when those realities threatened American lives and livelihoods. Indeed, it was prominent environmental catastrophes (Love Canal, etc) that led to

[37] EPA, 'The Safer Affordable Fuel Efficient (SAFE) Vehicles Final Rule for Model Years 2021–2026' Regulations for Emissions from Vehicles and Engines (updated 4 January 2023) <https://www.epa.gov/regulations-emissions-vehicles-and-engines/safer-affordable-fuel-efficient-safe-vehicles-final-rule> accessed 7 August 2023.

[38] Stacy Noblet, 'The Pillars of a Net-Zero Transportation Sector: EV Adoption and Clean Energy' (*Forbes*, 7 July 2022) <https://www.forbes.com/sites/stacynoblet/2022/07/07/the-pillars-of-a-net-zero-transportation-sector-ev-adoption-and-clean-energy/?sh=677c36bc324f> accessed 7 August 2023.

[39] See Coral Davenport, 'More automakers drop their support of Trump-era fuel economy standards' (*New York Times*, 2 February 2021) <https://www.nytimes.com/2021/02/02/business/more-automakers-drop-their-support-of-trump-era-fuel-economy-standards.html> accessed 7 August 2023.

[40] See 'The Trump-Putin summit in Helsinki' (*The Economist*, 5 July 2018) <https://www.economist.com/united-states/2018/07/05/the-trump-putin-summit-in-helsinki> accessed 7 August 2023.

[41] See Philip Bump, 'Trump on Kim Jong Un: Why shouldn't I like him?' (*Washington Post*, 1 March 2019) <https://www.washingtonpost.com/politics/2019/03/01/trump-kim-jong-un-why-shouldnt-i-like-him/> accessed 7 August 2023.

[42] Jorge Benitez, 'U.S. NATO Policy in the Age of Trump: Controversy and Consistency' (2019) 43(1) The Fletcher Forum of World Affairs 179–200 <http://www.jstor.org/stable/45289836> accessd 7 August 2023..

[43] Reuters, 'Merkel says Europe can't rely on U.S. to impose world order' (*Reuters*, 20 July 2018) <https://www.reuters.com/article/us-germany-merkel-usa/merkel-says-europe-cant-rely-on-u-s-to-impose-world-order-idUSKBN1KA1F9> ('We can't rely on the superpower of the United States') accessed 7 August 2023.

[44] See eg Angela Dewan and Stephanie Halasz, 'G20 closes with rebuke to Trump's climate change stance' (*CNN*, 9 July 2017) <https://www.cnn.com/2017/07/08/europe/g20-merkel-trump-communique/index.html> (recounting Chancellor Merkel's statement that she 'deplore[s]' President Trump's stance on the Paris Agreement and reaffirms the commitment of the other nineteen members of the G20 to go on without the United States) accessed 7 August 2023.

the bipartisan legislation that created the EPA and tasked the agency with cleaning up our nation's air and water.[45] Climate policy enjoys no such luxury of solidarity across political lines on the basis of objectively documented threats.

The COVID-19 pandemic revealed just how detached from scientific reality the partisan hold on issue positions was capable of going. Not even the threat of a deadly pandemic, highly salient to most of the country, could bring the fiercely defiant presidential administration together with members of the opposite party in the year of an election. Instead, President Trump downplayed COVID-19 with scepticism over scientific and medical assessments of the seriousness of the pandemic.[46] He objected to health mandates like business closures, the mandatory wearing of protective masks, and the avoidance of crowds. He predicted conditions would return to normal by Easter 2020.[47] President Trump further argued that the major responsibility for response to the disease fell on city and state officials, not the federal government. President Trump supported the search for a vaccine to control the disease, but resisted the idea of mandated implementation.[48] By November 2020, COVID-19 deaths had reached the thousands in the United States.[49] President Trump himself had been infected and hospitalized.[50]

More directly relevant to climate policy, 2020 brought numerous well-publicized extreme weather events across the country.[51] Tornadoes of greater than normal distance hit portions of the mid-South.[52] Forest fires in Colorado and California were of record intensity.[53]

Scientists described many of the disasters as a consequence of climate change especially in the intensity and frequency of the disasters.[54] Citizens around the country were forced to recognize that they faced the regular risk of catastrophic harm to themselves, their property, and their communities.

President Trump and his political allies remained steadfast in their scepticism of climate change and its suspected causes. Consequently, United States policy favoured businesses that promoted the extraction and use of fossil fuels and urged the opening of federally-owned lands for their resource development. Democratic legislators by contrast generally agreed with the science that recognized climate change and its consequences and with environmental policies that protected natural resources.

[45] See Lazarus (n 19).

[46] Juana Summers, 'Timeline: How Trump Has Downplayed The Coronavirus Pandemic' (*NPR*, 2 October 2020) <https://www.npr.org/sections/latest-updates-trump-covid-19-results/2020/10/02/919432383/how-trump-has-downplayed-the-coronavirus-pandemic> accessed 9 May 2023.

[47] Philip Ewing and Barbara Sprunt, 'Trump Sets Easter Goal for Reopening American Economy' (*NPR*, 24 March 2020) <https://www.npr.org/2020/03/24/820774378/trump-id-love-for-u-s-to-be-opened-up-by-easter-amidst-pandemic-response> accessed 9 May 2023.

[48] US Government Accountability Office, 'Operation Warp Speed: Accelerated COVID-19 Vaccine Development Status and Efforts to Address Manufacturing Challenges' (Report to Congressional Addresses, GAO-21-319, February 2021) <https://www.gao.gov/assets/gao-21-319.pdf> accessed 9 May 2023.

[49] Center for Disease Control, 'Covid Data Tracker' <https://www.covid.cdc.gov/covid-data-tracker/#datatracker-home>.

[50] BBC World, 'Trump flown to hospital after Covid-19 diagnosis' (*BBC World*, 3 October 2020) <https://www.bbc.com/news/world-us-canada-54396670> accessed 9 May 2023.

[51] NOAA National Centers for Environmental Information (NCEI), 'U.S. Billion-Dollar Weather and Climate Disasters' (2023) <https://www.ncei.noaa.gov/access/billions/> accessed 9 May 2023.

[52] ibid.

[53] ibid.

[54] See NOAA NCEI, 'U.S. Billion-Dollar Weather and Climate Disasters, FAQ' (2023) <https://www.ncei.noaa.gov/access/billions/faq> ('[T]he number and cost of disasters are increasing over time due to a combination of increased exposure (i.e., values at risk of possible loss), vulnerability (i.e., where we build; how we build) and that climate change is increasing the frequency of some types of extremes that lead to billion-dollar disasters').

As the US experience proves, it is extremely difficult to build solidarity against a common problem if the actors who might collaborate cannot even agree on the basic underlying facts. This is true on the global level as well. The age of dis- and misinformation has pushed decision-makers and constituents further apart, rather than helped them to identify common ground or shared values or objectives.

C. A New Administration?

The presidential election of 2020 put the true state of polarization in the United States on display. Political news coverage, debates, and campaigning reflected a lack of substance on important issues—including energy policy and climate change. It became clear during the election and its aftermath that the ability to build consensus had significantly deteriorated. Given the scope of the climate crisis and the comprehensive changes needed to create a net zero world, the political season of 2020 marked a low point. The election itself and its aftermath are described in detail because of how historically anomalous the decisions and events were. The prospects for American solidarity on anything looked extremely bleak. However, the results—electing President Biden and his promise of bipartisan collaboration—presented an opportunity for a return to a consensus-building approach.

Notwithstanding his mishandling of the pandemic and his apparent disrespect for even scientific consensus, President Donald Trump gathered a strong base within the Republican Party for the election of 2020. His influence was so strong that the party did not offer a detailed platform for the 2020 elections, rather simply issued a brief resolution endorsing the 'President's America-first agenda'.[55]

Democrats were generally distressed by President Trump's behaviour, his inexperience in government, and his apparent legislative, executive, and judicial agendas. In early winter of 2020 no Democrat stood out as the clear choice of the party to run against Trump in the November election.[56] Long-time Senator and former Vice President Joe Biden appeared to be the moderate favourite. Eventually, through a series of candidate exits coalescing support around the former Vice President, Biden wrapped up the Democratic nomination for President.

The fate of climate policy in the United States then hung in the balance of an election pitting two flawed septuagenarians against one another. By early evening on election night, the national vote total seemed certain to favour the Democrats. However, the Constitution made clear that the victor of the election would be decided by the 538 votes of the Electoral College who would be selected by the winners of the popular votes in their individual states.[57] Voting ended with the Electoral College in Biden's favour 306–232.[58]

In any other election year, the Electoral College vote would have resolved the election. The losing candidate would have conceded the result with greater or lesser grace. The

[55] See Republican National Committee, 'Resolution Regarding the Republican Party Platform' (2016) <https://www.prod-cdn-static.gop.com/docs/Resolution_Platform_2020.pdf>.

[56] FiveThirtyEight, 'Latest Polls: Democratic Primary, All States, 2020 Election Cycle' (polls ending 28 April 2020) <https://www.projects.fivethirtyeight.com/polls/president-primary-d/2020/> accessed 9 May 2023.

[57] US Constitution, art II, Section 1, Clauses 2 and 3.

[58] Mark Sherman, 'Electoral College makes it official: Biden won, Trump lost' (*AP*, 14 December 2020) <https://www.apnews.com/article/joe-biden-270-electoral-college-vote-d429ef97af2bf574d16463384dc7cc1e> accessed 27 February 2023.

winning candidate would have continued to assemble a new administration to take office on 20 January 2021. Donald Trump, however, continued to refuse to concede and started a visible campaign of objection to the 'stolen election' and a less public set of attempts to overturn the results.[59] The latter included efforts to promote slates of 'alternate electors' (who supported Trump) and to ask Republican Vice President Mike Pence to rule that President Trump had won re-election.[60]

What followed were the events of 6 January 2021. President Trump encouraged a gathering of his supporters in Washington, DC, on the day when the Congress would meet to confirm the Electoral College results. A mixture of organized and unorganized Trump supporters gathered outside the White House that morning. Trump spoke to them and encouraged a march on the Capitol Building which he promised to join. By early afternoon, thousands of Trump supporters had assembled outside the Capitol. Capitol Police were overwhelmed when some of the protestors became rioters and stormed the Capitol seeking to harm or kill government leaders and to prevent Congressional ratification of the Electoral College vote from taking place. By late afternoon, government reinforcements regained control of the Capitol. An evening session of the Congress then verified the election of Joe Biden and Vice President Kamala Harris.

On 20 January, Joe Biden and Kamala Harris were inaugurated as President and Vice President.[61] After Inauguration Day on 20 January 2021, the Democratic Party controlled the Presidency and both houses of Congress. However, control of the Senate depended on the votes of two independent Senators and the support of two Democratic senators one of whom, Joe Manchin of West Virginia, was a strong supporter of his state's coal mining industry with its sceptical views of climate change and opponents of fossil fuels.

Donald Trump's insistence that the 2020 election had been stolen from him and that he would remain active in Republican politics sharpened the partisan divide and left President Biden with little hope for Republican legislative support on many issues, including efforts to reduce GHG emissions and promote a net zero energy transition.

The continued dominance of the COVID pandemic as the most pressing challenge facing the new administration further sidelined the climate agenda. In sharp contrast to President Trump, President Biden declared that the pandemic was the responsibility of the national government, that scientific and medical evidence should drive efforts to control it, and that widespread vaccination of American citizens and control of citizen behaviour should drive the American response. President Biden made similar arguments with respect to addressing the climate crisis, as its effects were made more salient throughout his Presidency. The lack of consensus that a 'crisis' even existed to confront bogged down many of his efforts. Solidarity requires a common enemy and most Republicans refused to acknowledge that climate change was such an enemy.

[59] See Ed Kilgore, 'Trump's Long Campaign to Steal the Presidency: A Timeline' (*NY Magazine*, 14 July 2022) <https://www.nymag.com/intelligencer/article/trump-campaign-steal-presidency-timeline.html> accessed 27 February 2023.

[60] See eg President Donald J Trump's speech at 'Stop the Steal' rally prior to capitol riot on 6 January 2021. 'Transcript of Trump's speech at rally before US Capitol riot' (*AP*, 13 January 2021) <https://www.apnews.com/article/election-2020-joe-biden-donald-trump-capitol-siege-media-e79eb5164613d6718e9f4502eb471f27> accessed 27 February 2023.

[61] US Department of Defense, 'Biden, Harris Sworn in as America's New Leaders' (20 January 2021) <https://www.defense.gov/News/News-Stories/Article/Article/2477716/biden-harris-sworn-in-as-americas-new-leaders/> accessed 27 February 2023.

President Biden campaigned on his ability to work with leaders from the was elected and assumed office. Nonetheless, the governing mechanisms in kept people and politicians entrenched. One area where this was extremely salie mestic energy policy and any efforts to move the US economy away from fossil fu slowly. The accumulation of wealth and power over decades in the GHG-generating i tries, combined with the fervent division born in 2016, made the Biden administrati task of enacting meaningful net zero policy very difficult.

D. Unilateral and Collaborative Action on Net Zero

President Biden's efforts to advance the United States towards net zero fall into two categories—actions taken without bipartisan support (ie in the absence of solidarity) and actions taken with some modicum of bipartisan support, even if just among the populace (ie in solidarity with political opposition). Generally, actions in the former category had more explicit environmental aims but were less impactful, while actions in the latter category nominally targeted more consensus evils (eg inflation) and had more sweeping impact.

1. Executive and Administrative Action

In December President Biden signed Executive Order (EO) 14057, reestablishing the federal government's commitment to a net zero future.[62] The EO directed the federal government to lead by example to achieve a carbon pollution-free electricity sector by 2035 and net zero emissions economy-wide by no later than 2050.[63] It specifically directed federal agencies to meet the following goals:

- 100 percent carbon pollution-free electricity on a net annual basis by 2030, including 50 percent 24/7 carbon pollution-free electricity;
- 100 percent zero-emission vehicle acquisitions by 2035, including 100 percent zero-emission light-duty vehicle acquisitions by 2027;
- a net-zero emissions building portfolio by 2045, including a 50 percent emissions reduction by 2032;
- a 65 percent reduction in scope 1 and 2 greenhouse gas emissions, as defined by the Federal Greenhouse Gas Accounting and Reporting Guidance, from Federal operations by 2030 from 2008 levels;
- net-zero emissions from Federal procurement, including a Buy Clean policy to promote use of construction materials with lower embodied emissions;
- climate resilient infrastructure and operations; and
- a climate- and sustainability-focused Federal workforce.[64]

[62] The White House, 'Executive Order (EO) 14057: Catalyzing Clean Energy Industries and Jobs Through Federal Sustainability: President Biden' (8 December 2021) <https://www.whitehouse.gov/briefing-room/presidential-actions/2021/12/08/executive-order-on-catalyzing-clean-energy-industries-and-jobs-through-federal-sustainability/> accessed 7 August 2023.

[63] See ibid.

[64] ibid.

The Supreme Court in *West Virginia v EPA* ruled against environmental protection and scientific expertise and significantly hindered the ability of administrative agencies to follow through on Biden's promises.[65] There, the Supreme Court severely curtailed the ability of the US EPA from addressing GHG emissions from power plants through regulation under the existing Clean Air Act.[66] The Court solidified the creation of a new doctrine of administrative law—the Major Questions Doctrine—which requires 'something more than a merely plausible textual basis for the agency action' in cases of political and economic significance.[67] Instead, the agency must now point to 'clear congressional authorization' for the power it claims.[68] Because GHG emissions were not specifically mentioned in the subsection of the Clean Air Act at issue in the case,[69] the Court held that the EPA could not regulate them in the manner it had sought to since the Obama administration.[70]

2. Legislative Action

The Congress, with President Biden's strong support, reasserted its legislative role with the passage of several significant laws in August and September 2022. The most notable was the Inflation Reduction Act (IRA) enacted on 16 August 2022.[71]

The law gathered the support of all Democrats in both houses while all Republicans opposed.[72] One of the most significant sections of the Act addressed climate change. It committed approximately US$365 billion of the US$1.9 trillion bill to advance the goals of worldwide climate change control and the advancement of renewable energy.[73] While advocates for climate change control bemoaned shortcomings of the Act,[74] the adoption of the latter by the Biden administration clearly represent a strong signal in favour of environmental protection, in stark contrast with the Trump administration. The massive financial commitment also helped put the United States back into international environmental leadership.

The IRA represents the single largest investment in climate and clean energy in American history and puts the country on a path to a net zero economy by 2050. The law will have impacts economy-wide, but from a legal practitioner's perspective, two areas will demand increased focus: corporate finance and tax.

On the corporate side, the IRA funds loan guarantee programmes that will be available to help finance new investments in clean energy and energy infrastructure. Section 1703 extends US$40 billion of loan guarantee authority to the Department of Energy for new renewable energy projects.[75] The IRA recognizes that new sources of clean energy will be useless in the pursuit of net zero without improvements in grid infrastructure to carry the

[65] *West Virginia v Environmental Protection Agency*, 597 US 697 (2022).
[66] ibid.
[67] ibid.
[68] ibid.
[69] 42 US Code § 7411(d). 'Title 42 The Public Health and Welfare'. Standards of performance for existing sources; remaining useful life of source <https://www.govinfo.gov/content/pkg/USCODE-2021-title42/pdf/USCODE-2021-title42-chap85-subchapI-partA-sec7411.pdf>.
[70] *West Virginia v EPA* (n 65).
[71] *Washington Post*, 29 July 2022, A-1; *New York Times*, 31 July 2022, A-8; *New York Times*, 13 August 2022, A-1; *AP*, 14 August 2022, A-2; *Washington Post*, 17 August 2022, A-1.
[72] At A-1; *New York Times*, 24 August 2022, A-3; *New York Times*, 26 August 2022, A-4.
[73] *New York Times*, 24 August 2022, A-3; *New York Times*, 26 August 2022, A-4.
[74] The Santa Fe New Mexican, 'Poll: Most Americans Want More Action on Climate' (26 October 2022) A2 (popular support for action on climate change).
[75] IRA, Section 1703.

Table 20.1 IRA, Section 1706. Energy Infrastructure Reinvestment (EIR) Programme

Taxed Entity	Tax Credit
Business	• Renewable Electricity Production Tax Credit (PTC) • Business Energy Investment Tax Credit (ITC) • Energy-Efficient Commercial Buildings Tax Deduction • Alternative Fuel Vehicle Refuelling Property Tax Credit • Qualified Commercial Clean Vehicle Tax Credit
Individual	• Energy-Efficient Home Improvement Credit • Residential Clean Energy Tax Credit • Electric Vehicle Tax Credit

Sources: IRA; US Internal Revenue Service, 'Credits and Deductions Under the Inflation Reduction Act of 2022' (14 August 2023) <https://www.irs.gov/credits-and-deductions-under-the-inflation-reduction-act-of-2022>

power to the people who need it.[76] Thus, Section 1706 creates the Energy Infrastructure Reinvestment (EIR) Programme to guarantee loans to projects that renovate or replace energy infrastructure that has ceased operations, or enable operating energy infrastructure to reduce or sequester GHG emissions.[77]

On the tax code side, the IRA creates a substantial number of new deductions and credits for businesses and individuals. Table 20.1 outlines some of the most prominent.

If practitioners make full use of these incentives, the United States will make substantial progress towards net zero by 2030. According to a study from Princeton University's REPEAT project, a fully implemented IRA could cut annual GHG emissions by 42 per cent by 2030 (from 2005 levels), a reduction of about one billion metric tons. The primary drivers of those reductions are the growth of renewable generation prompted by the loan guarantee and tax credit provisions, as well as the accelerated electrification of transportation, buildings, and industrial loads. The renewable energy tax credits will contribute to a doubling of the pace of new projects within five years.

3. International Action

By early autumn 2022, the Biden administration had shaped a record of accomplishment in foreign, domestic, and environmental policy on which to contest the 8 November elections for Congress and state and local offices.

The November 2022 election results provided far better news for Democrats than had been expected a few months earlier.[78] The Republicans did gain control of the House of Representatives but with less than a ten-vote majority. The elections were a setback for Donald Trump.

[76] The REPEAT Project authors acknowledge that increasing transmission capacity is key to unlocking the IRA's benefits. According to their analysis, US transmission capacity growth needs to more than double from current levels to deliver the projected IRA benefits. If transmission expansion continues on its current trajectory, over 80% of the potential emissions reductions delivered by the IRA in 2030 will be lost.

[77] IRA, Section 1706.

[78] *New York Times*, 13 November 2022, A-4; *Washington Post*, 10 November 2022, A-5.

The results were a strong boost for President Biden both domestically and internationally. Biden's leadership in opposition to the Russian invasion of Ukraine drew solid domestic support and admiration from NATO and other free world leaders. The international boost came shortly before the COP27 to the UNFCCC gathering of world leaders to address net zero and other climate change issues at Sharm El-Sheikh in mid-November 2022.[79]

UN negotiations in Sharm El-Sheikh exhibited how factionalization and polarization operated on a global political scale, even outside of the Democrat–Republican dichotomy. On the world stage, negotiations settled into now-familiar patterns of entrenchment,[80] with the developing (Annex II) countries and groups (in particular AOSIS, the G77, China, and Independent Association of Latin American and Caribbean Countries) pushing for more action, particularly from developed (Annex I) countries (including the United States, Canada, and the United Kingdom). These lines emerged across multiple negotiation tracks, the most contentious of which had to do with compensation for climate harms, so-called 'loss and damage'. Indeed, the focus on compensation drowned out progress on other fronts, including net zero pledges. It also serves as an example of how solidarity might be built across seemingly unmovable lines and progress achieved on climate goals of tremendous importance.

Sometimes, including in this particular case, one compelling voice can reframe a question or a disagreement in such a way as to engender real empathy and identify a common cause. In this case, that may have been the combined voices of Molwyn Joseph, the Minister of Health, Wellness & The Environment for Antigua and Barbuda and Sherry Rehman, the Federal Minister for Climate Change for Pakistan. Minister Rehman reminded the parties of the devastating floods in her country, making salient the need for immediate assistance on loss and damage.[81] Minister Joseph not only spoke passionately about the immediate need for a loss and damage fund but made important concessions on how to get there on behalf of the Alliance of Small Island States (AOSIS). Around midday on the Thursday, with ostensibly one day to go, AOSIS, the G77, the Least Developed Countries, and the Independent Association of Latin American and Caribbean Countries held a joint press conference to discuss 'loss and damage finance inaction'. Minister Joseph spoke in the conference and afterwards, appealing directly to the developed world.[82] Importantly, he analogized opening a loss and damage fund to opening a bank account, conceding that deposits into it need not come immediately. This was a change in framing that amounted to a concession. A few hours later, the European Union (EU) had changed their tune, and professed willingness to open a fund. They had a new issue though—who would agree to be depositors and who would be beneficiaries.[83] The EU appeared to agree to developed countries depositing and developing countries withdrawing, as long as the countries agreed to use 2022 definitions of those terms (rather than 1992 Annex I and Annex II designations).[84]

[79] *Washington Post*, 18 November 2022, A-1; Sante Fe New Mexican, 21 November 2022, A-4.

[80] These conclusions are drawn from the author's (Anthony Moffa) notes, documentation, and recollection as a member of the University of Maine's observer delegation to the Conference of the Parties.

[81] Author's notes (n 80).

[82] ibid.

[83] ibid.

[84] ibid.

The focus on updated classifications could be attributed the world's largest emitter of GHGs *and* the world's second largest economy—China.

Unsurprisingly, the United States also had concerns, though less openly expressed at COP27, about China being able to take its money through a loss and damage fund (or really any other way). The ultimate landing zone was the opening at COP27 of a new loss and damage fund with details on how and in what amounts it would be funded, and by whom, to be worked out later. The signatories agreed:

> to establish new funding arrangements for assisting developing countries that are particularly vulnerable to the adverse effects of climate change, in responding to loss and damage ... [and] to establish a fund for responding to loss and damage whose mandate includes a focus on addressing loss and damage ... [and] to [e]stablish a transitional committee on the operationalization of the new funding arrangements for responding to loss and damage and the fund.

While compelling and vitally important, the ultimate agreement on establishing an international fund for climate harms only tangentially relates to the mitigation efforts, net zero or otherwise. Liability for loss and damage in theory serves the instrumental purpose of encouraging mitigation by developed countries. The market, with the cost signals in place, would shift from fossil fuels to renewable energy sources.[85] Put another way, one might view the agreed-upon loss and damage fund as a backdoor climate mitigation effort; a way to act on climate when direct regulation of emissions is difficult to achieve internationally.

Alongside the contentious finance negotiations, many nations, including the United States, publicly touted progress on net zero pledges. The US Department of Energy Secretary Jennifer Granholm appeared in multiple speaking engagements across COP27, armed with a laundry list of opportunities designed to benefit renewable energy transition projects (most stemming from the IRA). She also spoke at length about centring fenceline or frontline communities with the investment money, pointing to President Biden's Justice40 Initiative in particular.[86]

IV. Power Politics and the Search for Solidarity for Net Zero: Lessons Learned

The American experience with increasing polarization and political entrenchment is far from unique. Indeed, political extremism is on the rise globally.[87] The online information and social media age makes every issue highly visible and thus political. As a result, net zero policy depends on solidarity across political lines—without it, too little will be done too slowly. The Presidency of Donald J Trump is but one cautionary note demonstrating just that. The United States has moved on from that era of inaction and some important

[85] Richard A Posner, *Economic Analysis of Law* (6th edn, Aspen 2003) 206 (explaining that the ultimate goal, from an instrumentalist perspective, is 'to channel resource allocation through the market as much as possible').

[86] These conclusions are drawn from the author's notes (n 80).

[87] Heather Ashby, 'Far-Right Extremism Is a Global Problem and It Is Time to Treat It Like One' (*Foreign Policy*, 15 January 2021) <https://www.foreignpolicy.com/2021/01/15/far-right-extremism-global-problem-worldwide-solutions/>.

law- and policy-making lessons can be derived from that recent history so other nations may not stumble quite so spectacularly on the path to net zero.

First, we should be wary of unilateral action that lacks at least some marker of broad political support. In the United States, the regulatory and executive action, in the absence of new legislation, has been unable to rise to the task of addressing climate change. This is, at least in part, due to the political opposition finding ways to stymie progress, primarily through the courts.

Second, to build the needed broad-based solidarity for net zero, there is a need to identify a common enemy, and that enemy may not be, indeed likely should not be, 'climate change'. The United States' recent legislative success came literally in the name of addressing 'inflation'. The Inflation Reduction Act enjoys broader support than any legislation with climate change in the title likely could in the current political environment. Natural resource extraction and associated policy debates often involve taking from nature to generate wealth for a limited subset of humans. That dynamic necessarily fosters conflict, rather than cooperation. There exist other, more useful ways to frame important issues. Opportunities for consensus within fiercely divided nations and international coalitions exist around common causes that correlate with net zero and climate mitigation. To name just a few: grid infrastructure upgrades, national energy independence, and economic sanctions on oil-producing bad actors.

Third, tax and investment levers are the type of mechanisms that have the potential to garner support across otherwise warring factions—workers and corporate leaders, or environmentalists and pro-business groups. They also happen to generate a lot of new work for transactional lawyers. Training lawyers about the existence of new initiatives and how to maximize their usefulness to clients will be essential to full implementation of net zero initiatives designed to economically hasten the transition to renewable sources of energy. Given this essential role, it is best practice to involve transactional lawyers in the design of these laws.

If political leaders heed these lessons in domestic policy efforts, individual nations will progress more quickly towards net zero, doing so with some modicum of solidarity amongst citizens. If nations bring the same lessons to international negotiations, the global climate governance regime will similarly be more unified and more productive.

V. Conclusion

This chapter has highlighted how American politics have dictated, and will continue to dictate, legal and policy positions towards net zero, climate change, and environmental law in general. The increasing divisions, power politics, and the rise of nationalism and 'America first' policies in the United States all have significant implications for building the required international solidarity, especially multilateralism, cooperation, capacity development, as well as resource and technology exchange, needed to advance the global energy transition.

Only time will tell whether the US approach under President Biden will actually yield something close to a net zero national economy, or even whether it will continue into the next administration. At this point, reflecting on the sharp political divisions and increasingly vitriolic partisan rhetoric of the past two decades, one thing has been made clear. The path to net zero depends on some modicum of solidarity among the voting populace, the politicians, and, hopefully, both. It is extremely unlikely that one political party will accumulate enough power to unilaterally implement effective climate policy before it is far too late.

21

Towards Net Zero

A Cross-Sectoral Analysis of Australia's Energy Transition

Lee Godden

I. Introduction: Net Zero and Cross-Sectoral Energy Transition

As discussed in Chapter 1 of this book, advancing net zero and clean energy transition requires cross-sectoral solidarity and a multistakeholder governance approach across the natural resources sector. This chapter investigates the potential for climate legislation and a nexus of regulation and normative practices to drive decarbonization across the many sectors that are needed to progressively meet Australia's net zero emission targets. It explores the potential for climate litigation directed at natural resources development to propel faster and systemic change towards net zero, particularly in relation to Australia's high levels of natural resource exports.

In Australia in 2022, an incoming national Labor government introduced the Climate Change Act 2022 (C'th) after a long period of stagnation in national climate change policy.[1] An earlier government had rolled back national climate laws, including a carbon pricing mechanism.[2] This vacuum in national climate laws allowed state (subnational governments) some autonomy in how they regulated natural resources such as coal and gas, and whether they pursued energy transition. Many subnational governments, which have the powers under their respective constitutions to govern natural resources, including coal and gas, initiated legal frameworks for moving to renewable energy generation and developed plans for transition to net zero.[3] Typically, such governments have both legislation for the extraction and production of natural resources, and climate change laws setting relatively robust emission reduction targets and pathways. Other subnational governments remain major coal and liquified natural gas exporters, and relevant legislation lacks clear Nationally Determined Contribution (NDC) targets or transition pathways.[4]

In June 2022, the Australian Climate Change Minister announced that Australia would revise its NDC pledge under the Paris Agreement to reduce greenhouse gas (GHG) emissions by 43 per cent below 2005 levels by 2030.[5] Australia's target, whilst an encouraging

[1] The legislation was enacted soon after the government assumed office, with amendments proposed by the Greens party and 'Teal' Independents who conducted successful climate election campaigns.

[2] For discussion of the Clean Energy Act 2011 and associated regulation see Lee Godden, Jacqueline Peel, and Jan McDonald, *Environmental Law* (2nd edn, OUP 2018) 431–34.

[3] ibid 108–23.

[4] Lee Godden, 'Energy Law and Regulation in Australia' in Giuseppe Bellantuono and others (eds), *Handbook of Energy Law in the Low-Carbon Transition* (De Gruyter 2023) 369, 370–71.

[5] Chris Bowen, 'Address to the IGCC 2022 climate change investment and finance summit' <https://www.minister.industry.gov.au/ministers/bowen/speeches/address-igcc-2022-climate-change-investment-and-finance-summit> accessed 21 August 2023.

Lee Godden, *Towards Net Zero* In: *Net Zero and Natural Resources Law*. Edited by: Damilola S. Olawuyi, José Juan González, Hanri Mostert, Milton Fernando Montoya, and Catherine Banet, Oxford University Press. © International Bar Association 2024.
DOI: 10.1093/9780198925033.003.0021

improvement from the relatively weak NDC pursued by the previous government, still is not consistent with the level which the United Nations Environment Programme (UNEP) has indicated will be necessary to keep dangerous anthropocentric global warming below 1.5°C.[6] The Climate Change Act, though, ostensibly is designed to meet international mitigation targets and to drive energy transition to net zero. The Act embeds Australia's NDCs in a national domestic legal framework.[7] Its influence on natural resources law and regulation in Australia is not yet clear, but it is likely to drive faster energy transition in the states where the energy transition is well underway and where there is a coal phase-out already occurring.

Whilst the Climate Change Act offers a more certain basis on which to build energy transition, including transforming power generation, the legislation does not mandate specific pathways for energy transition, beyond setting relevant targets and embedding emissions reduction objectives into national government functions.[8] The Act is a 'Framework for Action' rather than a prescriptive regulatory transition scheme. It has no detailed requirements for directly regulating natural resources law as, under the Australian Constitution, it is state governments that have requisite powers over natural resources such as coal and petroleum.

At this subnational level, Australia has extensive legislation for fossil fuel exploration and production, as well as mineral and water resource governance legislation.[9] Given the importance of federalism in natural resources management in the nation, the national climate legislation seeks to set out principles and institute normative values that are predisposed to decarbonization across Australian society.[10] This 'soft' law federal model reflects the substantial past political difficulties in implementing more rigorous national climate laws that directly (ie through carbon pricing) control natural resources such as coal, petroleum, and minerals. Legal pathways towards net zero emissions in Australia thus comprise 'the set of (formal and informal, public and private) institutions, (formal and informal, public and private) legal tools and interpretative practices available in a specific legal system to pursue decarbonization goals'.[11] Climate law and policy, supported by robust financial incentives such as renewable energy subsidies, have already secured energy transition in residential, commercial, and some industrial settings.

In other sectors, such as natural resource contexts, there has been a lack of synchronization with climate law and policy, or substantial barriers to low-carbon transition. In respect of the primary legislation governing natural resources such as coal, typically, governments have not directly imposed net zero targets or similar energy transition measures in these statutory frameworks. As the national government can only indirectly 'regulate' natural resources, it seeks to do so through a nexus of laws relating to development control, environmental impact assessment laws, land sector, and biodiversity management legislation.

[6] United Nations Framework Convention on Climate Change (UNFCCC) opened for signature 4 June 1992 771UNTS 107 (entered into force 21 March 1994), art 2.

[7] Paris Agreement opened for signature on 22 April 2016, UNTS XXVII.7.d (entered into force 4 November 2016).

[8] The Climate Change Act implements Australia's net zero commitments and codifies Australia's net 2030 and 2050 emissions reductions targets under the Paris Agreement.

[9] Godden, Peel, and McDonald (n 2) 187–96, 203–09.

[10] ibid 425–37.

[11] Giuseppe Bellantuono and others (eds), *Handbook of Energy Law in the Low-Carbon Transition* (De Gruyter 2023) 4.

These laws that impinge on primary natural resource legislation thus provide the nexus for driving towards net zero; for example by regulating natural resources project developments. Indigenous land rights legislation provides for Aboriginal communities to be involved in natural resource decisions, such as whether new coal mines or shale gas projects should proceed. This type of legislation creates another set of stakeholders engaged in decisions relevant to energy transition. In this way, there is a dynamic tension between national climate change laws and related areas of environmental law and policy, and the natural resources laws that are all part of the cross-sectoral trends that need to be collated to move towards net zero in Australia.

Complicating matters is the continuation of the economic dependency of Australia on carbon-based natural resource exports, as well as Australia's long-term engagement with the transnational energy and natural resource corporations that facilitate that export. Regional geopolitical factors contribute to Australia's dependency on natural resources exports—a legacy from the nation's colonial history. In the twenty-first century, this path dependency on natural resources wealth in Australia remains a serious challenge that the national government will have to address to achieve decarbonization. Australia's commitment to meet net zero by 2050 will be tested by a dichotomy between its climate and natural resources law in domestic as opposed to transnational settings.

Accordingly, this chapter investigates the potential for national climate legislation to foster cross-sectoral solidarity and to continue the energy transition in Australian society to sufficiently meet net zero by 2050. Although the focus is on national government laws, the analysis considers the potential for climate litigation and financial regulation to indirectly govern natural resources such as coal and gas in order to propel faster emissions reductions in light of Australia's high levels of natural resource exports. This chapter has five sections. After this introduction, Section II examines the new climate legislation in the context of the net zero challenge. The section also references the law and constitutional position that is relevant to setting NDC targets in Australia. By reference to relevant literature, the section traces how a carbon-intense society in Australia was forged historically and the current challenges to coal phase-out. This cross-sectoral context explains in part why Australia is unlikely to meet net zero. Section III discusses the extent to which national energy laws in Australia are fostering a move to net zero. It examines how cross-sectoral law and regulation in the financial sector, aided by climate litigation, supports efforts to move to net zero. It explores how climate litigation in respect of coal and gas projects, in the context of the former government's inaction on climate targets is building community awareness and influencing cross-sectoral support for net zero. Section IV examines how the lessons from Australia's experience in cross-sectoral law and regulation may provide guidance for other jurisdictions. The chapter concludes in Section V.

II. The Legal and Historical Context to Climate Change in Australia

Australia has been occupied by Aboriginal peoples for approximately 60,000 years,[12] and these communities have over this time sustainably managed their environment.[13] Forced

[12] Christine Black, *The Land is the Source of the Law* (Routledge 2011) ch 1.
[13] Stuart Macintyre, *A Concise History of Australia* (4th edn, CUP) 9.

removal of Aboriginal people from parts of Australia following European settlement[14] has contributed to greatly increased emissions since colonization.[15] European settlement introduced extractive natural resource use (such as burning coal) with progressively higher levels of resulting GHG emissions over time.[16] The onset of the Anthropocene, that geologic era characterized by human-induced climate change, is coincidental with the substantial colonization of Australia.[17]

Currently, Aboriginal systems of natural resource management are less emissions-intensive,[18] and are being adapted across the continent to reduce the significant land sector emissions that form part of the baseline calculations for Australia's NDC targets. The national environment legislation, the Environment Protection and Biodiversity Conservation Act (EPBC Act), fosters co-management of these less emission-intense forms of natural resource management.[19] Such changes are part of cross-sectoral transitions required to meet net zero targets.

Concurrently, restoration of degraded native ecosystems to effectively sequester carbon to reduce emissions will be needed. The current legal frameworks are relatively weak.[20] Australia has a voluntary Emissions Reduction Fund (ERF) scheme.[21] Various natural resource activities related to native vegetation can create carbon offsets to be sold to meet their emission reduction targets, or to businesses which voluntarily offset emissions.[22] The EPBC Act requires those who clear vegetation for development to 'offset' the release of stored carbon.[23] In the past, Australia has met its international obligations under the Kyoto Protocol by using a combination of forest sector/natural resource and industrial emissions reductions. That emissions objective has been superseded by the NDCs set in 2022. Natural resource sequestration activities clearly can lower emissions, but collectively the measures are unlikely to substantially contribute to net zero by 2050.

Environmental laws have made some headway in curbing emissions, but climate-related legal and policy measures, have made relatively limited inroads into the prevention of escalating emission levels from natural resource project developments. Changing that orientation to meet net zero targets by 2050 remains partial and complex due to the federalism interplay in Australia. By contrast, laws that directly facilitate extraction of carbon-based natural resources have been in place for a surprisingly long time.

[14] ibid 57–62.

[15] Noel Butlin, *Forming a Colonial Economy: Australia, 1810–1850* (CUP 1994).

[16] Julia Dehm, *Reconsidering REDD+ Authority, Power and Law in the Green Economy* (CUP 2021) 1–2, 37–44.

[17] The Anthropocene is typically regarded as emerging with the 'Industrial Revolution' in the early nineteenth century. See eg Will Steffen and others, 'Trajectories of the Earth System in the Anthropocene' (2018) 115 (33) PNAS 8252, 8252. <https://doi.org/10.1073/pnas.1810141115>

[18] Marcia Langton and others, 'The Idea of a Treaty' in Anna Clark (ed), *The Knowledge Solution: Australian History: What Place Does History Have in a Post-Truth World?* (Melbourne UP 2019).

[19] Environment Protection and Biodiversity Conservation Act 1999 (C'th), s 3.

[20] Godden, Peel, and Mc Donald (n 2) 244–46.

[21] Eliza de Wit and Amy Quinton, 'Creating, Buying and Safeguarding Emissions Reductions Under the Emissions Reduction Fund' (2018) 92(1) Australian Law Journal 766.

[22] Ella Plumanns Pouton, Rod Keenan, and Lee Godden, 'An Australian Climate Accord: A New Way Forward for Climate Crisis Governance?' <https://apo.org.au/sites/default/files/resource-files/2022-04/apo-nid317943.pdf> accessed 30 August 2022.

[23] Australian Government Department of Sustainability, Environment, Water, Population and Communities Policy guiding the use of offsets under the Environment Protection and Biodiversity Conservation Act 1999 <https://www.dcceew.gov.au/environment/epbc/publications/epbc-act-environmental-offsets-policy>. [Accessed 2 December 2022.]

A. Dependency on Carbon Exploitation and Net Zero

From a small nucleus of penal colonies, the British colonial presence expanded rapidly in the early nineteenth century, especially in the southeastern part of the colony.[24] Assertion of British sovereignty secured the colonies' natural resources against other European powers. Appropriation of carbon-based natural resources was achieved at law, firstly through a nullification of the pre-existing indigenous relationship with 'country', and secondly, through importation of British legal and administrative regimes that had Crown vesting of resources at its centre.[25] Coal was utilized within twenty years of the first colony in Port Jackson (Sydney), with coal regularly shipped to that town. Natural resource use practices, set in place at colonization, reflected derived UK legal principles and local administrative frameworks.[26] The pattern of extraction and global export of natural resources such as coal, under British Imperial rule,[27] continued with formation of the Australian nation.[28]

By the early twentieth century, the resources law system had given rise to largely government-owned, fossil fuel energy extraction and associated infrastructure.[29] Coal and natural gas remain major power sources in Australia,[30] although liquified natural gas is predicted to rapidly overtake coal-based exports. Renewable energy is significant in domestic electricity generation, especially in southeastern Australia. Coal resources are widespread across the continent.[31] Coastal 'coal' ports are a major infrastructure along eastern Australia, with expansion of ports to facilitate exports such as that from the controversial Adani coal mine.[32] Coal-based industries remain key sources of economic prosperity for many Australian regional communities.[33]

B. The Coal 'Phase-Out'

The sheer size of coal reserves in Australia illustrates the barriers to a rapid decarbonization pathway to net zero. Australia's recoverable coal reserves are the third largest in the world.[34] Despite a relatively small population, Australia is responsible for approximately 5 per cent of total global emissions, if emissions from domestic and exported fossil fuel use are combined.[35] Australian per capita GHG emissions from coal typically are higher than any other

[24] Macintyre (n 13).

[25] Lee Godden, 'Wik: Feudalism, Capitalism and the State: Towards a Revision of Land Law in Australia?' (1997) 5 Property Law Journal, 162, 165.

[26] ibid.

[27] David Merrett, 'Big Business and Foreign Firms' in Simon Ville and Glenn Withers (eds), *The Cambridge Economic History of Australia* (CUP 2014).

[28] Cait Storr and Miranda Johnson, 'Australia as Empire' in Peter Cane, Lisa Ford, and Mark McMillan (eds), *The Cambridge Legal History of Australia* (CUP 2021).

[29] Anne Kallies, 'Regulating the Use of Energy Networks in Liberalised Markets' in Martha Roggenkamp, Kars de Graaf, and Ruven Fleming, *Energy Law, Climate Change and the Environment* (Edward Elgar Publishing 2021) 599, 600.

[30] John Wiseman, 'Accelerating the phase out of coal in Australia: Key trends and drivers' in Bellantuono and others (eds) (n 11) 183.

[31] ibid 185.

[32] When first proposed, the Adani coal mine would have been one of the world's largest. See the legal action challenging the mine: *Australian Conservation Foundation Inc v Minister for the Environment* [2016] FCA 1042.

[33] Wiseman (n 30) 185.

[34] Geoscience Australia, 'Coal' <https://www.ga.gov.au/digital-publication/aecr2021/coal> [accessed 12 July 2022.]

[35] Peter Christoff, 'Mining a Fractured Landscape: The Political Economy of Coal in Australia' in Michael Jacobs and Jan Steckel (eds), *The Political Economy of Coal: Obstacles to Clean Energy Transitions* (Routledge 2021) 233.

developed country.[36] Coal and gas projects under development in 2021 in Australia will result in 1.7 billion tonnes of emissions each year (equivalent to 200 coal-fired power stations)—or twice the annual emissions from global aviation.[37]

Given the Australian contribution to GHG emissions, there is concerted international and domestic pressure for it to reduce its coal-based emissions. To date, the legal and policy effort has been directed to phasing out coal mining and coal-fired power production, with less success in reducing exports. The contribution that the domestic coal phase-out will make to the net zero target remains uncertain. In the absence of a carbon pricing mechanism in Australian law, there are few direct legal drivers for a rapid transition from coal in the domestic system. This situation is compounded by subnational governments tending to approve mine developments in economically depressed regions.[38] Accordingly, progress in the phasing out of coal has remained reasonably slow.[39]

2. Coal as 'Stranded Asset'

Since 2015, the transnational tide has been slowly turning against coal. Mark Carney, then Governor of the Bank of England, drew attention to the risk that climate change posed to global financial systems.[40] This precipitated concern in the financial regulatory and investment sectors about global investments in natural resources and fossil fuel-based energy production, that these might become 'stranded assets'.[41] Several multinational natural resource and investment companies have already divested Australian coal assets. In national legal settings, this highlighted the legal liability and financial implications faced by businesses and investors in not addressing climate transition risks.[42] Ripples were felt in financial sectors in Australia, with anxiety expressed by financial organizations such as superannuation funds about the potential 'stranding' of assets in existing investments in coal mines and coal-fired power production. This resulted in financial regulators, including the national corporate regulators, issuing regulatory 'advices' for companies and professional bodies to attend to climate transition risks.[43] Even so, the nexus of coal and financial regulation in Australia are complex. The ambivalence is exemplified by the Labor government's post-election position. It has merged support for higher emission reduction targets, acceleration of renewable energy investment, with a commitment to protect coal industry employment.[44] Nonetheless, a combination

[36] Wiseman (n 30) 185.

[37] Mark Ogge, Audrey Quicke, and Rod Campbell, 'Undermining climate action the Australian way' (The Australia Institute 2021) <https://australiainstitute.org.au/wp-content/uploads/2021/11/P1163-Undermining-climate-action-the-Australian-way-WEB.pdf> accessed 21 August 2023.

[38] Laura Schuijers, 'Times have changed: why the environment minister is being forced to reconsider climate-related impacts of pending fossil fuel approvals' (*The Conversation*, 11 July 2022) <https://theconversation.com/times-have-changed-why-the-environment-minister-is-being-forced-to-reconsider-climate-related-impacts-of-pending-fossil-fuel-approvals-> accessed 21 August 2023.

[39] Christoff (n 35) 235.

[40] Mark Carney, 'Breaking the Tragedy of the Horizon—Climate Change and Financial Stability' (Speech, Bank of England, 29 September 2015) <http://www.bankofengland.co.uk/publications/Pages/speeches/default.aspx> accessed 21 August 2023.

[41] Stranded assets refer to the view that investment in carbon natural resources and fossil fuels could become 'stranded', ie non-productive given energy transition away from these resources.

[42] Neil Gunningham, 'A Quiet Revolution: Central Banks, Financial Regulators, and Climate Finance' (2020) 12(9596) Sustainability 1, 6–8.

[43] See discussion at section 111 B about company director's duties and disclosure of climate risk.

[44] Wiseman (n 30) 189.

of strategic measures, climate advocacy, and litigation are producing a tangible shift from coal.[45]

3. Just Transition and Coal

In Australia, as elsewhere, climate advocacy groups are successfully employing legal, financial, and corporate governance strategies to highlight the need to transition from fossil fuels, coal production and investment in coal.[46] However, the Australian government does not have a legal or policy position to cease coal export projects. A compromise policy position has been 'hammered out' with the need for respectful 'just transition' strategies to build community support for a planned shift away from coal resources.[47] There is public and political support for accelerating coal resource phase-out under just transition principles.[48] Australian experience reinforces international practice that emphasizes the need for well-managed and consultative regional transition strategies.[49]

In terms of net zero targets, a complete 'phase-out' of coal in Australia by 2050 is unlikely, given substantial existing investments in coal, and the planned economic life of such projects. A faster pathway for decarbonization is the accelerating retirement of coal-fired power stations assisted by various regulatory and financial incentives to enhance effective investment in solar and wind resources, to expand Australia's substantial renewable energy generation.[50] In turn, changes to rules governing national energy markets will be required to move more rapidly towards net zero.

III. Energy Market Regulation and Net Zero

A. Transition in Australia: The Current Legal Landscape

In light of the ongoing global clean energy transition, this section examines the extent to which national energy laws in Australia are fostering a systemic and coherent move to net zero.[51]

Australia's public system of energy resource extraction, and energy production and distribution initially developed under individual state laws. This pattern was disrupted in the 1990s by privatization of energy systems and introduction of liberalized energy markets. Energy transition began in the late twentieth century, alongside the emergence of 'national'

[45] John Wiseman and Linda Wollersheim, 'Building Just and Prosperous Zero Carbon Regions' (Melbourne Climate Futures, University of Melbourne 2021).

[46] Anita Foerster and others, 'Keeping Good Company in the Transition to a Low Carbon Economy? An Evaluation of Climate Risk Disclosure Practices in Australia' <https://papers.ssrn.com/sol3/papers.cfm?abstract_id=3018241>. [accessed 5 December 2022

[47] Wiseman (n 30) 189.

[48] Michael Jacobs and Jan Steckel (eds), *The Political Economy of Coal: Obstacles to Clean Energy Transitions* (Routledge 2021).

[49] Wiseman and Wollersheim (n 45).

[50] Anne Kallies, 'The Australian Energy Transition as a Federalism Challenge: (Un)cooperative Energy Federalism?' (2021) 10(2) Transnational Environmental Law 211–35, 213.

[51] Kylie Turner and Anna Skarbeck, 'Australia finally has a Net Zero Authority—here's what should top its agenda' (*The Conversation*, 5 May 2023) <https://theconversation.com/australia-finally-has-a-net-zero-authority-heres-what-should-top-its-agenda-205029> accessed 21 August 2023.

energy markets.[52] 'Cooperative' governance is characteristic of energy law and policy in Australia. [53] The national electricity market and the national gas market operate within complex multilevel and multiauthority statutory regulatory systems. The national government exercises certain intergovernmental powers in respect of energy, due to overlapping legislative regimes. Where there is overlap, the national laws take precedence.[54] Even so, energy law and policy typically operate in a separate register to environmental laws, except at the level of energy project development.

Reform efforts to better integrate natural resources laws, energy projects, and climate change laws (eg climate assessment in the EPBC Act) have produced mixed outcomes. The integration of stronger climate mitigation principles and transition policies into the energy regulation framework in Australia has been politically fraught for many years.[55] The previous conservative government maintained a regulatory focus on energy security, which tended to favour carbon-based generation systems, although there is substantial momentum towards net zero in the energy governance framework.[56]

1. New Climate Legislation and Net Zero

Australia now has national climate legislation, which seeks to implement the Australian government's NDC, although the emissions reduction target in the NDC is not likely to reach net zero by 2050. As noted, the Act's core functions relate to setting emissions reduction targets and to articulating future ambition around reduction targets.[57] An annual climate statement must be tabled in the national parliament, which must log progress towards reduction targets and assess the efficacy of policies in reducing emissions.[58] The Act requires the Climate Change Authority to advise the Minister for Climate Change regarding the annual climate statements,[59] and to provide advice on revised emissions reductions targets for any new or adjusted NDC. The legislative requirements for transparent national reporting on climate change goals will directly influence how energy market regulation contributes to emission reduction targets in the future.

Consequential amendments to other legislation were passed with the Climate Act 2022, which incorporated the emissions reductions targets into fourteen pieces of national legislation. The laws include climate change emissions reporting, renewable energy and carbon farming legislation, certain infrastructure, and financing statutes.[60] Of specific relevance to energy regulation, NDC targets were integrated into legislation governing agencies such as the Clean Energy Finance Corporation, Clean Energy Regulator, and the Australian Renewable Energy Agency.[61] To date, these agencies have been

[52] Penelope Crossley, 'Renewable Energy Law in the Context of a Transforming Australian Energy Market' in Tina Hunter and others (eds), *Routledge Handbook of Energy Law* (Routledge 2020) ch 26.

[53] Kallies, 'The Australian Energy Transition' (n 50) 212.

[54] Godden, Peel, and McDonald (n 2) 187–89.

[55] ibid 435.

[56] Lee Godden and Anne Kallies, 'Governance of the Energy Market in Australia' in Martha M Roggenkamp, Kars J de Graaf, and Ruven C Fleming (eds), *Energy Law, Climate Change and the Environment* (Edward Elgar Publishing 2022) 204–15, 205.

[57] Climate Change Act 2022, Part 2.

[58] ibid Part 3.

[59] ibid Part 4.

[60] Climate Change (Consequential Amendments) Act 2022 (C'th).

[61] ibid.

instrumental in the energy transition that has occurred in the national energy markets. While energy transition is gathering pace internally, the geopolitical context for Australia largely represents a business-as-usual profile for natural resource exports and energy markets internationally.

2. Geopolitical Context and Natural Resource Exports

The geopolitical situation in the Asia-Pacific region and Australia's trading relationships (typically based on coal and gas exports) introduce external uncertainties into any pathway to a transition away from coal exports. Whether the coal exports are 'replaced' by Liquid Nitrogen Gas (LNG) exports of similar volumes is also probable. Overall, the medium-term scenario is a mixed one. Australian coal exports (mainly going to Japan, China, India, South Korea, and Taiwan) are predicted to rise to over AU$110 billion in 2023.[62] The sharp increase is largely due to the Russia–Ukraine war and its effect on international coal prices. Alternatively, Australian coal exports could fall substantially if Australia's major trading partners adopt more robust UNFCCC targets.[63] Further, a 2021 Beyond Zero Emissions report for Australia identified the clear potential for renewable energy to drive investment in high-value, energy-intensive export industries including green hydrogen, green steel, and [64]green aluminium. Many business leaders in Australia, once in denial on climate change, now acknowledge that moving towards net zero by 2050 is necessary to develop a competitive advantage in new technologies and export industries.[65] Although governments typically advocate technological 'solutions', concurrent developments in law and regulation will be required to ensure that business and investments are channelled towards net zero targets. Climate litigation will be vital to ensuring that the financial sector is oriented towards net zero.

B. 'Gap Filling' Alternative Law and Regulation in the Move to Net Zero

1. Climate Financial Risk and Net Zero

Australia has now moved to firm up its legislative framework of NDC targets in a range of legislation. Given the previous weak NDC targets pursued by the former national governments, however, a range of private law, financial regulation measures, and climate litigation developed to provide cross-sectoral momentum for energy transition in lieu of robust legislative targets.[66] Whilst these indirect forms of governance may not be as clearly targeted

[62] Katrina Beaven, 'Coal exports forecast to smash record with value set to break $100 billion this financial year' (2022) <https://www.abc.net.au/news/2022-04-04/australian-coal-exports-to-break-record/> accessed 21 August 2023.

[63] Jonathon Kemp, Madeleine McCowage, and Faye Wang, 'Towards Net zero Implications for Australia of Energy Policies in East Asia' (*RBA Bulletin*, (2021) <https://www.rba.gov.au/publications/bulletin/2021/sep/towards-net-zero-implications-for-australia-of-energy-policies-in-east-asia.html> accessed 21 August 2023.

[64] Beyond Zero Emissions (2021) Export Powerhouse, Australia's $333 billion opportunity, 5 <https://bze.org.au/research_release/export-powerhouse/>accessed 20 September 2022.

[65] Rob Harris, 'Business Council calls for 46–50% emissions reduction by 2030 on path to net zero' (*Sydney Morning Herald*, 9 October 2021). https://www.smh.com.au/politics/federal/business-council-calls-for-46-50-percent-emissions-reduction-by-2030-on-path-to-net-zero-20211008-p58yed.html [accessed 14May 2024.]

[66] See Anita Foerster, 'Aligning Private Climate Risk Management to Paris Climate Goals? An Australian Perspective' (2022) 18(2) Utrecht Law Review 107.

as legislation, they have proved highly effectual in driving some energy transition in the Australian economy, including in natural resources projects. One of the central strategies has been to require greater transparency around how natural resources and associated projects are susceptible to climate impacts, including 'transition risk'. Transition risk is the failure to consider potential financial loss or liability due to not advancing transition with its consequent emission reductions.[67]

Calls for stronger climate risk disclosure by industry and financial institutions have grown in insistency. The aim of more robust discosure is to promote greater transparency and to reduce 'greenwashing' in the clean energy transition.[68] In Australia, attention has shifted from fiduciary and corporate duties to provide general information on climate impacts to specific measures on risk mitigation and pathways for energy transition.[69] Financial regulation of climate risk is well established.[70] It relies on legal disclosure, process-based regulation, and norm-setting codes of practice. Directors' duties under Australian corporations law now clearly require consideration of climate risk and comprehensive corporate disclosure obligations.[71] Given the importance of natural resources to the Australian economy, these corporate risk requirements touch many components of cross-sectoral regulation, including contract law and trade regulation. The Climate Change Act 2022 may reference net zero, but the 'legal risk of climate risk' is often passed by corporations through chains of contracts (eg in the coal and gas industries), by markets, and in the community by energy consumption. '[A] range of private regulatory initiatives have emerged to guide, support and pressure companies to identify and disclose climate-related risks to the market and demonstrate appropriate risk management'.[72] Concern has surfaced, though, around the efficacy of disclosure and information measures in driving decarbonization and in moving towards net zero targets. Australian experience with non-mandatory measures suggests a firmer stance by financial regulators may be advisable.

Financial regulators in Australia (and elsewhere) initially crystallized their role as requiring provision of market information, for example climate pricing to drive energy transition.[73] This regulatory model leaves substantive risk responses to the private sector.[74] Market measures are less prescriptive than legislation on how compliance is achieved, that is, they are more normative than prescriptive.[75] Private law and financial regulatory models

[67] Chris Barrett and Anna Skarbek, 'Climate Risk and the Financial System—Lessons for Australia from International Experience' (2019) 7 <https://www.monash.edu/sustainable-development/capabilities/climateworks-australia/climate-risk-and-the-financial-system> accessed 21 August 2023.

[68] See Chapter 12 of this book on EIA. See also Gernot Wagner and Martin Weitzman, *Climate Shock: The Economic Consequences of a Hotter Planet* (Princeton UP 2015).

[69] Barrett and Skarbek (n 67) 12–15.

[70] Jacqueline Peel and Hari Osofsky, 'Climate Change Litigation' (2020) 16 Annual Review of Law and Social Science 21; Jaqueline Peel and Rebekah Markey-Towler, 'Climate Change Risk and Sovereign Bond Investments: The Case of O'Donnell v Commonwealth of Australia' (2020) 14(3) Carbon & Climate Law Review 177.

[71] See eg Noel Hutley SC and Sebastian Hartford-Davis, 'Climate Change and Directors' Duties: Memorandum of Opinion' (Legal Opinion, The Centre for Policy Development and The Future Business Council, 7 October 2016).

[72] Foerster (n 66) 108.

[73] Cameron Holley, Neil Gunningham, and Clifford Shearing, *The New Environmental Governance* (Routledge 2012) 4.

[74] Lee Godden and others, 'Law, Governance and Risk: Deconstructing the Public/Private Divide in Climate Change Adaptation' (2013) 36 University of New South Wales Law Journal 224, 225.

[75] Fleur Johns, 'Drowning, Rescuing, and the Law in Between' (2020) 61(3) European Journal of Sociology 455, 456.

may not always achieve social equity in decarbonization pathways.[76] Climate litigation may, therefore, seek redress for vulnerable and marginalized social groups who experience climate harms. As natural resources such as coal are regarded as a 'source' of climate harms, it is not surprising that much climate litigation targets natural resources laws.

2. Climate Litigation

The Australian government has not substantially legislated in the climate risk financial space. In response to that legislative vacuum, Australian climate litigation has included actions against commercial banks, superannuation funds, and institutions responsible for issuing government bonds.[77] Thus, the attention of commercial banks,[78] central (reserve) banks,[79] and prudential and financial regulators[80] is now firmly oriented to the financial imperatives of energy transition.[81] Many of these financial institutions will have natural resources such as coal and gas (but increasingly renewable energy) within their management portfolios.

The transformation of climate change risk to a regulatory obligation has been rapid in Australia. The prospect of future liability such as negligence has catalyzed change in the financial sector, especially where climate impact is a material risk to investment returns. Superannuation investment strategies that include coal and gas holdings, for example, have come under intense scrutiny.[82] Given the strategic importance of the finance sector to other sectors in Australian society that will need to transition to meet net zero by 2050, these developments are significant. Even so, whilst many banks in Australia, for example, have lending policies that promote energy transition, changes in the financial sector to date are not far reaching enough to drive substantial decarbonization in natural resources, and energy transition in sectors such as transport, housing, and infrastructure. Where sustainable finance is driving stronger decarbonization is in project financing and renewable energy production.[83] This trend is running parallel to protest and litigation against fossil fuel projects.

C. Net Zero and Challenging Natural Resources Project Development

Australia has experienced a rapid escalation of climate litigation over the past decade designed to push policy-makers to set net zero targets. The litigation builds on public interest

[76] David Driesen, 'Legal Theory Lessons from the Financial Crisis' (2014) 40(1) Journal of Corporation Law 55, 56.

[77] *Abrahams v Commonwealth Bank of Australia* (Federal Court of Australia, VID879/2017); *McVeigh v Retail Employees Superannuation Pty Ltd* [2020] FCA 1698; *O'Donnell v Commonwealth of Australia* (Federal Court of Australia, VID482/2020, commenced 22 July 2020).

[78] See eg Joseba Eceiza and others, *Banking Imperatives for Managing Climate Risk* (McKinsey & Company 2020).

[79] See eg Patrick Bolton and others, 'The Green Swan: Central Banking and Financial Stability in the Age of Climate Change' (Bank for International Settlements and Banque de France, 2020).

[80] Australian Prudential Regulation Authority (APRA), 'Letter to all APRA-regulated entities' (APRA, 24 February 2020); Australian Securities and Investments Commission, '19-208MR ASIC updates guidance on climate change related disclosure' (ASIC, 12 August 2019).

[81] Jaqueline Peel and others, 'Governing the Energy Transition: The Role of Corporate Law Tools' (2019) 36(5) Environmental and Planning Law Journal 459.

[82] Foerster (n 66) 109.

[83] AEMO, 'Integrated System Plan 2022' (2022) <https://aemo.com.au/en/energy-systems/major-publications/integrated-system-plan-isp/2022-integrated-system-plan-isp> accessed 21 August 2023.

litigation that has, over many years, challenged government decision-making.[84] Natural resource and associated infrastructure projects frequently are the subject of government development approvals. Community groups, frustrated by a lack of action on climate change, have sought litigation avenues to challenge government decisions, institutional policies, and business operations that have entrenched carbon resource dependency in Australia.[85]

Early climate litigation in Australia was broadly directed to climate mitigation and energy transition by challenging government decision-making under planning, resources, and environmental laws.[86] Most of these legal actions have been applications for judicial review and merit review of government decisions that granted approvals for natural resources projects that substantially increased emissions.[87] Environmental impact assessment (EIA) laws in many Australian jurisdictions have relatively limited requirements for decision-makers to have regard to climate change impacts or energy transition priorities. The EPBC Act provides for judicial review of ministerial approvals of 'controlled actions' such as coal mines and petroleum projects,[88] as well as applications for injunctive relief where natural resource projects are likely to have a significant impact on a matter of national environmental significance. The Act has figured prominently in climate litigation.[89]

The peak conservation body, the Australian Conservation Foundation (ACF) supported by public interest legal organizations, has challenged government approvals of coal, conventional gas and petroleum projects, and unconventional (eg shale gas) projects under various legislative regimes.[90] The ACF brought judicial review challenges to the Adani coal mine at Federal Court and High Court levels.[91] Grounds for review included the failure of the Australian Environment Minister to have regard to relevant considerations including impacts of the mine on the World Heritage Great Barrier Reef due to the global emissions arising from overseas combustion of the coal from the mine. Central to the determination of 'no grounds for review' at various levels of the court hierarchy in which the ACF challenge was heard was a finding of insufficient evidence of a direct consequential linking of global emission impacts with the specific coal mine or gas/petroleum project. Similarly, other early judicial review challenges to coal and gas developments were not able to meet the causation threshold, that is, the linking of evidence of climate change impacts to a specific 'action' (ie the proposed mine of gas project. By contrast, in *Gloucester Resources Limited v Minister for Planning*,[92] the NSW Land and Environment Court, under a merits review procedure, confirmed an earlier rejection of an extension for

[84] Lee Godden and Anne Kallies, 'What Price Democracy? Blue Wedges and the Hurdles to Public Interest Environmental Litigation' (2008) 33(4) Alternative Law Journal 194.

[85] Laura Schuijers and Margaret Young, 'Climate Change Litigation in Australia: Law and Practice in the Sunburnt Country' in Ivano Alogna, Christine Bakker, Jean-Pierre Gauci (eds), *Climate Change Litigation: Global Perspectives* (Brill 2021).

[86] Jaqueline Peel, Hari Osofsky, Anita Foerster, 'Shaping the "Next Generation" of Climate Change Litigation in Australia' (2017) 41(2) Melbourne University Law Review 793.

[87] Godden, Peel, and McDonald (n 2) 145–50.

[88] Controlled actions have, or are likely to have, a significant impact on matters of national environmental significance including World Heritage places, Ramsar wetlands, and threatened species and communities.

[89] Laura Schuijers, 'Environmental Law: Climate of Change in the Courtrooms' (2021) 84 Law Society Journal 76, 78.

[90] See Australian and Pacific Climate Change Litigation, compiled by Melbourne Climate Futures, the University of Melbourne <https://law.app.unimelb.edu.au/climate-change/index.php> accessed 21 August 2023.

[91] *ACF v Minister for Environment* [2016] FCA 1042; *ACF v Minister for the Environment* [2021] FCA 550.

[92] *Gloucester Resources Limited v Minister for Planning* [2019] NSWLEC 7.

a thermal coal project.[93] Grounds for rejection included the contribution of the mine to global emissions (scope 3 emissions) and on local community values. This was a significant decision in building momentum for net zero targets. Another group of climate actions were linked to planning and environmental laws but sought relief for climate adaptation rather than climate mitigation.[94] Whilst this type of litigation is not directly focused on achieving net zero targets, it was significant in drawing attention to the widespread impacts of climate change and the urgency of stronger emission reduction targets.

1. Government Duties to Reduce Emissions

A distinctive feature of Australian climate litigation has been efforts to articulate a government duty to protect the population from climate change impacts. In 2020, the Bushfire Survivors for Climate Action commenced legal action against the EPA in the NSW Land and Environment Court.[95] The court found that the EPA had not fulfilled its statutory duty to protect the state's environment. The court ordered the agency to take action against climate change.[96] The case follows litigation brought against public authorities in Australia and around the world.[97] The Bushfire Survivors case demonstrates how the physical effects of climate change such as increased bushfire events are driving measures to reduce emissions.[98]

Nationally, whether the Environment Minister when approving projects under the EPBC Act might owe a duty of care to future generations to consider climate change impacts such as increased bushfire risk, has also been tested. Teenagers sought an injunction in advance of an approval by the minister for an extension to the Whitehaven coal mine project—a controlled action for EPBC Act purposes. In May 2021, Justice Bromberg of the Federal Court accepted the principle that a minister must have regard to a duty of care to prevent physical harm to at-risk children. [99] Justice Bromberg noted that, 'trauma will be far more common and good health harder to hold and maintain . . . It will largely be inflicted by the inaction of this generation of adults, in what might fairly be described as the greatest inter-generational injustice ever inflicted by one generation of humans upon the next'.[100] The injunctive relief that was granted, was reversed on appeal to the Full Federal Court.[101] The Full Federal Court offered different reasoning, although deference to the separation of powers principle and the need for legislative and executive government to lead on climate

[93] Merits review is a de novo proceeding where the court/tribunal rehears the factual evidence and reviews the law.

[94] See eg Tayanah O'Donnell, 'Legal Geography and Coastal Climate Change Adaptation: The Vaughan Litigation' (2016) 54(3) Geographical Research 301.

[95] Rachel Pepper, 'Environmental Law: Quartet of Recent Landmark Climate Change Cases' (2021) 95(11) Australian Law Journal 861.

[96] ibid.

[97] Matt Floro and others, 'Bushfire Survivors for Climate Action Inc v Environment Protection Authority: Australia's Massachusetts v EPA' (2022) 36(5) Australian Environment Review 10.

[98] Terri Janke, Clara Klemski, and Laura Melrose, 'Bushfires, Climate Change and Indigenous Ecological Knowledge: Healing Country through Holistic Environmental Management' (2021) 36(4) Australian Environment Review 93.

[99] Laura Schuijers, 'In a landmark judgment, the Federal Court found the Environment Minister has a duty of care to young people' (*The Conversation*, 27 May 2021) <https://www.theconversation> accessed 21 August 2023.

[100] *Sharma by her litigation representative Sister Marie Brigid Arthur v Minister for the Environment* (Sharma No 2) [2021] FCA 774, paras 72–73.

[101] See generally, *Sharma by her litigation representative Sister Marie Brigid Arthur v Minister for the Environment* (No 1) [2021] FCA 560 (Sharma (No 1); and Sharma (No 2). Note: both reversed on appeal in the Full Federal Court.

change law and policy reform figured prominently.[102] It was a disappointing outcome, as robust jurisprudence on 'duties to consider climate risks' would have been a catalyst for robust government decision-making in light of net zero targets when approvals of coal and gas projects were considered. Australian advocacy groups have continued their climate litigation strategies, even with the enactment of 2022 national climate legislation. In June 2022, the Environmental Defenders Office unsuccessfully sought a Federal Court injunction under the EPBC Act in relation to the proposed Scarborough offshore gas project.[103]

Climate change also threatens the right to life, water and sanitation, health, food, and housing, as well as civil and political rights.[104] Australia's human rights framework (there is no national human rights legislation) has been tested by climate litigation. Indigenous peoples have been proactive in respect of rights to life, home, and culture, where those have been threatened by weak climate mitigation targets.[105] Human rights claims have been litigated in state courts. The Queensland Land Court (Kingham J) considered whether the application by Waratah Coal for a mining lease and environmental authority to develop a thermal coal mine was in breach of the Human Rights Act 2019 (Qld). The legal issues included whether mine approval would be irreconcilable with human rights, such as the rights to recognition and equality before the law, right to life, property rights, the rights of children, and the cultural rights of Aboriginal and Torres Strait Islander peoples.[106] The climate change impacts of a colonial and post-colonial economy built on carbon-based natural resources are now inequitably burdening communities; a position compounded where net zero is an aspirational rather than an effective goal.

IV. Towards Nexus and Multisector Governance: The Role of Climate Litigation

Chapters 2 and 3 of this book have discussed the rise of climate legislation and net zero targets in many countries, as well as the assertion of resource sovereignty in the form of continued approval of carbon-intensive projects such as coal and oil and gas development. In Australia, climate legislation has been adopted at many levels of government and this has driven a strong internal energy transition in selected sectors such as power generation. The robustness of emission reduction targets in the national climate change legislation has varied significantly over the last fifteen years. The short-lived Clean Energy Act 2011 (C'th) had the potential to drive deeper transition. Following its repeal, the weak NDC targets in national climate-related laws created a hiatus in national momentum for energy transition with consequent expansion of coal and gas development projects (largely destined for export). The 2022 national climate change legislation is selectively driving energy transition and it only indirectly regulates these projects. As can be learned from the Australian

[102] *Minister for the Environment v Sharma* [2022] FCAFC 35.

[103] Environmental Defenders Office, 'Injunction sought against Woodside's Scarborough Gas project' (2022) <https://www.edo.org.au/2022/06/22/injunction-sought-against-woodsides-scarborough-gas-project-to-protect-great-barrier-reef/> accessed 21 August 2023.

[104] United Nations Human Rights Commission, Special Rapporteur on the promotion and protection of human rights in the context of climate change, Promotion and protection of human rights in the context of climate change A/77/226, 26 July 2022, 3.

[105] Schuijers and Young (n 85) 47, 48.

[106] ibid 79.

experience, however, climate litigation could propel faster and systemic change across various sectors to deter and reduce continuing high levels of fossil fuel exports.

In this context, climate litigation in Australia is stretching conventional forms of legal action to challenge coal and gas developments (and other natural resource projects with high emissions) in light of climate exigencies.[107] The outcomes in the courts have varied. In parallel, reforms have been sought to substantive legislation, such as the EPBC Act, which may provide a more robust mitigation framework for achieving net zero. These legal actions dovetail with litigation in the corporate and financial sectors that is also designed to challenge decisions in respect of natural resources development, but at the level of project finance and climate risk disclosure. Such trends in Australia and other countries seek to optimize transparency, integrity, and accountability for organizations when dealing with natural resources to ensure that climate risk information is taken into account. The intent is that such accountability will galvanize private sector actors to meet net zero emissions. This responsibility may even extend to legal professional responsibilities in terms of advice to clients around climate change accountability.[108] Thus there is a widening scope of law and regulation being brought into the realm of climate litigation in Australia. A similar trend is observable in many jurisdictions,[109] as litigants search for means to lift the ambition of government NDCs.

Climate litigation targeted to natural resource development and designed to ensure Australia reduces its emissions is well advanced. Like many jurisdictions, there are mounting claims for compensation due to climate change impacts. As communities face escalating extreme events such as floods and bushfires, the scale of litigation has expanded. Class actions and community-wide claims are now more evident in Australia, although most are still directed to governments or organizations with responsibility for natural resource development. Claims traverse a range of civil actions, human rights, and international law.[110] This is a pattern occurring in many jurisdictions where communities, impatient with the weak policy commitments on NDCs, are coming together to seek both redress for harms but also to put pressure on policy-makers to institute net zero targets.

A. Cross-Sector Outcomes

Australian climate change litigation is probing the legal parameters of the duties, responsibilities, liabilities for harm, and mitigation of risk that relate to the obligations of the Australian government (and arguably other organizations) to avoid dangerous anthropogenic climate change—the treaty obligation under the United Nations Framework Convention on Climate Change (UNFCCC) 1992. Litigation is building community awareness of the need to move rapidly to net zero by 2050.[111]

Climate litigation has been a catalyst for the longer-term statutory reform needed to achieve net zero in other natural resource sectors. The broader systemic effect of litigation

[107] See nn 70, 77, 91, 92, 95, 97, 100, 101.

[108] For discussion of lawyers' ethical duties see Christine Parker and Adrian Evans, *Inside Lawyers' Ethics* (3rd edn, CUP 2018).

[109] United Nations Environment Programme (UNEP), 'Global Climate Litigation Report: 2023 Status Review' (27 July 2023) <https://www.unep.org/resources/report/global-climate-litigation-report-2023-status-review>. [accessed 12 August 2023.]

[110] For an overview, see Jacqueline Peel and Rebekkah Markey-Towler, 'Recipe for Success? Lessons for Strategic Climate Litigation from the Sharma, Neubauer, and Shell Cases' (2021) 22 German Law Journal 1484–98.

[111] Schuijers and Young (n 85) 78.

in the acceleration of action on emissions reduction, especially in regard to coal and gas projects, should not be underestimated.[112] Climate litigation, whether successful or not, was an important normative influence for political change and the introduction of the 2022 Climate Change Act. Litigation is performing this parameter shift in many jurisdictions.[113]

Although the Australian Climate Act is principally target-setting, and not a prescriptive regulatory framework for attaining net zero, the legislation will provide a focus for more concerted national action on emissions reduction. It is significant that Australia's NDCs are incorporated into the Act, and via consequential amendments, into legislation that is central to natural resource and energy governance in Australia. This mechanism means progressively strengthened emission reduction targets will be integrated into the responsibilities of national government agencies. Two pivotal bodies, the Australian Renewable Energy Agency and the Climate Change Authority, will have proactive responsibilities for achieving NDCs and ultimately net zero. This model adopted in several other common law jurisdictions has the advantage of coordinating actions by top-level agencies in the hope of a 'trickle-down effect'.

In turn, this agency structure will indirectly 'regulate' natural resources laws and associated environmental management at the subnational level. In Australia's federal structure, this may (hopefully) act as a 'nexus' to better align the emission reduction objectives of the many national and subnational authorities towards effective energy transition. Over the last two decades, Australia's subnational governments have 'more or less' actively introduced legislative and policy incentives to promote renewable energy and energy transition.[114]

Given this complex nexus of legislation, legal action, financial regulation, policy, and practice, related to the embedded path dependencies on natural resources such as coal and gas, the pathway to net zero in Australia remains conflicted and uneven, despite new national climate legislation. This is one of the most compelling lessons from the Australian context. To achieve energy transition and to move to net zero, there needs to be multilayered legislation accompanied by cross-sector regulation. Law alone will not drive the normative shifts required to attain decarbonization. This can be demonstrated by the climate legislation that has directly targeted power generation as the 'heart' of energy transition. Although there has been a remarkable shift to renewable energy in the generation profile for power production, industrial production, infrastructure provision, housing, and transport show variable patterns of energy transition and emission reductions.

In Australia, stronger national environmental law requirements which are designed to propel energy transition are now proposed following a review of the EPBC Act. A similar strengthening of other environmental laws, particularly environmental impacts assessment and development controls, will be necessary in other countries. In the rural sector, where the climate impacts are pressing, there has been experimentation with market measures to reduce emissions from this sector using carbon sinks and revegetation projects as part of Australia's efforts to meet NDC targets. The inclusion of these type of ecosystem service models for emissions reductions is a recognizable trend across countries - but it is most apparent in countries with a high carbon-intense economy. Regulatory models for climate risk management, such as financial disclosure , have garnered modest but significant

112 Peel and Markey-Towler (n 89) 1496.
113 UNEP (n 109).
114 Godden and Kallies (n 54) 207.

results in the financial sector that funds natural resource developments.[115] Despite legislative measure such as the Climate Change Act, cross-sectoral energy transition in Australia in respect of coal and gas projects has proved to be the most difficult in terms of moving progressively to net zero targets.

V. Conclusion

Australia experimented with seeking to achieve cross-sectoral solidarity in the Clean Energy package of legislation and regulation in 2011. The political fallout was so severe that there is now a more selective governance approach to decarbonisation as exemplified by the Climate Change Act 2022.[116] Australia is slowly moving to develop the nexus style of governance that is required to achieve net zero and energy transition in the natural resources sector, especially in the licensing and approval of new fossil fuel development projects. Even so, climate litigation directed at stopping coal and gas projects in Australia to date has had mixed success, with some coal mines, mine extensions, and gas projects having been halted or altered in scale. Yet the nexus of legal and normative measures designed to put into effect energy transition has largely failed to stem the significant export of natural resources such as coal and gas. Australia, as a sovereign nation with its wealth of natural resources, exercises that sovereignty in continuing to be a large carbon energy exporter. Accordingly, if Australia is to seriously set a pathway to net zero emissions by 2050, governments must address the disparity between decarbonization that is gaining ground in national settings, and the failure to meet more ambitious emission reduction targets in the 'offshore'. While the new Climate Change Act has brought a consolidated focus on the function of Australia's NDC in driving the energy transition in Australia, its efficacy is limited in relation to Australia's transnational responsibilities for emissions reductions. In order to achieve the net zero target, will require governments, businesses, and communities to undertake an unflinching multilevel appraisal[117] of whether Australia can continue its exploitation of coal and other carbon-intensive resources to the detriment of its environment and peoples. Most urgently, it will require the national government to re-assess the extent to which, as a nation, we continue to engage in international trade of those fossil fuel resources.

[115] Peel and others (n 71).

[116] Barrett and Skarbeck (n 67) 17.

[117] Jacqueline Peel, Lee Godden, and Rodney Keenan, 'Climate Change Law in an Era of Multi-Level Governance' (2012) 1(2) Transnational Environmental Law 245.

22
Conclusion
Net Zero and the Future of Natural Resources Law

Damilola S. Olawuyi, José Juan González, Hanri Mostert, Milton Fernando Montoya, and Catherine Banet

I. Introduction

This volume examines the implications of the ongoing net zero and clean energy transition for natural resources law. With case studies from frontier natural resources hubs, the book discusses the overlapping sovereignty, security, and solidarity dimensions of the ongoing clean energy transition. The chapters also highlight emerging transformations in natural resources law aimed at balancing and addressing these challenges. In this concluding chapter, we offer some reflections on moving beyond fragmentation in addressing the net zero trilemma and towards holistic and nexus governance solutions.

For several decades, where law schools have committed to teach energy law, environmental law, climate change law, oil and gas and natural resources law, they have typically treated these courses as distinct from one another.[1] While environmental law is often taught as a foundation course, natural resources law is often offered as an advanced elective course that provides a path for specialization in a niche area of law, especially petroleum or mining law.[2] However, with the rapid development of environmental law, especially climate change law, the last decade has seen a rapid transformation in the study and practice of natural resources law. The global focus on halting the climate emergency through net zero targets means it is now difficult to study or practise natural resources law without a solid understanding of the legal, compliance, and human rights issues associated with climate change, net zero, and the clean energy transition. The rise of net zero as the organizing paradigm of natural resources law and policy means that decision-making on natural resource development and management must be explored from the lens of the potential implications for resource sovereignty, security, and solidarity.[3]

As discussed in Chapter 1, the net zero trilemma is the challenge of balancing resource sovereignty, security of supply, and solidarity in the clean energy transition. Considering the wide-ranging and overlapping impacts of net zero targets and policies on different natural resource sectors and actors, such as water, energy, agriculture, land use, infrastructure

[1] Unlike energy law that mainly covers the legal framework, rules, and regulation relevant to the efficient and sustainable production, commercialization, and distribution of energy, the discipline of natural resources law extends to the sustainable production, distribution, and sale of all natural resources including minerals, forests, water, energy, and biological resources amongst others. See n 1 in Chapter 1 of this book. See also Robert L Fischman, 'What Is Natural Resources Law?' (2007) 78 University of Colorado Law Review 717, Paper 197; and Raphael Heffron and others, 'A Treatise for Energy Law' (2018) 11 Journal of World Energy Law and Business 34.
[2] Fishman (n 1).
[3] See Chapter 1 of this book.

Damilola S. Olawuyi, José Juan González, Hanri Mostert, Milton Fernando Montoya, and Catherine Banet, *Conclusion* In: *Net Zero and Natural Resources Law.* Edited by: Damilola S. Olawuyi, José Juan González, Hanri Mostert, Milton Fernando Montoya, and Catherine Banet, Oxford University Press. © International Bar Association 2024. DOI: 10.1093/9780198925033.003.0022

development, oil, gas, and solid minerals, amongst others, integrated knowledge and co-ordinated actions are required at regulatory and practice levels. Systemic and integrated action will ensure that progress made in advancing net zero targets does not exacerbate energy insecurity, social exclusions, gender injustice, and adverse environmental, social, and governance (ESG) and human rights impacts in natural resource development. Yet, many of the case studies in this book paint a dismal picture in terms of balancing net zero targets with resource sovereignty, security, and solidarity. For instance, while several countries have announced net zero targets, the continued assertion of resource sovereignty through the approval of coal, oil and gas, and other carbon-intensive investments and projects continues to delay the path to net zero. Such incoherence also sends conflicting signals to investors in terms of regulatory environment, competitiveness, and investment climate.[4] At the same time, implementing net zero programmes without addressing their implications for energy security, decent employment and zero poverty, gender justice, resource efficiency, economic diversification, and human rights, amongst other crosscutting concerns, remain key concerns that may slow down the path to net zero and the attainment of all of the United Nations Sustainable Development Goals (UN SDGs).[5] It may also create social inequality, fuelling political instability. As investors seek greater certainty and guidance on what net zero and climate-aligned contracting practices are in a net zero era,[6] coherent legal frameworks at national, regional, and international levels, as well as bespoke legal advice, are required to clarify the scope of net zero and transitions-related obligations, including local content, ESG, and human rights due diligence requirements, across the entire natural resource value chain.[7]

The courtroom battles and arbitration challenges filed against net zero programmes and their implementation show the deep fragmentations, tensions, and gaps in the natural resource sector's overall regulatory governance of net zero.[8] Governments have been challenged for failing to align net zero plans with existing laws or contracts, a good example being the United Kingdom in which a court found that the UK government failed to comply with its legal duties under the Climate Change Act 2008 in the design and approval of its net zero strategy.[9] Some investors and governments have also been challenged for failing to act at all, for announcing inadequate net zero programmes, or for approving new investments that are inconsistent with their obligations under Paris Agreement.[10] Furthermore,

[4] See Chapters 2–3 of this book on the resource sovereignty risks and natural resource principles that are emerging in a net zero era.

[5] See Chapters 6–18 of this book for an extensive examination of the security and justice risks posed by net zero.

[6] See Chapter 4 of this book for a discussion of net zero and climate-aligned contracting practices in the natural resource sector.

[7] The UK Law Society, 'The Impact of Climate Change on Solicitors' (The Law Society, 19 April 2023) <https://www.lawsociety.org.uk/topics/climate-change/impact-of-climate-change-on-solicitors#h3-heading2> accessed 10 August 2023.

[8] See Chapters 1 and 4 of this book. See also United Nations Environment Programme (UNEP), 'Global Climate Litigation Report: 2023 Status Review', <https://wedocs.unep.org/bitstream/handle/20.500.11822/43008/global_climate_litigation_report_2023.pdf?sequence=3> accessed 04 May 2024, showing that more than 2000 climate and net zero-related cases have been filed in sixty-five jurisdictions and international or regional courts and tribunals as of December 2022.

[9] See *R (oao Friends of the Earth) v Secretary of State for Business Energy and Industrial Strategy*, High Court of Justice of England and Wales, EWHC 1841, 18 July 2022 (United Kingdom of Great Britain and Northern Ireland).

[10] A Dutch court held for the first time that a private company (Shell) has a duty under the Paris Agreement to mitigate greenhouse gas (GHG) emissions. See *Milieudefensie et al. v Royal Dutch Shell plc.*, The Hague District Court, C/09/571932/HA ZA 19-379, 25 April 2022 (Netherlands). See also the Italian case of *A Sud et al. v Italy*, Civil Court of Rome, 5 June 2021 (Italy); and French cases *Notre Affaire à Tous and Others v France* (2021), Administrative Court of Paris, Nos 1904967, 1904972, 1904976/4-1, 21 October (France) and

some natural resource operators have been challenged for greenwashing and misleading consumers on the scope and impact of their net zero programmes and products.[11] Tensions and conflicts on net zero and clean energy transition are only likely to increase as climate change alters the scope of regulations and guidelines in the entire natural resource value chain, ranging from project due diligence, licensing and approval, to operations, decommissioning, and end-of-lifetime closure. Complex legal disputes on net zero efforts will not only delay their implementation but may worsen energy insecurity and the supply of energy transition minerals (ETMs) needed to advance the clean energy transition. There is, therefore, an urgent need for all natural resource stakeholders to better align net zero and energy transition programmes with existing legal and contractual obligations, to avoid legal liabilities and risks.

Despite the impetus for greater coherence and coordination in the design, approval, financing, and implementation of net zero programmes, sectoral and piecemeal efforts and competitive geopolitics on net zero transition remain prevalent in several regions and countries. The rise of trade isolationism in the United States and other parts of the world, resource nationalism in the context of ETMs, the Russia–Ukraine war, economic sanctions, and the weakening of multilateralism continue to constrain the required international solidarity, especially trade cooperation and capacity development, as well as knowledge and technology exchange, needed to advance the global energy transition.[12] These have not fostered a holistic consideration of the interplay and trade-offs between net zero ambitions and sustainable resource governance across the entire natural resource sector value chain.

Achieving a just, inclusive, and orderly clean energy transition requires rapid and systemic transformations of natural resources law to ensure greater coherence in net zero ambitions and the regulatory structures needed to achieve them.[13] However, as the chapters of this book demonstrate, in several jurisdictions, such transformations are not easily forthcoming. Why is there such reluctance to change in natural resources law and practice? What are the required steps to address such reluctance? These questions are what we address in this chapter.

After this introduction, Section II discusses the drivers of—and sustainability risks posed by—fragmentation in response to the wide range of sovereignty, security, and solidarity challenges of net zero transition. Section III discusses the guiding principles of nexus and integrated resource governance that are required to promote coherence in addressing the net zero trilemma and advancing the clean energy transition. Natural resource actors will need to raise their ambition from net zero, unsustainable subsidies, and carbon offsets to implement zero carbon policies. They will also need to integrate clean energy transition into the entire natural resource value chain, ranging from project due diligence, licensing

Commune de Grande-Synthe v France (2021), challenging governments for failing to take action to meet the Paris Agreement's goals.

[11] See Clean Energy Wire, 'Environmental NGO wins greenwashing lawsuit against TotalEnergies' (5 April 2023) <https://www.cleanenergywire.org/news/environmental-ngo-wins-greenwashing-lawsuit-against-totalenergies> accessed 10 August 2023; see also *Advertising Standards Authority UK v Shell UK Ltd*, ASA Ruling on Shell UK Ltd. (Advertising Standards Authority, 8 July 2020) (United Kingdom of Great Britain and Northern Ireland) <https://www.asa.org.uk/rulings/shell-uk-ltd-g22-1170842-shell-uk-ltd.html> accessed 28 August 2023.

[12] See Chapter 20 of this book on power politics and the weakening of solidarity. See also Chapters 3 and 4 of this book on resource nationalism risks in the clean energy transition.

[13] See Kaisa Huhta and Seita Romppanen, 'Why Is Energy Law Resistant to Changes Required by Climate Policies?' (2023) 4 Energy and Climate Change 100096.

and approval, to operations, decommissioning, and end-of-lifetime closure. Section IV is the concluding section.

II. Net Zero and Regulatory Fragmentation: Drivers and Sustainability Risks

Regulatory fragmentation on net zero, meaning the existence of diverse standards, metrics, requirements, and supervisory structures and institutions—is currently pervasive, and has been identified as a threat to coherent implementation and progress.[14] The literature on energy policy failure recognizes regulatory fragmentation as one of the key causes of energy policy failure.[15] Without clear, comprehensive, and coherent legislation and policies, implementing net zero programmes will fail to effectively balance and achieve climate change and energy security goals set out in the Paris Agreement and the UN SDGs.

As demonstrated in this book, four key drivers of regulatory fragmentation on net zero in the natural resource sector exist. First, is the lack of a comprehensive global standard on net zero and the requirements for achieving it.[16] Under article 4(2) of the Paris Agreement, parties must prepare and submit their nationally determined contributions (NDCs) to the United Nations Framework Convention on Climate Change (UNFCCC).[17] While some NDCs include targets to achieve net zero, some do not.[18] Even in the NDCs that include net zero targets, a wide range of approaches, timelines, baselines, and measures have been developed to achieve net zero. While some countries express their net zero targets in legally binding terms, some only express such targets as voluntary and non-binding national visions and strategies. In contrast, some others make net zero targets conditional upon receiving international finance, technology, and capacity support for implementation under the Common but Differentiated Responsibilities and Respective Capabilities (CBDR-RC) principle.[19] Similarly, the wide range of net zero plans announced by non-state actors,

[14] Recognizing the lack of clear, transparent, and comprehensive regulatory standards on net zero, the United Nations Secretary-General, in 2022, established the High-Level Expert Group on the Net Zero Emissions Commitments of Non-State Entities (HLEG) to 'develop stronger and clearer standards for net-zero emissions pledges' and to speed up implementation. United Nations, Climate Action, 'Credibility and Accountability of Net-Zero Emissions Commitments of Non-State Entities' (2022) <https://www.un.org/en/climatechange/high-level-expert-group> accessed 10 August 2023. See also Robin K Craig, 'Climate Change, Regulatory Fragmentation and Water Triage' (2008) 79 University of Colorado Law Review 825.

[15] Energy policy failure has been defined as 'any energy policy which does not meet local, national, and international energy and climate goals across the activities of the energy life-cycle and where just outcomes are not delivered'. See Maciej Sokołowski and Raphael Heffron, 'Defining and Conceptualising Energy Policy Failure: The When, Where, Why, and How' (2022) Energy Policy 161, 112745; see also Pim Derwort, Nicolas Jager, and Jens Newig, 'Towards Productive Functions? A Systematic Review of Institutional Failure, Its Causes and Consequences' (2019) 52 Policy Science 281.

[16] UN HLEG (n 14).

[17] Conference of the Parties, Adoption of the Paris Agreement, 12 December 2015, Paris Agreement to the United Nations Framework Convention on Climate Change (the 'Paris Agreement') (12 December 2015) TIAS No 16-1104.

[18] For an in-depth analysis of the net zero targets, see International Energy Agency (IEA), 'Net Zero by 2050: A Roadmap for the Global Energy Sector' (October 2021). <https://iea.blob.core.windows.net/assets/deebef5d-0c34-4539-9d0c-10b13d840027/NetZeroby2050-ARoadmapfortheGlobalEnergySector_CORR.pdf> accessed 12 May 2024. See also World Bank, 'Net Zero Energy by 2060: Charting Europe and Central Asia's Journey Toward Sustainable Energy Futures' (22 February 2024) <https://www.worldbank.org/en/region/eca/publication/net-zero-energy-by-2060-charting-europe-and-central-asia-s-journey-toward-sustainable-energy-futures> accessed 12 May 2024.

[19] IEA, 'Net Zero by 2050', ibid.

especially investors in the natural resource sector, vary in terms of clarity, scope, and ambition.[20] The result is a proliferation of net zero targets and programmes with different ambitions, methodology, and scope.

The lack of clear international standards and requirements on net zero, including the process for verifying, enforcing, and monitoring implementation has not fostered the development of coherent and consistent methodology and taxonomy in the natural resource sector.[21] The pervasive inconsistency in the design and implementation of net zero standards results in market uncertainties and greenwashing, which impedes overall progress towards achieving the Paris Agreement's goals to limit global warming to 1.5°C.[22] As countries continue to clarify the modalities and rules for advancing the goals of the Paris Agreement, there is a need for clear, transparent, and comprehensive standards on net zero and just energy transition, including the methodology for measuring and reporting progress.[23]

A second driver of regulatory fragmentation is the disconnect between net zero targets and natural resource legislation, contracts, regulations, and risk management frameworks. While state and non-state actors are announcing net zero plans, failure to incorporate such targets into natural resource regulation and management frameworks mean that such ambitions most often do not align with actions. This situation continues to trigger litigation and disputes.[24] Chapter 4 of this book unpacks how, since 2015 when the Paris Agreement was adopted, many long-term natural resource contracts that include provisions that constrain the abilities of governments to enact net zero laws remain in place, while even new contracts adopted post-2015 have failed to address such gaps.[25] Furthermore, Chapter 4 discusses how natural resource legislation and contracts are yet to be infused with net zero-related provisions in many countries to enhance the effective implementation of net zero targets. Another example is the continued use of fossil fuel subsidies in many parts of the world, including countries with net zero targets. This exacerbates unsustainable consumption patterns and undermines the quest for net zero.[26] The result is that though net zero targets are increasingly announced, the development, financing, and implementation of new carbon-intensive coal and oil and gas projects continue in several jurisdictions, irrespective of reported progress made in reducing greenhouse gas (GHG) emissions intensity of such projects.[27] There is an urgent need for net zero and climate-aligned legislation and contracts in the natural resource sector to address the disconnect between net zero targets and the progress made in decarbonization and the clean energy transition.

20 UN HLEG (n 14).

21 ibid.

22 IEA, 'Net Zero by 2050' (n 18); UN HLEG (n 14).

23 UN HLEG (n 14).

24 ibid.

25 See also Natural Resource Governance Institute (NRGI), 'Tying Their Hands? How Petroleum Contract Terms May Limit Governments' Climate Policy Flexibility' <https://resourcegovernance.org/analysis-tools/publications/tying-their-hands-how-petroleum-contract-terms-may-limit-gov-climate-policy-flexibility> accessed 10 August 2023.

26 IEA, 'Fossil Fuel Subsidies in Clean Energy Transitions: Time for a New Approach? A "price gap-plus" approach could bring carbon prices and environmental costs into the equation' (February 2023) <https://www.iea.org/reports/fossil-fuel-subsidies-in-clean-energy-transitions-time-for-a-new-approach> accessed 10 August 2023; also UNEP, 'Calling time on fossil fuel subsidies' (7 December 2018) <https://www.unep.org/news-and-stories/story/calling-time-fossil-fuel-subsidies> accessed 28 August 2023.

27 See Chapter 7 of this book. See also IEA, Emissions from Oil and Gas Operations in Net Zero Transitions (May 2023) <https://www.iea.org/reports/emissions-from-oil-and-gas-operations-in-net-zero-transitions> accessed 10 August 2023.

Achieving net zero by 2060 or earlier requires deep transformations across the entire natural resource value chain, ranging from project due diligence, licensing and approval to infrastructure development, operations, decommissioning, and end-of-lifetime closure. The project due diligence stage should include stringent environmental impact assessment (EIA) and mandatory human rights due diligence (HRDD) requirements to screen out new investments that do not advance just energy transition, including the ethical and responsible sourcing of transition minerals.[28] At the contract negotiation, licensing, and approval stage, there is a need to carefully integrate just transition due diligence and HRDD provisions in natural resource contracts so as to ensure that the wide range of energy security, gender, local content, ESG, and human rights concerns in clean energy projects are properly anticipated and addressed by stakeholders.[29] The infrastructure development stage, which includes the development of physical and associated infrastructure for natural resource projects, should integrate climate-smart and resource-efficient buildings and infrastructure that advance climate change mitigation and adaptation objectives, including electricity from renewable energy sources (RES-E).[30] Furthermore, as RES-E is generated from decentralized energy sources, there will be a need to address network and grid balancing, energy storage, and integration to avoid grid overload and infrastructure collapse.[31] Similarly, at the end-of-lifetime closure stage, the need for clear legislation and contractual provisions on responsible exit and decommissioning is particularly important in the net zero era.[32] As net zero and low carbon transition programmes increase in scale, estimates indicate that about 10,000 redundant oil and gas infrastructures worldwide may be decommissioned by 2038 due to the rapid pace of net zero transition.[33] Clear and comprehensive legislation and industry guidelines are required to ensure that infrastructure decommissioning and repurposing proceed in a just and human rights-compatible manner, including putting in place financial assurance mechanisms for remediation and compensation.[34] Disputes on net zero and climate-aligned decommissioning and the duty-bearer in terms of decommissioning costs are already projected to increase exponentially as coal and oil and gas assets get phased out.[35] Without clear and comprehensive regulatory

[28] See Chapter 12 of this book. See also Theo Henckens, 'Mineral Resources Ethics' in Theo Henckens, *Governance of the World's Mineral Resources* (Elsevier 2021) 71–98; OECD Briefing Note, 'Responsible is reliable: How responsible sourcing can address disruption factors and geopolitical risks in the supply of transition minerals?' (October 2023) <https://media.business-humanrights.org/media/documents/Responsible_is_Reliable.pdf> accessed 23 October 2023.

[29] See Chapter 4 of this book.

[30] See Chapter 13 of this book.

[31] See Chapter 15 of this book.

[32] OHCHR, 'Business and Human Rights in Challenging Contexts: Considerations for Remaining and Exiting' (August 2023) <https://www.ohchr.org/sites/default/files/documents/issues/business/bhr-in-challenging-contexts.pdf> accessed 10 August 2023.

[33] Mintra, 'Decommissioning activities double as net zero gathers pace' <https://mintra.com/insights-and-news/08-02-22/decommissioning-activities-double-as-net-zero-gathers-pace> accessed 10 August 2023.

[34] See Chapter 11 of this book on ESG and human rights. See also OHCHR, 'Baseline Study on the Human Rights Impacts and Implications of Mega-Infrastructure Investment' (6 July 2017) 4–10. <https://www.ohchr.org/sites/default/files/2022-01/Baseline-Study-on-the-Human-Rights-Impacts-and-Implications-of-Mega-Infrastructure-Investment.pdf> accessed 10 August 2023.

[35] See David Jenaway and Christopher Mainwaring-Taylor, 'Fossil fuel decommissioning will drive disputes' (IFLR, 31 July 2023) <https://www.iflr.com/article/2bqbqugcf7j5rpm1f4mwx/decommissioning-of-fossil-fuel-infrastructure-will-drive-a-wave-of-commercial-disputes> accessed 04 May 2024. See also the English Commercial Court case, *Apache UK Investment Limited v Esso Exploration and Production UK Limited* [2021] EWHC 1283 (Comm), on the responsibility for future decommissioning costs.

and contractual frameworks in the natural resource sector, legal liabilities and delays from net zero and ESG disputes may slow down the clean energy transition.

A third driver of regulatory fragmentation is the rapid rise in protectionist and isolationist policies and mineral strategies that are undermining the international cooperation and solidarity needed to drive the clean energy transition.[36] Chapter 5 of this book discusses the evolution of critical mineral strategies in different jurisdictions. While these policies are designed to provide a national framework for developing ETMs, the introduction of localization, protectionist, and in-country value requirements, as well as the rise of resource nationalism related to ETMs may undermine global ambitions on net zero and clean energy transition.[37] As demonstrated in this book, announcing net zero plans without aligning them with existing domestic legislation, policies, and trade agreements, especially those relating to local content, ETMs, resource efficiency, and ESG, amongst others, may create negative outcomes for the host state in terms of regulatory cohesiveness, competitiveness, and investment climate. Chapter 18 specifically identifies the need for net zero and climate-aligned regional trade agreements with clear and comprehensive natural resource and environmental provisions, in order to promote regional solidarity for net zero.[38] Misaligned regulations and trade agreements could significantly undermine the exchange and flow of ETMs, raw materials, and technologies needed to drive the global energy transition. There is therefore a need to ensure that domestic legislation and trade agreements do not hinder global efforts to advance net zero and clean energy transition.

The need to align the design and implementation of nature-based solutions, emission trading, and carbon offset schemes with net zero ambitions is closely related to the foregoing.[39] The potential of nature-based solutions such as climate-smart agriculture, afforestation, reforestation, water management, ocean-based carbon removal, and sustainable land and forest use, to contribute to almost 40 per cent of climate change mitigation and the net zero transition has been identified in several studies.[40] Similarly, Chapters 17 and 19 of this book have examined the importance of regional emission trading and carbon border adjustment mechanism (CBAM) schemes as instrument choice for promoting solidarity for net zero. However, as these chapters demonstrate, there remains a need to address the risks of carbon leakage and greenwashing in implementing such schemes. Some United Nations (UN) reports call for a total stop to the use of offset schemes due to their high potential for

[36] See Donald Zillman and others (eds), *Innovation in Energy Law and Technology: Dynamic Solutions for Energy Transitions* (OUP 2018) 1–10.

[37] See Chapter 4 of this book. See also Damien Nyer and Silvia Marchili, 'A new wave of resource nationalism in the mining & metals industry' (15 September 2021) <https://www.whitecase.com/insight-our-thinking/new-wave-resource-nationalism-mining-metals-industry> accessed 10 August 2023.

[38] Chapter 18 of this book.

[39] See United Nations Environment Assembly (UNEA), 'Resolution on Nature-based solutions for supporting sustainable development' (2 March 2022) <https://wedocs.unep.org/bitstream/handle/20.500.11822/39864/NATURE-BASED%20SOLUTIONS%20FOR%20SUPPORTING%20SUSTAINABLE%20DEVELOPMENT.%20English.pdf> accessed 12 May 2024, para 2, which recognizes that although nature-based solutions may contribute significantly to climate action, 'they do not replace the need for rapid, deep and sustained reductions in greenhouse gas emissions, but can improve action for adaptation and resilience to and mitigation of climate change and its impact'.

[40] Javier Babí Almenar and others, 'Nexus between nature-based solutions, ecosystem services and urban challenges' (2021) 100 Land Use Policy 104898; World Bank, 'Climate Explainer: Nature-based Solutions' (19 May 2022) <https://www.worldbank.org/en/news/feature/2022/05/19/what-you-need-to-know-about-nature-based-solutions-to-climate-change> accessed 10 August 2023.

misuse and abuse.[41] Other studies emphasize the urgent need to address accountability, transparency, and integrity issues associated with carbon offset schemes.[42] Given the cross-border and extraterritorial nature of regional emission trading schemes and the CBAM, international cooperation, through knowledge and information exchange, is needed to ensure coherent implementation and avoid carbon leakage in nature-based offsets.[43]

A fourth driver of regulatory fragmentation is the lack of a clear legal framework in many jurisdictions to integrate and promote new technologies such as green hydrogen; carbon capture, utilization, and storage (CCUS); advanced batteries; biofuels; and artificial intelligence (AI) as part of the clean energy transition.[44] Chapter 14 of this book has unpacked the significant potential of green hydrogen to contribute to a just clean energy transition if adequate legal and institutional frameworks are implemented. Investment in clean energy technologies is required worldwide to drive the energy transition, especially in emission-intensive sectors such as the natural resource sector. As can be learned from the hydrogen case study in this book, clear and comprehensive legal frameworks are required to simplify the development, financing, and commercialization of climate and net zero-related technologies and to incentivize private sector participation. Yet, despite the rise of net zero targets, the deployment of clean energy technologies remains slow in the natural resource sector, especially in developing countries.[45] A reliance on technology transfer alone cannot effectively meet the significant technology requirements of decarbonization and the energy transition.[46] In addition to addressing the barriers to technology transfer, there is a need to dismantle all barriers to clean technology entrepreneurship at local levels.[47]

Coherent solutions to the multiple sovereignty, security, and solidarity challenges in reaching net zero must be based on a holistic transformation of natural resource law. Barriers to systemic integration and coherence must be acknowledged and addressed to succeed in the required transformation. The next section discusses the nexus governance approach as a functional framework for addressing the interdependencies and trade-offs in the governance of net zero in the natural resource industry.

III. Addressing Sovereignty, Security, and Solidarity Challenges of Net Zero: Roadmap for a Nexus Governance Approach

As demonstrated in this book, net zero's sovereignty, security, and solidarity risks are interconnected and cannot be effectively addressed in isolation. Therefore, systemic solidarity

[41] United Nations Working Group on Business and Human Rights (UN WGBHR), 'Information Note on Climate Change and the Guiding Principles on Business and Human Rights' (June 2023). See also UN WGBHR, 'Extractive Sector, Just Transition and Human Rights' (2023) UN General Assembly Report A/78/155.

[42] UN WGBHR, 'Extractive Sector Report' (n 41).

[43] Ben Filewod and Geoff McCarney, 'Avoiding carbon leakage from nature-based offsets by design' (Elsevier, 21 July 2023) 6 <https://www.cell.com/one-earth/pdf/S2590-3322(23)00258-0.pdf> accessed 10 August 2023.

[44] IEA, 'Technology needs for net-zero emissions' <https://www.iea.org/reports/energy-technology-perspectives-2020/technology-needs-for-net-zero-emissions> accessed 28 August 2023.

[45] See Chapter 4 of this book. See also Damilola Olawuyi, 'From Energy Consumers to Energy Citizens: Legal Dimensions of Energy Citizenship' in Ruven Fleming and others (eds), *Sustainable Energy Democracy and the Law* (Brill 2021) 101–23.

[46] IEA, 'Technology needs for net-zero emissions' (n 44).

[47] ibid.

and nexus governance are required at international, regional, and local levels to effectively mitigate transition risks in the natural resources sector.

The nexus governance approach emphasizes the need for hybrid, interconnected, and integrated resource management and governance to address regulatory fragmentation and to promote coherent outcomes.[48] Given the interconnectedness of the threats and challenges to the security of natural resources such as water, energy, food environment, and land use, studies highlight the nexus governance approach as a holistic framework to 'reduce trade-offs and boost synergies between sectors, resulting in greater policy coherence and better resource-use efficiency'.[49] To avoid regulatory fragmentation, overlap, and incoherence, nexus governance must harmonize and balance net zero ambitions with the wide range of sovereignty, security, and solidarity challenges discussed in this book.

The nexus approach to the integrated management of natural resources includes five core features.[50] These are the integration of: (1) instruments, laws, and policies to address trade-offs and exploit synergies; (2) institutions; (3) information-sharing; (4) infrastructure and technological solutions; and (5) international coordination and cooperation at regional levels (the '5-I Principles').[51] This section reflects on the strategies that have worked in some case studies in this book and the challenges that lie ahead as we strive for greater synergy and coherence in addressing the net zero trilemma.

A. Integration of Instruments, Laws, and Policies to Address Trade-offs and Exploit Synergies

To advance regulatory coherence in a net zero era, there is a need to integrate and harmonize the implementation of all applicable natural resource sector policy and economic and legal instruments to reduce trade-offs, duplication, and overlaps.[52] As demonstrated in this book, a multiplicity of laws, strategies, and policies relating to net zero and clean energy transition does not foster regulatory coherence and heightens the risk of non-compliance and legal liability for investors. Apart from primary natural resources specific laws such as (petroleum, mining, land use, energy and water legislation), legal obligations relating to just transitions, ESG and human rights due diligence are often found in a wide range of human rights legislation, National Action Plans on Business and Human Rights, and climate change and investment legislation.[53] Furthermore, due to the fact that legal regimes on net zero are still evolving in many countries and regions, obligations relating to transition

[48] Nina Weitz and others, 'Closing the Governance Gaps in the Water-Energy-Food Nexus: Insights from Integrative Governance' (2017) 45 Global Environmental Change 165; also Damilola Olawuyi, 'Sustainable Development and the Water-Energy-Food Nexus: Legal Challenges and Emerging Solutions' (2020) 103(1) Journal of Environmental Science & Policy 1.

[49] UNECE, 'Methodology for Assessing the Water-Food-Energy-Ecosystems Nexus in Transboundary Basins' 7–8 ECE/MP.WAT/WG.1/2015/8 (15 June 2015).

[50] For a detailed and excellent discussion of these five features, see UNECE, 'Reconciling Resource Uses in Transboundary Basins: Assessment of the Water-Food-Energy-Ecosystems Nexus', UN Doc ECE/MP.WAT/46 <https://www.unece.org/fileadmin/DAM/env/water/publications/WAT_Nexus/ece_mp.wat_46_eng.pdf> accessed 10 August 2023.

[51] UNECE, 'Methodology' (n 49) 62–63. See also Fitsum S Weldegiorgis, 'The Interplay of Mineral and Energy Security: A Nexus Approach to Africa's Economic Diversification' (2023) 106 Energy Research & Social Science 103336.

[52] UNECE, 'Methodology' (n 49).

[53] See Chapter 11 of this book.

minerals are found in mining strategies, national visions, and industry guidelines, and may change frequently.[54] Therefore, legal risk management in a net zero era requires a careful mapping of the wide range of laws relating to net zero when planning investments in the natural resource sector.

Failure to assess and understand the different interpretations, requirements, procedures, and sources of responsibility properly when meeting net zero standards could result in ambiguities. It is also important to understand laws on local content and procurements; repatriation of funds; the tax and customs regime; laws on the environment (gas flaring, reclamation, decommissioning, remediation, and clean-ups); labour and human rights law; competition law; contract law; transportation law; electricity law; and agricultural law relating to biofuels and trade laws.[55] The due diligence process allows natural resource investors to carefully evaluate the wide range of primary and secondary legislation and regulation on net zero that should be integrated into a holistic risk management and compliance framework. The risk of investing in countries with fuzzy and unclear standards on ESG and net zero and a high potential for resource nationalism should also be carefully evaluated.

To enhance the competitiveness and regulatory clarity that is required to boost clean energy investments across the entire natural resource value chain, countries and regulators should address regulatory fragmentation and its effects throughout the policy-making lifecycle. Regulators should implement clear, comprehensive, and integrated legislation on natural resource investments and net zero obligations. Natural resources law should provide clear standards and requirements on net zero, including coherent and consistent methodology and taxonomy for monitoring implementation. Chapter 11 of this book on ESG has elaborated on the wide range of ESG measurement and reporting standards emerging to promote a common methodology for rating and reporting net zero performance. Natural resource legislation can promote consistency by clearly identifying the applicable key performance indicators for measuring progress and success in terms of net zero targets and ESG, priority issues on net zero, the modalities for implementation, and clear responsibilities for all relevant ministries and entities to avoid trade-offs, overlap, and role duplication.

In aligning natural resources law relating to net zero and clean energy transition, a starting point is for regulators to conduct an extensive gap analysis that involves wide engagement of local communities and vulnerable groups in developing and implementing policies and programmes relating to the energy transition.[56] To achieve just transition, vulnerable groups such as indigenous communities, women, and youth need to be actively engaged in defining the scope of actions and measures that address vulnerability in the design and implementation of net zero and clean energy projects and programmes.

B. Integration of Institutions

To address regulatory fragmentation in the development of natural resources, especially ETMs needed to drive the clean energy transition, pragmatic and standardization

[54] See Chapter 5 of this book.

[55] ibid. See also Damilola Olawuyi, 'Legal Strategies and Tools for Mitigating Legal Risks Associated with Oil and Gas Investments in Africa' (2015) 39(3) OPEC Energy Review 247.

[56] UN WGBHR, 'Extractive Sector Report' (n 41).

approaches that foster cooperation and minimize duplication between different actors and ministries is essential.[57] As demonstrated in this book, a multiplicity of institutions with decision-making and oversight functions to approve licenses in the natural resource sector remains a key barrier to net zero and clean energy transition.[58] The fragmentation of project and permit approval responsibilities across different agencies and institutions, with distinct financial and resource allocations and often competing and conflicting priorities, could delay the approval and implementation of time-sensitive net zero and climate infrastructure projects, including the sourcing of ETMs. Furthermore, such institutional fragmentation does not foster regulatory coherence and heightens the risk of non-compliance and legal liability for investors. For example, compliance with guidelines issued by a mining ministry without complying with guidelines relating to ESG and human rights by a national human rights commission may result in regulatory fines and litigation. Also, in countries and regions where licensees and operators have to obtain a wide range of permits and licences across the value chain of natural resource projects such as water use permits, environmental permits, and technology permits, amongst others, the high cost of compliance may become a disincentive for private sector participation in clean energy investments.[59]

To minimize compliance risks, natural resource investors should carefully clarify the roles and responsibilities of national, regional, municipal, and local governments in project approval, licensing, and implementation. The due diligence stage allows investors to carefully evaluate the costs, in terms of time, financial payments, and local community expectations concerning natural resource investments, climate action, and environmental protection. Over the years, community development or impact benefit agreements (IBAs) have provided a contractual framework through which investors and local communities can collaboratively outline the benefits, responsibilities, and expectations for natural resource development projects.[60] To ensure that IBAs are net zero and climate-aligned, investors should ensure active consultation with local community leaders and representatives to clarify their expectations in terms of net zero, ESG, human rights, local content, and just transitions and ensure that such expectations are fully captured in the IBAs in a transparent and consultative manner.[61]

The role of regulators in improving coordination amongst the various national, regional, municipal, and local governments concerning net zero and natural resources law cannot be overemphasized. There is a need to put in place mechanisms to coordinate the design and implementation of strategies and policies relating to net zero and natural resource management across sectors at all levels of governance.[62] Such an enterprise will require building shared and common understanding by institutional actors in the diverse domains, sharing information and knowledge in open and linked systems, and constituting cross-sectoral panels and committees that can provide an informed picture of interdependencies and interplay.[63]

[57] ibid 62–63; also Olawuyi, 'Sustainable Development' (n 48).

[58] See Chapter 3 of this book on resource sovereignty.

[59] ibid.

[60] ibid. See also Chapter 4 of this book.

[61] Alastair R Lucas and David K Laidlaw, 'Oil and Gas Sector Local Content Decision Processes: Canadian Indigenous Participation' in Damilola Olawuyi, *Local Content and Sustainable Development in Global Energy Markets* (CUP 2021) 343–60.

[62] UNECE, 'Methodology' (n 49) 62–63.

[63] Olawuyi, 'Sustainable Development' (n 48). See also A Stirling, 'Developing "Nexus Capabilities": Towards Transdisciplinary Methodologies' (2015) ESRC Nexus Network 22.

A starting point is for regulators to conduct an extensive cross-sector analysis of the key institutions with oversight for addressing the wide range of resource sovereignty, security, and solidarity issues in the natural resource sector. Such analysis will examine to what extent the mandates of existing institutions are coherent, conflicting, or duplicative and whether there are linked platforms in place to support knowledge and information-sharing and intersectoral cooperation. Such analysis will reveal opportunities to share expertise, facilities, and best practices by engaging with staff and experts across sectors to review and assess projects in an integrated manner that advances net zero and clean energy transition objectives. Implementing joint knowledge-sharing initiatives on clean energy transition across ministries and agencies can also enhance synergy and build trust.[64]

C. Information-sharing

The risk of greenwashing in net zero and sustainability actions is pervasive in the natural resource sector.[65] Efforts to address greenwashing through consumer protection laws are currently high on regulatory agendas and will remain so for many years.[66] In addition to the greenwashing problem, the lack of transparent, accessible, and verifiable statistical data on the implementation of net zero projects and the levels of compliance with environmental standards remains a key barrier to just transition across the world. As demonstrated in this book, in many countries, members of the public are simply unable to access information on penalties assessed for non-compliance, and the number of operators that have been sanctioned or have lost their licences due to unabated GHG emissions and other human rights violations in their operations.[67]

As policies and legislation on ESG monitoring and reporting increase worldwide, investors need to improve transparent data collection on net zero and clean energy transition across their entire value chain, including pollution control measures by their subsidiaries, subcontractors, and suppliers. The rise of legislation and court decisions that hold investors liable for adverse ESG and human rights impacts of their subsidiaries, subcontractors, suppliers, and other third-party relationships abroad should lead to enterprise-wide risk control approaches that simplify data collection on net zero and ESG across their entire value chain.[68] Also, appointing ESG and human rights competent boards, officers, and advisors can improve risk management practices at the corporate level.[69]

[64] Stirling (n 63). See also UNECE (n 49) 62–63; Olawuyi, 'Sustainable Development' (n 48).

[65] UN WGBHR, 'Extractive Sector Report' (n 41); UN HLEG (n 14).

[66] See EU Directive on the substantiation and communication of explicit environmental claims <https://eur-lex.europa.eu/legal-content/EN/TXT/PDF/?uri=CELEX:52023PC0166> accessed 10 August 2023; also the Federal Trade Commission (FTC) Act, 15 USC, s 5; and the FTC Guides for the Use of Environmental Marketing Claims <https://www.ftc.gov/system/files/ftc_gov/pdf/GreenGuides-FRN-11-5-22.pdf> accessed 10 August 2023; also the UK Green Claims Code, Guidance: Making environmental claims on goods and services (20 September 2021) <https://www.gov.uk/government/publications/green-claims-code-making-environmental-claims> accessed 05 May 2024, which provides a set of guidance 'help businesses understand and comply with their existing obligations under consumer protection law when making environmental claims'.

[67] See Chapters 3, 10, and 11 of this book.

[68] See recent decisions such as *Okpabi v Royal Dutch Shell Plc* [2021] UKSC 3; *Vedanta Resources Plc and Another v Lungowe and Others* [2019] UKSC 20; *Begum v Maran (UK) Ltd* [2021] 3 WLUK 162; *Milieudefensie et al. v Royal Dutch Shell plc.*, The Hague District Court, C/09/571932/HA ZA 19-379, 25 April 2022 (Netherlands); *Lafarge case* (France) [2021] Cour de cassation Pourvoi no 19-87.367; Nevsun (Canada) 2020 SCC 5.

[69] See Chapter 11 of this book.

Regulators also need to enforce data reporting and verification requirements. Creating greater awareness of investors' obligations to be transparent in disclosing statistical data on the GHG emissions, identifying barriers to transparent information collection, and addressing such barriers is also necessary.[70] A starting point is for regulators to invest in system modernization tools and technologies to improve data collection and information-sharing in the natural resource industry. One important way to improve data transparency is to establish a searchable online enforcement and compliance database that can provide relevant information on enforcement actions concerning investigations and penalties.[71] Publicly accessible information on regulatory sanctions and fines for greenwashing can serve as a deterrents to other investors. Such an information platform can also provide regulators with reliable and searchable data on the success or failure of net zero policies.

D. Infrastructure and Technological Solutions

Chapter 13 of this book points out that net zero by 2060 or earlier cannot be achieved without major reductions in carbon emissions from physical and associated infrastructure in the natural resource sector, including building operations and carbon construction materials. With buildings responsible for over 21 per cent of global GHG emissions and over 31 per cent of global CO_2 emissions, the Intergovernmental Panel on Climate Change (IPCC) recognizes the need for substantial reductions of GHG attributable to buildings and infrastructure development.[72] The high intensity of GHG emissions from fossil fuel-powered water, energy, and desalination and cogeneration plants, still widely used in many parts of the world, raises the urgent need for measures to improve resource efficiency.[73]

To move net zero beyond rhetoric, regulators, investors, and other stakeholders in the natural resource sector need to measure and address the volume of GHG emissions in extant infrastructure, buildings, and power plants to effectively design decarbonization measures that limit the intensive carbon footprints of such infrastructure. Greater investment is needed in environmentally sustainable technologies (ESTs) and multipurpose climate-smart infrastructure projects that advance net zero.[74] Climate-smart infrastructure, such as buildings, structures, and systems that reduce GHG emissions can accelerate progress towards net zero, while also improving resilience and adaptation to risks posed by climate change.[75]

[70] UNECE, 'Methodology' (n 49) 62–63; UN General Assembly Report (n 41).

[71] A good example in this regard is the ruling database of the UK Advertising Standards Authority (ASA) for greenwashing investigations <https://www.asa.org.uk/codes-and-rulings/rulings.html> accessed 10 August 2023.

[72] Luisa F Cabeza and others, 'Buildings' in Preyadarshi R Shukla and others (eds), *Climate Change 2022: Mitigation of Climate Change: Working Group III Contribution to the Sixth Assessment Report of the Intergovernmental Panel on Climate Change*, 955 <https://www.ipcc.ch/report/ar6/wg3/downloads/report/IPCC_AR6_WGIII_FullReport.pdf> accessed 1 May 2023.

[73] Mohamed A Darwish, Fatimah M Al Awadhi, and Mahmoud Y Abdul Raheem, 'The MSF: "Enough is Enough"' (2010) Desalination and Water Treatment 193, calling for measures to reduce GHG emissions in the predominant and energy intensive multi-stage flash distillation (MSF) thermal plants.

[74] UNECE, 'Methodology' (n 49) 62–63.

[75] J Rydge, M Jacobs, and I Granoff, 'Ensuring new infrastructure is climate-smart' (2015) Contributing paper for *Seizing the Global Opportunity: Partnerships for Better Growth and a Better Climate. New Climate Economy* (Overseas Development Institute, October 2015) <http://newclimateeconomy.report/misc/working-papers/> accessed 28 August 2023; Joshua Meltzer, 'Financing Sustainable Infrastructure' (Brookings 2016) <https://www.brookings.edu/wp-content/uploads/2016/08/global_20160818_financing_sustainable_infrastructure.pdf> accessed 10 August 2023.

Furthermore, it is essential for natural resource sector operators to improve resource efficiency in production, distribution, and transportation processes, especially by reducing GHG emissions in water, energy, and electricity distribution networks. In this regard, 150 countries including the United States, Norway, Qatar, Oman, Nigeria, and the United Kingdom have joined the voluntary Global Methane Pledge which aims to reduce global methane emissions by at least 30 per cent between 2020 and 2030.[76] Achieving such reduction is projected to eliminate over 2°C warming by 2050.[77] Similarly, an alliance of major oil and gas corporations, including QatarEnergy, Exxon Mobil, Total, Shell, BP, and ENI, amongst others, have signed the Guiding Principles on Reducing Methane Emissions across the Natural Gas Value Chain.[78] Also, the Responsible Business Alliance, a coalition of business enterprises that are committed to responsible investment and ESG risk management, has released several tools to enable members to monitor and reduce GHG emissions.[79] By implementing such voluntary initiatives, natural resource industry operators can gain wider access to the technical knowledge, infrastructure requirements, capacity, and tools needed to address GHG emissions across their entire value chain.

A crucial element of improving resource efficiency in the natural resource sector is for countries to address barriers to clean technology entrepreneurship.[80] Chapter 3 of this book discusses the need to enhance the homegrown development of clean technologies needed to advance the clean energy transition. The starting point in this regard is to reform and address barriers to business registration, formalization, and financing which may hinder clean technology innovation.[81] By streamlining the requirements, time, and cost of business registration and project licensing, more citizens will be incentivized to develop soft ESTs to promote efficiency across the natural resource sector. Accelerator programmes that can enable the public, especially young innovators, to launch energy start-ups and move their energy innovations and projects from development to implementation are also very important aspects of placing citizens at the centre of the energy transition and governance.[82]

E. International Coordination and Cooperation

As discussed in Chapter 1, a successful energy transition regime calls for greater cooperation at international and regional levels to clarify the modalities and rules for advancing

[76] Global Methane Pledge <https://www.ccacoalition.org/en/resources/global-methane-pledge> accessed 10 August 2023.

[77] ibid.

[78] The document acknowledges that 'the transition to a low carbon future will be influenced by the extent to which the oil and gas industry reduces its methane emissions.' Climate and Clean Air Coalition, 'Guiding Principles on Reducing Methane Emissions across the Natural Gas Value Chain' <http://www.ccacoalition.org/en/resources/reducing-methane-emissions-across-natural-gas-value-chain-guiding-principles> accessed 10 August 2023.

[79] Responsible Business Alliance, 'Decarbonization: Advancing Sustainability Globally' <https://www.responsiblebusiness.org/initiatives/rei/decarbonization/> accessed 10 August 2023.

[80] See Zillman and others (n 36).

[81] See Olawuyi, 'Energy Consumers to Energy Citizens' (n 45); Mahmood Ahmad and Muhammad Y Raza, 'Role of Public-Private Partnerships Investment in Energy and Technological Innovations in Driving Climate Change: Evidence from Brazil' (2020) 27 Environmental Science & Pollution Research 30638.

[82] Olawuyi, 'Energy Consumers to Energy Citizens' (n 45). See also Evren Tok and others, 'Entrepreneurship in a Transformative and Resource-Rich State: The Case of Qatar' (2020) Extractive Industries and Society Journal 100708.

net zero, address carbon leakage, and remove barriers to the flow of ETMs, climate technologies, and other resources needed to advance net zero. Therefore coordination, cooperation, and knowledge-sharing must be improved across the wide range of trade, environment, water, and energy institutions to advance net zero objectives.[83] Yet, despite increased focus on the need for coherence and mutual supportiveness, concerns about 'regime complex' and the proliferation of potentially fragmented, conflicting, and overlapping obligations and rules at international and regional levels remain.[84] As shown in Chapter 18, infusing trade agreements with net zero and climate change provisions is a logical step that could bring about hybrid reasoning in harmonizing and integrating net zero with trade objectives to make them operate as part of a coherent and meaningful whole.

Trade organizations, such as the World Trade Organization (WTO), and multilateral environmental treaty bodies relating to net zero, such as the UNFCCC, will also need to collaboratively develop a set of common understandings or pact that clarifies key standards, tenets, and principles of net zero and clean energy transition. Such common understandings can enable trade and environment institutions to better understand the tensions that remain, such as cosmopolitan justice concerns relating to the definition of environmental goods, and how to better accommodate goods, services, and technologies from developing countries as part of a just and inclusive global energy transition.[85]

There is also a clear role for international energy and natural resources organizations and agencies such as the International Energy Agency (IEA), International Renewable Energy Agency (IRENA), the Organization of Petroleum Exporting Countries (OPEC), and the Gas Exporting Countries Forum (GECF) in clarifying an industry-wide common methodology on net zero. For example, in the aviation sector, the International Air Transport Association (IATA) has released a Net Zero Tracking Methodology to provide a consistent and industry-wide methodology and reporting mechanisms to track progress towards the net zero by 2050 goal.[86] Developing similar common methodology and guidance for the natural resource industry can provide industry-wide guidance on monitoring and measuring progress on the commitment to achieve net zero carbon emissions in the sector. By providing comprehensive methodology and industry-wide guidance on net zero, ESG and just transition reporting, common language, and best practices standards will emerge soon, thereby reducing the industry's currently pervasive greenwashing and fuzzy sustainability disclosures.

Addressing barriers to knowledge, technology, and information-sharing at regional and international levels is also important. Under the CBDR-RC principle, promoting solidarity for net zero will require developed countries to significantly increase technology development and transfer, capacity building, and financial resources to developing countries.[87]

[83] UNECE, 'Methodology' (n 49) 62–63.

[84] Kal Raustiala and David G Victor, 'The Regime Complex for Plant Genetic Resources' (2004) 58(2) International Organization 277, 279. Also United Nations (UN), 'Fragmentation of International Law: Difficulties Arising from the Diversification and Expansion of International Law: Report of the Study Group of the International Law Commission' (13 April 2006) A/CN.4/L.682 <https://legal.un.org/ilc/documentation/english/a_cn4_l682.pdf> accessed 28 August 2023.

[85] ILC (n 84); see also Damilola Olawuyi, 'Environment' in Isabelle Van Damme and others (eds), *Oxford Handbook of International Trade Law* (2nd edn, OUP 2022) 673–75.

[86] IATA, 'Net Zero 2050: Progress Tracking Methodology' <https://www.iata.org/contentassets/b3783d24c5834634af59148c718472bb/net-zero-tracking-progress-methodology.pdf> accessed 10 August 2023.

[87] See UNESCO Declaration on Ethical Principles Relating to Climate Change, art 6(4). See also the Paris Agreement, arts 9–12.

In implementing such cooperative measures, there is a need to integrate just transition principles to avoid the perpetuation of racial, gender, indigenous, capitalist, colonialist, and other forms of systemic social exclusions in the clean energy transition.[88] Knowledge-sharing between countries on net zero can help deepen harmonized, coherent, and rights-based implementation of net zero programmes at regional, national, and local levels. Knowledge-management platforms and institutions can also enable a full exchange of ideas, best practices, and knowledge on addressing trade and other barriers to clean energy transition in the natural resource sector.[89] Similarly, as discussed in Chapter 9 of this book, to address adverse environment and health and safety impacts associated with artisanal and small scale mining, states and businesses involved in the production and distribution of ETMs should support industry-wide training, capacity development, and formalization efforts required to address such risks.[90]

Higher education institutions also have key roles to play in promoting regional, North–South, and triangular research and scientific cooperation and knowledge exchange on net zero and just energy transition.[91] Regional associations are already emerging which aim to enhance the capacity and training for governments and business enterprises to better align their actions with net zero goals.[92] Governments, investors, and other stakeholders should continue to provide financial and technical support for such education and awareness programmes. Higher education institutions, in collaboration with all relevant natural resource stakeholders, should implement tailored ESG-focused programmes—masters, doctoral, and executive certificate programmes—that unpack human rights due diligence approaches for energy and climate planning in a net zero era.

IV. Beyond Fragmentation: The Future of Natural Resources Law

The ongoing clean energy transition worldwide calls for a reimagination and transformation of natural resources law to enhance coherence. Fragmented responses to the wide range of sovereignty, security, and solidarity risks of net zero programmes worldwide, and the associated rise in natural resource disputes and conflicts, could hinder a just, inclusive, and orderly clean energy transition.[93] Natural resources law and practice in a net zero era therefore requires an intricate understanding of resource ownership, energy security,

[88] Farhana Sultana, 'The Unbearable Heaviness of Climate Coloniality' (2022) 99 Political Geography 102638; Karen Bell, 'Can the Capitalist Economic System Deliver Environmental Justice?' (2015) 10 Environmental Research Letters 125017.

[89] For a list of knowledge sharing platforms on net zero, see <https://transparency-partnership.net/network/knowledge-platforms> accessed 10 August 2023.

[90] See also UN WGBHR, 'Extractive Sector Report' (n 41) paras 51–54. See also OECD, *OECD Due Diligence Guidance for Responsible Supply Chains of Minerals from Conflict-Affected and High-Risk Areas* (3rd edn, OECD Publishing 2016) 116–18.

[91] See UNESCO Declaration on Ethical Principles Relating to Climate Change, arts 7 and 14; also the Paris Agreement, art 12.

[92] eg the Association of African Environmental Law Lecturers (ASSELLAU) and the Association of Environmental Law Lecturers in the MENA region (ASSELLMU). See Elizabeth Mrema and Aphrodite Smagadi 'The United Nations Environment Programme: Promoting Climate Law Education in the MENA Region' in Damilola Olawuyi, *Climate Change Law and Policy in the MENA Region* (Routledge 2021) 21–42.

[93] International Monetary Fund (IMF), 'Fragmentation and Commodity Markets: Vulnerabilities and Risks' in World Economic Outlook (October 2023) 71–92 <https://www.imf.org/en/Publications/WEO/Issues/2023/10/10/world-economic-outlook-october-2023> accessed 10 November 2023.

climate change law, human rights, ESG and responsible contracting, resource politics, energy and resource ethics, trade, and environmental diplomacy, amongst other related legislation.

The nexus governance approach to resource management discussed in this book provides a starting point and roadmap for regulators, investors, and other stakeholders in the natural resource sector to better align their net zero targets with extant and emerging legislation in different sectors and disciplines. The nexus approach could also enable stakeholders to align their investment decision-making and risk management strategies with net zero and energy transition programmes in a manner that reduces fragmentation, trade-offs, and overlaps.

Integrated structural and non-structural reforms are fundamental to promote greater coherence between net zero ambitions and natural resources law. Structural measures such as investing in climate-smart infrastructure and ESTs that reduce pollution, improve resource efficiency, and simplify information sharing can enhance green and inclusive growth across the natural resource value chain. Similarly, non-structural measures such as clear, comprehensive, and more ambitious legislation on clean energy transition and net zero aligned licensing and contractual frameworks are important. Net zero-aligned laws and policies are required to integrate just energy transition into the entire natural resource value chain, ranging from project due diligence, licensing, and approval, to operations, decommissioning, and end-of-lifetime closure. There is also a clear need for governments, investors, and other stakeholders in the natural resource sector to raise their ambition through zero carbon policies and laws that eliminate the continued injection of GHGs into the atmosphere. Legal and institutional barriers that stifle clean technology entrepreneurship and the flow of ETMs needed for energy transition must also be carefully addressed. As investment in non-renewable natural resources progressively reduces, clear and comprehensive legal frameworks on all elements of nexus governance can stimulate the required financing, knowledge exchange, and multistakeholder cooperation needed to spur a just and inclusive energy transition that creates decent economic opportunities in the renewable natural resources sector.

In summary, considering the rapid pace of transformations currently taking place in light of the energy transition, there is a need for continuous knowledge exchange, professional development, and education for investors and regulators to boost capacity for ESG risk identification and management. There is also a need to significantly increase investment in research, education, and technology development programmes, to boost the development of homegrown clean technology solutions and green procurement practices across the entire natural resource value chain. Coherent natural resources laws and collaborative implementation will be essential in shaping these developments.

Index

For the benefit of digital users, indexed terms that span two pages (e.g., 52–53) may, on occasion, appear on only one of those pages.

Tables are indicated by an italic *t* following the page/paragraph number

The manufacturer's authorised representative in the EU for product safety is Oxford University Press España S.A. of el Parque Empresarial San Fernando de Henares, Avenida de Castilla, 2 – 28830 Madrid (www.oup.es/en or product.safety@oup.com). OUP España S.A. also acts as importer into Spain of products made by the manufacturer.

www.ingramcontent.com/pod-product-compliance
Lightning Source LLC
LaVergne TN
LVHW062205200926
848484LV00006B/1325
* 9 7 8 0 1 9 8 9 2 5 0 0 2 *